SECOND EDITION

Learning Success

THE WADSWORTH COLLEGE SUCCESS SERIES

Santrock and Halonen,
*Your Guide to College
Success: Strategies for
Achieving Your Goals*
(1999).
ISBN: 0-534-53354-X

Holkeboer and Walker,
*Right from the Start:
Taking Charge of Your
College Success*, 3rd Ed.
(1999).
ISBN: 0-534-56412-7

Petrie and Denson,
*A Student Athlete's Guide
to College Success: Peak
Performance in Class
and Life* (1999).
ISBN: 0-534-54792-3

Van Blerkom,
*Orientation to College
Learning*, 2nd Ed. (1999).
ISBN: 0-534-52389-7

Corey,
Living and Learning (1997).
ISBN: 0-534-50501-5

Campbell,
*The Power to Learn:
Helping Yourself to College
Success*, 2nd Ed. (1997).
ISBN: 0-534-26352-6

THE FRESHMAN YEAR EXPERIENCE™ SERIES

Gardner and Jewler,
*Your College Experience:
Strategies for Success*,
3rd Ed. (1997).
ISBN: 0-534-51895-8

   Concise Third Edition
   (1998).
   ISBN: 0-534-53749-9

   Expanded Reader
   Edition (1997).
   ISBN: 0-534-51898-2

   Expanded Workbook
   Edition (1997).
   ISBN: 0-534-51897-4

STUDY SKILLS/ CRITICAL THINKING

Longman and Atkinson,
*CLASS: College Learning
and Study Skills*, 5th Ed.
(1999).
ISBN: 0-534-54972-1

Longman and Atkinson,
*SMART: Study Methods
and Reading Techniques*,
2nd Ed. (1999).
ISBN: 0-534-54981-0

Sotiriou,
*Integrating College Study
Skills: Reasoning in
Reading, Listening, and
Writing*, 5th Ed. (1999).
ISBN: 0-534-54990-X

Smith, Knudsvig,
and Walter,
*Critical Thinking:
Building the Basics* (1998).
ISBN: 0-534-19284-X

Van Blerkom,
*College Study Skills:
Becoming a Strategic
Learner*, 2nd Ed. (1997).
ISBN: 0-534-51679-3

Kurland,
*I Know What It Says . . .
What Does It Mean?
Critical Skills for Critical
Reading* (1995).
ISBN: 0-534-24486-6

SECOND EDITION

Learning Success

Three Paths* to Being
Your Best at College & Life

* 1) Develop staying power
  2) Become a mindful learner & thinker
  3) Use information technology

Carl Wahlstrom
GENESEE COMMUNITY COLLEGE

Brian K. Williams

STUDENT PHOTOGRAPHS BY MICHAEL GARRETT,
GENESEE COMMUNITY COLLEGE

 Wadsworth Publishing Company

I(T)P® An International Thomson Publishing Company

Belmont, CA · Albany, NY · Boston · Cincinnati · Johannesburg · London · Madrid · Melbourne
Mexico City · New York · Pacific Grove, CA · Scottsdale, AZ · Singapore · Tokyo · Toronto

Publisher: Karen J. Allanson
Senior Editorial Assistant: Godwin Chu
Marketing Manager: Jennie Burger
Project Editor: Christal Niederer
Print Buyer: Barbara Britton
Permissions Editor: Bob Kauser
Production: Stacey Sawyer/Sawyer & Williams
Designer: Seventeenth Street Studios
Art Editor: Stacey Sawyer/Sawyer & Williams
Copy Editor: Richard Reser
Illustrator: Seventeenth Street Studios
Cover Design: Seventeenth Street Studios
Cover Image: The Stock Market
Dummy: Brian Williams/Sawyer & Williams
Compositor: Seventeenth Street Studios
Printer: Courier

Library of Congress Cataloging-in-Publication Data

Wahlstrom, Carl.
   Learning success : three paths to being your best at
college & life : 1). develop staying power, 2). become a
mindful learner & thinker, 3). use information technology
/ Carl Wahlstrom, Brian K. Williams ; student photographs
by Michael Garrett.
       p.   cm.
   Includes index.
   ISBN 0-534-53424-4 (alk. paper)
   1. College student orientation—United States.
   2. Study skills—United States.
   I. Williams, Brian K.   . II. Title.
   LB2343.32.W353   1999
   378.1'98—dc21   98–33220
                                          CIP

For more information, contact Wadsworth Publishing
Company, 10 Davis Drive, Belmont, CA 94002, or
electronically at http://www.wadsworth.com

International Thomson Editores
Seneca, 53
Colonia Polanco
11560 México D.F. México

International Thomson Publishing Asia
60 Albert Street
#15-01 Albert Complex
Singapore 189969

International Thomson Publishing Japan
Hirakawa-cho Kyowa Building, 3F
2-2-1 Hirakawa-cho, Chiyoda-ku
Tokyo 102, Japan

International Thomson Publishing Europe
Berkshire House
168-173 High Holborn
London, WC1V 7AA, United Kingdom

Nelson ITP, Australia
102 Dodds Street
South Melbourne
Victoria 3205 Australia

Nelson Canada
1120 Birchmount Road
Scarborough, Ontario
Canada M1K 5G4

International Thomson Publishing Southern Africa
Building 18, Constantia Square
138 Sixteenth Road, P.O. Box 2459
Halfway House, 1685 South Africa

Three important paths
to college and life-long success . . . begin your journey today!

With this motivating book, you'll soon discover that success is not some accidental or genetically endowed gift reserved for the lucky. You'll find that college and life-long success is the direct result of **skills that you can easily learn and practice.** Authors Carl Wahlstrom and Brian K. Williams guide you along three important paths that will be the cornerstones of your ultimate success:

Staying power

Developing staying power . . .
because persistence is the ultimate winner

Mindfulness

Becoming a mindful learner . . .
with creativity, openness, awareness, and critical thinking

Information technology

Using information technology . . .
tools that are vital to your success today and in the new millennium

Throughout **Learning Success,** *the authors help you keep these three paths on your horizon as you learn specific academic and personal success strategies. You'll be amazed at how versatile your skills are . . . not only paving your way to success in college, but also becoming an integral part of your success throughout your professional and personal life.*

Read on for important tips on using this book

Developing staying power . . . the backbone of your success

Developing Staying Power for Lifetime Success

Nothing Takes the Place of Persistence

IN THIS CHAPTER This chapter considers some of the changes you will face in college:

■ **The chief characteristic of college:** High school is a *structured* environment, college is more *unstructured*. College offers more freedom but also requires more responsibility—more *staying power.*

■ **The "why" of college and your values:** Why are you here? Your values, which have three characteristics, affect your reasons for going to college.

■ **The fears of college:** What are your fears about college? They are probably mostly the same fears everyone else has, such as flunking out.

■ **How college can better your life:** Compared to high-school graduates, college graduates usually make more money. They also experience gratifying personal growth during college. In addition, they probably have a better chance to discover what makes them happy. The skills that make you successful in college can make you successful in your career.

■ **The strengths that give you staying power:** You bring certain strengths that will give you the persistence to stay in college.

■ **Life goals and college goals:** There are six steps for translating your life goals into college goals and daily tasks.

Staying power

What goal or desire (or hypothetical desire) is the strongest in your life? Making your family (parents, spouse/lover, children) proud of you? Helping them be more comfortable? Saving them from harm? Making a lot of money? Seeing the world? Expressing yourself? Finding a true companion? Determining the most rewarding kind of work?

To what lengths would you be willing to go in order to achieve this goal? Put your life on the line? Work at a job you hated for 10 years? Give up television? Learn new skills that may be difficult to learn?

Could you exert this determination in the attainment of a college degree?

The Strengths That Give You Staying Power

PREVIEW & REVIEW Four qualities are helpful for giving one the persistence to achieve success in college—and in life: (1) sense of personal control and responsibility, (2) optimism, (3) creativity, and (4) ability to take psychological risks.

No matter what your worries about college, you have certain qualities of character that will help you to succeed. In this section, we'll look at strengths that can be cultivated for college success.

Successful people have the following:

■ Sense of personal control and responsibility

■ Optimism

■ Creativity

■ Ability to take psychological risks

PERSONAL CONTROL & RESPONSIBILITY. How much personal control do you feel you have over your destiny? **The term *locus of control* refers to your beliefs about the relationship between your behavior and the ___ of rewards and punishment.** ___ either an

---

In this important introductory chapter, you'll learn about the power of persistence in helping you achieve college and lifelong success. You'll discover the specific qualities of persistence and **how** to develop them. You'll also learn the true meaning of commitment, steadfastness, and discipline—**and** their tremendous influence on every academic and personal success strategy you master throughout this book.

In every chapter of this book, you'll find "Staying Power" icons and accompanying questions and activities that motivate you to stay the course.

PREVIEW & REVIEW

Appearing several times within each chapter, these section summaries help you preview—and later review—the material that follows for maximum reinforcement and retention. Watch for them!

Learning to "think smart" . . . because creative, **mindful thinking** means real learning

his unique chapter focuses your attention on the wonderful ability to think critically and learn actively. You'll discover a useful technique called **mindful learning** that helps you take active control of the thinking process—**and** helps you learn how to stay open to new information and different perspectives. You'll also see how different kinds of intelligence and learning styles can be successful, how to avoid incorrect reasoning traps, and how to take the chances that spark real creativity.

2 Becoming a Mindful Learner & Thinker

Learning Styles, Active Learning, & Critical & Creative Thinking

IN THIS CHAPTER How smart do you have to be to get through higher education? Or to get through life? While a high IQ may help, there's more to being smart than IQ. In this chapter, we consider different kinds of intelligence, the best kinds of learning, and ways to "think smart." We consider the following.

■ **Different kinds of intelligence:** There are perhaps seven kinds of intelligence, an important one being emotional intelligence.

■ **Your learning style:** Some people tend to favor some kinds of learning over others—sound, sight,

GROUP ACTIVITY #2.2

MINDLESSNESS VERSUS MINDFULNESS

With three to five other students in a group, discuss examples of how mindlessness is practiced in school. How would you bring a mindful approach to school subjects that you're less than thrilled about having to take?

USE YOUR SPARE TIME FOR THINKING. What do you think about when you're jogging, walking to class, standing in a bank line, inching along in traffic? It could be about anything, of course. (Many people think about relationships or sex.) However, there are three ways your mind can be made to be productive—to turn mindless behavior into mindful behavior:

Mindfulness

1. Try to recall points in a lecture that day.

2. Try to recall points in something you've read.

3. Think of ideas to go into a project or paper you're working on.

Again, the point of this use of idle time is to try to involve yourself with your schoolwork. This is equivalent to football players working plays in their heads or singers doing different kinds of phrasing in their minds. The superstars are always practicing mindfulness, always working at their jobs.

Beginning with Chapter 2, you'll find icons in every chapter accompanied by tips and activities that help you apply **mindful learning** and critical and creative thinking in practical ways.

YOURSELF THE EXTRA EDGE **113**

Using Information Technology

Leveraging Your
Success with
Computer &
Communications
Tools

Using computer and online tools to leverage your success

Learning to use the tools of information technology—computers, the Internet, and the World Wide Web—is absolutely critical to your success in college and beyond. That's why this information-packed chapter is another must read. It covers many practical items such as your options for getting the best computer for your needs, tips for saving on computers and accessories, leasing options, software choices, basic facts about getting on the Internet, all about the Web, directories, search engines, hyperlinks, bookmarks, and so much more. Very rarely will you find so much essential, useful information all in one place.

PANEL 3.2

Tips for buying a used computer. Buying from an individual means you have little recourse if something goes wrong. The following tips should help you to buy carefully.

- If possible, take someone who knows computers with you.
- Turn the computer on and off a few times to make sure there are no problems on startup.
- Use the computer and, if possible, try the software you want to use. Listen for strange sounds in the hard drive or the floppies.
- Turn the computer off and look for screen burn-in, a ghost image on the screen after the machine has been turned off. It can be a sign of misuse.
- Ask about the warranty. Some companies, including Apple and IBM, permit warranties to be transferred to new owners (effective from the date of the original purchase). A new owner can usually have the warranty extended by paying a fee.

Information technology

INTERNET ADDICTION. Don't let this happen to you: "A student e-mails friends, browses the World Wide Web, blows off homework, botches exams, flunks out of school."[19] This is a description of the downward spiral of the "Net addict," often a college student—because schools give students no-cost or low-cost linkage to the Internet—though it can be anyone. Some become addicted (although critics feel "addiction" is too strong a word) to chat groups, some to online pornography, some simply to the escape from real life.[20,21]

Stella Yu, 21, a college student from Carson, California, was rising at 5 A.M. to

Beginning with Chapter 3, every chapter includes these "Information Technology" icons. They call your attention to tips on use, or in this case, misuse of information technology.

Diversity & Differences

Preparing
to Meet the
21st Century

IN THIS CHAPTER In this chapter we describe the following important areas:

- **The new college student body:** Many students don't fit the profile of the traditional 18–24, full-time, residential student. They may be commuters, working, parents, older, and the like.

- **Race, culture, and stereotypes and why diversity matters:** Race, ethnicity, and culture all mean different things.

- **The multicultural "salad bowl":** How to see through the eyes of people different from you—in gender, sexual orientation, age, race, ethnicity, nationality, religion, and ability.

- **Commuter students:** Because 80% of students commute, they need to know how to adjust between the different sectors of their lives.

289

Cultures, races, genders, ages, disabilities . . . learning why **diversity** matters

Offering plenty of information and opportunities to help you sort out your feelings about diversity on campus, *Learning Success* devotes a comprehensive chapter to the many kinds of diversity you're likely to encounter. You'll explore how to talk to others about prejudice, what it's like to have a physical disability, how to watch for sexist behavior, and how to avoid stereotypical thinking about gender, age, race, and culture.

"As a commuter student, what things do you do to compensate for not living on campus?"

Name: Nancy Willis

Major: Human Services

Family & work situation: Married, two children, two stepchildren; work part time in grocery store

Interests: Floral arranging, Girl Scouts, wood crafts, cooking

Answer to question: "I planned my schedule so I have free time between classes. This allows me to use the library, the Center for Academic Progress [learning center], and the computer lab. Also, it allows me time to get tutoring, if necessary."

Appearing in this chapter and throughout the book, brief interviews with students representing different ages, ethnic backgrounds, and career fields help to broaden your thinking about diversity on campus— **and help you make meaningful personal connections to the strategies and material in each chapter.**

Get involved . . . because you learn best by interacting and doing

Real Practice Activities for Real People

REAL PRACTICE ACTIVITY #10.1: EXPOSING YOURSELF DELIBERATELY TO DIVERSITY. This practice activity is designed to get students to deliberately expose themselves to diversity. The activity is to be done outside of class and reported the following week, either in class discussion or as a reaction paper written for the instructor.

Staying power

Getting to know people who are different from you may require overcoming some shyness or discomfort. In other words, it requires a bit of persistence, but this kind of perseverence or staying power will probably be required throughout your life as you have to work with new and different kinds of people.

Outside of class make some attempt to get to know people different from

GROUP ACTIVITY #5.2

FINDING EXAMPLES OF THE SIX MEMORIZING STRATEGIES

Divide into six small groups with nearly equal numbers of people in each group. Each group should take one of the six memorizing strategies discussed: over-learning, distributed practice, avoiding interference, depth of processing, verbal memory aids, and visual memory aids.

With others in your group, come up with as many ways as possible to illustrate how you could use the particular learning strategy. Share your

Onward: Applying This Chapter to Your Life

PREVIEW & REVIEW Being exposed to multiple viewpoints enriches us all.

n this information age," writes Hugh Price, president of the National Urban League, "the quality of a nation's human capital is the key to its productivity. The more highly educated our growing minority population is, the more competitive our economy and cohesive our society will be."[51]

Being exposed to a multiplicity of viewpoints enriches not only one's educational experience but also prepares us for the highly diversified world we will have to deal with in the new century.

If you found only *one idea* important

REAL PRACTICE ACTIVITIES FOR REAL PEOPLE

These fun-to-do activities at the end of every chapter ask you to apply the three key paths to success that you'll be learning throughout the book to specific chapter topics. In this **Real Practice** from the diversity chapter, you'll apply staying power, mindful thinking, and information technology to diversity topics in three separate activities.

GROUP ACTIVITIES

Collaborative exercises that you can do in or outside of class, these **Group Activities** get you interacting with others to work through issues and topics raised in each chapter.

ONWARD: APPLYING THIS CHAPTER TO YOUR LIFE

This useful, end-of-chapter feature suggests that you write down something you've learned in the chapter that you can put into practice.

Personal contemplation to clarify your knowledge and goals

PERSONAL EXPLORATION #5.1

HOW'S YOUR MEMORY?

Honing your associative skills can boost short-term memory, says neurosurgeon Arthur Winter, director of the New Jersey Neurological Institute in Livingston and author of *Build Your Brain Power*.

Now cover the list and write down as many items as you can remember in the following space.

■ **WHAT TO DO**

To test your powers of association, look at the following word list for just 5 seconds.

Dog	Stone
Cat	Winter
Bird	White
Shovel	Will
Skill	Went
House	Ten
Horse	Star
Crag	Stair

PERSONAL EXPLORATION #2.1

HOW DO YOU LEARN BEST?

There are 12 incomplete sentences and three choices for completing each. Circle the answer that best corresponds to your style, as follows:

1 = the choice that is *least* like you.

2 = your second choice.

3 = the choice that is *most* like you.

1. When I want to learn something new, I usually . . .
   a. want someone to explain it to me. 1 2 3
   b. want to read about it in a book or magazine. 1 2 3
   c. want to try it out, take notes, or make a model of it. 1 2 3

2. At a party, most of the time I like to . . .
   a. listen and talk to two or

   c. make a fist or tense my muscles, take it out on something else, hit or throw things. 1 2 3

5. A happy event I would like to have is . . .
   a. hearing the thunderous applause for my speech or music. 1 2 3
   b. photographing the prize picture of an exciting newspaper story. 1 2 3
   c. achieving the fame of being first in a physical activity such as dancing, acting, surfing, or sports event. 1 2 3

6. I prefer a teacher to . . .
   a. use the lecture method, with informative explanations and discussions. 1 2 3
   b. write on the chalkboard, use visual aids and assigned readings.

9. When I cook something new, I like to . . .
   a. have someone tell me the directions, a friend or TV show. 1 2 3
   b. read the recipe and judge by how it looks. 1 2 3
   c. use many pots and dishes, stir often, and taste-test. 1 2 3

10. My emotions can often be interpreted from my . . .
    a. voice quality 1 2 3
    b. facial expression. 1 2 3
    c. general body tone. 1 2 3

11. When driving, I . . .
    a. turn on the radio as soon as I enter the car. 1 2 3
    b. like quiet so I can concentrate. 1 2 3

PERSONAL EXPLORATIONS

These learning activities ask you to examine your feelings and behaviors to help increase your self-awareness, with the ultimate goal of improving academic and personal success habits. There are more than 40 throughout the book.

The Examined Life

JOURNAL of your first year.

JOURNAL ENTRY #4.1: HOW'S YOUR MOTIVATION? How strongly motivated are you to pursue your life and college goals? What activities would you be willing to give up to achieve them?

JOURNAL ENTRY #4.3: WHAT CAN YOU DO TO MANAGE YOUR TIME BETTER? Just as business and professional people often look for ways to improve their time-management skills, so can students. What kinds of things did you note in this chapter that might help you manage your time better?

THE EXAMINED LIFE: JOURNAL OF YOUR FIRST YEAR

Located at the end of every chapter, **The Examined Life** asks you to explore your own thoughts on how to apply what you have just read in the chapter.

It's all here!
Every important academic & personal success strategy you need!

PART ONE of this book covers eight major academic success strategies —everything from time management, reading and study techniques, notetaking, class discussion, instructor relations, and making powerful written and oral presentations, to taking tests with confidence and integrity. Throughout these chapters the authors reinforce the three key paths to success—persistence, mindful thinking, and use of information technology—to help you solidly build and reinforce each skill.

PART TWO turns to the personal side of college and lifelong success with five comprehensive chapters dealing with resources and money management, diversity on campus, managing stress, looking and feeling good, dealing successfully with others, and choosing a major and career. These chapters also build on the authors' three paths to success—making these chapters an even more valuable learning experience.

Preface to the Instructor

We wrote this book to show students how to BE THEIR BEST—now, and for life. It is about *three paths to success in college,* which are also *paths to success in life:*

1) developing staying power;

2) becoming a mindful learner and thinker;

3) using information technology.

We hope students and instructors alike will find the strategies in this book useful and even inspiring.

THE AUDIENCE FOR THIS BOOK *LEARNING SUCCESS: Three Paths to Being Your Best at College & Life* is a college textbook intended for use in College Success and First-Year Experience courses. This text is designed to help students master the academic and personal skills needed in higher education—which in turn are skills needed for success in the workplace and in life.

THE KEY FEATURES OF THIS BOOK The key features of LEARNING SUCCESS are as follows.

SUCCESS TECHNIQUES FOR LIFE The techniques students learn for success in college can bring success outside of college, including careers. This book provides a *practical philosophy based on action* to help students:

■ *Be their best in college:* We show students how to master the academic and personal skills needed to succeed in higher education—how to manage their time, improve their reading and note-taking skills, handle finances, and work toward their career goals.

■ *Be their best in life:* We show students how the skills one needs for success in college are the same skills one needs for success in life—in work, in relationships, in stress management, in finances. We pay great attention to the connection between higher education and achieving one's goals in life.

STAYING POWER Persistence, commitment, and discipline are necessary for achievement—in college and out. *Staying power* as a key to college and life success is a dominant theme of the book, in the text, in activities, and in exercises throughout.

MINDFULNESS Becoming a mindful learner and thinker leads to greater success—in college and out. Starting with Chapter 2, "Becoming a Mindful Learner & Thinker," we give students an understanding of theories about multiple intelligences (based on Howard Gardner's *Frames of Mind* and Daniel Goleman's *Emotional Intelligence*) and different learning styles. We then show readers how to recognize "mindlessness" and learn to practice mindfulness or active learning (leaning on the theories of Ellen Langer as expressed in *Mindfulness* and *The Power of Mindful Learning*). We follow with discussions of how to practice critical thinking and creative thinking. Throughout the book, we continually show students how to bring the skills of mindfulness, critical thinking, and creative thinking to bear on their academic work—and how the skills of problem solving are much valued by employers in the world outside of college.

INFORMATION TECHNOLOGY Computers, the Internet, and the World Wide Web are essential productivity tools—in college and out. Starting with Chapter 3, "Using Information Technology," we show how information technology—the union of computers and telecommunications—are productivity tools that are essential to success. The proportion of colleges requiring students to demonstrate basic skills in computer or Internet use is rapidly climbing—up to 40% in 1997 from 32% in

1992. E-mail is now required in about a third of college courses, and about another third draw on the resources of the World Wide Web. In the belief that students should learn the benefits of information technology early (by now many have already been exposed before college), we show throughout the book how computers and the Internet may be used for college—and career—success.

DIVERSITY We direct this book to part-timers, working students, commuters, and other nontraditional students as well as to traditional students.
In this edition, we have expanded our section on diversity into a full chapter—Chapter 9, "Diversity & Differences." In this chapter, we consider not only diversity in gender, sexual orientation, age, culture, and race. We also consider all the various other differences that are now earmarks of most of today's college student bodies: part-timers, working students, parents, commuters, international students, and so on. For instance, we wrote this book with the full awareness that the majority of students today are commuters.

INTERACTIVE & EFFECTIVE PEDAGOGY

We offer a highly accessible, interactive, and engaging approach, with exceptional activities and exercises. *LEARNING SUCCESS* takes a focused approach in presenting material supported by interactive features, techniques to reinforce learning, and flexible organization for instructors. Here's how:

- *170 learning exercises and class activities, plus over 50 journal entry suggestions.* Past users of the book, both instructors and students, have praised the wealth of activities and exercises. Recognizing that most first-year classes are interactive ones, we provide a number of features that ask the student to become actively engaged with the material. Specifically:

(1) *Personal Explorations,* or learning exercises, ask students to examine their feelings and behaviors to help increase recognition and improvement of study habits. (Examples: "How Do You Spend Your Time?" "How Do You Learn Best?") There are over 40 Personal Explorations in the book, as listed in the Detailed Contents beginning on page xxi.

(2) *Classroom Activities* are collaborative exercises that instructors may elect to assign, in or out of the classroom. (Examples: "How's Your Memory?" "What Kinds of Negative Thoughts Do You Have During Tests?") There are 88 such Classroom Activities in this book, presented throughout each chapter.

(3) *Real Practice Activities for Real People* consists of three activities at the end of each chapter. These exercises reinforce our three major themes: staying power, mindfulness, and information technology. Examples are "How Have You Used Mindful Learning in Your Own Life?" "The Up Side & Down Side of Information Technology." "How Are You Going to Study Difficult Material?"

(4) *The Examined Life: Journal of Your First Year* is a regular end-of-chapter feature that asks students to explore their own thoughts on how to apply what they have just read in the chapter. There are over 50 journal entry suggestions that students may follow. If they wish, instructors may assign these as additional activities to be handed in.

(5) *Essentials for Time & Life Management* is a six-step strategy that shows students how to set daily tasks from life goals. It requires answering six questions: Why am I in school? What are my plans? What are my actions? What is my master timetable? What is my weekly timetable? What is on the To-Do list for today?

- *Techniques to reinforce student learning:* To help students learn and develop critical thinking, the following techniques help reinforce what students are learning:

(1) *Interesting writing,* studies show, significantly improves students' ability to retain information. We use high-interest strategies—such as the personal anecdote, the colorful fact, the apt direct quote—to make the material as interesting and memorable as possible.

(2) *Brief interviews with 27 students* representing different career fields, ages, and eth-

nic backgrounds help readers make a meaningful personal connection to the strategies and material.

(3) *Key terms and definitions are printed in bold-face* to help readers identify which terms are important and what they actually mean.

(4) *"Preview & Review"* is an "abstract" presented at the beginning of each section, which helps students preview, and later review, the material that follows.

(5) *Material is presented in "bite-size" portions and sentences are kept short and to the point.* Major ideas are presented in easily read, concise form, with generous use of advance organizers, bulleted lists, and new paragraphing when a new idea is introduced.

■ *Flexible organization:* Chapters may be taught in any sequence, or omitted, at the instructor's discretion. *LEARNING SUCCESS* covers both *academic success strategies and personal success strategies* in 13 chapters. Specifically:

Academic success strategies: The first eight chapters cover making the transition to higher education, goal setting, learning styles, mindful learning, critical and creative thinking, information technology, time management, note taking, memorizing and reading techniques, test taking, and researching and presenting written and oral reports.

Personal success strategies: The last five chapters cover diversity and differences; campus and community resources and money management; stress and wellness; and majors and careers. Instructors teaching abbreviated courses can skip any of these or teach them in any order.

Special topics: Instead of having a full chapter for each special-interest topic, as some other books do, we integrate coverage within the appropriate chapter to provide better context for material. *Values clarification,* for instance, is discussed in Chapter 1. *Learning styles* are considered in Chapter 2. *Math confidence* is discussed in Chapter 6. *Academic integrity* is covered in Chapters 7 and 8.

Supplements & Support

 complete resource package for instructors accompanies this text.

INSTRUCTOR RESOURCES

■ **Instructor's Resource Manual** This supplement provides instructors with additional activities and exercises, teaching suggestions and answers to commonly asked student questions for each chapter in the text.

■ **College Success PowerPoint** This cross-platform CD-ROM contains text and images to illustrate important concepts in the college success course. Use this CD in conjunction with your own PowerPoint program for the additional flexibility of adding your own slides, making changes or deleting existing slides and rearranging the slide order.

■ **College Success Transparency Acetates** 50 color transparencies featuring helpful checklists, charts, and key points about college success topics to help organize your classroom presentation.

■ **Test Bank** Quizzes and tests for each chapter topic.

■ **The Keystone** The exclusive newsletter of the Wadsworth College Success program. Published twice during the academic year, the Keystone brings you ideas and information about events and resources from colleagues around the country.

■ **The Wadsworth College Success Course Guide** This helpful resource covers a range of subjects, from building support for a freshman year course to administering the course and reshaping it for the future.

WORKSHOPS AND TRAINING

- **College Success Workshops** Wadsworth offers multiple training options to best meet your needs, including regional workshops and customized on-site workshops. Call 1-800-400-7609 for more information on creating a workshop just right for your program!

- **Teaching College Success: The Complete Resource Guide** *Exclusive* to Wadsworth, *Teaching College Success* is the perfect tool to create your own tailored training program for college success instructors! Designed as a stand-alone resource or as a reference, this training package focuses on faculty development and common issues related to teaching the freshman seminar across institutions. Contains a complete set of training modules and a PowerPoint CD-ROM.

VIDEO RESOURCES

- **CNN Today: College Success** *Exclusive* to Wadsworth, this innovative video program presents segments on key topics in college success, produced by the award-winning educational team at CNN. Perfect for "lecture launchers," these tapes are updated on a yearly basis.

- **Your College Experience: Strategies for Success Video Series** This 12-part video is designed to teach and stimulate lively group discussions. Based on the nationally acclaimed University 101 freshman seminar course directed by John Gardner and the University of South Carolina.

- **A World of Diversity** A powerful two-video set on communication and conflict resolution between cultures. Reviewed by African-American, Asian-American, Latino-American and other multicultural scholars for language authenticity and content accuracy.

- **Wadsworth Study Skills Videos** *Volume 1: Improving Your Grades* features students talking to students and involves viewers in the issues that contribute to their success. It is divided into five parts designed to help students get what they want out of college: Choosing an Approach to Learning, Making Decisions About Your Time,

Learning in Your Classes, Making Sense of Textbooks and Taking Tests. *Volume 2: Notetaking*, features a series of college lectures which provide students with the opportunity to practice their notetaking skills and instructors with the opportunity to assess student skills.

- **Wadsworth College Success Video Series** An extensive selection of videos from Films for the Humanities on stress management, reading improvement, time management, healthful eating and nutrition, substance abuse prevention, AIDS, maximizing mental performance, and many others.

INTERNET RESOURCES

- **InfoTrac College Edition** Designed to help your students make the best of the Internet, Wadsworth's *exclusive* InfoTrac College Edition provides them access to full-length articles from more than 700 scholarly and popular periodicals, updated daily. Four-month subscription free to adopting instructors.

- **Thomson World Class Course** The easy and effective way to create your own dynamic web site! Post your course information, office hours, lesson information, assignments, sample tests and links to web content, including student enrichment materials from Wadsworth. Updates are quick and easy and customer support is available 24 hours a day, seven days a week. More information is available at http://www.worldclasslearning.com.

- **Success Online** http://www.success.wadsworth.com
  This new Web service provides current and helpful professional resources including:

  - Training information for instructors of new and established college success courses

  - Faculty Forum for sharing ideas with your colleagues around the country

  - Course Tools to easily create a Website for your own course

  - InfoTrac College Edition—online access to more than 700 popular and scholarly periodicals, updated daily

- Online Instructor's Manuals and Power-Point slides
- The ability to create your own custom textbook online, by selecting individual chapters or sections from Wadsworth texts and combining them with your own campus materials
- Additional student resources

■ **College Success Internet-at-a-Glance** This handy one-page laminated pocket reference for students has a host of URL addresses related to college success—to give your students a guided tour of the Internet! Available free when packaged with many Wadsworth texts.

■ **College Success Guide to the Internet** Written especially for college success students, this practical guide includes step-by-step instructions and tips for learning to use the Internet and a substantial collection of sites grouped by key topics discussed in the college success course, such as health issues, study skills, time management, test taking and more.

■ **AT&T WorldNet Service** Get your students on the Internet with AT&T for a special low rate!

TIME MANAGEMENT RESOURCES

■ **Franklin-Covey Day Planner, Collegiate Edition** This is the ultimate daily planner to help students manage their college and professional careers! Includes a training audiotape for students that explains time management principles and how to use the planner. Available at an *exclusively* low price when packaged with Wadsworth College Success texts.

■ **College Life Calendar** This Windows™ program allows students to create and print their own personal calendar, customized to their class, work and vacation schedules. Available free when packaged with new copies of any Wadsworth College Success text.

Acknowledgments

Two names are on the front of this book, but there are a great many other talented people whose efforts helped to strengthen our own.

Foremost among the staff of Wadsworth Publishing Company were Karen Allanson, Susan Badger, Rob Zwettler, Lauren Larsen, Jennie Burger, and Godwin Chu, who did a terrific job of supporting us. In addition, we are deeply grateful to Christal Niederer and others in the production, permissions, and design departments: Pat Brewer, Kathy Carsen, Bob Kauser, Stephen Rapley, and Barbara Britton.

Outside of Wadsworth, we were ably assisted by a community of top-drawer publishing professionals. Directing the production of the entire enterprise was Stacey Sawyer—Brian's wife and an author herself, and thus fully equipped to understand authors' travails. Stacey, once again you've pulled a book out under challenging deadlines, and once again we're in your debt. Thanks for everything!

We also were extremely fortunate to be able to get the services of Seventeenth Street Studios and Lorrie Fink and Richard Whitaker, who came up with the inviting cover and also handled the composition and art preparation, and we greatly appreciate their efforts. In addition, we wish to thank copyeditor Rick Reser, proofreader Martha Ghent, and indexer James Minkin.

Carl Wahlstrom would like to acknowledge the support and encouragement of many friends and associates, including and most importantly his best friend and wife, Nancy, for her continued support, patience, and understanding; Don Green for his tremendous support, suggestions, and direct input; Glenn DuBois for his caring about this project and student success; Meredith Altman, Charley Boyd, and Brenda Beal for encouragement and being part of the team; Stuart Steiner for his continued support; and Pamella Schmitt for helping with information on financial aid. Kudos once again go to Michael Garrett, whose photographic help has helped to make this book once again a student-centered resource. Special thanks are due to the tremendous help from the faculty and staff at Rochester Institute of Technology, including J. Wixson Smith, Latty Goodwin, Maureen Berry, Enid Stevenson, Gail Gucker, Kris Mook, Jackie Czamske, Lorna Mittelman, Jo Cone, Ann Gleason, Audrey Debye, and Dottie Hicks. Carl would also like to thank all his friends and associates in the New York College Learning Skills Association. Last, but surely not least, he would like to express his gratitude to his students for providing him with a source of energy and warmth to help facilitate their growth and learning.

ACKNOWLEDGMENT OF REVIEWERS We are grateful to the following reviewers for their consultations and for their comments on drafts of the manuscript:

■ SECOND EDITION REVIEWERS

Britt J. Andreatta, University of California—Santa Barbara

Glenda A. Belote, Florida International University

Pamela J. Brown, Asheville Buncombe Technical Community College

Stephen J. Clarson, University of Cincinnati

Regina Grantham, State University of New York—Cortland

Lucinda Hawes, Tri-State Business Institute

Jeanne L. Higbee, The University of Georgia

Patricia A. Malinowski, Finger Lakes Community College

Merdis J. McCarter, Winston-Salem State University

Rosemary O'Grady, Trident Technical College

Alicia Pieper, Kent State University

Donna M. Smith, The University of Findlay

Joyce W. Twing, Vermont Technical College

■ FIRST EDITION REVIEWERS

David M. DeFrain, Central Missouri State University

Mary Annette Edwards, Trident Technical College

Margaret Ann Maricle, Cuesta College

Donna S. Sharpe, Bellevue Community College

Lester Tanaka, Community College of Southern Nevada

Pat Zeller, Defiance College

WE WANT TO HEAR FROM YOU! We welcome your response to this book, for we are truly trying to make it as useful as possible. Write to us in care of Editor, College Success, Wadsworth Publishing Company, 10 Davis Drive, Belmont, CA 94002 (fax: 1-800-522-4923). Or contact us directly at the following:

Carl Wahlstrom
Genesee Community College
One College Road
Batavia, NY 14020
Phone: 716-343-0055
Fax: 716-343-0433
e-mail: cmwahlstrom@sunygenesee.cc.ny.us
Wadsworth/ITP voice mail:
1-800-876-2350 ext. 339

Brian K. Williams
POB 10006, 771 Randall Avenue
Incline Village, NV 89450
Phone: 702-832-7336
Fax: 702-832-3026
e-mail: briankw@mindspring.com
Wadsworth/ITP voice mail:
1-800-876-2350 ext. 858

About the Authors

CARL WAHLSTROM is Professor of Intermediate Studies and Sociology at Genesee Community College, Batavia, New York. He has been the recipient of the State University of New York Chancellor's Award for Excellence in Teaching, the National Freshman Advocate Award, and several other teaching honors. He is past president of the New York College Learning Skills Association and a member of the State University of New York College Transition Course Development Council. He is an active presenter and educational consultant at the national, state, and local level.

Besides developing and teaching First-Year Experience courses, he has taught courses in human development, learning strategy, sociology, psychology, and human relations. He has a B.S. in Sociology and an M.S. Ed. in Counselor Education from SUNY Brockport and an M.A. in Sociology from the University of Bridgeport.

He lives with his wife, Nancy, an employee benefits consultant, in the Finger Lakes area of New York. He enjoys running, skiing, tennis, boating, mountain biking, karate, motorcycling, music, travel, and getting together with friends and students.

BRIAN K. WILLIAMS has a B.A. in English and M.A. in Communication from Stanford University. He has been Managing Editor for college textbook publisher Harper & Row/Canfield Press in San Francisco; Editor in Chief for trade book publisher J. P. Tarcher in Los Angeles; Publications & Communications Manager for the University of California, Systemwide Administration, in Berkeley; and an independent writer and book producer based in San Francisco and in Incline Village (Lake Tahoe), Nevada.

He has co-authored 17 books, including such best-selling college texts as *Computers and Data Processing* with H. L. Capron, *Microcomputing: Annual Edition* with Tim and Linda O'Leary, *Invitation to Health* with Dianne Hales, and *Using Information Technology* with Stacey Sawyer and Sarah Hutchinson.

He is married to author/editor and book producer Stacey Sawyer, and the two have a passion for travel and for experimenting with various cuisines. He enjoys reading four daily newspapers and numerous magazines and books, hiking in the Sierra, playing blues on the guitar, and getting together with his family, including two grown children, Sylvia and Kirk.

Brief Contents

Detailed Contents

5 RECALL & READING

6 MANAGING LECTURES

7 EXAMS

8 WRITING & SPEAKING

9 RESOURCES & MONEY

10 DIVERSITY & DIFFERENCES

I

Academic Success Strategies

Developing Staying Power for Lifetime Success

Nothing Takes the Place of Persistence

IN THIS CHAPTER This chapter considers some of the changes you will face in college:

- **The chief characteristic of college:** High school is a *structured* environment, college is more *unstructured*. College offers more freedom but also requires more responsibility—more *staying power*.

- **The "why" of college and your values:** Why are you here? Your values, which have three characteristics, affect your reasons for going to college.

- **The fears of college:** What are your fears about college? They are probably mostly the same fears everyone else has, such as flunking out.

- **How college can better your life:** Compared to high-school graduates, college graduates usually make more money. They also experience gratifying personal growth during college. In addition, they probably have a better chance to discover what makes them happy. The skills that make you successful in college can make you successful in your career.

- **The strengths that give you staying power:** You bring certain strengths that will give you the persistence to stay in college.

- **Life goals and college goals:** There are six steps for translating your life goals into college goals and daily tasks.

I wish I had the opportunity to talk with you personally.

I wish that you and I could sit down together and discuss what your hopes, concerns, and expectations are for college, as I've been able to do with other first-year students.

I teach a college-success course called *Transitions: The First-Year Experience* at a college in upstate New York, and I've been fortunate enough to have gotten to know a lot of students, including some probably much like you. I've taught and talked with students of both genders and of practically every age, race, religion, economic level, and physical ability. I've worked with foreign students of several different nationalities. I've taught inmates in nearby prisons. I've instructed high-school teachers, who in turn have passed on college-success techniques to their students. So, I wish that you and I could also get together and discuss what's on your mind about college.

However, a book is pretty much a one-way street. In this book, which I've cowritten with Brian Williams, I get to communicate with you, but you can't immediately communicate back as you would in conversation.

Fortunately, there are two ways around this:

■ ***This is an "interactive" book that you can use to gain important information about yourself:*** By "interactive" I mean that the book is not meant to be read passively, like a novel. Rather, it is designed so that you can *participate* in it and get feedback—as if you were sitting down with another person.

■ ***You have someone else to help you:*** This book can be used in a class on how to get the most out of college or other forms of higher education. That class, of course, is taught by an instructor. He or she is able to give you assistance that this book cannot.

So maybe we can't sit down and talk face to face. But we can try for the next best thing—a dialogue that *you* control through these pages.

The Chief Characteristic of College & the Importance of Staying Power

PREVIEW & REVIEW Each "Preview & Review" in this book gives you a brief overview of the information discussed in the section that follows. You can use it again as a review to test your knowledge. This is the first one.

Throughout life, one goes through stages of development—college being one of them—that require different behaviors and responsibilities and produce different stresses. First-year students often have to learn that college is not the same as high school. High school is a structured environment, offering less freedom but requiring less responsibility. College is a more unstructured environment, offering more freedom but in turn requiring more responsibility. The chief characteristic of college is that more is required of you. Thus, the secret to making it through college is staying power.

Throughout life most of us go through stages of development that represent major changes. We go from childhood to adolescence, to young adulthood, to middle age, and to old age. We go from grade school to middle school to high school to college or other forms of higher education. These changes of status are marked by a ***rite of passage,*** **some kind of associated ritual.** Sometimes the change is observed formally, as with a graduation ceremony, a first communion, a bar or bas mitzvah, a debutante ball. Sometimes it is observed informally, as in buying one's first razor or lipstick. Such changes continue throughout life. Some changes represent gains: getting one's own apartment or house, getting a job, getting a promotion, perhaps getting married, perhaps having children. Others represent losses: perhaps losing a job, perhaps getting divorced, and so on. The point is, *all such changes require us to take on new behaviors and new responsibilities.* They generate new stresses even as they open new doors.

Going to college is another such rite of passage. It will likely require you to act differently and could inject new kinds of tensions into your life. Yet it can provide a wealth of experiences and benefits you'll always be glad you had.

HOW HIGHER EDUCATION DIFFERS FROM HIGH SCHOOL. What kinds of changes and tensions arise during the rite of passage known as college? Here's one example: I have observed—and other college instructors have frequently told me—that many first-year students have one overriding difficulty in common. This difficulty is: *getting used to the fact that college is not high school.*

High school is required of all students. College is not.

High school has lots of rules. College has fewer rules.

High schools have homerooms. Colleges don't.

GROUP ACTIVITY #1.1

YOUR RITES OF PASSAGE

Some of the most powerful learning occurs during small-group discussion and projects. (A small group consists of about three to six students.) Thus, this book offers frequent suggestions for group activities. Here's the first one:

In a small group, you and others take turns describing rites of passage you have been through. (Examples: changing from a child to an adolescent, getting married, earning your first paycheck.) A *rite of passage* involves physical or emotional changes in your life, changes in how others view you, new behaviors you take on, and new responsibilities. It is often accompanied by stress. One person in your group, acting as recorder or secretary, should make a list of the different rites of passage, then copy the list onto the classroom blackboard.

With the whole class, discuss the lists developed by each group. What are the similarities? the differences? Were any possibilities overlooked? What are different ways of dealing with rites of passage (anger, avoidance, feelings of fight-or-flight, and so on)? Which of these ways are most appropriate?

In high school, you may have had the same daily class schedule. In college, the schedule can vary every day.

In high school, textbooks are given to you. In college, you have to buy your own.

In high school, teachers take class attendance. In college, instructors often do not.

High schools require a doctor's note saying you were ill if you miss a class. Colleges don't usually require this.

High schools emphasize teachers teaching. Colleges emphasize learners learning.

Often high-school students find they don't spend much time on homework. Most college students find they have to devote *a lot* of time to studying.

High schools are *structured environments:* they allow less freedom, but they make fewer demands and hence require less responsibility. Colleges are *unstructured environments:* they allow you much more freedom, but they make many more demands and hence require more responsibility.

The chief characteristic of college, therefore, is that MORE IS REQUIRED OF YOU.

THE IMPORTANCE OF STAYING POWER. If more is required of you in college than was in high school, what is going to pull you through? One important secret to college success is developing . . . *STAYING POWER.* Staying power is personal commitment, focus, persistence.

As the title page of this book states, the three paths to success in college are:

- Developing staying power

- Becoming a mindful learner and thinker

- Being able to use information technology

Mindful learning and thinking is discussed in Chapter 2, information technology in Chapter 3. Here let's talk about staying power, otherwise known as *perseverance* or *persistence.*

"Nothing takes the place of persistence," President Calvin Coolidge stated. "Talent will not. Nothing is more common than unsuccessful people with talent. Genius will not. Unrewarded genius is almost a proverb. Education will not. The world is full of educated derelicts. Persistence alone has solved and always will solve the problems of the human race."

Forget that Coolidge wasn't one of the greatest American presidents. His statement is probably still true: *Nothing takes the place of persistence.*

The importance of your ability to stay the course, to persevere, to hang on when the going gets tough, cannot be underestimated. If you had a less than privileged background, or went to a substandard high school, or have to juggle a job and children along with going to school, that's unfortunate. But the world does not reward those who wail and bemoan their fate. Others also have

those problems and still manage to get through school.

Having the quality of persistence, of staying power, will pay off not only in college but probably all the rest of your life. Consider the conclusions of a 1998 study of 1,000 U.S. executives by a human resources consulting firm, as reported by *Fortune* magazine columnist Anne Fisher. It seems, says Fisher, that "people who do the serious hiring in companies these days are desperate— and no, that's not too strong a word— for candidates with two traits: (1) A talent for problem solving. By which they mean: If I give you a Serious Situation to fix, can you figure it out? . . . And (2) conscientiousness. That is, do you know what a deadline is, and will you meet it? . . . Will you try to do a good job even when you're having a bad day?"[1]

Problem solving is an aspect of mindfulness, as we'll discuss. Conscientiousness is an aspect of staying power. Problem solving and conscientiousness were selected by the executives more than twice as often as any other quality, although "open to new ideas," "versatile," and "ability to handle stress" all ranked pretty high, too. All of these qualities are discussed in this book.

MOTIVATION. What is going to give you staying power? That comes down to your motivation for going to college. "Motivation depends not only on what you want to do," says a Columbia University psychiatry professor, "but what you think you'll have to *give up* to do it."[2]

Going to college means giving up some things. Some recreational activities, for instance. Or pay from a full-time job. Or time with your friends or family. Is college worth it? The extent to which you can answer yes indicates the strength of your motivation.

Your motivation is the spark plug that makes everything else happen. A college is not a jail. You can walk away from it at any time. And no doubt there will be times when you will *want* to. So what, ultimately, is going to make you determined not only to stay in but to do your best while you're there? The answer depends on how you deal with two important questions:

1. *Why are you here?*
2. *What is your fear?*

Why Are You Here? Values & Your Reasons for College

PREVIEW & REVIEW Your reasons for going to college reflect your values. Values, the truest expression of who you are, are principles by which you lead your life. A value has three characteristics: (1) It is an important attitude. (2) It is a matter on which you take action. (3) It should be consciously chosen.

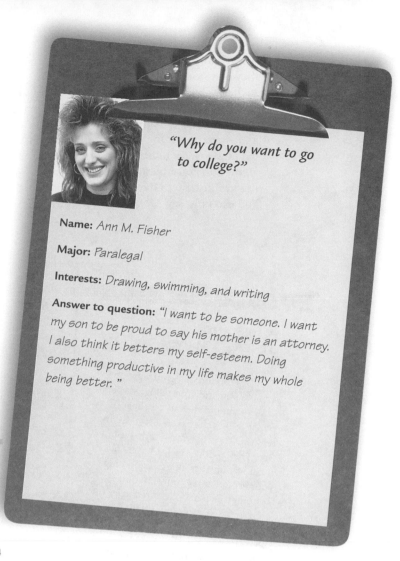

"Why do you want to go to college?"

Name: *Ann M. Fisher*

Major: *Paralegal*

Interests: *Drawing, swimming, and writing*

Answer to question: *"I want to be someone. I want my son to be proud to say his mother is an attorney. I also think it betters my self-esteem. Doing something productive in my life makes my whole being better."*

Being in college, some students have told me, makes them feel as though they exist in suspension, postponing real life.

But life cannot be postponed. It is lived today—not held off until the week-end, or vacations, or graduation. Or until you're in a relationship or settled in a career. Or until the children leave home or you retire.

Real life starts when you open your eyes in the morning, when you decide—that is, choose—what you will do today. And what you choose to do reflects your values.

WHAT VALUES ARE. Your values are the truest expression of who you are. **A *value* is a principle by which you lead your life. It is an important belief or attitude that you think ought to be (or ought not to be). Moreover, it is a belief that you feel strongly enough about to take action on and that has been consciously chosen.**

There are three important parts here:

1. *A value is an important attitude:* A value is an important attitude or belief that you hold. Examples: "College should help me get a good job." "Fairness means hiring according to ability, not family back-

ground." "Murder is wrong except in self-defense." "It's worth trying my hardest to get an 'A.'" ("Chocolate is better than vanilla" is a preference, generally not a value.)

2. *A value is a matter on which you take action:* You can *think* whatever you want, but if you don't back up your thought with some sort of action, it cannot be considered a value. If you really think it's wrong to cheat on an exam, then it's wrong for you to cheat on an exam. If you do, in fact, cheat, then your attitude that cheating is wrong is, for all practical purposes, not really a value.

3. *A value should be consciously chosen:* Values are not very strong if they are not truly your own. Many first-year students hold ideas or opinions received from their

parents or friends—ideas about which they may not have given much thought, such as religious beliefs. Or the belief that how much money you make is the main measure of happiness in life. For an idea to be a value rather than just a belief, you have to have thought enough about it to consider accepting or rejecting it. You have to have made it yours. You can't just say, "That's the way it is."

GROUP ACTIVITY #1.2

YOURS AND OTHERS' VALUES

Before breaking into groups, you and your fellow students should take out a sheet of paper and each make a list of 20 matters you consider important—your values. Then reduce the list to the five most important values. On joining your group (three to five people), appoint one person as a recorder or secretary. Go through and discuss your lists and agree (if possible) on what the top five values are for the group. The secretary should then write this list on the classroom blackboard.

In class discussion, consider the similarities and differences in values among the groups. How do your personal values compare to those on the group lists? Did you find it difficult in your group to come to agreement, and, if so, why?

If you had only a month or year to live, how would that fact influence your choices?

YOUR VALUES ABOUT COLLEGE. What kind of values do you hold? This is not a frivolous question, since values have a great bearing on how you view the whole subject of higher education. To see how your values affected your actions in going to college, try Personal Exploration #1.1[3] *(opposite page).*

What Is Your Fear? Anxiety as a Positive & Negative Motivator

PREVIEW & REVIEW Anxiety can motivate you to do well, but too much anxiety can motivate you to withdraw from competition. It's important to identify fears about higher education so they won't become motivators for dropping out. Common fears include fear of flunking out, of the pressure, of loneliness, of not finding one's way around, of running out of money.

Students who drop out of college sometimes do so for financial reasons but also for more personal ones. They include (1) academic underpreparedness, (2) academic overpreparedness, (3) feeling that college isn't useful, (4) unrealistic expectations about college, (5) uncertainty about major or career, and (6) lack of a personal support system.

As you know from playing video games or sports, a certain amount of anxiety can actually motivate you to accomplish positive results. Anxiety about losing a game (or the will to win) makes you alert, focuses the mind, and induces you to try and do well. Similarly, some fear of losing the game of higher education can motivate you to do your best.

YOUR VALUES ABOUT HIGHER EDUCATION

Take at least 10–15 minutes for this activity. The purpose is to see how your values and family background affected your actions in going to college.

■ A. FAMILY MATTERS

1. College is not a tradition in my family. (Family includes not only parents and grandparents or guardians but also uncles, aunts, and brothers and sisters.)

   ——— True ——— False
   ——— Somewhat true

2. My father/guardian completed (check one): ——— grade school ——— high school ——— college ——— graduate or professional school ——— other (identify)
   _____
   _____

3. My father/guardian (check one):
   ——— supports
   ——— does not support
   my decision to go to this college.

4. My mother/guardian completed (check one): ——— grade school ——— high school ——— college ——— graduate or professional school ——— other (identify)
   _____
   _____

5. My mother/guardian (check one):
   ——— supports
   ——— does not support
   my decision to go to this college.

6. My spouse/boyfriend/girlfriend (check one):
   ——— supports
   ——— does not support
   my decision to go to this college.

7. My spouse/boyfriend/girlfriend completed (check one):
   ——— grade school
   ——— high school ——— college
   ——— graduate or professional school ——— other (identify)
   _____
   _____

■ B. COLLEGE & FREE CHOICE

1. Regarding the influence of my parents/guardians or others, I'd say my going to college was the following (check one): (a) ——— It was mainly my decision but a little bit others' decision. (b) ——— It was mainly others' decision but a little bit my decision. (c) ——— It was about equally both mine and others' decisions. (d) ——— It was never talked about; it was just assumed I'd go.

2. If I wasn't going to college, I would do the following instead:
   _____
   _____
   _____
   _____
   _____
   _____
   _____
   _____

3. If I had the money and could do anything I wanted to this year, I would rather be doing the following:
   _____
   _____
   _____
   _____
   _____
   _____
   _____
   _____
   _____

4. Looking over my last three responses, I feel that I am going to college because of the following (check one): (a) ——— I am choosing to go and want to go. (b) ——— I don't really choose to go and don't really want to go, but others want me to. (c) ——— I don't feel I have a choice, but I want to go anyway. (d) ——— I don't know, I'm confused.

■ C. PUBLIC REASONS, PERSONAL REASONS

1. When people ask me why I chose this college, I tell them the following. (List three or four reasons.)
   a. _____
   _____
   b. _____
   _____
   c. _____
   _____
   d. _____
   _____

2. When people ask me why I am interested in a particular major or field of study (or why I am undecided), I tell them the following. (List three or four reasons.)
   a. _____
   _____
   b. _____
   _____
   c. _____
   _____
   d. _____
   _____

3. The reasons I chose (if I chose) the particular major or field of study mentioned in C.2 that I *don't* tell people about are as follows. (Examples: "My parents want me to do it." "I'm afraid I lack the talent or brains to do something else I might like better." "It's a matter of conscience.")
   a. _____
   _____
   b. _____
   _____

(continued on next page)

D. REASONS FOR GOING TO COLLEGE

The following is a list of reasons for attending college. Rank them in order of importance to you, with 1 meaning most important, 2 of secondary importance, 3 third in importance, and so on.
My reasons for going to college are . . .

a. ___ To please my parents.

b. ___ To have fun.

c. ___ To get a degree.

d. ___ To prepare for a career.

e. ___ To make friends.

f. ___ To better support my family/ help my children.

g. ___ To avoid having to work for a while.

h. ___ To find a girlfriend/ boyfriend/mate.

i. ___ To raise my economic level/ get a better job.

j. ___ To explore new ideas and experiences.

k. ___ To acquire knowledge.

l. ___ To gain maturity.

m. ___ To learn how to solve problems.

n. ___ To learn how to learn.

o. ___ To gain prestige.

p. ___ To become a better citizen.

E. IDENTIFYING YOUR VALUES REGARDING HIGHER EDUCATION

Look back over this Personal Exploration. Identify the top three values that influenced your decision to attend the college you are in. Write a brief essay in the following space. In the essay explain how each of the three values led you to take a particular kind of action in choosing the present college.

GROUP ACTIVITY OPTION

In a small group (three to five people), discuss some of the results of Personal Exploration #1.1. What role did your family or people close to you have in your decision to go to college? What would you do (or rather do, if you had the money) if you weren't going to college? What top three values influenced you to go to college? Discuss also your thoughts about "being the best" in the primary things you do. How do you feel about doing your "personal best" in college? What do you want to be? How would you like college to help you get there?

Too much anxiety, however, can motivate you to perform negatively. That is, you may be so overwhelmed by fear that you want to withdraw from the competition. This can and does happen to some college students. But it need not happen to you.

IDENTIFYING YOUR FEARS. Concerns and fears about higher education are actually normal. However, it's important to identify them so that you can take steps to deal with them. Take a few minutes to stop at this point and try Personal Exploration #1.2 *(opposite page).* Do this before you read the next section.

GOING TO COLLEGE: WHAT IS YOUR FEAR?

Identifying your fears about college is the first step in fighting them.

■ WHAT TO DO

For each of the following statements, circle the number below corresponding to how much you agree or disagree:

1 = strongly disagree
2 = somewhat disagree
3 = neither disagree nor agree
4 = somewhat agree
5 = strongly agree

I am afraid that . . .

1. College will be too difficult for me.　　　1 2 3 4 5

2. I will get homesick.　1 2 3 4 5

3. I might flunk out.　1 2 3 4 5

4. I won't be able to handle the amount of school work.　　1 2 3 4 5

5. My study habits won't be good enough to succeed.　1 2 3 4 5

6. I'll get lost on campus.　　1 2 3 4 5

7. I'll be a disappointment to people important to me, such as my parents, family, or children.
　　1 2 3 4 5

8. I won't have enough money and will have to drop out.
　　1 2 3 4 5

9. I won't be able to handle working and/or family responsibilities and college at the same time.
　　1 2 3 4 5

10. I will get depressed.　1 2 3 4 5

11. I won't be able to manage my time being on my own.
　　1 2 3 4 5

12. I'll oversleep or otherwise won't be able to get to class on time.
　　1 2 3 4 5

13. I won't be able to maintain the grade average I want.　1 2 3 4 5

14. The college will find out that I'm basically incompetent and will kick me out.　　1 2 3 4 5

15. I won't be able to compete with other students.　　1 2 3 4 5

16. I won't make any friends.
　　1 2 3 4 5

17. I won't be able to overcome my shyness.　　1 2 3 4 5

18. I'll have problems with my roommates.　　1 2 3 4 5

19. I won't be able to handle writing/spelling or math.
　　1 2 3 4 5

20. My professors will find out I'm inadequate.　　1 2 3 4 5

21. There will be no one to help me.
　　1 2 3 4 5

22. I'll choose the wrong major.
　　1 2 3 4 5

23. I'll have to cheat in order to survive the tough academic environment.　　1 2 3 4 5

24. My family or my job will complicate things, and I won't be able to keep up.　　1 2 3 4 5

25. Other (write in):

_____
_____
_____
_____
_____
_____

　　1 2 3 4 5

Add the number of points: _____

■ MEANING OF YOUR SCORE

100–125 *High*

You are very fearful or very concerned about your college experience. Although these concerns are not unusual, it would be a good idea to check into some college resources to assist you in dealing with your worries. Such resources include career and personal counseling, the college's learning center, and the financial aid office.

75–99 *Average*

You are somewhat fearful or somewhat concerned about your college experience. Welcome! Join the crowd! Your concerns are typical and are shared by the majority of college students. To assist you in addressing these issues, you may wish to identify the appropriate college resources—counseling center, learning center, financial aid—for assistance.

74 or less *Low*

You have few fears, perhaps are even laid back. Even so, it would be useful to identify college support services (such as counseling or learning center) in case you ever need them.

■ INTERPRETATION

We all tend to think that any one worry we have is unique, that it is ours alone, that no one else ever experiences it with the intensity that we do. This is not true! Indeed, the fears and concerns listed above are quite common. So also is the reluctance to seek help, to get support. But seeking support is probably what will help you overcome the fear. Resources such as counseling and financial aid are described in Chapter 9.

In a small group each student should discuss his or her top three concerns (unless they're considered too private to be shared), and others in the group should state whether they are experiencing the same concern. In addition, ask every person in the group to suggest (as tactfully as possible) a possible way to deal with each concern discussed.

GROUP ACTIVITY #1.3

YOUR GREATEST CONCERNS & ANXIETIES ABOUT COLLEGE

Take a few minutes to list, on a half sheet of paper or 3 × 5 card, your greatest concerns and anxieties about college. (If you wish, you can also list other concerns you have that your attendance at college may affect or aggravate.) Important: Don't sign your name to the card.

The instructor will collect your and other students' lists and shuffle them. Students will be called upon to come to the front of the class, pick a list at random, and copy the material on the blackboard. One area of the board should be saved; the instructor will write common themes there.

What are common themes or overlapping issues? What are your reactions to the most common themes? What techniques or resources do you have to cope with these concerns?

COMMON FEARS OF COLLEGE STUDENTS. What are common fears of college students?[4,5] They include the following:

- Fear of flunking out—this may be the biggest.

- Fear of not being able to manage everything.

- Fear of the pressure—of the work and responsibility, of not being able to compete.

- Fear of loneliness, of not finding supportive friends.

- Fear of not finding one's way around.

- Fear of running out of money.

Then there are all the specific fears—about being on one's own, about not having a good time, even about oversleeping. Many students express concerns about not being able to balance their college work and their family and/or job responsibilities.

WHY DO SOME PEOPLE HAVE TROUBLE WITH HIGHER EDUCATION? *Reality check:* Since we're discussing principal student fears, what do you think the dropout rate is for first-year college students? That is, what percentage fail to return to the same college the second year?

Answer: More than one in four students (26.9%), according to a report of 2,564 colleges. For community colleges, 44.3% of first-year students did not return the second year.[6]

Incidentally, it's important to know that, of first-year students who quit during school (rather than between terms), half drop out in the first six weeks. Thus, you should be aware that *the first two to six weeks can be a critical time of adjustment.*

Now, this doesn't mean that all first-year dropouts *flunk* out. Some simply transfer to another college. Others quit because of lack of money. Still, one reason for the great number of dropouts, it is speculated, is that college enrollment has skyrocketed and so there are "more people going to college who aren't prepared academically to deal with the work."[7]

Aside from lack of money, people who end up leaving school usually do so for the following reasons:[8]

- ***They are underprepared academically, which leads to frustration:*** Some students are underprepared—in reading, writing, and math skills, for instance—and find themselves in college courses that are too difficult for them. (Then they may be angry and resentful because they think someone has somehow set them up.) *It's important to know that your college offers all kinds of academic support services—for example, math tutoring. But it's best not to wait until you're in trouble to find them.*

If you sense even in the first couple of weeks of your first term that you're slipping, I recommend telling the instructor of the class for which you are reading this book. Or go to the student counseling center. Be honest also about telling your academic advisor if you're worried about being in over your head.

■ ***They are overprepared academically, which leads to boredom:*** Some first-year students complain that their courses repeat work they already covered in high school. This is why good academic advising by a counselor is important. Don't do as I did and take first-year chemistry in college after already taking it in high school (unless your academic advisor recommends it).

■ ***They perceive college as being not useful:*** First-year students who don't think their college work will be useful beyond the classroom can be high candidates for dropping out. This may be particularly so for first-year students who have not chosen a major. However, it also happens to those who do have career goals but who consider general-education requirements (normally a big part of the first year) irrelevant. It's important, then, to nail down the reasons *why* you're in college.

■ ***They have unrealistic expectations about college:*** Some first-year students don't have realistic expectations about themselves and college. For example, some come to campus expecting great things to happen without much investment on their part. Thus, they devote little effort to making higher education work for them.

■ ***They are uncertain about their major or career:*** It's okay to come into college undecided about your major or a career. Indeed, college is a great place to explore these possibilities. Even so, you should be aware that indecision about these important goals is a reason why some students drop out.

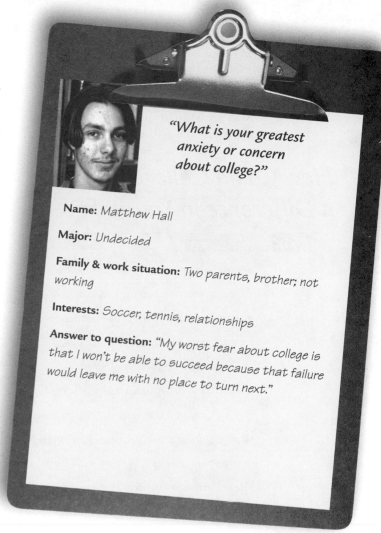

"What is your greatest anxiety or concern about college?"

Name: Matthew Hall

Major: Undecided

Family & work situation: Two parents, brother; not working

Interests: Soccer, tennis, relationships

Answer to question: "My worst fear about college is that I won't be able to succeed because that failure would leave me with no place to turn next."

■ ***They don't have a personal support system:*** Most first-year students have to start from scratch building an on-campus personal support system. This means making friends with other students, counselors, and professors or otherwise finding support. This may take more effort on a commuter campus than on a residential campus. Nevertheless, whoever you are, a support system *is* available (as I describe in Chapter 9).

Still, some students have difficulty seeking out support. Students who become only weakly involved in the college experience may stay in their rooms all the time, leave campus every weekend, or miss classes frequently.

In general, all these difficulties can be boiled down to three matters: (1) motivation, (2) support, and (3) skills achievement. With the help of this book and this course, however, you can get beyond your fears and make college the success you want it to be.

Now let's consider how going to college could change your life for the better—the benefits it will produce that will help you get past your fears and keep on going for college success.

How Could College Make a Difference in Your Life?

PREVIEW & REVIEW   College graduates usually make more money, are more knowledgeable and competent, and experience more personal growth. These factors may contribute to an increase in happiness.

The four principal ways of imparting knowledge in college are via lectures, readings, writing, and laboratories. The learning skills you develop for these activities can be used not only to improve your grades but also to further your career in the work world.

Suppose you were to decide right now NOT to continue on in college. What would you be missing if you didn't finish? Let's take a look.

INCREASED INCOME. With the widespread competitive and technological changes of the last few years, it has become clear that the rewards go to those with skill and education. There is all kinds of supporting evidence. Some examples:

■ *The more education, the more income:* The more education people have, the higher their income, according to studies by Princeton University economists Orley Ashenfelter and Alan Kreuger. From grade school through graduate school, *every year spent in school adds 16% to the average person's lifetime earnings.* This means, for instance, that a community

college degree—traditionally thought of as a two-year degree, though many students take longer—can be expected to increase an individual's earnings by about *one-third*. A college bachelor's degree—what has in the past been considered a four-year degree—would increase them by almost *two-thirds*.[9]

■ *Widening gap:* "Well-educated and skilled workers are prospering," says Robert Reich, former U.S. Secretary of Labor, while "those without education or skills drift further and further from the economic mainstream."[10] The gap between high-school graduates and college graduates has widened. In 1979, for example, a male college graduate earned 49% more than a man with a high-school diploma. In 1992, the average male college graduate was earning 83% more than his high-school graduate counterpart. In 1970, a woman with a college degree earned 50% more than a woman who had a high-school diploma. In 1995, she earned 75% more.[11]

■ *Growth in employer demands:* In the last decade of the 20th century, jobs requiring college degrees were expected to grow 1.5% per year, according to the head of one economic advisory firm. For high-school diplomas, the demand was predicted to grow only 0.6% per year.[12]

■ *Lifetime earnings:* According to the U.S. Census Bureau, a high-school graduate can expect to earn $821,000 over the course of a working life. By contrast, a college graduate with a bachelor's degree can expect to earn $1.4 million. And a person with a professional degree can expect to receive more than $3 million.[13]

Of course, a college degree won't *guarantee* you higher earnings—we all know there are college-educated cab drivers out there. Still, it provides better odds than just a high-school diploma. Moreover, I suspect, going to college will probably help you develop flexibility, so that whatever happens in the job market you'll be better apt to land on your feet.

INCREASED PERSONAL DEVELOPMENT. Money, however, is not the only reason for going

to college. Do you envy those high-school friends who skipped college and went directly to work? Don't. They are missing some of the most significant experiences possible in life—those having to do with personal growth and change.

The very fact that college serves up unfamiliar challenges and pressures can help you develop better adjustment skills, such as those of time management. The competition of different values and ideas—religious, political, and so on—can help you evaluate, modify, and strengthen your belief system.

Some of the positive changes that studies show are characteristic of college graduates are as follows.[14]

- *Increase in knowledge, competence, and self-esteem:* The college experience can increase people's knowledge of content, as you might expect, extending their range of competencies and providing them with a greater range of work skills. It can also help them develop their reasoning abilities. Finally, it can increase their self-esteem.

- *Increase in personal range:* College can help people to develop their capacity for self-discovery and to widen their view of the world. They can become more tolerant, more independent, more appreciative of culture and art, more politically sophisticated, and more future-oriented. Finally, they often adopt better health habits, become better parents, and become better consumers and citizens.

INCREASED HAPPINESS. Is there a relationship between educational level and happiness? A lot depends on what is meant by happiness, which is hard to measure. Still, wealthy people tend to be happier than poor people, points out one psychologist. "Does that mean that money buys happiness," he asks, "or that happy people are likely to succeed at their jobs and become wealthy?"[15]

Whatever the case, better-educated people do tend to make more money, as we have seen. They also have the opportunity to explore their personal growth and development in a way that less-educated people cannot. This gives them a chance to discover what makes them happy.

HOW COLLEGE CAN IMPROVE YOUR CAREER SKILLS. How is knowledge transferred to you in college? Can you apply the methods of learning in college courses—whatever the subject—to help you be successful in your career *after* college? The answer is: Absolutely!

Although European and other systems of higher education operate somewhat differently, in the colleges and universities of North America most first-year students acquire knowledge in four principal ways: through lectures, reading, writing, and laboratories. Let's consider these.

- *Lectures:* Students attend lectures by instructors and are tested throughout the school term on how much they remember.

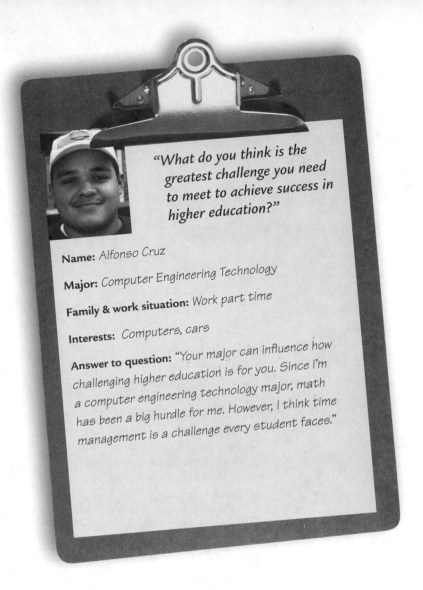

"What do you think is the greatest challenge you need to meet to achieve success in higher education?"

Name: Alfonso Cruz

Major: Computer Engineering Technology

Family & work situation: Work part time

Interests: Computers, cars

Answer to question: "Your major can influence how challenging higher education is for you. Since I'm a computer engineering technology major, math has been a big hurdle for me. However, I think time management is a challenge every student faces."

■ **Readings:** Students are given reading assignments in textbooks and other writings and are tested to see how much they recall. Quite often lectures and readings make up the only teaching methods in a course.

Relevance to your career: In the work world, comparable ways of communicating information are through reports, memos, letters, instruction manuals, newsletters, trade journals, and books. Here, too, the "test" will constitute how well you use the information to do your work.

■ **Writing:** Students are given assignments in which they are asked to research information and write it into a term paper. Generally, you need not recall this information for a test. However, it's important how you manage your time so that you can produce a good paper, which is usually an important part of the course grade.

Relevance to your career: In the work world, a research paper is called a report, memo, proposal, or written analysis. Police officers, nurses, salespeople, lawyers, teachers, and managers of all sorts all write reports. How well you pull together facts and present them can have a tremendous impact on how you influence other people and so are able to do your job.

■ **Laboratories:** Laboratories are practice sessions. You use knowledge gained from readings, and sometimes lectures, to practice using the material and you are graded on your progress. For example, in computer science or office technology you may take a lab that gives you hands-on instruction in word processing. In learning to speak Japanese, you may go to a lab to listen to, and practice repeating, language tapes. In chemistry, you may do experiments with various chemicals on a laboratory workbench.

Relevance to your career: In the world of work, your job itself is the laboratory, in which your promotions and career success depend on how well you pull together and practice everything you've learned about your work.

Relevance to your career: When you are out of school and go to work in the business or nonbusiness world, this method of imparting information will be called a "presentation" or a "meeting" or a "company training program." And the "test" will constitute how well you recall and handle the information in order to do your job. (Sometimes there's an actual test, as in government civil service, to see if you qualify for promotion. Lots of professionals—nurses, stockbrokers, accountants, doctors—also have to take periodic exams.)

There are also other instructional techniques. Instead of lectures, you may have *seminars,* or discussion groups, but you'll likely still be tested on what is said in them. Instead of readings, you may have to *watch films or slides or videotapes or listen to audiotapes,* on which you may be tested. Instead of term papers or laboratories, you may be assigned *projects.* For example, in psychology or geology, you may be asked to do a field trip and take notes. In music or drafting, you may be asked to create something. Still, most of these alternative methods of instruction make use of whatever skills you bring to bear in lectures, reading, writing, and laboratory work.

HOW LEARNING IN COLLEGE CAN HELP YOUR CAREER. I have pointed out that each of these instructional methods or situations has counterparts in the world of work. This is an important matter. Whenever you begin to think that whatever you're doing in college is irrelevant to real life—and I have no doubt you *will* think this from time to time (as I did in college)—remember that the *methods by which you learn can be important skills for success in the work environment.*

If you know how to take efficient notes of lectures, for example, you can do the same for meetings. If you know how to extract material from a textbook, you can do the same for a report. Moreover, these and other learning skills can be valuable all your life because they are often transferable skills between jobs, between industries, and between the for-profit (business) and nonprofit (education and government) sectors of the economy. They can also be valuable in nonwork areas, such as volunteer activities.

In sum: if you hone the skills for acquiring knowledge in college, these very same skills can serve you well in helping you live the way you want to live professionally and personally.

The Strengths That Give You Staying Power

PREVIEW & REVIEW Four qualities are helpful for giving one the persistence to achieve success in college—and in life: (1) sense of personal control and responsibility, (2) optimism, (3) creativity, and (4) ability to take psychological risks.

 o matter what your worries about college, you have certain qualities of character that will help you to succeed. In this section, we'll look at strengths that can be cultivated for college success.

Successful people have the following:

- Sense of personal control and responsibility
- Optimism
- Creativity
- Ability to take psychological risks

PERSONAL CONTROL & RESPONSIBILITY. How much personal control do you feel you have over your destiny? **The term *locus of control* refers to your beliefs about the relationship between your behavior and the occurrence of rewards and punishment.**

People are said to have either an external or an internal locus of control:

- *External:* Do you believe strongly in the influences of chance or fate or the power of others? **People who believe their rewards and punishments are controlled mainly by outside forces or other people are said to have an *external locus of control.***

- *Internal:* Do you believe that "I am the captain of my fate, the master of my soul"? **People who believe their rewards and punishments are due to their own behavior, character, or efforts are said to have an *internal locus of control.*** [16]

You may wish to try Personal Exploration #1.3 *(next page).*

WHO'S IN CHARGE HERE?

Are you in charge of your fate, or is a great deal of it influenced by outside forces? Answer the following questions to see where you stand.

1. Do you believe that most problems will solve themselves if you just don't fool with them?
   ❏ Yes ❏ No

2. Do you believe that you can stop yourself from catching a cold?
   ❏ Yes ❏ No

3. Are some people just born lucky?
   ❏ Yes ❏ No

4. Most of the time do you feel that getting good grades means a great deal to you? ❏ Yes ❏ No

5. Are you often blamed for things that just aren't your fault?
   ❏ Yes ❏ No

6. Do you believe that if somebody studies hard enough he or she can pass any subject?
   ❏ Yes ❏ No

7. Do you feel that most of the time it doesn't pay to try hard because things never turn out right anyway? ❏ Yes ❏ No

8. Do you feel that if things start out well in the morning, it's going to be a good day no matter what you do? ❏ Yes ❏ No

9. Do you feel that most of the time parents listen to what their children have to say?
   ❏ Yes ❏ No

10. Do you believe that wishing can make good things happen?
    ❏ Yes ❏ No

11. When you get punished, does it usually seem it's for no good reason at all? ❏ Yes ❏ No

12. Most of the time, do you find it hard to change a friend's opinion?
    ❏ Yes ❏ No

13. Do you think cheering more than luck helps a team win?
    ❏ Yes ❏ No

14. Did you feel that it was nearly impossible for you to change your parents' minds about anything?
    ❏ Yes ❏ No

15. Do you believe that parents should allow children to make most of their own decisions?
    ❏ Yes ❏ No

16. Do you feel that when you do something wrong, there's very little you can do to make it right?
    ❏ Yes ❏ No

17. Do you believe that most people are just born good at sports?
    ❏ Yes ❏ No

18. Are most other people your age stronger than you are?
    ❏ Yes ❏ No

19. Do you feel that one of the best ways to handle most problems is just not to think about them?
    ❏ Yes ❏ No

20. Do you feel that you have a lot of choice in deciding who your friends are? ❏ Yes ❏ No

21. If you find a four-leaf clover, do you believe that it might bring you good luck? ❏ Yes ❏ No

22. Did you often feel that whether or not you did your homework had much to do with the kind of grades you got? ❏ Yes ❏ No

23. Do you feel that when a person your age is angry with you, there's little you can do to stop him or her? ❏ Yes ❏ No

24. Have you ever had a good-luck charm? ❏ Yes ❏ No

25. Do you believe that whether or not people like you depends on how you act? ❏ Yes ❏ No

26. Did your parents usually help you if you asked them to?
    ❏ Yes ❏ No

27. Have you ever felt that when people were angry with you, it was usually for no reason at all?
    ❏ Yes ❏ No

28. Most of the time, do you feel that you can change what might happen tomorrow by what you do today? ❏ Yes ❏ No

29. Do you believe that when bad things are going to happen, they are just going to happen no matter what you try and do to stop them? ❏ Yes ❏ No

30. Do you think that people can get their own way if they just keep trying? ❏ Yes ❏ No

31. Most of the time, do you find it useless to try to get your own way at home? ❏ Yes ❏ No

32. Do you feel that when good things happen, they happen because of hard work? ❏ Yes ❏ No

33. Do you feel that when somebody your age wants to be your enemy, there's little you can do to change matters? ❏ Yes ❏ No

34. Do you feel it's easy to get friends to do what you want them to do?
    ❏ Yes ❏ No

35. Do you usually feel that you have little to say about what you get to eat at home? ❏ Yes ❏ No

36. Do you feel that when someone doesn't like you, there's little you can do about it? ❏ Yes ❏ No

37. Did you usually feel it was almost useless to try in school because most other children were just plain smarter than you were?
    ❏ Yes ❏ No

38. Are you the kind of person who believes that planning ahead makes things turn out better?
    ❏ Yes ❏ No

39. Most of the time, do you feel that you have little to say about what your family decides to do?
    ❏ Yes ❏ No

40. Do you think it's better to be smart than to be lucky?
    ❏ Yes ❏ No

(continued on opposite page)

▪ SCORING

Place a check mark to the right of each item in the key when your answer agrees with the answer that is shown. Add the check marks to determine your total score.

1. Yes ❑	2. No ❑	3. Yes ❑
4. No ❑	5. Yes ❑	6. No ❑
7. Yes ❑	8. Yes ❑	9. No ❑
10. Yes ❑	11. Yes ❑	12. Yes ❑
13. No ❑	14. Yes ❑	15. No ❑
16. Yes ❑	17. Yes ❑	18. Yes ❑
19. Yes ❑	20. No ❑	21. Yes ❑
22. No ❑	23. Yes ❑	24. Yes ❑
25. No ❑	26. No ❑	27. Yes ❑
28. No ❑	29. Yes ❑	30. No ❑
31. Yes ❑	32. No ❑	33. Yes ❑
34. No ❑	35. Yes ❑	36. Yes ❑
37. Yes ❑	38. No ❑	39. Yes ❑
40. No ❑		

Total score: _____

▪ INTERPRETATION

Low scorers (0–8):
Nearly one student in three receives a score of 0 to 8. These students largely see themselves as responsible for the rewards they obtain or do not obtain in life.

Average scorers (9–16):
Most students receive from 9 to 16 points. These students view themselves as partially in control of their lives. Perhaps they view themselves as in control academically but not socially, or vice versa.

High scorers (17–40):
Nearly 15% of students receive scores of 17 or higher. These students view life largely as a game of chance. They see success as a matter of luck or a product of the kindness of others.

What is *one area* in which you feel you can influence and control people and events? With others in a small group, discuss this area and the feelings of mastery and power it gives you. Discuss whether you think this control and influence could be applied to your academic work in college.

Studies have shown that people who have an internal locus of control—that is, low scores in the Personal Exploration—are able to achieve more in school.[17] They are also able to delay gratification, are more independent, and are better able to cope with various stresses.[18] Some people may have both an internal and external locus of control, depending on their situation. For instance, they may feel they can control their lives at home but not in the workplace.

OPTIMISM. "Mom, where are all the jerks today?" asks the young girl as she and her mother are driving along. "Oh," says the mother, slightly surprised, "they're only on the road when your father drives."

Therapist Alan McGinnis tells this story to make a point: "If you expect the world to be peopled with idiots and jerks, they start popping up."[19]

Are you an optimist, or are you what some people like to call a "realist" when they actually mean a pessimist? Perhaps optimism is related to matters of personal control. Pessimists may be overwhelmed by their problems, whereas optimists are challenged by them, according to McGinnis, author of *The Power of Optimism*.[20] "They think of themselves as problem-solvers, as troubleshooters," he says. This does not mean they see everything through rose-colored glasses. Rather they have several qualities that help them have a positive attitude while still remaining realistic and tough-minded. *(See ■ Panel 1.1.)*

CREATIVITY. The capacity for creativity and spontaneity, said psychologist Abraham Maslow, is an important attribute of the psychologically healthy person. This attribute is not limited to some supposed *artistic* class of people; it is built into all of us. <u>*Creativity*</u> **refers to the human capacity to express ourselves in original or imaginative ways.** It may also be thought of as the process of discovery. As Nobel Prize–winning biochemist Albert Szent-Györgyi expressed it, "Discovery consists of looking at the same thing as everyone else and thinking something different."[21]

Being creative means having to resist pressure to be in step with the world. It means looking for several answers, not the "one right answer," as is true of math problems. As Roger von Oech, founder of a creativity consulting company, puts it: "Life is ambiguous; there are many right answers—all depending on what you are looking for."[22]

It means forgetting about reaching a specific goal, because the creative

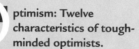

PANEL 1.1 ptimism: Twelve characteristics of tough-minded optimists.

OPTIMISTS . . .

1. Are seldom surprised by trouble.

2. Look for partial solutions.

3. Believe they have control over their future.

4. Allow for regular renewal.

5. Interrupt their negative trains of thought.

6. Heighten their powers of appreciation.

7. Use their imaginations to rehearse success.

8. Are cheerful even when they can't be happy.

9. Believe they have an almost unlimited capacity for stretching.

10. Build lots of love into their lives.

11. Like to swap good news.

12. Accept what cannot be changed.

process can't be forced. One should, in von Oech's phrase, think of the mind as "a compost heap, not a computer," and use a notebook to collect ideas.

We discuss creativity further in Chapter 2.

ABILITY TO TAKE PSYCHOLOGICAL RISKS.

What is risk taking? I am not endorsing the kind of risk taking (such as drug taking or fast driving) that might jeopardize your health. I'm only concerned with situations in which the main risk is to your pride. That is, where the main consequences of failure are personal embarrassment or disappointment. This kind of risk taking—having the courage to feel the fear and then proceeding anyway—is a requirement for psychological health.

Consider failure: none of us is immune to it. Some are shattered but bounce back quickly. Others take longer to recover, especially if the failure has changed our lives in a significant way. But what is failure, exactly? Carole Hyatt and Linda Gottlieb, authors of *When Smart People Fail,* point out that the word has two meanings:

■ *Failure can be an event:* First, "failure" is a term for an event, such as failing a test or not getting a part in a play or not making the team. This kind of failure you may not be able to do anything about.

■ *Failure can be a judgment about yourself:* Second, failure is a *judgment you make about yourself*—"so that 'failure' may also mean not living up to your own expectations."[23]

This kind of failure is a matter you can do something about. For instance, you can use your own inner voice—your "self-talk"—to put a different interpretation on the event that is more favorable to you. (For example, "I didn't get the part because I'm better suited to playing comedies than tragedies.")

One characteristic of many peak performers, according to psychologist Charles Garfield, is that they continually *reinvent* themselves. The late jazz musician Miles Davis, for example, constantly changed his musical direction in order to stay fresh and vital. Novelist James Michener took himself on a new adventure of travel and research with every book he wrote.[24] These are examples of psychological risk taking that lead toward success.

Setting College Goals from Life Goals

PREVIEW & REVIEW The six-step strategy called "Essentials for Time & Life Management" describes how to set daily tasks from life goals. The first step is to determine your ultimate goals.

We make decisions all the time. *Taking action* is making a decision. So is *not taking* action. There's nothing wrong with inaction and aimlessness, if that's what you want to do, but realize that aimlessness is a choice like any other. Most first-year students find out, however, that college works better if they have a program of aims—even if the aims are simply to try to find out what they want. The following pages tell you how to set up such a program.

ESSENTIALS FOR TIME & LIFE MANAGEMENT: SETTING DAILY TASKS FROM LIFE GOALS. Essentials for Time & Life Management is a six-step program for translating your life goals into daily tasks. *(See ■ Panel 1.2.)* The idea is to make your most important desires and values a *motivational force* for helping you manage your time every day.

In Chapter 4, you will see how you can apply these steps and employ them as strategies for time management. Here let us do just the first step.

STEP 1: WHY AM I IN COLLEGE? Why are you here? Even if you haven't picked a major yet—even if you're still a "searcher," which is perfectly all right—it's important to at least think about your long-range goals, your life goals.

These goals should be more than just "I want to get a college education" or "I want a degree so I can make a lot of money." You need ultimate goals but not goals that are too general. Better to state

---

PANEL 1.2 The six-step "Essentials for Time & Life Management."

The steps for transforming your life goals into daily tasks are as follows:

■ **Step 1:** The planning process starts when you answer the question "Why am I in school?"—that is, define your life goals or long-range goals.

■ **Step 2:** You then proceed to "What are my plans?"—setting your intermediate-range goals.

■ **Step 3:** This leads to "What are my actions?"—the steps you will take to achieve your goals.

■ **Step 4:** "What is my master time-table?" In this step you set your schedule for the semester or quarter.

■ **Step 5:** "What is my weekly time-table?" This is the schedule you follow from week to week.

■ **Step 6:** "What is on the To Do list today?" This is the errand list or "things to do" list that is no different from the To Do list that millions of people make every day.

Heroes: To follow in the footsteps of . . . (name a hero or heroine). (*Example:* an entertainer, political figure, someone you know—a teacher, a successful relative or family friend.)

Sacrifice: What is worth sacrificing for and what the sacrifice is. (*Examples:* giving up making a lot of money in order to help people; giving up close family life in order to travel the world.)

Values: What you hold to be most important and dear to you.

Love: How you would express it and to whom.

Family: What its importance is to you at present and in the future.

Security: What the least security is you would settle for financially, emotionally.

Principles: What you would stand up for and base your life on.

Creativity: What things you would like to create.

Curiosity: What questions you want to satisfy.

Personal challenges: What abilities you need to prove about yourself.

Death: What you hope to accomplish in the face of your own mortality.

the goals not in terms of surpassing other people—for there will always be people yet to be surpassed—but rather in terms of fulfilling your own potential. These goals should express your most important desires and values—not necessarily what your family wants you to do or what you think society expects of you. (*See* Panel 1.3. above.)

As I've mentioned, college is not an easy experience. In order to pull yourself through some difficult times, you need to know why you are doing all this. Now, then, is the time to set down your long-range goals. See Personal Exploration #1.4 below.

PERSONAL EXPLORATION #1.4

WHAT ARE YOUR LONG-RANGE GOALS?

Look back over your list of reasons for attending college. Do they include what might be considered *life goals*—things you hope college will help you achieve, say, 10 years from now? If not, add some life goals to the list below.

The top five goals I hope college will help me reach are . . .

1._____

2._____

3._____

4._____

5._____

Onward: Applying This Chapter to Your Life

PREVIEW & REVIEW College is about deciding what you want your life to be and how to achieve it. Three important keys to college success, as expressed throughout this book, are (1) developing staying power, (2) becoming a mindful learner and thinker, and (3) using information technology.

et a life!" everyone says.

But what, exactly, is a "life," anyway? And how do you "get" it? We pass this way only once. The calendar leaves fall away. And then it's over.

Some things just happen to us, but a lot of things we choose. How many people, though, wake up at the age of 60 or 70 and say: "I missed the boat; there were better things I could have chosen to do"?

Over a lifetime everyone acquires a few regrets. But the things that people regret the most, according to a survey of elderly people by Cornell University researchers, is not what they *have done* so much as what they *haven't done.* And chief among the regrets were (1) *missed educational opportunities* and (2) *failure to "seize the moment."* [25]

You are at a time and place to seize some splendid opportunities. College allows you to begin examining the choices available to you—about what you want your life to be. We're talking about the main event here, the Big Enchilada—deciding what is *truly* important to you.

The rest of this book emphasizes the following key themes, or paths to success, as identified by the symbols in the margins:

Staying power

- *Developing staying power:* Every chapter discusses how you can apply the techniques for being successful in college to being successful in the rest of your life, including careers. This, we hope, will help motivate you to stay the course—to give you staying power.

Mindfulness

- *Becoming a mindful learner and thinker:* Beginning with Chapter 2, every chapter shows you how to apply mindful learning and critical and creative thinking in practical ways.

Information technology

- *Using information technology:* Beginning with Chapter 3, every chapter shows you how to take advantage of information technology—computers and the Internet—to achieve college and life success.

A last thought before you leave this chapter: Was there anything you read that made you say, "I didn't know that!" Did you see anything that helped you discover something new about yourself? Was it something that you could *make useful in your life*? If so, what is it, and how could you make use of it? Write it down here:

_____

_____

_____

_____

Real Practice Activities for Real People

Three paths to success emphasized by this book are (1) developing staying power, or persistence; (2) becoming a mindful learner and thinker; and (3) using information technology. "Real Practice Activities for Real People" presents applications of these themes at the end of each chapter, identified by the symbols in the margin. This first instance of "Real Practice Activities" presents exercises having to do with staying power.

REAL PRACTICE ACTIVITY #1.1: DO OLD HIGH-SCHOOL HABITS DIE HARD?

Staying power

This activity may be used either as the basis for small-group or class discussion or it may provide the basis for an individual reaction paper (of a page or two) to be written and handed in to the instructor.

How can you learn to develop staying power—persistence, perseverance, conscientiousness—in the new environment of higher education? What old habits from high school might you have to modify? Take 15 minutes or more to brainstorm ways of effectively dealing with the new structure and relative freedom of college. Make lists that identify both your concerns and possible solutions, incorporating suggestions from the chapter.

If you're working with members of a group, can you identify common themes or issues of concern? What solutions appear do be most effective, and why?

REAL PRACTICE ACTIVITY #1.2: WHAT ARE LESSONS LEARNED FROM OTHER RITES OF PASSAGE IN YOUR LIFE?

Staying power

This activity is a variation on Group Activity #1.1 and is also designed for small-group or class discussion.

Identify some major rites of passage you have gone through in your life. What new roles and behaviors did you have to adopt as a result? What new responsibilities were required? Which rite of passage do you think you handled most successfully, and why? Which rites of passages have you handled less successfully, and why? What lessons did you learn that can now be transferred to the experience of going to college and to help you develop perseverance to make college a success?

REAL PRACTICE ACTIVITY #1.3: HOW POWERFUL IS YOUR MOST POWERFUL WANT, & WHAT ARE YOU WILLING TO DO TO FULFILL IT?

This activity may be carried out through small-group or class discussion or through individual reaction paper.

"What quality do you think you have for college success?"

Name: Robert Coulter

Major: Undeclared

Family & work situation: Mother a single parent, one brother

Interests: Ice hockey, basketball, cricket, break dancing

Answer to question: "I feel I will be successful in college because I am optimistic and determined. College was a big step for me because I have some types of learning differences (such as attention deficit disorder and dyslexia). High school was a struggle, but I got through it, and I will do the same in college."

Staying power

What goal or desire (or hypothetical desire) is the strongest in your life? Making your family (parents, spouse/lover, children) proud of you? Helping them be more comfortable? Saving them from harm? Making a lot of money? Seeing the world? Expressing yourself? Finding a true companion? Determining the most rewarding kind of work?

To what lengths would you be willing to go in order to achieve this goal? Put your life on the line? Work at a job you hated for 10 years? Give up television? Learn new skills that may be difficult to learn?

Could you exert this determination in the attainment of a college degree?

The Examined Life

The unexamined life is not worth living," the great Greek philosopher Socrates believed. If ever there was a time to examine your life, it is now, during the first year of college.

As you take this course, you should be considering such basic questions as these:

1. Why am I choosing the direction I've chosen?

2. How do I feel about the things I've seen, read, or heard?

3. What do I think of this idea, that person, those beliefs?

4. How can I *make use* of the experiences I'm having?

The place to express these thoughts and to keep track of the progress you are making is in a *journal*. By writing in a journal, you come to a better understanding of yourself. The form of the journal probably doesn't matter, although your instructor may make some suggestions. It may be a notebook, loose-leaf sheets in a three-ring binder, typed pages, or printed pages from a word processor.

Your journal may be entirely private. It's possible that, from time to time, your instructor will express interest in your thoughts or progress with the journal. However, you need not show him or her your actual journal unless you want to. Rather you can provide some sort of separate statement that summarizes some of those thoughts you feel like sharing.

At the end of each chapter, the book indicates some suggestions or assignments for journal entries. It also provides lines to write them on.

Here is the first group of journal entry suggestions.

JOURNAL ENTRY #1.1: WHY ARE YOU HERE?

This is the most important question you can answer about college. Write at least 25 words about this matter.

_____

_____

_____

_____

_____

_____

_____

_____

_____

_____

_____

JOURNAL ENTRY #1.2: WHAT IS YOUR FEAR?

This is probably the second most important question you can answer about college. Write at least 25 words about your two or three principal fears.

_____

_____

_____

_____

_____

_____

_____

_____

_____

_____

JOURNAL ENTRY #1.3: WHAT KINDS OF THINGS MAY CAUSE DIFFICULTY?

What kinds of things might cause you difficulty or create problems that may threaten your college success?

_____

_____

_____

_____

_____

_____

_____

_____

_____

_____

_____

JOURNAL ENTRY #1.4: HOW CAN YOU DEAL WITH DIFFICULTIES?

How can you effectively deal with the difficulties listed in entry #1.3? (We discuss various college and off-campus resources in Chapter 9.)

_____

_____

_____

_____

_____

_____

_____

_____

_____

JOURNAL ENTRY #1.5: WHAT SUPPORT DO YOU HAVE FOR COLLEGE? What kinds of support do you have that will help you succeed in college?

_____
_____
_____
_____
_____
_____
_____
_____
_____
_____

JOURNAL ENTRY #1.6: WHAT ARE YOUR STRENGTHS? Write about what you consider your strengths that will help see you through.

_____
_____
_____
_____
_____
_____
_____
_____
_____
_____

2

Becoming a Mindful Learner & Thinker

Learning Styles, Active Learning, & Critical & Creative Thinking

IN THIS CHAPTER How smart do you have to be to get through higher education? Or to get through life? While a high IQ may help, there's more to being smart than IQ. In this chapter, we consider different kinds of intelligence, the best kinds of learning, and ways to "think smart." We consider the following.

■ **Different kinds of intelligence:** There are perhaps seven kinds of intelligence, an important one being emotional intelligence.

■ **Your learning style:** Some people tend to favor one type of learning over another—sound, sight, or touch. Others are adept at all three.

■ **Mindful learning:** In mindful learning, facts are learned conditionally, not absolutely. Mindfulness has three characteristics: creation of new categories, openness to new information, and awareness of more than one perspective.

■ **Critical thinking:** Critical thinking, or clear thinking, takes a four-step approach; there are several types of incorrect reasoning to avoid.

■ **Creative thinking:** Creative thinking is sparked by being receptive to messiness, avoiding conceptual blocks such as stereotypes, and not being afraid to make mistakes.

"Genius" may be one of the most overused words in the English language.

Painter Vincent Van Gogh, composer George Gershwin, and discoverer of the law of gravity Sir Isaac Newton have all been called geniuses. But so also have comedian Bill Cosby, boxer Muhammad Ali, country-rock singer Jerry Lee Lewis, and Wal-Mart founder Sam Walton. Indeed, a computer search of major U.S. publications yielded 1,038 uses of the word "genius" in just one month![1]

Still, maybe this seemingly careless throwing around of the word is more or less appropriate. Geniuses are able to *think smart*, certainly, but their smartness reveals itself in far deeper and wider ways than can be summarized by the kind of analytical thinking reflected by a single number of IQ. This number, of course, is the "intelligence quotient" measured on traditional general-intelligence tests (such as the Stanford-Binet or Wechsler tests). Indeed, scientists now theorize that there are *several* different kinds of human intelligence.

Different Kinds of Intelligence— Including Emotional Intelligence or "EQ"

PREVIEW & REVIEW There are perhaps seven types of intelligence, which might be summarized as word smart, logic smart, picture smart, body smart, music smart, people smart, and self smart. Perhaps even more important than having a high IQ is having high "EQ," or "emotional intelligence"—the ability to cope, empathize with others, and be self-motivated.

How much does IQ buy you after you get out of school?" asks Yale University psychologist Robert Sternberg. "Not much," he concludes. "A high IQ doesn't make a better salesperson or a more creative artist or scientist, and it won't enable a doctor to work better with patients. Even college professors will fail if they don't know how to teach or get along with administrators."[2]

SEVEN KINDS OF INTELLIGENCE. In his book *Frames of Mind,* Harvard psychologist Howard Gardner suggested that there are seven types of intelligence. These might be summarized as *word smart, logic smart, picture smart, body smart, music smart, people smart,* and *self smart.*[3]

Do you think of yourself as being smarter in some of these areas than in others? Are you better at athletics ("body smart"), for example, than at writing ("word smart")? Or at reading your own emotions ("self smart") than at conceiving drawings ("picture smart")? Gardner suggests that you think of yourself as having multiple computers in your mind that process information. "We can all compute the information," Gardner says, "but some of us have better computers in one area than another."[4]

Maybe, then, you're not a genius at the kind of analytical, language, and memorizing skills best measured by IQ tests. But you might have exceptional musical, spatial, or social intelligence. Or perhaps you have qualities such as creativity, sense of humor, leadership, or— very important—*staying power* or *persistence* that, as one writer suggests, "today may propel a person with an undistinguished IQ . . . to extraordinary success and happiness."[5]

Staying power

EMOTIONAL INTELLIGENCE, OR EQ. One kind of intelligence that may be even more important than IQ is what has been called "EQ"—emotional intelligence. A term popularized by *New York Times* psychology and health journalist Daniel Goleman in his book by the same name, *emotional intelligence (EQ)* **is the ability to cope, empathize with others, and be self-motivated.**[6] High emotional intelligence, then, would seem to include being "people smart" and "self smart."

According to Goleman, EQ encompasses such traits as empathy (the ability to imagine and relate to other people's feelings), self-awareness, optimism, impulse control, and capacity to manage anxiety and anger. If you haven't begun to develop these traits, explains Goleman, you're apt to not be very popular. Not only will a lack of EQ affect your people skills and thus hinder your success in the workplace. It may also make it difficult for you to learn. "Our emotional state has a direct impact on our capacity to take in and act on information," he says.[7] Thus, if you're always angry, anxious, or frustrated, you can't think well, which can affect your academic performance.

I describe how to manage stress and conflict, which affect your EQ, in Chap-

ter 11, "Wellness." In the rest of the present chapter, let us consider what you can do to make yourself smarter in a way that could boost your academic success. We consider:

- Learning styles
- Mindfulness and mindful learning
- Critical thinking
- Creative thinking

Four Types of Learning Styles: Which Fits You?

PREVIEW & REVIEW Four types of learning styles correspond to the principal senses: auditory (hearing), visual (sight), kinesthetic (touch), and mixed modality (all three). You may favor one of these over others.

Educators talk about differences in *learning styles*—**the ways in which people acquire knowledge.** Some students learn well by listening to lectures. Others learn better through reading, class discussion, hands-on experience, or researching a topic and writing about it. Thus, your particular learning style may make you more comfortable with some kinds of teaching and learning, and even with some kinds of subjects, than with others.

To find out the ways you learn best, try Personal Exploration #2.1 *(next page).*

HOW DO YOU LEARN BEST?

There are 12 incomplete sentences and three choices for completing each. Circle the answer that best corresponds to your style, as follows:

1 = the choice that is *least* like you.

2 = your second choice.

3 = the choice that is *most* like you.

1. When I want to learn something new, I usually . . .

   a. want someone to explain it to me.   1 2 3

   b. want to read about it in a book or magazine.   1 2 3

   c. want to try it out, take notes, or make a model of it.   1 2 3

2. At a party, most of the time I like to . . .

   a. listen and talk to two or three people at once.   1 2 3

   b. see how everyone looks and watch the people.   1 2 3

   c. dance, play games, or take part in some activities.   1 2 3

3. If I were helping with a musical show, I would most likely . . .

   a. write the music, sing the songs, or play the accompaniment.   1 2 3

   b. design the costumes, paint the scenery, or work the lighting effects.   1 2 3

   c. make the costumes, build the sets, or take an acting role.   1 2 3

4. When I am angry, my first reaction is to . . .

   a. tell people off, laugh, joke, or talk it over with someone.   1 2 3

   b. blame myself or someone else, daydream about taking revenge, or keep it inside   1 2 3

   c. make a fist or tense my muscles, take it out on something else, hit or throw things.   1 2 3

5. A happy event I would like to have is . . .

   a. hearing the thunderous applause for my speech or music.   1 2 3

   b. photographing the prize picture of an exciting newspaper story.   1 2 3

   c. achieving the fame of being first in a physical activity such as dancing, acting, surfing, or sports event.   1 2 3

6. I prefer a teacher to . . .

   a. use the lecture method, with informative explanations and discussions.   1 2 3

   b. write on the chalkboard, use visual aids and assigned readings.   1 2 3

   c. require posters, models, or in-service practice, and some activities in class.   1 2 3

7. I know that I talk with . . .

   a. different tones of voice.   1 2 3

   b. my eyes and facial expressions.   1 2 3

   c. my hands and gestures.   1 2 3

8. If I had to remember an event so I could record it later, I would choose to . . .

   a. tell it aloud to someone, or hear an audiotape recording or a song about it.   1 2 3

   b. see pictures of it, or read a description.   1 2 3

   c. replay it in some practice rehearsal, using movements such as dance, play acting, or drill.   1 2 3

9. When I cook something new, I like to . . .

   a. have someone tell me the directions, a friend or TV show.   1 2 3

   b. read the recipe and judge by how it looks.   1 2 3

   c. use many pots and dishes, stir often, and taste-test.   1 2 3

10. My emotions can often be interpreted from my . . .

   a. voice quality.   1 2 3

   b. facial expression.   1 2 3

   c. general body tone.   1 2 3

11. When driving, I . . .

   a. turn on the radio as soon as I enter the car.   1 2 3

   b. like quiet so I can concentrate.   1 2 3

   c. shift my body position frequently to avoid getting tired.   1 2 3

12. In my free time, I like to . . .

   a. listen to the radio, talk on the telephone, or attend a musical event.   1 2 3

   b. go to the movies, watch TV, or read a magazine or book.   1 2 3

   c. get some exercise, go for a walk, play games, or make things.   1 2 3

■ SCORING

Add up the points for all the "a's," then all the "b's," then all the "c's."

Total points for all "a's": _____

Total points for all "b's": _____

Total points for all "c's": _____

(continued on next page)

■ INTERPRETATION

If "a" has the highest score, that indicates your learning style preference is principally *auditory*.

If "b" has the highest score, your learning style preference is principally *visual*.

If "c" has the highest score, your learning style preference is *kinesthetic*.

If all scores are reasonably equal, that indicates your learning style preference is *mixed*.

See the text for explanations.

GROUP ACTIVITY OPTION

Do Personal Exploration #2.1. This activity could result in a real sense of discovery for you. Maybe you vaguely suspected that you learn better by one method than another, but now's the first time you've had it demonstrated. This is extremely important knowledge.

Read the text (pp. 33–34) for an explanation of what your scores mean. Then in a small group take turns discussing what you learned from this Personal Exploration. Does your learning style suggest you will learn some subjects more easily than you will others? Will you have difficulty learning from lectures or from reading, probably the two principal means by which knowledge is conveyed in college—and in life? What should you resolve to do if you've found out that you have a harder time learning by some methods than others?

There are four ways in which people can learn new material: *auditory, visual, kinesthetic,* and *mixed*.[8] Let's consider these.

AUDITORY LEARNING STYLE. Auditory has to do with listening and also speaking. **_Auditory learners_ use their voices and their ears as the primary means of learning.** They recall what they hear and what they themselves express verbally.

"When something is hard to understand, they want to talk it through," write professors Adele Ducharme and Luck Watford of Valdosta State University in Georgia. "When they're excited and enthusiastic about learning, they want to verbally express their response. . . . These learners love class discussion, they grow by working and talking with others, and they appreciate a teacher taking time to explain something to them."[9]

If you're this type of person, it's important to know that such learners may be easily distracted by sounds. Thus, it may be best that they *not* listen to the radio while studying, because they attend to all the sounds around them. An effective study technique, however, is to repeat something aloud several times because that helps them memorize it. These types of learners may do well in learning foreign languages, music, and other areas that depend on a strong auditory sense.

VISUAL LEARNING STYLE. Visual, of course, refers to the sense of sight. **_Visual learners_ like to see pictures of things described or words written down.** "They will seek out illustrations, diagrams, and charts to help them understand and remember information," say Ducharme and Watford. "They appreciate being able to follow what a teacher is presenting with material written on an overhead transparency or in a handout."

For visual learners, an effective technique for reviewing and studying material may be to read over their notes and recopy and reorganize information in outline form. Elsewhere I'll discuss mind maps, pyramids, and other ways of organizing information in a visual way.

KINESTHETIC LEARNING STYLE. *Kinesthetic* ("kin-es-*thet*-ik") has to do with the sense of touch and of physical manipulation. <u>*Kinesthetic learners*</u> **learn best when they touch and are physically involved in what they are studying.** These are the kind of people who fidget when they have to sit still and who express enthusiasm by jumping up and down.

"These learners want to act out a situation, to make a product, to do a project, and in general to be busy with their learning," say Ducharme and Watford. "They find that when they physically do something, they understand it and they remember it."

MIXED-MODALITY LEARNING STYLE. Modality ("moh-*dal*-it-y") means style. As you might guess, <u>*mixed-modality learners*</u> **are able to function in all three of these learning styles or "modalities"—auditory, visual, and kinesthetic.** Clearly, these people are at an advantage because they can handle information in whatever way it is presented to them.

LEARNING STYLES, LECTURES, & READING. Lectures would seem to favor auditory learners. Textbooks would seem to favor visual learners. Lectures and readings are two of the principal pipelines by which information is conveyed in college.

However, suppose one or both or these methods don't suit you. Since you don't usually have a choice about how a subject is taught, it's important to get comfortable with both methods. This means you need to be able to *extract* the most information out of a lecture or textbook—that is, take useful notes, for example—regardless of your learning preference and the instructor's style. I show how to do this in later chapters. For now it's important that you be aware of which learning style or styles you tend to favor so that you can take advantage of those in which you are strong and compensate for those in which you are not so strong.

NOTE: Just because you seem to be superior in one form of intelligence or to favor one kind of learning, *IT'S VERY IMPORTANT THAT YOU NOT ASSUME YOU ARE THERE-FORE LIMITED OR DEFICIENT IN OTHER AREAS.* Despite a century of assumptions by earlier generations of psychologists, intelligence is *not* something defined by an absolute standard. Nor are people constrained by particular kinds of learning preferences. If you're less effective at one form of learning style than another, there are ways to bring about improvements, as discussed later in this book.

Mindfulness & Mindful Learning: Taking Active Control

PREVIEW & REVIEW In the mindful way of teaching, facts are taught conditionally; the instructor doesn't say "This is the answer" but rather "This is one answer." Mindfulness has three characteristics: (1) creation of new categories, (2) openness to new information, and (3) awareness of more than one perspective.

We've been learning things all our lives. But do we know what learning methods are best?

Dr. Ellen J. Langer, the first woman to become a tenured professor of psychology at Harvard University, has become well known for her studies of "mindlessness" versus "mindfulness," described in her two books *Mindfulness* and *The Power of Mindful Learning.*

We've all experienced *mindlessness*. We misplace our keys. We write checks in January with the previous year's date. We find ourselves standing in a room unable to recall our reason for being there. We talk to a clothing dummy in a store before we realize it isn't a sales clerk. Among college students, mindlessness can take the form of scribbling page after page of lecture notes without really paying attention. Or of underlining while reading a text with no particular strategy in mind. This kind of "automaticity," or automatic behavior, occurs because we are operating from preconceptions or mind-sets. *Mindfulness,* by contrast, is a form of *active engagement.*

Mindlessless, says Langer, "is like being on automatic pilot."[10] More specifically, **mindlessness is characterized by three features: (1) entrapment in old categories, (2) automatic behavior, and (3) acting from a single perspective.**

The key qualities of mindfulness are the opposite. **Mindfulness is characterized (1) by creation of new categories, (2) by openness to new information, and (3) by awareness of more than one perspective.**

Let's examine these three qualities.

ENTRAPMENT IN OLD CATEGORIES VERSUS CREATION OF NEW ONES. This quality has to do with inflexibility versus flexibility.

An avid tennis player, Langer says that at tennis camp she was taught *exactly* how to hold her racquet and toss the ball when making a serve. Indeed, all other students in the camp were taught to serve the ball the same way. Later, she said, when she watched a top tennis championship, the U.S. Open, "I noticed that none of the top players served the way I was taught, and, more importantly, each of them served slightly differently."[11]

The significance of this: because each person has different height, hand size, and muscle development, there can be *no one right way* of serving. Thus, Langer says, it is important to teach everything *conditionally.* For example, she says, an instructor can teach "Here is *one* way of serving," or "If an incoming ball has

backspin, here is *one* way that you can use to return it."

In this *conditional* way of teaching— the mindful way of teaching—the instructor doesn't say "This is *THE* answer" but rather "This is *ONE* answer." The method takes account of the fact that each case is different and a person's responses must change from day to day and moment to moment.

In college, you may well encounter instructors who will teach as though there *is* just one right answer. Nevertheless, as a student you should practice mindfulness by receiving the information *as though it were conditionally true,* not unconditionally (or absolutely) true. Even in the hard sciences, mathematics, and such subjects as grammar, where it may seem as though there is just one correct answer, you should regard such information with open-mindedness, since there may be exceptions. That is, you should act as though the information is true only for certain uses or under certain circumstances. Among the chief benefits is that this attitude may well *help you remember the information better.*

AUTOMATIC BEHAVIOR VERSUS OPENNESS TO NEW INFORMATION. In automatic behavior, says Langer, we take in and use limited signals from the world around us without letting other signals penetrate as well.

As an example of automatic behavior, Langer likes to tell the story of the time she used a new credit card in a department store. Noticing that Langer hadn't signed the card yet, the cashier returned it to her to sign the back. After passing the credit card through the imprinting machine, the clerk handed her the credit card receipt to sign, which Langer did. Then, says Langer, the cashier "held the form next to the newly signed card to see if the signatures matched."[12]

Mindfulness, then, is being open to new information—including information that has not been specifically assigned to you. Langer reports a study in which novice piano players were recruited to learn simple fingering exercises. The first group was taught to practice in a traditional memorization-through-repetition style. Members of the second group, the mindful instruction group, were instructed to be creative and vary their playing as much as possible. ("Try to change your style every few minutes, and not lock into one particular pattern. While you practice, attend to the context, which may include very subtle variations or any feelings, sensations, or thoughts you are having.") When independent evaluators (graduate students in music) listened to tapes of the students, without knowing which were

assigned to which group, they rated the mindful students as more competent and creative; these students also expressed more enjoyment of the activity.[13]

As a college student, you can see that mindfulness requires that you engage more fully with whatever it is you're studying. But, as with the mindful piano students, this may well have the benefit of *making the material more enjoyable for you.*

SINGLE PERSPECTIVE VERSUS SEVERAL PERSPECTIVES. The third feature of mindfulness is being open not only to new information but also to new perspectives—what Langer calls having "a limber state of mind."

Mindlessness is acting from a single perspective. Langer reports an experiment she conducted examining the effectiveness of different requests for help. A fellow investigator stood on a busy sidewalk and told passersby that she had sprained her knee and needed help. When someone stopped, he or she was asked to get an Ace bandage from the nearby drugstore, where the pharmacist had been enlisted to say he was out of Ace bandages. Not one subject out of the 25 studied thought to ask the pharmacist if he could recommend something else, and the helpful passersby all returned to the "victim" empty-handed. This seems to suggest that the request for help operated from a narrow perspective—a sprained knee needs an Ace bandage. Had the "victim" asked for less specific help, the passersby might have tried to find other kinds of assistance.[14]

Most people, Langer observes, typically assume that other peoples' motives and intentions are the same as theirs. For example, says Langer, "If I am out running and see someone walking briskly, I assume she is trying to exercise and would run if only she could," when actually she may only be trying to get her exercise from walking. For most situations, many interpretations are possible. "Every idea, person, or object is potentially simultaneously many things depending on the perspective from which it is viewed," says Langer. "A steer is steak to a rancher, a sacred object to a

Hindu, and a collection of genes and proteins to a molecular biologist."[15]

To a student, there are many benefits in trying out different perspectives. First, this gives you *more choices in how to respond*, whereas a single perspective that produces an automatic reaction reduces your options. Second, by applying an open-minded perspective to your own behavior, *personal change becomes more possible*.

HOW TO ENCOURAGE MINDFULNESS: ACTIVE LEARNING. Mindfulness means consciously adapting psychological states that are really different versions of the same thing:

1. Being open to novelty

2. Being alert to distinctions—seeing more sides of an issue or subject

3. Being sensitive to different contexts

4. Being aware of multiple perspectives

5. Being oriented in the present

In other words, you need to work at making inventive transformations of seemingly routine tasks.

All in all, then, mindful learning is *active learning*. Instead of simply reacting passively to what's in front of you—lectures, readings, or whatever—you should try to have your mind always working: questioning, criticizing, imagining, examining, speculating, hypothesizing. It means not always being oriented toward the *outcome* when you study something. (As in: "Got to memorize the date during World War II that America dropped the first atomic bomb on Japan if I'm going to pass my world history test.") It means keeping your mind limber so that you're paying attention to the *process*. (As in: "I wonder what would have happened in World War II if the U.S. had dropped the A-bomb on Germany first.") The payoff: with mindfulness you may well remember more and have more fun learning.

In the next two sections, I describe two aspects of mindfulness—critical thinking and creative thinking.

GROUP ACTIVITY #2.2

MINDLESSNESS VERSUS MINDFULNESS

With three to five other students in a group, discuss examples of how mindlessness is practiced in school. How would you bring a mindful approach to school subjects that you're less than thrilled about having to take?

Critical Thinking: What It Is, How to Use It

PREVIEW & REVIEW Critical thinking is clear, skeptical, or active thinking. It takes the approach that there is "no shame, no blame" in making and reducing errors.

Four steps in critical thinking are (1) getting an understanding of the problem, (2) gathering information and interpreting it, (3) developing a solution plan and carrying it out, and (4) evaluating the plan's effectiveness.

Critical thinking uses the tools of reasoning, as in determining when arguments are deductive or inductive. There are several types of incorrect reasoning, or fallacies. They include *jumping to conclusions, false cause, appeal to authority, circular reasoning, irrelevant attack on opponent, straw man argument, slippery slope, appeal to pity,* and *use of questionable statistics.*

C *ritical thinking* **means clear thinking, skeptical thinking, active thinking. It is actively seeking to understand, analyze, and evaluate information in order to solve specific problems.** You need to exercise critical thinking, for example, when you're trying to analyze the correctness of someone's point of view. Or of your own point of view when you're trying to solve an academic problem or personal problem.

Unlike passive thinking, in which you unquestioningly accept the information given you, critical thinking means you constantly question everything. You're curious to know more. You look further for answers. And, as a result, you experience what learning really is.

UNCRITICAL THINKING: THE MIND-SET AS ENEMY. The opposite of critical thinking is, of course, uncritical thinking. Uncritical thinking is all around us. People run their lives on the basis of horoscopes, numerology, and similar nonsense. They believe in "crystal healing" and "color therapy." They think cranks and quacks can cure cancer with apricot-pit extract or alleviate arthritis with copper bracelets. Otherwise intelligent people believe that mind power alone can be used to bend spoons.

These are not just bits of harmless goofiness, like wearing your "lucky" shirt to your final exam. James Randi, a debunker of claims made by supporters of the paranormal, suggests just why such uncritical thinking is dangerous.

"We live in a society that is enlarging the boundaries of knowledge at an unprecedented rate," he says, "and we cannot keep up with more than a small portion of what is made available to us. To mix our data input with childish notions of magic and fantasy is to cripple our perception of the world around us. We must reach for the truth, not for the ghosts of dead absurdities."[16]

The enemy of clear thinking is our *mind-sets.* By the time we are grown, our minds have become set in patterns of thinking that affect how we respond to new ideas. These mind-sets are the result of our personal experiences and the various social environments in which we grew up. Such mind-sets determine what ideas we think are important and, conversely, what ideas we ignore. As one book on clear thinking points out, we can't pay attention to all the events that occur around us. Consequently, "our minds filter out some observations and facts and let others through to our conscious awareness."[17] Herein lies the danger: "As a result we see and hear what we subconsciously want to and pay little attention to facts or observations that have already been rejected as unimportant."

Having mind-sets makes life comfortable. However, as the foregoing writers point out, "Familiar relationships and events become so commonplace that we expect them to continue forever. Then we find ourselves completely unprepared to accept changes that are necessary, even when they stare us in the face."[18]

REDUCING ERRORS: NO SHAME, NO BLAME.

One way to overcome mind-sets is to take a "no shame, no blame" approach to admitting errors. Says Gerard Nierenberg, whose book *Do It Right the First Time* advocates this approach to reducing errors in the workplace and in personal life, "30% to 40% of all workers' and executives' time is spent anticipating, correcting, and handling errors." By taking a no shame, no blame attitude toward our mistakes, he says, we can learn to make fewer of them.

How does one do this? "First you must determine exactly what is wrong, what the problem is," says Nierenberg. "Next,

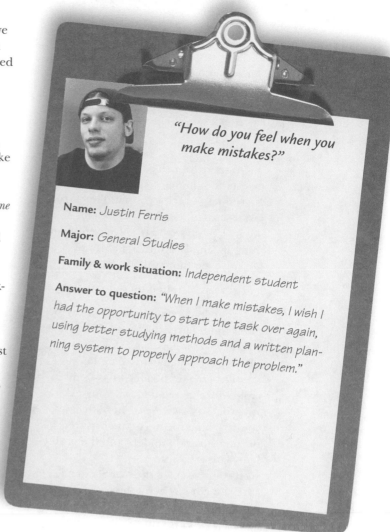

"How do you feel when you make mistakes?"

Name: *Justin Ferris*

Major: *General Studies*

Family & work situation: *Independent student*

Answer to question: *"When I make mistakes, I wish I had the opportunity to start the task over again, using better studying methods and a written planning system to properly approach the problem."*

GROUP ACTIVITY #2.3

USING THE "NO SHAME, NO BLAME" APPROACH TO MISTAKES

Nierenberg's "no shame, no blame" approach to error is as follows: "First you must determine exactly what is wrong, what the problem is. Next, you determine how extensive the damage is. Then you look at what caused the problem . . . [and] determine the best way to remedy it and how a reoccurrence can be best avoided."

Students should gather in small groups of three to five participants. Each student is to identify one or more incidents in which they encountered academic difficulties (such as doing poorly on a paper or a test or in a course). Individual students are to use the "no shame, no blame" approach to assess how they can prevent a recurrence of the problem, and other students may then comment.

you determine how extensive the damage is. Then you look at what caused the problem . . . [and] determine the best way to remedy it and how a reoccurrence can be best avoided."[19]

The most important factor in all this is *attitude:* You should learn to acknowledge an error as soon as it's discovered and not feel ashamed of having made it. Then you need to openly and honestly take responsibility, accepting criticism and advice from others without hiding behind self-justification or lies.

THE STEPS IN CRITICAL THINKING.
Fortunately, critical thinking can be learned just as you can learn, say, how to play the guitar, install a dishwasher, or explore the Internet.

The four steps in critical thinking are these:

1. Get an understanding of the problem.

2. Gather information and interpret it.

3. Develop a solution plan and carry it out.

4. Evaluate the plan's effectiveness.

Do these four steps seem rather obvious? (You'll notice some resemblance to Nierenberg's recipe for handling errors, just discussed.) Perhaps so, but it's amazing how often we try to solve or fix something by simply stumbling around, hoping everything will work out.

Let's run through these four steps.

1. *Get an understanding of the problem:* How many times have you been told, as for a test, to *read the directions*? How often, when looking at a manual on how to operate a new appliance or assemble a child's toy, have you found yourself *rereading the instructions*? In both cases, you're taking the necessary first step: making sure you understand the problem. This is basic.

If you *don't* take the trouble to make sure you comprehend the problem, you can waste a great deal of time trying to solve it and never do so. Getting an understanding may require you to read over the problem two or more times (as in math), ask someone for clarification (as an instructor), or seek alternative explanations (as in looking at a city road map instead of state road map).

Often you can get a better understanding of a problem just by talking about it, as in a discussion in a study group with other students.

2. *Gather information and interpret it:* Sometimes just by making sure you understand a problem you can see a solution to it. At other times, however, you may need to get additional information and interpret it. That is, you'll need to list resources that can give you help or identify areas that are preventing your solving the problem.

For instance, if the problem you're working on is what courses to take next quarter or semester, you're going to need the school's catalog and perhaps a curriculum worksheet (list of required courses) to see what courses you need to take in your major. Then you'll need a class schedule that describes what courses are offered and when.

As another example, if your problem is that you're required to write a paper on serial killers for a sociology or criminal justice course, you'll need to get books and other information on the subject from the library. Then you'll need to interpret it to make sure you know the difference between, say, serial killers and mass killers.

3. *Develop a solution plan and carry it out:* Developing a plan is sometimes the most difficult step. The reason: you may have to choose between several alternatives.

For example, you may have to choose among several courses you could take next term. And whatever course you *don't* take then, you'll have to take later—and hope that course will be offered some term at a day and hour that works out for you. Or, in writing about serial killers, you'll have to decide between several possible outlines and drawing on several possible examples.

Finally, you'll need to carry out the plan—which may or may not turn out to be workable. Maybe one course you sign up for turns out to require far more homework than you bargained for, and you can't handle it along with your other commitments. Maybe the direction of your paper can't be supported by the research you did.

4. ***Evaluate the plan's effectiveness:*** So you completed the semester of courses you planned or handed in your paper on serial killers. Maybe your experience was a disaster, in which case you'll want to know how to do it right next time. (Remember Nierenberg on reducing errors: you should look at what caused a problem for you and determine the best way to remedy it and how a recurrence can be avoided in the future.) Maybe your plan worked out okay, but there were things that might have been handled better.

Drawing lessons from your experience is part and parcel of critical thinking, and it's a step that should not be neglected. If the experience was successful, can it be applied to other, similar problems? If only partly successful, can you see ways to change the information-gathering step or the solution-planning step to make it work better? If the experience was a disaster, is there a slogan you can draw from it that you can post over your desk? (Example: NEVER TAKE MORE THAN ONE SCIENCE CLASS IN A SEMESTER, if you're not a science type. Or, LOOK FOR *RECENT* ARTICLES WHEN RESEARCHING CRIMINAL JUSTICE PAPERS.)

THE REASONING TOOL: DEDUCTIVE & INDUCTIVE ARGUMENTS. The tool for breaking through the closed habits of thought called mind-sets is reasoning.

Reasoning—**giving reasons in favor of this assertion or that**—is essential to critical thinking and solving life's problems. Reasoning is put in the form of what philosophers call *arguments*. ***Arguments*** **consist of one or more** ***premises***, **or reasons, logically supporting a result or outcome called a** ***conclusion***.

An example of an argument is as follows:

Premise 1: All instructors must grade students.

Premise 2: I am an instructor.

Conclusion: Therefore, I must grade students.

Note the tip-off word "therefore," which signals that a conclusion is coming. In real life, such as arguments on TV or in newspapers, the premises and conclusions are not so neatly labeled. Still, there are clues: the words *because* and *for* usually signal premises. The words *therefore, hence,* and *so* signal conclusions. Not all groups of sentences form arguments. Often they may form anecdotes or other types of exposition or explanation.[20]

The two main kinds of correct or valid arguments are inductive and deductive.

- ***Deductive argument:*** **A** ***deductive argument*** **is defined as follows: If its premises are true, then its conclusions are true also.** In other words, if the premises are true, the conclusions cannot be false.

- ***Inductive argument:*** **An** ***inductive argument*** **is defined as follows: If the premises are true, the conclusions are PROBABLY true, but the truth is not guaranteed.** An inductive argument is sometimes known as a "probability argument."

An example of a deductive argument is as follows:[21]

Premise 1: All students experience stress in their lives.

Premise 2: Reuben is a student.

Conclusion: Therefore, Reuben experiences stress in his life.

This argument is deductive—the conclusion is definitely true if the premises are definitely true.

An example of an inductive argument is as follows:[22]

Premise 1: Stress can cause illness.
Premise 2: Reuben experiences stress in his life.
Premise 3: Reuben is ill.
Conclusion: Therefore, stress may be the cause of Reuben's illness.

Note the word "may" in the conclusion. This argument is inductive. The conclusion is not stated with absolute certainty; rather, it only suggests that stress *may* be the cause. The link between premises and conclusion is not definite because there may be other reasons for Reuben's illness (such as a virus).

SOME TYPES OF INCORRECT REASONING. Patterns of incorrect reasoning are known as _fallacies_. Learning to identify fallacious arguments will help you avoid patterns of faulty thinking in your own writing and thinking. It will also help you identify them in others' thinking.

Some principal types of incorrect reasoning are as follows:

■ *Jumping to conclusions:* Also known as *hasty generalization,* the fallacy called **_jumping to conclusions_ means that a conclusion has been reached when not all the facts are available.**
    Example: Cab drivers may (illegally) refuse to take certain passengers to what they regard as dangerous neighborhoods merely on the basis of their skin color or looks, jumping to the conclusion that they are dangerous people. But what if that person turns out to be a city councilman, as happened in Boston a few years ago?

■ *False cause or irrelevant reason:* The faulty reasoning known as *non sequitur* (Latin for "it does not follow"), which might be better called **_false cause_ or _irrelevant reason_, means that the conclusion does not follow logically from the supposed reasons stated earlier.** There is no *causal* relationship.

Example: You receive an A on a test. However, because you felt you hadn't been well prepared, you attribute your success to your friendliness with the instructor. Or to your horoscope. None of these "reasons" has anything to do with the result.

■ *Appeal to authority:* Known in Latin as *argumentum ad verecundiam,* **the _appeal to authority_ argument uses an authority in one area to pretend to validate claims in another area in which the person is not an expert.**
    Example: You see the appeal-to-authority argument used all the time in advertising. But what does a champion golfer, for instance, really know about real-estate developments?

■ *Circular reasoning:* **The _circular reasoning_ argument rephrases the statement to be proven true. It then uses the new, similar statement as supposed proof that the original statement is in fact true.**
    Examples: You declare that you can drive safely at high speeds with only inches separating you from the car ahead. After all, you have driven this way for years without an accident. Or you say that paying student-body fees is for the common good because in the long run paying student-body fees benefits everyone.

- *Irrelevant attack on opponent:* Known as an *ad hominem* argument (Latin for "to the person"), **the _irrelevant attack on an opponent_ attacks a person's reputation or beliefs rather than his or her argument.**

  Example: Politicians frequently try to attack an adversary's reputation. Someone running for student-body president may attack an opponent's "character" or intelligence rather than the opponent's stand on the issues.

- *Straw man argument:* **The _straw man argument_ is when you misrepresent your opponent's position to make it easier to attack, or when you attack a weaker position while ignoring a stronger one.** In other words, you sidetrack the argument from the main discussion.

  Example: A politician might attack an opponent as a "socialist" for supporting aid to mothers with dependent children but not for supporting aid to tobacco growers. (This is because the politician also favors supporting tobacco growers.)

- *Slippery slope:* **The _slippery slope_ is a failure to see that the first step in a possible series of steps does not lead inevitably to the rest.**

  Example: The "Domino theory," under which the United States waged wars against Communism, was a slippery slope argument. It assumed that if Communism triumphed in Nicaragua, say, it would inevitably spread to the rest of Central America and finally to the United States.

- *Appeal to pity:* **The _appeal to pity_ argument appeals to mercy rather than an argument on the merits of the case itself.**

  Examples: Begging the dean not to expel you for cheating because your impoverished parents made sacrifices for your education exemplifies this fallacy.

- *Questionable statistics:* Statistics can be misused in many ways as supporting evidence. The statistics may be unknowable, drawn from an unrepresentative sample, or otherwise suspect.

  Example: Stating that people were less happy 10,000 years ago than today is an example of unknowable or undefined use of statistics.

Fallacies such as these are used every day in promotional pitches, legal arguments, news analyses, and appeals for money. Clearly, then, being aware of them will serve you well lifelong.

Creative Thinking

PREVIEW & REVIEW Creative thinking consists of being receptive to messiness, avoiding conceptual blocks such as stereotypes, not being afraid of making mistakes, and other techniques.

 reative thinking **consists of imaginative ways of looking at known ideas.** Creative thinking enables you to solve problems for which traditional problem-solving methods don't work.

Creative thinking doesn't just help you think up topics for research papers in school. In the workplace, employees burning with bright ideas are an employer's greatest competitive resource. "Creativity precedes innovation, which is its physical expression," says *Fortune* magazine writer Alan Farnham. "It's the source of all intellectual property."[23]

The popular notion of creative people is that they are oddballs, showboats, people who wear funny clothes. However, in reality anyone can be creative, whether wearing a beret or wearing a suit. And, contrary to the idea that people are born creative, creativity *can* be taught. For instance, creativity expert Edward de Bono, author of *Six Thinking Hats,* suggested the following exercise during one forum for executives. Five people were given a word, *party,* and challenged to use it to generate ideas for a new type of computer keyboard. After a moment, they began tossing out associations: Keyboards that connect through a party line. Keyboards that can be used only by peo-

ple "invited" (that is, authorized) to use them. Keyboards with "surprise" (preprogrammed) keys. Clearly, then, creativity can be induced in people who might not seem to have it.[24]

You don't have to have a high IQ or be well educated in order to think creatively. Rather, says Farnham, creative people "are self-motivated, love risk, thrive on ambiguity, and delight in novelty, twists, and reversals." In other words, they exhibit mindfulness.

So how do you begin to learn to think creatively? The following are some suggestions.

BE RECEPTIVE TO DISORDER & MESSINESS. Creativity is a messy process. There are people with an excessive fondness for order who cannot tolerate misleading and ill-fitting data and opinions. However, by allowing yourself to be receptive to such untidiness, you give yourself the chance for a new kind of order.

WATCH OUT FOR CONCEPTUAL BLOCKS. Conceptual blocks, or "mental walls" on creativity, keep you from correctly perceiving a problem or conceiving of its solution. One such block is *stereotyping*, **or selective perception.** This is when you see only what you *expect* to see. (When you see someone wearing a grey business suit, what kind of person do you expect? What about someone with a metal stud through his or her tongue?)

DON'T BE AFRAID OF MISTAKES. As I suggested earlier, the fear of making errors or mistakes, of failing, is quite common. It occurs because most of us have been rewarded while growing up for producing "right" answers. However, sometimes you *want* to permit yourself mistakes because that allows you to come up with fresh ideas.

By saying that no ideas are too risky or embarrassing, you allow yourself to consider information you'd normally ignore. Judgment and criticism are necessary later in the problem-solving process. However, if they occur too early, you may

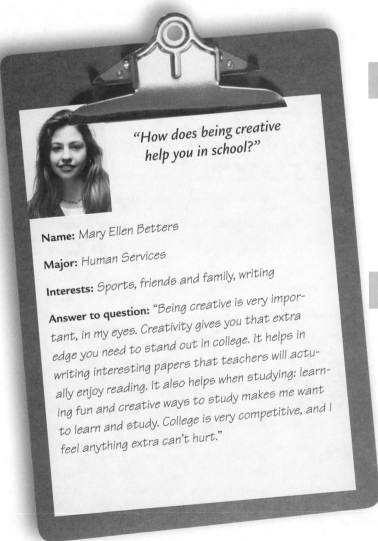

"How does being creative help you in school?"

Name: Mary Ellen Betters

Major: Human Services

Interests: Sports, friends and family, writing

Answer to question: "Being creative is very important, in my eyes. Creativity gives you that extra edge you need to stand out in college. It helps in writing interesting papers that teachers will actually enjoy reading. It also helps when studying: learning fun and creative ways to study makes me want to learn and study. College is very competitive, and I feel anything extra can't hurt."

reject many ideas, some of which are fragile and imperfect but may be made mature later.

TRY BRAINSTORMING. The word *brainstorming* was coined by advertising man Alex Osborn for a type of group problem solving in which several people work simultaneously on a specific problem. However, you can use this method by yourself. **In _brainstorming_, you express all the ideas that come to mind about a particular matter,** no matter how seemingly stupid or absurd.

Four rules govern the procedure, according to Osborn:

- **_No judgments allowed:_** No evaluations or judgments are permitted, which might cause people to defend rather than generate ideas.

- **_Be wild:_** Think of the wildest ideas possible, in order to decrease individual judgment among individual members.

- **_Go for quantity:_** The more ideas the better. Quantity is more important than quality and, in fact, quantity *leads to* quality.

- **_Build on others' ideas:_** Build on and modify the ideas of others whenever possible, which will lead to ideas superior to the original ones.[25]

TRY MIND MAPPING: BRAINSTORMING WITH PENCIL & PAPER. _Mind mapping_, sometimes called _clustering_, is brainstorming by yourself with the help of pencil and paper. To begin a mind-mapping session, suggests James M. Higgins, author of *101 Creative Problem Solving Techniques,* you write the name of the object or problem in the center of a piece of paper and draw a circle around it. Then you brainstorm each major aspect of the object or problem, drawing lines outward from the circle "like roads leaving a city."

As you brainstorm in more detail, you can draw branches from these "roads." "You can brainstorm all the main lines at once and then the branches for each," says Higgins, "or brainstorm a line and its branches, or jump from place to place as thoughts occur."[26] *(See* ■ *Panel 2.1.)*

PANEL 2.1 Example of mind mapping.

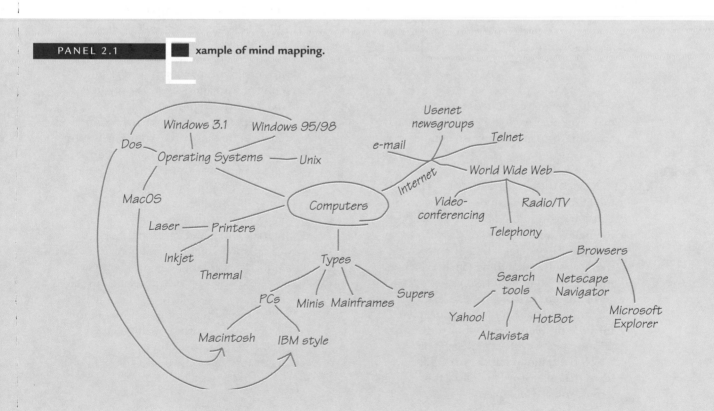

USING MIND MAPPING TO SOLVE PROBLEMS

Mind mapping is useful for identifying all the issues and subissues related to a problem. This is a group activity that can be done without the class having to break into small groups.

Each student should take out a sheet of paper and in the center of it write down a problem they want to solve. It can be an idea for a paper, a question about future plans, or a problem in personal relationships. Draw a circle around the problem, then take five minutes to brainstorm aspects of the problem, drawing "highways" and then smaller "roads" from the circle.

After five minutes, the instructor will ask students to discuss how well mind mapping seems to work for them. Questions for discussion: Do you find mind mapping useful? Or is it uncomfortable to use? (About half of people who learn it don't like it.) Do you find the lack of structure bothersome? Do you find it difficult to be spontaneous? What kinds of problems do you think it might be applied to successfully?

After you have finished your mind map, you can put your ideas and data into another form, such as a typed outline.

SURRENDER TO YOUR UNCONSCIOUS. The unconscious mind can be a terrific problem solver, point out Michael Ray and Rochelle Myers, authors of *Creativity in Business.* They suggest that when you're trying to solve something (such as picking a term-paper topic), you should let go of anxious striving. Instead, ask a clear question about the key issue, then turn the problem over to your unconscious, as in your sleep.[27] Relaxation allows the mind to wander over "silly" ideas that may prove to deliver the "Aha!" you are looking for.

ASK DUMB QUESTIONS. Ask questions the way a child would: "What's behind a rainbow?" "What color is the inside of my brain?" "Why are my toes in front of my feet?"[28] Such "dumb" questions have no expectations, assumptions, or illusions. Once you begin, questions will lead to more questions.

BE RECEPTIVE TO ALL YOUR SENSES. Some people are resistant to using *all* their senses—smell, taste, and touch, as well as the more favored sight and sound. Or some think verbally rather than visually, or vice versa. It's important to have access to all areas of imagination—to be able to smell and hear a ball park as well as visualize it. In addition, one must be able to manipulate and recombine ideas in the imagination—imagining a volcano in a ball park, for instance.

To see how creative you are in this respect, try Personal Exploration #2.2 *(opposite page).*

STUFF YOUR BRAIN, KEEP IDEA NOTES, & CULTIVATE LUCKY ACCIDENTS. Stuff your brain with all kinds of words, pictures, and sounds, whether or not they seem useful at the time. When in the library or before a magazine rack, pick up a magazine or journal you're not familiar with and scan it. Do anything that feeds the mind.

Keep a clipping file of articles and pictures that just strike your fancy. Carry a notepad or 3 × 5 cards and jot down ideas. Write down anything that interests you: insights, jokes, poems, quotes, songs, book titles, possible money-making ideas, and so on. Put in sketches, too, and cartoons.

The point of all this is to create a lot of lucky accidents, an event known as *serendipity.* Serendipity, according to the dictionary, is "the faculty of finding valuable or agreeable things not sought for." If you review your notes and idea files now and then, you'll be surprised how many turn out to be useful.

CREATIVITY: HOW GOOD ARE YOU AT DIFFERENT TYPES OF SENSORY IMAGES?

Rate the following to find out how good you are at different types of sensory images.

c = Clear

v = Vague

n = Nothing

This activity may help you develop your sensory imagery ability, if used extensively. Sight tends to be the predominant sense. However, it should not be allowed to overpower other modes—smell, sound, taste, and touch—which can increase the clarity of one's imagery.

IMAGINE:

		c	v	n
1.	The laugh of a friend.			
2.	The sound of thunder.	c	v	n
3.	The sound of a horse walking on a road.	c	v	n
4.	The sound of a racing car.	c	v	n
5.	The feel of wet grass.	c	v	n
6.	The feel of your wife's/husband's/ girlfriend's/boyfriend's/pet's hair.	c	v	n
7.	The feel of diving into a cold swimming pool.	c	v	n
8.	The feel of a runny nose.	c	v	n
9.	The smell of bread toasting.	c	v	n
10.	The smell of fish.	c	v	n
11.	The smell of gasoline.	c	v	n
12.	The smell of leaves burning.	c	v	n
13.	The taste of a pineapple.	c	v	n
14.	The taste of Tabasco sauce.	c	v	n
15.	The taste of toothpaste.	c	v	n
16.	The muscular sensation of pulling on a rope.	c	v	n
17.	The muscular sensation of throwing a rock.	c	v	n
18.	The muscular sensation of running.	c	v	n
19.	The muscular sensation of squatting.	c	v	n
20.	The sensation of being uncomfortably cold.	c	v	n
21.	The sensation of having eaten too much.	c	v	n
22.	The sensation of extreme happiness.	c	v	n
23.	The sensation of a long attack of hiccups.	c	v	n

GROUP ACTIVITY OPTION

With others in a small group share your findings from this Personal Exploration. Discuss which senses seem to be most fully developed. List some sensations, similar to those above, that represent some of your less developed senses. Share them with the class at large.

Onward: Applying This Chapter to Your Life

PREVIEW & REVIEW Learn to "incubate" to solve problems and generate ideas.

No doubt you've had the experience of sweating over a problem for hours only to have the answer pop into your head at some other time when your mind was on something else. What happened is known as *incubation*. When you take a break from something you're working on, the mind keeps on working subconsciously, unbeknownst to you.

Writer Mark Golin suggests you can use the incubation technique at the start of the week, for example, by picking a problem on Monday that needs to be solved by Friday. Look at the problem for an hour or so, then put it aside. On Wednesday afternoon, take out the problem again and look at it. "What might have taken you days to solve before may only take hours now that you've done some of the work in your subconscious."[29]

Incubation is, of course, a form of *persistence*. You continue to work on a problem even past the point where once you might have just given up.

Staying power

Mindfulness, critical thinking, and creative thinking can change your life. What two specific things did you find in this chapter that you found fascinating? practical? Write them down here.

_____

_____

_____

_____

_____

_____

_____

_____

Real Practice Activities for Real People

REAL PRACTICE ACTIVITY #2.1: IDENTIFYING YOUR FAVORED INTELLIGENCES & LEARNING STYLES, & DISCOVERING WHERE YOU NEED PERSISTENCE.

Staying power

This activity may take the form of a one-page reaction paper to be submitted to the instructor. Or it may be used as the basis for small-group discussion.

Which of the seven types of intelligence (*word smart, logic smart, picture smart, body smart, music smart, people smart,* and *self smart*) seem to apply best to you? Give examples.

Which of the four principal learning styles (*auditory, visual, kinesthetic,* or *mixed modality*) do you seem to favor? Give examples.

Do you see any relationships between the types of intelligence and learning styles you seem to favor and those courses you find easy and those you find difficult? What does this self-knowledge tell you about your need to make yourself more persistent in tackling those subjects that aren't easy for you? Most important, what you do you plan to do to boost your staying power to handle those areas where you may be weak?

REAL PRACTICE ACTIVITY #2.2: HOW HAVE YOU USED MINDFUL LEARNING IN YOUR OWN LIFE? This activity is to be performed in small groups and the results presented to the class at large.

Mindfulness

Review the three characteristics of mindful learners (being able to create new categories, being open to new information, and being aware of more than one perspective). With other students, take turns identifying examples in which you have practiced mindful learning. The situations may involve learning new skills (such as particular athletic or musical skills), resolving disagreements with people you know, or getting to know people who are quite different from you. Group members should discuss how well the examples reflect the three characteristics of mindful learning. They should then pick the example that best illustrates mindfulness, and one student should describe that to the class at large.

REAL PRACTICE ACTIVITY #2.3: EXPLORING PROBLEMS THROUGH MIND MAPPING. This activity is to be practiced by individual students, either in class or out of class, who are to develop mind maps (see Panel 2.1 in the text). On completion, students should get together in pairs to exchange maps for evaluation. Mind maps may be submitted to the instructor, who may pick an example or two for class discussion.

Mindfulness

Think of a problem you need to solve or task you need to complete. Examples: developing a topic on which to write a term paper, finding ways to make money while in school, exploring decisions to be made about your major. On a sheet of paper, explain the problem you're trying to solve. Beneath it draw a mind map (see Panel 2.1 and accompanying text for directions) to help you try to understand the various issues involved.

On completion, the instructor may ask you to meet with a fellow student for an exchange of maps. Using a different color pen, see if you can add additional lines and words that may suggest other factors your partner has overlooked. Discuss the results.

The Examined Life

JOURNAL ENTRY #2.1: WHAT IS YOUR BEST LEARNING STYLE? Which is your predominant learning style—sight, hearing, or touch? What kind of work can you do to improve your skills with other learning styles?

_____

_____

_____

_____

_____

_____

_____

_____

_____

_____

JOURNAL ENTRY #2.2: HOW HAS YOUR MIND-SET INFLUENCED YOU? Mind-set is everything. Identify a situation in your life where your mind-set led you to respond negatively to it.

_____

_____

_____

_____

_____

_____

_____

_____

_____

JOURNAL ENTRY #2.3: APPLYING CRITICAL THINKING TO YOUR LIFE. The four steps in critical thinking are (1) getting an understanding of the problem, (2) gathering information and interpreting it, (3) developing a solution plan and carrying it out, and (4) evaluating the plan's effectiveness. Apply these steps to some problem in your life.

_____

_____

_____

_____

_____

_____

_____

_____

_____

_____

_____

JOURNAL ENTRY #2.4: HOW CAN YOU EMPLOY CREATIVE THINKING? In what ways can you employ the techniques of creative thinking besides thinking up subjects for term papers?

_____

_____

_____

_____

_____

_____

_____

_____

_____

JOURNAL ENTRY #2.5: WHAT INTELLIGENCES OR KINDS OF SMARTNESS DO YOU THINK YOU HAVE? Which of the kinds of intelligence described on pages 30–31 seem to fit you? How do you think they might help you in college?

_____

_____

_____

_____

_____

_____

_____

_____

_____

_____

_____

JOURNAL ENTRY #2.6: HOW CAN MINDFUL LEARNING HELP YOU? Mindful learning has three characteristics: (1) creation of new categories, (2) openness to new information, and (3) awareness of more than one perspective (see pages 34–37). How could these characteristics help you outside of college?

_____

_____

_____

_____

_____

_____

_____

_____

_____

_____

_____

Using Information Technology

Leveraging Your Success with Computer & Communications Tools

IN THIS CHAPTER Information technology offers tools that are key to your future:

■ **Personal computers:** Most students find they benefit by having access to a personal computer (PC), either IBM-style or Macintosh, desktop or laptop.

■ **Computer software:** With a PC, you can use the following kinds of software to help you in your education and career: word processing, spreadsheets, database management systems, personal information managers, graphics programs, and integrated programs and suites.

■ **The Internet:** Using a PC with modem, you can use direct access, online information service, or an Internet service provider to connect to the Internet in order to take advantage of e-mail, Usenet newsgroups, mailing lists, FTP, and Telnet.

■ **The World Wide Web:** Because the Web is graphics-based, it is perhaps the easiest tool to use on the Internet. Using the Web requires a browser and access to directories and search engines.

■ **When copying software is allowed:** Commercial software makers allow you to make only one copy of their product. Public-domain software, freeware, and shareware have fewer or no such restrictions.

"Computers and communications: These are the parents of the Information Age," says one writer. "When they meet, the fireworks begin."[1]

Web—is vital to your future, both in college and afterward. In this chapter, I discuss the following:

- Personal computers
- Computer software
- The Internet
- The World Wide Web
- What's allowed and not allowed with computers

What kind of fireworks are we talking about? Maybe it is that portable computing and communications technologies are *changing conventional meanings of time and space.* As one expert pointed out (during a round-table discussion on an online network), "the physical locations we traditionally associate with work, leisure, and similar pursuits are rapidly becoming meaningless."[2]

The proportion of colleges that require students to demonstrate that they know basic skills for computer or Internet use is climbing rapidly—up to more than 40% in 1997 from 32% in 1992, according to a survey of 1,600 colleges nationwide.[3] E-mail, or electronic mail, is now required in almost a third of college courses—indeed, as high as 60% of courses at private universities. More than 14% of courses at all institutions put class materials on the World Wide Web, and more than 24% of other courses use other Web resources, the survey found.

Since the early 1990s, a monumental watershed has occurred: the Industrial Age has given way to the Information Age. "In 1991 companies for the first time spent more on computing and communications gear," says one report, "than on industrial, mining, farm, and construction machines. Info tech is now as vital . . . as the air we breathe."[4]

"Info tech"—information technology—is what this chapter is about. **_Information technology_ is technology that merges computers with high-speed communications links.** Learning to use the tools of information technology—computers, the Internet, the World Wide

---

GROUP ACTIVITY #3.1

WHAT ARE YOUR FEARS ABOUT COMPUTERS?

You and your fellow students should take a few minutes to list, on a half sheet of paper or 3 × 5 card, your concerns, frustrations, and anxieties about information technology—computers and communications devices. Are you worried about being unable to learn certain kinds of software? Are you frustrated by computers "crashing"? Important: You should not sign your name to the cards.

The instructor will collect all the lists and shuffle them. A student or students will then be asked to come to the front of the class, pick a list at random, and copy the material on the board. One area of the board should be saved; the instructor will write down common concerns here.

Questions for discussion: What are common themes? What are your reactions to the most common themes? What techniques or resources do you have to cope with these concerns? What are some horror stories about using computers?

Personal Computers

PREVIEW & REVIEW Most students find they benefit by having access to a personal computer (PC), either IBM-style or Macintosh, desktop or laptop. Buying a PC often requires making a trade-off between power (software that is flexible, hardware that is fast and has great data capacity) and expense.

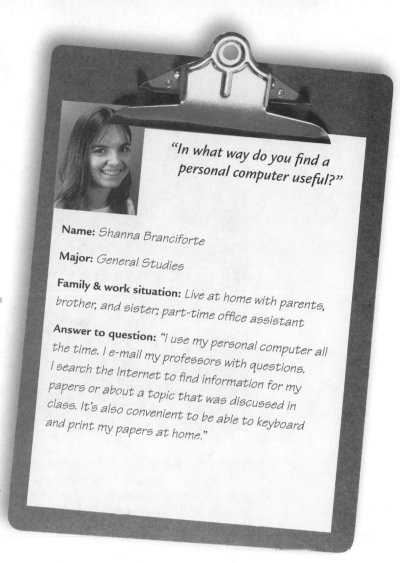

"In what way do you find a personal computer useful?"

Name: Shanna Branciforte

Major: General Studies

Family & work situation: Live at home with parents, brother, and sister; part-time office assistant

Answer to question: "I use my personal computer all the time. I e-mail my professors with questions. I search the Internet to find information for my papers or about a topic that was discussed in class. It's also convenient to be able to keyboard and print my papers at home."

A s an English Lit major at Swarthmore College, Dominic Sagolla hadn't much interest in computers. But after the college gave students access to the Internet from their dorms during his sophomore year, Sagolla found himself smitten. And after he took a number of computer-related courses, he landed a job upon graduation with computer maker Hewlett-Packard—as an information technology specialist.[5]

Given the direction of today's competitive job market, learning about information technology has become a must. "Any exposure to technology, whether through a class or self-teaching, is an additional set of tangible skills a student offers to an employer," says Simone Himbeault-Taylor, director of career planning and placement at the University of Michigan.[6] The first step is to learn how to use a computer.

Students who come to campus with a **_personal computer (PC)_—a desktop or portable computer that can run easy-to-use, personal-assistance software such as a word processing program**—are certainly ahead of the game. However, if you don't have one, there are other options.

IF YOU DON'T OWN A PERSONAL COMPUTER.
If you don't have a PC, you may be able to borrow someone else's sometimes. However, if you have a paper due the next day, you may have to defer to the owner, who may also have a deadline. When borrowing, then, you need to plan ahead and allow yourself plenty of time.

Virtually every campus now makes computers available to students, either at minimal cost or essentially for free as part of the regular student fees. This availability may take the following forms:

- **_Dormitory computer centers or dorm-room terminals:_** Residential campuses may provide dormitory-based computer centers (for example, in the basement). Even if you have your own PC, it's nice to know about these for backup purposes.

More and more campuses are also providing computers or terminals within students' dormitory rooms. These are usually connected by a campuswide local area network (LAN) to lab computers and administrative systems. Often, however, they also allow students to communicate over phone lines to people in other states.

- ***Library or computer labs:*** Both residential and commuter campuses may have computers available at the library or campus computer lab. Even students who have their own PCs may sometimes want to use these machines, which may have special software or better printers that they don't have.

- ***"Loaner" computers:*** On some campuses (such as mine), there are learning centers or special programs in which you can actually borrow a personal computer as a "loaner"—that is, take a portable computer home with you.

  Of course, if the system cannot accommodate a large number of students, all the computers may be in high demand come term-paper time. Clearly, owning a computer offers you convenience and a competitive advantage. Not having one, however, does not mean you are destined to fail in school.

IF YOU DO OWN A PERSONAL COMPUTER. Perhaps someone gave you a personal computer, or you acquired one, before you came to college. It will probably be one of two types: (1) an Apple Macintosh or (2) an IBM or IBM-compatible. IBM-compatibles go under such names as Acer, AST, Compaq, DEC, Dell, Gateway 2000, Hewlett-Packard, Micron, NEC, NCR, Packard Bell, Sony, and Toshiba.

If all you need to do is write term papers, nearly any microcomputer, new or used, will do. Indeed, you may not even need to have a printer, if you can find other ways to print out things. Some campuses (the University of Michigan, for instance) offer "express stations" or "drive-up windows." These allow students to use a diskette (floppy disk) or connect a computer to a student-use printer to print out their papers. Or, if a friend has a compatible computer, you can ask to borrow it and the printer for a short time to print your work.

You should, however, take a look around you to see if your present system is appropriate for your campus and your major.

- ***The fit with your campus:*** Some campuses are known as "IBM" (or IBM-compatible) schools, others as "Mac" (Macintosh) schools, although today Apple Macintosh accounts for only about 4% of new computers sold throughout the U.S.

Why should choice of machine matter? The answer is that diskettes generally can't be read interchangeably among the two main types of microcomputers. Thus, if you own the system that is out of step for your campus, you may find it difficult to swap files or programs with others. Nor will you be able to borrow their equipment to finish a paper if yours breaks down. (There are some conversion programs, but these take time and may not be readily available.) Call the dean of students or otherwise ask around to find which system is most popular.

■ *The fit with your major:* Speech communications, physical education, political science, biology, and English majors probably don't need a fancy computer system. Business, engineering, architecture, foreign language, and journalism majors may have special requirements.

For instance, an architecture major doing computer-aided design (CAD) projects or a journalism major doing desktop publishing might need reasonably powerful systems. A history or nursing major, who will mainly be writing papers, would probably not.

Of course, you may be presently undeclared or undecided about your major. Even so, it's a good idea to find out what kinds of equipment and programs are being used in the majors you are contemplating.

DESKTOP VERSUS PORTABLE. Look for a computer that fits your work style. For instance, you may want a portable if you spend a lot of time at the library. Some students even use portables to take notes in class. If you do most of your work in your room or at home, you may find it more comfortable to have a desktop PC. Though not portable, the monitors of desktop computers are usually easier to read.

Actually, however, portables have come so far along that you'll probably have no trouble reading the screens on the latest models. Keep in mind, however, that the keyboards on portables are smaller.

GETTING YOUR OWN PERSONAL COMPUTER: POWER VERSUS EXPENSE. Buying a personal computer, like buying a car, often requires making a trade-off between power and expense.

■ *Power:* Some students look for a personal computer system with as much power as possible. The word *power* has different meanings when describing software and hardware.

Applied to software, "powerful" means that the program is *flexible*. That is, it can do many different things. For example, a word processing program that can print in different typestyles (fonts) is more powerful than one that prints in only one style.

Applied to hardware, "powerful" means that the equipment (1) is *fast* and (2) has *great capacity*. A fast computer will process data more quickly than a slow one. With an older computer, for example, it may take several seconds to save, or store on a disk, a 50-page term paper. On a newer machine, it might take less than a second.

A computer with great capacity can run complex software and process voluminous files. *This is an especially important matter if you want to be able to run the latest versions of software.*

Will computer use make up an essential part of your major, as it might if you are going into engineering, business, or graphic arts? If so, you may want to try to acquire powerful hardware and software. People who really want (and can afford) their own desktop publishing system might buy a new Macintosh G3 with color inkjet or laser printer, scanner, and special software. This might well cost $7,000 or so. Most students, of course, cannot afford anything close to this.

Expense: If your major does not require a special computer system, a microcomputer can be acquired for relatively little. You can probably buy a used computer, with software thrown in, for under $500 and a printer for under $200.

What's the *minimum* you should get? Probably an IBM-compatible or Macintosh system with 4 megabytes of memory and two diskette drives or one diskette and one hard-disk drive. However, up to 16 megabytes of memory is preferable if you're going to run many of today's programs. Megabytes, along with kilobytes and gigabytes, are measures of storage capacity. A *kilobyte* is equal to about a thousand characters (letters and numbers) of information, a *megabyte* to a million characters, and a *gigabyte* to a billion characters.

As for printers, *dot-matrix printers* (the kind that use little pins to construct a letter out of small dots) are still in use on many campuses (24-pin printers are preferable to 9-pin). However, prices have plummeted for inkjet and laser printers, so that the cheap but noisy dot-matrix printer may well be going the way of the black-and-white TV set. Your choice in printers may come down to how much you print and whether you need color.

Inkjet printers, which spray ink onto the page a line at a time, can give you both high-quality black-and-white text and high-quality color graphics. The rock-bottom price for inkjets is only about $150. However, if you print a lot of color, you'll find color inkjets slower and more expensive to operate than color laser printers.

Laser printers, which print a page at a time, can handle thousands of black-and-white pages a month. Moreover, compared to inkjets, laser printers are faster and crisper (though not by much) at printing black-and-white copies and a cent or two cheaper per page. Finally, a freshly printed page from a laser won't smear, as one from an inkjet might. Low-end black-and-white laser printers start at about $200; color laser printers are considerably more expensive.

There are three ways to acquire a PC: buy new, buy used, or lease.

BUYING A NEW COMPUTER. There are several sources for inexpensive new computers, as follows:

- **Student-discount sources:** With a college ID card, you're probably entitled to a student discount (usually 10–20%) through the campus bookstore or college computer resellers. In addition, during the first few weeks of the term, many campuses offer special sales on computer equipment. Campus resellers also provide on-campus service and support.

- **Computer superstores:** These are big chains such as Computer City, CompUSA, and Microage. Computers are also sold at department stores, warehouse stores (such as Costco and Sam's Club), office-supply chains such as Staples and Office Depot, and electronics stores such as The Good Guys and Circuit City.

- **Mail-order houses:** Companies such as Dell Computer Corp. and Gateway 2000 found they could sell computers inexpensively while offering customer support over the phone. Their success inspired IBM, Compaq, and others to plunge into the mail-order business.

The price advantage of mail-order companies has eroded with the rise of computer superstores. Moreover, the lack of local repair and service support can be a major disadvantage. Still, if you're interested in this route, look for a copy of the phone-book-size magazine *Computer Shopper,* which carries ads from most mail-order vendors.

When buying a new computer, make sure the system software that comes with it is at least Windows 98 for a PC and at least System 8 for the Macintosh. Also, look to see if any applications software, such as word processing or spreadsheet programs, comes "bundled" with it. In this case, *bundled* means the software is included in the selling price of the hardware. This arrangement can be a real advantage, saving you several hundred dollars. Computer columnist Phillip Robinson offers several other suggestions for saving money in buying a new PC and software.[7] *(See ■ Panel 3.1.)*

Saving on computers, accessories, and software.

FIRST: Slow down the cycle. Don't buy every upgrade or even every other upgrade. . . .

Go from version 2.0 to 4.0, skipping right over 2.1, 3.0, and 3.1. Such version numbers are about as reliable indicators of feature changes as dress sizes from different manufacturers and countries, but at least they give some idea. Think about buying a new computer only as often as you buy a new car.

SECOND: Don't buy the absolute best the day it comes out. If you really, really want to have it, wait six months. Then it will only be second or third best, and will cost a fair amount less—because some other, glossier new "state of the art" tool will be available. . . .

THIRD: Avoid paying full price for software. Most important programs—especially for business and office "productivity"—are sold two ways: as full packages and as upgrades. The full package might cost $500 and the upgrade just $100. . . .

Read the fine print on the "upgrade" offer. Usually, you qualify for an upgrade if you use an earlier version or a long list of competing programs, one of which may already be on your hard drive or have come free with your scanner or modem. Maybe you can even buy it used at a swap meet: a $10 or $50 program could save you $400 or more. An old word processor from any of a dozen companies may be enough to get you the latest full office suite with word processor, spreadsheet, database, and more.

FOURTH: Buy technical support before technology. Unless you're an expert, you're better off with a 24-hour toll-free line than the fastest processor. Make sure that support line actually has live people on the other end, not just recordings or fax-back help. If you're doing a lot of home computing, look for weekend support hours.

Ask if the tech support covers everything, because some hardware companies are now excluding bundled software . . .

FIFTH: Look at the warranty. If it is 90 days, don't buy. If it is one year, ask the salespeople if the item is really worth the price if it will only last a year. If they assure you it will last longer, than why won't the warranty? . . .

SIXTH: Negotiate. Not all computer stores or mail-order companies will bargain with you, but some will. They'll cut the price, beef up some hardware component, throw in some software or supplies, extend a warranty, etc. Always be ready to go elsewhere, or to another 800 number, and do so if you can't make a deal. . . .

SEVENTH: Beware restockings. Some companies guarantee that you can return an item in 30 days for any reason, and then charge you a "restocking fee"—sometimes hundreds of dollars—to take it back. Don't buy if there's a restocking fee.

EIGHTH: Ask if batteries or other needed parts are included. This goes for cables, too. Are there any other elements you'll need? Each might only cost $10 to $20, but that adds up, and some companies toss them into the computer, printer, or software box at no extra charge.

NINTH: Check the price of consumables. Your computer system may soon feel like the hungriest mouth to feed in the house. The printer is the worst offender, with many of the latest printers intentionally designed to send you back to the store regularly to buy $40 ink cartridges and $1 sheets of special paper. . . .

BONUS CATEGORY: Rebates—I discovered, in talking with several tech companies, that only about 20% of buyers ever send in a manufacturer's rebate coupon—even if that coupon is for $50 or more. Companies love this because they can advertise those "Only $200" prices with small print saying "after manufacturer's rebate," and yet rarely have to pay the rebate. Send that coupon in as soon as you get home.

—Phillip Robinson, "There Are Many Ways to Pinch Pennies on PCs," *San Jose Mercury News*

BUYING A USED COMPUTER. Buying a used computer can save you 50%, depending on its age. If you don't need the latest software, this can often be the way to go. The most important thing is to buy recognizable brand names, examples being Apple and IBM or well-known IBM-compatibles (see the ones listed top of p. 54). Obscure or discontinued brands may not be repairable.

Among the sources for used computers are the following:

- *Retail sources:* A look in the Yellow Pages under "Computers, Used" will produce several leads. Authorized dealers (of IBM, Apple, Compaq, and so on) may shave prices on demonstration (demo) or training equipment.

- *Used-computer brokers:* There are a number of used-computer brokers, such as American Computer Exchange, Boston Computer Exchange, and National Computer Exchange.

- *Individuals:* Classified ads in local newspapers, shopper throwaways, and (in some localities) free computer newspapers and magazines provide listings of used computer equipment. Similar listings may also appear on electronic bulletin board systems (BBSs) on the World Wide Web.

One problem with buying from individuals is that they may not feel obligated to take the equipment back if something goes wrong. Thus, you should inspect the equipment carefully.[8] (See ■ Panel 3.2.) For a small fee, a computer-repair shop can check out the hardware for damage before you buy it. Be sure to check for a serial number, to help protect against buying stolen equipment. Also make sure the equipment comes with instruction books and other documentation.

LEASING A COMPUTER. Mail-order companies such as Dell and Gateway 2000, as well as retailers such as CompUSA, allow consumers to lease computers. Dell, for instance, provides a PC that would cost about $2,300 new but that can be leased for $106 a month for 24 months, which amounts to $2,544. This is more than the purchase price, but at that point you could choose to return the machine to Dell, buy it for fair market value, or trade it in for a new and more powerful machine at about the same lease rate.

PANEL 3.2

Tips for buying a used computer. Buying from an individual means you have little recourse if something goes wrong. The following tips should help you to buy carefully.

- If possible, take someone who knows computers with you.

- Turn the computer on and off a few times to make sure there are no problems on startup.

- Use the computer and, if possible, try the software you want to use. Listen for strange sounds in the hard drive or the floppies.

- Turn the computer off and look for screen burn-in, a ghost image on the screen after the machine has been turned off. It can be a sign of misuse.

- Ask about the warranty. Some companies, including Apple and IBM, permit warranties to be transferred to new owners (effective from the date of the original purchase). A new owner can usually have the warranty extended by paying a fee.

WHAT IS THE BEST WAY TO GAIN ACCESS TO A PERSONAL COMPUTER IN SCHOOL?

In class, discuss with other students various ideas for gaining access to a personal computer.

Questions for discussion: Are computers available in the library? Are there "loaners" from the learning center? What about student-use printers for printing out research papers? Does the bookstore sell personal computers? Is there a student discount? Where could one buy a used computer?

Computer Software

PREVIEW & REVIEW Personal computers provide the following kinds of productivity software to help you with educational and work tasks: word processing, spreadsheets, database management systems, personal information managers, presentation graphics, and integrated programs and suites.

There are thousands of software programs, available on floppy disks or CD-ROM disks, that will run on computer hardware. This section describes the following kinds, known as productivity software because they help you improve your personal productivity:

- Word processing
- Spreadsheets
- Database management systems
- Personal information managers
- Presentation graphics
- Integrated programs and suites

As a measure of the usefulness of these programs outside of school, small-business owners say the software they use most often is word processing (by 94% of those surveyed), spreadsheet (75%), and database management (67%).[9]

WORD PROCESSING. The typewriter, that long-lived machine, has gone to its reward. Today the usual alternative is a personal computer with word processing software and a printer.

Word processing software **allows you to use computers to create, edit, revise, store, and print text material.** Most current programs provide a number of **_menus_, or lists of choices, for manipulating aspects of your document.** Popular word processing programs are Microsoft Word, Lotus WordPro, or Corel WordPerfect, all for IBM-style PCs, and WordPerfect for the Macintosh. _(See ▪ Panel 3.3.)_

Word processing software allows you to use your computer to maneuver through a document with a cursor (a blinking symbol that shows where you are in the text) and _delete, insert,_ and _replace_ text, the principal correction activities. There are also additional features,

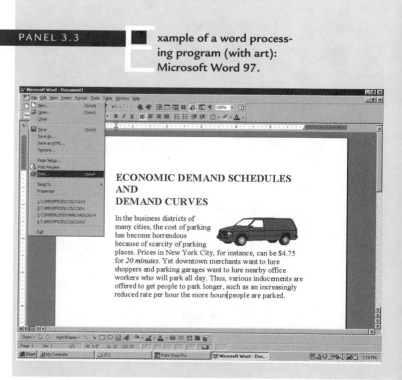

PANEL 3.3

Example of a word processing program (with art): Microsoft Word 97.

such as *search, replace,* and *cut-and-paste* commands; spelling checker; grammar checker; and a thesaurus (which gives alternate word suggestions when you're trying to think of the right word).

SPREADSHEET SOFTWARE. What is a spreadsheet? Traditionally, it was simply a grid of rows and columns, printed on special green paper, that was used by accountants and other financial types to produce financial projections and reports. A person making up a spreadsheet often spent long days and weekends at the office penciling tiny numbers into countless tiny rectangles. When one figure changed, all the rest of the numbers on the spreadsheet had to be recomputed—and ultimately there might have been wastebaskets full of old worksheets.

In the late 1970s, someone got the idea of computerizing all this. **The _electronic spreadsheet_ allows users to create tables and financial schedules by entering data into rows and columns arranged as a grid on a display screen.** The electronic spreadsheet quickly became the most popular small-business program. Today the principal spreadsheets are Excel, Lotus 1-2-3, and Quattro Pro. *(See* ■ *Panel 3.4.)*

Spreadsheets can be used to display data in graphic form, such as in pie charts or bar charts, which are easier to read than columns of numbers. One of the most important features, however, is the "what-if" or recalculation feature. That is, you can change one number in a calculation and see how all other numbers are affected.

DATABASE MANAGEMENT SYSTEMS. In its most general sense, a database is any electronically stored collection of data in a computer system. In its more specific sense, **a _database_ is a collection of interrelated files in a computer system. These computer-based files are organized so that those parts that have a common element can be retrieved easily.** The software for maintaining a database is a **_database manager_ or _database management system (DBMS)_, a program that controls the structure of a database and access to the data.** Thus, for example, the Registrar's Office can look for a record about you in different ways: by name, by major, by city or state, or by Social Security number.

Today the principal database managers are Microsoft Access, Microsoft Visual FoxPro, dBASE, Paradox, and Claris Filemaker Pro. *(See* ■ *Panel 3.5.)*

PANEL 3.4   Example of spreadsheet: Excel.

PANEL 3.5   Example of database manager: Microsoft Access.

Databases have gotten easier to use, but they still can be difficult to set up. Even so, the trend is toward making such programs easier for both database creators and database users.

PERSONAL INFORMATION MANAGERS. Pretend you are sitting at a desk in an old-fashioned office. You have a calendar, Rolodex-type address file, and notepad (items that could also be found on a student's desk). How would a computer and software improve on this arrangement?

Many people find ready uses for specialized types of database software known as personal information managers. **A _personal information manager (PIM)_ is software to help you keep track of and manage information you use on a daily basis, such as addresses, telephone numbers, appointments, To-Do lists, and miscellaneous notes.** Some programs feature phone dialers, outliners (for roughing out ideas in outline form), and ticklers (or reminders). With a PIM, you can key in notes in any way you like and then retrieve them later based on any of the words you typed.

Popular PIMs are Lotus Organizer, Microsoft Outlook, and ACT. *(See ▪ Panel 3.6.)*

PRESENTATION GRAPHICS SOFTWARE. Computer graphics can be highly complicated, such as those used in special effects for movies (such as *Twister* or *Titanic*). Here we are concerned with just one kind of graphics called presentation graphics.

Presentation graphics are part of presentation software, which uses graphics and data from other software programs to communicate or make a presentation of data to others, such as clients or supervisors. Presentation graphics are also used in information kiosks, multimedia training, and lectures.

Presentations may make use of some analytical graphics—bar, line, and pie charts—but they usually look much more sophisticated, using, for instance, different texturing patterns (speckled, solid, cross-hatched), color, and three-dimensionality. Examples of well-known presentation graphics packages are Microsoft PowerPoint, Aldus Persuasion, Lotus Freelance Graphics, and Compel. *(See ▪ Panel 3.7.)*

Presentation graphics are often output as 35-millimeter slides, which can be projected on a screen or displayed on a large monitor.

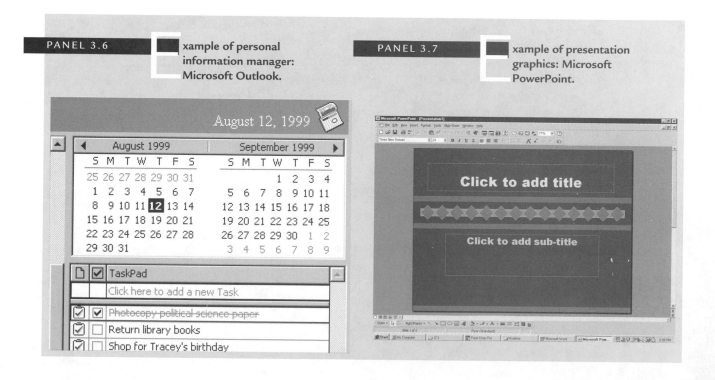

PANEL 3.6 Example of personal information manager: Microsoft Outlook.

PANEL 3.7 Example of presentation graphics: Microsoft PowerPoint.

INTEGRATED PROGRAMS & SUITES. What if you want to take data from one program and use it in another—say, call up data from a database and use it in a spreadsheet? You can try using separate software packages, but one may not be designed to accept data from the other. Two alternatives are the collections of software known as *integrated software* and *software suites*.

■ *Integrated software—"works" programs:* <u>Integrated software packages</u> **combine the features of several applications programs—such as word processing, spreadsheet, database, and graphics—into one software package.** These so-called "works" collections—the principal representatives are AppleWorks, ClarisWorks, Lotus Works, Microsoft Works, and PerfectWorks—give good value because the entire package often sells for $100 or less.

Some of these "works" programs have "assistants" that help you accomplish various tasks. Thus, Microsoft's Works for Windows 95 helps you create new documents with the help of 39 "task wizards." The wizards lead you through the process of creating a letter, for example, that permits you to customize as many features as you want.

Integrated software packages are less powerful than separate programs used alone, such as a word processing or spreadsheet program used by itself. But that may be fine, because single-purpose programs may be more complicated and demand more computer resources than necessary. You may have no need, for instance, for a word processor that will create an index. Moreover, Microsoft Word takes up about 20 megabytes on your hard disk, whereas Microsoft Works takes only 7 megabytes, which leaves a lot more room for other software.

■ *Software suites: "office" programs:* <u>Software suites</u>, **or simply** <u>suites</u>, **are applications— such as spreadsheets, word processing, and graphics—that are bundled together and sold for a fraction of what the programs would cost if bought individually.**

Three principal suites, sometimes called "office" programs, are available from Microsoft (with an estimated 93%

of the suite market in 1998), IBM Lotus (with 4%), and Corel (3%).[10] Microsoft's Office 97 is available in both "standard" and "professional" versions. IBM's Lotus SmartSuite 97 comes in one version. Corel's WordPerfect Suite 7 is the "standard" version and Office Professional is the "professional" version. Microsoft Office 97 consists of programs that separately would cost perhaps $1,500 but as a suite in the standard version costs $399 retail for new users.

Although lower price is what makes suites attractive to many customers, the software has other benefits as well. Software makers have tried to integrate the "look and feel" of the separate programs within the suites to make them easier to use.

A trade-off, however, is that such packages require a lot of storage capacity on your computer. The standard edition of Office 97 hogs 120 megabytes and Corel gobbles up 157 megabytes of hard-disk space—quite a lot if your hard disk holds, say, only 200 megabytes. (Compare with the "works" program ClarisWorks at 13 megabytes.)

GROUP ACTIVITY #3.3

FINDING HELP WITH COMPUTING

I n class discussion, share various ways to find help with problems related to computers.

Questions for discussion: What kind of assistance does the school offer in learning about computers? Is there a class you could take in how to use popular software? Is there a computer support center? A call-in number? A user support service? Are there some people who could serve as mentors? Is there an online place with FAQs—"Frequently Asked Questions"? Are there some helpful books?

The Internet

PREVIEW & REVIEW The Internet is the world's biggest computer network. Users can connect to the Internet via direct connections, online information services, and Internet service providers. The Internet provides a variety of tools: e-mail addresses, Usenet newsgroups, mailing lists, FTP, and Telnet.

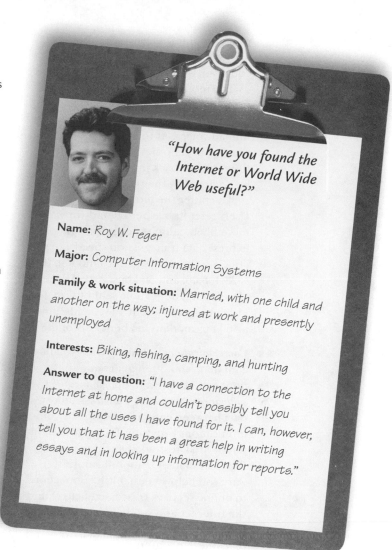

"How have you found the Internet or World Wide Web useful?"

Name: Roy W. Feger

Major: Computer Information Systems

Family & work situation: Married, with one child and another on the way; injured at work and presently unemployed

Interests: Biking, fishing, camping, and hunting

Answer to question: "I have a connection to the Internet at home and couldn't possibly tell you about all the uses I have found for it. I can, however, tell you that it has been a great help in writing essays and in looking up information for reports."

C alled "the mother of all networks," **the _Internet_, or simply "the Net," is an international network connecting approximately 140,000 smaller networks in more than 200 countries.** These networks are formed by educational, commercial, nonprofit, government, and military entities. The number of personal computers hooked up to the Internet jumped 71% between 1996 and 1997—to 82 million—and is expected to triple to 268 million by 2001.[11] The most popular part of the Internet, as I discuss in the next section, is the World Wide Web, which carries pictures, sounds, and video, as well as text. (The rest of the Net is strictly text-based.)

"Try as you may," says one writer, "you cannot imagine how much data is available on the Internet."[12] Besides offering electronic mail, chat rooms (discussion forums), bulletin boards, games, and free software, the Internet provides access to hundreds of thousands of databases containing information of all sorts. Here is a sampling:

> _The Library of Congress card catalog. The daily White House press releases. Weather maps and forecasts. Schedules of professional sports teams. Weekly Nielsen television ratings. Recipe archives. The Central Intelligence Agency world map. A ZIP Code guide. The National Family Database. Project Gutenberg (offering the complete text of many works of literature). The Alcoholism Research Data Base. Guitar chords. U.S. government addresses and phone (and fax) numbers. The Simpsons archive._[13]

And those are just a few droplets from what is a Niagara Falls of information.

MODEMS & COMMUNICATIONS SOFTWARE: WHAT YOU NEED TO CONNECT TO THE INTERNET. To connect with the Internet, you need a computer with a device called a _modem_, appropriate communications software, and access to a telephone line (or other network connection).

- _Modem:_ **A _modem_ (_moh_-dem) is an electronic device that allows computers to communicate with each other over a telephone line.** A modem may be purchased as a kind of small box that goes outside your computer. These days, however, nearly all new personal computers come equipped with a modem inside.

The modem translates the signals of the computer into signals that can be carried over telephone lines designed for human voices. At the other end of the phone line, another modem translates those signals back into signals that can be accepted by the receiving computer.

The faster the modem, the better. Users refer to bits per second (bps) or, more likely, kilobits per second (kbps) to express data transmission speeds. In general, you should try to get a modem that is 28.4, 33.6, and 56 kbps. A 10-page, single-spaced letter can be sent by a 28.4-kbps modem in about 10 seconds and by a 56-kbps modem in about 5 seconds.

Communications software: When you buy a modem, you often get communications software with it. *Communications software* **manages the transmission of data between computers.** Popular communications programs for personal computers are Crosstalk, QuickLink, and Procomm Plus. Communications software can help you establish connections to online services (discussed below) and the Internet and send fax messages from your computer to other people's fax machines or computers.

SERVICES FOR CONNECTING YOU TO THE INTERNET. There are three ways to connect your personal computer with the Internet:

- *Through school or work—dedicated access:* Universities, colleges, and most large businesses have high-speed phone lines that provide a direct connection to the Internet. This type of connection is known as dedicated access. *Dedicated access* **means a communication line is used that is designed for one purpose.**

    As a student, this may be the best deal because the connection is free or low cost. However, if you live off-campus and want to get this Internet connection from home, you probably won't be able to do so. You can find out from the Dean of Students office or perhaps your

instructor in this class how you can get dedicated access.

- *Through online information services:* Subscribing to a commercial online information service—such as America Online, CompuServe, Prodigy, or Microsoft Network—provides you with an electronic gateway to the Internet. (■ *See Panel 3.8.)* **An** *online information service* **provides access to all kinds of databases and electronic meeting places to subscribers equipped with telephone-linked personal computers.** This method may not be the cheapest way to connect to the Internet, but it is still one of the easiest. With this kind of connection, you are charged a

PANEL 3.8

Principal Internet service providers: online information services. There are thousands of ISPs in the United States, but the four principal online services—AOL, CompuServe, MSN, and Prodigy— have the most customers

America Online (AOL)
   10 million customers
   Rates: 50 free hours with download of trial software, then $21.95 per month.
   Toll-free phone: 1-800-827-6364
   Web address: *http://www.aol.com*

CompuServe
   5.5 million customers
   Rates: 1 month free with trial software, then $24.95 per month for unlimited use or $9.95 per month for 5 hours and $2.95 per hour thereafter
   Toll-free phone: 1-800-848-8199
   Web address: *http://www.compuserve.com*

Microsoft Network (MSN)
   3 million customers
   Rates: $69.50 per year for unlimited use or $19.95 per month for unlimited use, or $6.95 per month for 5 hours and $2.50 per hour thereafter
   Toll-free phone: 1-800-FREE-MSN
   Web address: *http://www.microsoft.com*

Prodigy
   1 million customers
   Rates: 1 month free, then $19.95 per month
   Toll-free phone: 1-800-776-3449
   Web address: *http://www.prodigy.com*

Internet service providers
   7.5 million customers

Others
   1 million customers

monthly or hourly fee for dialing into an intermediary source that then connects to the Internet.

As one of the hundreds of thousands of subscribers connected to an online service, you can have access to *e-mail, computer games* (both single-player and multi-player), *research, travel services,* and *shopping services.* The only restriction on the amount of research you can do online is the limit on whatever credit card you are charging your time to. Depending on the online service, you can avail yourself of several encyclopedias. Many online services store unabridged text from newspapers and magazines. Other features are book and movie/video news, contests, health reports, parenting advice, car-rental information, microwave cooking instructions, and on and on.

Before you can use an online information service, you need to open an account with it, using a credit card. Billing policies resemble those used by cable-TV and telephone companies. As with cable TV, you may be charged a fee for basic service, with additional fees for specialized services. In addition, the online service may charge you for the time spent while on the line. Finally, you will also be charged by your telephone

company for your time on the line, just as when making a regular phone call. However, most information services offer local access numbers. Thus, unless you live in a rural area, you will not be paying long-distance phone charges. All told, the typical user may pay $10–$20 a month to use an online service, although it's possible to run a bill of $100 or more. To keep costs down, many users go online only during off-hours (evenings and weekends), when the charges intended for business users are reduced.

■ *Through Internet service providers (ISPs):* **_Internet service providers (ISPs)_ are local or national companies that will provide unlimited public access to the Internet and World Wide Web for a flat monthly fee.** Essentially an ISP is a small network that hooks into the high-speed communications links (backbone) that make up the Internet—the major supercomputer sites and educational and research foundations within the United States and throughout the world. There are more than 5,000 ISPs in the United States, and the field is growing rapidly.[14]

Once you have contacted an ISP and paid the required fee, the ISP will provide you with information about phone numbers for connections and about how to set up your computer and modem to dial into their network. This will require dealing with some system software settings (which will be saved by the computer), using a user name ("user ID") and a password, and typing in some other specified information. After this, you can use a browser (such as Netscape Navigator or Microsoft Explorer, as I will explain) to find your way around the World Wide Web, the graphical part of the Internet.

So far, most ISPs have been small and limited in geographic coverage. Among the largest national companies are NET-COM, AT&T WorldNet, network MCI, SPRYNET, and EarthLink Network. Other ISPs are MindSpring Enterprises, UUNet Technologies, BBN Corporation, Pacific Bell Internet, and Tele-Communication Inc.'s @Home (pronounced "At Home").

Some national Internet service providers.

ISP company	Toll-free number
NETCOM	800-538-2551
AT&T WorldNet	800-967-5363
network MCI	800-550-0927
SPRYNET	800-777-9638
EarthLink Network	800-395-8425

(See ▪ Panel 3.9.) You can ask someone who already knows how to get on the World Wide Web to access the worldwide list of ISPs at *http://www.thelist.com.* This site presents pricing data and describes the features supported by each ISP.

INTERNET ADDRESSES. To send and receive e-mail on the Internet and interact with other networks, you need an Internet address. An Internet address (domain name) usually has two sections. Consider the address *president@whitehouse.gov.us*

The first section, the userID, tells "who" is at the address—in this case, *president* is the recipient. (Sometimes an underscore, or _, is used between a recipient's first name or initials and last name: *bill_clinton,* for example.) The first and second sections are separated by an @ (called "at") symbol. The second section—in this case, *whitehouse. gov.us*—tells "where" the address is. Components are separated by periods, called "dots." The second section includes the location (such as *whitehouse;* the location may have more than one part), the top-level domain (such as *.gov, .edu,* and *.com,* as I explain next), and country if required (such as *.us* for United States and *.se* for Sweden).

Among the top-level domains are *.com* for commercial organizations, *.edu* for educational and research organizations, *.gov* for governmental organizations, *.mil* for military organizations, *.net* for gateway or host networks, and *.org* for nonprofit or miscellaneous organizations.

FEATURES OF THE INTERNET. "For many people, the Internet has subsumed the functions of libraries, telephones, televisions, catalogs—even support groups and singles bars," says writer Jared Sandberg. "And that's just a sample of its capabilities."[15]

The leading online activities, ranked by the percentage of users who say they do each, are e-mail (32%), research (25%), news/information (22%), entertainment (19%), education (13%), and chat lines/chat rooms (8%).[16]

Let us consider the Internet tools at your disposal:

▪ *E-mail:* "The World Wide Web is getting all the headlines, but for many people the main attraction of the Internet is electronic mail," says technology writer David Einstein.[17] There are millions of users of e-mail in the world, and although half of them are on private corporate networks, a great many of the rest are on the Internet. **_E-mail_, or _electronic mail_, enables users to send letters and files from one computer to another.** Foremost among the Internet e-mail programs is Eudora (others are Microsoft Outlook, Lotus CC:Mail, and Pegasus Mail), which is used by the majority of the educational institutions on the Net. Nowadays you can also get e-mail as a free service, as we shall discuss in the section on the World Wide Web.

▪ *Usenet newsgroups—electronic discussion groups:* One of the Internet's most interesting features goes under the name *usenet,* short for "user network," which is essentially a giant, dispersed bulletin board. **_Usenet newsgroups_ are electronic discussion groups that focus on a specific topic.** They are one of the most lively and heavily trafficked areas of the Net.

Usenet users exchange e-mail and messages ("news"). "Users post questions, answers, general information, and FAQ files on Usenet," says one online specialist. "The flow of messages, or 'articles,' is phenomenal, and you can get easily hooked."[18] Pronounced "fack," **a *FAQ,* for *Frequently Asked Questions,* is a file that lays out the basics for a newsgroup's discussion.** It's always best to read a newsgroup's FAQ before joining the discussion or posting (asking) questions.

There are more than 15,000 Usenet newsgroup forums and they cover hundreds of topics. Examples are *rec.arts.startrek.info, soc.culture.african. american,* and *misc.jobs.offered.* The first part is the group—*rec* for recreation, *soc* for social issues, *comp* for computers, *biz* for business, *sci* for science, *misc* for miscellaneous. The next part is the subject—for example, *rec.food.cooking.* The category called *alt* news groups offers more free-form topics, such as *alt.rock-n-roll.metal* or *alt.internet.services.*

■ *Mailing lists—e-mail-based discussion groups:* Combining e-mail and newsgroups, mailing lists—called *listservs*—allow you to subscribe (generally free) to an e-mail mailing list on a particular subject or subjects. The mailing-list sponsor then sends the identical message to everyone on that list. Thus, the newsgroup listserv messages appear automatically in your mailbox; you do not have to make the effort of accessing the newsgroup. (As a result, it's necessary to download and delete mail almost every day, or your mailbox will quickly become full.) There are more than 3,000 electronic mailing-list discussion groups.

■ *FTP—for copying all the free files you want:* Many Net users enjoy "FTPing"—cruising the system and checking into some of the tens of thousands of so-called FTP sites offering interesting free files to copy (download). **FTP, for File Transfer Protocol, is a method whereby you can connect to a remote computer called an FTP site and transfer publicly available files to your own microcomputer's hard disk.** The free files offered cover nearly anything that can be stored on a computer: software, games, photos, maps, art, music, books, statistics.

Some 2,000-plus FTP sites (so-called *anonymous FTP sites*) are open to anyone; others can be accessed only by knowing a password. You can also use FTP to upload (transfer) your files to an FTP site. Many online information services and ISPs, as well as Web browsers, offer FTP programs to their users.

■ *Telnet—to connect to remote computers:* __Telnet__ **is a cooperative system that allows you to connect (log on) to remote computers.** This feature, which allows microcomputers to communicate successfully with big computers (mainframes), enables you to tap into Internet computers and public-access files as though you were connected directly instead of, for example, through your ISP site.

Although it is a text-only means of communication, the Telnet feature is especially useful for perusing large databases or library card catalogs. There are perhaps 1,000 library catalogs accessible through the Internet, and a few thousand more Internet sites around the world have Telnet interfaces. Telnet programs are also usually provided by ISPs and information services, as well as some operating systems.

There are some other Internet features (such as Gopher and WAIS) you may also wish to look into once you get some experience. One last feature of the Internet remains to be discussed—perhaps, for most general users, the most important one: the World Wide Web.

USING THE INTERNET

Some students in your class—or you yourself—may already have had great exposure to the Internet and the World Wide Web. In class discussion, this may yield some interesting insights in how to use these resources.

Questions for discussion: How do you gain access to the Net and the Web? Are there terminals or workstations on campus that all students may use? Where are they located? Are there rules for their use? Is there a way a student can connect his or her own modem-equipped personal computer for Internet access? What browsers are best? What search tools (directories and search engines) are most useful? Can the Internet and the Web be used for research for term papers? How?

The World Wide Web

PREVIEW & REVIEW The Web is one component of the Internet. However, because it's graphics-based, it's much easier to use than many of the other tools used to navigate the Internet. To use the Web, you need a browser. To find information, you use directories and search engines.

The Web is surely one of the most exciting phenomena of our time. The fastest-growing part of the Internet (growing at perhaps 4% per month in number of users), the World Wide Web is the most graphically inviting and easily navigable section of it. *The World Wide Web*, or simply "the Web," consists of an interconnected system of sites—computers all over the world that can store information in multimedia form—sounds, photos, and video, as well as text. The sites share a form consisting of a hypertext series of links that connect similar words and phrases.

Note two distinctive features:

1. *Multimedia form:* Whereas the rest of the Internet deals principally with text, the Web provides information in *multimedia* form—graphics, video, and audio as well as text. You can still access Usenets, FTP, and the like through the Web, but the Web offers more capabilities previously not offered by these more restricted Internet connection methods.

2. *Use of hypertext:* Whereas with other Internet tools you choose items from a menu (a list of choices), the Web uses a hypertext format. *Hypertext* **is a system in which documents scattered across many Internet sites are directly linked, so that a word or phrase in one document becomes a connection to a document in a different place.**

THE WEB: A WORKING VOCABULARY. If a Rip Van Winkle fell asleep as recently as 1989 (the year computer scientist Tim Berners-Lee developed the Web software), and awoke today, he would be completely baffled by the new vocabulary that we now encounter on an almost daily basis: *Web site. Home page. http://* Let's see how we would explain to him what these and similar Web terms mean.

- *HTML—instructions for document links:* The format, or language, used on the Web is called hypertext markup language. *Hypertext markup language (HTML)* **is the set of special instructions, called tags or markups, that are used to specify links to other documents.**

- *http://—communications standard for the Web:* HTML uses hypertext transfer protocol. *Hypertext transfer protocol*—**which is expressed as** *http://*—**is the communications standard (protocol) used to transfer information on the Web.**

When you use your mouse to point-and-click on a hypertext link—a highlighted word or phrase—it may become a doorway to another place within the same document or to another computer thousands of miles away.

- **Web sites—*locations of hyperlinked documents:*** The places you visit on the Web are called *Web sites,* and the estimated number of such sites throughout the world ranges up to 1,250,000. More specifically, **a *Web site* is the Internet location of a computer on which a hyperlinked document is stored.**

  For example, the Parents Place Web site (*http://www.parentsplace.com*) is a resource run by mothers and fathers that includes links to other related sites, such as the Computer Museum Guide to the Best Software for Kids and the National Parenting Center.

- **Web pages—*hypertext documents:*** Information on a Web site is stored on "pages." **A *Web page* is actually a document consisting of an HTML file.**

  The *homepage*, or *welcome page*, is the main page or first screen you see when you access a Web site, but there are often other pages or screens. "Web site" and "homepage" tend to be used interchangeably, although a site may have many pages.

  How fast a Web page will emerge on your screen depends on the speed of your modem or other connection and how many graphics are on the Web page. A text-only Web page may take only a few seconds. A page heavy on graphics may take several minutes. Most Web browsers allow you to turn off the graphics part in order to accelerate the display of pages.

- **Web browsers:** To access a Web site, you use Web-browser software and the site's address. **A *Web browser*, or simply *browser*, is software that translates HTML documents and allows you to view Web pages on your computer screen.** The two most popular Web browsers are *Microsoft Explorer* and *Netscape Navigator.* One or the other of these come bundled with new computers. Or you can obtain them from Microsoft's and Netscape's Web sites for free.

  With the browser you can browse (search through) the Web. When you connect with a particular Web site, the screen full of information (the home-

page) is sent to you. You can easily **_Web surf_—move from one page to another—** by using your mouse to click on the hypertext/hypermedia links.

- **The Web address:** To locate a particular Web site, you type in its address, known as a URL, for Universal Resource Locator. All Web page addresses begin with *http://*. Often an address looks something like this: *http://www.blah.blah.html*

  Here *http* stands for "Hypertext Transfer Protocol."

  www stands for "World Wide Web."

  html stands for "Hypertext Markup Language."

  The browsers Microsoft Explorer and Netscape Navigator automatically put the *http://* before any address beginning with *www.* So, from now on, throughout the rest of this book, I'm going to drop the *http://* from any Web addresses.

A Web address, I need to point out, is *not* the same thing as an e-mail address. Some people might type in *president@ whitehouse.gov.us* and expect to get a Web site, but it won't happen. The Web site for the White House (which includes presidential information, history, a tour, and guide to federal services) is *www.whitehouse.gov*

In both e-mail-type addresses and Web addresses, lowercase and capital letters should be typed *exactly.*

Web addresses often change. If you get a "Cannot locate server" message—a *server* is an online computer, often a database—try using a search engine (described below) to locate the site at its new address. Incidentally, many sites are simply abandoned because their creators have not updated or deleted them.

■ *Hyperlinks, history lists, and bookmarks:* Whatever page you are currently viewing will show the hyperlinks to other pages by displaying them in color or with an underline. (■ *See Panel 3.10.*)

When you move your mouse pointer to a hyperlink, you can then move to that link by clicking on the hyperlink or by typing its Web address.

Clicking your mouse pointer on the underlined items (hyperlinks) will take you to new Web pages.

Suppose you want to go back to some Web pages you have viewed. You can use either a history list or a bookmark.

A *history list* **records the Web pages you have viewed during what time session you are connected.** When you exit the browser, the history list is then canceled.

Book marks, **also called** *favorite places,* **consist of titles and URLs of Web pages that you might want to go back to; with these bookmarks stored in your browser, you can easily return to those pages in a future session.**

Some common examples of Web page components are shown on the opposite page. (■ *See Panel 3.11.*)

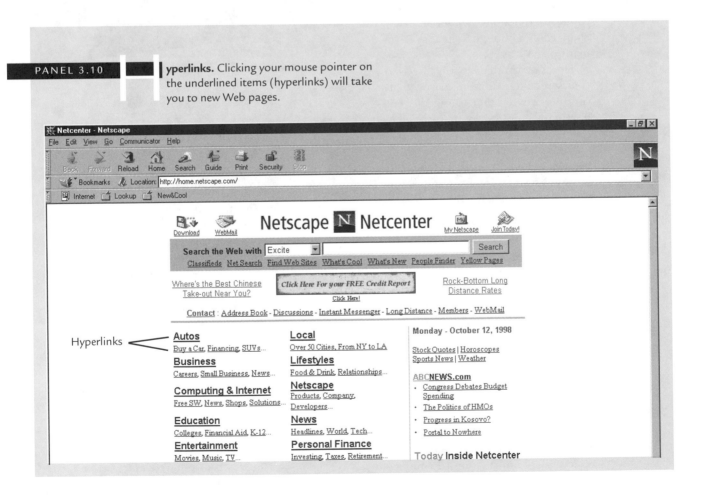

PANEL 3.10 **H**yperlinks. Clicking your mouse pointer on the underlined items (hyperlinks) will take you to new Web pages.

PANEL 3.11

Common examples of Web page components.

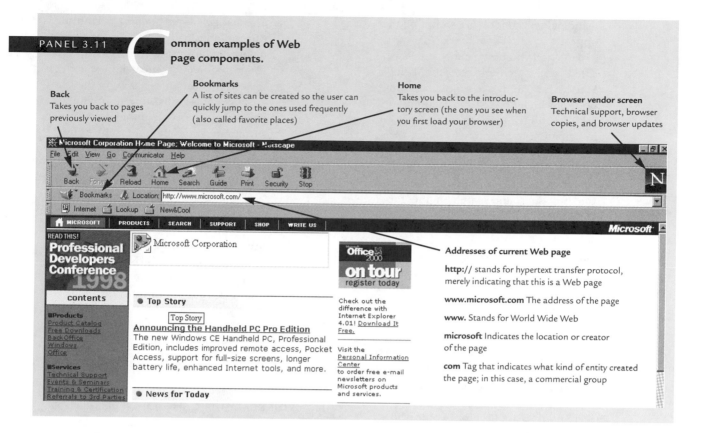

Back
Takes you back to pages previously viewed

Bookmarks
A list of sites can be created so the user can quickly jump to the ones used frequently (also called favorite places)

Home
Takes you back to the introductory screen (the one you see when you first load your browser)

Browser vendor screen
Technical support, browser copies, and browser updates

Addresses of current Web page

http:// stands for hypertext transfer protocol, merely indicating that this is a Web page

www.microsoft.com The address of the page

www. Stands for World Wide Web

microsoft Indicates the location or creator of the page

com Tag that indicates what kind of entity created the page; in this case, a commercial group

FINDING THINGS ON THE WEB: HOW TO USE DIRECTORIES & SEARCH ENGINES.

Unfortunately, there's no central registry that keeps track of the comings and goings and categories of Web sites. However, there are two ways to find information. First, you can buy books (such as *1001 Really Cool Web Sites*), updated every year, that catalog hundreds of popular Web sites. Second, and even better, you can use *search tools*—directories and search engines—to locate the Web addresses of sites on topics that interest you. *Directories* **are lists of Web sites clas-**sified by topic. Directories are created by people submitting Web sites to a group that classifies and indexes them. *Search engines* **allow you to find specific documents through keyword searches or menu choices.** Search engines find Web pages on their own. They use software indexers (called spiders) to "crawl" around the Web and automatically build indexes based on what they find.

Web browsers allow you to quickly use directories and search engines by clicking on the NET SEARCH button and then clicking on the icon of the directory or search engine you want to use. Some

principal search tools are shown on the opposite page. (■ *See Panel 3.12.*)

How can you best explore the Web? The key, says technology writer Michael Martin, is to apply two simple concepts, both of which derive from methods we are accustomed to using for finding information in other areas of life: *"browsing"* and *"hunting."* [19]

Using your browser (such as Navigator or Explorer), you can use directories for "browsing" and search engines for "hunting."

■ ***Directories—for "browsing":*** "Browsing," says Martin, "involves looking in a general area of interest, then zooming in on whatever happens to catch your attention." For example, he says, a basketball fan would head for the sports section of the newspaper, check the basketball news and scores on the front page, then skim other pages for related sports information.

Directories arrange resources by subject and thus are best for people who browse. Directories provide lists of Web sites covering several categories. These are terrific tools if you want to find Web sites pertinent to a general topic you're interested in, such as bowling, heart disease, or the Vietnam War. For instance, in Yahoo! you might click your mouse on one of the general headings listed on the menu, such as Recreation or Health, then proceed to click on menus of subtopics until you find what you need.

■ ***Search engines—for "hunting":*** "Hunting is what we do when we want specific information," Martin says. In his example, if you were hopelessly nearsighted and wanted to hunt up specifics on the latest advances in laser treatment, you might check with an ophthalmologist, a university library, the National Eye Institute, and so on.

Search engines such as Lycos and Infoseek are for those who want specifics. Search engines are best when you're trying to find very specific information—the needle in the haystack. Search engines are Web pages containing forms into which you type keywords to suggest the subject you're searching for. The search engine then scans its database and presents you with a list of Web sites matching your search criteria. The principal search engines add index information about new pages every day.

TIPS FOR SEARCHING. Here are some rules that will help improve your chances for success in operating a search engine:[20,21]

■ ***Read the instructions!*** Every search site has an online search manual. Read it.

■ ***Make your keywords specific:*** The more narrow or distinctive you can make your keywords, the more targeted will be your search. Say *drag racing* or *stock-car racing* rather than *auto racing,* for example. Also try to do more than one pass and try spelling variations: *drag racing, dragracing, drag-racing.* In addition, think of synonyms, and write down related key terms as they come to mind.

■ ***Use AND, OR, and NOT:*** Use connectors as a way of making your keyword requests even more specific. In Martin's example, if you were looking for a 1965 Mustang convertible, you could search on the three terms "1965," "Mustang," and "convertible." However, since you want all three together, try linking them with a connector: "Mustang AND convertible AND 1965." You can also sharpen the keyword request by using the word NOT for exclusion—for example, "Mustang NOT horse."

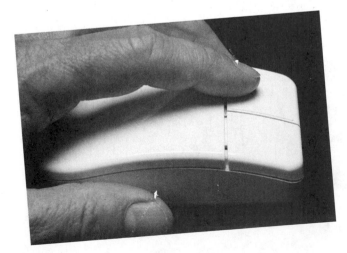

Some popular Web search tools. Using your browser (such as Navigator or Explorer), you can use directories for "browsing" and search engines for "hunting." (Go to *http://csuccess.wadsworth.com* for the most up-to-date Web addresses, or URLs.)

DIRECTORIES

Yahoo! *(http://www.yahoo.com)* is the most popular of the Web directories and lists half a million Web sites. The home page lists several topics, with some subtopics listed beneath. Among other things, Yahoo! features a weekly list of "cool sites" and Cool Links connections (look for the sunglasses "cool" icon). Unlike other directories, it does not review sites, and its decriptions are rather brief.

Magellan *(http://www.mckinley.com)* allows users to search 50 million Web sites. It also offers detailed overviews of more than 60,000 Web sites chosen and reviewed by Magellan's experts. Overviews include a short review and a percentage sign that rates a resource for relevance.

Netguide Live *(http://www.netguide.com)* has fewer Web site listings than Yahoo! but, unlike Yahoo!, offers reviews and evaluations of the sites listed.

The Mining Company *(http://www.miningco.com)* includes comprehensive Web sites for over 500 topics, run by outside experts who compile lists of sites that deal with their areas of expertise. Each site is devoted to a single topic, complete with site reviews, feature articles, and discussion areas.

Galaxy *(http://www.einet.net)* calls itself "the professional's guide to a world of information" and employs professional information specialists to organize and classify Web pages. It includes resources for professionals in nine categories, such as business, law, medicine, government, and science.

The Argus Clearinghouse *(http://www.clearinghouse.net/index.html)* is a directory of directories, or "virtual library"; that is, it is maintained by "digital librarians" who identify, select, evaluate, and organize resources. Argus provides a list of subject-specific directories on topics ranging from arts and entertainment to social science and social issues.

The Internet Public Library *(http://www.ipl.org)* is another "virtual library." It began in 1995 in the School of Information and Library Studies at the University of Michigan and has the goal of providing library services to the Internet community. Besides offering Web searches and lists of books and periodicals, it maintains its own collection of over 12,000 hand-picked and organized Internet resources.

SEARCH ENGINES

AltaVista *(http://www.altavista.digital.com)*, probably the largest and probably best known of the search engines, has over 100 million indexed Web pages, roughly twice as many as its competitors. It also takes care of all the searches that spill over from Yahoo! Thus, if you start your search on Yahoo! and can't find what you're looking for there, you'll automatically be switched to AltaVista. If you're worried you might miss a Web site, AltaVista is the search engine to use first. Along with HotBot, it should be one of the first Web searching tools you use.

Excite *(http://www.excite.com/)* is considered both a directory and a search engine and has 50 million indexed pages and 140,000 Yahoo!-style listings. Besides searching by exact words, it also searches by concept. For example, a query for "martial arts" finds sites about *kick-boxing* and *karate* even if the original search term isn't in the page. After you do a search, Excite will also suggest words to use to narrow the query. In addition, it ranks the documents as to relevancy—that is, as to how well they fit your original search criteria.

HotBot *(http://www.hotbot.com)* reindexes its 54 million Web pages every two weeks, which can often yield more recent material than is found using other search engines. In fact, you can find only up-to-date pages by limiting your search to those pages that have changed only in the last 3–6 months. Like Excite, HotBot offers relevancy rankings. Along with AltaVista, HotBot should be one of the first search tools you use when you're looking for something.

InfoSeek *(http://www.infoseek.com)* is a blend of search engine, directory, and news service. It has 60 million Web pages and an extensive directory and ranks results according to relevance to your search criteria. InfoSeek also searches more than the Web, indexing Usenet newsgroups and several non-Internet databases. Once you complete a search, you can search with those results, by constructing a new query and clicking on the "Search These Results" button.

Lycos *(http://www.lycos.com)*, which combines directory and search services, offers 30 million indexed pages. It also offers a list of interesting Web sites called A2Z, which indicates the most popular pages on the Web, as measured by the number of hypertext links, or "hits," from other Web sites pointing to them. The Lycos relevancy rankings are among the strongest of the search engines.

- **Don't bother with "natural language" queries:** Some search engines will let you do *natural language queries*, which means you can ask questions as you might in conversation. For example, you could ask, "Who was the Indianapolis 500 winner in 1999?" You'll probably get better results by entering "Indianapolis 500 AND race AND winner AND 1999."

- **Use more than one search engine:** "We found surprisingly little overlap in the results from a single query performed on several different search engines," says one writer who compared a number of them. "So to make sure that you've got the best results, be sure to try your search with numerous sites."

GROUP ACTIVITY #3.5

THE DIFFICULTIES OF USING COMPUTERS

Every computer user has some horror story, such as the computer "crashing" (failing) and losing vital information. Or the computer may turn out not to be as easy to use as advertised. Or going online has yielded some unfortunate experiences.

This activity is an opportunity for students to vent their feelings about computers. Questions for discussion: Ever had a nightmare experience with a computer? How did you resolve it? If not, have you heard of other computer users' bad experiences? How does this make you feel about becoming a computer user yourself? What are some of the best ways you can think of to express your staying power in learning about computers?

Staying power

What Do Colleges Want Students to Know About Copying Software?

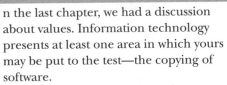

PREVIEW & REVIEW Commercial software, which is copyrighted, is licensed, rather than sold, to users; this gives them the right to make one copy only. Making copies of such software or of other copyrighted materials is not allowed, nor can copyrighted materials be posted on the Internet. Software known as public-domain software, freeware, and shareware can be copied.

In the last chapter, we had a discussion about values. Information technology presents at least one area in which yours may be put to the test—the copying of software.

Most of the software you'll be using will be commercial software with brand names such as Microsoft Word or Excel. In such cases, the software manufacturers don't sell you the software so much as sell you (or the college) a *license to become an authorized user* of it. What's the difference? In paying for a **_software license_, you in effect sign a contract in which you agree not to make copies of the software to give away or sell.** That is, you (or your college, in the case of a class full of students) have bought only the company's permission to use the software and not the software itself. This legal nicety allows the company to retain its rights to the program and limits the way its customers can use it.[22] The small print in the licensing agreement allows you to make one copy (backup copy) for your own use.

THE RULES AGAINST COPYING. Many colleges issue written policies about computer use, which they regard as important because they give notice and provide for due process if a student breaks a rule. Penalties for breaking the rules can include expelling offending students from school. (Companies may also sue both students and their institution for copyright infringement. Law-enforcement officials can follow with criminal prosecution.)

In general the rules regarding copying are as follows.

■ *Rule #1—You can't copy licensed software without permission:* Of the 523 million new business software applications used globally in 1996, according to the Business Software Alliance, nearly one in two were copied—that is, pirated.[23] Were it not for this widespread theft, software developers could cut the price of their wares in half.

Some students know that software piracy is against the law, but they do it anyway because they think they're getting back at "greedy" software companies, says Brian Rust of the division of information technology at the University

of Wisconsin.[24] In addition, he points out, some students may even observe instructors or staff members copying software programs, saying they're on a tight budget. "People will seek ways to justify their behavior," Rust notes.

Regardless, unless you have permission to do so, you're not allowed to copy and distribute diskettes of licensed applications software.

■ *Rule #2—You can't copy copyrighted music, photographs, videos, or text from the Internet or Web without permission:* Now that most music is in a digital format, a song can be posted to the World Wide Web and the quality of its sound will remain consistent no matter how many times the song is reproduced: the 100th digitized copy sounds as pristine as the first. Thus the temptation to copy.

Indeed, until now, it has not been at all difficult to use a search engine to locate a Web site that will yield a free but illegal album of, say, Smashing Pumpkins, U2, or No Doubt.[25] More and more, however, music publishers, film studios, software publishers, and law-enforcement units are using cybersleuths to track down Web sites offering bootleg goods.

■ *Rule #3—You can't post copyrighted materials online:* Students who post, say, "Dilbert" cartoons, *Playboy*'s Miss October, or the music of the Grateful Dead online may simply not realize that they are doing wrong. But the copyright owners of these materials have contacted campuses to complain about violations of copyright law. Universal Press Syndicate contacted Peter Edstrom, a student at the University of Minnesota at Duluth, and forced him to remove "Calvin and Hobbes" images from the home page he had created on the university-based network.[26]

The easy rationalization is to say that "I'm just a poor student, and making this copy or downloading only one digital recording isn't going to hurt anyone." But in reality, software copying is the same as shoplifting a software package off the shelf at the store.

THE USE OF PUBLIC-DOMAIN SOFTWARE, FREEWARE, & SHAREWARE. Fortunately, there are a number of software products—many available over the Internet—that have few or no restrictions regarding copying: *public-domain software, freeware,* and *shareware.*

■ *Public-domain software:* **Public-domain software is software that is not protected by copyright and thus may be duplicated by anyone at will.** Public-domain programs—usually developed at taxpayer expense by government agencies—have been donated to the public by their creators. They are often available through sites on the Internet. You can duplicate public-domain software without fear of legal prosecution.

■ *Freeware:* **Freeware is software that is available free of charge.** Freeware is distributed without charge, also usually through the Internet. Why would any software creator let the product go for free? Sometimes developers want to see how users respond so they can make improvements in a later version. Sometimes it is to further some scholarly purpose, such as to create a standard for software on which people are apt to agree. Freeware developers often retain all rights to their programs, so that technically you are not supposed to duplicate and distribute it further. Still, there is no problem about your making several copies for your own use.

■ *Shareware:* **Shareware is copyrighted software that is distributed free of charge but requires users to make a contribution in order to receive technical help, documentation, or upgrades.** Shareware, too, is distributed primarily through the Internet. Is there any problem about making copies of shareware for your friends? Actually, the developer is hoping you will do just that. That's the way the program gets distributed to a lot of people—some of whom, the software creator hopes, will make a contribution or pay a registration fee for advice or upgrades.

THE ETHICS OF USING INFORMATION TECHNOLOGY

Like everything else you do, how you use computers and the Internet is an indication of your values.

For class discussion: Why not make copies of commercial software? If you get skillful enough, why not learn to be a "hacker" and use the Internet to break into corporate, government, military, and university databases? What's wrong with accessing X-rated, sexually oriented Web sites?

Though copying shareware is permissible, because it is copyrighted you cannot use it as the basis for developing your own program in order to compete with the developer.

Onward: Applying This Chapter to Your Life

In a world of breakneck change, can you still thrive?

"Computer technology is the most powerful and the most flexible technology ever developed," says Terry Bynum, who chairs the American Philosophical Association's Committee on Philosophy and Computing. "Even though it's called a technical revolution, at heart it's a social and ethical revolution because it changes everything we value."[27]

In a world of breakneck change, can you still thrive? Clearly, information technology is driving the new world of jobs, leisure, and services, and nothing is going to stop it. Indeed, predicts one futurist, by 2010 probably 90% of the workforce will be affected by the four principal information technologies— computer networks, imaging technology, massive data storage, and artificial intelligence.[28]

Where will you be in all this? People pursuing careers find the rules are changing very rapidly. Up-to-date skills are becoming ever more crucial. Job descriptions of all kinds are being redefined. Even familiar jobs are becoming more demanding. Today, experts advise, you need to prepare to continually upgrade your skills, prepare for specialization, and prepare to market yourself. This is why, in the remaining chapters of this book, we show how you can use the skills of information technology for college success—skills that will translate into life success.

What information in this chapter did you find most useful to you? How do you plan to apply it? Write it down here.

_____

_____

_____

_____

_____

_____

_____

_____

_____

Real Practice Activities for Real People

Staying power

REAL PRACTICE ACTIVITY #3.1: INFORMATION TECHNOLOGY & PERSEVERENCE. This activity may take the form of a one-page reaction paper or mind map to be submitted to the instructor. Or it may be used as the basis for class or small-group discussion.

Are computers scary? frustrating? great fun? Make a list or a mind map of all the terms that reflect your feelings about information technology (computers and telecommunications) and the reasons for these feelings. It's important that you understand your attitudes here because information technology constitutes the most important revolution of our time, according to many observers, and one way or another you will have to deal with it.

Once you've identified your attitudes, describe what you need to do to persevere in learning about computers despite their drawbacks and frustrations. You might also indicate, based on Chapter 1, what strengths you think you have to give you staying power in what will probably turn out to be a lifelong learning experience.

Mindfulness

REAL PRACTICE ACTIVITY #3.2: USING A RATIONAL APPROACH TO ACQUIRING A PERSONAL COMPUTER. This project may be performed individually or collaboratively (in a small group) outside of class. The results may be used in a later class as a basis for class discussion or submitted to the instructor as a reaction paper.

The purpose of this practice activity is to apply a rational approach to buying a personal computer (the opposite of doing impulse buying). Even if you already own a PC, this exercise won't be a waste of time, since you'll probably have to purchase a new computer sometime in the near future.

Use whatever college or personal resources are available to you to come up with a *purchase plan* for acquiring a personal computer. Determine what you would want a computer for, what kind of hardware and software you would need, how long you would use the equipment, and what kind of financial arrangements (cash purchase, installment payments, or lease) are the best.

Once you have written up your purchase plan, describe how you have used a thoughtful approach to its development. That is, describe how you used some of the thinking tools discussed in Chapter 2 (mindful learning, critical thinking, creative thinking) to try to come up with the best plan possible.

Information technology

REAL PRACTICE ACTIVITY #3.3: EXPLORING ONLINE RESOURCES. This activity is to be practiced by students out of class, working either individually or in small groups. The results are to be submitted to the instructor as a short report (one to three pages).

This practice activity has two goals: (1) to enable you to find what online college resources are available that may be helpful to you in the future, and (2) to give you a look at future trends. Use a PC (your own or one at the library, computer lab, or elsewhere) to go online and find answers to the following question: *What future trend or trends in information technology might affect you?* Write up the results in a short report, being sure to list at least *four* online resources that you used.

Also answer the following questions: How difficult was it to research this topic? Were some resources more useful than others? What did you learn about your college's online resources?

The Examined Life

JOURNAL ENTRY #3.1: WHAT COMPUTER SKILLS WILL YOU NEED IN YOUR CAREER FIELD? Nearly every career field now uses information technology. What computer skills will be required in your career field? For example, what kinds of software should you become comfortable with? (If you don't know, find out from an instructor or your academic advisor.) At what point in your education will you begin learning these skills?

JOURNAL ENTRY #3.2: HOW GOOD ARE YOU AT KEYBOARDING—AND WHAT CAN YOU DO TO IMPROVE? Can you type using more than two fingers? Until you can type on a keyboard using all ten fingers, you won't be completely comfortable using a computer, since keyboarding is the skill most essential to this technology. If you need to upgrade your keyboarding skills, looking into inexpensive "typing tutor" software. (Look in the campus bookstore or go to the library and research some computer-magazine articles and ads.) Write what you plan to do to become a better keyboarder.

JOURNAL ENTRY #3.3: WHAT ARE SOME SOURCES OF ASSISTANCE IN USING COMPUTERS? What are some departments, offices, phone numbers, and online sites that offer support services in computing? Who are some people you could turn to for help?

JOURNAL ENTRY #3.4: WHICH COMPUTER SHOULD YOU GET—DESKTOP OR LAPTOP, IBM-TYPE OR MACINTOSH? Assume whatever personal computer you get will have to last you at least 2 years. What kind should you get?

_____

_____

_____

_____

_____

_____

_____

_____

_____

_____

JOURNAL ENTRY #3.5: WHAT ARE THE PRINCIPAL USES OF THE INTERNET TO YOU? The Internet could be a valuable resource, great entertainment, or a gigantic waste of time. What do you hope the Net and the Web can do for you?

_____

_____

_____

_____

_____

_____

_____

_____

_____

_____

4

Time Management as a Learned Skill

Setting Daily Tasks from Life Goals

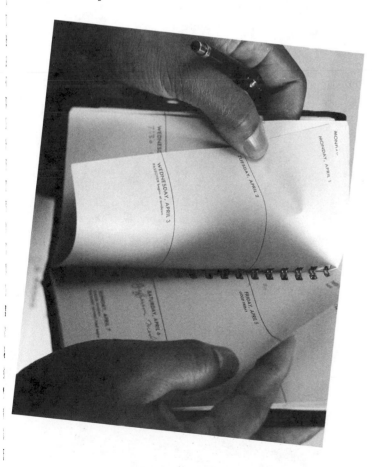

IN THIS CHAPTER One of the most important skills you can have is the ability to manage your time in order to fulfill your goals. We consider these subjects:

■ **Setting college goals:** We look at steps for translating your life goals into educational goals.

■ **Setting priorities:** How to set semester/quarter, weekly, and daily tasks.

■ **Beating the killer time wasters:** How to avoid distractions, delaying tactics, and procrastination.

■ **Being aware of really big time wasters:** Becoming aware of how much time TV, drinking, the Internet, commuting, and working can take.

■ **Improving study efficiency:** How to gain The Extra Edge in studying by using study groups and taking advantages of the time spaces in your day.

If you don't feel you're a terrific student or time manager, just fake it.

Seriously.

Even if you haven't done well in school in the past, pretend now that you're the ultimate student. Make as though you're a scholar. Play at being organized. Simulate being a good time manager.

There's a reason for all this: the chances are that if you *act* like the person you want to become, you will *become* that person. This is true whether it's being less shy, having a more optimistic outlook, having more self-esteem, or being a better student. Once you've become used to your new role, the feelings of discomfort that "This isn't natural for me" will probably begin to go away. In many kinds of behavior change, *you are more apt to ACT your way into a new way of thinking than to THINK your way into it.*[1]

If you have doubts that this works, just consider that people act their way into behavior change all the time. People may not feel as if they can handle the responsibilities of a promotion or a new job

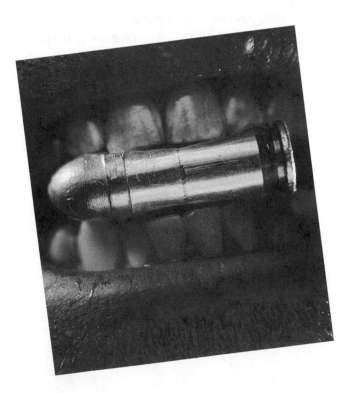

beforehand, but they usually do. Being a parent looks pretty awesome when you're holding a newborn baby, but most people in the world get used to it.

"If you want a quality, act as if you already had it," suggested the psychologist William James. "Try the 'as if' technique." In other words: *Fake it till you make it.* In this chapter, we'll examine how to fake your way into managing your time. As you might guess, this approach draws something from the active engagement or mindful learning that I described in Chapter 2.

Mindfulness

Getting Real About Studying

PREVIEW & REVIEW The universal advice is that students are expected to devote 2 hours of studying for every hour of class.

You may hear a fellow student say offhandedly, "Yeah, I got an A in the course. But I hardly had to study at all."

Don't believe it.

Sure, perhaps there really are some people who can get by this way (or courses that are really that easy). However, most people who talk like that just want to look as though they are brainy enough not to need to study. In general, though, in reality either they *are* studying a lot or they are *not* getting top grades.

Here is clearly an area in which you have to bite the bullet. Quite often, studying *is* hard work. It *does* take time. Most students probably *don't* like to do it. Learning can be fun, but studying *isn't* always something to look forward to. In short, studying may well be the first test of your ability to develop *staying power*—that is, persistence, commitment, discipline.

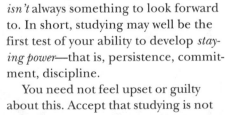

Staying power

You need not feel upset or guilty about this. Accept that studying is not always something you're going to do because you feel like it. Then you can begin to organize your time so that you can always get enough studying done.

The generally universal advice given on all campuses is this:

Students are expected to devote at least 2 hours of study for every hour of class.

By "study," I mean reviewing notes, reading assignments, writing papers—all the activity known as "homework." Some classes may require less than 2 hours, but some might require more. Indeed, some might require 3 or 4 hours of study for every hour in class, if you find the subject hard going.

Thus, suppose you have 16 hours of class time, a standard full-time course load. If to this you add 32 hours of study time, then *at least* 48 hours a week should be devoted to school work.

Compare that to the standard 40-hour week that your employed noncollege friends may be working. This means your *college work is more than a full-time job!*

"Oh, no!" you may say. "So where's the time for fun?" Consider, though, that there are 168 hours in a week, with 56 or so hours devoted to sleeping. Thus, most students usually find time enough left over for them to have fun and be with their friends.

But let's be honest. Are you commuting long distances? Are you working as well as studying? Are you on an athletic scholarship? Are you an adult returning student with family responsibilities? Then you simply won't have as much time now for leisure as you may have had in the past.

The bottom line is this: you're hoping that, as a result of your college efforts, there'll be *more* time for play later. It all comes back to your motivation. After all, as I said earlier, college is not jail; you don't have to be here. You're here, presumably, because you *want* to be here and hope the college experience will lead to your greater happiness later. College, I said, requires the development of *staying power.* That means it requires some sacrifices now for increased happiness in the future.

Staying
power

GROUP ACTIVITY #4.1

WHAT IS HAPPINESS? EDUCATING YOURSELF FOR THE WAY YOU WANT TO LIVE

You're in college, presumably, in the pursuit of your ultimate happiness—or something that will make you happier than you are now. But what, in fact, is happiness? If your instructor requests it, go to the library and read an article or part of a book on the subject of happiness. Make notes of the ideas that seem to speak directly to you. (If there's no time for research, take 5 minutes to write what you think happiness is and what would make you happy.)

In small groups (three to five people) discuss what happiness is. What is the way you want to live? How will education help you accomplish it? How does your definition of happiness differ from others' definitions? Could you be happy under others' terms?

The Six-Step Program for Improving Your Time Management: Steps 1–3

PREVIEW & REVIEW The six-step "Essentials for Time & Life Management" plan describes how to set daily tasks from your life goals. The six steps are: (1) Determine your ultimate goals. (2) Identify your plans for achieving them. (3) State the actions needed to realize your plans. (4) Lay out your master timetable for the school term. (5) Set your weekly timetable. (6) Do a daily or weekly To-Do list with reminders and priorities. This section describes the first three steps.

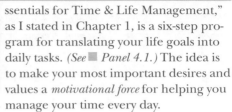

Essentials for Time & Life Management," as I stated in Chapter 1, is a six-step program for translating your life goals into daily tasks. *(See* ■ *Panel 4.1.)* The idea is to make your most important desires and values a *motivational force* for helping you manage your time every day.

The steps are as follows:

- ■ **Step 1:** The planning process starts when you answer the question "Why am I in college?"—that is, define your life goals or long-range goals.

- ■ **Step 2:** You then proceed to "What are my plans?"—setting your intermediate-range goals.

- ■ **Step 3:** This leads to "What are my actions?"—the steps you will take to achieve your goals.

- ■ **Step 4:** "What is my master timetable?" In this step you set your schedule for the semester or quarter.

- ■ **Step 5:** "What is my weekly timetable?" This is the schedule you follow from week to week.

PANEL 4.1 **T**he six-step program of **"Essentials for Time & Life Management."** Steps for transforming your life goals into daily tasks.

What you want school to help you do in life

1. Why am I in school? (Long-range goals)

2. What are my plans? (Intermediate-range goals)

3. What are my actions? (Steps to implement goals)

4. What is my master timetable?

5. What is my weekly timetable?

6. What is on today's To-Do list?

How you make it happen

- **Step 6:** "What is on the To-Do list today?" This is the errand list or "things to do" list that is no different from the To-Do list that millions of people make every day.

Two points need to be made before we proceed:

1. **Skipping steps:** It's possible you already know your life goals and how they translate into a college major and required courses. In that case, you may be interested only in how to get through the present quarter or semester most efficiently. If so, you will want to skip Steps 1–3 and go directly to Step 4, starting on page 91.

Alternatively, you may simply not feel like having to do Steps 1–3 right now. At some point, however, you will have to, because they have everything to do with why you're in college in the first place.

2. **Planning and spontaneity:** Does the idea of making such detailed plans bother you because it seems to rob life of its freedom and spontaneity? I would say that planning gives you *more* freedom. Planning allows you to focus on what's really important. Then you're less apt to spin your wheels—and waste time—on insignificant matters. As a result, you'll have more time left over to do the spontaneous things you want.

Now let's look at the program of "Essentials for Time & Life Management."

STEP 1: WHY AM I IN HIGHER EDUCATION?

You already answered this question in Personal Exploration #1.4 in Chapter 1, when you defined your long-range goals. Repeat them in Personal Exploration #4.1. If you've changed your mind about a few matters since then, that's fine.

PERSONAL EXPLORATION #4.1

WHAT ARE YOUR LONG-RANGE GOALS?

The top five goals I hope college will help me reach are . . .

1. _____
   _____
   _____
   _____
   _____
   _____

2. _____
   _____
   _____

3. _____
   _____
   _____
   _____

4. _____
   _____

5. _____
   _____
   _____

any event, now you need a plan, a rough strategy, of how to achieve or figure out your life goals.

We're talking here about career choices and your major field. "So soon?" you may say. "I just got here!" Nevertheless, you at least need to decide what you *don't* want to do. For example, a major in engineering, premedicine, music, or mathematics requires a sequence of courses that begins in the first year of college. If you think you might want to pursue these or similar fields, you need to be thinking about them now. Otherwise, you'll be required to make up courses later.

In making a plan, you need to take your thoughts about your life goals or long-range goals and then do the following things:

■ ***Decide on a major field (if only tentatively) and two or more alternatives:*** Looking at the college catalog, state what major will probably help you realize your life goals. Also state two or more alternative majors you think you would enjoy pursuing.

■ ***Think of obstacles:*** You need to think of the possible problems that may have to be overcome. Money possibly running out? Job and family responsibilities? Uncertainty about whether you're suited for this path? (Lack of motivation can be a killer.) Deficient math or language or other skills necessary for that major? Lack of confidence that you're "college material"?

■ ***Think of reinforcements:*** Think of what you have going for you that will help you accomplish your goals. Burning desire? Sheer determination? Parental support? Personal curiosity? Relevant training in high school? Ability to get along with people? Acquaintance with someone in the field who can help you? It helps to have positive reinforcement over the long haul.

To begin this process, do Personal Exploration #4.2.

STEP 2: WHAT ARE MY PLANS? Maybe you don't know what you want to do, but you know that you want to explore areas that express your values:

■ To help people

■ To make good products

■ To create

■ To educate

■ To exercise your curiosity

■ To entertain

■ . . . or whatever

Or maybe you already know what you want to do: journalism, engineering, acting, nursing, teaching, law, business. In

WHAT ARE YOUR PLANS? INTERMEDIATE-RANGE GOALS

The point of this exercise is not to lock in your decisions. You can remain as flexible as you want for the next several months, if you like. The point is to get you thinking about your future and what you're doing in college—even if you're still undecided about your major.

◼ WHAT TO DO: DETERMINING YOUR INTERMEDIATE-RANGE GOALS

Look at the five goals you expressed in Personal Exploration #4.1. Now determine how these goals can be expressed relating to college.

Example: Suppose your life goals or long-range goals include:

1. "To enter a profession that lets me help people."

2. "To find out how I can become a world traveler."

3. "To explore my interest in health and science."

4. "To meet interesting people."

You might list possible majors in Health, Nursing, and International Relations. In addition, you might list nonacademic activities— for instance, "Join International Club." "Go to a meeting of Premed Society" (for premedical students). "Look into study at overseas campus in sophomore or junior year."

Decide on Three or More Alternative Majors: Determine which major fields seem of particular interest to you. You can simply do this out of your head. However, it's better if you look through the college catalog.

Three possible majors that might help me fulfill my life goals are the following:

1. _____

2. _____

3. _____

Decide on Nonacademic Activities Supporting Your Goals: Determine what kind of extracurricular activities interest you. Again, you can make this up out of your head, or you can consult the college catalog or people in the campus community.

Five possible areas of extracurricular activities that might help me advance my college goals are the following:

1. _____

2. _____

3. _____

4. _____

5. _____

Identify Possible Obstacles: List the kinds of possible problems you may have to overcome in your college career.

Examples: Possible money problems. Conflict with job and family responsibilities. Temptation to pursue too active a social life. Uncertainty about a major. Lack of preparation in mathematics.

The five following obstacles could hinder me in pursuing my college career:

1. _____

2. _____

3. _____

4. _____

5. _____

Identify Reinforcements: List the kinds of things you have in your life that will support you in the achievement of your college goals when the going gets rough.

Examples: Support of your parents, husband/wife, or boyfriend/girlfriend. Personal curiosity. Knowing someone in a career you're considering. History of enjoying similar fields or activities in high school.

The five following facts or ideas could help sustain me in pursuing my college career:

1. _____

2. _____

3. _____

4. _____

5. _____

In a small-group situation, first report on your possible majors and extracurricular activities. Then take turns discussing the obstacles, followed by the positive things that will reinforce you in pursuing a college career. On a sheet of paper put the heading "I'M GOING TO MAKE IT BECAUSE . . ." Then list the things that will support you in realizing your college goals. Share some of your reasons with the class.

STEP 3: WHAT ARE MY ACTIONS? Step 2 provides you with the general guidelines for your college career. Step 3 is one of *action*. You have a plan for college; now you have to act on it. (Or why bother doing the preceding steps?)

As part of taking action, you need to look at what areas need to be improved in order for you to excel. Are your math, reading, or writing skills a bit shaky? Take advantage of the (often free) assistance of the college and get tutorial help. This is not something to be embarrassed about. Lots of people find they need practice of this sort to upgrade their skills.

In the next Personal Exploration you will need to accomplish the following:

■ *Determine the courses needed to accomplish your goals:* You need to know what courses you will probably take in what semester or quarter in order to make progress. Generally you can tell the courses you need to take for a particular major by looking in the college catalog. (Look for language such as the following: "Students seeking the bachelor of arts degree in Journalism must complete at least 128 credits, 40 of which will be in courses numbered 300 or higher . . ." Or, "The requirements for the degree of Associate in Applied Science in Criminal Justice are . . .")

Laying out course sequences will take some time. But, believe me, *students who don't do such planning could find themselves out of step on some course requirements. This could require extra semesters or quarters later on.* Such slippage is especially a hazard in colleges suffering from budget cutbacks, where it may be difficult to get the courses you want.

■ *Determine what extracurricular activities to pursue:* Some students, such as those on athletic scholarships, take their extracurricular activities as seriously as their coursework. (Some take them even *more* seriously than their courses.) Some students also are highly motivated to schedule in some study abroad at some point in college. In any event, you need to figure out how nonacademic activities fit with your academic activities, both in the short and long run.

■ *Determine how to overcome obstacles, if possible:* Money worries? Family problems? Work conflicts? See if you can identify some solutions or avenues that might lead to solutions (such as checking the Financial Aid Office).

■ *Get advice about your tentative plans, then revise them:* Take your plans (including your list of obstacles) to your academic advisor and discuss them with him or her. In addition, I strongly recommend taking them to a counselor in the career counseling center. Since all this advice is free (or included in your student fees or tuition), you might want to take advantage of it. You will end up with a reality-based plan that may help save you some semesters of misdirection.

To identify your courses of action, do Personal Exploration #4.3.

WHAT ARE YOUR ACTIONS? STEPS TO IMPLEMENT YOUR PLANS

This activity may take some time—perhaps an hour or so. However, *it is one of the most important Personal Explorations in this book*—maybe *the* most important.

■ WHAT TO DO

Here you list the *details* of how you will carry out your college plans. These include identifying courses to take, activities to pursue, and strategies for overcoming obstacles and getting appropriate advice.

Identify Courses to Take: Use the space below and/or a separate sheet of paper. List what courses (including prerequisites) you might need to take to realize your college degree and to fulfill your major and alternative majors. Indicate what years or semesters you will need to take them. These courses will be listed for the degree requirements in your college catalog. You may use a curriculum worksheet to complete this, as shown in Chapter 3, Panel 1.

The courses I will need to take to obtain my degree or degrees are as follows:

_____
_____
_____
_____
_____
_____
_____
_____
_____
_____
_____
_____
_____
_____

_____
_____
_____
_____
_____
_____
_____
_____
_____
_____
_____
_____
_____
_____
_____
_____
_____
_____
_____
_____
_____
_____

(Continue on a separate sheet of paper, if necessary.)

Identify Nonacademic Activities to Pursue: In the space below, list the nonacademic activities you want to try to pursue.

Examples: If you wish to play hockey, note how practice, game times, and travel may affect the rest of your schedule. If you wish to try to study abroad in your junior year, note the arrangements you need to make. (These include researching overseas programs, getting application forms, and noting deadlines for applying. In addition, note how overseas study will affect your course sequences on your home campus.)

The nonacademic activities I wish to pursue, and arrangements I will have to make, are as follows:

1. _____
   _____
   _____

2. _____
   _____
   _____

3. _____
   _____
   _____

4. _____
   _____
   _____

5. _____
   _____
   _____

(continued)

Identify Strategies for Overcoming Obstacles: If you're worrying about obstacles, now is the time to begin to deal with them. In the space below, indicate the steps you will take.

Examples: For "Possible money problems," you might state you will look into financial aid. For "Family conflicts," you might look into child-care possibilities.

The possible obstacles I need to overcome, and the steps I will take to begin to overcome them, are as follows:

1. _____
   _____
   _____
   _____
   _____
   _____

2. _____
   _____
   _____
   _____
   _____
   _____

3. _____
   _____
   _____
   _____
   _____
   _____

4. _____
   _____
   _____
   _____
   _____
   _____

5. _____
   _____
   _____

Get Advice About Your Plans: This section takes very little time, but it may involve using the telephone and then following up with a personal visit. The point of the activity is to identify and then follow through on courses of action you need to take.

Examples: With your list of prospective majors and course sequences in hand, call your academic advisor. Make an appointment to meet and discuss your concerns. If you're thinking about joining the student newspaper, call to find out what you have to do. If you're worried that money might be a problem, call the Financial Aid Office to discuss it. (Some kinds of action need not involve a telephone. For example, you could tell your family members that you need to sit down and talk about child-care arrangements and study time.)

Here are the telephone numbers I need to call, or people I need to see and when, about a certain matter. The date following signifies when I took the action.

1. PERSON TO CONTACT (AND PHONE NUMBER) AND MATTER TO BE DISCUSSED
   _____
   _____
   _____

   ACTION WAS TAKEN ON (DATE)
   _____

2. PERSON TO CONTACT (AND PHONE NUMBER) AND MATTER TO BE DISCUSSED
   _____
   _____
   _____

ACTION WAS TAKEN ON (DATE)
   _____

3. PERSON TO CONTACT (AND PHONE NUMBER) AND MATTER TO BE DISCUSSED
   _____
   _____
   _____

   ACTION WAS TAKEN ON (DATE)
   _____

4. PERSON TO CONTACT (AND PHONE NUMBER) AND MATTER TO BE DISCUSSED
   _____
   _____
   _____

   ACTION WAS TAKEN ON (DATE)
   _____

5. PERSON TO CONTACT (AND PHONE NUMBER) AND MATTER TO BE DISCUSSED
   _____
   _____
   _____

   ACTION WAS TAKEN ON (DATE)
   _____

The exercise in Personal Exploration #4.3 is a take-home activity that involves working with another student from the class, if possible. Make arrangements with someone in your class to meet in the next day or so and do this Personal Exploration together. With that person's help, work through the course requirements for your respective majors and their alternatives. Also explore together the exercises on nonacademic activities, strategies for overcoming obstacles, and obtaining advice. Put your name and date at the top of the assignments and turn them in to your instructor for evaluation.

■ **Step 5: "What is my weekly timetable?"** This is the schedule you follow from week to week.

■ **Step 6: "What is on the To-Do list today?"** This is the errand list or "things-to-do" list that is no different from the To-Do list that millions of people make every day.

STEP 4: WHAT IS MY MASTER TIMETABLE? Once you've determined your lineup of courses for the next few school terms, you need to block out your master timetable for the term you're now in. The reason for this is so you can establish your priorities.

Improving Your Time Management: Steps 4–6

PREVIEW & REVIEW This section describes Steps 4–6 in the six-step Essentials for Time & Life Management plan on how to set daily tasks from your life goals. We discuss (4) how to lay out your master timetable for the school term, (5) how to set your weekly timetable, and (6) how to do a daily or weekly To-Do list with reminders and priorities.

Here let me explain steps 4–6 of the "Essentials for Time & Life Management," which show how to translate your life goals and college goals into day-to-day tasks.

Step 4: "What is my master timetable?" In this step you set your schedule for the semester or quarter.

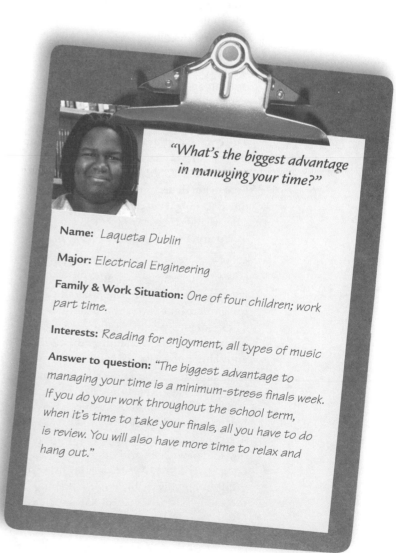

"What's the biggest advantage in managing your time?"

Name: Laqueta Dublin

Major: Electrical Engineering

Family & Work Situation: One of four children; work part time.

Interests: Reading for enjoyment, all types of music

Answer to question: "The biggest advantage to managing your time is a minimum-stress finals week. If you do your work throughout the school term, when it's time to take your finals, all you have to do is review. You will also have more time to relax and hang out."

To make a master timetable for the semester or quarter, do the following:

- **Obtain a month-at-a-glance calendar with lots of writing room:** You should use the blank calendar shown in Panel 4.3 on pages 93–94. (Or buy a month-at-a-glance calendar covering all the weeks in the school term. It should have big squares for all the days of the month, squares large enough to write five to ten words in.) When filled in with due dates and appointments, this will become your master timetable for the semester or quarter.

- **Obtain your institution's academic calendar:** The school academic calendar may be printed in the school's catalog. Sometimes it is sold separately in the bookstore. The academic calendar tells you school holidays, registration dates, and deadlines for meeting various academic requirements. It usually also indicates when final exam week takes place.

- **Obtain the course outline for each course:** The course outline or course information sheet is known as the _syllabus_ ("_sil_-uh-bus"). The syllabus tells you midterm and final exam dates, quiz dates (if any), and due dates for term papers or projects. The syllabus is given to you by your instructor, usually on the first day of class.

Now go through the school calendar and all your course outlines. Transfer to your master timetable calendar all class tests, important dates, and deadlines. These include pertinent due dates, dates for the beginning and end of the term, and school holidays. Also add other dates and hours you know about. Examples are those for part-time job, medical and dental appointments, concerts, football games, and birthdays. *(See ▪ Panel 4.2.)* Leave enough space for any given day so that you can add other entries later, if necessary. *Note:* Consider using a different, highly visible color—flaming red, say—to record critical dates such as test dates.

The master timetable. This is an example of one month of a student's semester or quarter. Note it shows key events such as deadlines, appointments, and holidays.

November

Sunday	Monday	Tuesday	Wednesday	Thursday	Friday	Saturday
			1	2	3 Poli Sci test	4
5	6 English essay	7	8 Dentist 3 p.m.	9	10	11 Sue's Party 8 p.m.
12	13	14 Math test	15	16	17 Poli Sci test	18
19 Band in Park 3 p.m.	20 English essay	21	22	23	24 ← Holidays	25
26	27 Poli Sci paper due	28 Math test	29 Thanksgiving	30		

To begin making up your own master timetable for the present semester or quarter, do Personal Exploration #4.4. After it is completed, you can three-hole punch it and carry it in your binder or notebook. Or you can post it on the wall above the place where you usually study.

YOUR MASTER TIMETABLE FOR THIS TERM

Make up your own master timetable for the present school term, using a blank calendar. *(See ▪ Panel 4.3 on pages 93–94.)*

Blank calendar for the school term.

Sunday	Monday	Tuesday	Wednesday	Thursday	Friday	Saturday

Sunday	Monday	Tuesday	Wednesday	Thursday	Friday	Saturday

Sunday	Monday	Tuesday	Wednesday	Thursday	Friday	Saturday

Sunday	Monday	Tuesday	Wednesday	Thursday	Friday	Saturday

This activity requires that you have (a) the college academic calendar for the present school term and (b) the course outline (syllabus) for each course you are taking. You should also have (c) knowledge of important extracurricular events (such as scheduled games if you are on a team).

Make up your own master timetable for this semester or quarter. Swap it with someone sitting next to you and discuss each other's efforts. Are there any circumstances to be particularly alert to, such as many deadlines coming all at once? What priorities should be established? (For example, what papers could be started early in order to avoid a crunch with exam preparation later on?)

WHAT IS MY WEEKLY TIMETABLE? Now we get down to the business end of the "Essentials for Time & Life Management": making up a weekly timetable. *(See ■ Panel 4.4.) The main point of creating a weekly timetable is to schedule your study time.*

PANEL 4.4

The weekly timetable. This is an example of the important activities in a student's weekly schedule. The most important purpose of this schedule is to program in study time. You may opt to program in other fixed activities, such as workouts, household responsibilities, and travel time to school.

	Monday	Tuesday	Wednesday	Thursday	Friday	Saturday	Sunday
7 a.m.							
8						Work	
9	English	Study	English	Study	English	Work	
10	History	Spanish	History	Spanish	History	Work	
11							
Noon					Psych		Study
1 p.m.	Psych	Study	Psych	Study	Study		Study
2	Study	Math	Study	Math	Study		Study
3	Study	Study	Study	Study	Study		
4							
5							Study
6	Study	Work	Study	Work			Study
7	Study	Work	Study	Work			Study
8	Study	Work	Study	Work			Study
9	Study	Work	Study	Work			
10		Work		Work			
11							

Some first-year students aren't sure what I mean by "study time." They think of it as something they do a day or two before a test. By *study time* I mean *everything connected to the process of learning.* This means preparing for tests, certainly, but also reading textbook chapters and other required readings, doing library research, writing papers, doing projects, and so on. Studying is *homework*, and it's an ongoing process.

By actually creating a weekly timetable to schedule their study time, students put themselves on notice that they take their studying *seriously.* They tell themselves their study time is as important as their classes, job, family meals, or other activities with fixed times.

They are also alerting others that they are serious. Some students post their weekly schedule on the door of their rooms. (Thus, if someone drops into your room to talk, you can point to the schedule and say, "I'm in the midst of studying now. Can I talk to you in another half hour?")

If you don't schedule your study time, you may well study only when something else isn't going on. Or you will study late at night, when your energy level is down. Or you will postpone studying until the night before a test.

The weekly master plan should include those activities that happen at fixed, predictable times. These are your classes, work, regularly scheduled student or family activities—and your regularly scheduled studying times. As mentioned, study time should amount to about 2 hours of studying for every hour of class time, perhaps more.

If you want, you can add meals, exercise, and commuting or transportation times. However, I believe that the fewer things you have on your calendar, the more you'll pay attention to the things that *are* there. Otherwise, you may get to feeling overregulated. You shouldn't schedule break times, for instance; you'll be able to judge for yourself the best times to stop for a breather. (I describe extended study time and breaks later in the chapter.)

To begin making up your own weekly timetable for this semester or quarter, do Personal Exploration #4.5. This, too, may be three-hole punched and carried in your notebook or prominently posted near your principal study place.

Blank timetable
for the week.

	Monday	Tuesday	Wednesday	Thursday	Friday	Saturday	Sunday
7 a.m.							
8							
9							
10							
11							
Noon							
1 p.m.							
2							
3							
4							
5							
6							
7							
8							
9							
10							
11							

WHAT IS MY DAILY TO-DO LIST? The final step is just like the informal To-Do lists that many people have, whether students or nonstudents. *(See ■ Panel 4.6.)*

The To-Do list can be made up every week or every evening, after referring to your master timetable and weekly timetable. It can be done on a notepad or 3 × 5 card. Either way, it should be easy to carry around so that you can cross things off or make additions. You can be as general or as detailed as you want with this piece of paper, but the main purpose of a To-Do list is twofold:

■ *Reminders:* Remind yourself to do things you might otherwise forget. Examples are doctor's appointments, things to shop for, and books to return to the library. Don't forget to write down promises you made to people (such as to get them a phone number or a photocopy of your class notes).

■ *Priorities:* Set priorities for what you will do with your day. It may be unnecessary to list your scheduled classes, since you will probably go to them anyway. You might want to list an hour or half hour for exercise, if you're planning on it. (It's good to exercise at least three times a week for 20 minutes or more.) You may wish to list laundry, shopping, and so on.

However, *the most important thing you can do is to set priorities for what you're going to study that day.* Thus, your To-Do list should have items such as "For Tues.—Read math chapter 13" and "Wed. p.m.—Start library research for Business Communication paper."

Most managers and administrators find a To-Do list essential to avoid being overwhelmed by the information overload of their jobs. Since you, too, are on the verge of drowning in information and deadlines, you'll no doubt find the To-Do list a helpful tool. Clearly also the To-Do list is another application that you can carry over from your educational experience to the world outside of school.

Now try doing Personal Exploration #4.6.

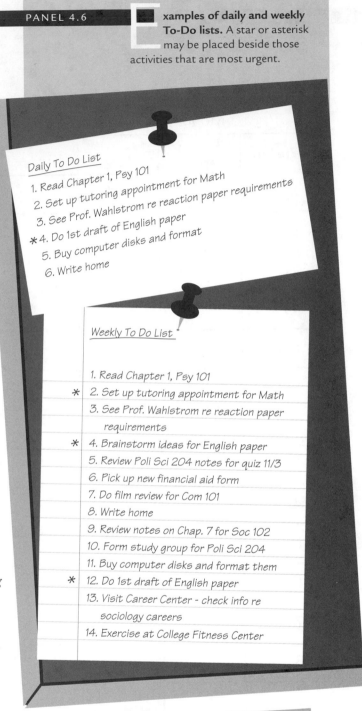

PANEL 4.6 **E**xamples of daily and weekly To-Do lists. A star or asterisk may be placed beside those activities that are most urgent.

Daily To Do List
1. Read Chapter 1, Psy 101
2. Set up tutoring appointment for Math
3. See Prof. Wahlstrom re reaction paper requirements
*4. Do 1st draft of English paper
5. Buy computer disks and format
6. Write home

Weekly To Do List
1. Read Chapter 1, Psy 101
* 2. Set up tutoring appointment for Math
3. See Prof. Wahlstrom re reaction paper requirements
* 4. Brainstorm ideas for English paper
5. Review Poli Sci 204 notes for quiz 11/3
6. Pick up new financial aid form
7. Do film review for Com 101
8. Write home
9. Review notes on Chap. 7 for Soc 102
10. Form study group for Poli Sci 204
11. Buy computer disks and format them
* 12. Do 1st draft of English paper
13. Visit Career Center - check info re sociology careers
14. Exercise at College Fitness Center

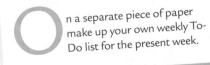

PERSONAL EXPLORATION #4.6

YOUR TO-DO LIST FOR THIS WEEK

On a separate piece of paper make up your own weekly To-Do list for the present week.

Make up a To-Do list for this week. Put your name at the top. Your instructor or another student will collect all the To-Do lists in the class and put them in a hat (or box). The hat will be circulated throughout the classroom and everyone will draw someone else's To-Do list. On the list that you get, write your reactions. When everyone is done, the lists are returned to their owners. A general discussion of To-Do lists may follow.

Battling the Killer Time Wasters

PREVIEW & REVIEW Consider how you spend your time, then try the following strategies to prevent wasting time. (1) Schedule study sessions that actually work. Study during the best times of day, don't schedule overly long sessions, allow short breaks, reward yourself afterward. (2) Fight distractions. Establish regular study sites, set up a good study environment, combat electronic and telephone distractions, and learn to handle people distractions. (3) Fight delaying tactics. Concentrate on boring assignments intensively for short periods; break long tasks into smaller ones, and tackle difficult tasks first. (4) Fight procrastination and other negative emotions.

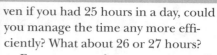

Even if you had 25 hours in a day, could you manage the time any more efficiently? What about 26 or 27 hours?

Everyone gets the same ration, a disappointingly small 24 hours a day. Although some people are indeed smarter, usually the ones who excel at school and at work simply *use* their time better. If you try Personal Exploration #4.7 on the next page—"How Do You Spend Your Time?"—for a week, you can begin to see where your time goes.

CONSIDERING HOW YOU SPEND YOUR TIME. You have 168 hours in a week (7 days of 24 hours each). Let's see where the time is apt to go.

- *Sleeping:* Everyone needs between 6 and 9 hours of sleep a night. (If you short yourself on sleep, you may find the "sleep deficit" causes you to doze off in class. But it's possible you may be able to make it up by, for example, napping on the bus.)

- *Showering, dressing, grooming:* This might take 30–60 minutes a day. It depends on how long you shower, whether you shave or not, if you put on makeup at home or on the bus, and so on.

- *Eating:* This might take at least an hour a day, perhaps 14–21 hours in a week. If you skip breakfast and even lunch, you still probably have at least a snack or two throughout the day. Dinner might just be a quick visit to Burger King or microwaving a prefab dinner pulled from the freezer. Or it might mean shopping for, preparing, cooking, eating, and cleaning up after a full-scale meal for your family. (And making lunches for others for the next day.) In any case, you'd be surprised the amount of time eating takes out of your week.

- *Commuting, travel time, errands:* Travel time—between home and campus, between campus and job, and so on—might take an hour or more a day, perhaps 10–16 hours a week. In 1990, the average commute to work by car was 10.4 miles and 19.7 minutes.[2] In some areas, travel may take much longer.

HOW DO YOU SPEND YOUR TIME?

The purpose of this activity is to enable you to see where your time goes. Honesty is important. The idea is to figure out how much time you *do* spend on studying. Then you can determine if you could spend *more* time.

■ KEEPING A LOG OF YOUR TIME

Record how many hours you spend each day on the following activities. (There are 168 hours in a week.)

	MON	TUES	WED	THUR	FRI	SAT	SUN
1. Sleeping							
2. Showering, dressing, and so on							
3. Eating							
4. Traveling to and from class, work, and so on							
5. Going to classes							
6. Working							
7. Watching television							
8. After-school activities (such as sports, band practice)							
9. Other leisure activities (such as movies, dating, parties)							
10. Other scheduled matters—church, tutoring, volunteering							
11. Other (such as "hanging out," "partying," "child care")							
12. Studying							
TOTAL HOURS							

■ YOUR INTERPRETATION

I put "Studying" at the bottom of the list so you can see how other activities in your life impinge on it.

Now consider the following:

1. Do you feel you are in control of your time? _____

2. Are you satisfied with the way you spend your time? _____

3. On what three activities do you spend the most time?

_____
_____
_____
_____
_____
_____
_____
_____

4. Do you feel you're giving enough time to studying? _____

5. If you had to give more time to studying, what two or three activities could you give up or cut down on?

_____
_____
_____
_____
_____
_____

This activity requires that you have kept an accurate record for a week on how you spent your time. In a group situation, large or small, discuss questions 1–5 in Personal Exploration #4.7.

When computing travel time, you have to remember to include waiting at bus or subway stops, hunting up parking places, and walking from bus stop or car to classes. You also have to total all the time involved in getting yourself not only to campus, job, and home but also, for example, in picking up children from day care, shopping, and running errands.

- **Classes and work:** Figuring out the amount of time you spend in class is easy. If you're enrolled in three courses, totaling 9 credit hours, you should be spending 9 hours a week in class.

  If you work while going to school, you can probably easily figure out the hours your job requires each week. (Two exceptions are if you're subject to unpredictable overtime hours or if you're working for a temporary-employment agency.)

  Incidentally, time researchers John P. Robinson and Geoffrey Godbey, authors of *Time for Life*, have found that, despite everyone's notion that they are overworked, the average work week has *shrunk* since 1965—about 6 hours less for working women and about 7 hours less for working men.[3]

- **Television:** Television, it turns out, takes up an enormous amount of most people's time. I discuss this in another few pages.

- **Studying:** As mentioned, on average you should devote 2 hours of studying outside of class for every hour you are sitting in class. With three courses requiring 9 hours a week in the classroom, for example, you should be spending 18 hours a week doing homework.

Add up the hours in these categories for the week, then subtract them from 168. What's left over is the time you have left for *everything else*. This means *EVERYTHING*: "hanging out," parties, sports, playing with or helping children, doing household chores (if not included above), religious activities, and so on.

Does it seem, then, that you're suddenly going to have to be more efficient about how you manage your time? What follows are some suggestions for battling the killer time wasters.

SCHEDULE STUDY SESSIONS THAT ACTUALLY WORK. As I've said, creating a schedule for studying *and sticking with it* are terribly important. Indeed, this is probably the single most valuable piece of advice anyone can give you.

There are, however, certain things to consider when you sit down to block out the master timetable that includes your study time:

- **Make study times during your best time of day:** Are you a morning person or a night person? That is, are you most alert before breakfast or most able to concentrate in the evening when it's quiet? When possible, schedule some of your study time for the times of day when you do your best work. These are particularly good times for doing difficult assignments, such as writing research papers.

for example, 50 minutes followed by a 10-minute break. Others are like sprinters and perform better by studying for 25 minutes followed by a 5-minute break.

Of course, you don't have to go exactly by the clock, but you should definitely permit yourself frequent, regularly scheduled breaks. Taken at regular intervals, breaks actually produce efficiencies. They enable you to concentrate better while studying, reduce fatigue, motivate you to keep going, and allow material to sink in while you're resting.

Breaks should be small ways of *pleasuring yourself*—going for a soft drink, taking a walk outside, glancing through a newspaper. I don't recommend getting on the phone, picking up your guitar, or dropping in on a friend, however, unless you can keep it short. You don't want the diversion to be so good that it wrecks your study routine.

■ *Reward yourself when you're done studying:* The end of the course is weeks away, the attainment of a degree months or years. What's going to keep you going in the meantime?

You need to give yourself as many immediate rewards as you can for studying, things to look forward to when you finish. Examples are a snack, phone talk with a friend, some music or TV time. Parts of your school career will be a grind, but you don't want it to be *just* a grind. Rewards are important.

If, after scheduling in your study time, you find it still isn't enough, you need to see where you can make adjustments. Can you reduce the number of courses? Work fewer hours? Get help with chores from family members? Whatever, the main thing is to make your scheduled study time effective when you're doing it.

■ *Don't schedule overly long sessions:* Imagine how you're going to feel at the start of a day in which you've scheduled 10 hours for studying. You'll probably take your time getting to work and won't do more than 7–9 hours of actual studying that day anyway.

To avoid setting yourself up for failure, I suggest programming *no more than* 8 hours of studying in a day. Also, divide that time block into two 4-hour sessions separated by perhaps a couple of hours of time off. (Actually, many students will find they just can't stand 8 hours of studying in a single day.) And if you do schedule long blocks of study time, mix the subjects you're working on so you'll have some variety. The point, after all, is not how *long* you study but how *effectively* you study.

Perhaps an even better strategy, however, is to schedule several short sessions rather than a handful of long sessions. I find, for instance, that I perform much better when I have several short stints of work rather than one long one.

■ *Allow for 5- to 10-minute study breaks:* Some people are like long-distance runners and do better by studying for long sessions—

FIGHT DISTRACTIONS! A phone call comes in while you're studying, and 20 minutes later you finish the conversation. Are you later going to tell yourself that you actually studied during your scheduled study time? Or are you going to pretend that you'll simply make up the work some other time?

There are many such possible interruptions, but it's important that you not lie to yourself—that you not play games with your study time. The following are some strategies for preventing or handling common distractions:

■ **Establish a couple of places where all you do is study:** When I was in college, I generally studied in two places—at a desk in my room, and here and there in the university library. This seems to be a reasonably commonplace arrangement. I also sometimes studied in the laundry room of my residence hall. (It was warm in the winter and the machine noises blotted out the noise of people talking.)

You see students studying just about everywhere, which is fine. However, it's important that *you establish a couple of places for regular studying* and, if possible, do nothing else there. Unless you can't

avoid it, don't routinely study on your bed, where you might fall asleep. Avoid studying at the kitchen table, where you may be inspired to eat. Don't work in the student lounge in front of the TV. If you use your study places only for studying, they will become associated just with that and will reinforce good study behavior.[4]

■ **Establish a good study environment:** For your principal study site, the best arrangement is a separate room, such as a spare room, that you treat as your home office. Otherwise, use a corner of your bedroom or dormitory room. Turn a desk or table to the wall to provide yourself with as much privacy as possible from others sharing the room.

Make this spot as comfortable and organized as you can. Make sure you have the right temperature, good lighting, and a comfortable chair. The desk

should have room for a computer or a typewriter, as well as reading and writing space. Books and supplies should be within reach. Having a personalized bulletin board is useful. Post important information, such as calendars, schedules, and announcements, on the wall nearby. (You can also post motivational slogans—EDUCATION: ONE ASSIGNMENT AT A TIME!—and notes nearby.)

Adult returning students in particular may have to be somewhat assertive with others in their household about their need for a quiet space. Sometimes having a "noise machine," such as an air purifier or electronic white-noise machine, can mask distracting sounds and help you concentrate better.

If your living area is too distracting, you can do as many students do and make the library your primary study place. Some libraries have small tables tucked away in quiet areas. Moreover, the entire atmosphere of quiet is supportive to studying.

■ **Fight electronic distractions:** Electronic equipment has completely taken over many households and residences. It has also taken over many student residence halls. Indeed, as one college administrator says, "the walls in some students' rooms look like the flight deck of the space shuttle."[5]

In some places, televisions, VCRs, powerful stereo systems, and CD players are considered basic furniture.[6] (This is in addition to computers, clock radios, microwave ovens, coffee machines, and refrigerators.) In fact, a two person-room at UCLA, for example, now requires 16 electrical outlets, compared to only three or four 25 years ago.[7]

One researcher found that even though college students may have television in their rooms, they watch less of it than the average adult.[8] Even so, you may need to deal with it and the other forms of noise-producing electronics if they interfere with your studying.

If the noise becomes too overwhelming and you can't get it turned down by common agreement, go somewhere else. Plan to do your studying in the library or other quiet place such as a laundry room.

I realize this is a tricky matter, because so many students think that they can study better with television or music as background noise. Indeed, it may be possible to study to certain kinds of music, such as music that doesn't have lyrics to it. However, the evidence suggests that the best studying is done when it's quiet.

■ **Fight telephone distractions:** Of course you don't have to make any outgoing calls during your scheduled study times, and you should resist doing so. As for incoming calls, there are four things you can do:

1. Be disciplined and don't answer the phone at all. (What kind of power is it that the telephone has over us? When it rings, do we *have* to pick it up?)

2. Answer the phone, but tell the caller you'll have to call back because "I'm studying for an important course right now" or "I have something important going on here."

3. Tell whoever answers the phone to take a message for you. You can then call back on your 5-minute study break, if you can manage to keep the conversation short. Even better, you can call back after you're done studying.

4. Let an answering machine or voice-mail system collect your calls, then call back later.

I personally suggest letting another person or a machine take the calls. You're then like businesspeople who have answering machines or secretaries hold their calls while they're doing important work, then return them all at once later.

- *Fight people distractions:* I remember my freshman-year dorm had one guy who restlessly wandered up and down the hall, dropping in to students' rooms to make conversation. He drove me crazy because he never seemed to sense that I had other priorities.

Eventually I realized that, by not telling him I was too busy to talk, I was simply being too polite for my own good. I then hit on the idea of hanging a hotel-room DO NOT DISTURB sign on the door knob whenever I was studying. It worked. (If you do this, you need to remember to take in the sign when you're not studying. Otherwise, people won't pay any attention to it.)

People interruptions can be a real problem, and eventually you have to learn to "just say no." You shouldn't be complaining or accusatory, but polite and direct. There's a piece of advice that says, *Don't complain, don't explain, just declare.* So when interrupted, you just declare: "Jackie, this is interesting, but I have to study right now. Can we talk later?"

Early on you need to develop some understanding with your housemates or family members about your study requirements. Show them your study schedule. Tell them when you're at your desk, you're supposed to be doing your schoolwork. Ask them for their assistance in helping you to accomplish this. One writer says that a student he knows always wears a colorful hat when he wants to study. "When his wife and children see the hat, they respect his wish to be left alone."[9]

What if you're a parent and have nowhere to put a young child (not even in front of a television set or in a room full of toys)? In that case, just plan on doing the kind of studying that is not too demanding, expecting to be interrupted. Or use your study breaks to play with the child. Or take a few minutes to play attentively with the child before you hit

the books, then say you have work to do. Or even read your textbook aloud to the child, making it sound interesting (a tactic that will probably last as long as the child's attention span). As long as the child feels he or she is getting *some* of your attention, you can still get some things done.

Of course, you can't control everything. Things will come up that will cut into your study time, as in the electricity going off or the flu wiping you out. That's why it's important to think of your scheduled study sessions as practically sacred.

FIGHT DELAYING TACTICS! All of us put off doing things sometimes. Delaying tactics can result when your prospective task is *boring, long,* or *difficult.* You need to look hard to see if one of these reasons applies, then fight back by applying the appropriate strategies:

- **Fight boring assignments with short concentrations of effort:** If the task is boring, you need to concentrate on seeing how fast you can get a portion of it done. That is, you need to concentrate on the benefits of completing it in a short time rather than on the character of the task itself.

  Thus, you can say to yourself, "I'm going to work on this for 15 minutes without stopping, applying my full concentration. Then I'm going to move along to something else." You can stand anything for 15 minutes, right? And this task may seem more acceptable if it's not seen as several hours of work—especially if you plan a little reward for yourself (getting a soft drink, say) at the end of that time.

- **Fight long assignments by breaking them into smaller tasks:** Most people have a difficult time tackling large projects, such as research papers. Indeed, most of us tend to take on simple, routine tasks first, saving the longer ones for later when we'll supposedly "have more time."[10] Thus, we often delay so long getting going on large assignments that we can't do an effective job when we finally do turn to them.

  The way to avoid this difficulty is to break the large assignments into smaller tasks. You then schedule each of these tasks individually over several days or weeks. (That's how this book got written—in small amounts over several weeks.) For example, when reading a chapter on a difficult subject, read just five or seven pages at a time.

- **Fight difficult tasks by tackling them first and making sure you understand them:** If you have one particular area of study that's difficult or unpleasant, *do that one first,* when your energy level is higher and you can concentrate best. For instance, if you find math problems or language learning more difficult than reading a psychology text, tackle them first. The easiest tasks, such as list-making and copying-type chores, can be done late in the day when you're tired.

  If a task seems difficult, you may also take it as a warning signal: maybe there's something about it you don't understand. Are the directions clear? Is the

material over your head? If either of these conditions is true, *run, do not walk,* to your instructor. Ask for clarification, if directions are the problem. Be frank with the instructor if you think the material (statistics? grammar? lab experiments?) is hard to comprehend or perform. It may be that what you need is to quickly get yourself the help of a tutor.

I cannot stress enough the importance of taking your own worries seriously if you find that what you're studying is too difficult. However, if you can deal with this before the school term is too far along, you'll probably be all right.

FIGHT PROCRASTINATION & OTHER NEGATIVE REACTIONS! Delaying tactics generally occur unintentionally or only occasionally. ___Procrastination___, **on the other hand, is defined as putting off things intentionally and habitually.**

While it's tempting to think of procrastinators as people who are disorganized or lazy, this is not the case, according to psychologist Linda Sapadin, author of *It's About Time.*[11] There are six styles of procrastinators, Sapadin says: perfectionists, dreamers, worriers, crisis makers, defiers, and overdoers.[12] *(See ■ Panel 4.7.)* Time-management tips, she says, won't help. Rather, what's required is that procrastinators understand the *emotional* problems that are hobbling them, then work to change the thinking behind them. If you don't understand why you delay time after time and always

Six styles of procrastinators.
Psychologist Linda Sapadin
has identified six types of procrastination and methods of coping
with them.

- **Perfectionists:** These types always worry they will fall short of their unrealistically high standards and become so involved in trying to avoid mistakes that they get stuck in details. They need to permit themselves to make accomplishments that will get something done.

  Recommendation: Sapadin suggests changing the self-talk voice in your head to say "I could" instead of "I should"—for example, " I could do this today." In addition, perfectionists need to have specific time limits set in order to complete a task.

- **Dreamers:** Unable to deal with details, dreamers tend to be vague and unrealistic, thinking in terms of "someday" or "soon."

  Recommendation: Dreamers need to make up short lists with specific tasks to do that day. They need to ask "who, what, how, when" questions when starting a project.

- **Worriers:** Worriers, always saying "What if . . . ?" lack confidence in their ability to make decisions; they become easily overwhelmed.

  Recommendation: Worriers need to learn it is better to make mistakes and learn from them than to avoid making decisions at all. They need to break up large projects into manageable chunks.

- **Crisis makers:** Crisis makers have low boredom thresholds and can't get motivated until the last minute. They prefer the adrenaline rush of life on the edge and so postpone projects until the crisis stage.

  Recommendation: Crisis makers need to realize that they need not be fascinated by a project in order to start or finish it. They should find another way to satisfy their need for excitement, such as competitive sports.

- **Defiers:** Defiers may be (1) people who are aggressive, argumentative, and sulky or (2) promisers who don't deliver (passive-aggressives).

  Recommendation: Both types need to avoid blaming and self-righteous indignation. Argumentative types need to become aware of their overreaction to suggestions or instructions. Promisers who don't deliver need to realize that "yes" constitutes an agreement to produce.

- **Overdoers:** Overdoers make extra work and don't focus on what really needs to be done. They also have difficulty saying no to requests.

  Recommendation: Overdoers need to learn to set priorities and to say no constructively. They need to delegate tasks when possible.

feel recurring regret but aren't confident you can change—an erroneous presumption—you need to consider this angle.

Procrastination is only one kind of emotional response to task avoidance. There are, however, several other reasons why students may blow an assignment or a course because something

about it is emotionally disagreeable or frightening.

Maybe, for instance, it's some aspect of *shyness*, so that you find making an oral presentation nearly unbearable. (Shyness, incidentally, is an extremely common condition, one afflicting 4 out of 10 people.)[13] Maybe it's some deep embarrassment about your writing or language skills. Maybe you think, "I'm no good at math." Maybe you're queasy about doing biology lab experiments. Maybe there's a former boyfriend or girlfriend in the class whose presence is upsetting you. Maybe the instructor turns you off in some way.

These and most similar situations can be helped, but *you have to reach out and get the help.* If you don't feel you can take the problem up with your instructor, then *immediately* go to the student counseling center. Counseling and tutoring are open to you, normally without any additional charge, as part of the support system available to you as a student. But try not to wait until you're overwhelmed.

The Really Big Time Wasters

PREVIEW & REVIEW Some time wasters that deserve separate discussion are television watching, partying (excessive drinking), Internet addiction, commuting, and working while going to school when it may not be necessary.

There are a handful of areas that, if you allow them to, can take vast tracts of time, putting college in serious jeopardy. They are *television watching, partying, Internet addiction, commuting,* and *unnecessary work.*

TELEVISION WATCHING. TV, say Robinson and Godbey, is "the 800-pound gorilla of free time."[14]

Since 1965, these sociologists have asked thousands of people to keep hour-by-hour diary accounts of what they do and for how long, from the time they wake up to the time they go to sleep. In the 32 years since their study began, they found that television has gobbled up ever more free time. In 1997 women watched 14.5 hours a week (up from 9.3 in 1965). Men watched 15.8 hours (up from 11.3).

Television is such an ingrained habit, says Robinson, that "people say they don't have any time because they're watching television. It's like some sort of . . . alien force out there, over which they have no control."

Paradoxically, although we spend far more time watching television than any other leisure activity (including reading books or magazines or listening to music), Americans report in surveys that TV is one of the first activities they would give up if they had to. Is this something you feel you could do?

If you're watching the standard 15 hours of television a week, that's equivalent to the time it's recommended you spend on a course that meets 5 hours a week (one 5-credit course)—both class and homework time.

PARTYING. Drinking is a big fact of life on a lot of campuses. "Partying starts on Thursday nights" and continues through the weekend, wrote a recent graduate of one major eastern university. He went on to explain: "You must understand that partying and getting drunk are synonymous to a college student."[15]

People in general—and college students in particular—tend to equate drinking alcohol with relaxation, good times, fellowship, and the easing of pain and problems. More than a third of first-year students, however, drink simply to get drunk. *(See ■ Panel 4.8.)*

Campus drinking is said to be less than it used to be.[16] Nevertheless, a Harvard University study of 17,592 students on 140 campuses reported that 50% of male college students and 39% of female students were *binge drinkers*. ***Binge drinking* is defined as consuming five (for men) or four (for women) or more drinks in a row one or more times in a two-week period.**[17] Among the results of heavy drinking: (1) Nearly two-thirds of binge drinkers reported having missed a class. (2) Students with D or F grade averages drink, on average, three times as much (nearly 11 drinks a week) as A students (3.4 drinks a week).[18]

PANEL 4.8

Why college freshmen drink. More than a third drink simply to get drunk.

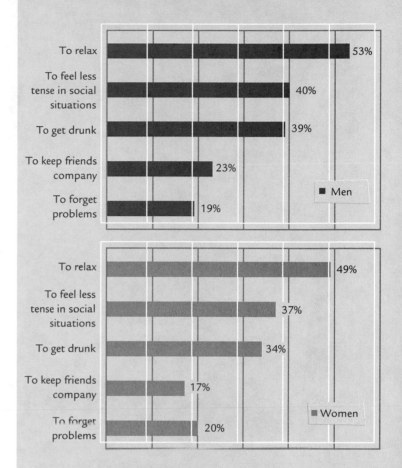

INTERNET ADDICTION. Don't let this happen to you: "A student e-mails friends, browses the World Wide Web, blows off homework, botches exams, flunks out of school."[19] This is a description of the downward spiral of the "Net addict," often a college student—because schools give students no-cost or low-cost linkage to the Internet—though it can be anyone. Some become addicted (although critics feel "addiction" is too strong a word) to chat groups, some to online pornography, some simply to the escape from real life.[20,21]

Information technology

Stella Yu, 21, a college student from Carson, California, was rising at 5 A.M. to get a few hours online before school, logging on to the Internet between classes and during her part-time job, and then going home to Web surf until 1 A.M. Her grades dropped and her father was irate

over her phone bills, some as high as $450: "I always make promises I'm going to quit; that I'll just do it for research. But I don't. I use it for research for 10 minutes, then I spend two hours chatting."[22]

Yu stopped short of calling herself an Internet addict. A case of denial?

College students are unusually vulnerable to Internet addiction, which is defined as "a psychological dependence on the Internet, regardless of type of activity once 'logged on,'" according to psychologist Jonathan Kandell.[23] The

course work.[27] A survey by Viktor Brenner of State University of New York at Buffalo found that some Internet addicts had "gotten into hot water" with their school for Internet-related activities.[28]

Personal Exploration #4.8 lists questions that may yield insights as to whether you or someone you know is an Internet addict.

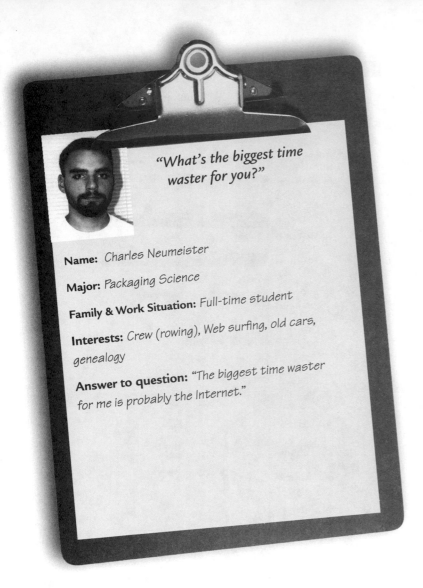

"What's the biggest time waster for you?"

Name: Charles Neumeister

Major: Packaging Science

Family & Work Situation: Full-time student

Interests: Crew (rowing), Web surfing, old cars, genealogy

Answer to question: "The biggest time waster for me is probably the Internet."

American Psychological Association, which officially recognized "Pathological Internet Use" as a disorder in 1997, defines an ***Internet addict*** **as anyone who spends an average of 38 hours a week online.**[24] (The average Interneter spends 5½ hours a week on the activity.[25])

What are the consequences of Internet addiction disorder? A study of the freshman dropout rate at Alfred University in New York found that nearly half the students who quit the preceding semester had been engaging in marathon, late-night sessions on the Internet.[26] The University of California, Berkeley, found some students linked to excessive computer use neglected their

THE COMMUTER RAT RACE. Eighty percent of college students are commuters.[29,30] Some take public transportation, but others come by car.

Commuting by car can be a wearing, time-consuming experience, especially during rush hour. "For those of you who do not know the commute pain, imagine sitting in bumper-to-bumper traffic, sucking up exhaust from cars and double-trailer trucks, watching out for lane jumpers and going only 10 miles in 30 minutes. Then imagine your commute is only one-third complete."

So writes a California man whose job changed from off hours to regular hours and as a result turned his 30-mile drive to work from 30 minutes to 90 minutes—one-way.[31] "I never had to go from 70 mph to a dead stop on the freeway every work day," he continues. "And then inch along and stop and inch along and stop and inch along and stop."

Commuting by bus, train, or subway can also consume a great deal of time. Although public transportation may be advantageous if you can study during that time, the use of public transit, particularly of bus service, is declining throughout the United States. In Chicago, for instance, the number of bus and train rides dropped 38% between

1980 and 1995.[32] Nationwide, car poolers dropped 19% between 1980 and 1990.[33] Thus, most people commute by car, usually alone, sometimes spending an hour or more every day.

Still, if you're a commuter, the question you have to ask yourself is: Is a car an absolute must? Often people think they *need* a car, but they really don't. For many people, particularly young people, it may really come down "to the difference between want and need," says one psychologist. "You would very much like to have a car: for independence, for status, and for the sense of power you feel when you drive," she says. "But you don't need one."[34]

Adds another writer, our dependence on a car "often has more to do with our lack of imagination and willingness to be flexible than it does on any real necessity." Indeed, he says, a simple shift in attitude—learning to view a car as a luxury rather than as a necessity—can save you a great deal of money.[35]

WORKING TOO MANY HOURS WHILE GOING TO COLLEGE. Eight out of 10 students work while pursuing an undergraduate degree, and they are of two types: "employees who study, and students who work," says Jacqueline King of the American Council on Education.[36]

Full-time employees who also go to college make up about a third of working undergraduates. They are usually older and attend part time.

The other two-thirds of working undergraduates are students who have jobs to meet college expenses. They are usually full-time students, under 24, and financially dependent on their parents. On average they work 25 hours a week. Often they are working because they want to lessen the need for student loans.

Working more than 15 hours a week can have a negative effect on students' chances of staying in college, according to a Department of Education study.[37] When full-time students work more than that, the competing demands can have unfortunate results. "Stressed-out students too often turn to drugs or binge drinking to 'blow off steam,'" says King, "with negative consequences for individual students as well as others on campus."

One reason that students work too many hours is that they are trying to avoid borrowing for college expenses. According to a study by the Department of Education of students at public four-year institutions in 1995–96:

1. 20% didn't take out loans and didn't work.

2. 15% took out loans, didn't work, or worked under 15 hours per week.

3. 40% didn't take out loans and worked 15 hours or more.

4. 25% took out loans and worked 15 hours or more.[38]

The best positions to be in, clearly, are 1 and 2. Borrowing money, incidentally, "does not seem to harm students' persistence in college or their academic success," King says. Better, then, to leave college owing some money than to work more than 15 hours a week and have no time left to really concentrate on your schoolwork. The various kinds of financial aid available are discussed in Chapter 9, "Resources & Money."

Maybe you can't do as much as you'd like about commuting and working while going to school. But you can at least not be *mindless* about how you approach these matters. And certainly you can bring an active awareness—*mindfulness*—to the other super time wasters: TV, partying, the Internet.

Mindfulness

GROUP ACTIVITY #4.4

BIG-TIME TIME WASTERS

The class will be divided at random into groups of five or six, each one taking the following topic as a subject for discussion: television watching, partying, Internet addiction, commuting, and unnecessary work.

Members of each group should take 15–20 minutes to discuss among themselves how important they think these are as major time wasters. What do you see fellow students doing in this regard? Have you sometimes felt yourself in a time crunch because of this drain on your time? What is the attraction for seeking this diversion (if that's what it is)? Are some of them really unavoidable (such as commuting and work)? What suggestions would you make to someone caught in one of these traps?

After 15 minutes, the class at large will meet to hear and discuss the results of the groups' conclusions.

Giving Yourself the Extra Edge: Developing Staying Power in Your Studying

Staying power

PREVIEW & REVIEW Techniques for developing staying power in your studying are: (1) Always carry some schoolwork and use waiting time. (2) Use your spare time for thinking. (3) Join a study group. (4) Review tapes you've made of lectures. (5) Review notes on a laptop computer.

We often read of the superstar athlete who spends many extra hours shooting baskets or sinking putts. Or we hear of the superstar performer who endlessly rehearses a song or an acting part. These people don't have The Extra Edge just because of talent. (There's *lots* of talent around, but few superstars.) They have put in the additional hours because they are in a highly competitive business and they want to perfect their craft. Students are in the same situation.

What do you think when you walk across campus and see students studying on the lawn or in a bookstore line or at the bus stop? Perhaps you could think of them as doing just what the superstar basketball player shooting extra hoops does. *They are making use of the time-spaces in their day to gain The Extra Edge.* This, of course, is another variation on what I have been talking about since the beginning—*developing staying power.*

Staying power

Here are some techniques that can boost your performance:

ALWAYS CARRY SOME SCHOOLWORK & USE WAITING TIME. Your day is made up of intervals that can be used—waiting for class to start, waiting for meals, waiting for the bus, waiting for appointments. These 5- or 10- or 20-minute periods can add up to a lot of time during the day. The temptation is to use this time just to "space out" or to read a newspaper.

There's nothing wrong with this kind of activity if you're trying to recharge your batteries in the midst of a stressful day—some mindlessness is allowable. However, these small bits of time can also be used to look over class notes, do some course-related reading, or review reading notes.

Mindfulness

As an exercise in beginning to apply mindfulness to everything you do, you could make a point of carrying 3 × 5 cards. These cards can contain important facts, names, definitions, formulas, and lists that you can pull out and memorize.

Students learning a foreign language often carry *flash cards,* with foreign words on one side and the English meaning on the other. **<u>Flash cards</u> are cards bearing words, numbers, or pictures that are briefly displayed as a learning aid. One side of the card asks a question, the other side provides the answer.** Flash cards are also sold in bookstores for other subjects, such as biology, to help you learn definitions. You can make up flash cards of your own for many courses.

The 5-minute ministudy session is far more valuable than might first seem. The way to better memorizing is simply to *practice practice practice,* or *rehearse rehearse rehearse.* Just as the superstars do.

Mindfulness

USE YOUR SPARE TIME FOR THINKING. What do you think about when you're jogging, walking to class, standing in a bank line, inching along in traffic? It could be about anything, of course. (Many people think about relationships or sex.) However, there are three ways your mind can be made to be productive—to turn mindless behavior into mindful behavior:

1. Try to recall points in a lecture that day.

2. Try to recall points in something you've read.

3. Think of ideas to go into a project or paper you're working on.

Again, the point of this use of idle time is to try to involve yourself with your schoolwork. This is equivalent to football players working plays in their heads or singers doing different kinds of phrasing in their minds. The superstars are always practicing mindfulness, always working at their jobs.

JOIN A STUDY GROUP. Some students find that it helps to get together with a friend in the same course to study boring or difficult subjects. By exchanging ideas about the subject matter, you may find the time goes faster. Indeed, an extremely valuable aid to learning is the _study group_, **in which a group of classmates get together to share notes and ideas.** In a study group you can clarify lecture notes, quiz each other about ideas, and get different points of view about an instructor's objectives. Being in a group also helps to raise everyone's morale. It makes you realize that you are not alone.

MAKE TAPES OF LECTURES & LISTEN TO THEM. This advice is particularly suitable for commuter students with a tape deck in the car or those with a portable tape player who ride the bus. At the end of a long day you might just want to space out to music. But what about at the beginning of the day, when you're fresh? That's the time for practicing some mindful behavior.

Mindfulness

Making tapes of lectures is no substitute for taking notes. But listening to the tapes can provide you with _additional reinforcement._ This is especially the case if the lecture is densely packed with information, as, say, a history or biology lecture might be.

Special note: Be sure to ask your instructors for permission to tape them. Some are uncomfortable having tape recorders in their classes. Some institutions, in fact, _require_ that you get the permission of instructors. At other schools, however, students are assumed to have the right to tape any instructor during class.

REVIEW NOTES ON A LAPTOP COMPUTER. If, as I discuss in the next few chapters, you have decided to give yourself the productivity advantages possible with information technology, you may learn to use a portable computer to take notes of lectures and readings. Thus, while you're waiting for class to start or on the bus, you can turn on your laptop and scroll through the notes you've made during the day.

Information technology

GETTING TOGETHER A STUDY GROUP

Research shows that students who study in groups often get the highest grades. The reasons are many: students in a group fight isolation by being members of a social circle, give each other support and encouragement, and help each other work through lecture notes and readings and prepare for exams. This activity shows you and other students how to organize and perform in a study group.

In a group with three to five other students (preferably a group that you've not been part of before), take turns introducing yourselves to each other, then consider the following questions, which have to do with this chapter.

What are the biggest problems you have in studying? What are your principal distractions or time wasters? What time-spaces in your day could you use for ministudying? What are the principal questions that will be asked about this chapter on the next exam? How do you feel about continuing this study group through the term for this course? What are some of your other, more difficult courses for which a study group would be helpful? Who would you ask to join in forming one?

Onward: Applying This Chapter to Your Life

PREVIEW Avoiding cramming is important, since it usually only produces stress without the grades to show for it.

Perhaps you have a sneaking suspicion that all this time-management stuff really isn't necessary. After all, perhaps in high school you put off a lot of studying, then at the last minute stayed up late *cramming*—studying with great intensity. Indeed, maybe you know that lots of college students seem to use this method.

Unfortunately, as a regular study technique, cramming leaves a lot to be desired. You'll probably find yourself greatly stressed without retaining much and without the grades to show for it. This is because in college there is so much more to learn.

Staying power

So we come back to one of the most important lessons one can learn about school—the importance of *STAYING POWER: persistence and commitment.* "It's said that good things come to those who wait," says Wilt Chamberlain, the basketball former superstar. "I believe that good things come to those who work."

Learning time and task management is one of the skills that is essential for success not only in school but in life. What information in this chapter did you find most useful in helping you develop this skill? How can you apply it outside of college? Write it down here:

_____

_____

_____

_____

_____

_____

_____

_____

Real Practice Activities for Real People

REAL PRACTICE ACTIVITY #4.1: WHAT ACTIVITIES MIGHT YOU HAVE TO GIVE UP? This practice activity is based on Personal Exploration #4.7 and may be performed either individually or collaboratively in small groups. The results are discussed in class.

Staying power

If you have not already done so, complete Personal Exploration #4.7, "How Do You Spend Your Time?" Be ruthlessly realistic, and do a thoughtful job.

Many first-year students are surprised how much the demands of academic life can affect their existing routines. Thus, now comes the true test of persistence in college, for you will probably have to confront the question, *What activity or activities might I have to give up?* Some things in your life are probably going to have to yield if you're really to demonstrate staying power in college. What is it? Television? Part-time work? Partying? Write down your conclusions in the form of a resolution that you might post over your desk. Discuss your findings with others in your group or with the class at large.

REAL PRACTICE ACTIVITY #4.2: DEVISING NEW TRICKS OF TIME MANAGEMENT. This project begins with individual efforts and is designed to produce rewards for individuals. The instructor may ask that the results be submitted as a short paper or made the basis for class discussion.

Mindfulness

Habits are powerful influences on us and sometimes hard to change, but there are times when we must make the effort. Some habits represent sheer mindlessness—automatic behavior, such as always turning on the TV after dinner or always turning on the CD player when you study.

Review Chapter 2 and use creative thinking and mindful learning (creating new categories, being open to new information, being aware of multiple perspectives) to develop a list of ways of how you can better use your time. You are encouraged to try out both low-tech and high-tech techniques of time management.

REAL PRACTICE ACTIVITY #4.3: THE UP SIDE & DOWN SIDE OF INFORMATION TECHNOLOGY. This activity is to be practiced by students out of class, working either individually or in small groups. The results are to be discussed in class.

Information technology

There's no doubt that the revolution of information technology has boosted personal productivity, allowing us to do many things faster and easier. But people have also found that there are things about computers and telecommunications (such as learning new software, dealing with hardware glitches) that can gobble up enormous amounts of time.

Visit campus staff (such as people in the library, learning center, or counseling center) to see what type of info-tech resources are available. List ways the technological tools can save you time. Then list pitfalls you need to be aware of that might cost you time.

The Examined Life

JOURNAL of your first year.

JOURNAL ENTRY #4.1: HOW'S YOUR MOTIVATION? How strongly motivated are you to pursue your life and college goals? What activities would you be willing to give up to achieve them?

_____

_____

_____

_____

_____

_____

_____

_____

JOURNAL ENTRY #4.2: HOW DO YOU WASTE TIME? Do you find, after keeping a record of your time usage for two or three days, that you waste time in certain specific ways, such as watching too much TV? Do these time-wasting ways serve some other purposes in your life, such as alleviating stress or furthering friendships? Give some thought to how these needs might be addressed in some other ways so that you can save more time for schoolwork.

_____

_____

_____

_____

_____

_____

JOURNAL ENTRY #4.3: WHAT CAN YOU DO TO MANAGE YOUR TIME BETTER? Just as business and professional people often look for ways to improve their time-management skills, so can students. What kinds of things did you note in this chapter that might help you manage your time better?

_____

_____

_____

_____

_____

_____

_____

_____

_____

_____

_____

_____

JOURNAL ENTRY #4.4: ARE YOU INTO PARTYING? Some students get so deeply into "partying" that they find it has a major impact on their time. Often the kind of escape sought in partying is brought about by the stresses of the constant academic demands of school. Is this a possible area of concern for you?

_____

_____

_____

_____

_____

_____

_____

_____

JOURNAL ENTRY #4.5: WHAT ARE YOUR OTHER RESPONSIBILITIES? What are some of the other responsibilities you have besides school? Are there some nonessential tasks that could be delegated to others?

_____

_____

_____

_____

_____

_____

_____

_____

_____

_____

Recall & Reading

Memorizing, Reading, & Study Techniques

IN THIS CHAPTER You discover one of the most valuable tools you own—your memory— and how to use it effectively in reading textbooks. We consider the following subjects:

■ **Memory and forgetting:** Understanding the drawbacks of cramming, the differences between short-term and long-term memory, and the "forgetting curve."

■ **What helps and hinders memory:** Lifestyle matters such as stress, alcohol, smoking, fatigue, and the like can negatively affect your memory. A good diet and sufficient exercise and sleep can help your memory.

■ **How to improve your memory—concerted memorization:** Learning through overlearning, studying a little at a time frequently, and avoiding interference.

■ **How to improve your memory—mindful learning:** Making material meaningful to you, using verbal memory aids, and using visual memory aids.

■ **Two reading systems—SQ3R and 3Rs:** The *SQ3R Method* consists of surveying, questioning, reading, reciting, and reviewing. The *3Rs Method* consists of reading, recording, and reciting.

■ **Dealing with special subjects:** How to handle difficult subjects by reducing anxiety, devoting more time to study, and using special study tools.

What would be your greatest wish to help you through college?

Maybe it would be for a photographic memory, a mind that could briefly look at something just once and later recall it in detail. Perhaps 5–10% of school-age children have this kind of memory, but it seldom lasts into adulthood.[1] Or maybe you'd like to be able to remember fantastic strings of numbers. Unfortunately, people who can do this are usually incapable of abstract thought.[2]

You can see, though, why a terrific memory would be so valuable. *If so much of instruction in higher education consists of testing you on what you remember, your ability to memorize great quantities of information becomes crucial.*

Memory & Forgetting: The Importance of Managing Long-Term Memory

PREVIEW & REVIEW Much of teaching in higher education consists of lectures and reading, which require memorization for testing. "Cramming" for exams—massive memorization at the last minute—is not advisable because there is too much to learn. Memory is principally immediate, short-term, or long-term. Boosting your long-term memory is better than favoring your short-term memory because of the "forgetting curve," whereby retention of information drops sharply after 24 hours.

How good is your memory? *Memory* **is defined as a mental process that entails three main operations: recording, storage, and recall.** More plainly, "memory is the persistence of information," as one scholar calls it.[3]

The main strategy at work seems to be *association*—**one idea reminds you of another.**[4] Actually, even though you may worry that you have a weak memory because you immediately forget people's names after being introduced to them at a party, it's probably just fine. (Remembering names is a skill you can quite easily develop, as I'll show.) To see how good your memory is—and let me prove a point—try Personal Exploration #5.1.

HOW'S YOUR MEMORY?

Honing your associative skills can boost short-term memory, says neurosurgeon Arthur Winter, director of the New Jersey Neurological Institute in Livingston and author of *Build Your Brain Power*.

■ WHAT TO DO

To test your powers of association, look at the following word list for just 5 seconds.

Dog	Stone
Cat	Winter
Bird	White
Shovel	Will
Skill	Went
House	Ten
Horse	Star
Crag	Stair
Robin	Life
Grant	Late
Elizabeth Taylor	Honor

Now cover the list and write down as many items as you can remember in the following space.

_____

_____

_____

_____

_____

_____

_____

_____

_____

_____

_____

_____

_____

_____

INTERPRETATION

"How many did you write down?" asks Winter. Probably no more than 10, he guesses, although undoubtedly you remembered *Elizabeth Taylor*. The better you are at creating associations among words—such as making a sentence using most of them—the sharper your short-term memory will be.

GROUP ACTIVITY OPTION

Take a few minutes to make up a list of 15 terms (not people) related to *one* subject with which you are familiar. (Examples: cars, health, your school.) Now add the name of a famous person, such as a movie actor.

Swap lists face down with someone else in the class. When everyone has someone else's list, turn it over and take 10 seconds (looking at the classroom clock or being timed by your instructor) to try to memorize the 15 terms. Then turn the piece of paper over and write as many terms as you can on the back.

Discuss with others, in either a large or small group setting, how many terms you were able to remember in 10 seconds. What tricks, if any, did you use to recall terms? What does this experiment say about your ability to remember new terms you will need to memorize in a subject you've never studied before? Was the subject on which the terms were based (for example, health) one you were already familiar with? Were you therefore able to remember more terms than you probably would have otherwise?

"I CRAM, THEREFORE I AM." Your mind holds a wonderful mishmash of names, addresses, telephone numbers, pictures, familiar routes, words to songs, and hundreds of thousands of other facts. How did you learn them—during several hours late one night or repeatedly over a long time? The answer is obvious.

When it comes to college, however, many students try to study for exams by doing a great deal of the work of a semester or quarter all in one night or in a couple of days. This is the time-dishonored memorizing marathon known as *cramming*. <u>**Cramming is defined as preparing hastily for an examination.**</u>

Many students have the notion that facts can be remembered best if they're *fresh*. There is indeed something to that, as I'll discuss. But does cramming work? Certainly it beats the alternative of not studying at all.

Suppose, however, you crammed all night to memorize the lines for a character in a play. And suppose also that the next morning, instead of going to an examination room, you had to get up on a stage and recite the entire part. Could you do it? Probably not. Yet the quarter or semester's worth of material you have tried overnight to jam into your memory banks for a test may be even more comprehensive than all the lines an actor has to memorize for a play.

In sum: even if you found cramming a successful exam-preparation technique in high school, I strongly recommend you begin now to find other techniques for memorizing. In higher education there is simply too much to learn.

TYPES OF MEMORY: IMMEDIATE, SHORT-TERM, & LONG-TERM. To use your memory truly effectively to advance your college goals—and life goals—it helps to know how it works. Memory is principally *immediate*, *short-term*, or *long-term*.

■ *Immediate perceptual memory:* <u>*Immediate perceptual memory*</u> **is defined as "a reflex memory in which an impression is immediately replaced by a new one."**[5] An example is in typing. As soon as a word is typed it is forgotten.

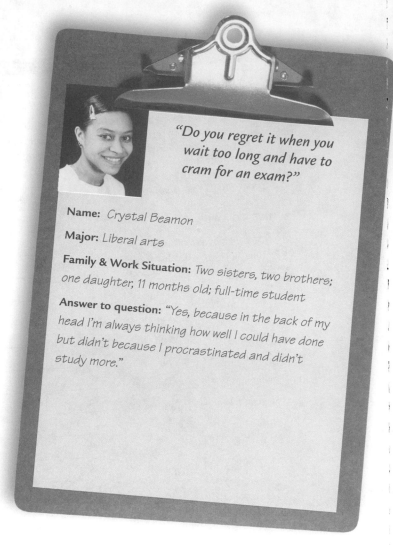

"Do you regret it when you wait too long and have to cram for an exam?"

Name: Crystal Beamon

Major: Liberal arts

Family & Work Situation: Two sisters, two brothers; one daughter, 11 months old; full-time student

Answer to question: "Yes, because in the back of my head I'm always thinking how well I could have done but didn't because I procrastinated and didn't study more."

■ *Short-term memory:* <u>*Short-term memory*</u> **is defined by psychologists as recording seven elements for a maximum of 30 seconds.** This is about the number of elements and length of time required to look up a telephone number and dial it. Short-term memory (sometimes called "working memory") has only limited capacity—for instance, about five to nine numbers for most people. To transfer such short-term information into your long-term memory requires reciting or other association techniques, as I'll describe.

The details of short-term memories fade unless you rehearse them. Or unless some emotionally charged event happens at the same time.

- **Long-term memory:** _Long-term memory_ **entails remembering something for days, weeks, or years.** Of course, long-term memories also fade, but they do so more slowly.[6]

Long-term memory often requires that _some kind of change be made in your behavior_ so that the information being learned makes a significant enough impression. This is why you're more apt to remember something that has some sort of _emotional significance_ or _relates to things you already know_—two key concepts you should know for memorizing things.

THE FORGETTING CURVE: FAST-FADING MEMORIES.

To understand why, from the standpoint of learning in higher education, long-term memory is so much more important, consider what psychologists call the _forgetting curve._ In one famous experiment long ago, Hermann Ebbinghaus found that, in memorizing nonsense syllables, _a great deal of information is forgotten just during the first 24 hours,_ then it levels out.[7] Although fortunately you need not memorize nonsense syllables, the rate of forgetting also occurs rapidly for prose and poetry. (See ▪ _Panel 5.1._) Interestingly, however, poetry is easier to memorize than prose because it has built-in memory cues such as rhymes, a trick you can use, as I'll show.

How good are people at remembering things in the normal course of events?

According to a survey from the National Institute for Development and Administration at the University of Texas, we remember only:

10% of what we read,
20% of what we hear,
30% of what we see,
50% of what we see and hear,
70% of what we say,
90% of what we do and say.[8]

One scholar, Walter Pauk, reports a study of people who read a textbook chapter in which it was found that they forgot:

46% of what they read after 1 day,
79% of what they read after 14 days,
81% of what they read after 28 days.[9]

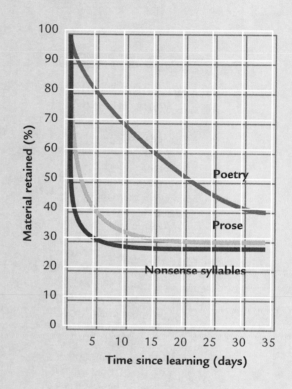

PANEL 5.1

The forgetting curve. Material is easily forgotten if you are exposed to it only once. The retention of information drops rapidly in the first 24 hours for nonsense syllables, which are not meaningful, and slightly less so for prose, which is meaningful. Poetry is remembered best because of helpful devices such as rhyming. Even so, only 40% of a poem is remembered after a month's time.

Chart: Material retained (%) vs. Time since learning (days), showing curves for Poetry, Prose, and Nonsense syllables.

As for remembering what one has heard, Pauk describes an experiment in which a group of psychologists who attended a seminar forgot over 91% of what they had heard after two weeks.[10]

If you were tested every other day on the lectures you attended and textbooks you read, memorizing wouldn't be much of a problem. But that's not the way it usually works, of course. Ordinarily an instructor will give you an exam halfway or a third of the way into the course. There may be another exam later, followed by a final exam at the end of the course. Each time you will be held accountable for several weeks' worth of lectures and readings. On the last exam, you're usually held responsible for the entire content of the course.

Memory is also important in writing papers. If you start your research or writing and then abandon it for a couple of weeks, it will take you some time to reconnect with your thoughts when you go back to it.

GROUP ACTIVITY #5.1

INTERVIEWING EACH OTHER: HOW'S YOUR MEMORY?

Divide into teams of two. Take 5 minutes or so each to interview each other, but *don't take notes*. Just try very hard to remember your team mate's answers.

Questions to ask: How good do you think your memory is? What subjects, hobbies, or interests are you able to memorize easily? What areas do you have trouble memorizing? Do you think cramming works? What memory tricks have you developed that you've found useful?

Now join with your partner in a small group consisting of four people. Report to the group on what your partner said, then let your partner comment on how well you recalled his or her answers. What kinds of conclusions can you draw from this experience?

How Your Lifestyle Affects Your Memory: What Hinders, What Helps

PREVIEW & REVIEW Lifestyle and health matters such as information overload, stress, alcohol, smoking, fatigue, and high blood pressure can negatively affect your memory. A good diet and sufficient exercise and sleep can help your memory.

As people of the Baby Boom generation move into their 50s, many have become concerned about increasing forgetfulness and memory lapses. While there is usually a gradual decline in short-term memory over the decades, this in no way foreshadows Alzheimer's disease. Indeed, most older adults are as capable of learning as younger ones. One study found in a comparison between young and middle-aged typists, for instance, that both groups typed at the same speed. Although the younger typists responded more quickly to new information, the older ones compensated by planning better, looking farther ahead in the text.[11] In any event, the evidence seems to be that staying mentally active will forestall or reduce memory decline.

The real problem—for people of any age—is the kind of lifestyle habits that will hinder or impair memory.

WHAT HINDERS YOUR MEMORY. There are various influences that can keep your brain from working at its full capacity and so impede your memory.[12–14]

Information technology

■ *Information overload:* A constant bombardment of information can overwhelm us to the point where we can't absorb everything. This is even more a problem now that so many of us are besieged by e-mail, the Internet, and other information technology, as well as phones, faxes, and multichannel television.

- **Stress:** Stress can directly affect our brain chemistry. Short-run stress can help us to do our best. After about 30 minutes, however, stress hormones affect the brain in such a way as to leave us low on energy. And over months or year, constant stress can literally shrink the hippocampus, the gland in the brain that acts as a kind of switching station that determines whether information will be retained or discarded. Anxiety and depression can be causes of stress.

- **Alcohol:** Studies have shown that two to three drinks consumed four times a week will lower our ability to accomplish thinking tasks, including remembering. And alcohol can lead to some memory loss, even among young people 21–30. People who are alternately drunk and sober find that things learned in one state are difficult to remember in the other—which is why so many people on sobering up the next morning can't recall what happened the night before.

- **Smoking:** Cigarette smoking may impair the blood supply carrying oxygen to the brain. One study has found that a non-nicotine group scored 24% higher than the nicotine group. Another found that nonsmokers were able to recall significantly more names 10 minutes after studying a list than smokers could.

- **Fatigue:** Too little sleep (and too many sleeping pills) can interfere with the formation of new memories. Fatigue also makes us shut off anything that will frazzle us further. Exhaustion means that you can't read a textbook correctly and recall the information later during a test.

- **High blood pressure:** Hypertension, or high blood pressure, can impair mental function. One study found that over 25 years men with hypertension lost twice as much cognitive ability as those with normal blood pressure.

WHAT HELPS YOUR MEMORY. Perhaps the best way to stay sharp is to stay healthy. This means getting enough sleep, eating right, and getting exercise. These matters are considered in Chapter 11, "Wellness." It's worth stating here, however, that any-thing that helps the circulatory system, such as not smoking and a heart-healthy diet, helps the brain. Researchers have found, for instance, an association between high test scores and high intake of fruits, vegetables, and fiber, the kind of diet recommended to curb heart disease. In addition, older people who stay physically fit are less inclined to slip mentally. Some health enthusiasts think that nutritional supplements such as ginkgo biloba (which may increase oxygen to the brain) may help brain function.[15]

The management of stress, a factor in the life of most college students, needs to be at the top of your list. Anxiety interferes with memorizing, distracting your recall abilities with negative worries. When you are relaxed, your mind captures information more easily. Thus, when you sit down to read a textbook, make notes of a lecture, or take a test, you should first take a few seconds to *become relaxed.* Close your eyes, take a deep breath, inhale, repeat. Say to yourself, "I plan to remember." If you're still tense, repeat this a few times.

I cover some stress-busting techniques in Chapters 7 and 11.

How to Improve Your Memory Power: Concerted Memorization

PREVIEW & REVIEW There are several principal strategies for converting short-term memory to long-term memory. This section discusses concerted memorization. (1) You can practice repeatedly, even overlearn material. (2) You can study a little at a time repeatedly (distributed practice) instead of cramming (massed practice). (3) You can avoid memory interference from studying similar material or being distracted.

As should be clear by now, *success in college principally lies with a strategy in which you convert short-term memories into long-term memories.* In this section, I'll describe some variations on the drill-and-practice type of learning.

PRACTICE REPEATEDLY—EVEN OVERLEARN MATERIAL.
How well could you play a part in a play or a movie after two readings? five readings? fifteen?

Clearly, you can't just speed-read or skim the script. You have to actively practice or rehearse the material. The more you rehearse, the better you retain information. Indeed, it has been found that *overlearning*—continued study even after you think you have learned material—will help you really commit it to memory.[16] *Overlearning* **is defined as continued rehearsal of material after you first appear to have mastered it.**[17]

A good way to learn is to repeatedly test your knowledge in order to rehearse it. Some textbooks come with self-testing study guides to help you do this, but you can also make up the questions yourself or form a study group with friends to trade questions and answers.

The more you rehearse, in fact, the better you may also *understand* the mate-rial.[18] This is because, as you review, your mind begins to concentrate on the most important features, thus helping your understanding.

The rule, then, is: Study or practice repeatedly to fix material firmly in mind. You can apply this rule to your social life, too. If you meet someone new at a party, for instance, you can repeat the person's name on being introduced, then say it again to yourself; then wait a minute and say it again.

STUDY A LITTLE AT A TIME FREQUENTLY: DISTRIBUTED PRACTICE VERSUS MASSED PRACTICE.
Learning experts distinguish between two kinds of learning or practice techniques: *massed practice* and *distributed practice.*

- *Massed practice:* Massed practice is what students do when they are cramming. *Massed practice* **is putting all your studying into one long period of time**—for example, one study session of 8 hours in one day.

- *Distributed practice:* Distributed practice takes no more time than cramming. **With** *distributed practice* **you distribute the same number of hours over several days**—for example, four days of studying 2 hours a day.

Distributed practice has been found to be more effective for retaining information than mass practice, especially if the space between practice periods is reasonably long, such as 24 hours.[19] One reason is that studying something at different times links it to a wider variety of associations.[20]

The rule here, therefore, is: Study or practice a little at a time frequently rather than a lot infrequently. If you're studying large amounts of factual material, try studying for 45 minutes, then take a break. Review the material, then take another break. You can also do this with small tasks of memorization. "Want to memorize the names of 10 bones? Study the list for several minutes," suggests one writer, "then go on to another task. Go back to the list, say it out loud, write it out. Review it. Then take another break and return to the list a third time, using whatever con-

centration techniques work best for you. Now test your recall. You'll find it much better than if you'd just studied for 25 minutes without a break."[21]

This rule suggests you can make use of the time-spaces in your day for studying. You can look over your notes or books or flash cards while on the bus, for example, or waiting for class to start. You can mentally rehearse lists while standing in line. It's like the difference between lifting weights once for 5 hours or five sessions of 1 hour each: the first way won't train you nearly as well as the second way.

AVOID INTERFERENCE. Learning some kinds of information will interfere with your ability to recall other kinds of information, especially if the subjects are similar. *Interference* **is the competition among related memories.** For example, if you tried to memorize the names of the bones in the human foot and then memorize the names of the bones in the hand, one memory might interfere with the other. And the more information

you learn, such as lists of words, the more you may have trouble with new information on successive days, such as new lists of words.[22]

Interference can also come from other things, such as distractions from background music, television, the people with whom you share your living space, and so on. The notion of interference also suggests why you do better at recalling information when it is fresh in mind. In other words, though I don't recommend cramming for exams, I do recommend giving information a thorough last-minute review before you go into the test. A last-minute review puts the "frosting on the cake" of helping you absorb the material, but it's no substitute for studying the material earlier.

The lesson here is: *When you're trying to memorize material, don't study anything else that is too similar too soon.* This is why it is often a good idea to study before going to sleep: there is less chance of the new information getting competition from other information.[23] It also shows why it's a good idea to study similar material for different courses on different days.[24]

How to Improve Your Memory Power: Mindful Learning

PREVIEW & REVIEW This section discusses learning mindfully. (1) You can make material personally meaningful to you. (2) You can use verbal memory aids—write out or organize information; use rhymes, phrases, and abbreviations; make up narrative stories. (3) You can use visual memory aids—make up a vivid picture or story of unusual images.

Mindfulness

Does practice make perfect? Probably it does for some things, as in repeatedly making basketball free throws. However, recall our discussion of *mindfulness* versus *mindlessness* in Chapter 2. Psychology professor Ellen Langer, author of *The Power of Mindful Learning,* contends that by simply drilling ourselves in a subject we are only learning to perform mindlessly. The result is less enjoyment in the learning experience and less flexibility later on when we call upon the skill we've practiced.

Instead, Langer proposes a more mindful approach, involving an openness to novelty, an awareness of different perspectives, an attention to fine distinctions. In line with these ideas, you might try the following techniques for making the subject matter you're studying meaningful to you.

MAKE MATERIAL MEANINGFUL TO YOU: DEPTH OF PROCESSING. Information in memory may be stored at a superficial level or at a deep level, depending on how well you understood it and how much you thought about it, according to the *depth-of-processing principle*.[25] The <u>*depth-of-processing principle*</u> **states that how shallowly or deeply you hold a thought depends on how much you think about it and how many associations you form with it.** The deeper the level of "processing" or thinking, the more you remember it.

This means that in memorizing something you shouldn't just mindlessly repeat the material; *you are better able to remember it when you can make it meaningful.*[26] It's important to somehow make the material your own—understand it, organize it, put it in your own words, develop emotional associations toward it, link it with information you already know or events you have already experienced. For example, if you are trying to remember that business organizations have departments that perform five functions—*accounting, marketing, production, personnel management,* and *research*—you can look for relationships among them. Which departments do or do not apply to you? Which ones do your relatives work in? Indeed, one way to make material meaningful to you is to *organize* it in some way, which is why outlining your reading can be a useful tool.

To repeat, **the rule here is:** *Make learning personally meaningful to you.* This is also a trick you can use in your social life. If you meet someone new at a party, you can try to remember the new name by associating it with the face of someone else with that name. (When you meet someone named Michael, remember that your uncle is named Michael too, or think of singer Michael Jackson or of basketball player Michael Jordan.) *(See ■ Panel 5.2.)*

Have trouble remembering names when you meet someone new? Here are some suggestions by psychologist Thomas Crook, Ph.D., author of the book *How to Remember Names*.

1. **Stay focused—concentrate and repeat the name:** Often we forget someone's name 10 seconds after an introduction because we are preoccupied with ourselves. Try to clear your thoughts during the introduction. Concentrate on hearing the name, then use it once or twice right away in your conversation. ("Well, Joan, are you from around here?")

2. **Pick an outstanding facial feature:** Focus on the new person's face. Note anything strange, interesting, or attractive. Or if nothing stands out, choose a feature and exaggerate it. If a person has red hair, for example, visualize it being on fire.

3. **Associate the name with a concrete image:** Once you've memorized a particular feature, transform the person's name into a memorable image. Use colors, occupations, places, animals, rhymes, celebrities, etc.: John *Black,* Lisa *Carpenter,* Carl *London,* Catherine the *Cat,* Bruce the *goose,* Fred *"Astaire"* Smith. If a name is uncommon, ask the person about it.

4. **Reinforce the image:** Put the face-name associations together. If the red-haired man's name is Bill, you would first visualize the red hair on fire, then visualize a dollar bill (for "Bill"), then visualize a dollar bill burning.

After meeting someone, you may wish to write down the name and the imagery associated with it.

USE VERBAL MEMORY AIDS. One way to make information more meaningful, and so retain it better, is to use memory aids—and the more you are able to personalize them, the more successful they will be. Psychologists call memory aids *mnemonic* (**"nee-*mahn*-ik") *devices,* tactics for making things memorable by making them distinctive.**

Some verbal devices for enhancing memory are as follows:

■ *Write out your information:* This advice may seem obvious. Still, the evidence is that if you write out a shopping list, for example, then if you lose the list, you are more apt to remember the items than if you didn't write them out.[27]

Clearly, this is a reason for taking notes during a lecture, quite apart from making a record: the very act of writing helps you retain information. Even better, if you don't simply write mindlessly but attempt to inject the material with personal meaning, you'll remember it even better.

■ *Organize your information:* People are better able to memorize material when they can organize it. This is one reason why imposing a ranking or hierarchy, such as an outline, on lecture notes or reading notes works so well, especially when the material is difficult.[28]

Thus, to learn lists, try grouping items that have similar meetings. "If you need to remember Queen Victoria, Charlotte Bronte, Prince Albert, and Charles Dickens," suggests one writer, "mentally split the group into males and females, or writers and royals."[29]

■ *Use rhymes to remember important ideas:* You may have heard the spelling rule, "I before E except after C" (so that you'll be correct in spelling "receive," not "recieve"). This an example of the use of rhyme as a memory aid. Another is "Thirty days hath September, April, June, and November . . . " to remember which months have 30 rather than 31 days.

Most of the time, of course, you'll have to make up your own rhymes. It doesn't matter that they are silly. Indeed, the sillier they are, the better you may be apt to remember them.

■ **Use phrases whose first letters represent ideas you want to remember:** Probably the first thing music students learn is "*Every Good Boy Does Fine*" to remember what notes designate the lines of the musical staff: *E G B D F*. This is an example of using a phrase in which the first letter of each word is a cue to help you recall abstract words beginning with the same letter.

What kind of sentence would you make up to remember that business organizations have departments performing five functions—*Accounting, Marketing, Production, Personnel* management, and *Research*? (Maybe it would be, "*Any Man Playing Poker is Rich*"—this also plants a picture in your mind that will help your recall.)

■ **Use a word whose first letters represent ideas you want to remember:** To remember the five business functions above, you could switch the words around and have the nonsense word *PRAMP* (to rhyme with "ramp," then think of, say, a wheelchair ramp or a ramp with a pea rolling down it), the letters of which stand for the first letters of the five functions.

A common example of the use of this device is the name *Roy G. Biv*, which students use to memorize the order of colors in the light spectrum: *r*ed, *o*range, *y*ellow, *g*reen, *b*lue, *i*ndigo, *v*iolet. *HOMES* is the device used to memorize the names of the Great Lakes: *H*uron, *O*ntario, *M*ichigan, *E*rie, *S*uperior.

■ **Make up a narrative story that associates words:** In a technique known as the <u>**narrative story method**</u>, **it has been found that making up a narrative, or story, helps students recall unrelated lists of words by giving them meaning and linking them in a specific order.**[30]
Suppose you need to memorize the words *Rustler, Penthouse, Mountain, Sloth, Tavern, Fuzz, Gland, Antler, Pencil, Vitamin*. This is quite a mixed bag, but if you were taking a French class, you might have to memorize these words (in that language). Here is the story that was constructed to help recall these unrelated words:

"A *Rustler* lived in a *Penthouse* on top of a *Mountain*. His specialty was the three-toed *Sloth*. He would take his captive animals to a *Tavern*, where he would remove *Fuzz* from their *Glands*. Unfortunately, all this exposure to sloth fuzz caused him to grow *Antlers*. So he gave up his profession and went to work in a *Pencil* factory. As a precaution he also took a lot of *Vitamin* E."[31]

In using verbal memory tricks, then, **the rule is:** *Make up verbal cues that are meaningful to you to represent or associate ideas*. In social situations, as when you are introduced to several people simultaneously, you can try using some of these devices. For example, "LAP" might represent Larry, Ann, and Paul.

USE VISUAL MEMORY AIDS. Some psychologists think that using visual images creates a second set of cues in addition to verbal cues that can help memorization.[32] In other words, it helps if you can mentally "take photographs" of the material you are trying to retain.

There are two visual memory aids you may find useful—*a single unusual visual image*, or *a series of visual images.*

■ **Make up a vivid, unusual picture to associate ideas:** The stranger and more distinctive you can make your image, the more you are apt to be able to remember it.[33]

Thus, to remember the five business functions (research, accounting, marketing, personnel management, production), you might create a picture of a woman with a white laboratory coat (research) looking through a magnifying glass at a man a'counting money (accounting) while sitting in a food-market shopping cart (marketing) that is being pushed by someone wearing a letter sweater that says *Person L* (personnel) who is watching a lavish Hollywood spectacle—a production—on a movie screen (production). (If you wish, you could even draw a little sketch of this while you're trying to memorize it.)

■ **Make up a story of vivid images to associate ideas:** A visual trick called the <u>*method of loci*</u> (pronounced "*loh*-sigh" and meaning "places") is to memorize a series of places and then use a different vivid image to associate each place with an idea or a word you want to remember.[34]

For example, you might use buildings and objects along the route from your house to the campus, or from the parking lot to a classroom, each one associated with a specific word or idea. Again, the image associated with each location should be as distinctive as you can make it. To remember the information, you imagine yourself proceeding along this route, so that the various locations cue the various ideas. (The locations need not resemble the ideas. For example, you might associate a particular tree with a man in a white laboratory coat in its branches—research.)

In short, when using visual memory tricks, **the rule is:** *the stranger you make the picture, the more you are apt to remember it.*

Reading for Pleasure Versus Reading for Learning

PREVIEW & REVIEW Reading for pleasure is different from reading for learning. With most pleasure reading you need only remember the information briefly, holding it in your short-term memory. With reading for learning, the information must be stored in your long-term memory, so that you can recall it for tests. This means you must read material more than once. Accordingly, you need to treat textbooks seriously. You also need to understand what their basic features are—title page, copyright page, table of contents, preface, glossary, appendix, bibliography, and index. Finally, you need to know what "advance organizers" are for purposes of surveying material.

What are your thoughts about the whole business of reading in higher education? To get an idea, try Practical Exploration #5.2 *(opposite page)*.

Maybe you already think you read pretty well. After all, you've been doing it for most of your life.

Or maybe you don't feel comfortable about reading. Perhaps you prefer television to print. Or perhaps you think you get information better when someone tells it to you. (A University of Colorado history professor who surveyed her class of traditional-age students found that 58% answered "true" to the question "True or false: I am better at retaining information when I hear it than when I read it."[35]) Or maybe you're an international student and find English a hard language to follow.

Whatever your skills, *there are techniques to improve your reading abilities so that you can better handle subjects at the level of higher education.* Some of them I'll describe in this chapter. If you don't find what you need here (for example, you feel you need help in reading English as a second language), you can probably get assistance through your school's learning center or reading lab.

TWO TYPES OF READING. Reading is principally of two types—for pleasure and for learning:

- *For pleasure:* You can read action-adventure, romances, sports, and similar material just one time, for amusement. This is the kind of material that appears in many novels, magazines, and newspapers. You don't have to read it carefully, unless you want to.

- *For learning:* Most of the other kind of reading you do is for learning of some sort, because you *have* to understand it and perhaps retain it. For instance, you certainly have to pay close attention when you're reading a cookbook or instructions on how to fix a car.

WHAT DO YOU KNOW ABOUT THE READING PROCESS?

Perhaps you regard the reading of textbooks as a reasonably straightforward activity. Or perhaps you find the whole process dreary or mysterious or scary. Answer "Yes" or "No" depending on whether you agree or disagree with the following statements.

1. Reading makes unusual or unique demands on a reader.

    _____ Yes   _____ No

2. Reading is a form of the thinking process. You read with your brain, not your eyes.

    _____ Yes   _____ No

3. Reading is a one-step process.

    _____ Yes   _____ No

4. Effective readers constantly seek to bring meaning to the text.

    _____ Yes   _____ No

5. Many comprehension problems are not just reading problems.

    _____ Yes   _____ No

6. Good readers are sensitive to how the material they are reading is structured or organized.

    _____ Yes   _____ No

7. Speed and comprehension are independent of each other.

    _____ Yes   _____ No

ANSWERS

1. *False.* Reading actually does not make unusual demands on a reader. The same mental processes you use to "read" people's faces or grasp the main idea of a situation you observe are used when you read.

2. *True.* Your eyes simply transmit images to the brain. Improving your reading means improving your thinking, not practicing moving your eyes faster or in a different way.

3. *False.* Reading includes three steps: (a) preparing yourself to read (thinking about what you already know about a subject and setting purposes for reading); (b) processing information; and (c) reacting to what you read.

4. *True.* When they are not comprehending, they take steps to correct the situation.

5. *True.* If you fail to understand something you are reading, it could be because it is poorly written. More likely, however, you lack the background information needed to comprehend—you wouldn't understand it even if someone read it aloud to you. Perhaps you need to read an easier book on the same subject first.

6. *True.* Good readers know the subject matter and main idea of each paragraph and understand how each paragraph is organized (for example, sequence, listing, cause and effect, comparison and contrast, definition).

7. *False.* The more quickly you can understand something, the faster you can read it. However, "speed" without comprehension is meaningless. Reading is more than just allowing your eyes to pass over lines of print.

GROUP ACTIVITY OPTION

In a group-discussion situation, consider which answers surprised you. Why did you think the opposite was true? Does anything you've learned change your previous attitude toward reading?

Reading for learning is something you will have to do all your life, whether it's studying to get a driver's license or finding out how much medicine to give an infant. Indeed, what many managers and administrators are doing all day, when they read reports, letters, and memos, is reading to learn.

But here's the difference between those kinds of reading for learning and reading textbooks:

In college, you'll often have to read the same material more than once.

The reason, of course, is that in college you have to *understand and memorize* so much of what you read.

ABOUT "SPEED READING." Before we go on, let me say a word about *speed reading,* like the kind of reading taught in the Evelyn Wood Reading Dynamics course.

Wouldn't it be great to read 700 words per minute (wpm), as opposed to a more normal rate of about 240 wpm? How about *100,000 wpm*? People have actually learned to skim at such blazing rates of speed. The problem is that they have substantially no comprehension during the process.

Back in 1987, psychologists compared three groups of readers: Evelyn Wood speed readers (700 wpm), "skimmers" (600 wpm), and average readers (240 wpm). The results: in general, speed hurts comprehension. While speed reading or skimming may work well with easy or familiar reading material, it can lead to problems with dense or unfamiliar material. For instance, when questioned about their reading of difficult material, average readers got half the questions right, while speed readers got only one in three. (Average readers also outscored speed readers in comprehending easy material—80% to 65% on general questions and 48% to 29% on specific questions.)[36]

The problem is that speed reading assumes that reading is only a *visual* task, that one can "take in a whole page in a single glance," that hand movement is important, or that reading is somehow independent of the content of the material to be read, as communications expert Phyllis Mindell points out. Mindell notes that researcher Ray Carver concluded that "one must read every word in order to understand the content of written material."[37]

So much for apparently easy solutions.

READING TO FEED YOUR LONG-TERM MEMORY. Thus, you may think, "Oh, boy. You mean there's no way I can just read stuff once and get it the first time?"

Perhaps you can if you're the sort who can memorize the code to a bicycle or locker combination lock with just one glance. Most people, however, need more practice than that.

This has to do with the notion of short-term memory versus long-term memory. As we discussed, the retention of information drops rapidly in the first 24 hours after you've been exposed to it (the "forgetting curve"). Short-term memory is roughly anything you can't hold in mind for more than 24 hours. Long-term memory refers to information you retain for a good deal longer than 24 hours.

Some students might try to make these facts an argument for cramming—holding off until the last day before a test and then reading everything at once. However, there is no way such postponement can really be effective. Many instructors, for instance, have *cumulative* final exams. They test you not just on the new material you're supposed to have learned since the last exam. Rather, they test you on *all* the material back to the beginning of the course. If you opt for cramming, this puts you in the position of having to cram for the *whole course.* In sum: you need to do the kind of reading that will feed your long-term memory.

TREAT TEXTBOOKS SERIOUSLY. Some students regard their textbooks as troublesome or uninteresting but unfortunately necessary (and expensive) parts of their instruction. Or they think of the books as being perhaps useful but not vital (and so they try to avoid buying them).

There's a likelihood, however, that *half or more of your study time will be devoted to such books.* Thus, when you think about what your education *is,* half of it is in your books. You need, then, to treat them as the tools of your trade (your trade being a student)—just as you would an instruction manual if your job required you, say, to fix motorcycles or lead a tour group of Great Britain.

With that in mind, here are a few tips for extracting some benefits from your textbooks:

■ **Look the text over before you take the course:** If you have any doubts about a course you're contemplating taking, take a look in the bookstore at the textbook(s) and any other reading materials that will be required for it. This way you can see what the course will cover and whether it is too advanced or too low-level in the light of your previous experience.

■ **Buy your books early:** In my first couple of semesters as a first-year student, I would dawdle as long as a week or 10 days before buying some of my books. Not a good idea. The school term flies by awfully fast, and I lost the advantage of a head start. (Also, sometimes when I waited too long the books were sold out.)

■ **Look the text over before the first class:** If you are familiar with the principal text before you walk into your first class, you will know what the course is going to cover and how to use the book to help you. Taking a couple of minutes to go from front to back—from title page to index—will tell you what resources the book offers to help you study better.

BECOME FAMILIAR WITH THE BASIC FEATURES. To get a sense of what a book is like, you need to look for eight particular features in the front and back of the book. (See ■ *Panel 5.3.*)

■ *Title page:* At the front of the book, **the <u>title page</u> tells you the title, edition number (if later than the first edition), author, and publisher.** Often the title can give you a sense of the level of difficulty of the book—for example, *Introduction to Business* (introductory level) versus *Intermediate Accounting* (higher level).

■ *Copyright page:* **The <u>copyright page</u> (on the back of the title page) tells you the date the book was published.** With some of the more rapidly changing fields, such as computer science, you hope for as recent a book as possible.

▼ Title page

POPULATION
An Introduction to Concepts and Issues
Fifth Edition

John R. Weeks
San Diego State University

Wadsworth Publishing Company
Belmont, California
A Division of Wadsworth, Inc.

▼ Copyright page

To Deanna

Editor: Serina Beauparlant
Editorial Assistant: Marla Nowick
Production: Greg Hubit Bookworks
Print Buyer: Randy Hurst
Permissions Editor: Peggy Meehan
Copy Editor: Kathleen McCann
Manuscript Editor: Deanna Weeks
Cover: Henry Breuer
Compositor: Bi-Comp, Incorporated
Printer: Arcata Graphics Fairfield

The cover illustration shows countries in proportion to population. Adapted by the author from United Nations data.

This book is printed on acid-free paper that meets Environmental Protection Agency standards for recycled paper.

© 1992 by Wadsworth, Inc. All rights reserved. No part of this book may be reproduced, stored in a retrieval system, or transcribed, in any form or by any means, without the prior written permission of the publisher, Wadsworth Publishing Company, Belmont, California 94002.

1 2 3 4 5 6 7 8 9 10—96 95 94 93 92

Library of Congress Cataloging in Publication Data

Weeks, John Robert, 1944—
    Population : an introduction to concepts and issues / John R.
Weeks. — 5th ed.
        p.   cm.
    Includes bibliographical references and index.
    ISBN 0-534-17346-2
    1. Population. I. Title.
HB871.W43 1992
304.6—dc20   92-6251
                                                      CIP

▼ Table of Contents

DETAILED TABLE OF CONTENTS

▼ Glossary

GLOSSARY

This glossary contains words or terms that appeared in boldface type in the text. I have tried to include terms that are central to an understanding of the study of population. The chapter notation in parentheses refers to the chapter in which the term is first discussed in detail.

abortion the expulsion of a fetus prematurely; a miscarriage—may be either induced or spontaneous (Chapter 4).

abridged life table a life table (see definition) in which ages are grouped into categories (usually five-year age groupings) (Appendix).

accidental death loss of life unrelated to disease of any kind but attributable to the physical, social, or economic environment (Chapter 6).

achieved characteristics those sociodemographic characteristics such as education, occupation, income, marital status, and labor force participation, over which we do have some degree of control (Chapter 9).

age/sex pyramid graph of the number of people in a population by age and sex (Chapter 8).

age/sex–specific death rate the number of people of a given age and sex who died in a given year divided by the total number of people of that age and sex (Chapter 6).

age-specific fertility rate the number of children born to women of a given age divided by the total number of women that age (Chapter 4).

age stratification the assignment of social roles and social status on the basis of age (Chapter 11).

age structure the distribution of people in a population by age (Chapter 8).

Agricultural Revolution change that took place roughly 10,000 years ago when humans first began to domesticate plants and animals, thereby making it easier to settle in permanent establishments (Chapters 2 and 14).

alien a person born in, or belonging to, another country who has not acquired citizenship by naturalization—distinguished from citizen (Chapter 7).

Alzheimer's disease a disease involving a change in the brain's neurons, producing behavioral shifts; a major cause of senility (Chapter 11).

ambivalence state of being caught between competing pressures and thus being uncertain about how to behave properly (Chapter 5).

amenorrhea temporary absence or suppression of the menstrual discharge (Chapter 4).

amino acids building blocks from which proteins are formed (Chapter 14).

anovulatory pertaining to a menstrual cycle in which no egg is released (Chapter 4).

antinatalist based on an ideological position that discourages childbearing (Chapter 3).

arable describes land that is suitable for farming (Chapter 14).

ascribed characteristics sociodemographic characteristics such as gender and race and ethnicity, with which we are born and over which we have essentially no control (Chapter 9).

average age of a population one measure of the age distribution of a population—may be calculated as either the mean or the median (Chapter 8).

521

▼ Preface

PREFACE

Population growth in the 1950s and 1960s could have been likened to a runaway train without an engineer, veering perilously close to a collision course with shortages of food and resources. That specter was altered somewhat by the events of the 1970s, especially by a few hopeful signs of a downturn in the birth rate of several large developing nations. In the 1980s and the 1990s the imagery has changed from the collision course to something equally terrifying. We are faced with a situation analogous to an immense locomotive hurtling down the track at a speed faster than the roadbed can tolerate. The engineer is groping for the brakes, but if and when those brakes are fully applied, the train will still cover a huge distance before it comes to a halt. How much havoc will the charging locomotive of population wreak before it stops, and what condition will we be in at that point? These are two of the most important questions that face the world.

Over the years I have found that most people are either blissfully unaware of the enormous impact that population growth and change have on their lives, or else they have heard so many horror stories about impending doom that they are nearly overwhelmed whenever they think of population growth. My purpose in this book is to shake you out of your lethargy (if you are one of those types), without necessarily scaring you in the process. I will introduce you to the basic concepts of population studies and help you develop your own demographic perspective, enabling you to understand some of the most important issues confronting the world. My intention is to sharpen your perception of population growth and change, to increase your awareness of what is happening and why, and to help prepare you to cope with (and help shape) a future that will be shared with billions more people than there are today.

▼ Appendix

APPENDIX
The Life Table,
Net Reproduction Rate,
and Standardization

▼ Bibliography

BIBLIOGRAPHY

Abelson, P.
14 1975a "The world's disparate food supplies." Science 187: editorial.
14 1975b "Food and nutrition." Science 188 (4188):501.
11 Adamchak, D., A. Wilson, A. Nyanguru, and J. Hampson
    1991 "Elderly support and intergenerational transfer in Zimbabwe: an analysis by gender, marital status, and place of residence." The Gerontologist 31:505–13.
4   Adelman, C.
    1982 "Saving babies with a signature." Wall Street Journal, 28 July.
5   Adlakha, A., and D. Kirk
    1974 "Vital rates in India 1961–71 estimated from 1971 census data." Population Studies 28(3):381–400.
7   Agassi, J., and I. C. Jarvie
    1959 Hong Kong. London: Oxford Press.
8   Ahlburg, D., and M. Schapiro
    1984 "Socioeconomic ramifications of changing cohort size: an analysis of U.S. postwar suicide rates by age and sex." Demography 21(1):97–105.
6   Ahonsi, B.
    1991 "Report on the seminar on anthropological studies relevant to the sexual transmission of HIV, Sonderborg, Denmark, 1990." IUSSP Newsletter 41:79–103.
4   Akin, J., R. Bilsbarrow, D. Guilkey, B. Popkin, D. Benoit, P. Cantrelle, M. Garenne, and P. Levi
    1981 "The determinants of breast-feeding in Sri Lanka." Demography 18(3):287–308.

Akpom, C., K. Akpom, and M. Davis
    1976 "Prior sexual behavior of teenagers attending rap sessions for the first time." Family Planning Perspectives 8:203–6.
12 Alba, R., and J. Logan
    1991 "Variations on two themes: racial and ethnic patterns in the attainment of suburban residence." Demography 28:431–53.
16 Allan, C.
    1981 "Measuring mature markets." American Demographics 3(3):13–17.
1,12 Alonso, W., and P. Starr
    1982 "The political economy of national statistics." Social Science Research Council Items 36(3):29–35.
16 Alsop, R.
    1984 "Firms still struggle to devise best approach to black buyers." Wall Street Journal, 25 October.
American Demographics
16 1982 "The demographic future." The Monthly Report of International Demographics (brochure).
16 1983 "Here comes 1984." American Demographics 5(6):11.
6   Anderson, B., and B. Silver
    1989 "Patterns of cohort mortality in the Soviet population." Population and Development Review 15:471–502.
6   Ankrah, E. M.
    1991 "AIDS and the social side of health." Social Science and Medicine 32:967–80.
8   Aries, P.
    1962 Centuries of Childhood. New York: Vintage Books.

530

▼ Index

Table of contents: The _table of contents_ lists the principal headings in the book. Sometimes a "brief contents" will list just parts and chapters, and a "detailed contents" will list other major headings as well.

Preface: The _preface_ tells you the intended audience for the book, the author's purpose and approach, why the book is different, and perhaps an overview of the organization. (The preface—which may also be called "Introduction" or "To the Student"—may go in front of the table of contents.)

Glossary: In the back of the book, **the _glossary_ is an alphabetical list of key terms and their definitions,** as found in the text. Quite often the same terms appear within the main body of the text in **boldface** (dark type) or _italics_ (slanted type).

Appendix: Also in the back of the book, **the _appendix_ contains supplementary material, material of optional or specialized interest.** Examples are tables, charts, and more detailed discussion than is contained in the text. Often there is more than one appendix. Engineering or business students, for instance, will often find time-saving tables contained in appendixes.

Bibliography: Appearing at the back of the book or at the end of each chapter, **the _bibliography,_ or "Notes" section, lists sources or references used in writing the text.** This section can be a good resource if you're writing a term paper for the course. Scanning the textbook's bibliography may suggest some valuable places to start.

Index: The _index_ is an alphabetically **arranged list of names and subjects that appear in the text, giving the page numbers on which they appear.** Sometimes there are two indexes—a name index and a subject index. The index is an _extremely_ useful tool. If you're not sure a topic is discussed in the book, try looking it up in the index.

UNDERSTAND WHAT "ADVANCE ORGANIZ-ERS" ARE. As I discuss shortly, one concept underlying many reading strategies is that of *surveying*. **A *survey* is an overview.** That is, you take a couple of minutes to look through a chapter to get an overview of it before you start reading it.

Surveying a chapter has three purposes:

1. ***It gets you going:*** Getting started reading on a densely packed 35-page chapter can be difficult. Surveying the material gets you going, like a slow warm-up lap around the track.

2. ***It gives you some familiarity with the material:*** Have you ever noticed that when you're reading on a subject with which you're familiar you read more rapidly? For example, you might read slowly about an event reported in the morning paper but read more rapidly a story about that same event in the evening paper or a different newspaper. When you survey a chapter in a textbook, you begin to make it familiar to you. Notice, then, that the survey is not a waste of time. *It enables you to read faster later.*

3. ***It gives you "advance organizers" to help you organize information in your mind:*** As you do your overview you pick up what are called "advance organizers." **Advance organizers are mental landmarks under which facts and ideas may be grouped and organized in your mind.** Thus, when you go to read the chapter itself, you already have some advance information about it.

Textbooks provide some or all of the following *advance organizers*. It's a good idea to pay attention to these when doing a survey of a chapter.

- ***Chapter table of contents:*** You can find a breakdown of the headings within the chapter at the front of the book (in the table of contents). Some textbooks repeat this outline of the contents at the beginning of each chapter.

- ***Learning objectives:*** Not all books do, but some texts have learning objectives. **Learning objectives are topics you are expected to learn, which are listed at the**

beginning of each chapter. This usually starts out with a sentence something like: "After you have read this chapter, you should be able to . . ." The list of objectives then follows.

For example, learning objectives in an introductory computer book might be: "Explain what desktop publishing is" or "Discuss the principal features of word processing software."

- ***Chapter summary:*** Many textbooks have a summary at the end of the chapter, describing key concepts of the chapter. *Be sure to read the chapter summary FIRST,* even though you probably won't understand everything in it. It will help you get an overview of the material so it will seem somewhat familiar to you later.

In this book, instead of having a summary at the end of each chapter, we have put a summary (called "PREVIEW & REVIEW") following every main section heading. This section-head summary describes ("previews") the material you are about to read in the section. You can also use it for reviewing purposes later.

- ***Review or discussion questions:*** These, too, may appear at the end of the chapter. Sometimes review or discussion questions can be quite important because *they ask some of the questions that will be asked on the test.* Be sure to skim through them.

- **List of key terms:** Key terms may appear in **boldface** type (dark type) or *italics* (slanted type) within the text of the chapter. Sometimes key terms also appear in a list at the end of the chapter.

- **Headings, subheadings, and first sentences:** Read anything that appears as a heading; then read the first sentence following the heading.

Of course, a lot of the advance organizers that you read during the survey step are not going to make complete sense. But some of them will. And most of the material will have a familiar, hence a somewhat comforting, feeling to it when you come back to it on subsequent steps.

In the rest of this chapter I describe some reading systems devised to help students get the most out of textbooks.

WHAT DO YOU THINK OF TEXTBOOKS?

f half of your education is in your textbooks, it's important to determine what your attitude is toward them. First list three negative things that come to mind about textbooks. Then list three positive things.

In class discussion, describe some of your feelings about textbooks, then consider some of the following questions. If you didn't have textbooks, what would you use instead to get the same information? Would it be more efficient? How much money in a quarter or term do you spend on recreation and how does that compare to the money spent on books? When you're learning something for work or personal interest, what kinds of sources of information do you use?

The Five-Step SQ3R Reading System

PREVIEW & REVIEW The five-step SQ3R method stands for: <u>S</u>urvey, <u>Q</u>uestion, <u>R</u>ead, <u>R</u>ecite, <u>R</u>eview. Its advantage is that it breaks down reading into manageable segments that require you to understand them before proceeding.

There's a war on! We must teach them to read faster!"

Maybe that's what psychologist Francis P. Robinson was told in 1941. In any event, Robinson then set about to devise an intensified reading system for World War II military people enrolled in special courses at Ohio State University. Since then, many thousands of students have successfully used his system or some variation.

The reason the system is effective is that it *breaks a reading assignment down into manageable portions that require you to understand them before you move on.*

Robinson's reading system is called *the SQ3R method.* **The _SQ3R reading method_ stands for five steps: Survey, Question, Read, Recite, Review.**[38] Let's see how you would apply these to the chapter of a textbook you are assigned to read.

STEP 1: S—SURVEY. As I said, a *survey* is an overview. You do a quick 1- or 2-minute overview of the entire chapter before you plunge into it. Look at the advance organizers—the chapter outline or learning objectives, if any; the chapter headings; and the summary, if any, at the end of the chapter. The point of surveying is twofold:

- **You establish relationships between the major segments:** Surveying enables you to see how the chapter segments go together. Understanding how the parts fit in with the whole helps you see how the chapter makes sense.

■ *You see where you're going:* If you know where you're going, you can better organize the information as you read. This is just like reading over directions to someone's house before you get there rather than bit by bit while traveling.

Next you apply Steps 2 through 4—Question, Read, Recite—*but only to one section at a time, or to an even smaller segment.* That is, you apply the next three steps section by section, or even paragraph by paragraph, if material is difficult. You apply the last step, Step 5, Review, after you have finished the chapter.

STEP 2: Q–QUESTION. Take a look at the heading of the first section and turn it into a question in your mind. For example, if the heading (in a book about computers) is "Basic Software Tools for Work and Study," ask "What does 'Basic Software Tools' mean?" If the heading is to a subsection, do the same. For example, if the heading is "Word Processing," ask, "How does word processing work?"

Questioning has two important effects:

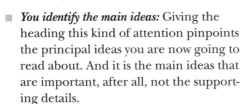

Mindfulness

■ *You become personally involved:* By questioning, you get actively involved in your reading. And personal involvement is one of the most fundamental ways to commit information to memory. This goes back to our discussion of mindful learning.

■ *You identify the main ideas:* Giving the heading this kind of attention pinpoints the principal ideas you are now going to read about. And it is the main ideas that are important, after all, not the supporting details.

If you are proceeding on a paragraph-by-paragraph basis because the material is difficult (as in technical courses such as physics), there may not be any heading that you can convert to a question. In that case, you'll need to put Step 3, Read, before Step 2: that is, you read the paragraph, then create a question about that paragraph.

Incidentally, it's perfectly all right (indeed, even desirable) at this stage to move your lips and ask the question under your breath.

STEP 3: R–READ. *Now* you actually do the reading—but only up to the next section heading (or paragraph). Note, however, that you do not read as though you were reading a popular novel. Rather, *you read with purpose—actively searching to answer the question you posed.* If you don't seem to understand it, reread the section until you can answer the question.

What is the difference between passive and active reading? If you were reading a murder mystery *passively,* you would just run your eyes over the lines and wait, perhaps mildly curious, to see how things came out. If you were reading that mystery novel *actively,* you would constantly be trying to guess the outcome. You would be asking yourself such questions as: Who was the killer? What was that strange phone call about? What motive would she have for the murder? What was that funny business in his background? And you would be searching for the answers.

Mindfulness

You don't need to do that with recreational reading. Reading a textbook, however, should *always* be an active, indeed *mindful,* process of asking questions and searching for answers. That's why you have to take study breaks from time to time (perhaps 5 minutes every half hour, or even every 15 minutes, if the material is difficult), because this type of reading is not effortless.

In addition, especially if the segment is somewhat long, you should read (perhaps on a second reading) for another purpose:

■ *You should determine whether the section asks any other questions:* The question you formulated based on the section heading may not cover all the material in the segment. Thus, as you read, you may see other questions that should be asked about the material.

■ *Ask those questions and answer them:* You probably get the idea: the Question and Read steps are not completely separate steps. Rather, you are continually alternating questions and answers as you read through the segment.

Some examples of questions you might frame in your mind as you read a textbook are:

What is the main idea of this paragraph?
What is an example that illustrates this principle?
What are the supporting facts?
Who is this person and why is he or she considered important?
What could the instructor ask me about this on the exam?
What about this don't I understand?

If necessary, as you stop and think about key points, you may want to write brief notes to trigger your memory when you get to Step 5, Review.

STEP 4: R—RECITE. When you reach the end of the section, stop and look away from the page. *Recite* the answer you have just discovered for the question you formulated. You should practice this in two ways:

■ *Recite the answer aloud:* When I say "aloud," I don't mean so loud that you have other students in the library looking at you. But there's nothing embarrassing about talking *subvocally* to yourself—that is, moving your tongue within your mouth while your lips move imperceptibly. When you move the muscles in your lips and mouth and throat,

this vocalizing or subvocalizing helps lay down a memory trace in your mind.

I can't stress enough the importance of reciting aloud or nearly aloud. As Walter Pauk writes, "Reciting promotes concentration, forms a sound basis for understanding the next paragraph or the next chapter, provides time for the memory trace to consolidate, ensures that facts and ideas are remembered accurately, and provides immediate feedback on how you're doing. . . ."[39] Pauk also mentions experiments that show that students who read and recite learn much better than students who just read.

■ *Say the answer in your own words:* When you formulate the answer in your own words (perhaps using an example) rather than just repeat a phrase off the page, you are required to *understand* it rather than just memorize it. And when you understand it, you *do* memorize it better.

If you did not take any notes for review earlier, you may wish to at this point. The notes should not be extensive, just brief cues to jog your memory when you move to Step 5, Review.

Don't move on to the next segment until you're sure you understand this one. After all, if you don't get it now, when will you? Once you think you understand the section, move on to the next section (or paragraph) and repeat steps 2, 3, and 4.

STEP 5: R—REVIEW. When you have read all the way through the chapter (or as far as you intend to go in one study session), section by section in Question-Read-Recite fashion, you are ready to test how well you have mastered your key ideas. Here's how to do it:

■ *Go back over the book's headings or your notes and ask the questions again:* Repeat the questions and try to answer them without looking at the book or your notes. If you have difficulty, check your answers.

■ *Review other memory aids:* Read the chapter summary and the review questions. Then skim the chapter again, as well as your notes, refreshing your memory.

GROUP ACTIVITY #5.4

PRACTICING THE SQ3R METHOD

At the instructor's discretion, this activity may be performed all in class or partly out of class and partly in class.

In a small group with three other students divide into two teams of two people each. Select two earlier chapters from this book on which to practice the SQ3R method. One team practices the method on one chapter, the other team on the other chapter. (Or use two chapters from another text on which the four of you can agree.) The method may be performed in or outside of class as the instructor suggests.

Next, without looking at the text, have the other team quiz you on the chapter you studied. Then take turns quizzing them on the chapter they studied. Finally, in class discuss how well the method worked for you. What would you do differently?

The Three-Step 3Rs Reading System

PREVIEW & REVIEW The three-step 3Rs Method stands for: <u>Read</u>, <u>Record</u>, <u>Recite</u>. The method has no survey step, but it helps you retain material through reading, rereading, underlining, making questions, and self-testing.

The *3Rs reading system* has three steps for **mastering textbooks: *Read, Record, Recite.*** This system was described by Walter Pauk, who says it "is perfect for students who like to move quickly into a textbook chapter, or for those who face exams with little time for intensive

study."[40] In other words, if (against all advice) you have to resort to cramming, use this method.

STEP 1: READ. There is no surveying or questioning of material first, as in the SQ3R Method. Rather, you just start reading and read a section or several paragraphs. Then do as follows:

- *Ask what you need to know:* Return to the first paragraph and ask yourself, "What do I need to know in this paragraph?"

- *Read and reread for answers and say aloud:* Read and reread the paragraph until you can say aloud what you need to know about it.

"Do you think writing in your textbooks helps you learn?"

Name: Jaratsunthonwong Pornchai

Major: Computer Science

Family & Work Situation: Family college-educated; worked four years before entering higher education.

Interests: Tennis, diving

Answer to question: "Yes, it helps me understand what topics or ideas are important in the reading. It also helps me emphasize topics that will probably go on the examination. Sometimes I will summarize all the information in a chapter so that it is easier for me to understand and remember."

STEP 2: RECORD. The SQ3R Method, previously discussed, says nothing about making marks or writing in the book, although you can do so if it helps. However, in Step 2 of the 3Rs Method you are *required* to mark up the book. Here's how:

- **Underline key information:** Once you can say aloud what you need to know, you should underline the key information in the book. It's important that you *underline just the key information—terms, phrases, and sentences*—not line after line of material. This is so that when you come back to review, you will see only the essential material.

- **Write a brief question in the margin:** After underlining, write a *brief question* in the margin that asks for the information you've underlined. *(See ■ Panel 5.4.)* Forming questions is extremely important to the 3Rs System, so you must be sure to do this.

PANEL 5.4 **Underlining & questions.** In Step 2, you underline key information and write questions in the margin.

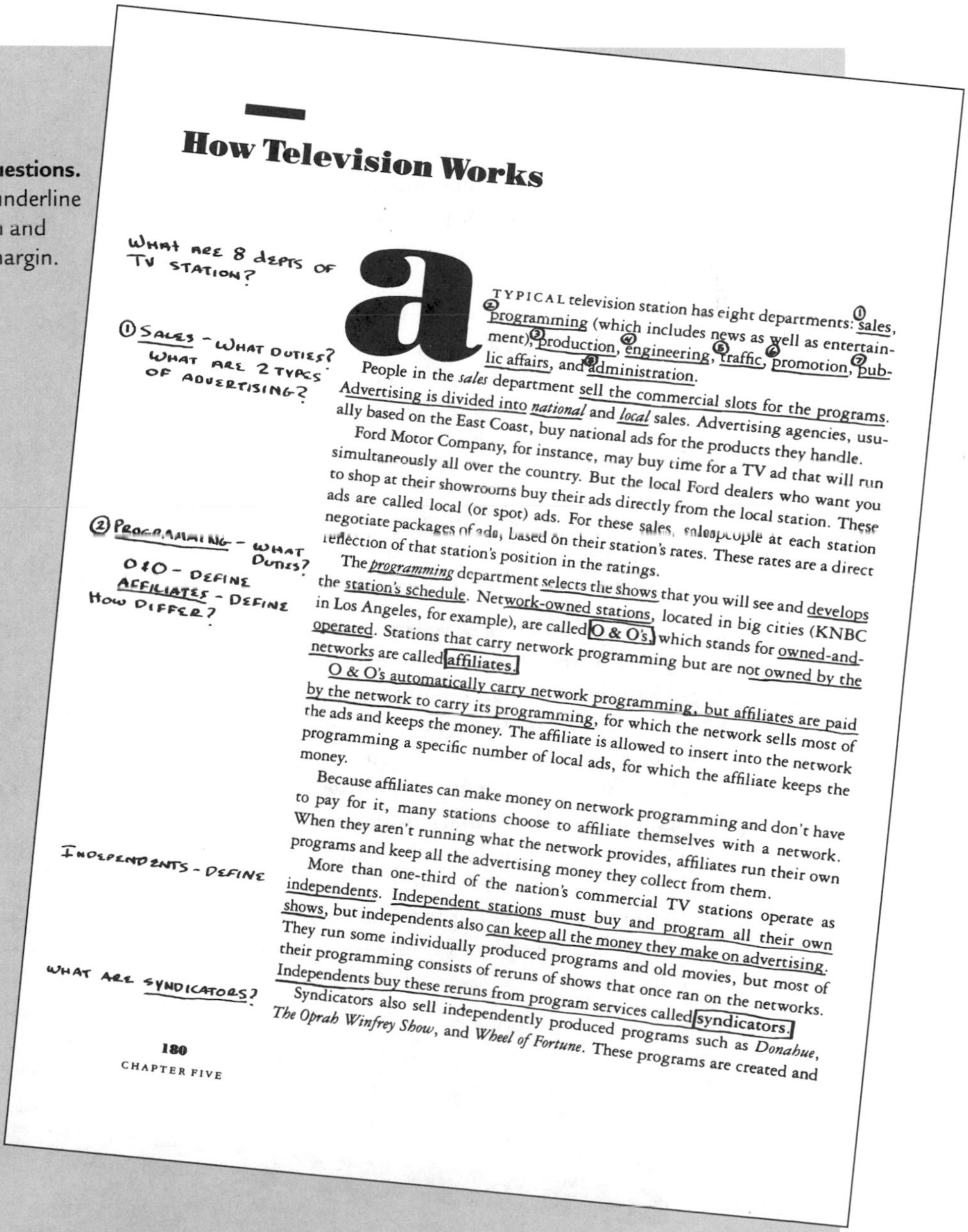

How Television Works

(margin questions):
WHAT ARE 8 DEPTS OF TV STATION?

① SALES - WHAT DUTIES? WHAT ARE 2 TYPES OF ADVERTISING?

② PROGRAMMING - WHAT DUTIES? O & O - DEFINE AFFILIATES - DEFINE HOW DIFFER?

INDEPENDENTS - DEFINE

WHAT ARE SYNDICATORS?

a TYPICAL television station has eight departments: sales, programming (which includes news as well as entertainment), production, engineering, traffic, promotion, public affairs, and administration.

People in the *sales* department sell the commercial slots for the programs. Advertising is divided into *national* and *local* sales. Advertising agencies, usually based on the East Coast, buy national ads for the products they handle. Ford Motor Company, for instance, may buy time for a TV ad that will run simultaneously all over the country. But the local Ford dealers who want you to shop at their showrooms buy their ads directly from the local station. These ads are called local (or spot) ads. For these sales, salespeople at each station negotiate packages of ads, based on their station's rates. These rates are a direct reflection of that station's position in the ratings.

The *programming* department selects the shows that you will see and develops the station's schedule. Network-owned stations, located in big cities (KNBC in Los Angeles, for example), are called O & O's, which stands for owned-and-operated. Stations that carry network programming but are not owned by the networks are called affiliates.

O & O's automatically carry network programming, but affiliates are paid by the network to carry its programming, for which the network sells most of the ads and keeps the money. The affiliate is allowed to insert into the network programming a specific number of local ads, for which the affiliate keeps the money.

Because affiliates can make money on network programming and don't have to pay for it, many stations choose to affiliate themselves with a network. When they aren't running what the network provides, affiliates run their own programs and keep all the advertising money they collect from them.

More than one-third of the nation's commercial TV stations operate as independents. Independent stations must buy and program all their own shows, but independents also can keep all the money they make on advertising. They run some individually produced programs and old movies, but most of their programming consists of reruns of shows that once ran on the networks. Independents buy these reruns from program services called syndicators.

Syndicators also sell independently produced programs such as *Donahue*, *The Oprah Winfrey Show*, and *Wheel of Fortune*. These programs are created and

180
CHAPTER FIVE

After you finish this step for these paragraphs, proceed to the next segment or paragraphs and again Read and Record.

Incidentally, a word about underlining: I've sat in libraries and watched students reading a chapter for the first time, underlining the text as they go. At the end, if they are using a green pen, say, the entire chapter looks like a mess of green paint. Obviously, this kind of underlining doesn't work. The point is to use your pen or highlighter to mark only *important* things, not *everything*. This is why it's best to read the chapter (or section) first without underlining, then reread it, doing your underlining on the second reading. (Note: Be sure to use pen or highlighter. If you use felt-tip markers or Magic Markers, the ink will go through the paper—indeed, perhaps through five or more pages.)

STEP 3: RECITE. After you've finished doing Steps 1 and 2 for the chapter, go back to the beginning. Now you will do the Recite step for the entire chapter, as follows:

- *Cover the page and ask yourself each question:* Use a folded piece of paper or your hand to cover the printed page of the text except for the questions you've written in the margins. Ask yourself the questions.

- *Recite aloud and check your answers:* Recite *aloud* the answer to each question. ("Aloud" can mean talking to yourself under your breath.) Then lift the paper and check your answer. If you're not clear on the answer, ask and answer again. Put a check mark in the margin if you need to come back and review again.

  Continue the Recite step until you get to the end of the chapter. Then go back and look at the places where you've left a check mark.

GROUP ACTIVITY #5.5

WHAT ARE THE PRINCIPAL MISTAKES MADE IN READING FOR LEARNING?

Along with others in a small group, make a list of examples of mistakes you have made in reading for learning (such as doing too much underlining or reading only once). Then identify specific techniques for correcting these mistakes. These may be whole systems such as SQ3R or specific techniques such as making diagrams. It's important that you show, through use of example, how the technique is being used.

With your group pick the best example of the use of a technique and share it with the class as a whole. Discuss which techniques appear to work best in which situations.

After several years of looking at various reading systems, I devised a system adapted from others' contributions, such as Walter Pauk's "Questions-in-the-Margin method."[41] The purpose of this system is *to produce an efficient study guide that you can use to effectively prime yourself the night before an exam.* I call this the Textbook–to–Study Guide method, and its purpose is to combine techniques of mindfulness and repetition so that you can imprint the reading material on your memory and get a grade of A on the exam. If you're interested in this, take a look at the accompanying box. *(See ■ Panel 5.5.)*

The **Textbook–to–Study Guide method.** This method is a seven-step system that produces a study guide you can use to prime yourself before exams. The seven steps are: (1) preview and question, (2) read actively, (3) reread and underline, (4) write keywords/questions in margins, (5) recite, (6) reflect, and (7) review.

Step 1: Preview & Question. A *preview* is a 2-minute or 5-minute skimming of the entire chapter to establish relationships between major segments and learn where you're going.

As you skim, make up *questions*. Use a pen to turn every heading into a question, adding words such as "What" or "How."

Step 2: Read Actively. Now actively read the chapter or section. Active reading is *reading to answer the questions* you posed in the headings.

Step 3: Reread & Underline. Now reread the material, using a pen (or highlighter) to underline (a) key terms, (b) main ideas, and (c) conclusions. (Don't mark examples, tables, and illustrations, unless they're important.)

Step 4: Write Keywords & Short-Answer Questions in the Margins. Now go through the material and write keywords and short-answer questions in the margins. (This will create a study guide for use later in preparing for tests.) *Keywords* are important terms or names, often in boldface or italics, that you're expected to know. *Short-answer questions* are those that might appear on a test; the answers appear in the text (underlined) near where you wrote the questions.

Step 5: Recite. Return to the beginning, and cover the text with a piece of paper, leaving keywords and questions exposed. Now go through and ask "What does the keyword mean?" and "What is the answer to the question?" *This reciting should be done aloud* (or almost aloud). Check your answers by lifting the paper.

Step 6: Reflect. After doing reciting for a section, raise your eyes and reflect on the knowledge you've acquired. Reflecting means thinking it over, bringing your own ideas to what you've learned, making your own personal associations with it.

Step 7: Review. Reviewing is of two sorts—immediate and later.

In *immediate reviewing*, before ending your study session, do one last leisurely sweep through the chapter. Use your newly created study guide to look at the keywords and questions you've written and visualize the definitions and answers. If you have difficulty, say the answer over one extra time, then put a check mark in the margin, so you'll know to pay particular attention to this question in the future.

In *later reviewing*, right before the test do a last run-through, doing reciting and reflection. Cover the text with a piece of paper and go through looking at the keywords and questions in the margins. *Recite aloud* the definitions and answers, then lift the paper to check your results. Pause and *reflect* as you go, trying to make a personal connection in your mind to the material you have just recited. Think particularly about material near which you've placed a check mark.

Dealing with Special Subjects: Math, Science, Languages, & Other

PREVIEW & REVIEW Mathematics, science, social science, history, foreign languages, and literature may be areas of study that require more study effort than you're accustomed to. The first step is to reduce your anxiety, using positive self-talk. The second step is to devote enough time and practice to the subject. The third step is to avail yourself of such tools as flash cards or index cards; diagrams, charts, and maps; and cassette tapes.

Some students, even though they may be smart in many ways, go into a panic when confronted with a particular subject—technical subjects such as math or chemistry or detail-oriented subjects such as foreign languages, history, or literature. The specific advice for coping here is:

■ *Take steps to reduce your anxiety.*

■ *Devote more time and practice to your assignments, and don't fall behind.*

■ *Use special tools for information organizing and study.*

Let's consider these matters.

REDUCING YOUR ANXIETY. "Math anxiety" is very real for a number of people, as is anxiety about the other subjects mentioned. Students may believe that math requires a logical ability or special knack that they don't think they have. With science they may think there is only one way to solve problems. With history, literature, or foreign languages, they may think they don't have a good enough memory for details.

Here's what to do:

■ **Learn your inner voice:** The first step is to learn what your inner voice is saying, to pinpoint those inhibiting pronouncements from within. This inner voice is often the *Voice Of Judgment (VOJ)*, the internal broadcast that goes on within all of us.

As one book describes it, the Voice Of Judgment "condemns, criticizes, attaches blame, makes fun of, puts down, assigns guilt, passes sentence on, punishes, and buries anything that's the least bit unlike a mythical norm."[42]

■ **Pinpoint your negative thoughts:** Once you've identified the negative thoughts ("I don't think I'm smart enough to get this stuff"), speak them aloud or write them down. Usually, such thoughts come down to two matters:

1. *"I don't understand it now, so I never will."* If you think about this, however, you'll realize that there have been many times in the past when you haven't understood something but eventually did. After all, there *was* a time when you couldn't read, ride a bicycle, drive a car, or whatever.

2. *"Everybody else is better at this subject than I am."* If you do a reality check—by asking your classmates—you'll find that this just isn't so. Probably a number of people will, if they're honest, say they aren't confident about this subject.

■ **Replace your negative thoughts with positive self-talk:** Now try to replace the VOJ and use your inner voice as a force for success. You do this by using *positive self-talk*, which can help you control your moods, turn back fear messages, and give you confidence.[43,44] **_Positive self-talk_ consists of giving yourself positive messages.**

The messages of positive self-talk are not mindless self-delusions. Rather they are messages such as "You can do it. You've done it well before" that correct errors and distortions in your thinking and help you develop a more accurate internal dialog.[45]

Stop and try Personal Exploration #5.3 to identify your negative thoughts, then figure out how to make them positive, using positive self-talk.

NEGATIVE THOUGHTS & POSITIVE THOUGHTS

Think of certain subjects you are anxious about and listen to what your inner voice (your Voice Of Judgment) says about you. (*Examples:* "My mind is always in confusion when I'm confronted with math problems." "I'm the kind of person who can barely change a light bulb, let alone operate a microscope." "I'm not as good as other people at figuring how a foreign language works." "If I ask the question I want to ask, people will think I'm dumb.")

1. _____
_____
_____
_____
_____
_____
_____

2. _____
_____
_____
_____
_____
_____

3. _____
_____
_____
_____
_____
_____
_____

4. _____
_____
_____

Now try to replace these negative thoughts with positive self-talk. (*Examples:* "I can solve math problems when I approach them calmly and deliberately and give myself time." "Just as I've learned [basketball, weaving, or some other skill] in the past, so I can learn a foreign language without having to compare myself to others." "Smart people ask questions rather than withhold questions.")

1. _____
_____
_____
_____
_____

2. _____
_____
_____

3. _____
_____
_____
_____
_____
_____

4. _____
_____
_____
_____
_____

GROUP ACTIVITY OPTION

With others in a group of three, develop a list of negative thoughts. Then replace them with a list of positive thoughts. Post a couple of examples of each on the board for class discussion. Are there some negative thoughts that seem to be fairly common? How are they hindrances to doing well in school and in life? What do you think of the idea of replacing "negative inner voices" with "positive inner voices"?

- **Deal with the stresses:** The sense of unpleasantness that the anxiety-provoking subject evokes may be felt in a physical way—as clammy hands, constricted breathing, headache, or other kinds of panicky reactions. Elsewhere in the book I describe ways to deal with stress, such as techniques of relaxation and visualization.

  For now, however, just try this: every time you have to deal with a troublesome subject, take a slow, deep breath and slowly exhale; then repeat. Then tell yourself, "Now I'm ready to deal with this subject calmly and methodically, taking however long it takes." If the anxiety begins to resurface, repeat the slow, deep breathing twice.

DEVOTE ENOUGH TIME. Once you've dealt with the emotional barriers, then be prepared to spend more time on the subject. It doesn't matter that it takes you longer to learn math, physics, French, or whatever than it will some other students; you're doing this for yourself. (The chances are, however, that a difficult subject for you is also a difficult subject for many others.)

Spending more time on the subject involves the following:

- **Keep up with the assignments:** Don't fall behind. Subjects such as math and foreign languages are *cumulative* or *sequential* kinds of knowledge: it's difficult to understand the later material if you don't understand the earlier material.

  Thus, if you feel yourself slipping, *get help right away.* Seek assistance from a classmate, the instructor, or a tutor. If you're worried about confiding your anxieties to someone involved with the subject, see your academic advisor. Or go to the campus counseling center and seek the advice of a counselor.

- **Review the previous assignment before starting the present one:** Precisely because later skills depend on having mastered earlier skills, it's a good idea to review the previous assignment. Being confident you understand yesterday's material will give you the confidence to move on to today's assignment.

- **Apply the SQ3R, 3Rs, or other reading method:** Difficult subjects are precisely the kinds of subjects in which you need to go over things several times, constantly asking questions and marking up the text. The reading methods I described earlier in this chapter will help here.

- **Work practice problems:** Math and foreign languages require that you learn specific skills as well as information. Accordingly, you should work all practice problems that are assigned, whether math problems or language exercises. For example, you should work practice problems at the end of every section within the book and also those at the end of every chapter.

- **Take frequent breaks—and remind yourself of why you're doing this:** Needless to say, studying difficult material is a frustrating business. Go easy on yourself. If you feel you're beating your head against the wall, take frequent breaks. Study some other material for awhile.

  When you come back to your original work, remind yourself why you're studying it—for example, "I need to study chemistry because it's important to my medical career."

- **Do lab assignments:** Some subjects require use of a laboratory. For biology or chemistry, for example, there is often a lecture portion, in which you take notes about concepts from a lecturer, and a lab portion, in which you do experiments or other hands-on tasks. *The two kinds of classes are not independent of each other:* what's learned in the lab reinforces what's learned in the lecture.

USE SPECIAL TOOLS FOR STUDYING. A whole bag of tools is available for helping to organize information and make special study guides to help you learn difficult subjects. Some of these tools, such as diagrams and charts, may be especially helpful if your learning style tends to be more visual than verbal.

The tools are as follows:

- **Flash cards or index cards: A _flash card_ is a card bearing words, numbers, or pictures that is briefly displayed as a learning aid.** A flash card may be a 3 × 5-inch index card that you make up yourself. Or it may be part of a set of cards that you buy

in the bookstore to use to study biological terms, foreign language vocabulary, or whatever.

If you're making up a flash card yourself, write the key term, concept, or problem that you are trying to grasp on the front and the explanation or answer on the back. Don't forget that you can put *several* terms on one side and their answers on the reverse. For example, for a history course you might list the name of a treaty followed by such questions as "Year?" "Signers?" "Purpose?" "Consequences?" You would list the answers on the back of the card.

Flash cards can be used for all kinds of subjects. For math or engineering, you can write a term or formula on one side and its definition, meaning, or calculations on the other. In science, you can state the theory or scientist on the front and the important principles or hypothesis associated with it or him/her on the back. For literature classes, you can write the name of a short story or poem on one side and its meaning on the other.

When you use flash cards, you can sort them into three piles according to how well you've memorized them: (1) cards you know well; (2) cards you know but respond slowly to or are vague about; (3) cards you don't know. You'll find it's pleasing to watch the "I know" pile grow. (And if you must cram for an exam, the first and second piles are the ones to concentrate on.)

Carry a few flash cards with you wherever you go. Then when you find yourself with a few minutes to spare you can take them out and practice answering the questions on them.

- *Cassette tapes:* Elsewhere we mentioned that taping lectures can provide a kind of reinforcement, particularly if the lecturer is hard to follow (though taping is no substitute for note taking). Listening to cassette tapes is also valuable for certain specific subjects such as language study. Since the heart of learning a foreign language is repetition and practice, during spare moments in your day you can use a Sony Walkman, for example, to listen to tapes on which you have recorded new vocabulary terms, verb forms, and idioms.

- *Diagrams, charts, and maps:* Drawing diagrams of concepts helps reinforce learning in two ways: (a) It helps your visual sense, because you can *see* the ideas.

(b) It helps your kinesthetic sense, or sense of touch, because you are actually creating something with your hand.

There are all kinds of ways to sketch out concepts and information. What follows are only a few ideas.

(a) **_Study diagrams_ are literal representations of things from real life,** which you have rendered in your own hand. This type of artwork is especially useful in the biological and health sciences: You can draw and label the parts of a cell, the bones in the head, the arteries and veins of the circulatory system. *(See ■ Panel 5.6a.)*

(b) **_Process diagrams_ are useful for representing the steps in a process** and thus are useful in such subjects as biology, geology, or environmental science. For example, you might sketch the process of photosynthesis, the process of global warming, or the geological formation of an ancient lake. *(See ■ Panel 5.6b.)*

(c) **_Concept maps_ are visual diagrams of concepts.** For example, you can make a drawing of psychologist Abraham Maslow's famous hierarchy of needs, the parts of a symphony, or the five departments of a typical business organization. *(See ■ Panel 5.6c.)*

(d) **_Time lines_ are sketches representing a particular historical development.** They are useful in memorizing historical processes, such as the buildup to the Civil War or the growth of computer technology. A time line consists of simply a vertical line with "tick marks" and labels, each indicating the year and its important event. *(See ■ Panel 5.6d.)*

(e) **_Comparison charts_ are useful for studying several concepts and the relationships among them.** Headings are listed across the top of the page and down the left side of the page; the concepts are then briefly described in a grid in the middle of the page. For example, you might compare various religions by listing their names across the top (such as *Christianity, Buddhism, Hinduism*), the principal categories of comparison down the side (*Deity, Holy book, Principal countries*), and then the specifics within the grid. *(See ■ Panel 5.6e.)*

Onward: Applying This Chapter to Your Life

PREVIEW & REVIEW Reading is half your education.

Reading, as I said, may well constitute half your education during the next few terms or years—reading textbooks, that is. There is also reading of another sort that you will do—namely, reading your lecture notes. Thus, some of the reading skills you have learned in this chapter will apply to the next chapter, in which I discuss lectures and note taking.

Consider two things you can take away from this chapter that you think will be useful lifelong. Describe them here:

_____

_____

_____

_____

_____

_____

Diagrams, charts, & maps for reinforcement.

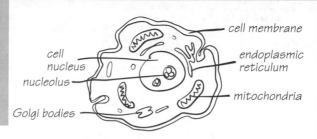

a. Study diagram—example of drawing and labeling a cell.

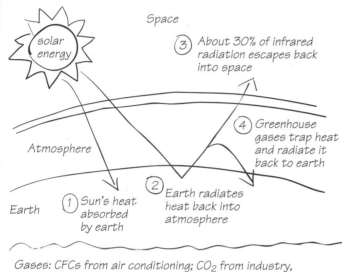

Space

③ About 30% of infrared radiation escapes back into space

④ Greenhouse gases trap heat and radiate it back to earth

Atmosphere

① Sun's heat absorbed by earth

② Earth radiates heat back into atmosphere

Earth

Gases: CFCs from air conditioning; CO_2 from industry, deforestation, & burning of fossil fuels; methane & nitrous oxide from cattle

b. Process diagram—example of representing steps in global warming.

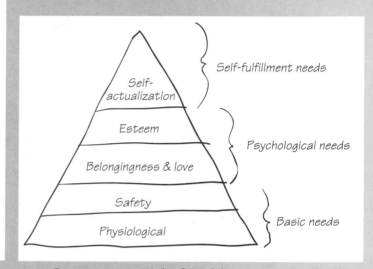

Self-fulfillment needs

Psychological needs

Basic needs

Self-actualization

Esteem

Belongingness & love

Safety

Physiological

c. Concept map—example of visual diagram of concepts in Maslow's hierarchy of needs.

1832	1843	1890	1930	1946	1952	1964	1970	1977	1981
Babbage's analytical engine	First programmer – Ada Lovelace publishes notes	Electricity used with punched cards	General theory of computers	ENIAC – first computer in U.S.	UNIVAC predicts presidential election (Eisenhower)	IBM 360 line of computers introduced	Micro-processor chips	Apple II computer – first personal computer in assembled form	IBM introduces PC

d. Time line—example of historical development of the computer.

	Hinduism	Judaism	Christianity	Islam
Principal geographic locations	India	Israel, Europe, Americas	Especially Europe & Americas; adherents worldwide	Asia, North Africa, Central Africa
Type (number of gods)	Polytheistic	Monotheistic	Monotheistic	Monotheistic
Holy book(s)	Mahabharata, Ramayana	Torah	Bible	Koran

e. Comparison chart—example of concepts of various world religions.

151

Real Practice
Activities for Real People

Staying
power

REAL PRACTICE ACTIVITY #5.1: HOW ARE YOU GOING TO STUDY DIFFICULT MATERIAL? This practice activity may be performed either individually or collaboratively in small groups. The results are to be written up in a short reaction paper for the instructor.

If you have not already completed the six-step "Essentials for Time & Life Management," you should now do Step 3, "What Are My Actions?" In this step, you use the college catalog to determine the courses you need to accomplish your college goals.

You will no doubt see some courses on this list that look like they won't be easy for you, because you lack the interest or think you lack the aptitude. In a one-page paper, list which courses you think these are. Then, using material from this chapter and earlier ones, describe what strengths you have and what techniques you will use to develop the persistence to succeed at these courses.

Mindfulness

REAL PRACTICE ACTIVITY #5.2: DEVISING NEW TRICKS OF TIME MANAGEMENT. This practice activity is to be performed by all students individually for the next week or two, or whatever length of time is suggested by the instructor, and the results are to be shared in class.

From Chapter 2, you know that people have different learning styles and know which style is most comfortable for you. Chapter 5 presents a variety of memorization, reading, and study techniques, some of which may be better suited to certain learning styles (for example, visual as opposed to auditory).

In this activity, you are to select one or two study techniques from this chapter and practice using them in some of your other courses for the period of time indicated by your instructor. (For example, you might try using the SQ3R method or special study diagrams to help you with your history and biology courses.) How well do these techniques work for you? Be prepared to discuss in class.

Information
technology

REAL PRACTICE ACTIVITY #5.3: LEARNING HOW TO BUY BOOKS BY GOING ONLINE. This activity is to be practiced by students out of class, working either individually or in small groups. The results are to be discussed in class.

When you buy books, probably most of the time you buy them at the campus bookstore or off book racks where you often shop. But what if you're searching for books on a particular subject and can't find them in the library or in a local bookstore? Here's where it helps to know about going online. This practice activity will show you how to do that, although you won't be required to buy anything.

Pick a topic that interests you, one that you would like to explore further. Now go online and try each of the following six online "bookstores" to find possible books on the subject:

www.amazon.com
www.barnesandnoble.com
www.borders.com
www.books.com
www.varsitybooks.com
www.abebooks.com

(Go to *http://csuccess.wadsworth.com* for the most up-to-date Web addresses, or URLs.)

Print out (or make handwritten notes about) what you find. Jot down your thoughts about this method of finding books for class discussion.

The Examined Life

JOURNAL ENTRY #5.1: WHAT ARE THE TOUGH-EST SUBJECTS TO MEMORIZE? What subjects do you worry you will have the most trouble memorizing? Why is this? What tricks can you use from this chapter to change this?

_____

_____

_____

_____

_____

_____

_____

_____

_____

_____

JOURNAL ENTRY #5.2: WHAT HAVE YOU HAD TO MEMORIZE IN THE PAST? In what kind of areas have you had to do extensive memorizing in the past? Examples might be music, athletic moves or plays, dramatic roles, or skills in conjunction with a job. What motivated you to remember? How did you go about doing the memorization?

_____

_____

_____

_____

_____

_____

_____

_____

JOURNAL ENTRY #5.3: WHAT HAVE YOU LEARNED FROM READING IN THE PAST? No doubt at some point in the past you had to learn a lot of material from reading. (Examples: material necessary to do your job, religious studies, government paperwork.) What was it? How did you go about absorbing it?

_____

_____

_____

_____

_____

_____

_____

_____

_____

JOURNAL ENTRY #5.4: HOW COULD YOUR PRESENT READING SYSTEM BE IMPROVED? What is your present system for marking up and reviewing textbooks? What mistakes have you made (for example, doing too much underlining or reading only once)? What specific techniques could you use to correct these mistakes?

_____

_____

_____

_____

_____

_____

_____

_____

_____

_____

JOURNAL ENTRY #5.5: HOW DO YOU STUDY ESPECIALLY CHALLENGING MATERIAL? Do you do anything different in studying more challenging material—such as mathematics, foreign language, or history—than you do in studying "regular" subject matter? How is your approach different? What does your Voice Of Judgment tell you about your inadequacies in handling certain types of material (such as math, for example)?

_____

_____

_____

_____

_____

_____

_____

_____

JOURNAL ENTRY #5.6: HOW DOES YOUR LIFESTYLE HELP OR HINDER YOUR MEMORY? Stress, alcohol, smoking, fatigue can affect your memory negatively and good diet, exercise, and sleep can affect it positively. Can you think of any lifestyle matters that might be improved?

_____

_____

_____

_____

_____

_____

_____

_____

_____

_____

_____

Managing Lectures

Note Taking, Class Discussion, & Instructor Relations

IN THIS CHAPTER Now we come to some techniques that will truly benefit you for the rest of your life:

- **Making lectures work:** Whatever you think of lectures, they can be made to work for you.

- **Optimizing the classroom game:** How to focus your attention and overcome classroom obstacles.

- **Participating in class:** Shyness about speaking up is a problem for many students; however, class participation not only helps your memory but prepares you for life.

- **Memorizing material:** How to use the "5R steps" to memorize information from a lecture.

- **Getting to know your instructors:** Instructors, most of whom love to teach, can be a resource.

- **Information technology in the classroom:** Computers, e-mail, and the Internet are becoming more essential to this aspect of education.

Lecturing may be an efficient way for instructors to convey information. Is it a good way for students to receive it?

I do a great deal of teaching through discussion and small-group activities, but I also do a fair amount of lecturing, as do most instructors. Lecturing is certainly an easy way for instructors to transfer knowledge—they talk and students listen. Perhaps this is why the lecture system is one of the mainstays of college teaching. Whether it is efficient for any given student, however, depends a lot on his or her preferred learning style.

Lectures, Learning Styles, & Life

PREVIEW & REVIEW Because you can't control the way information is conveyed to you, either in college or in your career, it's important to become comfortable with the lecture method. This means discovering how to extract material from the lecture and learn it.

Of the four learning styles I described in Chapter 2—auditory, visual, kinesthetic, and mixed-modality—lectures would seem to favor auditory learners. Auditory learners, you'll recall, use their voices and their ears as the primary means of learning.

But suppose you're not an auditory learner. That is, suppose you're a *visual learner* and favor pictures or words written down. Or you're *kinesthetic* and favor touching and physical involvement. (If you're *the mixed-modality type,* you can function in all three learning styles.)

In the work world, too, you don't always have a choice about the method by which information is conveyed to you. You may often have to attend a meeting, presentation, speech, or company training program. There, as I pointed out earlier, the "examination" will consist of how well you recall and handle the information in order to do your job.

It's important, therefore, that you learn to get comfortable with the lecture method of teaching. Thus, you have two tasks, as I'll describe in the rest of this chapter:

- **Be able to extract material:** You need to be able to *extract* the most information out of a lecture—that is, take useful notes, regardless of your learning preference and the instructor's style.

- **Be able to learn material:** You need to be able to *learn* the lecture material so that you can do well on tests.

Information technology

If you're into computers, you may be interested to know that there is a software program called Learning Styles (available from Education Information Systems, Ridgewood, NJ; 800-253-3828) that the publisher claims can help any student improve grades and test scores by identifying strengths and weaknesses, both yours and the instructor's. The program asks you to rate the accuracy of 54 statements about your learning style (such as whether you prefer to read something or to hear about it, to study in a group or alone). At the end, the program will tell you, for example, that you are a visual learner—that you learn better from written than oral material, should use a highlighter pen, and should frequently rewrite material that you want to learn. The program will also diagnose the strengths and weaknesses of any particular instructor.

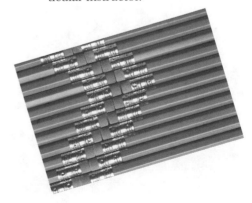

HOW WELL DOES YOUR LEARNING STYLE SUIT THE LECTURE METHOD?

In a group situation, look back at Personal Exploration #2.1 in Chapter 2. Determine which learning style—auditory, visual, kinesthetic, or mixed-modality—you seem to favor. Then discuss the following questions.

What experiences have you had that make you think you like one learning style better than others (if that's the case)? How well does your learning style relate to the lecture method of presenting information? In a work situation, have you had any difficulty with retaining information from presentations and meetings? Since not everything in life is delivered to you in an easy manner, what kinds of strategies would you recommend for getting the most out of the lecture system?

Making Lectures Work: What They Didn't Tell You in High School

PREVIEW & REVIEW Cutting classes has been found to be associated with poor grades. Being in class, even a boring one, helps you learn what the instructor expects. It also reflects your attitude about your college performance—whether you want to get successfully through school or merely slide by. Being an active participant means bringing syllabus and textbooks to class, doing the homework, and reviewing previous assignments in order to be ready for each new lecture.

How do you approach the whole matter of going to class? Many of your classroom habits may have been picked up while you were in high school. Do you sit in the back, find yourself constantly distracted during lectures, have difficulty taking notes? To get an idea of your present performance in the classroom, try Personal Exploration #6.1, next page.

CLASS ATTENDANCE & GRADES. In high school, I was required to attend every class every school day. What a surprise, then, when I got to college and found that in many classes professors didn't even take attendance and that I was free to cut if I chose. Of course, it was easy to be selective about which classes to go to and which not. In the wintertime, for instance, it wasn't hard to choose between staying in a warm bed and getting up for an 8:00 A.M. class—particularly if I thought the instructor or the subject was boring.

However, in those early days I was not aware of an important fact: *poor class attendance is associated with poor grades.* According to one study, "unsuccessful" students—those defined as having grades of C– or below—were found to be more commonly absent from class

LISTENING QUESTIONNAIRE: HOW'S YOUR CLASSROOM PERFORMANCE?

Read each statement and decide how the habit reflects your listening. Answer as follows:

"Yes"—if you use the habit over half your listening time.
"No"—if you don't use the habit very much at all.
"Sometimes"—if you use the habit periodically.

1. Do you often doodle while listening?
   - ❑ Yes
   - ❑ No
   - ❑ Sometimes

2. Do you show attending behaviors through your eye contact, posture, and facial expressions?
   - ❑ Yes
   - ❑ No
   - ❑ Sometimes

3. Do you try to write down everything you hear?
   - ❑ Yes
   - ❑ No
   - ❑ Sometimes

4. Do you listen largely for central ideas as opposed to facts and details?
   - ❑ Yes
   - ❑ No
   - ❑ Sometimes

5. Do you often daydream or think about personal concerns while listening?
   - ❑ Yes
   - ❑ No
   - ❑ Sometimes

6. Do you ask clarifying questions about what you do not understand in a lecture?
   - ❑ Yes
   - ❑ No
   - ❑ Sometimes

7. Do you frequently feel tired or sleepy when attending a lecture?
   - ❑ Yes
   - ❑ No
   - ❑ Sometimes

8. Do you mentally review information as you listen to make connections among points?
   - ❑ Yes
   - ❑ No
   - ❑ Sometimes

9. Do you often call a lecture boring?
   - ❑ Yes
   - ❑ No
   - ❑ Sometimes

10. Do you recall what you already know about a subject before the lecture begins?
    - ❑ Yes
    - ❑ No
    - ❑ Sometimes

11. Do you generally avoid listening when difficult information is presented?
    - ❑ Yes
    - ❑ No
    - ❑ Sometimes

12. Do you pay attention to the speaker's nonverbal cues?
    - ❑ Yes
    - ❑ No
    - ❑ Sometimes

13. Do you often find yourself thinking up arguments to refute the speaker?
    - ❑ Yes
    - ❑ No
    - ❑ Sometimes

14. Do you generally try to find something of interest in a lecture even if you think it's boring?
    - ❑ Yes
    - ❑ No
    - ❑ Sometimes

15. Do you usually criticize the speaker's delivery, appearance, or mannerisms?
    - ❑ Yes
    - ❑ No
    - ❑ Sometimes

16. Do you do what you can to control distractions around you?
    - ❑ Yes
    - ❑ No
    - ❑ Sometimes

17. Do you often fake attention to the speaker?
    - ❑ Yes
    - ❑ No
    - ❑ Sometimes

18. Do you periodically summarize or recapitulate what the speaker has said during the lecture?
    - ❑ Yes
    - ❑ No
    - ❑ Sometimes

19. Do you often go to class late?
    - ❑ Yes
    - ❑ No
    - ❑ Sometimes

20. Do you review the previous class lecture notes before attending class?
    - ❑ Yes
    - ❑ No
    - ❑ Sometimes

(continued)

■ SCORING

Count the number of "Yes" answers to *even-numbered* items: _____

Count the number of "Yes" answers to *odd-numbered* items: _____

■ INTERPRETATION: The even-numbered items are considered *effective* listening habits.

The odd-numbered items are considered *ineffective* listening habits.

If you answered an item as "Some-times," determine how often and under what circumstances you find yourself responding this way. Identify the areas where you have written "Yes" or "Sometimes" to odd-numbered items and write an explanation here:

_____
_____
_____
_____
_____
_____
_____
_____
_____
_____
_____
_____

GROUP ACTIVITY OPTION

In a small group situation, go through Personal Exploration #6.1 and discuss some of the items you answered "Yes" to. What things are you doing right? What things need changing? Since changing one's behavior is not always easy, what kinds of prompts or reinforcement will you give yourself to help you change negative behavior to positive behavior?

than "successful" students, those with a B average or above.[1] *(See* ■ *Panel 6.1.)*

It may come as no surprise that research shows that college students who think their instructors are prepared and organized actually learn a lot better than students who think otherwise. That is, students who believe their teachers present their material well, use class time effectively, and clearly explain course goals and requirements do significantly better on tests of reading comprehension, math, and critical thinking, according to the National Study of Student Learning.[2]

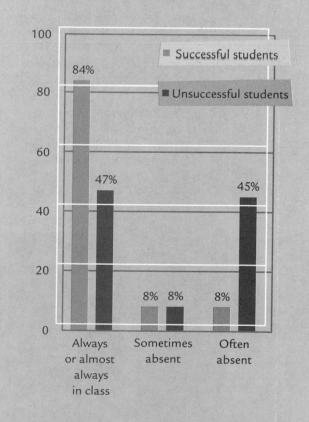

PANEL 6.1

Successful and unsuccessful **students' class attendance.** According to one study, attendance was much better among successful students (B average or above) than unsuccessful students (C– or below).

■ Successful students

■ Unsuccessful students

84%

47%

45%

8% 8%

8%

Always or almost always in class

Sometimes absent

Often absent

"But," you may say, "what if the lecturer knows the material but can't present it in an organized way so that I can comprehend it? Why should I waste my time going to class?"

There are two answers to this—things they don't usually tell you in high school:

■ *Being in class helps you learn what the instructor expects—and to anticipate exams:* Even if the instructor is so hard to follow that you learn very little from the lectures, it's still important to go to class. "If nothing else," one set of writers points out, "you'll get a feel for how the instructor thinks. This can help you to anticipate the content of exams and to respond in the manner your professor expects."[3]

■ *Going to class goes along with a can-do attitude about college in general:* Students who try to *slide by* in school are those who look for all the ways to pass their courses with the least amount of effort: they cut class, borrow other students' notes, cram the night before exams, and so on. This is the mindless approach to learning.

Students like you, I hope—who are intent on active, mindful learning—take the attitude that, sure, there are certain shortcuts or efficiencies to making one's way through college (this book is full of such tips). However, they realize that always trying to cut corners is not productive in the long run. Thus, among other things, they try to attend every class.

Which one would an employer want to hire? Recall from Chapter 1 that I reported that people who do the hiring in companies are interested in finding

Staying power

workers who are *conscientious*—who will do the work regardless of the obstacles. These are the people who learned how to develop staying power in college.

So, here again we have the relevance of college to life outside college: A can-do attitude in higher education is the kind of quality needed for you to prevail in the world of work.

BEING AN ACTIVE PARTICIPANT: PREPARING FOR CLASS. Being an active rather than passive student means taking a *mindful,* involved approach to the course. Besides attending regularly and being on time for class, try to prepare for your upcoming classes, doing the following:

Mindfulness

■ *Use the course syllabus as a basic "roadmap":* The *syllabus* is a *very* important document. **The <u>syllabus</u> (pronounced "*sill*-uh-buss") is a course outline or guide that tells you what readings are required, what assignments are due when, and when examinations are scheduled.** This basic roadmap to the course is a page or more that the instructor hands out on the first class day.

It's a good idea to three-hole punch the syllabus and include it in the front of your binder or staple it inside the front of your notebook. That way you will automatically bring it to class and can make any changes to it that the instructor announces (such as a new date for a test).

■ *Do the homework before the lecture:* A syllabus will often show that certain readings coincide with certain lectures. It usually works best if you do the readings

before rather than after the lectures. Like putting your toe in the water, this will help you know what to expect. If you do the homework first, you'll understand the instructor's remarks better.

- **Anticipate the lecture:** Not only will doing the required readings before class prepare you for the lecture, so will reading over your lecture notes from the last class. Often the next lecture is a continuation of the last one. In addition, you can look at the syllabus to see what's expected.

    When doing the homework, develop questions on the readings. Bring these to class for clarification.

- **Bring the textbook to class:** Some people come to class carrying only a notebook and pen (and some don't even bring those). Are they the "A" and "B" students? I'd guess they are not.

    Students who are successful performers in college don't feel they always have to travel light. Besides their notebook they also carry the principal textbook and other books (or supplies) relevant to the course. This is because instructors often make special mention of material in the textbook, or they draw on the text for class discussion. Some instructors even follow the text quite closely in their lectures. Thus, if you have the text in the classroom, you can follow along and make marks in the book, writing down possible exam questions or indicating points of emphasis.

Optimizing the Classroom Game

PREVIEW & REVIEW   The best way to fight boredom and fatigue in the classroom is to make attending class a game. Two ways to improve your classroom game are to learn (1) to focus your attention and (2) to overcome classroom obstacles.

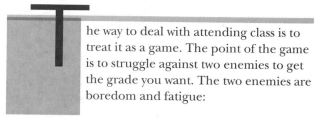

The way to deal with attending class is to treat it as a game. The point of the game is to struggle against two enemies to get the grade you want. The two enemies are boredom and fatigue:

- **Boredom:** Boredom is a very real factor. Television may have raised our expectations as to how stimulating education ought to be. However, many instructors—indeed, most people in general—can't be that interesting all the time.

- **Fatigue:** Fatigue can also be a real factor. This is particularly so for students who are struggling with other demands, such as those of work and family, or who short themselves on sleep.

    As a student, then, you need to turn yourself into an active listener and active participant in the classroom to get past these two hurdles.

    Two ways to improve your classroom game are:

- Learn to focus your attention

- Learn to overcome classroom obstacles

LEARNING TO FOCUS YOUR ATTENTION. Once you've come to class, what do you do then? You learn to pay attention. Being attentive involves *active listening,* which is different from the kind of passive listening we do when "listening" to television. Active listening is, in one writer's description, "paying attention so that your brain absorbs the meaning of

Mindfulness

Staying power

words and sentences."[4] Active listening, then, is mindful listening.

Being an active listener requires that you do the following:

■ **Take listening seriously:**[5] Make up your mind you *will* listen. Everything begins with your attitude—hence this decision. Students can coast through the college classroom experience yawning, day-dreaming, and spacing out, thereby missing a lot, or they can *decide* to listen.

Making the commitment to learn and taking an active part in obtaining information also improves your ability to remember the material. If you find your mind wandering, pull your thoughts back to the present and review mentally what the speaker has been saying.

■ **Sit up front and center:** For a variety of reasons, some students don't want to sit at the front of the class. However, when you go to a musical event or stage performance, you probably *want* to sit down front—because you're interested and you want to see and hear better.

Sitting in the front and center rows in the classroom will also help you hear and see better, of course. Moreover, the very act of sitting in that place will actually stimulate your interest. This is because you have taken the physical step of *making a commitment*—of putting yourself in a position to participate more. (Also, you'll be less likely to talk to classmates, write letters, or fall asleep if you're where the instructor can see you.)

■ **Stay positive and pay attention to content, not delivery:** If you *expect* a lecture to be boring or lacking in content, I guarantee you it will be. By contrast, if you suppress negative thoughts, ignore distractions about the speaker's style of delivery or body language, and *encourage the instructor with eye contact, interested expression, and attentive posture,* you will find yourself much more involved and interested in the subject matter.

If you find yourself disagreeing with something the speaker says, don't argue mentally, but suspend judgment. (Maybe make a note in the margin and bring the matter up later during class discussion.) Assess the instructor's reasoning, then make up your mind.

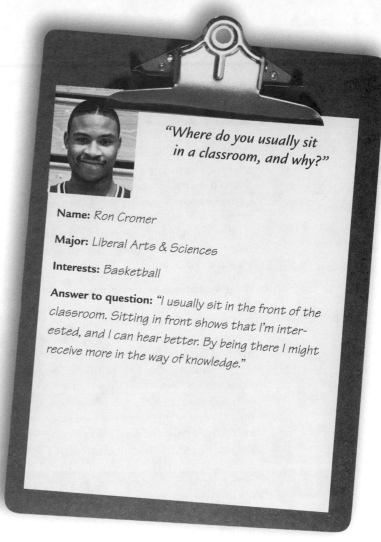

"Where do you usually sit in a classroom, and why?"

Name: *Ron Cromer*

Major: *Liberal Arts & Sciences*

Interests: *Basketball*

Answer to question: *"I usually sit in the front of the classroom. Sitting in front shows that I'm interested, and I can hear better. By being there I might receive more in the way of knowledge."*

■ **Listen for "bell" phrases and cues to determine what is important:** All lecturers use phrases and gestures that should "ring a bell" and signal importance.

A _bell phrase_—also called a _signal word_ or _signal phrase_—is an indicator of an important point. Bell phrases are important because they indicate you should note what comes after them and remember them. Examples of bell phrases are: "Three major types . . ."; "The most important result is . . ."; "You should remember . . ."; "Because of this . . ."; "First . . . second . . . third . . ." *(See Panel 6.2.)*

Some bell phrases. Also known as "signal words" and "signal phrases," these indicate an important point that should be remembered.

Additive words: These say, "Here's more of the same coming up. It's just as important as what we have already said."
Examples:
also
and
besides
further
furthermore
in addition
moreover
too

Equivalent words: They say, "It does what I have just said, but it does this too."
Examples:
as well as
at the same
equally important
likewise
similarly
time

Amplification words: The author is saying, "I want to be sure that you understand my idea; so here's a specific instance."
Examples:
as
for example (e.g.)
for instance
like
specifically
such as

Alternative words: These point up, "Sometimes there is a choice; other times there isn't."
Examples:
either/or
other than
otherwise
neither/nor

Repetitive words: They say, "I said it once, but I'm going to say it again in case you missed it the first time."
Examples:
again
in other words
that is (i.e.)
to repeat

Contrast-and-change words: "So far I've given you only one side of the story; now let's take a look at the other side."
Examples:
but
conversely
despite
even though
however
in spite of
instead of
nevertheless
notwithstanding
on the contrary
on the other hand
rather than
regardless
still
though
whereas
yet

Cause-and-effect words: "All this has happened; now I'll tell you why."
Examples:
accordingly
because
consequently
for this reason
hence
since
so
then
therefore
thus

Qualifying words: These say, "Here is what we can expect. These are the conditions we are working under."
Examples:
although
if
provided that
unless
whenever

Concession words: They say, "Okay, we agree on this much."
Examples:
accepting the data
granted that
of course

Emphasizing words: They say, "Wake up and take notice!"
Examples:
above all
indeed
more important

Order words: The author is saying, "You keep your mind on reading; I'll keep the numbers straight."
Examples:
finally
first
last
next
second
then

1, 2, 3.

Time words: "Let's keep the record straight on who said what and especially when."
Examples:
afterward
before
formerly
meanwhile
now
presently
previously
subsequently
ultimately

Summarizing words: These say, "I've said many things so far; let's stop here and pull them together."
Examples:
for these reasons
in brief
in conclusion
to sum up

A *bell cue* is an action or gesture that indicates important points. Examples are (1) diagrams or charts; (2) notes on the blackboard; (3) pointing, as to something on the board or a chart; (4) underlining of or making a check mark by key words; (5) banging a fist; and (6) holding up fingers.

When a class is long or tedious, you can turn it into a game by telling yourself you will try to detect as many bell phrases and cues as possible. Then, every time you pick up one, put a check mark in your notes. I've found when I do this I become more actively involved. Not only does it fight boredom and fatigue but it also increases the quality of my note taking.

LEARNING TO OVERCOME CLASSROOM OBSTACLES. You now know what to do if the instructor or subject matter is boring. What do you do if the instructor speaks too fast or with an accent? If your shorthand or ear is not good enough to keep up, here are some strategies:

■ *Do your homework before class:* If you keep up with the reading assignments, doing them before the lecture rather than afterward, you'll often be able to mentally fill in gaps and select key points.

■ *Leave holes in your notes:* Whenever you miss something important, leave spaces in your notes, with a big question mark in the margin. Then seek to fill in the missing material through other methods, as explained below.

■ *Trade notes with classmates:* If you and others in class take readable notes (even using private shorthand), you can easily make photocopies of your notes and exchange them. Two or three students may find that among them they are able to pick up most of a lecture.

■ *Use a tape recorder:* The trick here is not to make a tape recorder a *substitute* for note taking. Then you'll merely be taking the same amount of time to listen to the lecture again—and perhaps still be confused. Use the tape recorder as a backup system, one in which you can use the fast-forward and reverse buttons to go over material you had trouble follow-

ing in class. (Remember to get permission from the instructor to use a tape recorder in his or her class.)

■ *Ask questions—in class or after:* If the instructor has a question period, you can ask questions to clarify what you missed. Or see the instructor after class or during his or her office hours.

Learning to focus your attention and overcome classroom obstacles aren't the only way to optimize the lecture experience. There's also another activity: class participation. This deserves separate discussion.

GROUP ACTIVITY #6.3

WHAT ARE EXAMPLES OF BELL PHRASES & BELL CUES?

This activity requires that you look at your lecture notes from other classes this week. (Alternatively, the instructor may have students monitor two of their lectures in other classes this week in preparation for this class discussion.)

What bell phrases and bell cues do you observe your instructors using? Write them down (in your lecture notes) as you hear and see them. Observe what effect, if any, paying attention to these cues has on your levels of boredom and fatigue.

In your First-Year Experience class, share with the class or with a small group some of the bell phrases and bell cues you observed. How did putting yourself in a state of alertness to these cues affect your levels of boredom and fatigue? What are some questions you might see on an exam that are suggested by these cues?

Participating in Class Discussion & Overcoming Shyness

PREVIEW & REVIEW Class participation reinforces memorization. You should do your homework beforehand, follow your curiosity, and respect the opinions of others. Whether one is publicly shy or privately shy, shyness is a painful hindrance to class participation, as well as other aspects of life. However, you can analyze your shyness, take steps to build self-confidence, and build your social skills to overcome this problem.

"What do you do to fight boredom in the classroom?"

Name: Erin Loomis

Major: Hotel Technology/Hospitality Management

Interests: Sports (volleyball, basketball, softball), music, dancing

Answer to question: "I doodle little notes and/or pictures. I usually doodle something about what we are discussing in the class. For example, in a history class we might be talking about the U.S. presidents. I try to draw a picture of what I think they look like. Then when I study I look at the picture, and I seem to remember what was said in class."

Are you the type of person who prefers to be invisible in the classroom? No doubt you've noticed many students are. They sit in the back row, never ask questions, and can go an entire semester without talking to the instructor.

In doing this, one can probably scrape by. However, life does not reward the passive. If you ever need a reference from a professor for a job or for graduate or professional school, how will you know whom to ask if you've never given the instructor an opportunity to get to know you? When you're starting on your career, what skills will you be able to draw on to speak up in meetings, give presentations, or persuade authority figures of your point of view? As I've said all along, the skills you practice in the college classroom, regardless of subject, really are practice for life outside of college.

HOW TO PARTICIPATE IN CLASS. Class participation, whether in a lecture or a discussion section, further reinforces memorization because it obliges you to become actively engaged with the material and to organize it in your mind. Once again, then, I'm talking about taking a *mindful* approach to learning.

Mindfulness

Some suggestions regarding participation are as follows:

- *Do your homework:* There is an understood contract—namely, that you should have kept up with the homework assignments, such as the textbook readings. That way you won't embarrass yourself by asking questions or making remarks about something you are already supposed to have read.

- *Follow your curiosity:* We've all had the experience of holding back on asking a question, then hearing someone else raise it and be complimented by the professor with "That's a very good question!" Follow your instincts. You have a right to ask questions, and the more you do so, the more you will perfect this particular art.

- **Respect the opinions of others:** If the questions or remarks of others seem off-the-wall or biased, don't be scornful (at least openly). Civility is important. A spirit of cordiality and absence of intimidation is necessary to keep learning channels open and tempers cool.

BUT I'M SHY! For many students, shyness is a very real, even incapacitating problem. Some shy students stare down at their notebooks or desks to avoid making eye contact with the instructor, thus hoping to escape his or her attention. Sooner or later, however, most people are called upon to speak in class—and, for some, this can be an anxious, even terrifying experience.

Some shyness is situation-specific, such as discomfort about being the focus of attention or interacting in large group settings. Some people, however, find themselves constantly tormented by feelings of shyness, regardless of the situation in which they find themselves. Shyness, then, can range from occasional awkwardness in social situations to a complex condition that can completely disrupt a person's life. "To be shy is to be afraid of people," writes psychologist Philip Zimbardo in *Shyness,* "especially people who for some reason are emotionally threatening: strangers because of their novelty or uncertainty, authorities who wield power, members of the opposite sex who represent potential intimate encounters."[6]

Shy people may feel they are practically the only ones so afflicted, but the reality is quite different. According to one study, about 80% of those questioned reported they were shy at some point in their lives, either presently, in the past, or always. Of those, over 40% considered themselves presently shy. About 25% reported themselves chronically shy, now and always. A mere 7% of all Americans sampled reported that they have never, ever experienced feelings of shyness.[7]

Zimbardo has identified two types of shy people:

- **Publicly shy:** The *publicly shy* are those who stutter, slouch, blush, avoid eye contact, and similarly show that they are unable to conceal their shyness.

- **Privately shy:** The *privately shy* cover up their shyness and may actually seem somewhat outgoing—or, alternatively, bored and aloof—but they suffer the same inhibitions and fearfulness as shy people.

Zimbardo suggests that those who are shy may unknowingly elicit the very criticism and rejection they fear. Because they are so preoccupied with being judged and rejected, and imagine that others will consider them stupid or inept, for example, they take the defensive action of withdrawing from social interaction. Their discomfort and withdrawal may prompt people to avoid them.

COPING WITH SHYNESS. There are three key elements to coping with shyness:

- **Analyze your shyness:** Identify the situations in which you feel most shy and try to understand what is causing your anxiety.

- **Take steps to build self-confidence:** Making use of the college counseling center is a good way to start. Some of the techniques for conquering shyness consist of putting oneself directly into the situation that makes one uncomfortable. For instance, people who have difficulty with public speaking may go to a group such as Toastmasters to practice speaking to one another. People who have trouble with social encounters can expand their confidence and skills by introducing themselves to classmates or to other guests at a party.

- **Build your social skills:** Building communication skills will help here. Learn to be a great listener or to be an expert in one of your personal areas of interest. At least half of those who were once shy have been able to overcome their anxiety.

The main hurdle shy people have to overcome is the fierce perfectionism about themselves. As one woman who had difficulty with speaking in group situations learned, the most important thing is "right before you get up [to speak], to mentally forgive yourself if you blow it. The degree to which you don't forgive yourself is the degree to which you [become anxious]."[8] In short, you have to give yourself permission not to be perfect.

There comes a time in life when, *if you can't let go of the fear of "being laughed at," the feeling that you must always be "perfect," there is a real question as to whether you will be able to get what you want in your career and in your relationships.* Learning to participate in a public dialogue is simply part of the growth process. This is where your staying power, your willingness to try to overcome your fear of uncomfortable situations, can really pay off.

Staying power

DISCUSSING SHYNESS

In a small group situation, each person should make a list of occasions when he or she has felt shy. Each should then take turns describing these to other group members.

After everyone has made a report, discuss the following questions: Are there certain common situations in which a lot of people are shy? Are there some people in the group who don't seem shy but who (from their report) clearly experience shyness sometimes? Are there some people who find certain situations nearly devastating because of their shyness? What is it about participating in class discussion (especially in large classes) that makes people so uncomfortable? How can people begin to overcome shyness in class participation? Would a "buddy system," in which a shy person pairs with another shy person and each takes turns asking questions, be workable?

The 5R Steps: Record, Rewrite, Recite, Reflect, Review

PREVIEW & REVIEW Because the greatest amount of forgetting happens in the first 24 hours, you need not just a note-*taking* system but also a note-*reviewing* system. Five steps for committing lecture notes to long-term memory are: Record, Rewrite, Recite, Reflect, and Review.

Many students have the idea that they can simply take notes of a lecture and then review them whenever it's convenient—perhaps the night before a test. Certainly that was the way I started out doing it in college. And it's easy to think you are doing well when you attend every class and fill page after page of your notebook.

However, simply writing everything down—acting like a human tape recorder—by itself doesn't work. *The name of the game, after all, is to learn the material, not just make a record of it.* Writing things down now but saving all the learning for later is simply not efficient. As I discussed in Chapter 5, research shows that the most forgetting takes place within the first 24 hours, then drops off. The trick, then, is to figure out how to reduce the forgetting of that first 24 hours.

Effective learning requires that you be not only a good note *taker* but also a good note *reviewer*. This may mean you need to change the note-taking and note-learning approach you're accustomed to. However, once these new skills are learned, you'll find them invaluable not only in college but also in your career.

One method that has been found to be helpful in note taking and note learning consists of five steps known as **the _5R steps_, for Record, Rewrite, Recite, Reflect, Review.** They are:

- ■ *Step 1—Record:* Capture the main ideas.

- ■ *Step 2—Rewrite:* Following the lecture, rewrite your notes, developing key terms, questions, and summaries.

- ■ *Step 3—Recite:* Covering up the key terms, questions, and summaries, practice reciting them to yourself.

- ■ *Step 4—Reflect:* To anchor these ideas, make some personal association with them.

- ■ *Step 5—Review:* Two or three times a week, if possible, review your notes to make them more familiar.

"Too much!" I hear students say. "I've got a lot of things to do. I can't be forever rehashing one lecture!"

Actually, the system may not take as much time as it first looks. Certainly it need not take much more *effort* than if you try to learn it all by cramming— absorbing all the material in one sitting.

In any event, studies show that increased practice or rehearsal not only increases retention. It also improves your *understanding* of material, because as you go over it repeatedly, you are able to concentrate on the most important points.[9] You probably can appreciate this from your own experience in having developed some athletic, musical, or other skill: the more you did it, the better you got. Like an actor, the more you practice or rehearse the material, the better you

will be able to overcome stage fright and deliver your best performance on examination day.

Let's consider these five steps:

STEP 1: RECORD. You'll see many of your classmates with pens racing to try to capture every word of the lecture. Don't bother. You're not supposed to be like a court reporter or a secretary-stenographer, recording every word. You should be less concerned with taking down everything than in developing a *system* of note taking. Here is how the system works *(See ■ Panel 6.3.).*

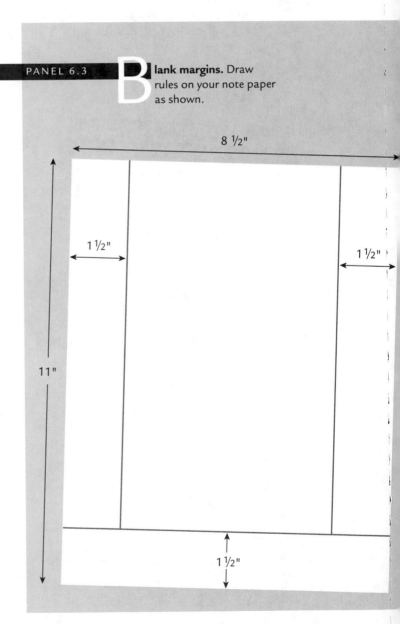

PANEL 6.3

Blank margins. Draw rules on your note paper as shown.

8 ½"

1 ½"

1 ½"

11"

1 ½"

■ **Leave blank margins on your note page:** This is a variation on what is known as the *Cornell format* of note taking. Draw a vertical line, top to bottom, 1½ inches from the left edge of the paper, a similar line 1½ inches from the right side, and a horizontal line 1½ inches up from the bottom. As I explain, you will use these blank margins for review purposes.

■ **Take notes in rough paragraph form:** At some point you may have been told to take notes in outline form, using the standard "I, A, 1, a," format. If you're good at this, that's fine. However, most professors don't lecture this way, and you should not have to concentrate on trying to force an outline on the lecture material.

Simply take your notes in rough paragraph form. Put extra space (a line or two) between new ideas and divisions of thought. Don't try to save on the cost of notepaper by cramming notes onto every line of the page.

■ **Try to capture the main ideas:** Don't try to take down everything the instructor says. Not only will this create a mass of information that you will have to sort through later, it will also interfere with your learning. Instead of forcing you to pay attention and concentrate on what's important, you become simply a mindless tape recorder. You want to be a *mindful* note taker. An extremely important part of your note-taking system, then, is to try to capture just the key ideas. More on this below.

Mindfulness

■ **Develop a system of abbreviations:** Some people take highly readable notes, as though preparing to let other people borrow them. You shouldn't concern yourself primarily with this kind of legibility. The main thing is that *you* be able to take ideas down fast and *you* be able to read them later.

Thus, make up your own system of abbreviations. For example, "w.r.t" means "with regard to"; "sike" means "psychology"; "para" is borrowing the Spanish word for "in order to." *(See* ■ *Panel 6.4.)*

By adopting these practices, you'll be well on your way to retaining more information than you have in the past.

PANEL 6.4

Personal shorthand. These are some commonly used abbreviations. If you wish, you can tear out or photocopy this list and tape it inside the cover of your binder or notebook.

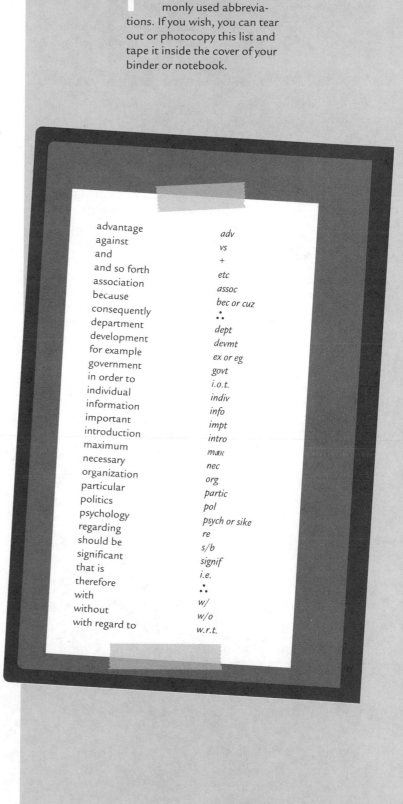

advantage	adv
against	vs
and	+
and so forth	etc
association	assoc
because	bec or cuz
consequently	∴
department	dept
development	devmt
for example	ex or eg
government	govt
in order to	i.o.t.
individual	indiv
information	info
important	impt
introduction	intro
maximum	max
necessary	nec
organization	org
particular	partic
politics	pol
psychology	psych or sike
regarding	re
should be	s/b
significant	signif
that is	i.e.
therefore	∵
with	w/
without	w/o
with regard to	w.r.t.

STEP 2: REWRITE. *This is extremely important.* The point of this step is to counteract the brain's natural tendency to forget 80% of the information in the first 24 hours.

As soon as possible—on the same day in which you took lecture notes—you should do one of two things:

1. *Either recopy/rewrite your notes, or*

2. *At least go over them to familiarize yourself and to underline key issues and concepts and make notations in the margins.*

Of course, it's not *necessary* to recopy your notes. The point I must emphasize, however, is that this very activity will give you the extra familiarization that will help to imprint the information in your mind. If you have a personal computer with a word processing program, the rewriting is not as time consuming as it sounds. *(See ■ Panel 6.5.)*

Information technology

Alternatively, if you don't have time or aren't strongly motivated to rewrite your notes, you should take 5 or 10 minutes to make use of the blank margins you left around your notes. (You should also do this if you rewrite your notes.) Whichever method you use, by rewriting and underlining you reinforce the material, moving it from short-term into long-term memory.

Here's what to do:

■ *Read, rewrite, and highlight your notes:* Read your notes over. If you can, rewrite them—copy them over in a separate notebook or type them up on a word processor—with the same margins at the left, right, and bottom as I described above. Now read the notes again, using highlighter pen or underlining to emphasize key ideas.

Information technology

If you have a personal computer with word processing capability on it, here's how to use it to rewrite your notes. As with the pen-and-paper method of rewriting notes, you should try to do this *within 24 hours* of the lecture, in order to head off the "forgetting curve."

Open a word processing file for each course: Open a file with a readily recognizable file name (such as "PSYCH101" or "ECON130") for each course you're taking.

Reset margins: After opening a new file, look in the instruction manual for the word processing program (or get assistance through the "Help" command) and find out how to reset the left and right margins. You want to have margins on both sides that are 1½ inches wide. You may wish to reset the bottom margin to 1½ inches also; otherwise, simply leave extra space at the bottom as you are typing in material.

Identify the lecture: At the top of the page, put the date of the lecture and a title that describes the topic or topics discussed that day (for example, "SCHOOLS OF PSYCHOLOGY: FREUD AND JUNG").

Type in your notes: Copy your handwritten notes from class into the computer. Don't just copy blindly, but focus on the main ideas and key questions. Use CAPITAL LETTERS, **boldface,** and <u>underlining</u> to emphasize important points.

Print out a copy and write in the margins: Print out a final version of the lecture—single space if you want to be able to see more things on a page or double space if you want to write between the lines. Then, using pencil or pen, write key terms and main concepts in the left margin. Write questions in the right margin. Write a summary in the bottom margin.

- *Write key terms in the left margin:* In the left margins, write the key terms and main concepts. *(See ■ Panel 6.6.)* Reviewing these important terms and concepts is a good way of preparing for objective questions on tests, such as true-false or multiple-choice questions.

- *Write one or two questions in the right margin:* On the right side of each page, write two questions about the material on the page. *(See ■ Panel 6.6 again.)* Reviewing these questions later will help you prepare for tests featuring essay questions or subjective questions.

- *Write a summary on the last page:* At the bottom of the last page of that day's notes, summarize in a few words the material in the notes. *(See ■ Panel 6.6 again.)* Some students write these summaries in red or green ink. With this eye-catching color, they can then flip through their notes and quickly take in all the summary information.

I cannot stress enough how important it is to take time—*absolutely no later than one day after your class*—to go over your notes, rewriting them if you can but certainly writing key terms, questions, and summaries at the end.

STEP 3: RECITE. Another reinforcement technique is *recitation*. This consists of covering up your detailed notes and using the key terms or concepts in the left margin to say out loud (or under your breath to yourself) what you understand your notes to mean. You can also do this with the questions in the right margin and the summary in the bottom margin.

Recitation is an activity you can do at your desk when you're doing homework or when you have 5 or 10 minutes between classes. It is a particularly effective reinforcing technique because the activity of verbalizing gives your mind time to grasp the ideas and move them from short-term to long-term memory.

STEP 4: REFLECT. Reflecting is something you can do in the few minutes as you sit in class waiting for the next lecture to begin.

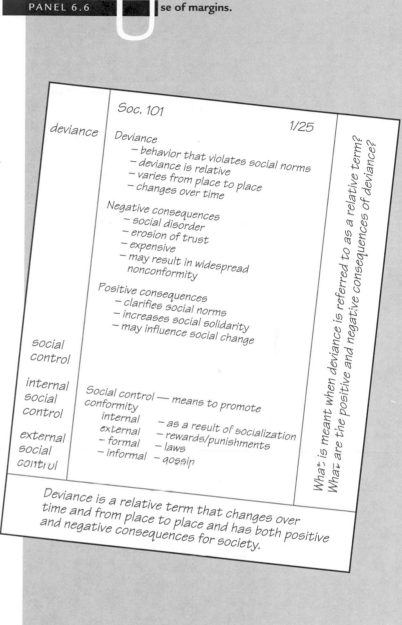

Look over your notes from the previous class period in the course and try to make some *personal associations* in your mind with the material. Such personal associations will help to anchor the material. For example, if you're learning about European history, imagine how you might link some of these facts on a tour of Europe or to a movie you've seen that was set in that period.

STEP 5: REVIEW. Two or three times a week, review all your notes, using the techniques of recitation and reflection to commit the information to memory. At first you may find that the review takes longer, but as you get more familiar with the material the review will get easier. At the end of the semester or quarter you will then have perhaps 80% of the lecture information stored in your long-term memory. The remaining 20% can be learned in the days before the exam. Unlike the process of cramming, having this much material already memorized will give you much more confidence about your ability to succeed on the test.

GROUP ACTIVITY #6.5

STUDYING YOUR NOTES: PRACTICING THREE OF THE FIVE R'S

This activity requires that you have the notes of the last lecture from one of your other courses. Pair up with another student in your First-Year Experience class. Take your lecture notes and follow the procedures in Step 2, Rewrite. Then take a few minutes to follow Step 3, Recite, and Step 4, Reflect.

Now trade your rewritten notes with your partner. Take turns quizzing each other on your respective notes. How well does this experience help you retain information? Discuss with the class at large.

Understanding the Instructor

PREVIEW & REVIEW Most college instructors love teaching. Compared to high-school teachers, college instructors may have had less training in teaching but usually more years of academic study and degrees. In some institutions, research is stressed over teaching. Instructors can be valuable resources, and it's important to get to know some of them.

High student evaluations of instructors do not necessarily mean they are easier graders. Most instructors are not sympathetic to making grade changes after the final exam.

How do college teachers *feel* about their jobs, about teaching, about their students?

Here's university professor John Bravman, who teaches the branch of engineering known as materials science. Although he has won seven awards for his teaching, he doesn't yet consider himself a great lecturer. "I can't keep people spellbound for 50 or 90 minutes and I'm not an actor," he says.[10] His secret is extensive preparation for lectures, high-quality handouts, putting key information on a blackboard in organized fashion, and trying to get students engaged through class demonstrations. Does he care about the reactions of his students? He says he used to worry that students looked bored but finally concluded that "their expressions do not represent what they are thinking." To support this contention, he tells about one student who "could have won an Academy Award for her sour face. I tried to avoid looking at her, but I couldn't do it. I can't tell you how relieved I was when that course ended." A few months later, to his surprise, she came to his office and told him that she had enjoyed his course so much that she had decided to major in materials science.

Here's Professor Tim Dave, physics instructor, inching along in evening rush-hour traffic. Most of the other drivers have finished their workday; Dave is on the way to starting the second shift of his, having left one California community college to get to another one. By the time he returns home, after being away for 12 hours, he will have driven 170 miles. Dave is one of the 40% of college faculty who are classified as part-time instructors. He manages to work full time by teaching part time at more than one college. "I live on the hairy edge," he says. "You truly have to love teaching to live this life."[11]

I, too, am in my car a lot. The college at which I teach is 60 miles from where I live, so I spend 2½ hours every workday on the road. While, unlike Tim Dave, I'm an instructor there full time, I also teach elsewhere from time to time, such as at a nearby four-year institution or nearby state prison. Why do I, and many college instructors like me, do this? The additional income is only part of it. Most of us simply love to teach.

Of course, you may well have some instructors who *don't* appear to enjoy teaching. Regardless of their likeability, however, your instructors can be valuable resources to you.

HIGH-SCHOOL VERSUS COLLEGE TEACHERS.
High-school teachers and instructors in higher education often have different kinds of training, as follows:

- *Training in teaching:* You may have been bored by some of your high-school teachers, but, believe it or not, all such teachers have actually had training in how to teach. Instructors in higher education, on the other hand, often have not, although recently research-oriented universities ranging from Cornell to the University of Washington to Arizona State have begun creating programs aimed at preparing graduate students to teach undergraduates.[12]

- *Years of study:* Most high-school teachers have earned a teaching credential on top

of a bachelor's degree (B.A. or B.S.), representing a minimum of four to five years of schooling.

Some instructors with whom you will study now may have a master's degree (M.A. or M.S.), which represents one or two years of study after the bachelor's degree. These instructors may be addressed as "Mr." or "Ms." or "Professor." (Sometimes instructors will invite students to address them by their first names.)

Some instructors—those you might address as "Doctor"—have a *doctorate* or *Ph.D.* or *Ed.D.* degree. (Ph.D. stands for "Doctor of Philosophy," although the degree is given for all subject areas in addition to philosophy. Ed.D. stands for "Doctor of Education.") To earn this degree, they have spent several years researching and writing a doctoral dissertation, a book-length investigation of a specific subject.

Part-time college instructors may also have master's or doctoral degrees. Or they may be graduate students (called *teaching assistants,* or "TAs"). Or they may be people from another campus or the nonacademic world (called *adjunct professors*) teaching special courses. Their years of study may be about the same as those of most high-school teachers. (These instructors may be addressed as "Mr." or "Ms." or "Professor.")

■ **Mission—teaching or research?** High-school teachers teach—that's their principal job. That's also the principal mission of *some,* but not all, college instructors. It depends on what kind of institution of higher learning you're attending.

For example, professors in two-year colleges—community colleges or junior colleges—are hired mainly to teach. A full-time instructor may teach four or five courses a week.

However, the teaching demands for professors in four-year institutions may not be so explicit. Teaching may indeed be the main mission of an instructor at a private liberal-arts college or even at some state universities. (These are institutions that grant bachelor's and master's degrees and sometimes doctorates.) However, for the really large and/or top-flight state or private universities, teaching is *not* the main emphasis for professors. Rather, research, writing, and publishing are, or at least that has been the emphasis for many years.

■ **Teaching versus learning:** As I suggested in Chapter 1, the biggest difference between taking courses in high school and in college is: *more is expected of you in college.* College, after all, is designed more to treat you as an adult. Thus, you have more adult freedoms than were probably allowed you in high school. For example, many instructors do not take daily attendance. Moreover, they may not check your assignments on a daily basis. Thus, you are expected to do more of your work on your own.

THE INSTRUCTOR AS RESOURCE. Instructors are among the academic resources available to you. College faculty members are supposed to be in their offices during certain hours (although part-time instructors may be harder to find, since at some colleges they don't even have offices). Hours are posted on their office doors or are available through the department secretary. In addition, many are available for questions a minute or so after class. You may also be able to make appointments with them at other times.

The instructor is the one to see if you have a question or problem about the course you are taking. These include which books to buy, what readings a test will cover, anything you don't understand about an assignment or a test question. Don't be afraid to ask. And if you begin to have trouble in a course, don't wait until the test. See your instructor as soon as possible.

How do you get to know an instructor? One way is to try Personal Exploration #6.2. *(opposite page).*

STUDENT EVALUATIONS & GRADES. Toward the end of a semester's classes, instructors not only get to evaluate you, through your course grade. On many campuses, you get to evaluate them—through the tool known as the *student evaluation* form. In 1973, 23% of 600 colleges and universities surveyed were using student evaluations; today 88% are.[13]

INTERVIEWING AN INSTRUCTOR

The purpose of this 10- to 15-minute Personal Exploration is to introduce you personally to one of your instructors. This will give you practice in talking to faculty members. The interview will enable you to see what kind of people they are and what their expectations are of students.

■ WHAT TO DO

Select one of the instructors at the college. It can be one in a course you are now taking. Or it can be someone in a field that you are thinking of majoring in. Or it can be your faculty advisor.

Telephone that instructor, and explain that you are doing a class assignment for the course. Ask if he or she can spare 10 or 15 minutes of time for a brief interview. Make an appointment to meet. Review the interview questions below and add two of your own.

Note: Instructors are busy people, so be sure to hold your interview to 10–15 minutes.

■ QUESTIONS FOR THE INTERVIEW

Fill in the following blanks.

Name of instructor being interviewed:

_____

_____

Department in which instructor teaches. (Example: Business.)

_____

_____

1. What is your particular discipline? (Example: Management.)

_____

_____

2. What is your area of specialization or research?

_____

_____

_____

_____

3. What are your other interests or hobbies?

_____

_____

_____

_____

_____

_____

_____

4. Why did you choose to teach in this particular discipline?

_____

_____

_____

_____

_____

_____

5. What kind of undergraduate and graduate degrees do you have, and where did you receive them?

_____

_____

_____

_____

_____

6. Why did you decide to teach at this college?

_____

_____

_____

_____

7. Ask a question of your own. (Example: "What do you think are the characteristics of a good student?")

Your question:

_____

_____

_____

_____

The instructor's answer:

_____

_____

_____

_____

_____

_____

_____

_____

_____

_____

_____

_____

8. If there's time, ask another question of your own. (Example: "What do you think are the characteristics of a bad student?")

Your question:

_____

_____

_____

_____

The instructor's answer:

_____

_____

_____

_____

_____

_____

_____

_____

_____

_____

_____

_____

Thank the instructor for his or her time.

Conduct Personal Exploration #6.2 in teams of two. Report back to the class two of the most interesting questions and their answers. Or write up your results as a report.

There has been some concern among colleges and universities that student evaluations affect instructors' grading patterns. That is, college administrators are afraid that instructors "who want high ratings [think] they must dumb down material, inflate grades, and keep students entertained."[14]

These evaluations aren't necessarily good guides to teaching effectiveness. For instance, one psychology professor, on the advice of a media consultant, added more hand gestures to his teaching style, varied the pitch of his voice, and generally tried to be more exuberant. Even though he covered the same material as in the previous semester and used the same textbook he had used for years, the change in student evaluations was astounding. "Students' ratings . . . soared," says one account. "They even gave higher marks to the textbook, a factor that shouldn't have been affected by differences in his teaching style."[15]

In addition, you can't bank on the notion that instructors who have high student evaluations are easier graders. "Some high graders receive low evaluations," says one English department chair about his faculty, "some low graders receive high evaluations, and some professors receive evaluations similar to the grades they give. . . . [H]igh-grading graduate-student instructors . . . are particularly likely to receive low evaluations."[16]

What if you've let things slide and received a poor final grade in a course?

University physics professor Kurt Wiesenfeld sadly describes students who try to wheedle better grades after getting a D or an F in his course and "don't think it's fair that they're judged according to their performance, not their desires or 'potential.'"[17] In the last several years, he says,

some students have developed a disgruntled-consumer approach. If they don't like their grade, they go to the "return" counter to trade it in for something better. . . . Many, when pressed about why they think they deserve a better grade, admit they don't deserve one but would like one anyway. . . . There's a weird innocence to the assumption that one expects (even deserves) a better grade simply by begging for it.

What should an instructor do in the face of pleas that "If you don't give me a C, I'll flunk out," or "If my grade isn't raised to a D, I'll lose my scholarship"? Or even, "If I don't pass, my life is over"? This is difficult for an instructor to deal with, even though it's invariably the students' fault that they let slide three months of midterms, quizzes, and lab reports. But it's not desirable that the instructor dispense grades like popcorn.

Grades by themselves intrinsically have no more value than gold stars on a child's toothbrush chart, but added together they translate into something worthwhile: a college degree, which is supposed to represent *competence,* even *excellence.*

Thus, there is a very good reason why Professor Wiesenfeld routinely ignores all pleas to change failing or dismal grades. Most of his students are science and engineering majors. If they haven't studied well enough to get the answer right, "then the new bridge breaks or the new drug doesn't work. . . . These are real-world consequences of errors and lack of expertise." Indeed, as he points out, construction failures and product recalls often reflect exactly these faults. Though some low-performing students may indeed flunk out or lose their scholarships, consider what's at stake: the grading system is necessary to help our society maintain the minimum standards of quality needed to maintain safety and integrity.

GROUP ACTIVITY #6.6

WHAT DO YOU WANT TO SEE IN AN INSTRUCTOR?

Take a piece of paper and list five positive qualities you'd like to see in an instructor and five negative qualities you'd like to avoid. Don't sign your name to the list. The instructor will collect your and your classmates' lists and will read aloud from some of them.

Questions for class discussion: What qualities seem to be most favored? What qualities are most to be avoided? What high-school teacher have you had in the past that embodied the best qualities? the worst qualities? What would attract you to the profession of teaching, college or non-college? What would put you off?

Information Technology in the Classroom

PREVIEW & REVIEW Laptop computers are useful because they can be carried all over campus. At many colleges, computers, e-mail, and the World Wide Web are being used in conjunction with certain classes. Online classes are catching on as a form of distance learning.

Information technology

Maybe, if you're at a college that has become wired and computerized, you'll get your grades via the World Wide Web, as students at the University of Oregon do. By now computers and the Internet are a fact of life at many colleges. But the use of information technology in the classroom—or as an adjunct to the classroom—varies widely from campus to campus. Let's look at some uses.

THE USES OF A LAPTOP. How do you tell first- and second-year students from juniors and seniors at Wake Forest University? By looking at their backpacks. The newer students are carrying the bulky, specially padded packs designed to protect laptop computers. For two years, the campus at Winston-Salem, North Carolina, has required its new students to have a laptop, which is paid for as part of the tuition.[18]

Other colleges and universities also require some or all of their students to have portable computers—for example, Bentley, Case Western, Columbia, Drew, Hartwick, Mississippi State, Nichols, UCLA, the University of Florida, the University of Minnesota's Crookston campus, and Virginia Tech. Portable computing, many students find, offers more convenience than the larger desktop models. They can take their computers not only to class but also to the cafeteria, to a campus bench, or on a bus.

Portable computers—laptops, notebooks, and sub-notebooks—are easy targets for thieves. Obviously, anything conveniently small enough to be slipped into your briefcase or backpack can be slipped into someone else's. Never leave a portable computer unattended in a public place.

It's also possible to simply lose a portable, as in forgetting it's in the overhead-luggage bin in an airplane. To help in its return, use a wide piece of clear tape to tape a card with your name and address to the outside of the machine. You should tape a similar card to the inside also. In addition, scatter a few such cards in the pockets of the carrying case.

Desktop computers are also easily stolen. However, for under $25, you can buy a cable and lock, like those used for bicycles, that secure the computer, monitor, and printer to a work area. For instance, you can drill a quarter-inch hole in your equipment and desk, then use a product called LEASH-IT (from Z-Lock, Redondo Beach, California) to connect them together. LEASH-IT consists of two tubular locks and a quarter-inch aircraft-grade stainless steel cable.

If your hardware does get stolen, its recovery may be helped if you have inscribed your driver's license number, Social Security number, or home address on each piece. Some campus and city police departments lend inscribing tools for such purposes. (And the tools can be used to mark some of your other possessions.)

Finally, insurance to cover computer theft or damage is surprisingly cheap. Look for advertisements in computer magazines. (If you have standard tenants' or homeowners' insurance, it may not cover your computer. Ask your insurance agent.)

At Hartwick College, for example, student Amy Grenier was able to work on a paper during a trip of several hours to see friends. "I did some work in the car, which I couldn't do with a large computer," she said. "You get to utilize more time to get your work done."[19]

One problem to be aware of with portable computers: they are easily stolen—and often are. (See ■ Panel 6.7.)

USING COMPUTERS IN CONJUNCTION WITH CLASSES. These days, says one writer, "class notes are more likely to be taken electronically than in anything spiral bound."[20] Actually, this is not exactly true.

It might be efficient to take lecture notes on a portable computer if the class is English or history, assuming you're a reasonably good typist. But it might be difficult to use a laptop in math (equations are hard to type), physics or biology (where you need to stop and make drawings), or certainly Russian or Japanese. In addition, the batteries in some laptops may last only 3 hours or so. If you have a full day of classes, then, your computer might not stay charged up the entire time.

Where a laptop does come in handy is when you have time between classes and you want to retype your lecture notes—I see lots of students doing this in my college library. It's also helpful for exchanging e-mail with other students when you're working on a joint project. Finally, as I'll show in the next chapter, it's useful for connecting to the Internet to do research for a term paper.

Colleges in which the majority of students live off campus and are commuters may well have computers available for student use (in various labs and libraries around campus). However, they may be less apt to require that students maintain an e-mail account, and so instructors may be less apt to transact classroom business through e-mail. Colleges in which most students reside in campus housing, on the other hand, may be in the forefront of using computers and communications as adjuncts to the normal classroom experience. At some schools, class assignments are posted on the World Wide Web and discussions are held online. Lecture notes and study aids may be posted online. Students may be asked to submit papers to a class Web site or to solve science problems on an interactive Web site.[21]

Some techno-savvy instructors may use multimedia, or "presentation technology," to spice up lectures. Presentation technology has caught on in business training (as with sales promotions and speeches) and is now coming into education as well. Presentations "are no longer just linear stories with a supportive collection of charts and pretty pictures," says one promotional piece on the topic. The concept "involves a dazzling array of attention-grabbing, information-delivering sight and sound equipment designed to get the message across."[22]

However, before we embrace multimedia learning uncritically, we need to ask: How well does it work? Stanford University economics and education professor Henry Levin agrees that multimedia learning is "splashy and attractive." However, he points out that there has been "no truly rigorous study that compares the effectiveness of CD-ROM training to more traditional classroom training."[23] Multimedia programs may be sufficient for teaching "do this, do that" basic information, but they aren't good "at picking up subtle behavior cues for evaluating thought processes," Levin states. "Multimedia may be the flavor of the month," says Richard Clark, professor of educational psychology at the University of Southern California, "but there's no evidence of it—even if very well designed—having a performance benefit over other types of training."[24]

What about using a book instead of a CD-ROM? Books have endured for a number of reasons, point out intellectual-property lawyer Richard Hsu and former multimedia producer William Mitchell. Compared to computers, books are easier to read, are more portable and durable, cost less, last longer, and often (because of limited capacity) are more carefully edited and more succinctly written.[25]

But the times they are a'changing. "Students love working with [multimedia] computer technology: computer ranks with lunch as their favorite part of the day," says a Connecticut middle-school teacher. "The shape and process of knowledge have changed, and today's students know it."[26]

DISTANCE LEARNING: ONLINE COURSES. For a number of years, colleges have offered so-called *telecourses*—televised or videotaped courses, in which an instructor lectures to a TV camera, which then transmits the lecture to television sets in remote classrooms or elsewhere. (I've taught a number of telecourses myself.) This is one form of *distance education*.

The newest kind of distance education consists of courses offered online. If, say, you were to take a course in economics, you would buy the assigned textbook, but other aspects of the course would be unlike the normal classroom situation. Your instructor would send the syllabus and reading and term-paper assignments either to your e-mail address or to a Web site that you would then connect to with

your computer. Lectures would appear in typed form the same way. If there was something you didn't understand, you would type in a query to the instructor, then wait for a typed response. (Classes are not usually conducted in "real time"—that is, with students and instructor all online together at the same time—so responses may be a day or two later.) Tests could also be handled online.

College administrators and instructors have found some surprises about online courses:

■ *Concerns about quality of education:* Administrators wonder about students who sign up for online courses but then don't communicate. Students who neither send e-mail messages nor participate in discussions, says biology professor William D. Graziadei, of the State University of New York at Plattsburgh, "simply are not there."[27] In addition, some students who are connected through their own Internet service providers (rather than through a campus network) may worry about the per-minute fees charged by their ISPs and thus not fully engage in their online courses.

■ *The nature of online students:* Originally, the University of Colorado at Denver offered Internet distance learning for "a reportedly vast population of time-strapped adult learners who live too far away to come to the campus but would pay good money to get an education online," according to one account.[28] Instead, administrators found a surprisingly large number of students (500 of 609 distance-education students) who were already enrolled in regular classes who wanted to ease their schedules by taking online courses. Other institutions, particularly those with large populations of commuter students, are finding the same kind of response.

■ *What students feel about online courses:* The main attraction, of course, is convenience, which appeals to students holding down full- or part-time jobs while earning degrees. "I love it," says Carol Craig, a 30-year-old English major at Denver. "I can get more credits this way and dial in from anywhere at any time."[29]

Craig also finds it easier to frame her thoughts on e-mail than in a classroom. Other students feel they get more attention from instructors in online courses, and can spend more time thinking about questions their instructors pose. Some like online courses because they like to sleep past 8:00 A.M. and feel they will never miss a class.

On the other hand, some students feel that online courses entail more work. Others prefer face-to-face classes where they can meet people and bounce ideas off each other.

One last note: Some instructors identify students by their Social Security numbers. But if an instructor uses these numbers when posting examination or course grades on the World Wide Web, students' privacy can be jeopardized.[30] A criminal could use this to open a checking account, get a driver's license, or otherwise commit what is known as "identity theft."

GROUP ACTIVITY #6.7

BENEFITS & PROBLEMS OF COMPUTERS

Questions for wide-ranging class discussion: If you had a laptop computer, what benefits would you put it to in order to aid your education? What concerns do you have about using this technology? Which do you prefer, classroom learning or online learning, and why?

Onward: Applying This Chapter to Your Life

For your entire life the lecture format will be enacted over and over again in different settings. If it's not a college professor speaking, it could be your boss, or an expert in an area of particular interest to you, or a speaker at a neighborhood meeting, or a political leader on televi-

sion. Thus, the skills you've learned in this chapter will be of value well beyond your time in college.

What is the single most important thing you learned in this chapter that you can "own" and use for the rest of your life? Write it down here:

_____

_____

_____

_____

_____

Real Practice Activities for Real People

Staying power

REAL PRACTICE ACTIVITY #6.1: HOW DIFFI-CULT IS CLASS PARTICIPATION FOR YOU? This practice activity, to be performed in class, is designed to help students increase their participation in class.

Take 5 minutes to write out notes to yourself about how you feel about participating in class. If participation is difficult (because you're shy, for example), describe what makes it so. Also describe what you can do to overcome this difficulty—what will give you the staying power to continue on in college class participation. When the instructor calls on you, take a minute or two to discuss what you've written. (You may read from your notes if you find that helpful.)

Mindfulness

REAL PRACTICE ACTIVITY #6.2: REACTING MINDFULLY TO INSTRUCTORS WHOSE LECTURING STYLE YOU FIND DIFFICULT. This practice activity takes 10–15 minutes in or out of class and is to be performed by students individually. The results may be shared in class discussion or submitted to the First-Year Experience course instructor as a reaction paper.

Take a few minutes to describe the characteristics of some instructors you had in the past or have now that really bother you—traits that put you off in some way and made or make it difficult for you to learn. (Don't identify the instructors.) Try to distinguish *instructor difficulties* from *subject matter difficulties.* (For example, you might have difficulty learning because the instructor talks too fast or too quietly, not because the subject being taught is Russian or statistics.)

Consider your reactions: Are you reacting mindlessly because the instructor's attributes put you off? What can you do to overcome them? What would you do if you found the same attributes in someone else who was important to you, such as a boss or an important client or customer?

Information technology

REAL PRACTICE ACTIVITY #6.3: USING A PERSONAL COMPUTER TO HELP LEARN FROM LECTURES. This activity is to be practiced by students out of class individually. Later the results are discussed in class.

Use a computer word processing program to do one of the following activities: (1) Using a laptop computer, take lecture notes of one of your courses. Do this for at least one class, more than one if possible. (2) Using a personal computer— your own, a friend's, or one available from the college—copy or rewrite your handwritten lecture notes for a couple of your classes. (You may use a pen to write key terms and questions in the margins.)

Afterward apply the rest of the 5R memorization techniques described in the chapter to these notes. Be prepared to discuss your reactions in class. How well does the experience help you retain information? Is using a computer and word processing program efficient for you?

The Examined Life

JOURNAL ENTRY #6.1: HOW DO YOU RATE YOURSELF AS A STUDENT PER-FORMER? For each of the following activities, rate yourself according to the following standard:

A Excellent

B Above average

C Average

D Below average

F Poor

1. Active listener in class
   A B C D F

2. Consistent attendance
   A B C D F

3. Participate and ask questions
   A B C D F

4. Involvement in study groups
   A B C D F

5. Use of bell cues and bell phrases
   A B C D F

6. Do readings prior to class
   A B C D F

7. Effectively and consistently use 5 Rs in note taking
   A B C D F

JOURNAL ENTRY #6.2: SHOULD YOU CHANGE YOUR NOTE-TAKING BEHAVIOR? How should you change your note-taking habits from your accustomed methods?

_____

_____

_____

_____

_____

_____

JOURNAL ENTRY #6.3: WHICH INSTRUCTORS DO YOU HAVE TROUBLE WITH? What kinds of instructors, or what particular instructors, do you have trouble following when they lecture? Why, and what can you do about it?

_____

_____

_____

_____

_____

_____

_____

_____

_____

JOURNAL ENTRY #6.4: ARE YOU TOO SELF-CONSCIOUS ABOUT OTHER STUDENTS? Are you afraid other students will laugh at you for being too obviously engaged in the lecture and learning process? Are you afraid they will consider you some sort of wimp because you're not obviously detached, indifferent, or supposedly cool? Why does this bother you? What does this self-consciousness—this tremendous concern about how people think about you—imply for your future in school or in a career?

_____

_____

_____

_____

_____

_____

_____

_____

JOURNAL ENTRY #6.5: WHAT DO YOU THINK ABOUT DISTANCE LEARNING?

You've probably been taking lecture classes all your life. What do you think of the idea of taking a class via television or online computer?

_____

_____

_____

_____

_____

_____

_____

_____

_____

_____

_____

Exams

Taking Tests with Confidence & Integrity

You are not a victim.
You are here by choice.
You hope higher education
will help you be your
best and lead to your
ultimate happiness.

Perhaps this is the outlook to have the next time you're facing exams. Remember why you're seeking an education in the first place. You are not a prisoner. You're here because you expect school to enhance your life. Exams may not be fun, but they are simply part of the experience of higher education—an experience you have *chosen* to undertake.

Thus, perhaps the attitude to take is "Since I'm here in school voluntarily and want it to better my life, I might as well become good at one of the important things school requires—taking tests." This is part of the attitude of staying power.

Staying
power

Taking Charge of Taking Tests

PREVIEW & REVIEW Becoming expert at tests means psyching out the instructor, learning how to prepare for specific tests, knowing what to bring to the test, and getting off to the right start in the testing room.

Taking charge of taking tests has four components:

- Psyching out the instructor
- Learning how to prepare for specific tests
- Knowing what to bring to the test
- Getting started right in the testing room

Let's consider these.

PSYCHING OUT THE INSTRUCTOR. Instructors not only have different ways of teaching, they have different ways of testing. Some test mainly on the textbook, some mainly on the lecture material, some on both. It's up to you to be a *detective*—to figure out the instructor's method of operating and plan accordingly. This is usually not hard to do. The aim of an instructor, after all, is not to trick you but to find out what you know.

Following are some ways to get a jump on the test by finding out what the instructor will do:

- ***Look at the course syllabus:*** The syllabus handed out by the instructor on the first class day is often a good guide for test preparation. As mentioned earlier, the *syllabus* ("*sill*-uh-buss") is a course outline or guide that tells you what readings are required, when assignments are due, and when examinations are scheduled.

  This basic road map to the course may tell you a lot about testing. It may tell you what kind of weight testing has in the overall course grade. It may indicate if low grades can be made up. It may describe what happens if the test is missed. It may indicate if the lowest grade on a series of tests is dropped when the instructor is determining your average grade for all tests.

- ***Look at instructor handouts:*** Frequently instructors hand out potential essay questions in advance, or they prepare study guides. Handouts show what the instructor thinks is important. Like an actor learning your lines, you can use such material to practice taking the test. This can not only help prepare you by giving you sample material, it may also help reduce the stage fright–like condition known as test anxiety.

- ***Ask about the specific test:*** Particularly before the first test in a class, when you don't know what's coming, make a point to ask the instructor (in class or during office hours) the following:

1. How long will the test last?

2. How much will the test results count toward the course grade?

3. What types of questions will appear on the test? Will they be true-false? multiple-choice? fill-in? essay? all of these? Different questions require different test-taking strategies, as I'll explain later.

It's also fair to ask the instructor what is most important for you to know. Some instructors may emphasize certain subject areas over others, or they may emphasize the lecture or laboratory material over the textbook.

■ *Ask to see copies of old tests:* Some instructors may be willing to provide you with copies of old tests or with the kinds of questions they are inclined to ask. Don't feel it's somehow impolite or incorrect to ask to see old tests. (Sometimes old tests are on file in the library.)

■ *Consult students who have taken the course:* If you know others who have already taken the course, ask them about their test experiences. See if you can get them to share old exams so you can look at the kinds of questions the instructor likes to ask. Indeed, an item from an old test may even reappear on the one you will take, since there are only so many ways to ask a question. (But don't count on it.)

■ *In lectures watch for "bell phrases" and "bell cues":* As I mentioned in Chapter 6, all lecturers use phrases and gestures that should "ring a bell" and signal importance.

A *bell phrase* **is a verbal indicator of an important point.** Examples: "Three major types . . . ," "The most important result is . . . ," "You should remember . . ."

A *bell cue* **is an action or gesture that indicates important points.** Examples are pointing, as to something on the board or a chart; underlining or making a check mark by key words; and holding up fingers.

LEARNING HOW TO PREPARE FOR A SPECIFIC TEST. In addition to the foregoing suggestions, there are strategies to employ when preparing for a specific test.

■ *Rehearse study-guide or other practice questions:* Some textbook publishers produce a separate study guide, which you can buy at the campus bookstore. A *study guide* **is a booklet that contains practice questions, along with their answers, covering material in the textbook.** For a fairly modest price, the study guide represents an excellent investment because *it gives you a trial run at types of questions similar to those apt to be asked on the test.*

A variation on the paper-and-print study guide now being seen more frequently is the electronic study guide. **An** *electronic study guide* **is a floppy disk that students can use on their personal computer (IBM-style or Apple Macintosh) to rehearse practice questions and check their answers.**

Information technology

Some textbooks also have practice questions at the end of chapters, with answers to some or all of them in the back of the book.

■ *Form study groups with other students to generate practice questions:* Forming study groups with some of your classmates is an excellent way to generate possible test questions—especially essay questions—and quiz one another on answers. Moreover, study groups offer reinforcement and inject a bit of social life into your studying.

■ *Develop self-study practice sessions:* Besides study guides and study groups, a useful preparation strategy is simply to have your own periodic practice sessions. Every week set aside time to go through your notes and textbooks and compose practice tests. Specifically:

1. Practice reviewing material that is emphasized. This includes anything your instructor has pointed out as being significant. Practice defining key terms, the terms presented in *italics* or **boldface** in the text. This is an area, incidentally, where you can make excellent use of flash cards. **A *flash card*, as you may recall, is a card bearing words, numbers, or pictures that is briefly displayed as a learning aid.**

2. Practice reviewing material that is presented in numbered lists (such as the 13 vitamins or warning signs for heart disease). Enumerations often provide the basis for essay and multiple-choice questions.

3. Practice answering questions on material on which there are a good many pages of coverage, either in text or lecture notes. Answer questions you've written in the text margins and in your lecture notes. Formulate essay questions and outline answers.

■ *Study throughout the course:* The best way to prepare for exams is *not* to play catch-up. In Chapter 5 I mentioned the idea of overlearning—continuing to repeatedly review material even after you appear to have absorbed it. Of course, to overlearn you must first have learned. This means keeping up with lecture notes and textbooks, rereading them so that you really get to know the material. Space your studying rather than cramming, since it is *repetition* that will move information into your long-term memory bank.

■ *Review the evening and morning before the test:* The night before a test, spend the evening reviewing your notes. Then go to bed without interfering (as by watching television) with the material you have absorbed. Get plenty of rest—there will be no need to stay up cramming if you've followed the suggestions of this book. The next morning, get up early and review your notes again.

KNOW WHAT TO BRING TO THE TEST. Asking to borrow a pencil or pen from the instructor on exam day because you forgot to bring one will not get you off to a good start. It makes you feel and look as though you're not exactly in charge. Thus, be sure to bring some sharpened pencils (#2 if the tests are machine-scored) or pens (preferably blue or black ink; no red, a color instructors often use for grading).

Besides pencils or pens, other items you should bring are these:

■ *A watch:* If the examination room has no clock, you'll need a watch to be able to budget your time during the test.

■ *Blue book or paper and paper clips:* Some instructors will hand out "blue books" for examinations or require that you bring some along. (They're usually for sale in the campus bookstore.) Otherwise, bring some paper to write on and some paper clips (or small stapler) to attach pages together.

■ *Calculator, dictionary, formulas, or other aids:* Some instructors allow you to bring items to assist test taking. Be sure to give yourself The Extra Edge by availing yourself of these learning aids if they're permitted!

In math, business, and science courses, you may be allowed to have a calculator.

In foreign language or literature courses, you may be permitted a dictionary.

In some math, statistics, business, engineering, and science courses, instructors may allow you to jot down formulas on index cards and bring them to the test.

GETTING STARTED RIGHT IN THE TESTING ROOM. It's important to extend the feeling of "taking charge" to the environment of the testing room. Here's how:

■ *Arrive on time:* Have you ever been sitting in an exam room and watched some fellow students arrive late, perhaps having overslept? You have to feel sorry for them. They're clearly starting at a disadvantage, and their faces show it.

Arrive early. Or if arriving early makes you nervous because it means listening to other students talk about the test, then arrive on time.

■ *Find a good test-taking spot:* Find a spot where you won't be distracted. Sitting near the front of the room is good, where you won't see a lot of other people. Or sitting in your normal spot may make you feel comfortable.

GROUP ACTIVITY #7.1

WALKING IN YOUR INSTRUCTOR'S SHOES: PREPARING FOR AN EXAM

This activity requires that you and everyone else in the class have a copy of this text plus notes from the First-Year Experience course. In small groups (three to five people), you and other group members are to come up with four possible long-answer essay questions that you might be asked on the next test. Use the kinds of tips mentioned previously to try to "walk in the instructor's shoes" and psych out what kinds of questions are apt to be asked.

A long-answer essay question requires three or more paragraphs to answer. It may ask you to compare and contrast (show how things are similar and different), take a position for or against, and discuss in detail.

Then, with other group members, share with the larger class the questions you developed. Explain the reasoning behind your choices. If time permits, outline your response to one of the questions.

How to Cope with Test Anxiety in the Classroom

Five short-term strategies exist for helping you cope with test anxiety in the classroom. (1) Press fists against your closed eyes and squint. (2) Drop your head forward and slowly roll it left and right. (3) Alternately tense your muscles, then let go. (4) Concentrate on breathing slowly in and out. (5) Try positive self-talk.

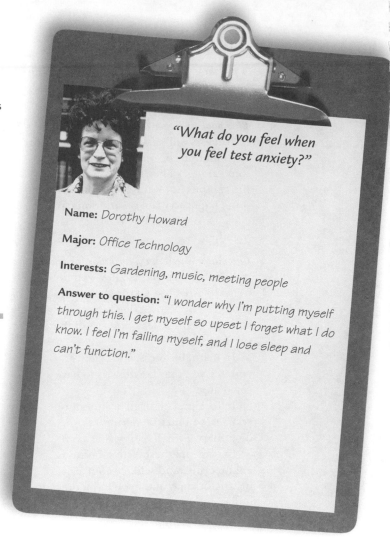

"What do you feel when you feel test anxiety?"

Name: *Dorothy Howard*

Major: *Office Technology*

Interests: *Gardening, music, meeting people*

Answer to question: *"I wonder why I'm putting myself through this. I get myself so upset I forget what I do know. I feel I'm failing myself, and I lose sleep and can't function."*

Dry mouth. Rapid breathing. Quickened pulse. Taut muscles. Sweating. Nausea. Headache. These are just some of the *physical* symptoms—which I well recall myself—associated with test anxiety.

Then there are the *mental* aspects—panic, mental blocks, foreboding, dread. "You're going to freeze up," the inner Voice Of Judgment says. "You *know* you're going to flunk!"

Test anxiety consists of thoughts and worries (the mental component) and feelings and sensations (the physical component) of stress linked to test taking. Test anxiety has much in common with other kinds of *performance anxiety*—the stresses associated with first dates, public speaking, job interviews, pregame nervousness, stage fright, and the like.

Anxiety is an indicator of the importance we attach to an event and of our concern that we may not succeed. Anxiety is *normal* under these circumstances; indeed, a certain amount can actually be *helpful.* As you've probably noticed in other challenges (games, for example), some anxiety makes you focus your attention and get up to perform. The problem lies in the kind of test anxiety that hinders your performance. What can be done about it?

The best recipe for alleviating feelings of panic is to be prepared. If you've reviewed the material often enough, you can have butterflies in your stomach and still feel confident that you'll pull through. Beyond that, there are various techniques for coping with stress (such as relaxation training and visualization, which I describe in Chapter 10).

Here are five techniques for handling test anxiety in the classroom.

PRESS FISTS AGAINST YOUR CLOSED EYES & SQUINT. This exercise will give you a moment to blank out tensions and distractions. Here's how it works (best not to try this if you wear contact lenses):

Press your fists against your closed eyes. Squint or tightly close your eyes at the same time.

After a few seconds, take your hands away and open your eyes.

DROP YOUR HEAD FORWARD & SLOWLY ROLL IT LEFT & RIGHT. Do the following exercise five times:

Drop your head forward on your chest. Roll it slowly over to your left shoulder, then slowly over to your right shoulder.

ALTERNATELY TENSE YOUR MUSCLES & THEN LET GO. If a particular part of your body, such as your shoulders, is tense, try this tense-and-relax activity. The effect is to make you aware of the relaxed feeling after you have released the tension.

Take a deep breath and hold it.
Make the muscles in the tense place even more tense.
Hold tightly for a few seconds.
Then let out your breath and release the tension.

You can do this for other parts of your body (chest, neck, and so on) or for all parts simultaneously.

CONCENTRATE ON BREATHING SLOWLY IN & OUT. This activity will calm some of the physical sensations in your body. Do this for 2–5 minutes.

Focus your mind on your breathing.
Breathe slowly through your nose.
Deeply and slowly inhale, filling your lungs.
Then slowly exhale through your mouth.
Avoid taking short breaths.

Once your breathing is calm and regular, you can concentrate on the test.

TRY POSITIVE SELF-TALK. When the Voice Of Judgment within you says "You're going to flunk!" make an effort to replace this and other negative thoughts with positive ones. Say to yourself: "Nonsense! I studied enough, so I know I'll be okay." See Personal Exploration #7.1 below.

PERSONAL EXPLORATION #7.1

MORE ON NEGATIVE THOUGHTS & POSITIVE THOUGHTS

What kinds of negative thoughts do you have during tests? Pretend you are sitting in an examination room. Listen to what your inner voice (the Voice Of Judgment) is saying, and write down the thoughts below. *Examples:*

"My mind is a blank; I can't remember anything!"
"I'm going to flunk, and my life will be ruined!"
"Everyone else is leaving early; they're smarter than I am!"

1. _____
_____
_____

2. _____
_____
_____

3. _____
_____
_____

Now try to replace these negative thoughts with positive thoughts, using positive self-talk. Write your responses below. *Examples:*

"Breathe easy, and you'll start to remember some things. If not, come back to the question later."
"Even if you flunk, you'll survive. But don't get distracted. Just concentrate on each step of the test."
"Leaving early doesn't mean they're smarter, maybe the reverse. Just focus on the test, not other students."

1. _____
_____
_____

2. _____
_____
_____
_____
_____

3. _____
_____
_____
_____

With others in a small group write down a list of negative thoughts, like those in Personal Exploration #7.1, that you sometimes have during test situations. Also describe the circumstances that generate such negative thoughts.

Next generate a list of positive thoughts, like those above, to replace the negative thoughts. Share your responses and conclusions with the class and with your instructor.

The Six-Step Examination Approach

PREVIEW & REVIEW The six-step examination approach consists of the following: (1) Unload. (2) Review subjective questions. (3) Do objective questions. (4) Do subjective questions. (5) Do questions left undone. (6) Proofread.

Once you have settled your nerves with some of the exercises described in the previous section, you need to apply a strategy for taking the test itself. The six-step system discussed here has three purposes. First, it is a very efficient method for tackling a test. Second, it helps you stave off panic because it gives you a plan to follow. Third, it helps you build confidence. The six steps are these:

1. Unload on the back of the test.
2. Review, but don't answer, the subjective questions.
3. Answer the objective questions.
4. Answer the subjective questions.
5. Answer questions left undone.
6. Proofread the examination.

STEP 1: UNLOAD ON THE BACK OF THE TEST. The first thing you should do after getting the test from your instructor is to *put your name on it.* (You'd be surprised how many students simply forget to sign their exam, baffling the instructor and delaying posting of the final grade.)

After signing it, *without looking at any of the questions,* flip the examination sheet over and simply *unload.* **_Unloading_ means taking 2–3 minutes to jot down on the back of the exam sheet any key words, concepts, and ideas that are in your mind.** These are things that you think might be on the test, and things you feel a bit shaky about—that is, things you've only recently studied and need to get down on paper while you still have them in mind.

Unloading is important for two reasons:

- *It relieves anxiety:* Just "blowing out" all the information pent up in you at the outset of the test can be extremely useful in helping overcome test anxiety.

- *It helps prevent forgetting:* One term or one idea can be like a string attached to a whole train of ideas that make up an entire essay. Unloading may well produce a key term or idea that leads to a mental string that you can pull on later in the test.

There is nothing illegal or unethical about unloading. It is not cheating so long as the things you unload are the product of your own brain and not cribbed from elsewhere.

STEP 2: REVIEW, BUT DON'T ANSWER, THE SUBJECTIVE QUESTIONS. After unloading, flip the test over. Skip over any objective questions (true-false, multiple-choice) and go to the subjective questions. **_Subjective questions_ are those that generally require long answers,** such as essay-type questions or those requiring lists as answers. Examples:

Compare and contrast the main schools of psychology.

Describe the principal methods of textile making.

List the four operations of a computer system.

You should also take 2–3 minutes to do a form of unloading: Write *key words* in the margins next to each question. These key words will help to serve as a rough outline when you start answering. Don't, however, immediately begin writing answers to the subjective questions (unless these are the only kinds of questions on the exam). Rather, proceed next to the objective questions on the test.

STEP 3: ANSWER THE OBJECTIVE QUESTIONS. <u>**Objective questions**</u> **are those that are true-false, multiple-choice, matching, and fill-in.** There's a good reason for answering objective questions before subjective questions: *the very process of answering may supply details that will help you answer the subjective questions.* It may also help you answer a subjective question you didn't know when you reviewed it in Step 2.

This method of operating shows how you can use the test as a tool. That is, your recognition of the answer to an objective question may help you to recall other material that may help you later in the test.

Answer the objective questions as quickly as you can. Don't spend any time on questions you're not sure of. Rather, circle or star them and return to them later.

STEP 4: ANSWER THE SUBJECTIVE QUESTIONS. When grading the test, instructors often assign more importance to some subjective questions than to others. That is, they will judge the answer to one question to be worth, say, 30% of the test grade and another to be worth 10%. Quite often the point values are mentioned on the examination sheet. If not, raise your hand and ask. It's your right as a student to know.

To make efficient use of your time, do the following:

- **Read the directions!** This is obvious advice, and it applies to all types of test questions. However, since subjective questions usually have more point values than objective questions do, you want to be sure you don't misunderstand them.

- **EITHER answer the easiest first . . . :** Answer the *easiest* subjective questions first.

- **. . . OR answer the highest-value questions first:** Alternatively, answer the subjective questions with *the greatest point values* first.

STEP 5: ANSWER QUESTIONS LEFT UNDONE. By this point you will have answered the easiest questions or the ones that you have most knowledge about. As you get toward the end of the test period, now is your chance to go back and try answering the questions you left undone—those you circled or starred.

A word about guessing: *Unless the directions say otherwise*, often an *unanswered* question will count off just as much as an *incorrectly answered* question, especially on objective questions. Thus, *unless the instructor or test says there's a penalty for guessing*, you might as well take a guess.

STEP 6: PROOFREAD THE EXAMINATION. If you get through all your questions before the end of the examination period, it's tempting to hand in your test and walk out early. For one thing, you'll be dying to find relief from the pressure cooker. Secondly, you may think it somehow looks as if you're smarter if you're one of the first to leave. (However, it's not so. Often it's the ones who don't know the answers and have given up who leave early.)

The best strategy, however, is: *if you have any time left, use it.* By staying you give yourself The Extra Edge that the early leavers don't. During this remaining time, look over the test and *proofread* it. Correct any misspellings. Reread any questions to make sure you have fully understood them and responded to them correctly; make any changes necessary to your answers.

Mastering Objective Questions

PREVIEW & REVIEW   Different strategies may be employed for the different types of objective questions—for true-false, multiple-choice, matching, or fill-in-the-blank questions.

As mentioned, *objective questions* are true-false, multiple-choice, matching, or fill-in-the blank questions. Objective questions can often be machine-scored. Such questions are called "objective" because, for the instructor who is doing the grading, there is no need for interpretation or judgment calls. By contrast, with "subjective," essay-type questions, the grader has some leeway in how to judge the worth of the answer.

Here are three general strategies to apply to objective questions:[1]

- *Guess, unless there's a penalty:* With objective questions, *never leave an answer blank*, unless the instructor or test says there's a

penalty for guessing. Some instructors have grading systems for objective tests that penalize guessing (for example, a correct answer that counts +1, a nonresponse –1, and a wrong answer –2). Thus, be sure you know the ground rules before you guess.

■ *If there are penalties for guessing, guess anyway if you can eliminate half the choices:* If the instructor does take points off for guessing, take a guess anyway when you can eliminate half or more of the options—for example, two out of four choices on a multiple-choice test.

■ *Allow second thoughts, if you've prepared:* Answer objective questions reasonably quickly, and make a check mark for any answer that you're unsure about. You may decide to change the answer when you do a final survey, based on information suggested to you by later items on the test.

"Contrary to the popular advice about never changing answers, *it can be to your advantage to change answers*," say educators Tim Walter and Al Siebert (emphasis theirs). "The research evidence shows that when students have prepared well for an examination, the number of students who gain by changing answers is significantly greater than the number of students who lose by changing answers."[1]

The key here is "prepared well." If you've studied well for the test, your second thought may be more apt to be correct.

HANDLING TRUE-FALSE QUESTIONS. *True-false questions* are statements that you must indicate are either "true" or "false." With such items, you have a 50% chance of getting each one right just by guessing. Thus, instructors may try to put in statements that seem true but on close reading actually are not.

Here are some strategies for handling true-false questions:

■ *Don't waste a lot of time:* Go through the true-false items as quickly as you can. Don't spend time agonizing over those you don't know; they usually aren't worth a lot of points compared to other parts of the test. Moreover, later questions may jog your memory in a way that suggests the correct answers.

■ *Be aware that more answers are apt to be true than false:* True-false tests generally contain more true answers than false ones. Thus, mark a statement true unless you know for sure it is false.

■ *Be aware longer statements tend to be true:* Statements that are longer and provide a lot of information *tend* to be true, though not always. Read the statement carefully to be sure no part of it is false.

■ *Read carefully to see that every part is true:* For a statement to be true, every part of it must be true. Conversely, it is false if *any part of it* is false. (Example: "The original Thirteen Colonies included Massachusetts, Virginia, and Illinois" is a false statement because the last state was not among the thirteen, though the first two were.)

■ *Look for qualifier words:* Qualifier words include *all, none, always, never, everyone, no one, invariably, rarely, often, usually, generally, sometimes, most.*

Two suggestions to follow are these:

1. Statements that use *absolute* qualifier words, such as "always" or "never," are usually false. (Example: "It's always dry in Nevada" is false because it does rain there sometimes.)

2. Statements that use *moderating* qualifier words, such as "usually" or "often," tend to be true more often than not. (Example: "It's generally dry in Nevada" is true.)

HANDLING MULTIPLE-CHOICE QUESTIONS. *Multiple-choice questions* allow you to pick an answer from several options offered, generally between three and five choices. The question itself is called the *stem.* The choices of answers are called the *options.* Incorrect options are known as *distractors* because their purpose is to distract you from choosing the correct option. Usually only one option is correct, but check the test directions (or ask the instructor) to see if more than one answer is allowed.

Two kinds of strategies apply to multiple-choice questions—*thinking strategies* and *guessing strategies.* Here are some *thinking strategies:*

- **Answer the question in your head first:** Read the question and try to frame an answer in your mind before looking at the answer options. This will help you avoid being confused by "distractor" options.

- **Eliminate incorrect answers first:** Read *all* the options, since sometimes two may be similar, with only one being correct. (Beware of trick answers that are only partly correct.) Eliminate those options you know are incorrect. Then choose the correct answer from those remaining.

- **Return to questions that are difficult:** Mark those questions that are difficult and return to them later if time permits. Spending time mulling over multiple-choice questions may not pay off in the points the instructor allows per question. Moreover, later questions in the test may trigger a line of thought that helps you with answers when you come back.

- **Try out each option independently with the question:** If you're having trouble sorting out the options, try reading the question and just the first option together. Then try the question and the second option together. And so on. By taking each one at a time, you may be able to make a better determination.

- **Be careful about "all of the above" or "none of the above":** "All of the above" or "none of the above" is often the correct choice. But examine the alternatives carefully. Make sure that *all* the other options apply before checking "all of the above." Make sure *no one* other option is correct before marking "none of the above."

- **Look for opposite choices:** If two choices are opposite in meaning, one is probably correct. Try to eliminate other choices, then concentrate on which of the opposite options is correct.

Here are some *guessing strategies* for multiple-choice questions:

- **Guess, if there's no penalty:** Unless the instructor has indicated he or she will take points off for incorrect answers, you might as well guess if you don't know the answer.

- **Choose between similar-sounding options:** If two options have similar words or similar-sounding words, choose one of them.

- **If options are numbers, pick in the middle:** If the alternative options consist of numbers, high and low numbers tend to be distractors. Thus, you might try guessing at one of the middle numbers.

- **Consider that the first option is often not correct:** Many instructors think you should have to read through at least one incorrect answer before you come to the correct answer. Thus, when you're having to guess, consider that there's a high probability that the first option will be incorrect.

- **Pick a familiar term over an unfamiliar one:** An answer that contains an unfamiliar term is apt to be a distractor, although many students tend to assume otherwise. If you have to guess, try the familiar term.

As I said of true-false questions, when you go back and review your answers, don't be afraid to change your mind if you realize that you could have made a better choice. The idea that you should always stick with your first choice is simply a myth.

HANDLING MATCHING QUESTIONS. *Matching questions* **require you to associate items from one list with items from a second list.** For example, on a history test you might be asked to associate eight famous political figures listed in Column A with the time period in which each lived, as listed in Column B.

Strategies for handling matching questions are as follows:

- **Ask if items can be used more than once:** With most matching-questions tests, each item in one column has its unique match in the other column. However, it's possible that items can be used for more than one match. That is, an item in Column B may fit several items in Column A. If you're not sure, ask the instructor.

- **Read all choices before answering, then do the easy matchings first:** Before making your choices, read all options in both columns. Then work the easy items first. Matching the easier items first may help you match the tougher ones later by a process of elimination.

If you can use an item only once, cross off each item as you use it. (If items can be used more than once, put a check mark next to the ones you have used rather than crossing them out.)

Put a question mark next to the matchings you're not sure about. If time permits, you can go back later and take another look at them.

HANDLING FILL-IN-THE-BLANK QUESTIONS.

Also known as *sentence-completion questions*, _fill-in-the-blank questions_ **require you to fill in an answer from memory or to choose from options offered in a list.** Often the answers are names, definitions, locations, amounts, or short descriptions. Frequently there are clues contained within the incomplete sentence that will help you with your answer.

Strategies for working fill-in-the-blank tests are as follows:

- *Read the question to determine what kind of answer is needed:* Reading the question carefully will tell you what kind of fact is needed: a key term? a date? a name? a definition? By focusing on the question, you may be able to trigger an association from your memory bank.

- *Make sure the answer fits grammatically and logically:* Be sure that subject and verb, plurals, numbers, and so on are used grammatically and logically. For example, if the statement says "a ____," don't put in "hour" and if it says "an ____," don't put in "minute." "*A* hour" and "*An* minute" are not grammatical.

As suggested for other types of objective questions, put a star or question mark beside those items you're not sure about. Later material on the test may prompt your memory when you come back to review them.

Mastering Written Examinations: Short & Long Essays

PREVIEW & REVIEW Two types of written examinations are short-answer essay and long-answer essay. The strategy for the short-answer essay is to determine the amount of detail needed, depending on time available, point value, and your knowledge. The strategy for the long-answer essay is to meet the standards for relevance, completeness, accuracy, organization, logic, and clarity. This means reading the directions; looking for guiding words; determining choice of essay question; brainstorming ideas and making an outline of your position, supporting details, and summary; writing the three parts of the essay; making sure the essay is clear; and watching your time.

Written examinations generally require you to write essays, either short or long. Both types of essays may be on the same exam.

- *Short-answer essay:* A _short-answer essay_ **may be a brief one-word or one-sentence answer to a short-answer question, a one- or two-paragraph essay, or a list or diagram.** Usually you are asked to write a response to just one question.

- *Long-answer essay:* A _long-answer essay_ **generally requires three or more paragraphs to answer.** You may be required to answer one question or several questions, all in the same essay.

Let's consider strategies for both of these.

HANDLING THE SHORT-ANSWER ESSAY.
Frequently tests contain questions that require only a short answer—anywhere from a single word to two or three paragraphs. Examples:

State the name of a particular theory. *(This might be a one- or two-word answer.)*

Define a certain term. *(Could be done in a sentence.)*

List the basic steps in a process. *(Could be several words or sentences or a list.)*

Describe a particular scientific study. *(Might require a paragraph.)*

Identify and describe three causes of a particular event. *(Might be done in two or three paragraphs.)*

Your strategy here is to provide the instructor with enough information (but not too much) to show that you understand the answer—whether it's a list, some brief sentences, or a few paragraphs.

How much detail should you provide? This is sometimes difficult to determine. After all, to identify and describe three causes of the First World War could take several pages. To decide how much detail is appropriate, consider three factors:

■ *Time available:* How much time do you have for other questions on the exam? You may need to allow for an upcoming long essay question, for example.

■ *Point value:* What is the relative weight (number of points) the instructor assigns to short-answer questions compared with other questions?

■ *Your knowledge:* How much do you know about the topic? The instructor might mark you down if you volunteer erroneous information.

In general, it's best to write the minimum you think necessary. If in doubt, respond to one short-answer question, then take it up to the instructor and ask if it's long enough.

HANDLING THE LONG-ANSWER ESSAY. The long-answer essay (and to some extent the short-answer essay) is sometimes considered a *subjective* test. This notion would seem to imply there are no objective facts and that it's up to the grader to deter-mine how good your answer is. Actually, there usually *are* objective facts, and the instructor looks for them in your answer.

What strategy should you follow on a long-answer question? According to one clinical psychologist and instructor of first-year seminar courses, research shows that instructors award the greatest number of points when an essay answer meets the following six standards:[3]

1. *Relevance:* The answer sticks to the question. That is, the facts and points set down are relevant to the question.

2. *Completeness:* The question is answered completely.

3. *Accuracy:* The information given is factually correct.

4. *Organization:* The answer is organized well.

5. *Logic:* The answer shows that the writer can think and reason effectively.

6. *Clarity:* Thoughts are expressed clearly.

Basically, then, two things are important in answering essay questions: First, *you need to know your facts.* Second, *you need to present them well.*

Let me now proceed to outline a strategy for answering long-answer essay questions.

■ *Read the directions!* This is important for *all* test questions, of course, but especially here because of the amount of time you're required to invest in responding to long-answer essay questions and the high point values attached to them.

In failing to read the directions carefully, students may answer only one question when three have been asked. Or they may answer three when only one has been asked (thereby depriving themselves of time to respond adequately to later test questions). Or they may go off on a tangent with an answer that earns no credit. I don't know how many times I've written in the margin of a test, "Nice response, but it misses the point. Did you read the directions?"

Reading the directions will help you stay on the topic, thereby helping you to meet Standard #1 above—making the answer *relevant.*

- **Look for guiding words in the directions:** When you read the directions, look for guiding words—key task words such as *discuss, define,* or *compare*—which may guide your answer. <u>*Guiding words*</u> **are common words that instruct you in the task you are to accomplish in your essay-question answer.**

Common guiding words are *analyze, compare, contrast, criticize, define, describe, discuss, enumerate, explain, evaluate, illustrate, interpret, outline, prove, relate, state, summarize,* and *trace.* A list of guiding words and their definitions appears below. *(See ■ Panel 7.1.)*

 uiding words. These key words appear in essay-question directions as part of the examination vocabulary. As you read the instructions, circle or underline such words so that you will be sure to focus your answer.

When an examination states . . .	You should . . .
Analyze	Explain the major parts or process of something.
Apply	Show function in a specific context.
Compare	Show similarities.
Contrast	Show differences.
Criticize (Critique, Evaluate, Examine)	Present your view (positive or negative) of something, giving supporting evidence for your position.
Define	Give the meaning of a word or expression. (Giving an example often helps.)
Demonstrate	Show function.
Describe	Present major characteristics.
Differentiate	Distinguish between two (or more) things.
Discuss (Review)	Give a general presentation of the question. (Give examples or details to support the main points.)
Enumerate	Present all the items in a series, as on a numbered list or outline.
Experiment	Try different solutions to find the right one.
Explain	Show how and why; clarify.
Formulate	Devise a rule workable in other situations; put together new parts in several ways.
Identify	Label or explain.
Illustrate	Present examples.
Interpret	Explain the meaning of one thing in the context of another.
Justify	Give reasons why; argue in support of a position.
Organize	Put together ideas in an orderly pattern.
Outline	Present main points and essential details.
Perform (Solve, Calculate)	Work through the steps of a problem.
Propose	Suggest a new idea of your own for consideration.
Restate	Express the original meaning of something in new words.
Revise	Put together items in new order.
Sketch (Diagram)	Outline; draw picture or graph.
Summarize	Present core ideas.
Trace	Present a sequence; start at one point and go backward or forward in order of events.
Translate	Convert from one system to another.

As you read the directions, *circle or underline the guiding words* so that you know exactly what is required of you. This will help you achieve Standards #2 and #3—making your answer *complete* and *accurate*.

Often, for instance, I will ask students to "compare and contrast" two ideas. However, some students will show only the similarities ("compare") and not the differences ("contrast"), thus answering only half the question and getting only half the points. Circling guiding words will help you avoid such oversights.

■ *If you have a choice of essay questions, read them all:* Some tests will allow you to choose which of, say, two or three essay questions you want to answer. In order to take your best shot, read *all* such questions, circling the guiding words. Then pick the essay question you think you can answer best.

■ *Brainstorm ideas:* Now it's time to go to work by doing some brainstorming and then making an outline. It's best to make your notes on a separate sheet of scratch paper. (If you use a part of the exam-questions sheet or blue book, be sure to cross them out afterward. You don't want to confuse the grader and have your notes figured into your point values— unless you're attaching the outline because you've run out of writing time.)

Here's how to proceed:

1. Do a little brainstorming. *Brainstorming* **means jotting down all the ideas that come to mind** in response to the directions in the question. Just blow out as many ideas as you can that seem to be pertinent. Do this for a minute or two. This will help ensure that you haven't left anything out—helping you to achieve Standard #2, *completeness*.

2. Next, read through your notes and *underline the important ideas*. These will become the basis for your outline and your essay.

■ *Make an outline of your prospective answer:* At this point you may feel under extreme pressure to simply begin writing. However, by taking another minute to make an outline you will help achieve Standard #4—your answer will be *organized*.

Many students find that a certain formula for an outline seems to help them organize their thoughts and touch on the main points of the answer. The outline formula consists of three parts— Your Position, Supporting Details, and Summary. (See ■ Panel 7.2.)

PANEL 7.2 **O**utline of the parts of a long-answer essay.** The answer consists of three parts: (1) Your Position, (2) Supporting Details, and (3) Summary. This is the response you might make to a question in a criminal justice course: "Criticize or defend the proposition that capital punishment benefits society."

THE ESSAY QUESTION:
CRITICIZE OR DEFEND THE PROPOSITION THAT CAPITAL PUNISHMENT BENEFITS SOCIETY.

POSSIBLE OUTLINE FOR ANSWER:

Part 1, Your Position:
State your position in response to essay question.

1. Doesn't benefit.

Part 2, Supporting Details:
List key words representing 3 or so facts supporting your position.

2. Why not:
   a. Doesn't deter murders (FBI stats—compare states)
   b. Innocent executed (names)
   c. C.P. applied more to poor than rich (names)

Part 3, Summary:
Restate your position; include supporting "mini-fact."

3. C.P. not mark of civilized society. Canada, England, Japan lower murder rate, no C.P.

Part 1, *Your Position,* states your position or viewpoint in response to the question being asked. It says what you are going to write about.

Part 2, *Supporting Details,* lists the supporting evidence for your position. These might be three or more facts. In your outline, jot down key words that represent these facts.

Part 3, *Summary,* restates your position. It may include an additional supporting "minifact."

One reason for making an outline is that *if you run out of time and can't finish, you can attach the outline to your test answer and get partial credit.*

■ ***Do Part 1, Your Position, by rewriting or restating the test question, stating your position, and listing the evidence:*** Begin writing Part 1 of the essay. If you follow the for-mula for the first paragraph that we describe, you will show your instructor that you are achieving Standard #5—your answer is *logical.*

1. In the first sentence, include part of the examination question in your answer (without using the exact same words the instructor used). This will help you overcome inertia or anxiety and get going.

2. Next, state the position or point of view you will take.

3. Then list, in sentence form, the facts you will discuss as evidence to support your position, starting with the strongest points in order to make a good impression.

Your first paragraph might read as shown in the accompanying example. *(See* ■ *Panel 7.3.)*

PANEL 7.3

Example of a first paragraph for a long-answer essay. The first sentence restates the examination question or direction. The second sentence states the position you will take. The third, four, and fifth sentences list the facts you will discuss as evidence to support your position.

THE ESSAY QUESTION OR DIRECTION:

CRITICIZE OR DEFEND THE PROPOSITION THAT CAPITAL PUNISHMENT BENEFITS SOCIETY.

THE FIRST PARAGRAPH OF YOUR LONG-ANSWER ESSAY:

Whether capital punishment actually benefits society has long been a controversial issue in the United States.

[This first sentence somewhat restates the test question.]

I will argue that in the long run it does not.

[This second sentence states your position.]

As evidence, I offer the following supporting facts: First, capital punishment has not been found to deter future murders. Second, some innocent prisoners have been executed by mistake. Third, capital punishment is applied disproportionately to poor people.

[These last three sentences list the supporting facts for your position, which you will develop in subsequent paragraphs.]

Let us consider these three facts . . .

[This is a transition sentence. You will now develop each of the three facts into a full paragraph.]

Do Part 2, Supporting Details, by expanding each fact into a paragraph: Now you take the supporting facts you stated in sentence form in the first paragraph and address them separately. Take each fact and expand it into a full paragraph with supporting details. *(See ■ Panel 7.4.)* Use transitional sentences to connect the supporting details so that the reader can follow the progress of your discussion.

■ **Do Part 3, Summary, by writing a paragraph summarizing your position and adding a supporting minifact:** The conclusion is basically a summary paragraph in which you simply restate your position. If you have an additional supporting minifact (or a supporting detail you've forgotten until now), this can punch up your ending a bit and bring your essay to a dramatic close. *(See ■ Panel 7.5.)*

■ **As you write your essay, make sure it's clear:** Here are some tips to help you achieve Standard #6—*clarity.*

1. *Write legibly,* using a pen rather than a pencil (which is difficult to read) and writing neatly rather than using a frantic scrawl. Because, as we said, grading of essay questions is somewhat subjective, you don't want to irritate the instructor by making your answer hard to read and risk lowering your points.

2. *Write on one side of the paper only.* Writing on both sides will make the ink show through. Writing on one side also leaves you the opposite side of the page as a place to write an insert later in case you've forgotten something.

3. *Leave generous space between paragraphs and in the margin.* Leaving space gives you an opportunity to add material later in such a way that you don't have to cram it in and make it hard to read.

4. *Proofread.* If you have time, go back over your answer and check for grammar, spelling, and legibility so as to boost the clarity of your effort.

■ **Watch your time:** Throughout the test you should keep track of your time, periodically checking to see how much time you have left. Answer the easy questions first to build confidence, but after that give more time to questions that are worth more points.

PANEL 7.4 — **Example of expansion of supporting fact into a paragraph.**

Let us consider these three facts. One of the strongest arguments for capital punishment is that the example of execution of murderers deters others from committing murders themselves. Thus, we would expect homicide rates to be lower in states with capital punishment laws than in states without them. However, this is not always the case. According to FBI crime statistics,

[Notice the supporting detail.]

homicide rates in Southern states, most of which feature capital punishment, are higher than they are in many states in the Midwest, in which the strongest penalty for a homicide conviction is a life sentence. For instance, Georgia, which has capital punishment, has a higher murder rate than Minnesota, which does not.

[Notice additional supporting detail.]

Proponents of capital punishment also assume that the criminal justice system doesn't make mistakes . . .

[Notice the transition sentence to the next paragraph of supporting evidence.]

PANEL 7.5 — **Example of summary paragraph.**

In conclusion, I believe capital punishment is not the mark of a civilized society but rather its opposite.

[This first sentence restates your position.]

Other nations of the developed world, with far lower homicide rates than ours—Canada, England, Japan—have long since abolished this extreme form of punishment.

[This second sentence adds a last supporting mini-fact.]

It's time that we join them.

The Important Matter
of Academic Integrity

PREVIEW & REVIEW Academic integrity or honesty is very important. Types of dishonesty include the following: (1) Cheating, or using unauthorized help. (2) Plagiarism, or presenting someone else's ideas as one's own. (3) Fakery, or inventing material. (4) Lying, by omission or commission. People commit such dishonest behaviors for several reasons: (1) They think what they're doing is a "white lie that won't hurt anyone." (2) They are in a crisis and are desperate. (3) They think "everyone does it." You can determine whether behavior is ethical by looking at yourself in the mirror, asking what your parents or friends would say, or asking if you could defend the behavior in court. Penalties for dishonesty in higher education could be a failing grade, suspension, or expulsion. Alternatives to cheating are (1) being prepared or (2) negotiating with the instructor.

As a student I used to think test taking was often a matter of luck or having some sort of inherited smarts. However, you can see from the foregoing that it's pretty much a *learned* skill. And there's no question you're capable of learning it.

GROUP ACTIVITY #7.2

APPLYING EXAM STRATEGIES

Take a few minutes to look through Chapter 5 (on recall and reading) and write out five examination-style questions based on that material: *one example each* of true-false, multiple-choice, matching, fill-in, and subjective (essay) questions. Join with four other people and exchange all your questions (25 in all) with another team.

With the four people in your team, work through all the 25 questions you've received. Apply the techniques learned in this section to try to solve them. Share your strategies with the rest of the class.

At some point in this book we need to consider the matter of academic integrity or honesty. This is as good a place as any, since one of the areas where problems arise is cheating on tests.

There are all kinds of ways to be less than honest in higher education: use crib sheets for tests, exchange signals with other test takers, give instructors false reasons for being late ("I was ill"; "I had car problems"), plagiarize term papers (pass off others' material as your own), buy "canned" term papers prepared by commercial firms—the devices are endless.

HOW WOULD YOU RESPOND TO CHALLENGES TO HONESTY?

College can throw you into situations that pose basic ethical conflicts. To see how you might fare, answer the following:

1. If I were in a classroom taking a final exam and saw two friends exchanging secret signals about the answers, I would do the following:

   a. Tell them afterward that I was ticked off because I'd studied hard and they hadn't, and their cheating might affect my grade.

   ❑ Yes   ❑ No

   b. Probably say nothing to them.

   ❑ Yes   ❑ No

   c. Report them in an unsigned (anonymous) note to the instructor.

   ❑ Yes   ❑ No

   d. Complain personally to the instructor.

   ❑ Yes   ❑ No

2. If I saw two students who were unknown to me exchanging secret signals in a test situation, I would do the following:

   a. Do nothing about it, although I might be contemptuous of them or even upset.

   ❑ Yes   ❑ No

   b. Report them in an unsigned (anonymous) note to the instructor, identifying their location in the classroom and what I saw.

   ❑ Yes   ❑ No

   c. Complain personally to the instructor.

   ❑ Yes   ❑ No

3. I wouldn't cheat on a test myself, but I would not turn in a friend who cheated.

   ❑ Yes   ❑ No

4. Lying about why I am late with a paper or missed a class is just a "white lie" that harms no one.

   ❑ Yes   ❑ No

5. Higher education (and the world) is so competitive that sometimes you have to bend the rules just to survive.

   ❑ Yes   ❑ No

6. So many people cheat. Cheating is wrong only if you get caught.

   ❑ Yes   ❑ No

7. If you don't cheat, you're just an honest loser in a world where other people are getting ahead by taking shortcuts.

   ❑ Yes   ❑ No

8. I try to be honest most of the time, but sometimes I get in a jam for time and am forced to cheat.

   ❑ Yes   ❑ No

9. There's nothing wrong with buying a term paper written by someone else and passing it off as my own.

   ❑ Yes   ❑ No

10. If instructors look the other way or don't seem to be concerned about cheating, then I'd be a fool not to take advantage of the system and cheat.

    ❑ Yes   ❑ No

■ MEANING OF THE RESULTS

See the discussion in the text.

GROUP ACTIVITY OPTION

The class is divided into small groups. Each group is asked to consider a different question from this Personal Exploration. After debating the question, share your conclusions and reasoning with the rest of the class.

A good place to examine one's values is in the area of academic honesty. To get a sense of some of the areas you may well encounter, take a look at Personal Exploration #7.2.

TYPES OF ACADEMIC DISHONESTY. Academic dishonesty is of several principal types—cheating, plagiarism, fakery, and lying:

■ *Cheating: Cheating* **is using unauthorized help to complete a test, practice exercise, or project.** This can mean writing

crib notes of critical dates and names for a history test on one's shirt cuff or under the bill of a baseball cap. It can mean arranging a signal with other test takers to exchange answers. It can mean stealing a look at someone else's exam booklet or of a copy of the test before it is given out. It can mean copying someone else's laboratory notes, field project notes, or computer project.

■ *Plagiarism:* _Plagiarism_ **means presenting another person's ideas as one's own.** For example, some students, having no opinions of their own about, say, a novel they've been assigned to write a report about in English, may try to pass off the comments of a literary critic as their own. (If you can't come up with any ideas of your own but simply *agree* with the critic's ideas, that's okay. Only be sure to *cite* the critic.)

■ *Fakery:* _Fakery_ **is when a person makes up or fabricates something.** Inventing data for a science experiment, for example, is fakery.

■ *Lying:* _Lying_ **is misrepresentation of the facts. Lying may be by omission or commission.**

In lying by *omission,* crucial facts are left out. For example, a student might explain a late paper with "I had computer problems" when really the person whose computer she often borrows had to use it.

In lying by *commission,* facts are changed. For example, a student might say his paper was late "because I was sick" when in fact he was just partying.

The most outrageous—and risky— form of lying is passing off work as your own on which you have expended very little or no effort—for example, a term paper bought from a commercial firm or recycled from a former student in the course.

WHY TO PEOPLE LIE OR CHEAT? According to Sissela Bok, professor of ethics at Brandeis University and author of the book *Lying,* people lie or cheat for one of three principal reasons:[4]

■ *Just a little white lie:* People say to themselves they're just telling a little white lie. "It doesn't hurt anybody," they say, "so who cares?" Often, however, the lie *does* hurt somebody. In a course in which students are graded on a curve, for example, the honest term-paper writers who gave up their weekends to meet a course deadline may be hurt by the person who stayed up partying, then lied about being sick when handing in the paper late.

■ *Desperation:* People may feel obliged to cheat because of a crisis. To save face with themselves they may say, "I don't usually do this, but here I really have to do it." This is the rationalization of students handing in a phony research paper bought from a term-paper factory because they didn't allow themselves enough time to research and write the paper themselves.

■ *"Everyone does it":* This is a very common excuse. As one graduate student at the Massachusetts Institute of Technology said, commenting on a cheating scandal attributed to extreme academic pressures, students see cheating take place and "feel they have to. People get used to it, even though they know it's not right."[5]

People who cheat in higher education, suggests University of Southern California psychology professor Chaytor Mason, are those "who don't think they're smart enough to make it by themselves. One of the greatest threats people feel is being considered unacceptable or stupid."[6]

Many people who are bent on cheating, then, are probably less concerned with looking like a crook than with looking like a schnook. And that certainly shows *their* values. Clearly, this dilemma can be avoided by developing adequate study skills and scheduling enough time for studying.

I discuss term-paper cheating further in Chapter 8.

IMAGINING YOU'RE FOUND OUT. If cheating seems to have been widespread in some places, ethics appear to be making a comeback. According to Michael Josephson, head of the Los Angeles–based Joseph and Edna Josephson Institute for the Advancement of Ethics, studies show that "90% of adults say they want to be considered ethical."[7] According to an executive for The Roper Organization, polls show that students in higher education are deeply concerned with "the moral and ethical standards in our country."[8] Thus, the place for ethics and morality starts with you.

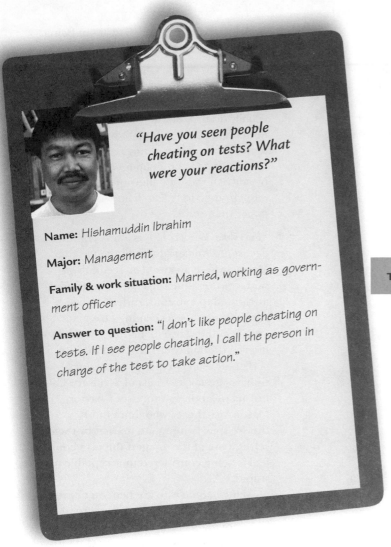

"Have you seen people cheating on tests? What were your reactions?"

Name: Hishamuddin Ibrahim

Major: Management

Family & work situation: Married, working as government officer

Answer to question: "I don't like people cheating on tests. If I see people cheating, I call the person in charge of the test to take action."

If you have any doubt about the ethical question of something you're doing, you might put yourself through a few paces recommended by a crisis-management expert for business people who are worried about whether they are committing fraud:[9]

■ **The Smell Test:** Can you look yourself in the eye and tell yourself that the position you have taken or the act you are about to undertake is okay? Or does the situation have a bad smell to it? If it does, start over.

■ **The What-Would-Your-Parents-Say Test:** This is far more demanding. Could you explain to your parents (or family) the basis for the action you are considering? If they are apt to give you a raised eyebrow, abandon the idea. (You might actually have to deal with your parents or family, of course, if you were found to be cheating and were expelled from school.)

■ **The Deposition Test:** A deposition is testimony taken under oath by lawyers. Could you swear in court that the activity you are doing is right? Or if a future employer or graduate or professional school asked if your grades were satisfactory, could you show them a transcript of your courses containing no F's—the automatic failing grade given students caught cheating?

THE PENALTIES FOR CHEATING. No matter how much you might be able to rationalize cheating to yourself or anyone else, ignorance of the consequences is not an excuse. Most schools spell out the rules somewhere against cheating or plagiarizing. These may be embodied in student codes handed out to new students at the beginning of the year. Where I teach, instructors frequently give students a handout, as I do, at the first class that states that "If reasonable evidence exists that indicates you have cheated, you will receive a failing grade."

In general, the penalties for cheating are as follows:

■ **Failing grade:** You might get a failing grade on the test, the course, or both. This is the slap-on-the-wrist punishment. Actually, it's usually automatic with a cheating or plagiarism offense and is given out *in addition to* other penalties.

Of course, if you think you might fail the course anyway, you might be inclined to think, "Why not take the chance and cheat?" The reason not to do it is the *additional penalties,* which could vitally affect your future—as well as your feelings about yourself.

■ **Suspension:** <u>Suspension</u> **means you are told you cannot return to school for a given amount of time,** usually a semester or quarter or a year.

■ **Expulsion:** <u>Expulsion</u> **means you are kicked out of school permanently;** you are not allowed to return. This penalty is especially bad because it could make it very difficult to transfer to another school.

ALTERNATIVES TO CHEATING: PREPARATION & NEGOTIATION. Some students cheat routinely, but most do so only once, probably because they are desperate.[10] Let me make some suggestions on how one can avoid cheating at all:

- **Be prepared:** The obvious advice is simple: be prepared. This usually comes down to a matter of developing your time-management and study skills. Overcoming bad habits such as procrastination or spending too much time on nonacademic matters will probably keep you from even thinking of cheating. Getting the assistance of a tutor may also help.

- **Negotiate with the instructor for more time:** So your instructor is an intimidating figure? You assume he or she won't listen to an explanation of your situation? As an instructor myself, I understand how it's possible to fall behind and I'm always open to a reasonable explanation from my students.

Note that there may be other times in your life when you'll have to nervously explain to some authority figure why something you were responsible for didn't work out. Explaining to an instructor why you need more time to study for a test or to write a paper is simply practice for those other occasions. It's possible you could push back the deadline a couple of days, which may be all you need. Or you might need to take an "Incomplete" in the course, which would allow you to make it up the following term. (Some schools, however, allow "Incompletes" only for medical reasons.)

Of course it's possible the instructor may deny your request, but at least you made the effort. If that's the case, grit your teeth, pull an all-nighter, do the best you can in the short time you have, and make a resolution never to put yourself in this bind again. Learning from experience is the first step toward change.

But don't cheat. That could really mess up your future. And it certainly reflects poorly on the values you would like to think you hold.

GROUP ACTIVITY #7.3

HAVE YOU EVER CHEATED? WHAT DO YOU THINK OF CHEATERS?

This is a classwide discussion activity. On a piece of scratch paper describe in 25 words or less one of the following: (a) an incident in which you cheated in school; (b) an incident of cheating you observed in school; (c) an incident of cheating you observed in some other situation.

Don't put your name on the paper. Carefully fold up your answer, which will be collected along with those of everyone else in the class. Students will then take turns coming to the front of the class, drawing one of the folded comments from a hat or box, then reading it aloud. Discuss the comments.

What are the rules of your school's academic integrity standards? (If you don't know, look them up in the school's catalog.)

Onward: Applying This Chapter to Your Life

PREVIEW & REVIEW This important chapter covered test-taking techniques and honesty.

This is an important chapter because it shows you valuable techniques for being successful on tests. It also asks you to take a hard look at matters of academic honesty and how they relate to your core values. What did you find in this chapter that you can apply in the world outside of higher education? Write it down here:

_____

_____

_____

_____

_____

Real Practice Activities for Real People

Staying power

REAL PRACTICE ACTIVITY #7.1: WHAT SPECIFIC TEST-TAKING TECHNIQUES WILL HELP YOU MOST ON FUTURE QUIZZES & EXAMS? This practice activity is to be performed in class in small groups, with individuals completing lists of goals designed to help them in their test taking. Later, after students have taken a test in this course or other courses, there may be class discussion in which students describe the impact of their lists on their test-taking performance.

College requires that students demonstrate more perseverence, more staying power than was probably required of them in high school. That means taking more responsibility for their actions, such as in determining what kind of information and questions they anticipate on tests and how to handle them.

Using the information in this chapter, list ten test-taking techniques that you feel would help you most in taking quizzes and exams in the future (and thereby help you persist in college). Express the techniques as goals to achieve when taking tests from now on.

Mindfulness

REAL PRACTICE ACTIVITY #7.2: USING CRITICAL THINKING TO APPLY TEST RESULTS TO FUTURE TESTS. This practice activity may be performed in small groups in class or by individuals out of class in the form of reaction papers. The results may be shared in class discussion.

Frequently, when students receive their marked-up tests back after a quiz or exam, they take a quick look at the grade and then either rejoice in their accomplishment or grimly put the test away, learning little from the experience.

This practice exercise requires that you evaluate the results of a quiz or exam you have taken recently. First, identify your strengths and weaknesses regarding the material covered. (That is, how well did you know the content on which you were being tested?) Second, evaluate your test-taking skills. (For example, do you have more difficulty with certain types of objective questions, or did the short-answer or essay questions give you problems?) Finally, apply the steps in critical thinking presented in Chapter 2 to help you improve your test-taking skills.

Information technology

REAL PRACTICE ACTIVITY #7.3: USING A PERSONAL COMPUTER TO HELP PREPARE FOR TEST ESSAY QUESTIONS. This activity should be practiced individually by students outside of class. The instructor may ask that the results be handed in as reaction papers or discussed in class.

Significant accomplishments—such as those realized by athletes, musicians, actors, and, yes, test takers—usually come about because of continual rehearsal and practice. One kind of test question for which most students unfortunately do little practicing is the essay question. This practice activity is designed to give you a head start in this area.

At your instructor's direction, prepare for your next exam in this course or some other course by identifying three areas in which (to judge from the emphases and clues given by the instructor) you are apt to be asked an essay question. Using the word processing program on a personal computer, ask yourself the essay questions you might expect. Beneath each question make an outline of the response you plan to give, following the technique discussed in this chapter.

The Examined Life

JOURNAL ENTRY #7.1: HOW HAVE YOU PRE-PARED FOR TESTS IN THE PAST? Consider how you have prepared for tests in the past. How successful has your routine been? Which techniques would you take from this chapter that you would use in the future?

_____

_____

_____

_____

_____

_____

_____

_____

_____

_____

JOURNAL ENTRY #7.2: HOW AFFECTED ARE YOU BY TEST ANXIETY? How big a roadblock is test anxiety for you? Which techniques will you try to employ to reduce it next time?

_____

_____

_____

_____

_____

_____

_____

_____

_____

_____

JOURNAL ENTRY #7.3: WHAT TYPES OF TESTS ARE DIFFICULT FOR YOU? What kinds of tests do you do the worst on—true-false, multiple-choice, matching, fill-in-the-blank, short-answer essay, or long-answer essay? How will you change your approach in the future?

_____

_____

_____

_____

_____

_____

_____

_____

_____

_____

_____

_____

_____

_____

JOURNAL ENTRY #7.4: WHAT ABOUT CRAMMING FOR TESTS? Are you used to cramming for tests? How do you feel about this method? How will you break this habit in the future?

_____

_____

_____

_____

_____

_____

_____

_____

_____

_____

_____

_____

JOURNAL ENTRY #7.5: WHAT PROBLEMS OF ACADEMIC INTEGRITY HAVE YOU COME UP AGAINST? Everyone gets in a jam for time now and then. What difficulties have you encountered where you were tempted to cheat? What did you do? What would you do in a similar situation in the future?

_____

_____

_____

_____

_____

_____

_____

_____

_____

_____

Writing & Speaking

Making Powerful Written & Oral Presentations

IN THIS CHAPTER Does the idea of having to write a paper or give a speech make you ill? Maybe that's because you don't have a formula for doing it. You'll probably have to write a number of papers in school—and in your career (when they're called "reports"). Now's your chance, then, to develop a strategy for writing papers. This chapter shows the following:

■ **How to target your audience:** What instructors look for in a written presentation, such as a research paper.

■ **Making a written presentation:** The five phases of conceptualizing, researching, and writing a paper.

■ **How to use information technology:** How to use computers and the Internet—and how not to use them.

■ **Making an oral presentation:** Giving a talk or speech.

Writing papers and giving oral reports is mainly just academic busywork and not required much outside of college—right?

That's what I used to think. I thought doing papers and reports were temporary skills I had to learn so instructors would have some basis for grading me.

After I graduated, however, I found out otherwise. The ability I had developed in researching, writing, and speaking, I discovered, was *very* important in building a career. If you need to research a business report, make a presentation to clients, or contribute to a newsletter, for instance, you'll be glad you learned how.

Indeed, the new companies in the computer industry consider so-called "soft skills"—the ability to communicate well with others and to work effectively in teams—essential for all but the most technical jobs. Because of the way today's organizations work, "you can have the smartest person, but if they can't get along in a group or a team, or if they don't have self-managing capabilities, they'll fail," says Mary Ann Ellis, director of human resources for Raychem Corp. in California.[1]

For now, though, it's a great benefit to learn how to think creatively and critically. It's also a benefit to learn how to use the library, pull information together, and present your research well. These are vital skills for success in higher education. In this chapter, we'll consider the following:

- What instructors look for in a term paper

- How to use computers and the Internet for research

- How to write a paper

- How to give an oral presentation

What Do Instructors Look for in a Term Paper?

PREVIEW & REVIEW Instructors grade term papers according to three criteria: (1) demonstration of originality and effort; (2) demonstration that learning took place; (3) neatness, correctness, and appearance of the presentation.

Writing may be something you do for yourself. For instance, you can keep a journal or diary about your feelings, observations, and happenings (as I've urged throughout this book); this is *personal writing*. Or you can write songs or poetry or musings; this is *expressive writing*. Or you can keep private notes about something you're working on, to help you sort out what you think. Here, however, let us consider a kind of writing you do for other people: term papers for instructors.

Think about the meaning of the word "term" in *term paper*. Doing the paper is supposed to take the greater part of a school *term*—that is, a semester or quarter. Thus, it is supposed to be a paper based on extensive research of a specific subject. When finished it should probably run 10 or more double-spaced pages done on a typewriter or word processor (equivalent to about 20 handwritten pages). Sometimes you may have to give an oral presentation instead of writing a paper, but much of the work is the same. Because so much effort is required, no wonder instructors often consider the term paper to be worth *50% of the course grade*. This suggests why it's worth giving it your best shot, not just knocking it out over a weekend (equivalent to cramming for a test).

Perhaps the best way to get oriented is to ask, *How do instructors grade term papers?* There are probably three principal standards:[2]

- Demonstration of originality and effort

- Demonstration that learning took place

- Neatness, correctness, and appearance of the presentation

DEMONSTRATION OF ORIGINALITY & EFFORT. Are the ideas in your paper original and does the paper show some effort? Instructors are constantly on the lookout for papers that do not represent students' own thoughts and efforts. These papers can take three forms, ranging from most serious (and dangerous to the student) to least serious:

- *"Canned" or lifted papers:* Canned papers are those bought from commercial term-paper-writing services or rewritten or lifted from old papers, as from those in a fraternity-house file.

    Beware of submitting a paper that is not your own. The instructor might recognize it as the work of a student who was there before you or suspect the style is not yours. If you're found out, you'll not only flunk the course but probably will be put on some form of academic probation. This means you might be suspended or expelled from school.

- *Plagiarized papers:* The ideas or expressions in a paper are ***plagiarized*** **if they are another person's passed off as one's own**—copying passages from another source without giving credit to the source, for instance.

    Most instructors have a sensitivity to plagiarism. They can tell when the level of thought or expression does not seem appropriate for student writing. Moreover, lifting others' ideas goes against the very nature of why you're supposed to be in college to begin with. That is, you're supposed to be here to learn ways to meet challenges and expand your competence. In any case, plagiarism can also result in an F in the course and possible suspension from school.

- *Unoriginal, no-effort papers:* Quite often students submit papers that *show no thought and effort.* They consist of simply quoting and citing—that is, rehashing—the conflicting ideas of various experts and scholars. There is no evidence that the student has weighed the various views and demonstrated some critical thinking. A 10-page paper that shows original thinking is always better than a 20-page paper with lots of footnotes but no insights of your own.

    This leads us to the second point, about learning.

DEMONSTRATION THAT LEARNING TOOK PLACE. Instructors want to see you demonstrate that you've learned something—the very reason you're supposed to be in college in the first place.

How do you show that you're learning? My suggestion: ask a question for which the term paper provides the answer. Examples of questions are as follows:

"Do men and women view 'date rape' differently?"

"Are alcohol and cigarettes really gateway drugs to illegal drug use?"

"How did the Vietnam War affect the U.S. approach to the war in Bosnia?"

"What's the best way to dispose of radioactive waste?"

Always try, if you can, to make the question one that's important or interesting to you. That way you'll be genuinely motivated to learn something from the answer. At the end of your paper, you'll be able to demonstrate that learning took place. For example, you might conclude: "When I first looked into the question of date rape, I wondered whether men and women view the matter differently. As the research in this paper has shown, I have found that . . ."

NEATNESS, CORRECTNESS, & APPEARANCE OF PRESENTATION. Like most readers, instructors prefer neatness over messiness, readability over unreadability. Studies show that instructors give papers a higher grade if they are neat and use correct spelling and grammar. The third standard, then, involves form. Is your paper typed and proofread and does it follow the correct form for footnotes and references?

Consider these points:

■ **Typed versus handwritten:** All instructors *prefer*—and many *require*—that you hand in a paper that has been produced on a word processor or a typewriter rather than handwritten. Even if you're only a hunt-and-peck typist, try to render the final version of your term paper on a word processor or typewriter. (A word processor is easier for people who make lots of typing mistakes.) Or hire someone else to type it.

■ **Correct spelling and grammar:** As you write, look up words in the dictionary to check their spelling. Proofread the final version to correct any mistakes and bad grammar. If you're using a word processor, run the final draft through spelling-checker and grammar-checking programs, but also read it over yourself, since those programs won't catch everything.

You may be sick and tired of your paper when you finally get done with it. Nevertheless, you would hate to blow it at the end by allowing the instructor to mark it down because you overlooked the small stuff.

■ **Follow correct academic form:** Different academic disciplines (English and psychology, for example) have their preferred footnote and bibliography styles. Be sure to follow any directions your instructor gives for these and any other requirements for the form of the paper.

Now you know what you're aiming for. Let's see how to achieve it.

Information technology

Writing a Term Paper: Five Phases

The five phases of producing a term paper are as follows. (1) Pick a topic. (2) Do initial research and develop an outline. (3) Do further research. (4) Sort notes, revise the outline, and write a first draft. (5) Revise, type, and proofread the paper.

The audience for a term paper, I said, is an instructor. Writing for instructors is different from other writing. It's not the same, for example, as an essay accompanying an application for admission to university, college, or vocational-technical school. Nor is it the same as an article for the school paper or a letter of complaint to a landlord or government official. Nor is term-paper writing the same as writing an article for an academic journal; it is usually less formal and rigorous.

In this section I explain how to prepare a term paper for an instructor. There are five principal phases:

- *Phase 1:* Picking a topic

- *Phase 2:* Doing initial research and developing a preliminary outline

- *Phase 3:* Doing your research—using the library

- *Phase 4:* Sorting your notes, revising the outline, and writing a first draft

- *Phase 5:* Revising, typing, and proofreading your paper—employing critical thinking

Be aware that the grade on the term paper will count heavily toward the grade in the course. Thus, you should try to spread these phases over the semester or quarter—not do them all in one week or a few days.

Phase 1: Picking a Topic

The first phase, *picking a topic,* has four parts. (1) Set a deadline for picking a topic. (2) Pick a topic important to the instructor and interesting to you. (3) Refine proposed topics into three questions. (4) Check topics with the instructor.

Phase 1 consists of picking a topic. This has four parts:

- Set a deadline for picking the topic

- Pick a topic important to the instructor and interesting to you

- Refine your proposed topics into three questions

- Check with your instructor

SET A DEADLINE FOR PICKING YOUR TOPIC. Students often procrastinate on this first step. However, the most important advice I can give you about writing papers is: START EARLY. By beginning early, you'll be able to find a topic that interests you. Moreover, you'll avoid pitfalls such as picking a subject that is too narrow or too large.

Thus, *as soon as you get your instructor's guidelines for the term paper, set a deadline for picking the topic.* In your lecture notes, on a page by itself, write a big note to yourself:

*** *DEADLINE:* PICK TERM PAPER TOPIC BY TUESDAY NOON! ***

In addition, put this on your To-Do list and your weekly planner.

PICKING A TOPIC: TWO CRITERIA. There are two criteria for picking a topic: pick something that is (1) important to your instructor and (2) interesting to you.

- **Topics important to the instructor:** You need to determine what is important to your instructor because he or she is the sole audience for your paper.

  How do you find out what the instructor believes is significant? First, if he or she has provided written guidelines, read them carefully. If the assignment is given verbally, take precise notes. You'll also get a better idea of what's important when you meet with the instructor to discuss your proposed topics.

- **Topics interesting to you:** Motivation is everything. Whenever possible, try to choose a topic that interests you. It also helps if you already know something about it. To determine what might be suitable, look through your lecture notes to see what things pop out at you.

  If you're having trouble nailing down a topic idea, it's good to know how to stimulate creative thinking. As I mentioned in Chapter 2, *creative thinking* consists of imaginative ways of looking at known ideas. Creative thinking not only helps you dream up topics for term papers but also to solve problems for which traditional problem-solving methods don't work. See Chapter 2 for suggestions on how to stimulate ideas.

Mindfulness

EXPRESSING PROPOSED TOPICS AS THREE QUESTIONS. By the time your self-imposed deadline arrives for choosing your topic, you should have three alternative ideas. Because your purpose is to demonstrate that you're learning, these should be expressed as questions.

For example, for an introductory health course, you may decide on the following possible topics.

> *"What diets are most effective for weight loss?"*
>
> *"Does meditation prolong life in cancer patients?"*
>
> *"Does wearing helmets reduce motorcycle injuries?"*

Are some of these questions too broad (diets) or too narrow (helmets)? In the next step, you'll find out.

CHECKING TOPIC IDEAS WITH YOUR INSTRUCTOR. It's now a good idea to take your topic questions and show them to your instructor (after class or during office hours). Questions to ask are the following:

- **Is it important enough?** Ask, "Do you think any of these topics are important enough to be worth exploring in a term paper?" The answer will indicate whether you are meeting the first criterion in selecting a topic—does the instructor think it's significant?

- **Is the scope about right?** Ask, "Do you think the topic is too broad or too narrow in scope?" The instructor may suggest ways to limit or vary the topic so you won't waste time on unnecessary research. He or she can also prevent you from tackling a topic that's too advanced. Equally important, the instructor may be able to suggest books or other resources that will help you in your research.

  What if you're in a large class and have difficulty getting access to your instructor or teaching assistant? In that case, go to the library and ask a reference librarian for an opinion on the topic's importance and scope. In addition, of course, he or she will be able to steer you toward good sources of information for your research.

GROUP ACTIVITY #8.1

GETTING GOING ON A RESEARCH PAPER

With three to five other students, select one of the following topics: horse racing, magnetic resonance imaging (MRI), information literacy, population control, Christmas-tree farming, long-distance running, retirement planning, Mayan ruins. (Or consult with your instructor about another topic.) Develop a number of questions on the topic. Now use the questions to produce an outline. Write your names at the top of the outline and turn it in to the instructor.

Phase 2: Doing Initial Research & Developing an Outline

PREVIEW & REVIEW The beginning of Phase 2, *doing initial research*, consists of using the library's card catalog and guide to periodicals to determine the scope of research material. The second part of Phase 2, *developing an outline,* means doing a tentative outline suggesting the paper's beginning (introduction), middle (body), and end (conclusion). The beginning and middle pose questions you hope your research will answer.

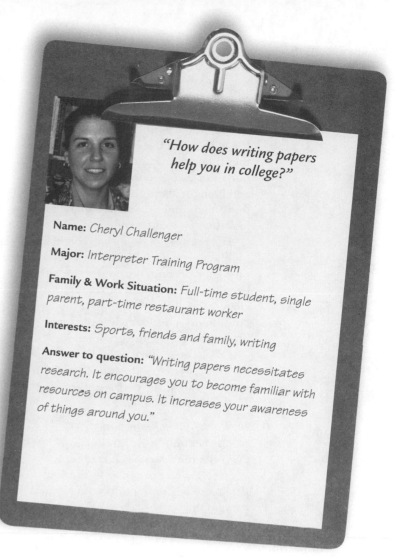

"How does writing papers help you in college?"

Name: *Cheryl Challenger*

Major: *Interpreter Training Program*

Family & Work Situation: *Full-time student, single parent, part-time restaurant worker*

Interests: *Sports, friends and family, writing*

Answer to question: "*Writing papers necessitates research. It encourages you to become familiar with resources on campus. It increases your awareness of things around you.*"

Phase 2 consists of doing initial research and developing an outline. If it took you one week to decide on a topic, it should take you another week to do Phase 2. Here, too, you should write a big note to yourself (and also put it on your weekly calendar and To-Do list):

*** *DEADLINE:* CHECK OUT RESEARCH FOR TERM PAPER BY WEDNESDAY 5 P.M.! ***

The idea here is to satisfy yourself about two things:

- *Research material:* Is enough material available to you so that you can adequately research your paper?

- *Rough outline:* Do you have a rough idea of the direction your paper will take?

INVESTIGATING RESEARCH MATERIAL. This step need not take long—perhaps a half hour in the library. The idea is to look in a handful of places to get a sense of the research material available to you. Here are two possibilities:

- *Card or online catalog:* Look under the subject listing in the library's card catalog or online catalog to see what books

exist on your topic. Don't assume, however, that just because the books are listed that they are easily available. (They may be checked out, on reserve, or in another campus library. An online catalog may tell you if they're checked out.) Look up some call letters for relevant titles, then visit the shelves and see what books you can find.

- *Guide to periodicals:* Magazines and journals are apt to be more up to date than books. Check the *Reader's Guide to Periodical Literature* to see what articles are available in your topic area. Jot down the names of the periodicals, then check with the reference librarian to see if they are available.

Further information about the library, including use of the card catalog and guide to periodicals, is given in Phase 3, Research. This preliminary investigation, however, gives you an overview of the subject.

DEVELOPING AN OUTLINE. While you're in the library doing your first research you should also do a preliminary outline.

Many people resist doing an outline because they think, "I don't know where I'm going until I've been there." That is, they think they won't know their direction until they've done all the research and thought about the material. Or they think an outline is somehow going to lock them in to the wrong approach.

The purpose of doing a preliminary outline now is twofold. First, it saves you time later. Second, it provides you with a general road map. You can always change the outline later. But if you set out without one, you may waste time before you get a sense of direction.

Take a sheet of paper and write *OUTLINE #1* across the top. Then fill in the following three parts—*I. Beginning, II. Middle,* and *III. End.*[3]

I. *BEGINNING—the introduction*

The beginning or introduction describes the *one or two main questions your paper will try to answer.* In the final paper, the beginning will be one or two paragraphs.

Examples: "How smart are college athletes?" "Are college athletics dominated by 'dumb jocks'?"

II. *MIDDLE—the body*

The middle or body of the outline describes *some specific questions your paper will try to answer.* These detailed questions help you answer the main questions.

Examples: "What's the grade-point average (GPA) of college football, baseball, and basketball players?" "What's the GPA of competitive swimmers, gymnasts, and tennis players?" "What percentage of athletes graduate compared to other students?" "What percentage drop out?" "What proportion of athletes in pro sports are college graduates?" "Are top athletes usually top scholars, such as Phi Beta Kappa, magna cum laude, Rhodes Scholars?" And so on.

III. *END—the conclusion*

You won't know the end or conclusion, of course, until you've done the research and answered your questions. For now, *just state that you will write a conclusion based on your answers.*

Here are some techniques for developing your outline:

■ *Write questions on index cards:* Get a stack of 3 × 5 index cards or cut sheets of notepaper into quarters. On each card or quarter-page, write a question you want to answer about your topic. *Write as many questions as you can think of, both general and detailed.*

■ *Organize index cards into categories:* Now sort your 3 × 5 cards into stacks by category. One stack might contain a few general questions that will make up your introduction; the others could comprise the body of the outline.

What categories might you have? Some stacks may be of similar kinds of questions. Some might be advantages and disadvantages, causes and effects, or comparisons and contrasts. Do whatever kind of grouping seems sensible to you.

■ *Write out your outline:* Copy the categories and questions into the outline form shown above. You now have a road map to follow to begin your research.

Note: If you are used to computers, you may find an *outlining program* useful rather than 3 × 5 cards. This kind of software allows you to brainstorm and sort out ideas onscreen.

Information technology

After developing it, show your outline to your instructor. He or she will be able to determine at a glance whether you seem to be headed in the right direction.

Phase 3: Doing Your Research—Using the Library

PREVIEW & REVIEW Phase 3, doing research, usually means using the library. This requires learning the parts of the library; discovering how to use librarians and the catalog; knowing how to locate books, periodicals and journals, and reference materials; and finding out how to use other libraries. Low-tech ways of collecting information involve use of 3 × 5 cards. High-tech ways involve the use of photocopiers and computers.

P hase 3 consists of doing your research, which usually means making use of the library. In this section, let us consider these aspects:

- Parts of the library
- Using librarians and the catalog
- Locating books
- Finding periodicals and journals
- Finding reference materials
- Using other libraries
- Low-tech ways to collect information: 3 × 5 cards
- High-tech ways to collect information: photocopiers and personal computers

FINDING YOUR WAY AROUND THE LIBRARY. Particularly at a large university, you may find that the library is a lot larger than those you're accustomed to. Indeed, there may be several libraries on campus, plus access to libraries elsewhere. The most important one for first-year students is the *central library*, the principal library on campus.

The central library has several parts:

- **Main section:** The main section includes six parts:

1. The desk where you check books out

2. The catalog (card or computerized) listing books

3. A reference section, with dictionaries, encyclopedias, and directories

4. A periodicals section displaying current newspapers, magazines, and journals

5. A section (perhaps called the "stacks") housing books

6. A section housing back issues of periodicals

- **Other sections:** In addition, the central library usually has some special sections:

1. A media center, or section containing audiotapes and videotapes

2. A section for reserve books set aside by instructors for certain courses

3. A vertical file containing pamphlets on special topics

4. A government documents section

- **Other services—study areas and machines:** Most campus libraries also provide study areas. Indeed, because the whole purpose of the library is to enable students to do serious work, there are relatively few distractions.

Finally, there may be several machines available for your use. Examples are machines for reading microfilm and microfiche (materials on film), terminals for accessing databases, and indexes and machines for making photocopies. Some libraries provide typewriters or word processors. Some also have machines providing access to audiotapes, CDs, videotapes, slides, films, filmstrips, videodiscs, computer floppy disks, or CD-ROM disks.

If you have not had a formal orientation to the library, whether on videotape or through an actual tour, now is the time. If possible, do it *before* you're under a tight deadline for a research paper, so you won't have to do your research under panic conditions. Some institutions offer a credit course in how to use the library—something I would recommend to anyone.

The principal resource—the trained navigators, as it were—are the *reference librarians*. Don't hesitate to ask for their help. That's what they're there for. They can tell you if the library has what you need and show you how to get started. Reference librarians are also the people to hunt up when you have exhausted other resources. They may refer you to special sources within the library or to different libraries on or off campus.

HOW TO FIND WHAT YOU WANT IN BOOKS.

Books may be found on open shelves in the main section of the library. In some places, they may also be in the "stacks," requiring a library page or runner to go get them. Or they may be in special libraries located elsewhere on campus, such as those attached to the business school or the law school. Or they may be available by means of *interlibrary loan*, **a service that enables you to borrow books from other libraries.** Allow extra time— several days or even weeks—and perhaps expect to pay a small fee when obtaining a book through interlibrary loan.

To find a book, you will probably use a *CD-ROM catalog* or *online computerized cat-* *alog*, both of which have supplanted the old-fashioned card catalog.

Information technology

■ *CD-ROM computerized catalog:* **_CD-ROM_** **_catalogs_ look like music compact disks (CDs), but they store text and images. CD-ROM stands for Compact Disk— Read Only Memory.** To use a CD-ROM, put the disk into the microcomputer's CD-ROM drive, then follow directions (perhaps on Help screens) for searching by title, author, or subject.

An advantage of CD-ROMs is that you can use key words to search for material. **_Key words_ are words you use to find spe- cific information.** For example, you could use the key words "National Social- ism" to look for books about Hitler and the Nazi Party.

Information technology

■ *Online computerized catalog:* **_Online comput-_** **_erized catalogs_ require that you use a com- puter terminal or microcomputer that has a wired connection to a database.** Online catalogs have all the advantages of CD-ROMs, including the ability to do key- word searches. However, they are more quickly updated. The instructions for using online catalogs appear on the com- puter keyboard or on the display screen (in Help screens). *(See* ■ *Panel 8.1.)*

PANEL 8.1 Online computerized library catalog. Example of a screen showing response to subject or key-word search—in this case, the key words are "National Socialism."

```
                                                              LIBCAT

Your search: S=NATIONAL SOCIALISM
LINE
  #      ------Author---------      ------------------Title------------------   Date
                                                                                1965
  1    Allen, William Sherida    The Nazi seizure of power; the experience      1961
  2    Bossenbrook, William J    The German mind.                               1968
  3    Butler, Rohan d'Olier.    The roots of national socialism, 1783-1933     1986
  4    Engelmann, Bernt, 1921    In Hitler's Germany : daily life in the Th     1970
  5    Fest, Joachim C., 1926    The faces of the Third Reich; portraits of     1978
  6    Glaser, Hermann.          The cultural roots of national socialism /     1988
  7    Herzstein, Robert Edwi    Waldheim : the missing years / Robert Edwi     1965
  8    McRandle, James Harrin    The track of the wolf; essays on national      1966
  9    Mosse, George L. (Geor    Nazi culture: intellectual, cultural, and      1959
 10    Snell, John L., ed.       The Nazi revolution: Germany's guilt or Ge
(More)

Enter:  Line #      (1, 2, 3, etc.) to see more information.
        N           to see Next screen.         P    to see previous screen.
        B           to Backup.                   ST   to start over.
        (UP ARROW)  to view previous commands.

                                              Enter ? for HELP

     >>
```

Note: *Books in Print* is an annual reference work—organized by title, author, and subject—that lists most books currently in print in the United States. By using the subject category you can also find books in your area of research, although they won't necessarily be in your school's library.

Most schools' libraries use the Library of Congress system of call numbers and letters. Get the call numbers from the card or computerized listing, then use a map of the library to find the appropriate shelves. Once you've found your book, look at other books in the general vicinity to see if they could be useful.

If you can't find a book on the shelves and decide you really need it, ask a librarian for help. It may be in the reference section or on reserve for a class. If it has been checked out, ask the library to put a hold on it for you when it's returned. Or ask for help getting another copy through interlibrary loan.

HOW TO FIND WHAT YOU WANT IN NEWSPAPERS, MAGAZINES, & JOURNALS. You can see what general newspapers, magazines, and journals are available by simply looking at the open shelves in the periodicals reading room. A list of the library's holdings in periodicals should also be available at the main desk.

Here are some avenues for finding articles in the research area you're interested in. *(See ■ Panel 8.2.)*

PANEL 8.2 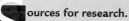 **S**ources for research.

Newspaper indexes: Examples of newspapers printing indexes about articles appearing in their pages are *The New York Times Index* and *The Wall Street Journal Index.* Look also for *Newspaper Abstracts* and *Editorials on File.*

Examples of computerized databases providing information about newspaper articles are *Data Times, Dialog, CompuServe, America Online, Prodigy,* and *Nexis.*

Magazine indexes: The *Readers' Guide to Periodical Literature* lists articles appearing in well-known American magazines.

Other indexes, available in printed, microfilm, or CD-ROM form, are *Magazine Index, Newsbank, InfoTrac, Business Index,* and *Medline.*

Journal indexes and abstracts: Examples of indexes and databases for specialized journals are *Accountants' Index, Applied Science and Technology Index, Art Index, Business Periodicals Index, Computer Data Bases, Education Index, Engineering Index Monthly, General Science Index, Humanities Index, Medline,* and *Social Science Index.*

Examples of indexes called abstracts are *Biological Abstracts, Chemical Abstracts, Historical Abstracts, Psychological Abstracts,* and *Sociological Abstracts.*

Some computerized online indexes to journals are available, such as *PsycLit,* a bibliographic database to *Psychological Abstracts.*

Specialized dictionaries: Examples of specialized dictionaries for technical subjects are *Dictionary of Biological Sciences, Dictionary of Film Terms, Dictionary of Quotations, Dorland's Illustrated Medical Dictionary, Grove's Dictionary of Music and Musicians, Mathematical Dictionary,* and *Webster's New World Dictionary of Computer Terms.*

Encyclopedias, almanacs, and handbooks: Examples of encyclopedias on specialized subjects are *Cyclopedia of World Authors, Encyclopedia of Associations, Encyclopedia of Banking and Finance, Encyclopedia of Bioethics, Encyclopedia of Religion and Ethics, Encyclopedia of Sports, Encyclopedia of World Art, Thomas Register of American Manufacturers,* and *The Wellness Encyclopedia.*

Examples of specialized almanacs, handbooks, and other reference sources are *The Business Writer's Handbook, Comparisons, The Computer Glossary, Facts on File, The Guinness Book of World Records, Keesing's Record of World Events, Literary Market Place, The Pacific Rim Almanac,* and *The Secret Guide to Computers.*

Government literature: Publications published by the U.S. government are listed in *The Monthly Catalog* and *PAIS (Public Affairs Information Service).*

Computer networks: Examples of guides to computerized information networks are *Directory of Online Databases, Encyclopedia of Information Systems and Services,* and *Guide to the Use of Libraries and Information Services.*

- *Newspaper indexes:* In the United States, the newspapers available nationally and in many campus libraries are *The New York Times, The Wall Street Journal,* and *USA Today.* Some schools may also subscribe to other respected newspapers such as *The Washington Post* or *The Los Angeles Times.* Some newspapers print indexes that list information about the articles appearing in their pages. Examples are *The New York Times Index* and *The Wall Street Journal Index.* Look also for *Newspaper Abstracts* and *Editorials on File.*

  In addition, your library may subscribe to computerized databases providing bibliographical information about articles appearing in hundreds of magazines and newspapers. Ask the librarian how you can use *Data Times, Dialog,* or the reference services of *America Online, CompuServe, Microsoft Network, Prodigy,* or *Nexis.*

- *Magazine indexes:* The index for the 100 or so most general magazines, many probably available in your library, is the *Readers' Guide to Periodical Literature.* This lists articles appearing in such well-known magazines as *Time, Newsweek, Reader's Digest,* and *Psychology Today.*

  Other indexes, available in printed, microfilm, or CD-ROM form, are *Magazine Index, Newsbank, InfoTrac, Business Index,* and *Medline.*

- *Journal indexes and abstracts:* Journals are specialized magazines, and their articles are listed in specialized indexes and databases. Examples range from *Applied Science and Technology Index* to *Social Science Index.*

  In addition, there are indexes called **_abstracts_, which present paragraphs summarizing articles along with bibliographical information about them.** Examples range from *Biological Abstracts* to *Sociological Abstracts.*

  Some journal indexes are accessed by going online through a computer. For example, *PsycLit* is a bibliographic database to *Psychological Abstracts.*

HOW TO FIND OTHER REFERENCE MATERIALS. Among other wonderful reference materials available are:

- *Dictionaries, thesauruses, style books:* Need to look up specialized terms for your paper? The reference section of the library has not only standard dictionaries but also specialized dictionaries for technical subjects. Examples range from *Dictionary of Biological Sciences* to *Webster's New World Dictionary of Computer Terms.*

  In addition, you may find a thesaurus helpful in your writing. **A _thesaurus_ lists synonyms, or words with similar meanings.** This is a great resource when you can't think of the exact word you want when writing. Many computers now come with a thesaurus built in.

  Finally, there are various style books for helping you do footnotes and bibliographies, such as *The Chicago Manual of Style.*

- *Encyclopedias, almanacs, handbooks:* No doubt the library has various kinds of standard encyclopedias, in printed and CD-ROM form. As with dictionaries, there are also encyclopedias on specialized subjects. Examples range from *Cyclopedia of World Authors* to *The Wellness Encyclopedia.*

There are also all kinds of specialized almanacs, handbooks, and other reference sources. Examples range from *The Business Writer's Handbook* to *The Secret Guide to Computers*.

Nowadays there are a number of encyclopedias available as software:

■ **Government literature:** A section of the library is probably reserved for information from both the federal government and state and local governments. The most prolific publisher in the world is the United States government. To find out publications pertinent to your subject, look in *The Monthly Catalog* and *PAIS (Public Affairs Information Service).*

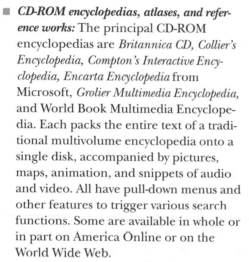

Information technology

■ **CD-ROM encyclopedias, atlases, and reference works:** The principal CD-ROM encyclopedias are *Britannica CD, Collier's Encyclopedia, Compton's Interactive Encyclopedia, Encarta Encyclopedia* from Microsoft, *Grolier Multimedia Encyclopedia,* and World Book Multimedia Encyclopedia. Each packs the entire text of a traditional multivolume encyclopedia onto a single disk, accompanied by pictures, maps, animation, and snippets of audio and video. All have pull-down menus and other features to trigger various search functions. Some are available in whole or in part on America Online or on the World Wide Web.

CD-ROMs are also turning atlases into multimedia extravaganzas. Mindscape's *World Atlas & Almanac,* for instance, combines the maps, color photos, geographical information, and demographic statistics of a traditional book-style atlas with video, sounds, and the ability to immediately find what you want. Maps, for example, may include political charts showing countries and cities, three-dimensional maps showing mountain ranges, and even satellite maps. An audio feature lets you hear the pronunciation of place names. There are also street atlases (*Street Atlas U.S.A., StreetFinder*), which give detailed maps that can pinpoint addresses and show every block in a city or town, and trip planners (*TripMaker, Map 'n' Go*), which suggest routes, attractions, and places to eat and sleep.

Examples of other types of CD-ROM reference works are *Eyewitness History of the World, Eyewitness Encyclopedia of Nature, Skier's Encyclopedia,* and *The Way Things Work.* You can get the full text of 1,750 great works of literature and other books and documents on *Library of the Future.*

There are now hundreds of other resources available on CD-ROMs. *(See ■ Panel 8.3, page 224.)*

Information technology

■ **Computer networks:** This is a vast subject in itself. Now many libraries subscribe to computerized information networks, such as DIALOG, ERIC, ORBIT, and BSR. Directories and guides exist to help you learn to use these services. Examples are *Directory of Online Databases, Encyclopedia of Information Systems and Services,* and *Guide to the Use of Libraries and Information Services.*

I describe some of the problems of using the Internet and the Web in the next major section.

HOW TO USE OTHER LIBRARIES. In big universities, various departments and schools often have their own libraries. Thus, the libraries of, say, the business school or medical school will have material that the main library does not. In addition, you may find a visit to local city or county libraries worthwhile or the libraries of other colleges nearby. Although you probably won't be allowed to check out materials, you can certainly use the materials available to the general public.

LOW-TECH WAYS TO COLLECT INFORMATION: 3×5 CARDS. Some materials (principally books) you'll be able to check out and have access to at your usual writing desk. However, most libraries won't let you take out magazines, encyclopedias, and general reference materials. Thus, you'll need to be able to take notes in the library.

Traditional 3 × 5 index cards are useful because you can write one idea on each card, then later sort the cards as you please. Index cards should be used

More infotech: other CD-ROM information sources.

Clearly CD-ROMs are not just a mildly interesting technological improvement. They have evolved into a full-fledged mass medium of their own, on the way to becoming as important as books or films.

Information technology

- **Education and training:** Want to learn photography? You could look for a pair of CD-ROMs by Bryan Peterson called *Learning to See Creatively* (about composition) and *Understanding Exposure* (discussing the science of exposure). When you pop these disks in your computer, you can practice on screen with lenses, camera settings, film speeds, and the like. Or you could learn history from such CD-ROMs as *Critical Mass: America's Race to Build the Atomic Bomb* or *The War in Vietnam*. CD-ROMs are also available to help students raise their scores on the Scholastic Aptitude Test (*Score Builder for the SAT*, *Inside the SAT*).

- **Edutainment:** Edutainment software consists of programs that look like games but actually teach, in a way that feels like fun. *Multimedia Beethoven: The Ninth Symphony*, an edutainment program for adults, plays the four movements of the symphony while the on-screen text provides a running commentary and allows you to stop and interact with the program.

    You may also explore the inner workings of the human body in *Body Voyage*, a 15-gigabyte CD-ROM package based on Joseph Paul Jernigan, a condemned prisoner executed in 1993. Jernigan gave scientists permission to freeze his body and then cut it into 1,878 slices, 1 millimeter each, which were then photographed and scanned into a computer.

- **Music, culture, and films:** Want to experience a little "rock 'n' ROM"? In *Xplora 1: Peter Gabriel's Secret World*, you can not only hear rock star Gabriel play his songs but also create "jam sessions" in which you can match up musicians from around the world and hear the result.

    Other examples of such CD-ROMs are *Bob Dylan: Highway 61 Interactive*; *Multimedia Beethoven, Mozart,* *Schubert*; *Art Gallery*; *American Interactive*; *A Passion for Art*; and *Robert Mapplethorpe: An Overview*.

    Developers have also released several films on CD-ROM, such as the 1964 Beatles movie *A Hard Day's Night*, *This Is Spinal Tap*, and *The Day After Trinity*.

- **Books and magazines:** Book publishers have hundreds of CD-ROM titles, ranging from *Discovering Shakespeare* and *The Official Super Bowl Commemorative Edition* to business directories such as *ProPhone Select* and *11 Million Businesses Phone Book*.

    In 1993, photographer Rick Smolan pioneered the splashy CD-ROM book with *From Alice to Ocean*, which used text, audio, digital photos, and video clips to tell the story of a young woman's 1,700-mile lone journey by camel through the Australian Outback. In 1995, Smolan and 70 international photographers produced a CD-ROM and accompanying book called *Passage to Vietnam*.

    Examples of CD-ROM magazines are *Blender*, on the subject of music; *Medio*, a general-interest monthly; *Go Digital*; and *Launch*, which aims to offer a look at new music, movies, and computer games.

- **Data storage:** Among the top-selling titles are road maps, typeface and illustration libraries for graphics professionals, and video and audio clips. Publishers are also mailing CD-ROMs on such subjects as medical literature, patents, and law.

    Want to have access to 1,235-plus back issues of *National Geographic* magazines? They're available on 30 CD-ROMs that include every article, photograph, and even advertisement that has appeared in the magazine during its 108-year history.

Three uses of 3 × 5 cards: sources, information, ideas.

---

d. Source card: Use source cards to keep track of bibliographical information.

Anderson, Dave. "Real College Champions Are
the Ones Who Graduate."
New York Times July 6, 1995, p. B5.

---

b. Information card: Use information cards to write down information to be used in the paper; put quoted material in quotation marks.

Anderson 1995 p. B5   Graduation Rates
NCAA issued graduation rates at its 302 Division I
schools for all 1st-year students compared with student-
athletes (men & women) who entered college in 1988-89
school year. No breakdown of sports documented.

"Based on its graduation numbers, Penn State (77% student-athletes, 79% all students) deserved to be the top-
ranked football team last season..."

"Of basketball's Final Four teams, North Carolina had the
best rates (76% student-athletes, 85% all students)."

Idea card: Use idea cards to jot down ideas that occur to you.

IDEA #1

Find out: Do many college athletes not graduate
because they don't have time-management skills
to handle both studies and sports?

---

in three ways—as *source cards, information cards,* and *idea cards.* (See ■ *Panel 8.4.*)

■ **Source cards:** Use *source cards* to keep track of bibliographical information. At the time you're looking up your sources, you can jot down the call letters on these cards. Specifically:

1. For each *journal article:* Write down the author's last and first name (for example, "Wahlstrom, Carl"), title of article, title of journal, month and year, volume and issue number, and page numbers.

2. For each *book:* Write down the author's (or editor's) name, book title, edition, city and state of publication, name of publisher, year of publication (listed on the copyright page), and pages you referred to, if necessary.

   Later, when you type your references, you'll be able to arrange these source cards in alphabetical order by authors' last names.

■ **Information cards:** Use *information cards* to copy down information and quotations. This is the actual research material you will use. The card will have three areas:

1. *Source abbreviation:* At the top of each card, put an abbreviated version of the source, including the page number. (Example: "Wahlstrom 1998, p. 23." If you have two 1998 Wahlstrom references, label them *a* and *b.*) If you use more than one card for a single source, number the cards.

2. *Information:* In the lower part of the card, write the information. If it's a direct quote, enclose it in quotation marks.

3. *Key-word zone:* Reserve the top right corner of the card as a "key-word zone." In this area put one or two key words that will tie the card to a place on your outline. (Example: "Graduation rates.") The key word can also tie the card to a new subject, if it is not on the outline.

■ **Idea cards:** Use *idea cards* to jot down ideas that occur to you. To make sure you don't mix them up with information cards, write "IDEA #1," "IDEA #2," and so on, at the top.

To keep the cards organized, keep them in three separate stacks each wrapped in a rubber band.

HIGH-TECH WAYS TO COLLECT INFORMATION: PHOTOCOPIERS & LAPTOP COMPUTERS. Using 3 × 5 cards is a traditional though low-tech way of collecting information. They can also be somewhat time-consuming, since you're required to write out everything by hand.

Two high-tech ways to collect information in the library are the use of photocopiers and portable computers.

■ *Photocopiers:* When you find an article from which you'd like to quote extensively, it may make sense to simply use the library's photocopying machines. Sometimes this means feeding the machine a lot of dimes, but the time saving may still be worth it. Some libraries allow students to open charge accounts for use of these machines.

For organizing purposes, you can then take scissors and cut up the photocopied material. Then write the source abbreviation and page number in one margin and the "key words" in the other.

Information technology

■ *Laptop computers:* Having a portable computer with a word processing program can be a godsend in collecting library information. (If your library has desktop word processors installed on the premises, you might also be able to use them.) Some researchers also use hypertext programs. An example is the HyperCard software on the Apple Macintosh, which electronically simulates 3 × 5 "cards" and "stacks" that can be manipulated.

Even if you're not very fast on the keyboard, it may still be faster than writing out your information by hand. Follow the same format as you would for 3 × 5 cards.

Personal Exploration #8.1 *(opposite page)* lets you try your hand at researching a topic or author.

Phase 4: Sorting Your Notes, Revising the Outline, & Writing the First Draft

PREVIEW & REVIEW In Phase 4, you first determine your writing place, then sort your notes, revise your outline, and write a thesis statement and working title. You next write your first draft—middle first, then beginning, then end. In writing, you should make your point and give support, quoting experts, avoiding irrelevancies, and giving sources.

P*hase 4 consists of sorting your notes, revising your outline, and writing a first draft of the paper.* The research phase may have taken a lot of work, but now it's time to put it all together.

ESTABLISHING YOUR WRITING PLACE. What kind of writing environment suits you best is up to you. The main thing is that it *help you avoid distractions.* You may also need room to spread out, even be able to put 3 × 5 cards and sources on the floor. If you write in longhand or use a laptop, a table in the library may do. If you write on a typewriter, you may need to use the desk in your room.

Some other tips:

■ *Allow time:* Give yourself plenty of time. A first draft of a major paper should take more than one day.

■ *Reread instructions:* Just before you start to write, reread the instructor's directions regarding the paper. You would hate to find out afterward that you took the wrong approach because you overlooked something.

Ready? Begin.

SORTING YOUR NOTES & REVISING YOUR OUTLINE. In gathering your information, you may have been following the

RESEARCH: LOOKING UP A TOPIC IN THE LIBRARY

Think of a topic that you are required to research for another class or just for your own interest. (Or, if your instructor assigns this as a group activity, you might use the topic you developed in Group Activity #8.1.) Then use three methods to locate three different sources of information about it.

■ A. YOUR TOPIC

The topic for which I am doing research is _____
_____
_____

■ B. FINDING SUBJECT HEADINGS

Check the *Library of Congress Subject Headings* for two subject headings that will lead to information about your topic. Write them down here:

1. _____
_____
_____

2. _____
_____
_____

■ C. FINDING BOOKS

Look in the subject section of the library's card catalog or electronic catalog. Write down information for three books on your subject. Information should include authors' names, book titles, city and name of publisher, year of publication (look on copyright page), call number.

1. Book #1:
_____
_____
_____
_____

2. Book #2:
_____
_____
_____
_____

3. Book #3:
_____
_____
_____
_____

■ D. FINDING MAGAZINE, JOURNAL, AND NEWSPAPER ARTICLES

Use three sources to find three different articles. One should be from a magazine, one from a journal, and one from a newspaper.

1. **Article from a Magazine:** Use the *Reader's Guide to Periodical Literature* to find an article on your topic. Write down the authors' names, article title, name and date of magazine, volume number, article page numbers, and call number. Find the article and write down the first and last sentence in it.
_____
_____
_____
_____
_____
_____

2. **Article from a Journal:** Use another periodical index to find another article on your subject, this time from an academic journal. (An example is *Applied Science and Technology Index;* see other examples in Panel 8.2.) Write down the periodical index used,

the authors' names, article title, name and date of journal, volume and issue number, article page numbers, and call number. Find the article and write down the first and last sentence in it.
_____
_____
_____
_____
_____
_____

3. **Article from a Newspaper:** Use a newspaper index to find an article on your topic. (Examples are the *New York Times Index* and the *Wall Street Journal Index.*) Write down the newspaper index used, the authors' names, article title, name and date of newspaper, section and page numbers, and call number. Find the article and write down the first and last sentence in it.
_____
_____
_____
_____
_____
_____

■ E. FINDING OTHER SOURCES

Use other sources to find more information—for example, government literature, encyclopedias, or computer networks.

1. _____
_____
_____
_____

2. _____
_____
_____
_____

This activity involves out-of-class time because it requires a visit to the library. You may develop the topic agreed on by your group in Group Activity #8.1 or use a topic required for a paper in another class.

In the library research the sources requested above, either by yourself or with other students in your team from Group Activity #8.1. In class discuss the following questions. What types of information were the easiest to locate and why? Which the most difficult? Is your approach to locating sources low-tech or high-tech and how? How could searching for information be improved? What did you learn about the library?

questions that appeared on your preliminary outline. However, the very process of doing research may turn up some new questions and areas that you hadn't thought of. Thus, your 3 × 5 cards or source materials may contain information that suggests some changes to the outline.

Here's what to do:

■ *Sort your information cards:* Keeping your eye on the key words in the upper right corner of your 3 × 5 cards (or other source material), sort the information material into piles. *Each pile should gather together information relating to a similar question or topic.* Now move the piles into the order or sequence in which you will discuss the material, according to your preliminary outline.

■ *Revise your outline:* The piles may suggest some changes in the order of your outline. Thus, you should now take a fresh sheet of paper, write *OUTLINE #2* at the top, and redo the questions or categories.

By now you will be able to write answers to some or all of your questions. *As you rework the outline, write answers to the questions you have listed.* Refer to the sources of your information as you write.

For example, suppose you have the question "What percentage of basketball players graduate compared to most students?" You might write "NCAA 1995 study: No breakdown by sports. However, at basketball Final Four schools, graduation rates were as follows: North Carolina 76% student-athletes, 48% all students; UCLA 56% and 77%; Arkansas 39% and 41%; Oklahoma State 38% and 40% (Anderson 1995, p. B5)."

Resequence the topics so that they seem to follow logically, with one building on another.

■ *Write a thesis statement and working title:* When you get done with reworking and answering questions in *II. Middle* of your outline, go back up to *I. Beginning.* Revise the main question or questions into a thesis statement. **A _thesis statement_ is a concise sentence that defines the purpose of your paper.** For example, your original main questions were "How smart are college athletes?" and "Are college athletics dominated by 'dumb jocks'?" These might now become your thesis statement:

"Though graduation rates of college athletes are lower than those for other students, some individual athletes are among the best students."

The thesis statement will in turn suggest a working title. **A _working title_ is a tentative title for your paper.** Thus, you might put down on your outline: *Working title: "How Smart Are College Athletes?"*

WRITING YOUR FIRST DRAFT. The first draft has one major purpose: *to get your ideas down on paper.* This is not the stage to worry about doing a clever introduction or choosing the right words or making transitions between ideas. Nor should you concern yourself about correct grammar, punctuation, and spelling. Simply write as though you were telling your findings to a friend. *It's important not to be too judgmental about your writing at this point.* Your main task is to get from a blank page to a page with *something* on it that you can refine later.

Proceed as follows:

Write the middle: Skip the beginning, letting your thesis statement be the introduction for now. Instead, follow Outline #2 for *II. Middle* to write the body of your paper, using your information cards to flesh it out. Set down your answers or ideas one after the other, without worrying too much about logical transitions between them. Use your own voice, not some imagined "scholarly" tone.

Follow some of the writing suggestions mentioned in the next section, "Some Writing Tips."

Write the beginning: When you have finished setting down the answers to all the questions in the middle, go back and do *I. Beginning.* By starting with the middle, you'll avoid the hang-up of trying to get your paper off the ground or of writing an elegant lead. Also, having done the middle, you'll have a solid idea, of course, of what your paper is about. You'll know, for instance, which questions and answers are the most important. These may be different from the questions you asked before you did your research.

Now, then, you'll be able to write the introduction with some confidence. An example might be:

"A common image many people have of college athletes is that they are 'dumb jocks.' That is, they may be good on the playing field but not in the classroom. Is this true? The facts vary for different sports, colleges, class levels, and other factors. This paper examines these differences."

Write the end: Finally, you write *III. End.* The end is the conclusion. It does not include any new facts or examples. It provides just the general answer or answers to the main question or questions raised in the beginning. This is the answer you've arrived at by exploring the questions in the middle section. It's possible, of course, that your conclusion will be incomplete or tentative. It's all right to state that further research is needed.

An example of the end of a paper might be as follows:

"As we have seen, although the dropout rate is higher for players in some sports and in some schools, it is not in others. Moreover, college athletes often graduate with honors, and some go on not only to professional sports but also to Rhodes scholarships, Fullbright and Wilson fellowships, and graduate and professional schools. Today the 'strong-back, weak-brain' athlete of the past is largely a myth."

SOME WRITING TIPS. In writing the first draft of the middle, or body, of the paper, you should try to get something down that you can revise and polish later. Thus, don't worry too much if this initial version seems choppy; that's why a first draft is called a "rough" draft.

As you write, try to follow these guidelines:

Make your point and give support: The point you want to make is the answer to each question. (For example, your question might be "Does football require more intelligence than other major sports?") In your writing, this answer will become a statement. Example:

"It's possible that football requires greater intelligence than other major sports do."

Then support the statement with evidence, data, statistics, examples, and quotations. Example:

> "*Memorizing and executing scores or hundreds of different plays, for instance, takes a lot of intelligence. When scouts for pro football teams look over college players, one question they ask is, 'How is he at learning the playbook?'*" (Then footnote the source.)

■ *Quote experts:* It makes your statements or arguments much more convincing when you can buttress them with brief quotes from experts. Quoting authorities also can make your paper much more interesting and readable to the instructor. One caution, however: don't overdo it with the quotations. Keep them brief.

■ *Avoid irrelevancies:* Don't think you have to use all your research. That is, don't feel you have to try to impress your instructor by showing how much work you've done in your investigation. Just say what you need to say. Avoid piling on lots of irrelevant information, which will only distract and irritate your reader.

■ *Give the source of your data and examples:* Your instructor will want to know where you got your supporting information. Thus, be sure to provide sources. These can be expressed with precision on the final draft, following the particular footnote and bibliography ("works cited") style you've decided on. For now put some sort of shorthand for your sources in the first draft.

For instance, at the end of the sentence about the football playbook, you could provide the author, year, and page for the source in parentheses. Example: "... learning the playbook?' (Wahlstrom 1998, p. 23)."

■ *Jot down ideas:* As you proceed through the first draft, jot down any ideas that come to you that don't immediately seem to fit anywhere. You may find a place for them later.

■ *Take breaks:* Professional writers find that physical activity gives the mind a rest and triggers new ideas. The brain needs to disengage. Take short breaks to relax. Go get a soda, stroll down the corridor, take a walk outside, or otherwise move your body a bit. Take pen and paper and jot down thoughts.

LETTING THE DRAFT SIT. Many students write papers right up against their deadlines. It's far, far better, however, if you can get the first draft done early and let it sit in a drawer for a day or so. This will allow you to come back and revise it with a fresh perspective.

Phase 5: Revising, Finalizing, & Proofreading Your Paper

PREVIEW & REVIEW Ideally the fifth phase should take as much time as the first four. This final phase consists of seven parts. (1) Read the paper aloud or have someone else read it. (2) Delete irrelevant material. (3) Write transitions and do reorganizing. (4) Do fine-tuning and polishing. (5) Type the paper. (6) Proofread the paper. (7) Make a copy.

The last phase, Phase 5, consists of *revising, finalizing, and proofreading your paper.* How much time should revising take? One suggestion is this: Phases 1–4 should take half your time, and Phase 5 should take the other half of your time. This rule shows the importance that is attached to revision.

The steps to take in revision are as follows:

- Read the paper aloud or get someone else to read it.

- Delete irrelevant material.

- Write transitions and do any reorganizing.

- Do fine-tuning and polishing.

- Type the paper.

- Proofread the paper.

- Make a copy.

Mindfulness

Also, whereas at the beginning of the term-paper process you needed to do creative thinking, now you need to do critical, or analytical, thinking. See the section in Chapter 2, "Critical Thinking: What It Is, How to Use It."

READ ALOUD OR HAVE SOMEONE ELSE READ DRAFTS OF YOUR PAPER. It's hard for us to spot our own mistakes, particularly during a silent reading. To better catch these, try the following:

- *Read your draft aloud to yourself:* If you read aloud what you've written, whether first draft or revised draft, you'll be able to spot missing words, awkward usage, and missing details.

- *Get feedback from another person:* By having a friend, family member, or the instructor read any of your drafts, you can get the help of an "editor." (You can offer to read friends' papers in exchange.) Any additional feedback can be valuable.

   SPECIAL NOTE: *Don't take the criticism personally.* If your readers say your paper is "illogical" or "vague," they are not implying you're stupid. When people criticize your draft, they are not criticizing you as a human being. Moreover, remember you don't *have* to do what they say. You're looking for suggestions, not commandments.

DELETE IRRELEVANT MATERIAL. The best way to start the revision is to take a pencil and start crossing out words. Like a film maker cutting scenes so a movie won't run too long and bore the audience, you should cut your paper to its essentials.

   This is what editors call "blue penciling." Strive for conciseness and brevity. As a mental guideline, imagine someone writing "Repetitious!" or "Redundant!" or "Wordy!" in the margin. Be ruthless. First cut unnecessary sections, pages, and paragraphs. Then cut unnecessary sentences, phrases, and words. Cut even your best ideas and phrases—those gems you're proud of—if they don't move the essay along and advance your case.

WRITE TRANSITIONS & DO ANY REORGANIZING. You may have written the first draft fairly rapidly and not given much thought to making transitions—logical connections—between thoughts. You may also have deleted such connections when you blue-penciled material above. Now's the time to make sure the reader is able to move logically from one of your ideas to another.

   You may well discover while doing this that your paper needs to be reorganized, that your outline isn't working right. There are two ways to handle this:

- **Low-tech reorganizing—scissors and glue:** You can use scissors to cut up your paper, then move the cut-up sections around. Use glue (paste) or transparent tape to attach the sections to blank pieces of paper. This activity is known as "cutting and pasting."

Information technology

- **High-tech reorganizing—word processing:** The same kind of resequencing can be done electronically with a word processing program by using the "cut-and-paste" (or "block move") function. You use the "cut" command to mark the beginning and end of a section. Then you go to another location in the document and use the "paste" command to transfer that marked-off section to it.

DO FINE-TUNING & POLISHING. Now you need to take a pencil and do a final editing to make sure everything reads well. Some suggestions:

- **Have a thesis statement:** Make sure the introduction to the paper has a thesis statement that says what the main point of your paper is.

- **Guide the reader:** Tell the reader what you're going to do. Introduce each change in topic. Connect topics by writing transitions.

- **Present supporting data:** Make sure you have enough examples, quotations, and data to support your assertions.

- **Don't be wordy:** Don't be infatuated with the exuberance and prolixity of your own verbosity. Don't use big words when short ones will do. Delete unnecessary words.

- **Check grammar and spelling:** Check your paper for grammatical mistakes. Also check for spelling. Look up words you're not sure about.

- **Follow correct style for documentation:** Follow the instructor's directions, if any, for documenting your sources. The humanities, for example, follow the style developed by the Modern Language Association. The social sciences follow the style developed by the American Psychological Association. Guidebooks are available in the campus bookstore or at the library.

A popular style nowadays is to identify the author's last name and the page reference within parentheses. For example:

"As one _New York Times_ reporter summarized the NCAA study, white male athletes and nonathletes graduated at the same rate. But athletes had a better graduation rate than nonathletes among black women, black men, and white women (Litsky C19)."

You then present a complete description of each source in an alphabetical listing at the end of the paper entitled "Works Cited." (See ■ Panel 8.5.)

PANEL 8.5

Documentation. The preferred style of documentation is to identify the author's last name with the page reference within parentheses in the text. The complete source is then presented at the end of the paper in a "Works Cited" section.

Example of citation in text:

As one _New York Times_ reporter summarized the NCAA study, white male athletes and nonathletes graduated at the same rate. But athletes had a better graduation rate than nonathletes among black women, black men, and white women (Litsky C19).

Example of "Works Cited" section:

WORKS CITED
Litsky, Frank. "Athletes' Graduation Rate Surpasses Nonathletes'." _New York Times_ 27 June 1997, C19.
Rice, Philip L. _Stress and health_. 2nd ed. Pacific Grove, CA: Brooks/Cole, 1992.
Thurow, Roger. "Duh . . . NFL Players Really Aren't So Dumb." _Wall Street Journal_ 19 April 1996, B11.

THE PRESENTATION: DO YOUR PAPER ON A WORD PROCESSOR OR TYPE-WRITER. Presentation is important. Some instructors accept handwritten papers, but they'd rather not, since they're harder to read. In a job interview situation, you have to sell yourself not only with your experience but also by the way you dress and present yourself. Similarly, you have to sell your paper not only by its ideas but by its presentation.

Thus, you should type your paper or have it typed. You need not be expert; using two fingers instead of ten just means typing will take a little longer. With a personal computer, you'll find typing is even less of a chore, because it's easier to fix mistakes. You can type (keyboard) on the machine, print out a draft, and make corrections on the draft with a pencil. Then you can type in the corrections and print out a clean draft.

Information technology

PROOFREADING. In the past have you had papers come back from the instructor with red ink circling spelling and grammatical mistakes? Those red circles probably negatively affected your final grade, marking you down from, say, an A– to a B+.

With your paper in beautiful final-typed form (and the hand-in deadline perhaps only hours away), it may be tempting not to proofread it. You may not only be supremely tired of the whole thing but not want to "mess it up" by making handwritten corrections. Do it anyway. The instructor won't have any excuse then to give you red circles for small mistakes. If you're using a word processor, providing a completely clean final draft is very easy.

MAKE A COPY. Papers do get lost or stolen after they've been handed in (or on a student's way to handing it in). If you typed your paper on a word processor, make sure you save a copy on a floppy disk. If you typed it on a typewriter or hand-wrote it, use a photocopying machine at the library or an instant-printing shop to make a copy.

Important note: Another good reason for retaining a copy of your paper is that you may be able to expand on the subject in subsequent papers later. I've known students who gradually explored a particular topic to the point where in graduate school it finally became the subject of their doctoral dissertation.

ANOTHER APPROACH: 14 STEPS. Some students find it more manageable to approach term-paper research and writing by breaking the five phases discussed above into 14 steps. These are presented in the box on the next page. (*See* ■ *Panel 8.6, page 234.*)

GROUP ACTIVITY #8.2

HANDLING FOOTNOTES & REFERENCES

Finding the correct form for footnotes and references may seem somewhat daunting. With a bit of out-of-class time for research and in-class time for discussion, however, you can learn to feel comfortable with these important matters.

You need to be able to do correct references for three kinds of source material: (1) books, (2) articles from periodicals, and (3) other sources (such as encyclopedias and government publications). Different academic disciplines have their own preferred reference and footnoting or reference styles. In the library, find and copy out footnote and reference styles for books, articles, and other sources. Find sources that will appear in (a) papers you will submit in most of your courses and (b) papers you will submit in courses in your major or prospective major.

The instructor will select some examples to put on the board. Discuss the differences between the various forms.

The **14-step term paper approach: 10 weeks**. The following 14 steps show you how to research and prepare a research paper in 10 weeks.

2 WEEKS: Pick a Topic

1. Start early. Set a deadline for picking your topic.

2. Pick your own topic, if possible, in order to make it interesting to you. In addition:

    a. Make sure the scope or focus is narrow enough. (Check with your instructor.)

    b. Make sure you have sufficient resources. (Check the library's online catalog and guide to periodicals.)

1 WEEK: Do Initial Research & Develop a Preliminary Outline

3. Brainstorm a working or preliminary outline. (Use mind-mapping or similar creativity-enhancing techniques.)

4. Gather resources and review them. (Use the library or Internet.)

5. Revise your outline. (Change your working outline to reflect any new information you've gathered.)

1 WEEK: Do Further Research

6. Gather additional resources (articles, books), if necessary.

7. Review each resource and make your source cards. (Write on 3 × 5 note cards. These are bibliography cards, with author name, book/article title, publication date, page numbers, etc.)

3 WEEKS: Sort Note Cards, Revise the Outline, & Write a First Draft

8. Review each resource in detail and make your information cards. (These are 3 × 5 note cards containing actual information—facts, statistics, quotations, paraphrasing—and source abbreviations.)

9. Sort and sequence your information cards

    a. Sort your information cards corresponding to categories of your outline.

    b. Then sequence these same cards by choice, to reflect your preference for which cards you will lead off with within categories.

10. Write the first draft. (Handwrite or use a word processor to do a rough draft of the paper.)

3 WEEKS: Revise, Final-Type, & Proofread the Paper

11. Read over the first draft and edit it. (Read for understanding. Have other people read it too, if you can.)

12. Prepare your final draft. Use a typewriter or word processor (and use a spelling and grammar checker).

13. Prepare the bibliography. (This goes at the end of the paper; it follows the style appropriate for the discipline you're writing in.)

14. Do a final proofreading. (Correct errors by hand or with word processor. Make sure you have a copy of the paper.)

TOTAL TIME: 10 WEEKS

Term Papers, Web Research, & Cheating

PREVIEW & REVIEW The Internet can provide good sources of research material, although you should first check with online library catalogs for reliability of Web sites. Some students are tempted to use the Web to acquire term papers written by others to pass off as their own. Others may misuse the Web and write low-quality term papers.

Information technology

tuck for a topic for a research paper? Word processing software and electronic spell-checkers and dictionaries are great tools for student writers, but they won't unblock a writer's block. Maybe you need something to help you brainstorm ideas. Maybe you need Paradigm Online Writing Assistant.

Developed by Chuck Guilford, an English professor at Boise State University in Idaho, Paradigm is a World Wide Web site *(www.idbsu.edu/english/cguilfor/paradigm/)* that offers exercises to stimulate creative juices. "While style and grammar are important considerations for writers," says Guilford, "I want Paradigm to emphasize larger conceptual issues, such as discovering, exploring, and shaping ideas."[4]

Striking creative sparks is not the only thing you can use the Web for, of course. As I indicated back in Chapter 3, it can be a tremendous source of research material. The box below, for instance, offers some Web sites that may yield valuable materials. *(See ■ Panel 8.7.)*

Nevertheless, there are a lot of things wrong with the data available on the Web, as I shall describe. Librarians have not assessed the reliability of all of it. However, some librarians and instructors

---

PANEL 8.7 ome useful Web sites. Go to *http://csuccess.wadsworth.com* for the most up-to-date Web addresses (URLs).

Information technology

U.S. Government. Federal agencies ranging from the White House to the Supreme Court, from the CIA to the IRS, have their own Web sites. Try accessing some of the following:

- **The White House** *(http://whitehouse.gov)* or *(http://sunsite. unc.edu/white-house/white-house.html)* offers information and details about the White House, including e-mail system, press conferences, and the federal budget.
- **Supreme Court Decisions** *(http://www.law.cornell.edu/supct)* allows you to search by topics or key words for summaries of High Court decisions since 1990.
- **Thomas: Legislative Information** *(http://thomas.loc.gov)* offers an electronic version of the Congressional Record plus full text of all House and Senate bills.
- **The Library of Congress** *(http://lcweb.loc.gov/homepage/lchp. html)* provides links to tons of interesting material, including the library's vast card catalog.
- **The Smithsonian** *(http://www.si.edu)* has several collections. The Smithsonian gem and mineral collection *(http://galaxy. einet.net/images/gems/gems-icons.html)*, for example, offers nearly 50 images and descriptions of different types of gems and minerals.
- **U.S. Bureau of the Census** *(http://www.census.gov)* provides up-to-the-minute population projections and some access to census data. Try the POPclock (population clock) Projection at *http://www.census.gov/cgi-bin/popclock* to see latest U.S. population estimates.
- **Internal Revenue Service** *(http://www.ustreas.gov/treasury/bureau/irs/irs.html)*—Dial this for a really good time.
- **Central Intelligence Agency** *(http://www.ic.gov/)* offers a look at declassified spy photos from the 1960s, CIA maps, and other facts.
- **DefenseLink** *(http://www.dtic.dia.mil/defenselink)* offers the latest in military news and briefing transcripts from the Department of Defense.

Canadian Government. This Web site *(http://debra.dgbt.doc.ca:80/opengov/)* enables you to explore (in both English and French) segments of the Canadian federal government: House of Commons, the Senate, the Supreme Court, and federal departments and agencies.

News. The news offerings of the commercial online services—America Online, CompuServe, Prodigy—are generally superior to those on the Web, but you might want to try the following:

- **Online Newspapers** *(http://marketplace.com/e-papers.list.www/e-papers.links.html)* provides a list of links to the major newspapers that are available online.
- **Daily Sources of Business and Economic News** *(http://www. helsinki.fi/~lsaarine/news/html)* offers links to free sources of daily news on the Internet.
- **Electronic Newsstand** *(http://www.enews.com)* shows tables of contents from the latest issues of several magazines, plus ordering information.
- **Sports Information Server** *(http://www.netgen.com/sis/sports. html)* covers football, basketball, and hockey.
- **GNN NetNews** *(http:gnn.com/gnn/news/index.html)* is a general news service; Internet issues are emphasized.
- **Canadian Broadcasting Corporation (CBC) Radio Trial** *(http://debra.dgbt.doc.ca/cbc/cbc.html)* offers CBC radio transcripts of daily news broadcasts, program listings, and sample radio programs.

Science. Because the Internet and World Wide Web originated in science and research, there is an abundance of Web sites having to do with science.

- **National Academy of Sciences** *(http://www.nas.edu/)* includes information and news from the National Research Council, Institute of Medicine, and National Academy of Engineering.
- **National Science Foundation** *(http://http:/www.nsf.gov)* presents NSF news and information on science trends, research, statistics, education, and grants.
- **NASA Information Services** *(http://www.gsfc.nasa.gov/NASA_homepage.html)* offers links to the space centers and research labs of the National Aeronautics and Space Administration.
- **National Centers for Environmental Prediction** *(http://grads. iges.org/pix/head.html)* offers weather maps, satellite images, and movies of the Earth.
- **Physics News** *(http://www.het.brown.edu/news/index.html)* presents news from physical sciences.
- **Web-Elements** *(http://www.cchem.berkeley.edu/Table)* gives you an online table of the elements.
- **National Center for Atmospheric Research** *(http://http.ucar. edu/metapage.html)* presents research on climate, weather, and the atmosphere.
- **Space Telescope Science Institute** *(http://www.stsci.edu)* offers a look through the Hubble Space Telescope archives.
- **Project Bluebook** *(http://www.cis.ksu.edu/psiber/substand/bluebook/html)* presents UFO reports.

Culture and the Arts. Although a lot of "culture" on the Web is just silly entertainment, here are some alternatives to try:

- **Internet Underground Music Archive** *(http://www.luma.com/)* is a music archives concentrating on up-and-coming bands.
- **Cardiff's Movie Database Browser** *(http://www.msstate.edu/Movies/)* is a large database (that Internet users can add to themselves) in which you can find out almost any movie-related fact.
- **World Arts Resources** *(http://www.cgrg.ohio-state.edu/Newark/artsres.html)* is a guide to online art exhibitions, galleries, and museums.
- **Shakespeare Homepage** *(http://the-tech.mit.edu/Shakespeare/works.html)* offers the complete works of Shakespeare, for searching or downloading.
- **Philosophy on the Web** *(http://www.phil.ruu.nl/philosophy-sites.html)* is a listing of sites having to do with philosophical big questions.

have created Web sites that have authoritative bibliographies, full texts of primary sources, and other legitimate information. Others have created Web pages for certain academic disciplines that refer users to the best online sites for research. Finally, these Web pages and scholarly sites have been evaluated by librarians—for accuracy, currency, and authoritativeness—who have listed them in many online library catalogs.[5] These can save you a lot of time that might be wasted in just random searching.

HOW THE WEB CAN LEAD TO CHEATING.

Some students may be tempted to use the Web to cheat, as in trying to pass off as their own all or part of a term paper written by someone else. No matter how much students may be able to rationalize such behavior, ignorance of the consequences is not an excuse. As I stated in Chapter 7, most instructors announce the penalties for cheating at the beginning of their course—usually a failing grade in the course and possible suspension or expulsion from school.

Even so, probably every college student becomes aware before long that the World Wide Web contains sites that offer term papers, either for free or for a price. Some dishonest students may download (transfer or copy) papers and just change the author's name to their own. Others are more likely to use the papers just for ideas. Perhaps, suggests one writer, "the fear of getting caught makes the online papers more a diversion than an invitation to wide-scale plagiarism."[6]

Two types of term-paper Web sites are these:

- **Sites offering papers for free:** An example is Cheater.com, which requires users to fill out a membership form, then provides at least one free student term paper.

- **Sites offering papers for sale:** Commercial sites may charge $6 to $10 a page, which users may charge to their credit card. An example is Termpapers-on-File, which allows users to search their files and to view excerpts from papers.

"These paper-writing scams present little threat to serious students or savvy educators," says one writer. "No self-respecting student will hand in purchased papers; no savvy educator will fail to spot them and flunk the student outright."[7] English professor Bruce Leland, director of writing at Western Illinois University, points out that many Web papers are so bad that no one is likely to benefit from them in any case.[8]

How do instructors detect and defend against student plagiarism? Leland says professors are unlikely to be fooled if they tailor term-paper assignments to work done in class, monitor students' progress—from outline to completion—and are alert to papers that seem radically different from a student's past work.

Eugene Dwyer, a professor of art history at Kenyon College, requires that papers in his classes be submitted electronically, along with a list of World Wide Web site references. "This way I can click along as I read the paper. This format is more efficient than running around the college library, checking each footnote."[9]

The World Wide Web, points out Mitchell Zimmerman, also provides the means to detect cheaters. "Faster computer search programs will make it possible for teachers to locate texts containing identified strings of words from amid the millions of pages found on the Web."[10] Thus, a professor could input passages from a student's paper into a search program that would scan the Web for identical blocks of text.

HOW THE WEB CAN LEAD TO LOW-QUALITY PAPERS. Besides tempting some students to plagiarize, the Web also creates another problem in term-paper writing, says William Rukeyser, coordinator for Learning in the Real World, a nonprofit information clearinghouse. This is that it enables students "to cut and paste together reports or presentations that appear to have taken hours or days to write but have really been assembled in minutes with no actual mastery or understanding by the student."[11]

This comes about because, as I described in Chapter 3, the Web features *hypertext*—highlighted words and phrases that can be linked online to related words and phrases. Students use hypertext to skip to isolated phrases or paragraphs in source material, which they then pull together, complains Rukeyser, without making the effort to gain any real knowledge of the material.

Philosophy professor David Rothenberg, of New Jersey Institute of Technology, reports that as a result of students doing more of their research on the Web he has seen "a disturbing decline in both the quality of the writing and the originality of the thoughts expressed."[12] The Web, he says, makes research look too easy:

> *You toss a query to the machine, wait a few minutes, and suddenly a lot of possible sources of information appear on your screen. Instead of books that you have to check out of the library, read carefully, understand, synthesize, and then tactfully excerpt, these sources are quips, blips, pictures, and short summaries that may be downloaded magically to the dorm-room computer screen. Fabulous! How simple! The only problem is that a paper consisting of summaries of summaries is bound to be fragmented and superficial, and to demonstrate more of a random montage than an ability to sustain an article through 10 to 15 double-spaced pages.*

How does an instructor spot a term paper based primarily on Web research? Rothenberg offers four clues:

- **No books cited:** The student's bibliography cites no books, just articles or references to Web sites. Sadly, says Rothenberg, "one finds few references to careful, in-depth commentaries on the subject of the paper, the kind of analysis that requires a book, rather than an article, for its full development."

- **Outdated material:** A lot of the material in the bibliography is strangely out of date, says Rothenberg. "A lot of stuff on the Web that is advertised as timely is actually at least a few years old."

- **Unrelated pictures and graphs:** Students may intersperse the text with a lot of impressive-looking pictures and graphs that may look as though they were the result of careful work and analysis but actually bear little relation to the precise subject of the paper. "Cut and pasted from the vast realm of what's out there for the taking, they masquerade as original work."

- **Superficial references:** "Too much of what passes for information [online] these days is simply *advertising* for information," points out Rothenberg. "Screen after screen shows you where you can find out more, how you can connect to this place or that." And a lot of other kinds of information is detailed but often superficial: "pages and pages of federal documents, corporate propaganda, snippets of commentary by people whose credibility is difficult to assess."

Once, points out Brian Hecht, the Internet was a text-only medium for disseminating no-frills information. The World Wide Web added a means of delivering graphics, sound, and video, but as access has widened, says Hecht, "legitimate information has been subsumed by a deluge of vanity 'home pages,' corporate marketing gimmicks, and trashy infomercials . . . It is impossible to know where [a given piece of] information comes from, who has paid for it, whether it is reliable, and whether you will ever be able to find it again."[13]

In sum: having access to the Internet and the Web doesn't provide miracles in research and term-paper writing.

GETTING RESEARCH FROM THE WEB & ELSEWHERE

Kari Boyd McBride is a lecturer in women's studies and Ruth Dickstein is a social sciences librarian at the University of Arizona. They have been concerned about students' uncritical use of Web resources. To teach students how to read research material critically—from *all* sources, both regular print materials and Internet materials—they have developed an exercise that goes as follows.

With four other students in a group, do research on a topic of mutual choosing using the following five resources—a book, an article, a reference work, material found through a CD-ROM index, and a Web site. Each of you should then report on one resource, summarizing the information it contains and evaluating the reliability and the plausibility of his or her argument.

After you have met with your own group, choose a member of that group to summarize the results and report them to the class at large. The focus of your group effort is to try to see where the biases lie.

Making an Oral Presentation

PREVIEW & REVIEW An oral presentation can involve the same kind of research and writing as is required for a written presentation (term paper). Beyond that, an oral presentation has the following aspects. (1) You need to prepare readable speaker's notes, either full text or notes only. (2) You need to prepare a beginning that goes right to the point, a middle that expands on that, and an ending that repeats the middle points. (3) You need to understand the attention cycle of the audience. (4) You need to know how to reduce your nervousness through rehearsal and preparation, breathing, and mind control. (5) You need to make the delivery while coping with your nervous energy, focusing on the audience, and pacing yourself.

The material you've gathered and organized for a written paper can also be used for an oral presentation. If you're one of the millions of people who are anxious—indeed, panicked—about speaking on your feet before several other people, take heart. I used to be that way myself, but I've since found some ways to make it easier—and to reduce the panicky feelings.

It's possible to go all the way through school and not have to make an oral presentation. Some instructors, however, may require it. More important, outside school, the ability to speak to a room full of people is one of the greatest skills you can have. This is supported by a study conducted by AT&T and Stanford University. It found that the top predictor of success and professional upward mobility is how much you enjoy public speaking and how effective you are at it.[14] No doubt you'll need to draw on this skill at some point. Maybe it will only be to make a toast at a wedding. But maybe it will be to present ideas to clients or supervisors on a matter that could profoundly affect your future.

PREPARING YOUR NOTES: TWO METHODS.

Obviously, your notes have to be readable. If you have to squint or bend over to read them, you'll be undermining the effect of your presentation. Thus, unless you'll be sitting down when you deliver your speech, assume you'll be reading your notes from about 2 feet away.

Whether your speech takes 10 minutes or an hour, there are two ways to prepare your notes:

- **On 4 × 6 cards:** You can prepare your final text or your notes on 4 × 6 note cards (better than the smaller 3 × 5 cards). Number the cards so that you can put them back in order if they are dropped. Move the cards from front to back of the stack as you go through them.

  If you'll be standing up (or if your vision is not perfect) while you speak, print your notes in large block letters. If you'll be sitting down, type them in all-capital letters.

- **Outlined on paper:** You can also prepare your text or notes on standard size (8½ × 11) paper. The advantage of this method is that you won't distract your audience by shuffling cards.

  When you type your text, type all capital letters, triple-spaced, and allow generous margins to the left and right. One public-speaking expert, Ed Wohlmuth, recommends using standard proofreader's marks in red for emphasis. Put "a triple underline under the first letter of each sentence and circle around each period," he says. "This will help you find the location of each complete sentence very quickly. . . ."[15]

  If you use a word processor for typing, most programs will allow you to enlarge the type. Thus, to enhance readability, you can produce notes in a type size two or three times as large as normal typewriter type.

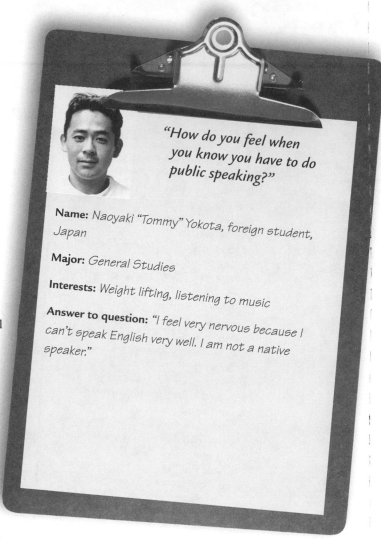

"How do you feel when you know you have to do public speaking?"

Name: Naoyaki "Tommy" Yokota, foreign student, Japan

Major: General Studies

Interests: Weight lifting, listening to music

Answer to question: "I feel very nervous because I can't speak English very well. I am not a native speaker."

FULL TEXT OR NOTES ONLY?

Should you type out the full text of the speech or should you just do notes? Wohlmuth recommends that you write out the entire speech, even if later you convert to notes only. The reason is that doing a word-for-word text will help you ingrain the speech in your memory.[16]

A full text is particularly recommended if you are doing a stand-up speech to an audience of 30 people or more. If you're talking to a small group, whether you're standing up or sitting down, a full-text delivery is probably inappropriate. You want to *interact with* the people in the audience, not talk to them.

THE BEGINNING, MIDDLE, & END. Speech writer Phil Theibert says a speech comprises just three simple rules:[17]

1. Tell them what you're going to say.

2. Say it.

3. Tell them what you said.

These correspond to the three parts of a paper—beginning, middle, and end (or introduction, body, and conclusion).

- **Beginning:** The introduction should take 5–15% of your speaking time, and it should prepare the audience for the rest of the speech.

  Should you begin with a joke? Probably not. If it bombs, your audience will be uncomfortable (and will wonder if more mediocre material is to come) and so will you. Unless you're David Letterman or Jay Leno—whose jokes fail surprisingly often, you'll notice—it's best to simply "tell them what you're going to say."

  Also I suggest avoiding phrases such as "I'm honored to be with you here today. . . ." Because *everything* in your speech should be relevant, try to go right to the point. For example:

  > *"Good afternoon. The subject of computer security may seem far removed from the concerns of most of us. But I intend to describe how our supposedly private computerized records are routinely violated, who's doing it, and how you can protect yourself."*

  If you wish, you might tell a *true* story (not a joke) as a way of hooking your audience.[18] For example:

  > *"My topic this morning is computer security. In a few seconds I'm going to explain how our supposedly private computerized records are routinely violated, who's doing it, and how you can protect yourself. First, however, I'd like to tell you a true story about a student, his father, and a personal computer. . . ."*

- **Middle:** In the main body of the speech, the longest part, which takes 75–90% of your time, you "say what you said you were going to say."

  The most important thing to realize is this: your audience won't remember more than a few points anyway. Thus, you need to decide *what three or four points must be remembered.*[19] Then cover them as succinctly as possible.

  The middle part generally follows the same rules as were explained for the middle part of a term paper. Use examples, quotations, and statistics (don't overdo it on the statistics) to support your assertions and hold your listeners' attention.

  Be particularly attentive to transitions. Listening differs from reading in that the listener has only one chance to get your meaning. He or she cannot go back and reread. Thus, be sure you constantly provide your audience with guidelines and transitional phrases so they can see where you're going. Example:

  > *"There are four ways the security of computer files can be compromised. The first way is . . ."*

- **End:** The end might take 5–10% of your time. Don't drop the ball here. You need a wrap-up that's strong, succinct, and persuasive. Indeed, many professional speakers consider the conclusion to be as important as the introduction.

  The conclusion should "tell them what you told them." You need some sort of signal phrase that cues the audience you are heading into your wind-up. Examples:

  > *"Let's review the main points we've covered. . . ."*

  > *"In conclusion, what CAN you do to protect against unauthorized invasion of all those computerized files with your name on them? I pointed out three main steps. One . . ."*

  Give some thought to the last thing you're going to say. It should be strongly upbeat, a call to action, a thought for the day, a quotation, a little story. In short, you need a solid finish of some sort. Examples:

  > *"I want to leave you with one last thought . . ."*

  > *"Finally, let me close by sharing something that happened to me. . . ."*

"As Albert Einstein said, 'Imagination is more important than knowledge.'"

Then say "Thank you" and stop talking.

UNDERSTANDING THE AUDIENCE. As you yourself know, your attention can wander when you're a member of an audience. Thus, you have to understand the basics of the attention cycle and tailor your speech accordingly—particularly the middle part. As Tony Alessandra and Phil Hunsaker, authors of *Communicating at Work*, point out:

> *Studies have shown that material at the beginning and end of a presentation will be remembered more than the material in the middle. Our attention span lasts only for a short time and then it tapers off. When we sense the end of a message, we pull back in time to catch the last material. Fluctuation of the attention cycle is one of the main reasons we put such emphasis on the introduction and conclusion.*[20]

So how do you hold people's attention during the middle of your speech? Alessandra and Hunsaker recommend putting in a lot of minicycles with beginnings, middles, and ends, changing the pace every 10–15 minutes. You can do

this by including appropriate humor, stories, analogies, examples, comparisons, personal testimony, and variation in tone of voice. You can even have activities and exercises that ask for the audience's involvement.

HOW TO REDUCE YOUR NERVOUSNESS: REHEARSAL & PREPARATION. It may be true that the number one fear of most adults—even more than death—is speaking in public.[21] You can't do anything about death, of course, but you can about your fear of public speaking.

Professional speaker Lilly Walters suggests that 75% of your fear can be reduced by rehearsal and preparation. The remaining 25%, she says, can be reduced by breathing and mind control.[22] Stage fright is *normal.* Every professional speaker, actor, musician, and performer gets that feeling of weak knees, sweaty palms, and butterflies in the stomach. The best way to reduce this nervousness is through rehearsal and preparation—in other words, practice practice practice.

Here are some tips for rehearsing the speech:

■ *Read silently:* Read the speech over several times silently. Edit the manuscript as you go to smooth out awkward passages.

- **Read aloud:** Read the speech several times aloud. Use a loud voice (unless you'll be using a microphone when you speak). Your voice sounds different to you when you talk loudly; you want to be used to this when you give your address. Time yourself so you won't run too long.

- **Memorize the opening:** Memorize the opening *word for word*. This is essential.

- **Practice on a spot:** Practice your speech while staring at a spot on the wall. This is particularly good advice for the opening. You are most nervous during the first few minutes. Thus, one professional speaker suggests, you should memorize a dynamite opening and practice it while staring at a spot on the wall. As a result, he says, "you develop such fantastic confidence that it carries you through the rest of the speech."[23]

- **Practice in a mirror:** Practice delivering the speech while standing in front of a mirror. Observe your gestures, expressions, and posture. Don't worry too much about gestures: the main thing is to do whatever comes naturally.

- **Practice on audiotape, videotape, or in front of friends:** Any other rehearsal activities are bound to help. Read your speech into an audiotape recorder and listen to the results. Or do the same thing with a videotape recorder, which may be available at the school's media center. Notice voice inflections and mannerisms (such as *you know*s, *umm*s, *ah*s). Watch for your voice trailing off at the end of sentences or phrases.

  Try out your address in front of friends or family members. It's possible they will be heavy on the positive ("I think your speech is quite good"). However, you should solicit and listen to any criticism ("Do you know you rock from side to side a lot?").

HOW TO REDUCE YOUR NERVOUSNESS: BREATHING & MIND CONTROL.

When we're nervous, we forget to breathe normally, which makes us more nervous. To control your breathing, Lilly Walters suggests the following 5-second exercise:

Think, "Deep breath and hold, 1, 2, 3, 4, 5." (Add a "Mississippi" onto the end of each number—it's pretty tough to figure out how long a second is when your adrenaline is racing.) Tell yourself, "Slow release, and inhale 1, 2, etc."[24]

Mind control consists of self-talk. Your inner Voice Of Judgment may be saying a lot of negative things. ("They're going to *hate* me." "I'm going to look like a *fool*." "I'll look *fat*.") You can take comfort, then, from what Walters says:

Have you ever gone to a presentation and really wanted the presenter to be terrible? Most of the time you'd much rather have a good time than a bad time. The same is true for your audience. Most listeners are sitting there, ready and willing to make allowances for your mistakes. In fact, a few mistakes make you human and just that much more lovable.[25]

Instead of letting negative thoughts take over, try positive affirmations that are important to you: "I know what I know." "I'm glad I'm here." "I can do it!" Using self-talk, let your thoughts direct you to success!

DELIVERING THE ORAL PRESENTATION.

Come the day of the big speech, there are a few things to concentrate on:

- **Dress appropriately:** Dress to look your best—or at least appropriate to the occasion. Even if you're just doing a report in a classroom, audiences like it when you look a little special (though not out of place).

- **Deal with your nervous energy:** Almost every speaker, even professionals, experiences stage fright. This is actually your body preparing for a big event; in fact, you need the edge in order to be your best. The trick is to manage your nervous energy and avoid expressing it in ways— foot tapping, fiddling with eyeglasses, swaying back and forth—that can be annoying to an audience.

  Ed Wohlmuth suggests buying a kid's rubber ball that's large enough to cover most of your palm. During your waking hours before the speech, squeeze it frequently in each hand. From then on, when you feel nervous energy start to mount, think of the rubber ball.[26]

Whatever you do, don't use tranquilizers or alcohol. Eat in moderation before your talk. Drink some water (but not gallons) before the speech to ease the dryness in your mouth.

- **Try out the speaker's position:** Get to the classroom or hall early, or go a day or two before. Step behind the podium or wherever the speaker's position is. If the room is empty, speak your introduction aloud, aiming it at the last seat in the room. You might even deliver the entire speech.

  If you plan on using audiovisual aids, flip charts, or a microphone, it's especially recommended you do a dry run. (Do this with the help of others managing the equipment.)

- **Focus on the audience:** When your speech is under way, *focus on the audience.* Maintain eye contact, shifting your attention among a few friendly faces in the room. When you look at people, the audience becomes less intimidating. If you see people talking among themselves, talk directly to them; this may impel them to stop.

- **Pace yourself and watch your time:** Try to stick to the timetable you set during your rehearsals. You can lay a watch face up on the podium. Or you can position it on the inside of your wrist, where it's easier to glance at it without calling attention to the act.

  Pace yourself. Your instinct may be to rush through the speech and get it over with. However, your listeners will appreciate a pause from time to time.

  Remember that it's better to end early than to run long. Because the conclusion is so important, you don't want to have to be rushed at the end because you're squeezed for time.

It may be that you won't have to do much in the way of stand-up oral presentations. But it's important to learn to speak in public anyway. By learning to speak up in class, for example, you'll become comfortable with getting answers to questions that come to mind during lectures. Through your involvement and interaction you'll increase your learning ability—and probably your grades.

GROUP ACTIVITY #8.4

THE 1-MINUTE ORAL PRESENTATION

Perhaps the prospect of giving a half-hour oral presentation to a large group fills you with terror. A way to begin to overcome your fears is to start by doing something very short before a small group. The instructor may ask you to take some time to prepare this 1-minute oral presentation ahead of time, speaking on whatever topic you choose. Or you may be asked to speak without preparation—doing what is called "extemporaneous" speaking.

The class will be divided into groups of seven or eight people each. The groups will assemble in corners of the room. Give your 1-minute speech to this group. When it's your turn to listen to others, take notes listing positive and negative points about each person's speech. After everyone has finished speaking, take turns giving a brief analysis of the presentation. *Important:* Begin your analysis by giving *positive feedback,* then give *negative feedback,* then conclude with *more positive feedback.* This is the best form in which to give criticism.

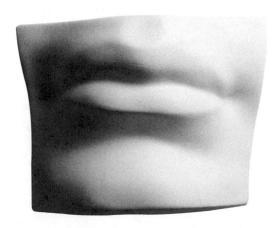

Onward: Applying This Chapter to Your Life

Education is more than memorizing subjects.

Learning to conceive, research, and write papers and speeches is learning how to think. American education has been criticized because students are required to memorize subjects rather than to understand and analyze them. However, as Wisconsin student James Robinson points out, future survival lies in knowing how to solve problems. "If we do not know how to analyze a problem," he says, "how are we ever going to compete in the real world? The problems we are going to face are not all going to be written down in a textbook with the answers in the back. . . . As students, we must realize that we need to come up with our own solutions."[27]

Mindfulness

This is *mindful learning,* and Robinson is right. And the final payoff is this: It has been found that students who learn how to think do better not only in school but in life.[28]

Writing and speaking are among the most useful skills you will ever learn. What two specific things did you find in this chapter that you can use during your career? Write them down here:

_____

_____

_____

_____

_____

_____

_____

_____

_____

_____

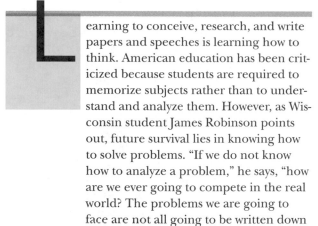

Real Practice
Activities for Real People

Staying
power

REAL PRACTICE ACTIVITY #8.1: HOW CAN IMPROVING YOUR WRITTEN & ORAL COMMUNICATION SKILLS HELP YOU? This practice activity is to be performed in class in small groups, with each group listing as many ways as possible how writing and speaking skills are relevant to other aspects of life. The results may be described later in class discussion.

Often students don't see the connection between real life and some of the subjects they must take to fulfill college requirements. (For example, business majors may question a sociology requirement and communications majors a math requirement.) Actually, *every* subject can be made relevant to real life if you make the effort to discover the connections.

The goal of this practice activity is to help you see the connection between written and oral communication and other parts of your life. The purpose is to help you motivate yourself in order to develop the staying power needed to get through the kinds of courses in college that at first may seem to not have much value to you. In a small group, discuss how becoming better at writing and speaking can benefit you in your career and in your personal relationships.

Mindfulness

REAL PRACTICE ACTIVITY #8.2: USING CREATIVE THINKING TO DEVELOP WRITING TOPICS. This practice activity is to be performed in small groups of five people each. The purpose is to help individuals explore and outline a topic for a research paper.

Take turns with other group members identifying a topic each of you would like to know more about, and giving and getting feedback. This may be a topic for a research paper in another class or simply a subject you would like to explore.

As described in Chapter 2, use the techniques of brainstorming and mind mapping to elaborate on the topic. Circulate the results to others in the group for comments. Later translate your mind map into an outline form that could be the basis for a paper. Turn in both the mind map and the outline to your instructor.

Information
technology

REAL PRACTICE ACTIVITY #8.3: FINDING OUT THE LIMITATIONS OF THE SPELLING & GRAMMAR CHECKERS IN A WORD PROCESSING PROGRAM. This activity should be practiced individually by students outside of class during the course of writing a paper, using a word processing program with spelling and grammar checker. The results of the exercise are to be handed in to the instructor.

One of the first things students discover in a word processing program is the spelling-checker and grammar-checker features. However, some students don't realize that these programs are not perfect—that they still need to proofread their papers. The purpose of this activity is to help you learn to use these features and, more importantly, to recognize their limitations.

This activity requires that you write a paper and then use a personal computer with a word processing program that includes a spelling and grammar checker. The paper may be a short reaction paper, a long research paper, or some other kind of original writing that you've typed on the word processor.

After you've typed in the first draft of the paper, employ the spelling and grammar checker features and make any necessary corrections. Now print out the paper, then *proofread* it—that is, read it over with pen in hand, looking for further mistakes. Do you see any things that the program missed? Examples are words that are correctly spelled but incorrectly used (such as "there," "their," "they're," or "hair" and "hare") or names or dates that are incorrect. Use a dictionary, if necessary. Make corrections in ink, then hand in the paper to your instructor.

The Examined Life

JOURNAL ENTRY #8.1: WRITING ABOUT SOMETHING IMPORTANT TO YOU Write a few words about something that is very important to you, such as a particular person or event that profoundly affected you. (Use a separate sheet of paper, if you wish.) Describe how writing helps you understand it.

_____

_____

_____

_____

_____

_____

_____

_____

_____

JOURNAL ENTRY #8.2: WHAT MORE DO YOU NEED TO FIND OUT ABOUT THE LIBRARY? How comfortable are you with using the school's library? For each of the following library resources, rate yourself on your confidence in using that resource for research. Use the following system:

A = Very comfortable
B = Comfortable
C = Somewhat uncertain
D = Very uncertain
F = Totally unfamiliar

1. Online card catalog   A B C D F

2. Microfiche   A B C D F

3. Interlibrary loan   A B C D F

4. Newspaper, magazine, and journal indexes   A B C D F

5. Specialized dictionaries   A B C D F

6. Internet and other computerized networks   A B C D F

Look at those you rated C, D, or F. What specific steps could you take to become more comfortable with them?

_____

_____

_____

_____

_____

_____

_____

_____

_____

JOURNAL ENTRY #8.3: WHAT DO YOU NEED TO FIND OUT ABOUT TEXT CITATIONS AND WORKS-CITED (BIBLIOGRAPHY) STYLES? One subject that might have been discussed in more detail in this chapter was the proper form for text citations and bibliographies. Is this an area in which you need further help? Who can give you the assistance you need?

_____

_____

_____

_____

_____

_____

_____

_____

JOURNAL ENTRY #8.4: WHAT ARE YOUR WORRIES ABOUT PUBLIC SPEAKING?

What worries do you have about public speaking? Besides the techniques described in this chapter, what other means are available to help you do better at giving stand-up speeches? For instance, the counseling services may offer assistance, or you could join the group known as Toastmasters, which helps amateur speakers achieve proficiency.

_____

_____

_____

_____

_____

_____

_____

_____

II

Personal
Success Strategies

9 Resources & Money

Finding Assistance & Opportunity on Campus

IN THIS CHAPTER In this chapter discover the treasure trove to be found on your campus in these important areas:

- *Assistance:* How to find help—for your studies, health, emotions, finances, and other matters.

- *Opportunity:* How to get extra value with your education—in activities, student life, and living arrangements.

- *Managing costs:* Getting and spending.

- *Important record keeping:* Money plans and expense records.

- *Money handling:* A crash course in strategies.

- *Financial aid:* How to get financial help for education.

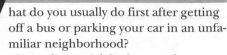

HELP!

hat's a word we've all used at some point. Or certainly wanted to.

Often help is easy to ask for and easy to get. ("Am I in the right line?") At other times, however, Help! may be the silent cry of a student overwhelmed by homesickness, loneliness, test anxiety, family problems, or money worries. Is help available for these sorts of matters? The answer is: you bet!

Unfortunately, sometimes people with a problem can't imagine there's a way out. Or they're too timid or too proud to ask for help. That's why I put this chapter in the book. Its purpose is to show what kind of assistance is available when you need it.

In addition, I want to give you the chance to find out what a gold mine higher education is outside of the classroom. For instance, many former students value lifelong friendships and job contacts they made while in school. To help you realize the same benefits, we will look at opportunities that school gives you.

A Look Around the Campus

PREVIEW & REVIEW Finding out about campus services is like looking over an unfamiliar neighborhood. The orientation program and campus tour for new students is a good way to start. Helpful publications include the college catalog, campus map, student handbook, campus newspaper and bulletins, course lists and instructor evaluations, brochures and posters. Areas of assistance include academic help; physical, emotional, and spiritual help; other college help; activities and campus life; and community services.

hat do you usually do first after getting off a bus or parking your car in an unfamiliar neighborhood?

You take a quick look around.

You check out the area to get a sense of the layout of things. You get a picture of what your options are.

That's what we're going to do in this chapter—take a quick look around the campus, so you can see what your options are. You'll learn how to check out various campus facilities to find out what services and opportunities are available to help you survive, enjoy, and profit from school.

THE ORIENTATION PROGRAM & CAMPUS TOUR. Many colleges offer an orientation program and tour of the campus for new students. However, some facilities and services may be left off the tour (because of time). Or you may not find some of them personally interesting or currently valuable to you. Still, if you have a chance to take the tour, I urge you to do so. You may sometime need to know where to go to get permission to skip a course or get into one already filled. Or you may need to get information to resolve a tenant-landlord hassle or other problem.

PUBLICATIONS: INSTRUCTION MANUALS FOR HIGHER EDUCATION. Many jobs have instruction manuals, briefing books, and similar publications to help employees understand what they are supposed to do. College has them too, as follows:

■ *College catalog:* Publications are a great way to learn about all aspects of campus life. Probably the most valuable is the college catalog, which is the playbook or rule book for the game of higher education. **The _college catalog_ contains requirements for graduation, requirements for degree programs, and course descriptions.** It also may contain a history of the school, information about faculty members, and various programs and services. In addition, it may contain information about financial aid.

The college catalog is most likely available in the Admissions Office, Counseling Office, or campus bookstore.

- *Campus calendar:* Of particular value is the *campus calendar,* **which lists the deadlines and dates for various programs.** You'll particularly want to note the last days to *enroll* in a new course and to *drop* a course without penalty. The campus calendar may be included in the college catalog.

- *Campus map:* Many college catalogs include a map of the campus, but if yours does not, pick up one. You might wish to have a one-page map anyway because it's easier to carry around.

- *Student handbook:* Some colleges publish a *student handbook,* **which summarizes many of the college's policies and regulations.** This may duplicate information in the catalog but be written so as to be more accessible to students.

- *College newspaper and campus bulletins:* The *college newspaper* **is a student-run news publication that is published on some campuses.** The college newspaper may be the single best source of ongoing information. Depending on the campus, it may be published daily, twice a week, weekly, or every two weeks. Because its readership is the entire college community—students, staff, faculty, and possibly townspeople—the news may cover topics of broad interest. In addition, some colleges publish a special "Orientation Edition" of the paper as a service to new students.

  On some campuses, there may also be a student bulletin. **The** *student bulletin,* **or** *campus bulletin,* **is helpful in keeping you informed of campus activities and events,** as well as other matters. This periodical, appearing occasionally throughout the term, may be published by the student government or by an office of the administration.

- *Course lists and instructor evaluations:* The *course list* **is simply a list of the courses being taught in the current school term.** Published before each new term, the course list states what courses are being taught. The list states on what days at what times courses are given, for how many units, and by what instructor.

Sometimes the instructor is simply listed as "Staff." This may mean he or she is a teaching assistant (often a graduate student). Or it may mean that the instructor was simply unassigned at the time the course list was printed. Call the department if you want to know who the instructor is.

As I mentioned in Chapter 6, on many campuses, students publish instructor evaluations. *Instructor evaluations* **consider how fairly instructors grade and how effectively they present their lectures.** If your campus does not have such evaluations, you may be able to sit in on a potential instructor's class. You can also talk with other students there to get a feel for his or her style and ability. In addition, you can find out what degrees an instructor has and from what institutions, usually by looking in the college catalog.

- *Brochures, flyers, and posters:* Especially during orientation or when registering, you may find yourself flooded with brochures. You may also see flyers and posters on campus bulletin boards.

  Some of these may be on serious and important personal subjects. Examples are security and night escorts to parked cars, alcohol and drug abuse, and date rape. Some may be on campus events and club offerings. Some may simply list apartments to share or rides wanted. Some may list upcoming concerts, political rallies, or film festivals.

Most of this kind of information has to do with the informal or extracurricular side of your college experience. Much of this is as important as the purely academic part. Indeed, many prospective employers look at this extracurricular side to see how well rounded a student's educational experience has been.

To begin to get familiar with the college catalog, do Personal Exploration #9.1 *(opposite page).*

SOME PARTICULARLY IMPORTANT PLACES TO KNOW ABOUT. There are three places on campus that, in my opinion, a newcomer should get to know right away:

- **The library:** Most new students don't understand how to use the library and are unaware of the scope of its services. When it comes to writing papers, this is the place to know about.

- **The learning center:** This is the place for learning specific subjects or skills (for example, word processing or math help). You can also get tutoring in most subjects here. The learning center is an invaluable resource.

- **The career counseling center:** If you're undecided about your major, the career counseling center is the place to go. This can save you from going down a lot of blind alleys. Even students who have already chosen a major can benefit from this place, which can help them focus their efforts.

FIVE ADDITIONAL IMPORTANT SERVICES OR CENTERS. There are five additional areas of services or centers, as I will describe in this chapter. They are:

- *Academic help:* Examples are instructors, academic advisors and counselors, librarians, and tutors.

- *Physical, emotional, and spiritual help:* Examples are health and fitness professionals, counselors, psychotherapists,

security personnel, and chaplains. In addition, there are probably support groups (as for adult returning students or single parents, for example).

- *Other help:* Examples are financial affairs, housing office, career counseling and placement, child care, and legal services. There are also various community services, such as post office, laundry, and bank.

- *Activities and campus life:* Examples are athletics, clubs, bands and other musical groups, and fraternities and sororities.

- *Multicultural centers:* Examples are centers for racial and ethnic groups, women, international students, gays and lesbians, nontraditional students, and students with disabilities.

GROUP ACTIVITY #9.1

GOING ON A SCAVENGER HUNT

A scavenger hunt is a party game. People are sent out to acquire, within a time limit and without paying money, items that take some difficulty to obtain. The list is provided by the party's host.

Divide into teams of two. Visit at least one advisor, service, facility, or center from each of the five areas mentioned above. You're urged to follow your curiosity. Visit areas that you would probably not visit were it not for this opportunity. Find out what the facility or center offers or does.

Bring back evidence of your visit for your instructor. (For example, you might bring back a free leaflet, someone's business card, or a one-sentence note from someone you met.) Attach the evidence to a one-page report (composed by both of you) of where you went and what you learned.

LEARNING TO USE YOUR COLLEGE CATALOG

Obtain a copy of your college catalog. Fill in the answers in the following lines.

A. GENERAL

1. How many undergraduate students are enrolled?_____

2. When was the college founded?_____

3. What is the mission, orientation, or specialization of the college? (Examples: liberal arts, religious values, teacher training.)
_____
_____
_____

4. How is the institution organized? (Example: schools, with divisions and departments.)
_____
_____
_____

5. What are three graduate or professional programs offered by the college, if any, that interest you? (Examples: teacher certification, business, law.)
_____
_____
_____

6. What are some other campuses or sites the college has, including extension divisions, if any?
_____
_____
_____

7. Look at the lists of majors and minors offered by the college. Which three majors might interest you?
_____
_____
_____

Which three minors might interest you?
_____
_____
_____

8. Is it possible to graduate with more than one major? If so, which two might interest you?
_____
_____
_____
_____

B. THE CAMPUS CALENDAR

1. *Cut-off dates:* What is the last date this semester on which you may ... (specify month and day)

   Add a course?_____

   Drop a course?_____

   Drop a course and receive partial tuition refund? _____

   Ask for a grade of "Incomplete," if offered?_____

   Withdraw from a course?_____

2. *Holidays:* On what holidays is the college closed this semester?
_____
_____
_____

3. *Registration:* What are the dates for registration for next semester?
_____
_____

4. *Exams:* When are final exams scheduled for this semester?
_____
_____

5. *Class end and start dates:*

   What is the last day of classes for this semester?_____

   What is the first day of classes for next semester?_____

C. TUITION & FINANCIAL AID

1. What is the annual tuition for in-state students at the college?
_____ For out-of-state students? _____

2. What financial aid is available? (Examples: loans, scholarships, work/study.)
_____
_____
_____

D. GRADES

1. Grades instructors give (such as A, B, C, D, F) and what they mean:
_____
_____
_____

2. Meaning of "Pass/fail," if offered:
_____
_____

3. Meaning of "Incomplete," if offered:
_____
_____

4. Meaning of "Audit":
_____
_____

5. What minimum grade point average do you need to maintain in order to be considered in satisfactory academic standing?
_____
_____

6. What happens if you fall below that minimum?
_____
_____

E. CREDITS

1. What is the definition of a credit (or unit)?
_____
_____

2. Does your college give credit for advanced courses taken in high school? _____ For courses taken at other colleges? _____

   For some life experience outside of college? _____

(continued on next page)

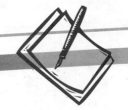

■ F. GRADE-POINT AVERAGE & GRADUATION REQUIREMENTS

1. Explain the formula for computing students' grade-point average:

_____
_____
_____
_____

2. List the courses you are taking this semester or quarter and the number of credits (units) for each.

_____
_____
_____

For each course assign a hypothetical grade according to the following formula: A = 4.0, B = 3.0, C = 2.0, D = 1.0, F = 0.0. Then compute the grade points earned for each course. (Example for one course: "First-Year Experience, 3 credits, grade of A = 4.0; 4.0 x 3 credits = 12 grade points.")

Now add up your grade points earned for all courses. Finally, divide them by the total number of credits (units) attempted to derive your hypothetical grade-point average for the semester or quarter.

_____
_____
_____
_____

3. What minimum grade-point average is required for graduation?

_____

4. Besides completing a major, what are the other requirements for graduation?

_____
_____
_____
_____
_____

■ G. MISCONDUCT

1. _Academic matters:_ How does the college deal with cheating and plagiarism? (Plagiarism is passing off someone else's work as your own, as when writing a paper.)

_____
_____
_____

2. _Nonacademic matters:_ How does the college deal with nonacademic matters such as sexual harassment, drunkenness, property damage, or off-campus arrests?

_____
_____
_____
_____
_____

■ H. SPECIAL PROGRAMS

1. _Academic honors:_ What forms of recognition does the college offer for academic excellence? What are the standards for achieving such honors? (Examples: honors programs, dean's list, Phi Beta Kappa, scholarships.)

_____
_____
_____
_____

2. _Other special programs:_ What other special programs are offered, and what are the criteria for participation? (Examples: study-abroad programs, internships.)

_____
_____
_____
_____
_____

GROUP ACTIVITY OPTION

Complete Personal Exploration #3.1. Then on a separate piece of paper list a feature or two of the college that you're still not quite clear on. Also list some resources you might be interested in. They may include matters related to grades, majors, and graduation. They may also include nonacademic matters that will help you enjoy your college experience.

In a small-group setting discuss anything you're still unsure or confused about. Ask other members of the group what their understanding is. Also discuss those matters you'd like to investigate further.

Which things discussed by your group are particularly interesting or noteworthy? Designate someone to describe them to the class.

Academic Help

PREVIEW & REVIEW People who can assist you with academic problems are academic advisors, instructors, librarians and media center staff, and tutors and study-skills staff. Other academic services include the computer center, music practice rooms, and the Dean of Students Office. Academic advising—which is principally about degrees, majors, and courses—is extremely important because it affects your college, career, and life plans.

Some day you may return to college as a retired person and *actually take some courses for the fun of it.* Older people often do this. I assume, however, that you are the type of student for whom "fun" is not the main priority of the college experience. That is, you are here on the serious mission of getting a degree.

Obtaining a college degree—whether Associate's, Bachelor's, Master's, or other—is the goal, of course, of the academic part of college. The degree signifies that you have passed certain courses with a minimum grade. Completing the courses means that you have passed tests, written research papers, done projects, and shown staying power. To accomplish all these, you must have attended classes, listened to lectures, gone to the library, and read a lot.

Staying power

POSSIBLE ACADEMIC DIFFICULTIES. The problem with accomplishing these tasks is that there are many places where hangups can occur—and where you might need some help. Here are some possibilities: You can't get the classes you want. You wonder if you can waive some prerequisites. You don't know what you still need to do to graduate. You're having trouble with your writing, math, or study skills. You're sick and can't finish your courses. You don't know how to compute your grade-point average. You need recommendations for an employer or a graduate school.

Knowing how to find help, get good advice, and cut through bureaucratic red tape aren't skills that become obsolete after college. They are part and parcel of being A Person Who Can Get Things Done, which is what we all wish to be. Learning how to find your way around the college academic system, then, is training for life. Outside college, these skills are called *networking* and *troubleshooting*—and they are invaluable in helping you get where you want to go.

To get help or advice in college, you may need to consult the following academic services or people:

- Academic advisors
- Instructors
- Librarians and media center staff
- Tutors and study-skills staff
- Some other academic services
- When all other help fails: the Dean of Students office

ACADEMIC ADVISORS. What people will you deal with the most for academic matters? Probably your instructors. But there is another individual who, in the grand scheme of things, could be *more* important: your academic advisor. Why? "For most freshmen, the first year of college is both exciting and crisis oriented," say one pair of writers. "New students are unfamiliar with college resources, their major field, the faculty, course work, academic expectations, and career applications of their major."[1] Thus, *academic advising is important because it affects your planning for college and, beyond that, for your career and for your life.*

The *academic advisor* counsels students about their academic program. The academic advisor is either a full-time administrative employee or a faculty member, often in the field in which you'll major. What does he or she do that I think is so important? There are two principal activities:

■ *Gives information about degrees, majors, and courses:* The academic advisor explains to you what courses are required in your degree program. **The *degree program* consists of all the courses you must take to obtain a college degree in a specific field.** Courses will be of two types:

1. *General education courses* are those specified in the college catalog that all students have to take to obtain a degree. Examples are a choice of some courses in social science (as in sociology, political science) or in humanities (as in English, philosophy).

2. *Courses in your major* will be those offered, from another list, that are needed for you to complete your major. **Your *major* is your field of specialization.** Perhaps a third of the courses you need to graduate will be in this category. Some colleges also require a *minor*, **a smaller field of specialization,** which will entail fewer courses.

Both general-education courses and the courses for your major are identified on a *curriculum worksheet* available to you and your advisor. **The *curriculum worksheet* lists all the courses required for the major and the semesters in which it is recommended you take them.** It may also list additional courses you might have to take if you transfer from a community college to a university. The accompanying example shows a curriculum worksheet for Hotel Technology: Hospitality Management, which is offered at the college at which I teach. (See ■ *Panel 9.1.*)

A curriculum worksheet. This example, which shows the courses required and their recommended order, is for a major in Hotel Technology: Hospitality Management.

- *Provides information, advice, and support in general:* Academic advisors are usually also available to talk about other matters important to you. These include difficulty keeping up with course work, uncertainty about your major, worries about fair treatment by an instructor, and personal stresses. If an advisor does not feel capable of helping you directly, he or she can certainly suggest where to turn. (You may be directed to a counselor, who is different from an advisor.)

Here's an important fact: *poor academic advising is a major reason students drop out of college.*[2] Conversely, students who receive good academic advising are not only more apt to graduate but also are happier while in college. For students in community colleges planning to go on to a university, seeing an academic advisor can save them headaches later. This is because different colleges and universities sometimes have different transfer requirements. Thus, it's possible to end up spending extra semesters taking courses at the junior or senior level that you could have completed earlier. An academic advisor can help you avoid such time wasters.

When you enter college, your academic advisor will be assigned to you. Later, if you change majors or if you go from being "Undecided" or "Undeclared" to declaring your major, you may change advisors. When I was in college, I changed from being a philosophy major to undeclared to sociology major. Each time I was assigned a new academic advisor.

Students should see their academic advisor *at least* once a semester or quarter. You should also see him or her whenever you have any questions or important decisions to make about your college career. (See ■ *Panel 9.2.*)

INSTRUCTORS. Probably the paid representatives of the college that you will see most are the instructors. As mentioned in Chapter 6, in most institutions, instructors are required to be in their offices during certain hours (posted on their office doors or available through the department secretary). In addition, many are available for questions for a minute or so after class.

---

  sing your advisor for college success.

Like everything else in higher education, you get out of academic advising what you put into it. Here are some tips for using your advisor to make school work best for you:

Be aware of the advising period—see the catalog: The school requires students at least once a semester or quarter to see their advisors about which courses they will take the next term. The period for doing this, often about two weeks, is usually listed on the academic calendar in the school catalog and is announced in campus notices. *Put the dates of the advising period on your personal calendar and be sure to make an appointment to see your advisor.*

See your advisor more than once a term to establish a relationship: Your advisor is not just a bureaucrat who has to sign off on your courses and should not be treated as such. See him or her at least one other time during the semester or quarter to discuss problems and progress. Ask about interesting courses, interesting instructors, any possible changes in major, and difficult courses and how to handle them. Discuss any personal problems affecting your life and work. *In short, if possible, make your advisor a mentor—a person you can trust.*

If your advisor isn't right for you, find another one: If you feel your advisor is distant, uncaring, arrogant, ignorant, or otherwise unsuitable, don't hesitate to make a change. You have this right, although you have to be your own advocate here. *To make a change, ask another instructor or staff person to be your advisor.* Depending on the arrangements on your campus, you may get another advisor by going to the Advisement Center, the Registrar, the Office of Student Services, or the Dean of Students.

LIBRARIANS & MEDIA-CENTER STAFF. Perhaps you think the library is just a quiet place with books and magazines where you can go to study. Actually, there is more to it than that. *One of the first things you should do in college is find out how to use the library.* Often the library has a room or section in it called the *media center.*

The library is one of the most important buildings on campus. Don't be intimidated by all the staff, books, and machines (computer terminals, microfilm readers). Instead, I suggest doing the following:

- *Tour the facilities:* Go to the library/media center and simply walk around every place you are allowed to go. *Actively* scan the titles on the shelves, looking for books or magazines you're interested in. *Actively* take note of the desks and study areas available, picking out a couple of spots you might favor using later. *Actively* read the directions on how to use machines, such as computers, microfilm readers, and copiers.

- *Ask how to use the facilities:* Have you ever noticed how some people are so concerned with how they look to others that they never ask directions? Some drivers, for instance, would rather "figure it out for themselves" than stop and ask a local person how to get somewhere.

    These folks really limit themselves. People shut off a major source of personal growth when they can't ask for assistance or help.

    If you're the kind of person who's reluctant to seek help, here's a good exercise. Ask the librarians or media center staff for a *demonstration* on how to use the facilities to do research. Sometimes there is a standard guided tour. Ask how to use the computer-based catalog for books and periodicals and how to use microfilm equipment. Ask how to play videotapes or audiotapes in the media center. Ask about other research libraries and facilities on campus.

    Libraries and media centers were described in detail in Chapter 8, "Writing & Speaking."

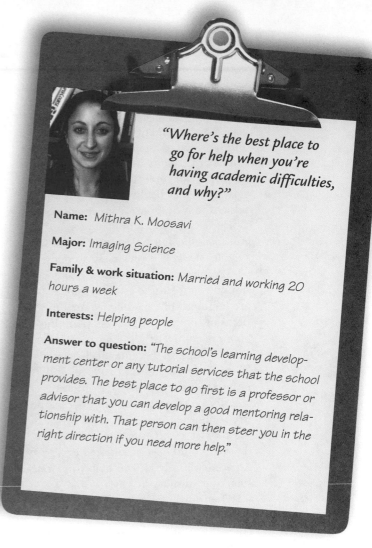

"Where's the best place to go for help when you're having academic difficulties, and why?"

Name: Mithra K. Moosavi

Major: Imaging Science

Family & work situation: Married and working 20 hours a week

Interests: Helping people

Answer to question: "The school's learning development center or any tutorial services that the school provides. The best place to go first is a professor or advisor that you can develop a good mentoring relationship with. That person can then steer you in the right direction if you need more help."

TUTORS & STUDY-SKILLS STAFF. *This is an important, probably underused resource.*

Most colleges offer courses or services for improving your reading, writing, math, or study skills. The place for doing this may be located in a learning center. A _learning center_, or _learning lab_, **is a special center where you go to learn a specific subject or skill.** Sometimes these are located in a special building on campus. Sometimes they are attached to various departments, such as foreign language departments. For example, some foreign-language learning centers have computer terminals or booths with television monitors and earphones for practice purposes.

In addition, you can arrange through the learning center or through academic departments (ask the department secretary) for tutoring help. **A _tutor_ is essentially a private teacher or coach.** This person will help you, through a series of regularly scheduled meetings, to improve a particular skill.

SOME OTHER ACADEMIC SERVICES. Other on-campus resources are available to help you with your academic work, ranging from photocopiers to music practice rooms. For example, your campus may have several art resources: museums, art galleries, archives, and special libraries. Most campuses have computers or a lab in which you may use a personal computer. Computer centers offer courses that teach valuable computer skills, such as word processing.

WHEN ALL OTHER HELP FAILS: THE DEAN OF STUDENTS OFFICE. If you can't seem to find help for whatever your difficulty is, try the Dean of Students office. It is the *job* of the staff here to see that you are taken care of in college. If they can't handle the problem themselves, they will find someone who will.

Physical, Emotional, & Spiritual Help

PREVIEW & REVIEW People to help you take care of your physical, emotional, and spiritual well-being are found in several places. They include the health service, counseling center, security office, chapel, wellness/fitness services, and on-campus and off-campus support groups.

The academic help I described has to do with taking care of your mind. Now let's consider the services offered to take care of your body, heart, and spirit.

The basic facilities and services are these:

- Health service
- Counseling center
- Security
- Chapels and religious services
- Wellness/fitness services
- Support groups

HEALTH SERVICE: THE CLINIC OR INFIRMARY. Most colleges have some sort of health or medical service. Treatment is often free or low-cost for minor problems.

If you are attending a large residential campus, there is probably a clinic, health-care center, or infirmary staffed by nurses and physicians. If you go to a college that mainly serves commuters, it may be just a nurse's office. The college assumes that most students' health care will be han-

dled by community hospitals and other resources. However, you can at least get first aid, aspirin, and advice and referrals.

The health service is a good place to go to if you need help with physical problems, of course. In addition, it can help with anxiety, birth-control information, sexually transmitted diseases, and alcohol or other drug problems.

COUNSELING CENTER: PSYCHOLOGICAL SERVICES. All of us have stresses in our lives, and going to college unquestionably adds to them. If you're sleeping through classes because you dread the subject or are panicky with test anxiety, *don't hesitate to seek help at the counseling center.* Certainly if you feel you're on the verge of flunking for whatever reason, get to the center as quickly as you can. Such counseling is often free or low-cost.

In addition, problems arise that may not have much to do with the academic side of college. These include love relationships, problems with parents and with self-esteem, "Who am I?" identity concerns, pregnancy, and worries about sexually transmitted diseases. Most psychological counselors are familiar with these problems and are able to help.

Psychological distress is as real as physical distress and should not be ignored. Some students worry that it is not cool or it will be seen as an admission of weakness to seek

counseling help. Nothing could be further from the truth. People who are unwilling to admit they need help often find their problems "leak out" in other ways. These could include oversleeping, alcohol or other types of drug abuse, or anger toward family or roommates. By refusing to get help, they compound their problems until later they need help even more. Believe me, I speak from experience on this because, besides teaching first-year college-experience courses, I also work as a counselor.

SECURITY: CAMPUS POLICE. Campus security personnel or police may be most visible in their roles of enforcing parking control—a problem on almost every college campus. However, they do far more than that.

Afraid to walk across campus to your car after a night class? Call campus security to ask for an escort. It's done all the time on many urban campuses. Locked out of your car, residence hall, or locker? Call the campus police. Lost your watch, discovered your room burglarized, been hassled by a drunk, or found yourself dealing with someone who's been raped? Such problems are the reasons why, unfortunately, campus security exists. *(See ▪ Panel 9.3.)*

CHAPELS & RELIGIOUS SERVICES. Residential campuses often have chapels that students may attend for religious services. Even nonreligious students are welcome to go in during quiet times just to meditate. Or they may wish to talk about personal or spiritual problems with the chaplain.

In addition, many campuses have organizations serving students of different religious affiliations. Examples are the Newman Club for those of the Catholic faith and Hillel House for those of the Jewish faith.

WELLNESS/FITNESS SERVICES: ATHLETIC & FITNESS CENTERS. If you think gymnasiums, field houses, and athletic centers are just for athletes (as I did in my

Safety is a major issue on many campuses. At your college, you may see posters, brochures, and newspaper articles concerned with such matters as dormitory security, date rape, and use of nighttime escorts to parked cars. The basic piece of advice is: Use common sense about your safety; be alert for trouble. Other safety tips are as follows:

WHEN WALKING, TRAVELING, OR OUT IN PUBLIC:

1. At night or early morning, don't walk alone or jog alone. Stay with groups. Take advantage of campus escort services. Travel in well-populated, well-lighted areas.

2. Don't show money or valuables in public. Discreetly tuck away your cash after using an automated teller machine.

3. On foot: Walk rapidly and look as though you're going somewhere; don't dawdle. If someone makes signs of wanting to talk to you, just keep on going. It's less important that you be polite than that you be safe.

4. In a car: Make sure all doors are locked. Don't open them for anyone you don't know.

WHEN IN YOUR RESIDENCE OR CAMPUS BUILDINGS:

1. Lock your dorm-room or residence doors, even when you go to the shower. Theft is a big problem in some residence halls.

2. Don't let strangers into your residence hall. Ask any stranger the name of the person he or she wants to see.

3. Don't leave backpacks, purses, or briefcases unattended, even in your residence lounge.

IF YOU SENSE YOU MIGHT BE ATTACKED:

1. If you are facing an armed criminal, the risk of injury may be minimized by cooperating with his or her demands. Avoid any sudden movements and give the criminal what he or she wants.

2. If you sense your life is in immediate danger, use any defense you can think of: screaming, kicking, running. Your objective is to get away.

3. In a violent crime, it is generally ineffective for the victim to cry or plead with the attacker. Such actions tend to reinforce the attacker's feeling of power over the victim.

Other Kinds of Assistance

PREVIEW & REVIEW Questions about your academic record can be resolved at the registrar's office. Other assistance is available to help with financial aid, housing, transportation, check cashing, job placement, career counseling, day care, and legal services. Alumni organizations can also be interesting resources. Finally, services not found on campus, ranging from post offices to gas stations to church-sponsored student centers, are available in the community.

oing to a college campus is almost like going to a one-industry town, the industry in this case being education. Fortunately, the town's administrators also care about students. Thus, they have set up services to deal with those of your needs that are not academic, physical, emotional, or spiritual.

Among the services available:

- Registrar
- Financial aid
- Housing
- Transportation
- Cashier/Business office
- Job placement
- Career counseling
- Child care
- Legal services
- Community services

first year), think again. They are supposed to be available for all students, including physically challenged students.

You can use not only lockers, showers, and spas but also pools, fitness centers, weight equipment, racquetball courts, and basketball courts. If your campus is anything like mine, you'll see hundreds of students jogging or playing or working out every day. And many of them did not take up such activities until they got to college.

SUPPORT GROUPS. Most colleges offer some sort of connection to support groups of all kinds. There are, for example, support groups for people having difficulties with weight, alcohol, drugs, gambling, incest, spouse abuse, or similar personal problems. There are also support groups or "affinity" groups. (They may exist for women, men, the physically challenged, gays, ethnic and racial minorities, returning students, foreign students, and so on.) The counseling center can probably connect you with one of interest to you. Or you may see meeting announcements in campus publications.

REGISTRAR. The _registrar_ **is responsible for keeping all academic records.** This is the office you need to seek out if you have questions about whether a grade was recorded correctly. The people there can also answer your inquiries about transcripts, graduation, or transfer from or to another college.

FINANCIAL AID. This is one of the most important offices in the college. If you're putting yourself through school or your family can't support you entirely, you need to get to know this office. Just as its title indicates, **the _financial aid office_ is concerned with finding financial aid for students.** Such help can consist of low-interest loans, scholarships, part-time work, and other arrangements.

I discuss the workings of financial aid later in this chapter.

HOUSING. No doubt you already have a roof over your head for this semester or quarter. If you're living in a campus residence hall, you probably got there through the housing office when you accepted your admission. However, most college students—80% of them—live off campus or at home.

The campus _housing office_ helps students find rooms in campus housing (except fraternities and sororities). It also provides listings of off-campus rooms, apartments, and houses for rent in the community. Because landlords probably must meet standards for safety and cleanliness, the housing office may be a better source than advertisements for rentals.

TRANSPORTATION. The transportation office may be part of campus security or the campus police. **The _transportation office_ issues permits for parking on campus and gives out information on public transportation and car pools.**

CASHIER/BUSINESS OFFICE. The _cashier's office_ or _business office_ is where you go to pay college fees or tuition.** On some campuses you may also be able to cash checks here.

JOB PLACEMENT. The _job placement office_, or _employment office_, provides job listings from local or campus employers looking for student help.** Most of the jobs are part time. They may range from waiting tables, to handing out equipment in the chemistry lab, to working behind a counter in a store.

CAREER COUNSELING. The _career counseling center_ is the place to find help if you're having trouble deciding on career goals or a major.** (It may also be called the _career development center_ or the _career center_.) We consider the process of selecting a major and a career in Chapter 13, "Majors & Careers."

CHILD CARE. Some colleges offer child-care or day-care facilities for children of adult students and faculty. The centers are usually staffed by professional child-care specialists. They may be assisted by student interns or helpers studying child-related disciplines, such as education or psychology.

LEGAL SERVICES. Larger colleges and universities have a legal-services office to provide information and counseling to students. Naturally, I hope you'll never have to use it. Still, it's good to know where to call if problems such as landlord-tenant disputes, auto accidents, drunk driving, or employment discrimination arise.

COMMUNITY SERVICES. You'll probably want such services as post office, laundromats, copy centers, automated teller machines, eating places, service stations, and bicycle repair shops. These may exist right on campus, at least at larger colleges. In other places they exist in the community close by the college. You may also be able to find help in consumer organizations, political and environmental organizations, city recreation departments, and YMCAs and YWCAs. Finally, you may need to find such services as off-campus counseling, child care, and legal assistance.

Activities & Campus Life

PREVIEW & REVIEW   A great deal of student life centers on the student union, the book store, college residences, and clubs and activities.

I f colleges consisted only of lecture halls, laboratories, and libraries, they wouldn't be much fun. Much of the fun and energy on a college campus come from the places that are student-centered. These include the student union, the bookstore, student residences, and other centers of student life.

STUDENT UNION. This is often the "crossroads of the campus," the place where you go to hang out after class, to find your friends. **The _student union_, often called the _student center_ or _campus center_, is different on every campus. However, it most certainly includes a cafeteria or dining hall and probably some recreation areas.** Recreation may include television rooms, Ping-Pong tables, pool tables, video games, and maybe even a bowling alley. There may also be a bookstore, study lounges, a post office, convenience store, barbershop or hairdresser, and bank or automated teller machine. Here's where you will find bulletin boards advertising everything from films to shared rides.

BOOKSTORE. Often located in the student center, the campus bookstore's main purpose is to make textbooks and educational supplies available for students. Beyond that, it may carry anything from candy, coffee mugs, and college sweatshirts to general-interest books and personal computers. The bookstore also often sells the _college catalog_ and the _course list_ (if these are not free).

In most college bookstores, you can find textbooks for the courses you're taking by looking for the course number on the shelves. Three tips I try to pass along to my students regarding textbooks are as follows:

- _Check out the books for your courses:_ If ever there was a way of getting a preview of your academic work, it is here. Want to know how hard that course in physics or German is going to be? Go to the bookstore and take a look through the textbooks.

- _Buy the books early:_ Many students do a lot of course adding and dropping at the beginning of the school term. Thus, they may wait to buy their textbooks until they are sure of what their classes are. Big mistake. Books may be sold out by the time they make up their minds, and new ones may take weeks to arrive. Better to buy the texts, but don't write in them. Hang on to your receipts so that you can return the books later and get your money back.

- _Buy the right edition:_ As material becomes outdated, publishers change the editions of their books. If you buy a used version of the assigned text, make sure you get the most recent edition. An out-of-date edition (even for a history book) won't have all the facts you need to know.

In some communities, off-campus bookstores also carry textbooks, both new and used.

COLLEGE RESIDENCES. Some first-year students live at home or in off-campus housing, particularly for commuter schools, such as many two-year colleges. However, at residential colleges, many first-year students—particularly those of the traditional student age of about 18 or so—live in a campus dormitory. **A _dormitory_ or _residence hall_ is a facility providing rooms, or suites of rooms, for groups of students.** In a typical case, you might share a room with another student. Each dormitory floor would have one community bathroom, if the dorm is single-sex, or two, if it's shared by both sexes.

One good source of advice is the resident assistant. **The _resident assistant_, or _RA_, is an advisor who lives in the residence hall who is usually a student also.** RAs have been through the same kinds of experiences you are presently undergoing, so they can readily relate to your problems.

Fraternities and sororities may be open to first-year students. However, you probably will have to have "pledged" (chosen to join) during the summer or by the end of the first fall term. I'd advise finding out the _purpose_ of a fraternity or a sorority before joining, since they are not all alike. Some, for instance, are more service-oriented than others. Once you're in, however, you may have a network of friends and connections that will be invaluable later in life.

STUDENT LIFE. Whatever your background, there is probably some club, association, or activity on or near the campus that will interest you. Through these you can continue to develop talents discovered before college, such as in music or sports. You can also use them to develop new talents and interests, such as in theater, politics, or camping.

You can join groups not only simply to have fun but also for two other important reasons. The first is to make friends. The second is to get some experience related to your major. For instance, if you major in journalism, you'll certainly want to work in whatever media are available on campus—newspaper, radio, film, tele-

vision. The same is true with other majors. This is not just "pretend" stuff. It is valid experience that you'll want to put on your career résumé when you go job hunting later.

You may wish to try Personal Exploration #9.2 (_opposite page_).

Managing Costs: Getting & Spending

PREVIEW Students get their money from parents, jobs, grants and loans, and other sources. They spend it not only on college and living expenses but also in some unpredictable ways. Handling your money is a matter of constantly balancing your income and your expenses.

ollege is a financial struggle for many people. Is it worth it?

Many students are doing whatever it takes financially to get a college education. More first-year students than ever before are now basing their choice of college not on educational reasons but on financial reasons. For example, they

CAMPUS SERVICES & EXTRACURRICULAR ACTIVITIES

This Personal Exploration has two parts. In Part A, you take a walking tour of the campus. In Part B, you explore extracurricular activities of possible interest to you.

A. A WALK AROUND CAMPUS: FINDING IMPORTANT SERVICES

Find the following places, and write down the location and the telephone number for contacting them. (If these places do not exist on your campus, indicate *None* in the space.) Unless your instructor asks you to turn this in, post the list over your desk or near your bed.

LEARNING/TUTORING CENTER

Building name & room number

_____

_____

Telephone _____

LIBRARY/MEDIA CENTER

Building name & room number

_____

_____

Telephone _____

YOUR ACADEMIC ADVISOR

Building name & room number

_____

_____

Telephone _____

DEAN OF STUDENTS

Building name & room number

_____

_____

Telephone _____

HEALTH SERVICE OR INFIRMARY

Building name & room number

_____

_____

Telephone _____

COUNSELING CENTER

Building name & room number

_____

_____

Telephone _____

SECURITY OR CAMPUS POLICE

Building name & room number

_____

_____

Telephone _____

CHAPEL

Building name & room number

_____

_____

Telephone _____

REGISTRAR

Building name & room number

_____

_____

Telephone _____

FINANCIAL AID OFFICE

Building name & room number

_____

_____

Telephone _____

HOUSING OFFICE

Building name & room number

_____

_____

Telephone _____

TRANSPORTATION OFFICE

Building name & room number

_____

_____

Telephone _____

CASHIER/BUSINESS OFFICE

Building name & room number

_____

_____

Telephone _____

JOB PLACEMENT CENTER

Building name & room number

_____

_____

Telephone _____

CAREER COUNSELING CENTER

Building name & room number

_____

_____

Telephone _____

CHILD CARE

Building name & room number

_____

_____

Telephone _____

LEGAL SERVICES

Building name & room number

_____

_____

Telephone _____

STUDENT UNION OR CENTER

Building name & room number

_____

_____

Telephone _____

BOOKSTORE

Building name & room number

_____

_____

Telephone _____

(continued on next page)

B. LOOKING INTO EXTRA-CURRICULAR ACTIVITIES

Choose three extracurricular activities that you are interested in getting involved in. They might be a club, an athletic event, a community-service organization. The catalog, student newspaper, bulletin, or other information will indicate what's available. Then, for one of the three activities, attend one event or meeting this week. In the following lines, describe what you did, including the names of club officers, performers, or other principals involved.

_____

_____

_____

_____

_____

_____

_____

_____

GROUP ACTIVITY OPTION

Do the first part of this project with another person from your class—someone you don't know. Turn in your written results to your instructor.

may choose an institution because it charges low tuition, offers financial aid, or enables them to live at home.[3] Many students are also having to borrow in order to meet their college expenses. Half the students graduating from college have debts, such as student loans, that have to be repaid.[4] Indeed, the number of students in debt has doubled over the past 10 years.[5]

In addition, more and more students are taking longer than four years to graduate from college. In part this is because many need to work and go to school part time. At the University of Texas in Austin, for instance, fewer than half of the first-year students graduate in four years. At San Francisco State University in California, fewer than a quarter of students graduate within _five_ years.[6]

These facts are evidence that a lot of students are willing to go to great lengths to get a college education. Are the sacrifices worth it? As Chapter 1 showed, the evidence is that it is. Most college graduates make incomes sufficient to repay their investment in college. As a group, college graduates have always done better than high-school graduates, but in recent years they have widened the gap significantly. During the 1980s, college grads earned about 30% more than high-school graduates. Now they earn _60% more._[7]

Thus, even if you leave school owing $10,000—the debt of the average student finishing today—you'll probably be able to handle it. Indeed, a year after graduation, college graduates will be making an average (median) annual income of $18,600.[8,9]

Add to this the fact that college graduates usually have happier, more fulfilled lives than noncollege graduates, and the costs seem worth it.

GROUP ACTIVITY #9.2

WHAT ARE COMMON CONCERNS ABOUT MONEY?

On a sheet of paper, write down some things that come to mind about money—your five principal thoughts or worries. Don't put your name on the paper, but fold it up for collection by the instructor. The instructor will read aloud some of the responses to the class for discussion purposes.

Questions for discussion: How common are some of these concerns? What can you do about them? Does it make you feel better knowing that others have the same worries you have?

PAYING ATTENTION TO YOUR MONEY. Probably the best advice that can be given about money is that *you have to pay attention.* "Our inattentiveness toward money is enough of a misperception of reality that it can lead us into trouble," says an economist and former banker. In this way it is dangerous in the same sense that "any misperception of reality can lead to trouble."[10]

Thus, he says, the most important rule is that "you have to keep track of your money. You have to know approximately how much you have, how much you are spending, how much is coming in, what the general direction of your dollar flow is."[11] Once again, this means applying mindfulness to what you're doing.

Mindfulness

If you can add and subtract, that's all that's required to keep track of your money while in college. After all, there are only three parts to basic money management:

- *Getting*—determining your **income, or where the money comes from**

- *Spending*—determining your **outgo, or what your expenditures are**

- *Balancing*—determining that you have the income *when you need it* to balance the spending

Let's take a look at these.

THE GETTING: YOUR INCOME. Most people would not consider gambling and robbery efficient sources of income. (Neither are predictable nor look good on a career résumé.) However, there are a variety of other sources. Most students have a mix, as follows:[12]

- *Family assistance:* Nearly three-quarters of students have this resource.

- *Employment:* More than half of all students work during summers. Nearly a third work part-time during the school year.

- *Grants or scholarships:* A good portion of college costs are supported by college, federal, or state grants or scholarships, and nearly half of students have access to this resource.

- *Loans:* Many college costs are supported from the Guaranteed (Stafford) Student Loan.

- *Other sources:* Savings not derived from summer or part-time work earnings and other sources make up the rest of the income sources. More than a quarter of all students draw on nonwork-related savings as a resource.

Do you have more control over your sources of income than of your expenses? That's up to you to decide. Some students get a regular allowance from their parents. Others, such as many adult returning students, may have to earn or borrow every cent they get—more evidence of how the world is unfair. On the other hand, those who must go out and scrape up their income themselves have one advantage. They often develop a better sense of the value of money than those who simply have it given to them.

THE SPENDING: YOUR OUTGO. An important moral is: *It's important to distinguish between your needs and your wants.* Sure, you might want to go out and party, to dress right, to treat your friends, but do you need to? You might like to move off campus or away from home and have your own apartment, but do you have to? With the constant drumming of advertising on us from television and other mass media (18,000 messages a day, supposedly), we are always being made to *want* all kinds of things. But, when you think about it, we *need* very little. This can be a healthy point of view to take when you consider your expenses.

Expenses are of the following types:

- **One-time educational expenses:** These are one-shot expenses for items that you need to buy only once and that might serve you for most of your college years. Examples are bicycle (for getting to or around campus), computer or typewriter, furniture and linens, and dictionary and other reference books. Some of these you (or your family) may already have at home.

- **Recurring educational expenses:** These are educational expenses that are repeated every quarter or semester. Examples are tuition, registration fees, books and educational supplies, and laboratory fees. Many of these figures you can get from your college catalog.

- **Housing, food, and clothing expenses:** These are the expenses that it takes just to live: housing, utilities, food. Don't forget to add insurance, such as fire and theft insurance of your possessions. You also need to determine your clothing expenses—even if you wear only T-shirts and jeans half the time.

  NOTE: Don't underestimate the cost of food. Besides the college-cafeteria ticket, if that's your arrangement, you'll need to allow for meals out and snacks— possibly a big item.

- **Transportation:** If you have a car, this can be a big expense, because you'll need to allow for car insurance, maintenance, and repairs, as well as gas and oil. Parking fees can also be a big item. Many students don't have cars, of course, but need to allow for bus or other commuting fees.

- **Personal and health expenses:** These include expenses for your laundry, toothpaste and other personal-care products, medicines, and health insurance or health-center fees.

- **Telephone expense:** This expense can get tricky, depending on your living arrangements, but it should be budgeted for.

- **Entertainment:** If you didn't budget up above for expenses for snacks and eating out, put them here. Dating, going to musical or athletic events, movies or theater, skiing, whatever seems to be fun— add these expenses here. Also add as many other entertainment expenses as

you can think of. These include television, CDs and tapes, athletic gear, musical instruments, travel and hotels during spring break, and so on.

- **Emergencies and other expenses:** Bad stuff happens, and you need to allow for it. I'm talking about car breakdowns, emergency trips home, roommates skipping out and sticking you with their telephone bills, and so on. You may also want to plan for some good stuff—a summer trip, for example.

THE BALANCING ACT. What if you get in most of your money at the beginning of the fall term, but your expenses will go on for the next nine months? One of my students, on picking up his financial-aid money at the start of the school year, thought the check looked so big that he went and bought an expensive CD player. Later he found himself short when the telephone bill came in.

One problem that people who don't have a regular allowance or paycheck have to face is *uneven cash flow.* That is, many bills (rent, phone, credit cards) tend to come due at regular intervals. However, the income does not flow in on the same timely basis. Thus, some short-range saving is necessary. Of course, saving money may not be as much fun as spending it. However, short-range saving sure beats the desperate feeling of not having the funds there when the rent is due. Managing your money, in short, is a constant balancing act between income and outgo.

For many of us, money has a way of just dribbling through our fingers, and we're not really sure where it goes. That's why credit counselors, who help people in debt, have clients keep detailed records of all expenses, even for candy bars and newspapers. Even if you don't have money troubles, before you can *plan* how to manage your money, you need to *observe* your present money patterns. To do this, I suggest doing Personal Exploration #9.3 for a week, longer if you can. From this information, you can draw up some spending categories and projections, as we will show.

THE MONEY DIAGNOSTIC REPORT:
WHERE DOES IT COME FROM, WHERE DOES IT GO?

Tear out or photocopy this page and carry it around with you in an accessible place for a week.

Every time you receive a check or cash (*Money in*), write down its source and the amount. (Example: "Loan from Susie, $10.") Every time you spend money—whether cash, check, or credit card (*Money out*)—write down the expenditure and the amount. (Example: "Movie, food: $12.")

■ **MONEY IN:** Examples of sources of funds: job, parents, grant, savings, loan, friend, tax refund.

MONEY IN FROM	SUNDAY	MONDAY	TUESDAY	WEDNESDAY	THURSDAY	FRIDAY	SATURDAY

Total received for week: _____

■ **MONEY OUT:** Examples of expenditures: books, meals, bus fare, snacks, phone, rent, entertainment, clothes, laundry.

MONEY OUT FOR	SUNDAY	MONDAY	TUESDAY	WEDNESDAY	THURSDAY	FRIDAY	SATURDAY

Total spent for week: _____

Money Plans & Expense Record

A money plan, or budget, is of two types. The yearly *money plan* helps you look at the big picture of your income and outgo. The *monthly money* plan helps project ordinary monthly expenses. The money *expense record* tells you what your expenses actually were.

To effectively balance your getting and spending, you need to know where you're going. This requires formulating a *money plan,* the name we prefer rather than *budget,* although they are the same. **A *money plan*, or *budget*, is simply a plan or schedule of how to balance your income and expenses. It helps you see where your money is going to come from and where it is going to go.**

Most students find it useful to have two kinds of money plans:

- *Yearly:* A yearly money plan helps you visualize the big picture for the school year.

- *Monthly:* A monthly money plan, which includes "Money in" and "Money out" columns, helps you keep track of your ongoing financial situation.

Let's take a look at these.

THE YEARLY MONEY PLAN. The yearly money plan is your big-picture estimate of your income and expenses for the academic year (for example, September to June). You may be able to obtain much of your financial information from the college catalog. Examples of sources of "Money in" are the dollar amounts coming to you from loans or grants. Examples of kinds of "Money out" are tuition and dormitory room and board.

Other information you may have to estimate. If you have already established a record of expenses, as in Personal Exploration #9.3, you can use that. You can also collect a month or two of old bills and receipts, canceled checks, and credit card statements. Then you can estimate what these expenses would amount to over the course of the school year. If you have not already made out a Yearly Money Plan, I strongly suggest you spend some time on Personal Exploration #9.4 *(opposite page).*

THE MONTHLY MONEY PLAN. The monthly money plan is a smaller version of the yearly one. It is particularly useful if you don't live in an on-campus dormitory or residence hall (thus appropriate for adult returning students). Then you are more apt to have several monthly bills, such as rent, phone, water, electricity, gas, and garbage. Even students living on campus, however, may have monthly credit-card and telephone bills for which they need to plan.

Developing a monthly money plan requires three steps:

- *Subtract large one-time expenses from yearly income:* First you need to take your *yearly* income and subtract all your *large one-time* expenses: college tuition, registration fees, housing fees, meal ticket, textbooks and supplies (total for all terms), and insurance premiums. Some students also subtract their transportation from home to campus and back at the beginning and end of the school year.

  Example: Using round figures, suppose you have $18,000 coming in from all sources. This includes loans, grants, part-time and summer work, and parents' help. Suppose your tuition and registration fees are $10,000. Add your on-campus housing fee ($3,000), meal ticket ($1,500), insurance ($300), and textbooks and supplies ($300 for two semesters). Add your round-trip plane ticket from home ($400). The total comes to $15,500. You then subtract $15,500 from $18,000, which leaves $2,500.

- *Divide the remaining sum by the number of months to determine how much you have to spend on everything else:* After subtracting one-time large expenses from your yearly income, you can see how much you have left for other requirements.

THE YEARLY MONEY PLAN: HOW MUCH MONEY COMES IN & GOES OUT DURING A SCHOOL YEAR?

■ INCOME (FOR 10 MONTHS)

Examples of money sources: grants/scholarships, loans, salary, parents, refunds, sale of unneeded belongings, other.

INCOME	SEP	OCT	NOV	DEC	JAN	FEB	MAR	APR	MAY	JUN

Total income: _____

■ OUTGO (FOR 10 MONTHS)

Examples of expenses: rent/mortgage, food, tuition, college fees, books/supplies, transportation (including parking), clothes, phone, insurance, medical, child care, personal items, entertainment, other.

OUTGO	SEP	OCT	NOV	DEC	JAN	FEB	MAR	APR	MAY	JUN

Total outgo: _____

Example: Suppose you figure you had $2,500 left over after subtracting one-time expenses from yearly income. You would divide that by the number of months in the academic year—that is, nine months. This would give you about $278 a month to spend. This may seem like a lot if you just need to cover snacks and an occasional movie or meal out. However, if you have to support a car or buy a lot of clothes and heavy entertainment, it may not be enough.

■ **Determine other categories of expenses and decide how much to spend each month:** Only you can determine the expenses remaining after your one-time "big ticket" expenses are taken out. The cost of your monthly transportation expenses will differ depending on whether you drive a car or ride a bicycle to class. Expenses for clothing, phone calls, CDs, video rentals, and meals off campus can vary tremendously, depending mainly on your personal restraint.

One category many students are glad they've created: *savings.* This category will help you keep a fund for emergencies or special expenses. It may also help you restrain your spending.

Example: Your monthly categories for spending $278 might be as follows, ranging from large to small expenses. *Car* (gas and oil, repairs, parking—insurance is included above): $80. *Entertainment* (including dates): $45. *Personal* (personal-care products): $33. *Meals out:* $30. *Clothes:* $30. *Snacks:* $25. *Phone:* $25. *Savings:* $10.

To set up your Monthly Money Plan, spend a few minutes with the "A. To Plan" portion of Personal Exploration #9.5.

YOUR MONTHLY MONEY PLAN— & YOUR RECORD OF ACTUAL INCOME & OUTGO

Tear out or photocopy the form on the opposite page. Use this form (1) to plan and (2) to record your income and outgo for the next month.

■ The left side of the form is for *planning and recording Income*—money in.

■ The right side of the form is for *planning and recording Outgo*—money out.

■ **A. TO PLAN**

On the left side of the form ("Income") indicate your predicted sources and amounts of money you expect to receive. *Examples:* "Family," "Job," "Loan," "Grant," "Scholarship," "Tax refund," "Aunt Gladys." Put the amounts in the column headed *Planned.*

On the right side of the form ("Outgo"), first indicate your categories of expenses, from left to right. *Examples:* "Rent," "Phone," "Utilities," "Credit card," "Car payments," "Food," "Transportation," "Clothing," "Entertainment," "Savings," "Miscellaneous." For each category, put in the *predicted* expenses. Put these amounts in the columns headed *Planned.*

■ **B. TO RECORD**

On the left side ("Income"), record the date/source and amount of money coming in. Example: "9/30 job— $200." Record these data in the *Actual* column.

On the right side ("Outgo"), record the date/expenses, amounts, and method of payment ($$ for cash, CK for check, CC for credit card) of your expenditures within each category. *Example:* Within the category of "Entertainment," you could record "10/15 video rental—$6.00 CK"; "10/18 dinner Amelio's—$12.30 CC"; "10/18 crackers—$1.10 $$."

■ **AT MONTH'S END**

Total up your *predicted* Income and Outgo and compare it with the *actual* Income and Outgo. Use the information to adjust your predicted Money Plan for the next month.

MONTHLY MONEY PLAN & RECORD

INCOME: MONEY IN

Date/Source	Planned Amount	Actual Amount

OUTGO: MONEY OUT

Category Date/Expense/Amount	Category Date/Expense/Amount	Category Date/Expense/Amount	Category Date/Expense/Amount	Category Date/Expense/Amount

MONTHLY MONEY PLAN & RECORD

INCOME: MONEY IN

Date/Source	Planned Amount	Actual Amount

OUTGO: MONEY OUT

Category Date/Expense/Amount	Category Date/Expense/Amount	Category Date/Expense/Amount	Category Date/Expense/Amount	Category Date/Expense/Amount

Mindfulness

THE EXPENSE RECORD. How do you know if you're overspending in some expense categories? In accordance with the advice about mindfulness at the beginning of this discussion ("Pay attention to your money"), you keep an expense record. The expense record has two parts, daily and monthly:

■ *The daily expense record:* This can be very simple and can be carried around as a shirt-pocket spiral-bound notebook or even as a 3 × 5 card in your wallet or purse. The point is to make this easy so you won't mind doing it.

You need to write down only three things: *date, item, cost.* (If you wish, you can also indicate if you paid with cash, check, or credit card—$$, CK, CC.) Examples are:

3/15	Snack	1.50
3/15	Gas	8.33
3/16	Toothpaste	2.00
3/16	Movie & popcorn	9.50

■ *The monthly expense record:* At the end of the month, you can sort the daily expenses into the different categories of your Monthly Money Plan under the "Actual" column. The categories might be: *Housing & utilities, Meals & snacks, Transportation, Entertainment, Personal supplies, Books & supplies, Savings,* and *Other.* When you add up the different columns, you can then see if you are staying within your budget.

To record your expenses in the coming month, follow the "B. To Record" portion of Personal Exploration #9.6.

Does all this record keeping seem like a lot of boring work? Actually, it's just a series of easy mechanical tasks. The whole reason for doing them is to give you *peace of mind.* After all, disorganization around money and consequent financial problems can affect your emotional well-being in other ways, making it difficult to study. Using these tools can help you avoid those difficulties.

GROUP ACTIVITY #9.3

HOW CAN YOU REDUCE EXPENSES?

Bring completed Personal Explorations #9.5 and #9.6 to class. With others in a small group, generate a list of largest monthly expenses. Also list expenses that you might be able to reduce. Share the lists and money-saving strategies with the rest of the class. Which areas are the easiest to reduce spending in and why? Which areas most difficult? What have you learned about your needs and your wants? Do you control your emotions or do they control you regarding spending? What can you do to exercise more control over your financial affairs?

A Crash Course in Money Handling

PREVIEW & REVIEW Controlling spending starts with managing big-ticket purchases, such as housing and transportation, which are often trade-offs. You can also find ways to get inexpensive furniture and computers. Tactics exist for controlling telephone charges and food and clothing purchases. Students need to investigate good banking and ATM sources. They need to know how to manage charge cards and credit cards. They also need to make arrangements to be covered by insurance—health, tenants, and automobile.

t's almost impossible to grow up in this society and not want to spend more than one's income. The television and print ads just never let us forget life's endless possibilities for parting with our money. Maybe you can't increase your income, but you can almost always find ways to cut spending.

CONTROLLING YOUR SPENDING. Here are some money-saving tips, ranging from big-ticket items to everyday small expenditures:

■ *Housing and transportation:* Housing and transportation often represent a trade-off. You might find a cheap apartment off campus, but it might require a car to get there, an expensive mode of transport. On-campus housing might cost more, but you can get around on foot or bicycle.

If you desperately want a car, maybe you can swing it by living at home or by sharing living space with roommates. For short periods of time, you might even live rent-free by house-sitting someone's place, taking care of plants and pets. A good place to look for these connections is the campus housing office.

When comparing prospective rents, be sure to determine if the rent does or doesn't include utilities, such as electricity, water, and garbage collection. Try to take care of your rental unit by fixing things yourself when possible and making sure to keep up the yard. This will help you get back any security deposits when you move out. It will also help you get a favorable reference from the landlord that will assist you in lining up the next rental.

Cars can be expensive. The purchase price of a car is only the beginning. Compared with gas, oil, tires, repairs, insurance, and parking, a bicycle may turn out to be a real bargain.

■ *Computers, furniture, refrigerators:* Things that cost the most are also those on which you can cut costs. Remember you won't be in college forever. Thus, you don't need to go first-class on such big-ticket items as computers and furniture. Do you need a television set, CD player, radio, heater, or fan? Check with your housemates or roommates, who may have these. Do you need a bed, a desk lamp, a dresser? All of these may be bought used.

You don't need *both* a typewriter and a computer, but you're well advised to have one or the other. (You might be able to borrow someone else's machine. But what if he or she needs it when you're up against a tight deadline to get a paper done?) Computers may be bought used, especially if all you need them for is typewriter-like purposes, such as writing papers.

Some students like to have a refrigerator in their rooms, either the 2.8 cubic-foot size or the smaller 1.6 cubic-foot size. These may be rented from local organizations (for perhaps $50–$75) or bought outright for $100–$150 from local discount appliance stores.[13] When these costs are shared with housemates, they become manageable.

Information technology

■ *The telephone:* Probably there's not much hazard in making a lot of local calls—unless you're tying up your family or housemates' phone, too. However, homesickness, cross-country love affairs, and talks with friends at other schools can produce massive long-distance charges. (Recently, though, many people have found making telephone calls on the Internet considerably cheaper. You might want to look into this. E-mail is also cheaper.)

If you're the one originating the calls, you may find a telephone timer will help you hold calls to 10–15 minutes instead of 2 hours. Also, don't feel you have to answer every incoming call, especially if you're studying. Tell others in your living unit to take a message, then call back later.

■ *Food and clothing:* Food can be a great hidden magnet for cash. Consider what the minimum wage is in this country (around $5 an hour before deductions). Then consider how *little* that will buy in the way of soft drinks, potato chips, and other packaged snacks. Even meals at fast-food places can rapidly drain your money. Meals at fancier restaurants can be a major hit on your wallet.

Clearly, learning how to cook will save you money, even if it's just spaghetti. So will learning how to shop. Shop from a list, which keeps you disciplined. Don't shop when you're hungry; it tends to make you reach for convenience foods and snacks. Shop for fresh fruits, vegetables, grains, and other foods that are not processed; they are less expensive. Use clip-out coupons from newspapers if they will really save you money. (Don't use them to buy expensive processed foods you would not otherwise buy.)

Some people are hyperconscious about the way they dress, which is fine,

so long as they aren't hooked into following every fashion. There are ways to buy clothes cheaply: at the end of the season, other sale times, or at used-clothing stores. If you build your wardrobe around one or two colors, you can do a lot of mixing and matching.

You might consider entering into a contest with housemates to find ways of saving money: turning down the thermostat, turning off unnecessary lights, keeping doors and windows closed in winter, buying toilet paper and paper towels in large lots at discount prices.

BANKS & ATMS. One student who, with friends, wrote a guide to college survival, suggests keeping two things in mind when choosing a bank.[14] First, find a bank that has automated teller machines (ATMs) that are handy for you. Second, consider all possible hidden costs of the bank in question.

There are many kinds of checking and savings accounts. On standard checking accounts, some banks charge you a monthly fee, some a fee for every check you write, some both. Some checking accounts pay interest if you maintain a high balance, but often the fees will eat up the interest. If you don't write a lot of checks, you might do better with a savings account, which pays interest. Finally, some banks offer a basic banking account, geared to low-income or retired customers. This allows you to write six checks per month or so without additional charge.

ATMs are popular with those who want fast spending money. Indeed, customers who are 18–24 years old conduct a higher share of their transactions at ATMs than any other age group. Most of the youngest ATM users are college students.[15] Clearly, there are some advantages to having an ATM card. For example, with shared banking networks, family members can make a deposit in one state and you can make a withdrawal in another. In addition, you can do transactions during evenings and weekends, when most banks are closed.

CHARGE CARDS, CREDIT CARDS, & DEBIT CARDS. Studies have shown banks and credit-card companies that students are as responsible with credit as most adults. Consequently, campuses have been deluged with ads and applications, trying to entice thousands of students into The Way of Plastic. Indeed, credit-card companies often waive credit histories and income requirements.[16] As a result, 82% of college students have at least one credit card.[17]

Charge cards **are those that require that the bill be paid off every month.** Examples are charge cards given out by American Express and many oil companies. _Credit cards_ **are those that allow the charges to be paid off in installments plus interest, provided you make a minimum payment every month.** Examples are those given out by MasterCard, Visa, and Discover. A third kind of card is the debit card, which can be used at certain stores such as some grocery chains. **The**

debit card **enables you to pay for purchases by withdrawing funds electronically directly from your savings or checking account.** That is, the debit card acts in place of a paper check.

The advantage of all three types of cards is convenience: you don't have to carry cash. Such cards also allow you to rent cars, buy plane tickets, and book hotel rooms, transactions difficult to do with cash or check. Credit cards can also give you a loan when you need it.

There are, however, some disadvantages:

■ *It's easy to forget you're spending money:* "We'll just put it on plastic," students say. Somehow it's easy to spend $80 on that great shirt in the store window when you only have to sign a charge slip. It's a lot more difficult when you have to hand over four Andrew Jacksons. With plastic, you get what you want now without the pain of feeling as if you're paying for it.

■ *Debts can pile up:* With debit cards, the money is gone from your checking account as soon as you use it. With American Express and other charge cards, you have to pay the bill every month, just like the phone bill. With Visa, MasterCard, Discover, and other credit cards, however, debts can be carried over to the next month. Credit limits for students typically start at $500. Many students find this line of credit too much of a good thing.

A survey of students at three Michigan universities found that 10% had outstanding credit card bills of more than $700. A handful had bills as high as $5,000 or $6,000.[18] One student was reported to have an $1,100 bar tab on his Visa. One first-year law student was $40,000 in debt but unable to stop using her cards.[19]

■ *Interest rates can be high:* Credit-card interest rates can be much higher than the rates banks charge for other kinds of loans, such as car loans. (And that's all that a credit card is—a loan.) Many cards charge 18–20% a year. And every month interest is added to the interest.

NOTE: If you carry a $6,297 credit-card balance and make only the minimum $200 payment every month, you'll be paying off that debt for—the next 23 years and 10 months! (And that cost could include over $9,570 in interest.)[20]

If you have trouble restraining yourself on your credit cards, there's only one solution: take some scissors and cut them in half.

INSURANCE. A dull subject, you may think, but it's important. Murphy's Law states, "If anything can go wrong, it will."

For a college student, there are two or three important kinds of insurance:

■ *Health insurance:* This is absolutely essential. The United States is not a country where it's wise to be without health insurance. If something goes wrong, a hospital somewhere (maybe not a good one) will probably admit you. However, without health insurance you might not get the level of care you need. Moreover, the hospital's business office will bill you anyway. This could lead to financial disaster, either for yourself or, if you're a minor, for your parents.

Parents' employer health plans can often be extended to cover college-age children up until the age of around 24. In addition, most colleges offer student health plans, and you should check to see what their benefits cover. Are lab tests, surgery, hospital stays, long-term care included? If necessary, pay for supplemental health insurance to cover care not provided on campus.

■ *Tenant's insurance:* You should make sure your possessions are covered by insurance against fire and theft. Students who are still dependents of their parents may be covered by their parents' insurance. This is so even if the students live in a dormitory or off-campus apartment. It assumes, however, that they still live at home during the summer, are registered to vote there, or carry a driver's license with parents' address. Your coverage usually amounts to 10% of your parents' coverage, minus the deductible. Thus, if your parents' plan covers $150,000 and has a $250 deductible, you are covered up to $15,000. If a $2,000 computer system is stolen out of your room, you'll get that back minus $250. Check with your insurance company to make sure you're covered as you should be. If not, you should be able to get a special policy for additional premiums.

If you're self-supporting or emancipated or older than about 23, you'll need to get your own tenants' policy.

- **Car insurance:** If you have a car and are under age 25 (especially if you're an unmarried male), perhaps you've already found that car insurance is one of the most expensive things you can buy. Indeed, it and all other car expenses should seriously make you think about whether you really need a car at school.

  If you have an older car, as so many students do, it may not be worth carrying collision insurance. This is the kind of insurance that covers any repairs (usually with a deductible) should anyone run into you. However, you'll want to carry as much comprehensive insurance as you can in case you run into another car, bicyclist, or pedestrian. You should also be covered for hospitalization for any passengers riding in your car.

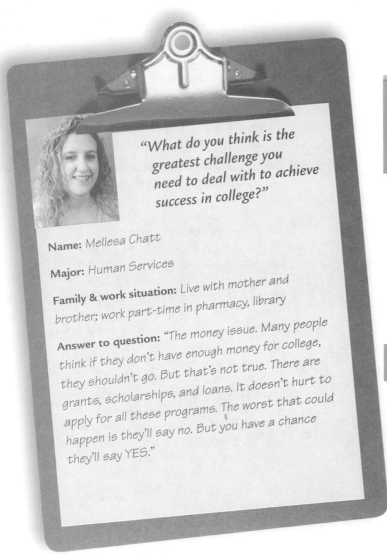

"What do you think is the greatest challenge you need to deal with to achieve success in college?"

Name: Mellesa Chatt

Major: Human Services

Family & work situation: Live with mother and brother; work part-time in pharmacy, library

Answer to question: "The money issue. Many people think if they don't have enough money for college, they shouldn't go. But that's not true. There are grants, scholarships, and loans. It doesn't hurt to apply for all these programs. The worst that could happen is they'll say no. But you have a chance they'll say YES."

Financial Aid

PREVIEW & REVIEW Financial aid may consist of gifts, such as grants and scholarships. Or it may consist of self-help assistance, such as loans, part-time work, and college work-study. Most financial aid is considered "need-based," in which you show economic need. However, some aid is "merit-based," such as academic, music, or sports scholarships. To demonstrate financial need, you or your family must fill out a needs analysis document. Aid is available for parents of students, self-supporting students under 24, and older students.

Student need for financial aid has shot up in recent years. This is partly because colleges have raised their tuition rates but also partly because of changes in the kinds of students going to college. For instance, over the past decade, three-quarters of colleges have reported taking more students over 25 years old. Because most of them are part time, they are not eligible for federal financial aid, so they have turned to the schools themselves to cover their aid requirements.[21]

The purpose of this section is to show you the different sources of financial aid available to you.

GIFTS & SELF-HELP, NEED-BASED & MERIT-BASED. The term _financial aid_ refers **to any kind of financial help you get to enable you to pay for college.** There are two ways to distinguish financial aid:

- *Gifts versus self-help assistance: Gift assistance* **is financial aid you do not have to pay back.** It includes *grants* and *scholarships.*

  Self-help assistance **is financial aid that requires something in return.** *Loans,* which must be repaid, are one example. *Part-time work* and *college work-study* is another.

- *Need-based versus merit-based:* Most financial aid is need-based. With *need-based financial aid*, you or your parents fill out forms stating your resources. The college then determines how much aid needs to be made up from somewhere else.

  Merit-based financial aid is based on some sort of superior academic, music, sports, or other abilities.

CAN YOU SHOW YOU NEED IT? *Demonstrated financial need* means that you have proven you need financial aid according to a certain formula, such as the Congressional Methodology. To begin to apply for need-based financial aid, you must ask your institution for an application form called a needs analysis document. **The *needs analysis document* is a form for helping people prove their financial need to colleges.** The *two federal forms you are most likely to encounter are the FAF and the FAFSA.* Financial aid is available whether you are or are not getting money from your family. It is also available whether you are going it alone as a young person or are going back to school as an older person.

- *Aid for parents of students:* The Congressional Methodology formula considers your family's size, income, net worth, and number of members now in college. It then considers your anticipated costs of attending a particular college. From these two factors, the formula arrives at an estimated family contribution. Colleges then make their own calculations based on this formula. If the results show your family's resources are insufficient, you'll get some help.

- *Aid for self-supporting students under 24:* If you're self-supporting, the Congressional Methodology formula counts just your income and assets, not your family's. You must show that you are single, under age 24, and without dependents. You must also show you have not been claimed as a dependent by your parents for two years. Finally, you must show you have had annual resources of at least $4,000 during each of these two years.[22]

- *Aid for returning adult students:* Even returning adult students can obtain financial aid based on need. It's a matter of minimizing one's income and assets. (For example, older people can move their savings into retirement plans, which are sheltered from financial aid computations.) Believe it or not, it may also help to apply to an expensive college, according to one piece of advice. The reason is that the more expensive the college is, the more aid one is eligible for.[23]

TYPES OF FINANCIAL AID. We may classify financial aid as grants, scholarships, loans, and work. These are available from several sources: federal, state, college, and private.

- *Grants: Grants* **are gifts of money;** they do not have to be repaid.

  One large need-based grant program from the federal government is the *Pell Grants,* given to undergraduates on the basis of need. Normally Pell Grants are given to families with an annual income of less than $25,000, although there are special exceptions. You should apply in any case. Many colleges will not consider you for other grants unless you've been turned down for a Pell Grant.

  Another need-based federal grant program is the *Supplemental Educational Opportunity Grants (SEOG), which are designed to augment other forms of financial aid.*

  Some companies also offer their employees grants in the form of educational benefits that allow them to attend school while working. For example, a hospital may pay one of its employees to go to nursing school while he or she continues working.

- *Scholarships: Scholarships* **are usually awarded on the basis of merit,** often academic merit. Sometimes the scholarships are for merit in other areas as well, such as proficiency in a certain sport or musical activity. Examples are various *Reserve Officer Training Corps (ROTC)* scholarships.

  Sometimes scholarships are available for reasons you couldn't possibly predict, and they seem to have nothing to do with merit. For instance, you have a certain last name, have a parent who worked for a certain organization, or are from a certain geographical area. You'll never know what these are unless you start looking. Go the financial aid office or library and ask for help.

■ *Loans:* **A *loan* is money you have to pay back, either as money or in some form of work.** There are three well-known federal loan programs.

The *Perkins Loans* allow students to borrow up to $4,500 for their first and second years. They can borrow up to $9,000 for all undergraduate years. The interest rate is 5%. Repayment begins nine months after graduation (unless you quit or become a student less than half time). The repayment may be spread over 10 years.

The *Stafford Loan Program,* also known as the Guaranteed Student Loans, allows you to borrow money up to $2,625 per year for the first and second year. You can borrow up to $4,000 for the third year and beyond. Thus, you can accumulate up to $17,250 for your undergraduate years. Loans are made by banks or other private lenders. Repayment doesn't start until six months after you graduate, quit, or drop below half-time student status.

The *Parent Loans for Undergraduate Students (PLUS)* program allows parents to borrow from a private lender for their children's education. They can borrow up to $4,000 a year, up to $20,000 for each student and at a rate up to 12%. To be eligible, you have to have applied for a Pell or Stafford first. Parents begin repayment 60 days after receiving the money. Students taking out the loan may wait until 60 days after quitting or graduating from college before beginning repayment.

A more recent kind of loan, to include 1,500 campuses in 1995, is a direct-loan program by the U.S. government, designed to cut out bankers' profits, streamline procedures, and help students predict and organize their debts. Depending on their circumstances, graduates can repay their debt over 10–30 years. (Most student loans are structured for repayment over 10 years.)[24]

■ *Work:* Many colleges offer part-time work opportunities, usually on campus, for money or for room and/or board. Of course, you may also be able to line up part-time work off-campus. In addition, a federally funded need-based program

called *College Work-Study* helps colleges set up jobs for students. Typically College Work-Study covers 12–15 hours a week, or up to 40 hours a week during the summer.

Cooperative education programs **allow you to improve your marketability upon graduation by giving you work experience in your major.** The work may go on at the same time as the course work or as part-time school and part-time work. Or the work may alternate with course work—for example, one semester in school and the next semester at work. Pay is often modest, but the experience is what counts. Cooperative education programs are offered at about 1,000 schools.

GETTING GOING. Even if you don't think you're eligible for financial aid right now, it might be advisable to go through the application process. At least then you'll know where you stand. And you'll be prepared if something happens to the college funds that you're presently counting on. Help in obtaining financial assistance is offered through a couple of toll-free numbers. Call the Federal Student Aid Information Center at 800-4-FEDAID or the Federal Student Aid Advisory Center at 800-648-3248.

One caution, however: Allow *lots* of time. No one's going to give you any money if you didn't follow their rules and apply within the deadlines posted. Applying for money is just like applying to get into college itself—these things do not happen instantaneously. It will take time for you (or your parents) to fill in the forms, to meet a filing deadline far in advance of the first day of the school term. Then it will take college officials time to approve the paperwork before they can send you a check. Be sure to keep copies of all your paperwork in case something gets lost.

Staying power

Applying for financial aid is just as much a test of adult responsibility—of staying power—as filing an income-tax return. Or applying to college, and you remember how long that took. Just as the burden is on you to meet the deadlines and proofs of the admissions office or the tax collector, it's the same with financial aid.

THERE'S MONEY OUT THERE SOMEWHERE

This activity, which requires some out-of-class time, is to be done in a group with three to five other students. Many students are familiar with the basic state and federal programs offering financial aid. The purpose of this exercise is to locate less obvious sources of financial assistance. With your group members, use the campus library to identify *five* new potential sources of financial aid. (If possible, prepare a typed list of potential resources, to be distributed to each person in the class.)

In class report on your findings or distribute your list. What were your reactions to the sources of financial assistance available? Do you feel these funds are readily accessible? Have you identified new sources of monetary aid that are directly applicable to your own financial situation?

Onward: Applying This Chapter to Your Life

Don't always pretend "everything's cool" when it's not.

ften people wear a mask to hide their feelings. Sometimes it's an "Everything's cool" expression. Sometimes it's a stone-faced "Don't mess with me" look. However, *I* know and *you* know that behind the mask is often a human being in need of help and friendship.

When the pressures of school begin to be overwhelming, that's the time to take another look at this chapter. It's clear that all kinds of support are available to students. The main thing is to decide that *you're not alone* and go after it.

The principal lesson of this chapter has a great deal of value outside of school. That lesson is: *find out everything you can about the organization you're in.* The more you understand about the departments and processes of your work world, for instance, the better you'll be able to take control of your own life within it. The same is true with the world outside of work.

In addition, I hope you have found at least one thing in this chapter that you didn't know about money matters. Write it down here:

_____

_____

_____

_____

_____

_____

_____

Real Practice Activities for Real People

REAL PRACTICE ACTIVITY #9.1: WHAT ARE USEFUL CAMPUS RESOURCES TO HELP YOU SUCCEED IN COLLEGE? This practice activity, which is designed to identify important college resources, can be performed by individuals out of class, who then submit a reaction paper to the instructor. Or it may be performed in class in small groups, with the results being shared with the class at large.

Staying power

For individuals: with the awareness that your life experiences, strengths, and weaknesses may differ from those of other people, use the college catalog and other campus publications to identify five college resources that could help you make a success of higher education. Submit your findings to your instructor as a one-page reaction paper.

For small groups: in discussion with other members of your group, identify as many college resources as you can, using the college catalog and other campus publications. Identify the function and location of these resources. If the college seems to lack important resources, identify possible alternatives within the local community. Later the instructor may ask your group to share results with the class at large.

REAL PRACTICE ACTIVITY #9.2: USING THE FOUR-STEP CRITICAL THINKING APPROACH TO SOLVE AN IMPORTANT ACADEMIC OR PERSONAL PROBLEM. This practice activity, which is designed to apply critical thinking to a student's important academic or personal issue, is to be performed by individuals out of class, who then submit their results in a reaction paper to the instructor.

Mindfulness

Problem solving works best when it is done in a systematic, organized way. Identify an important problem, either academic or personal, that you really would like to come to grips with. Then use the four-step approach to critical thinking (problem solving) discussed in

Chapter 2 to come up with a plan for handling the problem. Include in your plan campus (or community) resources available to you. While developing your plan, try to identify any previously held opinions or mind-sets that initially made formulating the plan difficult.

Write up your findings as a one-page paper for the instructor. Identify the problem, the solution, how the solution was realized, and the college (and community) resources you can use.

REAL PRACTICE ACTIVITY #9.3: USING A PERSONAL COMPUTER & SPREAD-SHEET SOFTWARE TO ANALYZE YOUR INCOME & EXPENSES. This activity should be practiced individually by students outside of class, using a personal computer with a spreadsheet program. The results may be discussed in class afterwards.

Information technology

In this practice activity, you are to use a personal computer and a spreadsheet software program to identify what your income and expenses are for the present month and the coming month. (If you are unable to find or use a computer, do this exercise by hand.) Use the categories suggested in this chapter for various types of expenses.

After you have completed the activity, consider the following questions for class discussion: What was your reaction to the history of the income and outgo of your money? Does the exercise suggest areas where you need to cut expenses or refigure your budget? How difficult was it for you to use the spreadsheet software?

The Examined Life

JOURNAL ENTRY #9.1: WHAT PROBLEM MIGHT YOU NEED HELP SOLVING? What problem can you think of that might occur during school for which you might need help? It could be lack of money, conflicts in a personal relationship, dealing with child care, or difficulty in keeping up with a course. What kind of assistance could you get to ease the problem?

_____

_____

_____

_____

_____

_____

_____

_____

_____

JOURNAL ENTRY #9.2: FINDING IMPORTANT SCHOOL SERVICES. Find the following places, and write down the location and the telephone number for contacting them. (If these places do not exist on your campus, indicate _None_ in the space.) Unless your instructor asks you to turn this in, post the list over your desk or near your bed.

Services	Building name & room number	Telephone
Learning/tutoring center		
Library/media center		
Your academic advisor		
Dean of students		
Health service or infirmary		
Counseling center		
Security or campus police		

Registrar		
Financial aid office		
Housing office		
Transportation office		
Cashier/business office		
Job placement center		
Adult services		
Career center		
Child care		
Legal services		
Student union or center		
Bookstore		

JOURNAL ENTRY #9.3: WHAT'S AN IMPORTANT EXTRACURRICULAR ACTIVITY? If any extracurricular activity _could be considered as important as your major,_ what would it be? How would you go about becoming involved, if you haven't done so already?

_____

_____

_____

_____

_____

_____

_____

_____

_____

JOURNAL ENTRY #9.4: WHAT IS UPSETTING ABOUT MONEY? What do you find particularly upsetting to you about money? What does this chapter suggest you might be able to do about it?

_____

_____

_____

_____

_____

_____

_____

_____

JOURNAL ENTRY #9.5: PAYING ATTENTION: HOW MUCH MONEY DO YOU OWE? Some students are only vaguely aware of how much money they owe, including both student loans and credit card debts. Indeed, they may be off by as much as $5,000. Do you know how much you need to repay? How long will it be before you're debt free?

_____

_____

_____

_____

_____

_____

_____

_____

_____

JOURNAL ENTRY #9.6: WHAT DO YOU KNOW ABOUT STUDENT LOANS? Some students talk almost like bankers, computing which loans and repayment schedules are better than others. Have you done comparisons of the various loans available? If not, what kind of action might you take here?

_____

_____

_____

_____

_____

_____

_____

_____

_____

_____

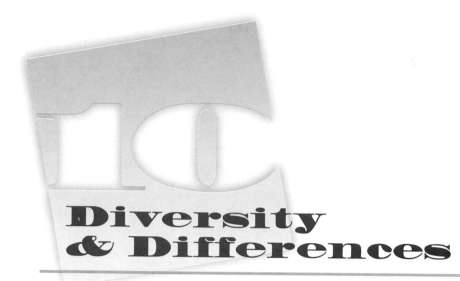

Diversity & Differences

Preparing to Meet the 21st Century

IN THIS CHAPTER In this chapter we describe the following important areas:

- *The new college student body:* Many students don't fit the profile of the traditional 18–24, full-time, residential student. They may be commuters, working, parents, older, and the like.

- *Race, culture, and stereotypes and why diversity matters:* Race, ethnicity, and culture all mean different things.

- *The multicultural "salad bowl":* How to see through the eyes of people different from you—in gender, sexual orientation, age, race, ethnicity, nationality, religion, and ability.

- *Commuter students:* Because 80% of students commute, they need to know how to adjust between the different sectors of their lives.

Tiger Woods, the fantastic golf pro, may have "learned to swing a club before he learned to walk," as his father said, but he's also distinctive in another way: his ancestry is Asian, black, and native American.

This may make him unusual in a sport long dominated by white faces. However, he actually is representative of a trend in North America: whites are becoming less the majority population. In the United States and Canada, we are becoming more _multicultural_, **or racially and culturally diverse countries.** _Diversity_ **means variety—in race, gender, ethnicity, age, physical abilities, and sexual orientation.** This diversity is reflected on many college campuses. To get a sense of how you feel about diversity, try taking Personal Exploration #10.1 (_opposite page_).

The New College Student Body

PREVIEW & REVIEW A great many students don't fit the profile of the traditional student between 18 and 24, attending college full time, living in a dormitory, and engaging in extracurricular activities. Instead, they may be a commuter, working, a parent, older, and struggling to meet ends meet.

If you consider the picture of college students that emerges from television and magazines, it seems to be something like this: they are in their late teens or early twenties. They attend school full time, mostly supported by their parents. Their college education consists of a lot of sitting in classrooms. They live in college dormitories, fraternities, or sororities. They go to football games during the fall and head for the beaches during spring break.

Of course, many college students _do_ fit this profile of what is considered a _traditional_ college student: between 18 and 24, attending college full time, living in a college residence hall, and engaging in extracurricular activities. This book is intended for them as well.

However, there is a good possibility you may not fit this profile. Instead, you may share some or all of the following characteristics. You may be a student . . .

who works full or part time while attending college,

who lives off campus and commutes,

who is of a racial or ethnic minority,

who is older than 24,

who is a parent (and worries about day care),

who goes to college part time,

who has little time for extracurricular activities,

who is struggling to make ends meet,

who often takes evening classes or online classes,

who is the first in his or her family to go to college,

who comes from outside the United States.

Even if only one or two things on this list describe your situation, this book is for you also. The fact of the matter is that a greater proportion of students these days are not apt to fit the picture of the traditional student.

The City College of New York, for instance, is a true urban commuter school that shows a great deal of diversity. For generations, City College has reflected the changing population of New York City. From 1920 to 1950, its enrollments consisted largely of the children of Jewish

THE QUICK DISCRIMINATION INDEX

This inventory is intended to help you become more aware of your beliefs and attitudes. Circle the number that most closely corresponds to your thinking.

1   Strongly disagree

2   Disagree

3   Not sure

4   Agree

5   Strongly agree

1.   I do think it is more appropriate for the mother of a newborn baby, rather than the father, to stay home with the baby during the first year.

1 2 3 4 5

2.   It is as easy for women to succeed in business as it is for men.

1 2 3 4 5

3.   I really think affirmative action programs on college campuses constitute reverse discrimination.

1 2 3 4 5

4.   I feel I could develop an intimate relationship with someone from a different race.

1 2 3 4 5

5.   All Americans should learn to speak two languages.

1 2 3 4 5

6.   It upsets (or angers) me that a woman has never been president of the United States.

1 2 3 4 5

7.   Generally speaking, men work harder than women.

1 2 3 4 5

8.   My friendship network is very racially mixed.

1 2 3 4 5

9.   I am against affirmative action programs in business.

1 2 3 4 5

10.   Generally, men seem less concerned with building relationships than women.

1 2 3 4 5

11.   I would feel OK about my son or daughter dating someone from a different race.

1 2 3 4 5

12.   It upsets (or angers) me that a racial minority person has never been president of the United States.

1 2 3 4 5

13.   In the past few years, too much attention has been directed toward multicultural or minority issues in education.

1 2 3 4 5

14.   I think feminist perspectives should be an integral part of the higher education curriculum

1 2 3 4 5

15.   Most of my close friends are from my own racial group.

1 2 3 4 5

16.   I feel somewhat more secure that a man rather than a woman is currently president of the United States.

1 2 3 4 5

17.   I think that it is (or would be) important for my children to attend schools that are racially mixed.

1 2 3 4 5

18.   In the past few years too much attention has been directed toward multicultural or minority issues in business.

1 2 3 4 5

19.   Overall, I think racial minorities in America complain too much about racial discrimination.

1 2 3 4 5

20.   I feel (or would feel) very comfortable having a woman as my primary physician.

1 2 3 4 5

21.   I think the president of the United States should make a concerted effort to appoint more women and racial minorities to the country's Supreme Court.

1 2 3 4 5

22.   I think white people's racism toward racial-minority groups still constitutes a major problem in America.

1 2 3 4 5

23.   I think the school system, from elementary school through college, should encourage minority and immigrant children to learn and fully adopt traditional American values.

1 2 3 4 5

24.   If I were to adopt a child, I would be happy to adopt a child of any race.

1 2 3 4 5

25.   I think there is as much female physical violence toward men as there is male physical violence toward women.

1 2 3 4 5

26.   I think the school system, from elementary school through college, should promote values representative of diverse cultures.

1 2 3 4 5

27.   I believe that reading the autobiography of Malcolm X would be of value.

1 2 3 4 5

(continued)

28. I would enjoy living in a neighbor-hood consisting of a racially diverse population (Asians, blacks, Latinos, whites).

                      1 2 3 4 5

29. I think it is better if people marry within their own race.

                      1 2 3 4 5

30. Women make too big a deal out of sexual harassment issues in the workplace.

                      1 2 3 4 5

■ SCORING

For these items fill in your circled scores and add them up:

4_____	12_____	22_____
5_____	14_____	24_____
6_____	17_____	26_____
8_____	20_____	27_____
11_____	21_____	28_____

Subtotal: _____

For the other items, reverse the circled scores as follows:

Score of 1 = 5

Score of 2 = 4

Score of 3 = 3

Score of 4 = 2

Score of 5 = 1

1_____	10_____	19_____
2_____	13_____	23_____
3_____	15_____	25_____
7_____	26_____	29_____
9_____	18_____	30_____

Subtotal: _____

Total score: _____

Your score may range from 30 to 150. Higher scores show greater sensitivity to and knowledge of minority and gender equality issues.

immigrants. Now its students, as one writer states, have "names such as Abukar and Hyunsun and Fernando."[1] In a recent year, its racial composition was found to be 39% black (often as not Dominican or Haitian), 28% Hispanic, 18% Asian, and 14% white (often from the Middle East or former Soviet republics). Half were born abroad. Many are single parents, work at several jobs, and live on meager budgets.[2]

Other campuses aren't as multicultural even though they, too, may be in a city. State urban campuses in Milwaukee and St. Louis, for instance, have fewer than 15% black or Hispanic students. At the University of Oregon's Portland campus, the black or Hispanic enrollment is 5%.[3] Still, such students share many similarities with minorities at more multicultural urban schools.

Some colleges have a high proportion of transfer students and of older students who are taking longer to complete their educations. "Each semester I teach at [New York's] Queens College I have students, now in their thirties, who had dropped out of college a dozen years earlier," says one professor. "The registrar tells me that almost half of the bachelor's degrees we award are to people who started elsewhere."[4]

Whatever kind of college you attend, diversity is important. Let's find out why.

WHAT'S THE COMPOSITION OF YOUR CLASS?

Every student in the class should take 10 minutes to make a list on a sheet of paper answering how he or she fits the following questions. (If some make you uncomfortable, you need not answer them.)

Questions: (1) Male or female? (2) Age (or approximate age)? (3) Country of citizenship or state of residence? (4) Racial heritage or heritages? (5) On-campus resident or commuter? (6) Working full time, part time, or not at all? (7) Going to school full time or part time? (8) Marital status (single, married, divorced, widowed)? (9) If parent, how many children? (10) College major? (11) First in family to go to college? (12) Extracurricular activities. (13) Anything else you want to mention. (For example, do you have a disability or tattoos, piercings, or other characteristics that make you different?)

Don't put you name on the paper (unless you want to). The instructor will collect them and, class size and time permitting, will total the results and post them on the board. (This activity may be continued at the next class meeting.)

Questions for discussion: How does your class vary from the usual idea held by the public of what a college student is supposed to be? Do you feel like you have a lot in common with other students? Or do you feel as if you're in the minority? Are there other students you feel you could seek out that, based on the class inventory, you might want to be friends with?

Race, Culture, & Stereotypes & Why Diversity Matters

PREVIEW & REVIEW Race, ethnicity, and culture all mean different things. Race refers to how a group of people are distinguished by certain obvious inherited characteristics. Ethnicity refers to how people can be distinguished by national origin, language, religious tradition, and the like. Culture refers to the intangible and tangible products of a society. A stereotype is an expected or exaggerated expectation about a category of people, which may be completely inaccurate when applied to individuals.

Deirdre Howard, 25, of San Francisco, is proud of both parts of her heritage—from her Irish-American father and from her Japanese-American mother. But in the past it's been a dilemma for her when a government form asking her to list her race has forced her to choose between the two.

The U.S. year 2000 census, however, allows people to mark off as many races as they want. Under the new rules, forms with a race question have the usual five basic categories of race: (1) Asian, (2) black, (3) white, (4) Native Hawaiian or Pacific Islander, and (5) American Indian or Alaskan Native. (Latinos are not classified by the government as a separate racial group, nor are Jews or Arabs.) But now there is a sixth category: "Other," which allows 63 possible combinations. "It's going to be nice not having to pick which parent and heritage I love most when I fill out some form," says Howard. "This finally allows multiracial people to be counted fairly."[5]

While the change in the census has political considerations that I haven't the space to go into, it can be argued that it reflects today's realities. For instance, the number of children in mixed-race families was estimated at 2 million in 1990.[6]

But what, exactly, do we mean by "race," and how does it differ from "ethnicity" and "culture"?[7]

- **Race:** *Race* **refers to how a group of people are distinguished by certain obvious inherited characteristics.** Skin color is often the principal indicator used, but so also are hair color and characteristics, facial features, and body build. This is how a dark-haired, black-skinned African American ("black") is supposed to be distinguished from a white-skinned, red-haired Irish American ("white"), for example.

  The notion that humans are divided into three races of people—Caucasian, Negroid, and Mongoloid—is a half century out of date, although many students still come to college with this idea in mind. Moreover, the distinctions among races are generally graded, not abrupt, points out anthropologist Mark Nathan Cohen. Skin color is not just black or white; it varies on a range from dark to light. Nose shapes may vary along a spectrum from broad to narrow. Persons of black skin may even have blond hair, as is found among some natives of Australia.

- **Ethnicity:** *Ethnicity* **refers to how people can be distinguished by national origin, language, religious tradition, and the like.** Such people may be of the same race or of different races. Thus, a Latino, someone who himself is (or whose parents were) from Latin America who speaks Spanish and is from a Catholic background is of Hispanic ethnicity. Someone from Russia who speaks Russian and belongs to the Russian Orthodox church is of Russian ethnicity. Both may be members of the white race, but then again they could be from, say, the black race.

- **Culture:** *Culture* **refers to the intangible and tangible *products* of a society.**

  Among the *intangible products* are language, values, beliefs, and norms, which are important in defining how an individual sees the world—what is considered "reality." Certain societies may believe that men are superior to women, and this is expressed in the culture by urging women to dress a certain way, be ineligible for certain kinds of education

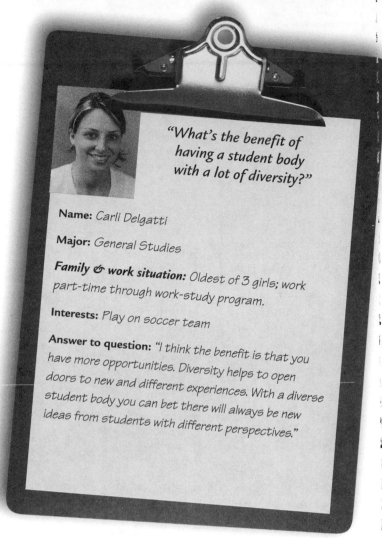

"What's the benefit of having a student body with a lot of diversity?"

Name: Carli Delgatti

Major: General Studies

Family & work situation: Oldest of 3 girls; work part-time through work-study program.

Interests: Play on soccer team

Answer to question: "I think the benefit is that you have more opportunities. Diversity helps to open doors to new and different experiences. With a diverse student body you can bet there will always be new ideas from students with different perspectives."

or work, not be allowed in the company of a man not related to them, and not be allowed to drive a car.

Among the *tangible products* of a culture are particular foods, furniture, musical instruments, art, houses, and so on: tortillas, bag pipes, prayer rugs, and the like. A coat is a tangible product, but the way it comes out (flashy looking but shoddily made, say, versus plain looking but well made) reflects intangible values and norms.

Lots of people believe that race explains some human differences. It's true that variation in skin color could affect how susceptible one is to sunburn and skin cancer, for example, and genetic differences may protect some people from malaria but predispose others to smallpox. But so many other attributes that people have erroneously said are caused by race are, in fact, based on racial stereotypes. **A _stereotype_ is an expected or exaggerated expectation about a category of people, which may be completely inaccurate when applied to individuals.** An example of a stereotype is that black people inherit characteristics that make them inherently better as dancers or basketball players, or that Asians are hard-working and "cunning," among other wrongheaded ideas. Variations among "races," says anthropologist Cohen, "cannot possibly explain the differences in behavior or intelligence that people think they see. . . . [N]o genes are known to control differences in specific behavior or intelligence among human groups."

What _does_ make a difference in variations in behavior—and this cannot be stressed strongly enough—is _culture._ Says Cohen:

> _[Like human language,] culture structures our behavior, thoughts, perceptions, values, goals, morals, and cognitive processes—also usually without conscious thought. Just as each language is a set of arbitrary conventions shared by those who speak the language, so each culture is made up of its own arbitrary conventions. . . . All of us—Americans as well as members of remote Amazonian tribes—are governed by culture. Our choices in life are circumscribed largely by arbitrary rules, and we have a hard time seeing the value of other people's choices and the shortcomings of our own._[8]

Thus, if a particular "race" of people seems to score lower on certain standardized tests, this has nothing to do with inherent I.Q. based on race. Because such tests are generally biased in favor of students in the mainstream, some minority students—especially if they have experienced health and educational deprivations—won't do well because they may not be familiar with certain conventions and subtleties of the majority culture that are reflected in the tests.

WHY A MINORITY PERSPECTIVE MATTERS. Pollsters have long been baffled as to why some (not all) white people, say, will give conservative views to white pollsters and more moderate views to black pollsters. Or why black people will give different opinions to black pollsters than to white pollsters. This is known as the "race of interviewer" effect. Does this mean people are lying to gain the pollsters' approval?

UCLA political scientist John Zaller theorizes that people don't have fixed opinions about many specific issues. Rather, he argues, people have many different "considerations" about any given issue, and when they are asked to express a political opinion they call upon _some_ of these considerations and use them to construct a response. Individuals are highly suggestible, so that the "consideration" can vary depending on all sorts of things—how the question is phrased, the personal characteristics of the pollster, what they saw on the news, and so on. Thus, when whites are interviewed by African American pollsters about programs intended to support minority groups, they are likely to use "considerations" about black interests. That is, in the words of Heather C. Hill, "white people are more likely to consider the interests of blacks when they talk to a black pollster."[9]

Hill, a graduate student in political science at the University of Michigan, found an echo of these ideas in two American government classes that she taught. Her afternoon class had no minority students; her morning class included several African American students (as well as an Asian and Middle Eastern student). Discussion in her afternoon class "was tinged with racial misunderstandings and stereotypes," she said. Students in the afternoon class did not hear the perspectives of black students (because none were present) and were not prompted by the presence of black students to take African American interests into account.

However, students in her morning class, just by looking around them, "were prompted to think about African Americans and their interests. These students then used these thoughts as they selected evidence and formed opinions that they voiced in classroom discussions." As it happened, the African American students were not outspokenly liberal themselves. Even so, "the result was a class in which racial issues were dealt with thoughtfully and more generously than in the afternoon section."[10]

From this, Hill sees an important reason why it's important to have a minority perspective in the classroom:

> *We should not overlook the tangible gains that come from having classes in which not everyone is the same color. For whites, these gains include being prompted to think from a perspective not one's own—a critical skill that needs to be learned during the college years.*

GROUP ACTIVITY #10.2

HOW OFTEN HAVE YOU BEEN EXPOSED TO MEMBERS OF GROUPS UNLIKE THE ONE YOU BELONG TO?

In small groups of no less than five people, students should take turns describing their experiences with members of groups unlike those they have grown up with, played with, gone to school with, or worked with. How do you think such people differ from you, and why? Now describe groups with whom you have had *no* experience. How do you think they differ?

One member of each group should be designated a "recording secretary" and make notes of some of the comments. After 20 minutes of discussion, the recording secretaries of the various groups should report some of the remarks made (without designating who made them) to the class at large.

Discuss some of the results. Are some of them stereotypes? Why?

The Multicultural "Salad Bowl": Diversity of Genders, Ages, Cultures, Races, & So On

PREVIEW & REVIEW Because of the changing "melting pot," global economy, and electronic communications, you will live in a world that is increasingly culturally and racially more diverse. Higher education gives you the opportunity to learn to live with diversity in gender and sexual orientation, age, race and culture, and disabilities.

Three developments ensure that the future will not look the same as the past:

- **Changing "melting pot" (or "salad bowl"):** By 2000, it is estimated that white males will make up less than 10% of newcomers to the American workforce. Most new workers will be women, minorities, and recent immigrants.[11] America has always been considered a "melting pot"—or maybe "salad bowl" is a better description—of different races and cultures, of course. However, it seems it will become more so in the near future.

- **Changing world economy:** The American economy is becoming more a part of the world economy. "We are in an unprecedented period of accelerated change," point out John Naisbitt and Patricia Aburdene. Perhaps the most breathtaking, they say, is "the swiftness of our rush to all the world's becoming a single economy."[12] The American economy is now completely intertwined with the other economies of the world—and therefore with the world's people.

Information technology

- **Changing information technology and communications:** Electronic communications systems—telephones, television, fax machines, computers—are providing a wired and wireless universe that is bringing the cultures of the world closer together. For example, millions of people already communicate with each other through the Internet. Communications satellites and cell phones and pagers are also extending the range of communications.

Many people are not prepared for these changes. Fortunately, as I mentioned, many institutions of higher education are becoming more multicultural and more diverse. Thus, college gives you the opportunity to learn to study, work, and live with people different from you. While you need not approve of other people's lifestyles, it's in your interest to display respectful behavior toward others. In this way you prepare yourself for life in the 21st century.

In this section, we look at the following kinds of diversity:

■ Gender and sexual orientation

■ Age

■ Race and culture

■ Disabilities

GROUP ACTIVITY #10.3

DO THE MASS MEDIA POR-TRAY GENDER, AGE, RACIAL, & CULTURAL STEREOTYPES?

No doubt you enjoy watching television or reading magazines and newspapers. But do these mass media show old people, young people, women, men, and people of color as they *really are*? Here's your chance to find out.

Divide into groups of three to five students (preferably a mix of genders, ages, races, and cultures). Over the next few days, look closely at print ads, television commercials, and TV programs. Do you see any instance of people being shown in roles that don't correspond to the way things are? For example, are nurses and teachers always shown as women and doctors and plumbers always shown as men? Discuss your findings with the others in your group. Vote on which one is the worst example of stereotyping for reporting to the class.

GENDER & SEXUAL ORIENTATION. After steady increases over two decades, enrollments of women in higher education now greatly exceed those of men. In 1970 women made up 42% of those in higher education. By 1990, however, that figure had risen to 55%. Why the dramatic change? One reason, perhaps, is the surge of interest among older women who postponed or never considered higher education and now are enrolling. Indeed, 49% of women in higher education are over 24 years old, compared with 24% of men.[13]

Women have reasons to feel proud of their accomplishments. They get higher grades on the average than men do, are awarded more scholarships, and complete degrees at a faster pace.[14, 15] However, traditionally they also suffer lower pay and slower advancements after leaving school. Still, with so many women in higher education, the increased numbers of female graduates could put pressure on employers to change.

Colleges have experienced considerable pressures to develop policies for countering sex stereotypes, sexism, and sexual harassment:

- **Sex stereotype:** As mentioned, a *stereotype* is an expectation or exaggerated expectation about a category of people, which may be completely inaccurate when applied to individuals. A sexual stereotype, for example, is that men are better than women in science, or women are better than men in child care.

- **Sexism: _Sexism_ is discrimination against individuals based on their gender.** An example is instructors who call more often on men than women (as is frequently the case) to answer questions in class.

- **Sexual harassment: _Sexual harassment_ consists of sexually oriented behaviors that adversely affect someone's academic or employment status or performance.** Examples are requests for sexual favors, unwelcome sexual advances, or demeaning sexist remarks.

To get a sense of what sexist behavior is, try taking Personal Exploration #10.2.

Higher education has also been trying to improve the climate for homosexuals, or gays and lesbians. In recent times, surveys have found first-year students more accepting of gay rights. For example, in 1987 60% of male freshmen said there should be laws prohibiting homosexuality, but four years later only 33% of them still supported such laws.[16] Among Americans of all groups, disapproval of homosexuality dropped from 75% in the late 1980s to 56% in 1996.[17]

Most students keep their views on homosexuality to themselves. However, on some campuses, homophobia still exists and may be expressed in active ways. _Homophobia_ **is fear of, or resistance to, the idea of homosexuality or of homosexuals.** Students may express their opposition by harassing gay rights activists or even physically assaulting students whose sexual orientation they do not accept. In many states, the law now allows prosecutors to file charges against those accused of such harassment.

PERSONAL EXPLORATION #10.2

OBSERVING SEXIST BEHAVIOR

During the next week, write down five instances you've observed personally, or discovered in writing or films, of sexist behavior or attitudes. (Some examples: Males who talk principally to males when in conversation with a male-and-female couple. Male instructors who call on male students more often than female students or call on "good-looking" rather than average-looking female students.)

1._____

2._____

3._____

4._____

5._____

AGE. About 12 million Americans are college undergraduates. However, just 67% of them are so-called **_traditional students—_ that is, 18 to 24 years old**.[18] *(See* ■ *Panel 10.1.)* The shift from students in their late teens and early 20s occurred because of the rising number of nontraditional students. **_Nontraditional students_—sometimes called adult students or returning students—are those who are older than 24.** As mentioned, nearly half the women students and nearly a quarter of the men students in higher education are over age 24. Many of these also attend part time. (Actually, about half of the students in higher education, regardless of age, are enrolled part time.)

Who are these nontraditional students? There is no easy way to categorize them. Large numbers are women entering the labor force, displaced workers trying to upgrade their skills, people switching careers, managers taking courses to gain advancement, others seeking intellectual stimulation. Some are retirees: in a recent year, according to the Census Bureau, 320,000 Americans age 50 and over were enrolled in higher-education courses.[19]

Whatever their reasons, nontraditional students often bring a high level of motivation, a wealth of life experience, and a willingness to work hard. Younger students often find that adult students make valuable team or study-group members. After they get over the initial fear "Am I smart enough?" mature students often turn out to be the best students, says one career planning counselor—"purposeful and excited about learning again."[20] Moreover, whereas students coming out of high school might be continuing their education only because of their parents' wishes, says another counselor, older students tend to be self-driven—often by economic necessity.[21]

Nontraditional students also bring a number of concerns. They worry that their skills are rusty, that they won't be able to keep up with younger students. They worry that their memory is not as good, that their energy level is not as high. Single parents worry that they won't be able to juggle school and their

Age of U.S. college undergraduates. Of the 12 million Fall 1997 U.S. college undergraduates, according to the U.S. Census Bureau, the ages and their percentages were as follows.

Age	Percentage
17	1%
18 - 19	26%
20 - 21	24%
22 - 24	17%
25 - 29	11%
30 - 34	7%
35 and up	14%

other responsibilities. They are concerned about scant or nonexistent child care. They may feel greater pressure regarding employment security.

Strategies for adult learners.

Some strategies for students who are over age 24 or attending college part time:

Ask for support: Get your family involved by showing them your textbooks and giving them a tour of the campus. Hang your grades on the refrigerator right alongside those of the kids. Or get support from friends (such as other adult students), a counselor, or an instructor. See if the college sponsors an adult support group.

Get financial aid: See Chapter 9, on money. You may be able to get loans, scholarships, or fellowships.

Enroll part time: Going part time will ease the stresses on your time and finances. Start with just one course to test the waters.

Arrange for child care: If you have young children, you'll need child care not only for when you're away at class but also when you're home doing homework.

Learn time-management skills: See the other chapters in this book, particularly Chapter 4, on how to manage your time.

Get academic support: If you're worried about being rusty, look for review courses, one-on-one free tutoring, and similar support services.

Avoid grade pressure: Unless you're trying to get into a top graduate school, don't put yourself under undue pressure for grades. Just do the best you can in the time you have to devote to school.

Have fun: College should also be enjoyable for itself, not just a means to a better life. If you can't spare much time for campus activities, at least spend some time with other nontraditional students. Some campuses, for example, even have a "resumers lounge." Or experiment with your image, dressing in ways (hip? professional? sexy?) that will allow you to reinvent yourself a bit.

Form or join a returning students group: Get together with others in your classes who seem to be in similar circumstances for study and other mutual support.

Fortunately, most campuses have someone whose job is to support adult students. There are also a number of other strategies that adult learners can employ. (*See ■ Panel 10.2, above.*)

RACE & CULTURE. Past generations of the dominant culture in the United States felt threatened by the arrival of Irish, Italians, Germans, Eastern Europeans, Catholics, and Jews. (And some people are still uncomfortable with them today.) Now the groups considered prominent racial minorities are people of African, Hispanic, and Asian descent or Native American and Alaskan Native. Indeed, four of these groups (African Americans, Hispanic Americans, Native Americans, and Alaskan Natives) presently make up

20% of Americans. By the year 2000 they are expected to make up nearly a third of students in higher education.

Let us briefly consider some of these groups:

■ *African Americans:* The largest nonwhite minority, African Americans make up 12% of the population of the United States, comprising 30 million people. By almost any measure, African Americans continue to face disadvantages resulting from the burden of slavery and three centuries of racial discrimination. Indeed, one survey found that 80% of African Americans who responded reported some form of racial discrimination during their years in higher education.[22]

Gains in civil rights and voting rights during the 1960s increased the numbers

FORM A STUDY GROUP WITH OTHERS LIKE YOU

Many students feel as if they are somehow "out of step" with other students. However, nontraditional students—those over age 24—are especially apt to feel this way. One effective morale booster is to form study groups with other students who are like you. (This activity can also be done by students of any group, not just nontraditional students.)

Note: The principal reason for forming a study group with others like you is to get *support*. You want to be careful, however, that it doesn't lead to your isolating or "ghettoizing" yourself from the other students. A goal of college should be to *seek out* diversity, not avoid it.

In this or any other course, approach two or more other students with whom you think you might feel comfortable. Ask them if they would like to set aside an hour or two once a week for a study group. Suggest that the purpose could be to share study techniques, compare lecture notes, practice math problems, or review for exams. In the course of your meetings you can also discuss the problems peculiar to being a non-traditional student. (Examples are holding a full-time job, child care, divorce, or whatever.)

For each class for which you've formed a study group, list members' names and telephone numbers below. Also list the day, time, and place where you've arranged to meet every week.

Name & phone

Day, time, & place

1._____

_____

2._____

_____

3._____

_____

4._____

_____

5._____

_____

of African Americans in elective office sixtyfold during the last 30 years. Outlawing discrimination in education and employment has helped establish a third of African Americans in the middle class (up 10% from the 1960s). Still, unemployment rates for African Americans continue to be double those of whites. Moreover, they continue to suffer disproportionately from serious health problems, crime, and poverty.

Many African Americans go to school in the large system of black colleges and other black institutions of higher learning. Still, perhaps 80% of African American students attend institutions of higher education in which the majority of students are white.[23]

- **Hispanic Americans:** People originally from Spanish-speaking cultures make up the second largest minority group in the United States, and they are expected to surpass African Americans as the largest minority group by 2005.[24] (Presently, one in nine Americans is Hispanic, and it's projected to be one in four by 2050.) A common Latino subculture doesn't exist in the U.S.; for example, many of these 29 million people speak only English.

    Still, among the various subcultures that are considered Hispanic, 75% currently live in only five states: California, Texas, Florida, Illinois, and New York. However, they are growing fast in other states. Two-thirds of Hispanics are Mexican Americans. Puerto Ricans and Cubans are the next largest group, followed by others from Caribbean, Central American, and South American countries.

    One article identifies 17 major Latino subcultures: Californians (divided among immigrant Mexicans, middle-class Mexicans, barrio dwellers, and Central Americans); Tejanos (South Texans, Houston Mexicans, Texas Guatemalans); Chicago Latinos (Chicago Mexicans, Chicago Puerto Ricans); Miamians (Cubans, Nicaraguans, South Americans); New York Hispanics (Puerto Ricans, Dominicans, Colombians); and elsewhere in the U.S. (New Mexico's Hispanos, migrant workers all over).[25]

- **Asian Americans:** There are 28 separate groups of Asian-Americans, according to census studies, ranging from Chinese to Japanese to Pacific Islanders. Asian Americans are the fastest-growing minority in the United States, with 40% living in California and most of the rest in Hawaii and New York.[26] The two largest groups are Chinese and Filipino who, along with the Japanese, are descendants of earlier tides of immigration. However, the fastest-growing groups of recent years have been those from Vietnam, India, Korea, Cambodia (Kampuchea), and Laos. Asian Americans continue to suffer discrimination, as reflected in lower income levels compared to whites.

- **Other races, cultures, religions:** Of course there are many other groups of ethnic and religious minorities. Those with the longest history of habitation in the United States are those considered native—Indians, Alaskans, and Hawaiians. In 1990 there were nearly 2 million Native Americans and Alaskan Natives, according to the U.S. census. Since 1968, 24 institutions of higher education have been established in the United States that are owned and operated by Native Americans.[27]

    The dominant religion in the U.S. is Protestant. Nevertheless, there are numerous minority religions: Catholic, Jewish, Muslim, Buddhist, Hindu, and so on. And, of course, many people have no formal religion or no religion at all.

- **International students:** Many campuses are enriched by the presence of international students, who make up 3.2% of all postsecondary enrollment in the United States.[28] These are foreign visitors who have come to the United States to pursue a course of study.

    Some of them may find themselves especially welcomed. Others, however, may find that their skin color, dress, or accent expose them to no less bias than American-born minorities experience. Some Americans worry that, with so much overseas talent in science and engineering programs, we are offering a kind of foreign aid. In fact, however, over half of all foreign graduate students in science and engineering choose to remain in the

United States after completing their schooling. Thus, they form an important part of our high-tech work force.[29]

It's worth noting, incidentally, that the immigrant population as a whole is rising in the United States. Almost 10% of Americans were born elsewhere, according to the Census Bureau, and nearly one in three foreign-born residents have become naturalized citizens. Half of foreign-born residents were from Central America, South America, or the Caribbean. One in four was born in Asia, one in five was European. About a fourth of foreign-born residents 25 years and older had completed four or more years of college, about the same as native-born Americans.[30]

To get more information about cultural or racial prejudices, try Personal Exploration #10.3.

PERSONAL EXPLORATION #10.3

TALKING TO OTHERS ABOUT PREJUDICE

Whatever group you belong to, majority or minority, this activity is intended to give you more information about cultural or racial prejudice.

■ IF YOU'RE A MEMBER OF THE MAJORITY CULTURE . . .

Find someone on campus who is of a *different* culture or race from yours. Ask if you may speak to him or her for a minute or so. This person may be a student in a class above you (sophomore or junior) or an instructor or a staff member. Ask him or her the following two questions and write down the answers.

1. Can you give an example, large or small, of an instance of racial discrimination or prejudice on this campus? (Example: No white student has asked to borrow his or her notes.)

   _____
   _____
   _____
   _____

   _____
   _____
   _____
   _____

2. What advice do you have for members of the majority culture about dealing with members of the minority culture on this campus?

   _____
   _____
   _____
   _____
   _____

■ IF YOU'RE A MEMBER OF A MINORITY CULTURE . . .

Find someone on campus who is of the *same* culture or race as yours, if possible. Ask if you may speak to him or her for a minute or so. This person may be a student in a class above you (sophomore or junior) or an instructor or staff member. Ask him or her the following two questions and write down the answers.

1. Can you give an example, large or small, of an instance of racial discrimination or prejudice on this campus? (Example: No white student has asked to borrow his or her notes.)

   _____
   _____
   _____
   _____

2. What advice do you have for members of your culture about how to succeed in college on this campus?

   _____
   _____
   _____
   _____
   _____

GROUP ACTIVITY OPTION

Report some of your findings as the basis for class discussion.

a result of the 1990 Americans With Disabilities Act, colleges have had to change policies and remodel buildings to accommodate students with disabilities. For instance, the law bars discrimination against the disabled in public accommodations and transportation. This means that new and renovated buildings and buses must be accessible to people with handicaps.

People with disabilities include not only those who are physically handicapped (for example, wheelchair users) or the visually or hearing impaired. They also include those with any type of learning disability. For example, people with dyslexia have difficulty reading. In any case, people with disabilities resent words that suggest they're sick, pitiful, childlike, or dependent or, conversely, objects of admiration.[32]

Try Personal Exploration #10.4 to get a sense of what it's like to have a physical disability.

DISABILITY. Nearly one in eleven first-year students in higher education report some kind of physical disability.[31] **A _physical disability_ is a health-related condition that prevents a person from participating fully in daily activities,** including school and work. As

PERSONAL EXPLORATION #10.4

WHAT IT IS LIKE HAVING A PHYSICAL DISABILITY

How does it feel to be physically handicapped? If you're young and healthy, you can try doing as students in a college class on aging and human development did. You can use earplugs to reduce hearing and use or discard glasses to impair eyesight. You can wrap your joints in elastic bandages to simulate stiffness.[33] Or you can do as medical students do in a program training them in better communication skills with the elderly. That is, you can try wearing wax earplugs and fastening splints to your joints. Or you can put raw peas in your shoes to simulate corns and callouses. Or you can don rubber gloves to diminish the sense of touch.[34]

■ **WHAT TO DO**

Devise a project you will undertake to simulate a disability, and describe how you will go about it. (Examples: Borrow a wheelchair and try getting around campus, wear earplugs all day, use duct or masking tape to immobilize your fingers.)

_____
_____
_____
_____
_____
_____
_____
_____
_____
_____

■ **REPORT YOUR EXPERIENCES**

Briefly describe what you learned.

_____
_____
_____
_____
_____
_____
_____
_____
_____
_____
_____

GROUP ACTIVITY OPTION

Report some of your experience to the rest of the class.

Commuter Students

PREVIEW & REVIEW Eighty percent of college students are commuters, which often requires adjustment between the different sectors of their lives. Car ownership may not be necessary.

To see how far American colleges have moved from the model of residential campuses, consider that today about 80% of college undergraduates commute from housing beyond the borders of their campuses.[35,36] Almost half of students—most commuters—attend college part time, many of them older adults who are working at full-time jobs and engaged in raising families.[37] As a result, only about two in five students complete a bachelor's degree within four years after entering college; some take as long as nine years to graduate.[38]

Many people live this way, getting back and forth either by car or by public transportation—bus, train, subway, streetcar. In the New York, Chicago, and Washington, D.C. metropolitan areas, the average commute to work one way is about a half hour, and more than 10% of commuters take more than an hour. Nationwide the aver-age work commute—again, one way—is now 22.3 minutes, and it's usually done by car. Moreover, because the suburbs accounted for 70% of all new jobs between 1980 and 1990, suburb-to-suburb travel is now the largest category, accounting for 44% of commuting. City-to-suburb commutes also have increased, from 9% to 12%.[39,40] But not only are most workers commuters, so are most students.

ADJUSTING TO THE TRANSITION BETWEEN THE PARTS OF LIFE. If you're a commuter, how well do you make the transition between the different sectors of your life? All of us have to deal not only with the *physical* separation between home, school, and (often) work but also with the way we *think and act* in each realm. Some people (called "segmenters"), according to Christena Nippert-Eng, draw wide boundaries between the compartments of their lives. For example, at home they avoid all thoughts of work; at work they completely shut out their personal life. Others ("integrators") blend their different worlds. For example, some may go back and forth several times during the day between work (or school) and home, or they may invite coworkers (or fellow students) to their homes.[41]

The problem for some commuter students is that being on campus or at work may be manageable, because these realms are fairly orderly. Home, however,

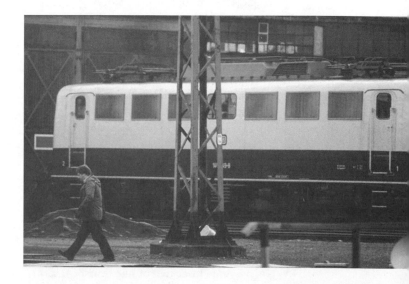

may be full of noisy housemates or children, yet you have to do your studying there anyway. How do you make the mental transitions across these boundaries?

What's required is to figure out your personal style. It may be best, for example, to stay on campus after class and do your studying there, where it's quiet. Or, if this is impossible, you keep a To-Do list—a "road map of the day"—to provide the organizing boundaries you need to make transitions.[42] You religiously follow the study schedule you drew up according to the description in Chapter 4.

CARS & THEIR ALTERNATIVES. If you get a used car for $3,000, say, that's equivalent to approximately 600 hours of labor at minimum wage. That's about like taking a semester off and working full time at that pay rate. Most new cars, of course, cost much more—$10,000 and up. And they'll cost you a lot more than that if you make monthly payments on an auto loan or lease rather than buying one for cash saved in advance.[43] In general, the less you pay for a car, the less it will cost in sales taxes and motor-vehicle fees and the less you will pay to insure it.

But buying a car is just the beginning. The average cost of owning and operating a car—including gas, tires, battery, repairs, and so on—works out to 45 cents a mile, according to the American Automobile Manufacturers Association.[44] Thus, if you drive an average of 12,000 miles a year, you are spending $5,400 annually on the car. And this *does not* include parking fees or bridge or turnpike tolls.

Besides public transit and ride-sharing, what is the alternative to driving your own car? An obvious one is to live close to campus or job, which can allow you to walk or ride a bicycle. Many people, says Eric Tyson, author of *Personal Finance for Dummies*, never consider this option. "Most assume that it would be too expensive," he says. "But a decrease in transportation costs by living close to work [and school] might more than make up for an increase in housing costs."[45] If you can't move closer to campus or work, you might also consider moving closer to a public-transportation

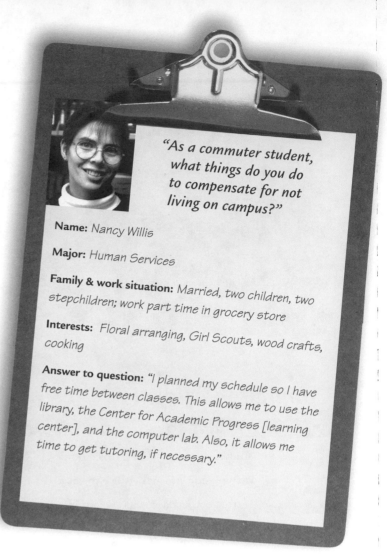

"As a commuter student, what things do you do to compensate for not living on campus?"

Name: Nancy Willis

Major: Human Services

Family & work situation: Married, two children, two stepchildren; work part time in grocery store

Interests: Floral arranging, Girl Scouts, wood crafts, cooking

Answer to question: "I planned my schedule so I have free time between classes. This allows me to use the library, the Center for Academic Progress [learning center], and the computer lab. Also, it allows me time to get tutoring, if necessary."

route. As I've mentioned elsewhere, from a student's point of view, public transit may provide a bonus in that you may be able to get some studying done while you're traveling.

If moving is out of the question and the travel time and crowds on public transit are too inconvenient, you might also consider a motorcycle or motor scooter. Motorcycles have become enormously popular—so much so, in fact, that they are more apt to be stolen than cars. This means you should chain your bike to an immovable object such as a lamp post, since thieves often use freon to freeze the handlebar lock, then smash it with a hammer.[46] Motor scooters are less expensive and easier to drive. However, motorcycle and scooter insurance isn't as competitive as car insurance.[47] Moreover, if you're involved in an accident, the outcome may be a lot more serious than if it happened to you in a car.

Information technology

DISTANCE LEARNING. I mentioned distance learning in Chapter 6. Here students take courses given at a distance, using television or a computer network, and the teacher may be close by in another room or on the other side of the world.

Of course, there are drawbacks to this process. "Some courses just don't translate well at a distance," says Pam Dixon, author of *Virtual College*. "Sometimes it's better to get your hands dirty and experience the course in a physical setting. Would you have wanted your dentist to have learned his or her craft entirely by videoconferencing?"[48] But, Dixon points out, business, writing, computers, mathematics, and library science, to name just a few courses and career paths, are well suited to teaching from afar. Indeed, students may get more attention from teachers online than they would from teachers in a large classroom with hundreds of students. In addition, says tele-education entrepreneur Glenn Jones, distance learning has the capability of offering computer access to virtual libraries of print, photos, recordings, and movies.[49]

To be sure, distance learning may take a bit of getting used to, as Joseph Walter, professor of communication studies at Northwestern University, found in studying the subject. "We learned a lot," says Walter, "including such things as the fact that the computer changes the dynamics of communication. It takes four or five times as long as speaking when you have to type out what you want to say."[50]

But in return for giving up being in a live classroom—and perhaps a long commute—students gain the convenience of being able to take courses not offered locally, often at times that suit their own schedules, not the space needs of an educational institution.

Onward: Applying This Chapter to Your Life

PREVIEW & REVIEW Being exposed to multiple viewpoints enriches us all.

In this information age," writes Hugh Price, president of the National Urban League, "the quality of a nation's human capital is the key to its productivity. The more highly educated our growing minority population is, the more competitive our economy and cohesive our society will be."[51]

Being exposed to a multiplicity of viewpoints enriches not only one's educational experience but also prepares us for the highly diversified world we will have to deal with in the new century.

If you found only *one idea* important in this chapter, what would it be? Write it down here:

_____

_____

_____

_____

_____

_____

GROUP ACTIVITY #10.5

COMMUTER SOLUTIONS

How about a contest to see which student has the longest commute? Each student should take a slip of paper and write down how many *total* minutes he or she spends on commuting—to and from school, home, work, day care, or whatever.

The instructor will ask students to call out their commute times, and will ask by what method they commute (private car, car pool, bus, and so on).

Questions for discussion: Can you get any school work done during your commute? Assuming you didn't have your present method of transportation, how would you commute? Are there any ways to make your commuting time productive? Could you move closer to school or work?

Real Practice
Activities for Real People

REAL PRACTICE ACTIVITY #10.1: EXPOSING YOURSELF DELIBERATELY TO DIVERSITY. This practice activity is designed to get students to deliberately expose themselves to diversity. The activity is to be done outside of class and reported the following week, either in class discussion or as a reaction paper written for the instructor.

Staying power

Getting to know people who are different from you may require overcoming some shyness or discomfort. In other words, it requires a bit of persistence, but this kind of perseverence or staying power will probably be required throughout your life as you have to work with new and different kinds of people.

Outside of class make some attempt to get to know people different from you. You could do this by attending a meeting of an extracurricular organization (criminal justice club, returning adult student support group, single-parent group, students with disabilities group, and so on). Or you could make arrangements to meet for coffee with someone with whom you share a class. Or you could contact someone through the college alumni association.

Following the directions of your instructor, next week report on the results of this activity either in class discussion or in a reaction paper. Some questions to consider: What are your reactions about your involvement? What are the benefits? What are the similarities with the person or people you met? How could you continue the involvement?

REAL PRACTICE ACTIVITY #10.2: WHAT KIND OF STEREOTYPING HAVE YOU EXPERIENCED? This practice activity, which is designed for class discussion, requires that students take 15–20 minutes to write up a particular experience regarding stereotyping.

Mindfulness

Stereotyping is a particular kind of mindlessness. Using a half sheet of paper or a note card, describe a past or present situation in your life in which a stereotype held by you or by others led to a negative experience. Don't put your name on the paper, but hand it into the instructor.

Drawing at random from the class contributions, the instructor will initiate class discussion about the types of stereotypes involved and their effects. What can be done to avoid such distortions in the future?

REAL PRACTICE ACTIVITY #10.3: FINDING OUT WHAT DISTANCE-LEARNING COURSES ARE AVAILABLE TO YOU. This activity may be performed by individuals out of class, who then submit a reaction paper to the instructor.

Information technology

As mentioned in the chapter, distance learning, in which an instructor instructs students through a computer or television network, gives students more options than were previously available. In particular it offers commuter students some relief from the hassles of fighting traffic or public transportation to get to campus. However, even on-campus students may find that distance learning offers them more types of courses or courses that better suit their time schedules.

Does your college offer distance learning? Using the college catalog, library, academic counseling, or other resources, find out what distance-learning courses are available to you. Write a one-page reaction paper to submit to the instructor in which you describe how you would take distance-learning courses, what kind of equipment you would need, and which of the courses offered are most suitable for you. In addition, discuss whether such courses are convenient for you and their possible advantages and disadvantages.

The Examined Life

JOURNAL ENTRY #10.1: WHAT IS YOUR CULTURAL HERITAGE? Many people have never taken the time to learn about their cultural heritage. Using library research and interviews with family members and relatives, answer the following questions:

1. What factors brought your family to this country?

_____
_____
_____
_____

2. What are the unique characteristics of your cultural background?

_____
_____
_____
_____

3. How has your family's living in North America changed the influences of your cultural heritage?

_____
_____
_____
_____

4. What would you like others to know about your cultural background that you feel they don't understand?

_____
_____
_____
_____

JOURNAL ENTRY #10.2: HOW ARE YOU DIFFERENT FROM OTHER STUDENTS? Looking around your classes or campus, how do you think you differ from most other students? How many students do you see that are sort of like you? What could you do to get to know them?

_____
_____

JOURNAL ENTRY #10.3: WHAT INFORMATION IN THIS CHAPTER WAS A SURPRISE TO YOU? Lots of people come to college with stereotypes in mind—about race, about gender, about ethnicity, and so on. What have you learned so far that has changed your mind about these kinds of matters?

JOURNAL ENTRY #10.4: WHAT DIFFERENCES ARE MOST DIFFICULT FOR YOU TO IDENTIFY WITH? Do you find it difficult to imagine yourself, say, an old person (if you're young), a homosexual (if you're heterosexual), with a physical disability (if you're able-bodied), or a foreign student (if you're American)? Identify someone who is totally different from you and try to describe what kinds of difficulties that person experiences.

_____

_____

_____

_____

_____

_____

_____

_____

_____

_____

Wellness

Managing Stress, Looking Good, & Feeling Good

Don't eat this. Don't drink that. Do more of this. Do less of that.

We are all exposed to conflicting messages about health, and I'll be the first to tell you I get confused myself. Still, a great deal of agreement exists about many aspects of health.

One thing I recall about being a student was feeling almost invulnerable: "Hey, I'm young, what could happen?" Health professors tell me this attitude drives them crazy. It's extremely frustrating, they say, to try to convince students of traditional college age that the habits they establish now will affect them in the future.

For example, many students whose drinking behavior is pretty excessive seem to think they will reduce their alcohol consumption once they are out of college. Many will, but others will have established drinking patterns that are tough to change. Many students say their alcohol and other drug use is related to *stress,* which college provides in abundance. What they may not know, however, is that the overuse of alcohol and other drugs only leads to *more* stress.

In this chapter, I describe some health practices that have several benefits: they are stress-busters, they make you look good, and they make you feel better.

Stress: Causes & Manifestations

PREVIEW & REVIEW Three principal worries of college students are (1) anxiety over wasting time, (2) anxiety over meeting high standards, and (3) feelings of being lonely. Stress is the body's reaction, stressors are the source of stress. Stressors may be small irritating hassles, short-duration crises, or long-duration strong stressors. A source of stress may be negative and cause "distress" or positive and cause "eustress." Stress may produce certain physical reactions: skin problems, headache, gastrointestinal problems, and high blood pressure. Stress may also produce emotional reactions such as nervousness, anxiety, and burnout.

A great deal of the college experience, unfortunately, consists of *stress.* Indeed, at one point for me in college, things were so stressful—because of academic pressures, financial worries, and my stormy love life—that I considered dropping out. I'm glad I didn't, because of course I've found since that stress certainly doesn't end with graduation. Indeed, I've learned there's even a *good* kind of stress, one that propels you to accomplish the things you want to do.

I've read that stress or burnout is one of the greatest causes of students leaving school without graduating.[1] I say that not to alarm you but simply so you'll know that any feelings of anxiety or tension you have are *commonplace* for college students.

THE WORRIES OF STUDENTS. College students, says one psychologist, are most hassled by three things:[2]

Staying power

- *Anxiety over wasting time:* To be in college is to always feel like you should be studying—particularly if you haven't yet set up a time-management system. Students who don't draw up a schedule of their study times and stick to it—demonstrate staying power—are particularly apt to suffer constant anxiety over wasting time.

- *Meeting high standards:* Another worry for students is whether or not they can meet the high standards of college. They may worry that they won't do well enough to get top grades. Or they may worry that they won't do well enough even to get passing grades and will flunk out.

- *Being lonely:* Many college students feel lonely from time to time. They may be lonely because they presently have no friends with common interests, no one with whom to share their worries, or no current love relationship.

TYPES OF STRESSORS: THE CAUSES OF STRESS. To understand how to fight stress, you need to understand the difference between *stress* and *stressors*. **Stress is the reaction of our bodies to an event. The source of stress is called a _stressor_.** Stressors may be specific and may range from small to large. That is, they may cover everything from a question you don't understand on a test all the way up to a death in your family.

Some characteristics of stressors are:

- *Three types:* There are three types of stressors—*hassles, crises,* and *strong stressors.* **A _hassle_ is simply a frustrating irritant,** such as a term-paper deadline. **A _crisis_ is an especially strong source of stress,** such as a horrible auto accident. Though it may be sudden and not last long, it may produce long-lasting psychological (and perhaps physical) effects. **A _strong stressor_ is a powerful, ongoing source of extreme mental or physical discomfort,** such as a back injury that keeps a person in constant pain. It can dramatically strain a person's ability to adapt.

From these terms, it would appear the stressors of college aren't so bad compared to other things that can happen. That is, your main experience is one of *hassles* rather than crises or strong stressors.

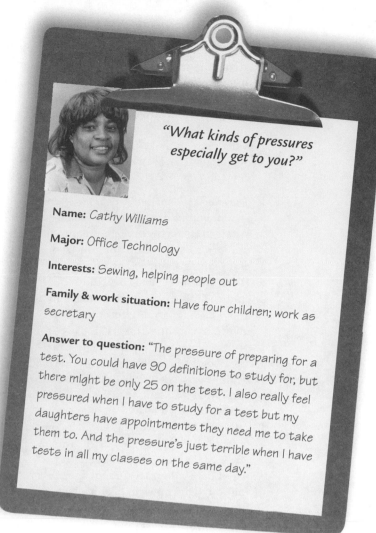

"What kinds of pressures especially get to you?"

Name: Cathy Williams

Major: Office Technology

Interests: Sewing, helping people out

Family & work situation: Have four children; work as secretary

Answer to question: "The pressure of preparing for a test. You could have 90 definitions to study for, but there might be only 25 on the test. I also really feel pressured when I have to study for a test but my daughters have appointments they need me to take them to. And the pressure's just terrible when I have tests in all my classes on the same day."

- *Distressors or eustressors:* One famous expert on stress, Canadian researcher Hans Selye, points out that stressors can be either negative or positive.[3]

  When the source of stress is a negative event, it is called a _distressor_ and its effect is called _distress_. An example of a distressor is flunking an exam or being rejected in love. Although distress can be helpful when one is facing a physical threat, too much of it may result in depression and illness.

  When the source of stress is a positive event, it is called a _eustressor_ and its effect is called _eustress_ (pronounced *"you-*stress"). An example of a eustressor is getting an A on an exam or falling in love. Eustress can stimulate a person to greater coping and adaptation.

We can't always prevent distressors. However, we can learn to recognize them, understand our reactions to them, and develop ways of managing both the stressors and the stress. Eustressors, on the other hand, are what impel us to do our best. Examples are the pressure to win games, to make the dean's list, to try out a new activity, to ask out someone new for a date.

■ *The number, kind, and magnitude of stressors in your life can affect your health:* When stressors become cumulative they can lead to depression and illness. Several years ago, physicians Thomas Holmes and Richard Rahe devised a "future illness" scale.[4] The scale, known as the Holmes-Rahe Life Events Scale, identifies certain stressors (life events), both positive and negative. These are stressors that the physicians found could be used to predict future physical and emotional problems.

You may wish to try Personal Exploration #11.1 *(opposite page)*, which contains a version of this scale, the Student Stress Scale. This was designed for people of the traditional student age, 18–24 (although anyone can take it). Note that the scale includes both negative and positive sources of stress.

TYPES OF STRESS: YOUR PHYSICAL & PSYCHOLOGICAL REACTIONS TO THE STRESSORS. Stress—your internal reactions to the stressor—has both physical and emotional sides. Physically, according to researcher Selye, stress is the "nonspecific response of the body to any demand made upon it."[5] Emotionally, stress is the feeling of being overwhelmed. According to one authority, it is "the perception that events or circumstances have challenged or exceeded a person's ability to cope."[6]

Specifically, stress reactions for you and for most other students could take the following forms:

■ *Physical reactions:* All diseases are to some extent disorders of adaptation.[7] Often, however, an adaptation to stress appears in a particular part of the body—what doctors call a person's *stress site*. My own

stress site, for instance, is the neck or back, where tension is felt as a knot in the muscles—a familiar stress reaction for many people. Some people I know grind their teeth. Others develop nervous tics or perspire excessively.

Do you have a stress site? Some physical reactions to stress are *skin problems, headaches, gastrointestinal problems, susceptibility to colds and flus,* and *high blood pressure.*[8–11]

■ *Psychological reactions:* Individual emotional reactions to stress cover a wide range. Among them are *nervousness and anxiety,* expressed as irritability, difficulty concentrating, and sleep disturbances. Nervousness and anxiety also is expressed in feelings of dread, overuse of alcohol and other drugs, and mistakes and accidents. Another emotional reaction is *burnout,* a state of physical, emotional, and mental exhaustion. [12,13]

Managing Stress

PREVIEW & REVIEW You can adapt to or cope with stress. Adaptation is not changing the stressor or stress. Some ways of adapting are use of drugs and other escapes such as television watching, junk-food eating, or sleeping. Coping is changing the stressor or your reaction to it. There are five strategies for coping: (1) Reduce the stressors. (2) Manage your emotional response. (3) Develop a support system. (4) Take care of your body. (5) Develop relaxation techniques.

 egardless of your age, you have already found ways to deal with stress in your life. The question is: Are these ways really the best? For instance, on some campuses students drink a lot of alcohol—and I mean *a lot.* Why? "Stress!" seems to be the answer. Actually, however, heavy alcohol use only leads to *more stress.*[14]

THE STUDENT STRESS SCALE

In the Student Stress Scale, each event, such as beginning or ending school, is given a score that represents the amount of adjustment a person has to make in life as a result of the change. In some studies, people with serious illnesses have been found to have high scores on similar scales.

■ DIRECTIONS

Check off the events you have experienced in the past 12 months.

POINTS

1. Death of a close family member	❏ 100
2. Death of a close friend	❏ 73
3. Divorce of parents	❏ 65
4. Jail term	❏ 63
5. Major personal injury or illness	❏ 63
6. Marriage	❏ 58
7. Firing from a job	❏ 50
8. Failure of an important course	❏ 47
9. Change in health of a family member	❏ 45
10. Pregnancy	❏ 45
11. Sex problems	❏ 44
12. Serious argument with close friend	❏ 40
13. Change in financial status	❏ 39
14. Change of scholastic major	❏ 39
15. Trouble with parents	❏ 37
16. New girl- or boyfriend	❏ 37
17. Increase in workload at school	❏ 36

18. Outstanding personal achievement	❏ 36
19. First quarter/semester in school	❏ 31
20. Change in living conditions	❏ 30
21. Serious argument with an instructor	❏ 30
22. Lower grades than expected	❏ 29
23. Change in sleeping habits	❏ 29
24. Change in social activities	❏ 29
25. Change in eating habits	❏ 28
26. Chronic car trouble	❏ 26
27. Change in the number of family get-togethers	❏ 26
28. Too many missed classes	❏ 25
29. Change of college	❏ 24
30. Dropping of more than one class	❏ 23
31. Minor traffic violations	❏ 20

Total points: _____

■ SCORING

To determine your stress score, add up the number of points corresponding to the events you checked

■ INTERPRETATION

If your score is 300 or higher, you are at high risk for developing a health problem.

If your score is between 150 and 300, you have a 50-50 chance of experiencing a serious health change within two years.

If your score is below 150, you have a 1-in-3 chance of a serious health change.

The following can help you reduce your risk:

■ Watch for early signs of stress, such as stomachaches or compulsive overeating.

■ Avoid negative thinking.

■ Arm your body against stress by eating nutritiously and exercising regularly.

■ Practice a relaxation technique regularly.

■ Turn to friends and relatives for support when you need it.

GROUP ACTIVITY OPTION

On a sheet of paper list your Top Ten Stressors, drawing on the Personal Exploration, if necessary. Then, in a small group (three to five students), designate a secretary or recorder and develop a master list from your separate lists. Identify the top five stressors for the group. Discuss how the stressors affect your behaviors and feelings and how you have ineffectively coped with such stressors in the past. Discuss how you would hope to deal with them in the future. If time permits, share your experiences with the class as a whole.

DO YOU CONTROL STRESS OR DOES STRESS CONTROL YOU? Unfortunately, we can't always control the stressors in our lives, so we experience stress no matter what we do. Thus, which is more important—what happens to you, or how you handle it? Clearly, learning how to *manage* stress—minimize it or recover from it—is more important.

There are two principal methods of dealing with stress—adaptation and coping:

■ *Adaptation:* **With _adaptation_, you do not change the stressor or the stress.** An example is getting drunk. Adaptation is the *bad* way of handling stress.

■ *Coping:* **With _coping_, you do change the stressor or change your reaction to it.** For example, if you're feeling stressed about handing in a paper late, you go talk to the instructor about it. This is the *good* way of handling stress.

ADAPTATION: THE NONPRODUCTIVE WAYS OF HANDLING STRESS. Some of the less effective ways in which people adapt to stress are as follows:

■ *Drugs, legal and illegal:* Coffee, cigarettes, and alcohol are all legal drugs. However, too much coffee can make you tense, "wired." Cigarettes also speed up the heart rate and may make it difficult to get going in the morning. Moreover, they put you under the stress of always having to reach for another cigarette.

Alcohol is perceived as being a way of easing the strain of life temporarily, which is why it is so popular with so many people. The down side, however, is what heavy drinking makes you feel like the next morning—jittery, exhausted, depressed, all conditions that *increase* stress.

Other legal drugs, such as tranquilizers, and illegal drugs, such as marijuana and cocaine, may seem to provide relaxation in the short run. However, ultimately they complicate your ability to make realistic decisions about the pressures in your life.

■ *Food:* Overeating and junk-food snacking are favorite diversions of many people.

The act of putting food in our mouths reminds us of what eased one of the most fundamental tensions of infancy: hunger.

■ *Sleep and social withdrawal:* Sleep, too, is often a form of escape from exhaustion and depression, and some individuals spend more than the usual 7–9 hours required in bed. Withdrawal from the company of others is also usually an unhealthy form of adaptation.

How do you adapt to stress now? Consider the kinds of responses you habitually make to the tensions in your life.

COPING: THE PRODUCTIVE WAYS OF HANDLING STRESS—FIVE STRATEGIES. Now let me turn from negative adaptations to stress to positive coping mechanisms. There are five strategies for coping with stress:

1. Reduce the stressors.

2. Manage your emotional response.

3. Develop a support system.

4. Take care of your body.

5. Develop relaxation techniques.

STRATEGY NO. 1: REDUCE THE STRESSORS.
Reducing the source of stress is better than avoidance or procrastination.

Reducing the stressors seems like obvious advice. However, it's surprising how long we can let something go on being a source of stress—usually because dealing with it is so uncomfortable. Examples are falling behind in your work and having to explain your problem to your instructor; having misunderstandings with your family, lover, or people sharing your living space; and running up debts on a credit card. It may not be easy, but all these problems are matters you can do something about. Getting the advice of a counselor may help. Avoidance and procrastination only make things worse.

STRATEGY NO. 2: MANAGE YOUR EMOTIONAL RESPONSE.
You can't always manage the stressor, but you can manage your reactions. Techniques include understanding and expressing your feelings, acting positively, and keeping your sense of humor and having hope.

Learning how to manage your emotional response is crucial. Quite often you can't do anything about a stressor (being stuck having to read a dull assignment, for example). However, you can do something about your *reaction* to it. (You can tell yourself that resentment gets you nowhere, or choose to see a particular stressor as a challenge rather than a threat.) Some techniques for managing your emotional response are the following:

■ *Understand and express your feelings:* Understanding pent-up feelings is imperative. This advice is supported by a study of students at Southern Methodist University. It was found that those who kept a journal recounting traumatic events and their emotional responses had fewer colds and reported fewer medical visits.[15]

Are you one who believes it's not appropriate to cry? Actually, crying helps. In one study, 85% of women and 73% of men reported that crying made them feel better.[16]

■ *Act positively:* To keep their spirits up, some people put up signs of positive affirmation on their bathroom mirrors or over their desks. For example:

DON'T SWEAT THE SMALL STUFF.

ONE DAY AT A TIME.

"NEVER GIVE UP"—Winston Churchill.

Can you actually *will* yourself to feel and act positively and affirmatively? There is some evidence this is so. Some studies have found that putting a smile on your face will produce the feelings that the expression represents—facial action leads to changes in mood.[17-19]

You can also make your "inner voice" a force for success. Positive "self-talk" can help you control your moods, turn back fear messages, and give you confidence.[20,21] Positive self-talk is not the same as mindless positive thinking or self-delusion.[22] Rather, it consists of telling yourself positive messages—such as "You can do it. You've done it well before"—that correct errors and distortions in your thinking and help you develop a more accurate internal dialogue.

■ *Keep your sense of humor and have hope:* A growing body of literature seems to show that humor, optimism, and hope can help people conquer disease or promote their bodies' natural healing processes.[23-26] There is some disagreement as to how much effect laughter and hope have on healing. Still, so many accounts have been written of the positive results of these two qualities that they cannot be ignored.

STRATEGY NO. 3: DEVELOP A SUPPORT SYSTEM.
Finding social support is vital for resisting stress. Sources of support are friends—in the true sense—counselors, and self-help and other support groups.

It can be tough to do things by yourself, so it's important to grasp a lesson that many people never learn: *You are not alone. No matter what troubles you, emotional support is available—but you have to reach out for it.*

Some forms of support are as follows:

■ *Talk to and do things with friends:* True friends are not just people you know. They are people you can trust, talk to honestly, and draw emotional sustenance from. (Some people you know quite well may actually not be very good friends in this sense. That is, the way they interact with you makes you feel competitive, anxious, or inferior.) Friends are simply those people you feel comfortable with, regardless of age or social grouping.

It's vital to fight the temptation to isolate yourself. Studies show that the more students participate in activities with other students, the less they suffer from depression and the more they have feelings of health.[27]

■ *Talk to counselors:* You can get emotional support from counselors. Paid counselors may be psychotherapists, ranging from social workers to psychiatrists. Unpaid counselors may be clergy or perhaps members of the college student services.

Sources of free counseling that everyone should be aware of are telephone "hot lines." Here, for the price of a phone call, callers can find a sympathetic ear and various kinds of help. (Hot lines are listed under the heading of CRISIS INTERVENTION SERVICE in the Yellow Pages. Other forms of stress counseling are listed under the heading STRESS MANAGEMENT AND PREVENTION.)

Information technology

■ *Join a support group:* This week an estimated 15 million Americans will attend one of about 500,000 meetings offered by some form of support group.[28] Self-help organizations cover all kinds of areas of concern. There are many on various types of drug addiction and others that offer help to adult children of alcoholics. Others range from single parenting to spouse abuse to compulsive shopping to "women who love too much" to various forms of bereavement. Some of these groups may exist on or near your campus. There are also now various kinds of support forums on the Internet.

In the true self-help group, membership is limited to peers. There is no professional moderator, only some temporarily designated leader who makes announcements and calls on people to share their experiences. This is in contrast with group-therapy groups, in which a psychologist or other therapist is in charge.

STRATEGY NO. 4: TAKE CARE OF YOUR BODY. *Taking care of the body helps alleviate stress in the mind. Techniques include eating, exercising, and sleeping right and avoiding drugs.*

The interaction between mind and body becomes particularly evident when you're stressed. If you're not eating and exercising well, short on sleep, or using drugs, these mistreatments of the body will only make the mind feel worse.

STRATEGY NO. 5: DEVELOP RELAXATION TECHNIQUES. *There are three relaxation techniques for de-stressing yourself. One is progressive muscular relaxation, which consists of tightening and relaxing muscle groups. A second is mental imagery, which consists of visualizing a change. A third is meditation, which consists of focusing on removing mental distractions.*

There is an entire body of extremely effective stress reducers that most people in North America have never tried at all.[29] They include the following:

■ *Mental imagery:* <u>*Mental imagery*</u>, **also known as** <u>*guided imagery*</u> **or** <u>*visualization*</u>, **is a procedure in which you essentially daydream an image or desired change, anticipating that your body will respond as if the image were real.** The box below shows how to do mental imagery. *(See ■ Panel 11.1.)*

PANEL 11.1 **M**ental imagery. It's recommended that you devote 10 minutes or so to this procedure.

■ *Progressive muscular relaxation:* The technique of <u>*progressive muscular relaxation*</u> **consists of reducing stress by tightening and relaxing major muscle groups throughout your body.** If you like, take 10 minutes to try the following.

1. *Get comfortable and quiet.* Sit down or lie in a comfortable setting where you won't be disturbed. Close your eyes.

2. *Become aware of your breathing.* Breathe slowly in through your nose. Exhale slowly through your nose.

3. *Clench and release your muscles.* Tense and relax each part of your body two or more times. Clench while inhaling. Release while exhaling.

4. *Proceed through muscles or muscle groups.* Tense and relax various muscles, from fist to face to stomach to toes. (A good progression is: Right fist, right biceps. Left fist, left biceps. Right shoulder, left shoulder. Neck, jaw, eyes, forehead, scalp. Chest, stomach, buttocks, genitals, down through each leg to the toes.)

Get comfortable and quiet: Remove your shoes, loosen your clothes, and sit down or lie in a comfortable setting, with the lights dimmed. Close your eyes.

Breathe deeply and concentrate on a phrase: Breathe deeply, filling your chest, and slowly let the air out. With each breath, concentrate on a simple word or phrase (such as "One," or "Good," or a prayer) Focus your mind on this phrase to get rid of distracting thoughts. Repeat.

Clench and release your muscles: Tense and relax each part of your body, proceeding from fist to face to stomach to toes.

Visualize a vivid image: Create a tranquil, pleasant image in your mind—lying beside a mountain stream, floating on a raft in a pool, stretched out on a beach. Try to involve all five senses, from sight to taste.

Visualize a desired change: If you're trying to improve some aspect of your performance, such as improving a tennis serve, visualize the act in detail: the fuzz and seam on the ball, the exact motion of the serve, the path of the ball, all in slow detail.

■ *Meditation:* *Meditation* **is concerned with directing a person's attention to a single, unchanging or repetitive stimulus. It is a way of quelling "mind chatter"**—the chorus of voices that goes on in the heads of all of us. An age-old technique, the purpose of meditation is simply to eliminate mental distractions and relax the body. The box below shows one method.[30] *(See* ■ *Panel 11.2.)*

PRACTICING A RELAXATION TECHNIQUE

How self-conscious are you? How aware are you of others around you? In order to practice a relaxation technique, you need to learn to shut out distracting thoughts. Although it's not easily done, this is an opportunity to try out such a technique.

The instructor will select *one of the three relaxation techniques—progressive muscular relaxation, mental imagery,* or *meditation*—for 10 minutes of practice by the class. He or she will read aloud from this book the steps for the particular method. *Important: Whenever everyday thoughts occur, disregard them and return to the relaxation procedure.*

After the 10 minutes are up, discuss your experience. Do you actually feel more relaxed? Did you almost fall asleep? Was it difficult to disregard the intrusion of everyday thoughts? Were you too aware of others in the room? Do you think the technique might work in private?

PANEL 11.2 **M**editation. Meditation includes the repetition of a word, sound, phrase, or prayer. Whenever everyday thoughts occur, they should be disregarded, and you should return to the repetition. The exercise should be continued for 10 minutes or so.

Herbert Benson, M.D., author of *The Relaxation Response* and *Your Maximum Mind,* offers the following simple instructions for meditation:

■ Pick a focus word or short phrase that is firmly rooted in your personal belief system. For example, a Christian person might choose the opening words of Psalm 23, "The Lord is my shepherd"; a Jewish person, "Shalom"; a nonreligious individual, a neutral word like "One" or "Peace."
■ Sit quietly in a comfortable position.
■ Close your eyes.
■ Relax your muscles.
■ Breathe slowly and naturally, and as you do, repeat your focus word or phrase as you exhale.
■ Assume a passive attitude. Don't worry about how well you're doing. When other thoughts come to mind, simply say to yourself, "Oh, well," and gently return to the repetition.

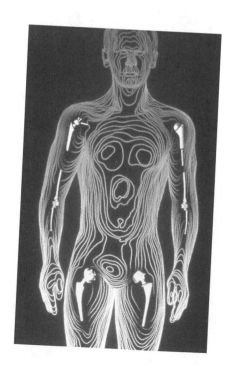

Alcohol: Are you Partial to Partying?

PREVIEW & REVIEW Since alcohol is a big part of campus life, one needs to learn the art of drinking. This includes learning what "a drink" is and what "BAL" means, how to reduce the effects of alcohol, and what the risks of drinking are.

People in general—and college students in particular—tend to equate drinking with relaxation, good times, fellowship, and the easing of pain and problems. However, as I mentioned in Chapter 4, a 1993 Harvard University study of 17,592 students on 140 campuses found some depressing news. It reported that 50% of male college students and 39% of female students were binge drinkers. *Binge drinking*, you'll recall, is defined as consuming five (for men) or four (for women) or more drinks in a row one or more times in a two-week period.[31] White male students were found to drink far more than white females and more than blacks and Hispanics of both sexes. (There was positive news, however: 35% of men and 45% of women drank at nonbinging levels. And 15% of men and 16% of women said they had abstained for the last two weeks.)

What are the results of excessive drinking on campus? Here's what the research says:

- **Effects on selves:** Nearly two-thirds of binge drinkers reported having missed a class. Over half forgot where they were or what they did. Forty-one percent engaged in unplanned sex, and 22% had unprotected sex. Twenty-three percent said they got hurt, 22% damaged property, and 11% got into trouble with police.

- **Effects on others:** On the 43 campuses with the greatest number of heavy drinkers, 68% of the lighter drinkers said they had had their study or sleep interrupted by an intoxicated student. Over half had to care for a drunken student. About a third said they had been "insulted or humiliated." One in four women said she had experienced an unwanted sexual advance. Other sober students reported serious arguments, having property damaged, or having been pushed or assaulted.

- **Suicides, accidents, and violence:** According to other sources, two-thirds of student suicides were legally drunk at the time, and 90% of fatal fraternity hazing accidents involved drinking. In addition, 95% of violent crime on campus has been found to be related to alcohol or other drugs. Moreover, 73% of assailants and 55% of victims of rape had used alcohol or other drugs.[32]

- **Lower bank account, lower grades:** Students spend $5.5 billion on alcohol annually, *more than they spend on nonalcoholic drinks and books combined.*[33] Students with D or F grade averages drink, on average, three times as much (nearly 11 drinks a week) as A students (3.4 drinks a week).[34]

Interestingly, in the 1993 Harvard study of college drinking, few students reported themselves as having a drinking problem. Asked to characterize their alcohol use, only 0.2% of all students surveyed and only 0.6% of the binge drinkers designated themselves as problem drinkers.

What about you? What are your drinking habits? You might want to try Personal Exploration #11.2 *(opposite).*

Being part of a hard-drinking social circle is difficult because of the powerful influence of the group over the individual. Still, throughout life we will always have to deal with the power of the group, and certainly this power is not always worth giving into. Here, then, are some suggestions on how to drink successfully:

■ ***Understand what a "drink" is:*** Think some drinks are stronger than others—whiskey more than beer, for example? That may be so, but a typical *serving* of the major types of alcoholic beverages—beer, wine, distilled spirits—contains about the same amount of alcohol. That is, 1 beer = 1 glass of table wine = 1 shot of distilled spirits. In terms of pure 100% alcohol, they're all approximately the same.

We're talking about a *standard* size drink here, which is equivalent to the following:

1. A 12-ounce can of light beer that is 4.8% alcohol. *(Total alcohol content per serving: 0.58 ounce.)*

2. A 4-ounce glass of table wine, such as chablis or burgundy, that is 12% alcohol. *(Alcohol content: 0.48 ounce per serving.)*

3. A 1-ounce shot of distilled spirits ("hard liquor"), such as scotch, bourbon, vodka, gin, rum, or tequila, that is 40% or 50% (80 or 100 proof) alcohol. *(Alcohol content: 0.40 or 0.50 ounce per serving.)* Actually, a standard bar shot is 1.5 ounces; thus the average bar drink contains 0.60 ounces of alcohol.

Many drinks, however, are not standard: distilled liquors or spirits can range from 40% to 75% alcohol. Mixed drinks or poured drinks may have more alcohol than those in bottles or cans. Some distilled fruit-based liqueurs are 20% alcohol.

■ ***Understand how to determine when you're legally drunk:*** The <u>blood alcohol level (BAL)</u> **is a measure of the amount of alcohol in the blood.** Thus, 10 drops of alcohol in 1,000 drops of blood is expressed as .10% BAL. (Think of 10 black marbles in 1,000 red marbles.) *If you have a .08%*

BAL, you are legally drunk in most states. If it's .10% BAL, you're legally intoxicated in all states and the District of Columbia. These are the levels, for example, at which the police establish whether someone is guilty of drunken driving ("driving under the influence").

How long will it take you to achieve these BALs? To determine that, you need to know how much you weigh and the number of drinks you've consumed in a 1-hour period. Find your approximate weight in the accompanying chart. *(See* ■ *Panel 11.3.)* Then look down the column to see what your estimated BAL would be for a given number of drinks consumed in 1 hour.

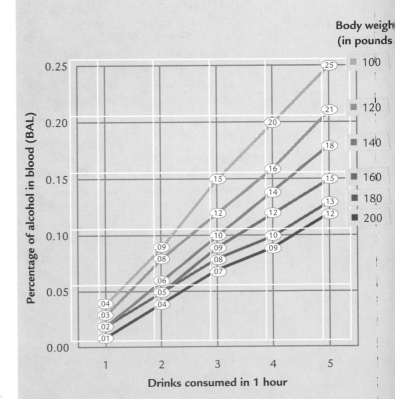

| PANEL 11.3 | **C**alculating your BAL. This table presents the approximate blood alcohol level (BAL) according to your body weight and the number of drinks consumed during 1 hour. |

WHAT KIND OF DRINKER ARE YOU?

Answer each of the following questions by placing a check next to the appropriate answer.

1. Do you feel you are a normal drinker? (If you are a total abstainer, check "Yes.")

   ❑ Yes   ❑ No

2. Have you ever awakened the morning after some drinking the night before and found that you could not remember a part of the evening before?

   ❑ Yes   ❑ No

3. Does your spouse [boyfriend/girl-friend] (or a parent) ever worry or complain about your drinking?

   ❑ Yes   ❑ No

4. Can you stop drinking without a struggle after one or two drinks?

   ❑ Yes   ❑ No

5. Do you feel bad about your drinking?

   ❑ Yes   ❑ No

6. Do friends or relatives think you are a normal drinker?

   ❑ Yes   ❑ No

7. Do you ever try to limit your drinking to certain times of the day or to certain places?

   ❑ Yes   ❑ No

8. Are you always able to stop drinking when you want to?

   ❑ Yes   ❑ No

9. Have you ever attended a meeting of Alcoholics Anonymous (AA)?

   ❑ Yes   ❑ No

10. Have you gotten into fights when drinking?

    ❑ Yes   ❑ No

11. Has drinking ever created problems with you and your spouse [boyfriend/girlfriend]?

    ❑ Yes   ❑ No

12. Has your spouse [boyfriend/girl-friend] (or other family member) ever gone to anyone for help about your drinking?

    ❑ Yes   ❑ No

13. Have you ever lost friends or dates because of drinking?

    ❑ Yes   ❑ No

14. Have you ever gotten into trouble at work because of drinking?

    ❑ Yes   ❑ No

15. Have you ever lost a job because of drinking?

    ❑ Yes   ❑ No

16. Have you ever neglected your obligations, your family, or your work for two or more days in a row?

    ❑ Yes   ❑ No

17. Do you ever have a drink before noon?

    ❑ Yes   ❑ No

18. Have you ever been told you have liver trouble? Cirrhosis?

    ❑ Yes   ❑ No

19. Have you ever had delirium tremens (DTs) or severe shaking, heard voices, or seen things that weren't there after heavy drinking?

    ❑ Yes   ❑ No

20. Have you gone to anyone for help about your drinking?

    ❑ Yes   ❑ No

21. Have you ever been in a hospital because of drinking?

    ❑ Yes   ❑ No

22. Have you ever been in a psychiatric hospital or on a psychiatric ward of a general hospital where drinking was part of the problem?

    ❑ Yes   ❑ No

23. Have you ever gone to a psychiatric or mental health clinic or to a doctor, social worker, or clergy

man for help with an emotional problem in which drinking had played a part?

   ❑ Yes   ❑ No

24. Have you ever been arrested, even for a few hours, because of drunk behavior?

    ❑ Yes   ❑ No

25. Have you ever been arrested for drunk driving or driving after drinking?

    ❑ Yes   ❑ No

■ SCORING

Give yourself points for your answers as follows.

QUESTION NUMBER	"YES" ANSWER	"NO" ANSWER
1	0	2
2	2	0
3	1	0
4	0	2
5	1	0
6	0	2
7	0	0
8	0	2
9	5	0
10	1	0
11	2	0
12	2	0
13	2	0
14	2	0
15	2	0
16	2	0
17	1	0
18	2	0
19	2	0
20	5	0
21	5	0
22	2	0
23	2	0
24	2	0
25	2	0

(continued next page)

INTERPRETATION

0–3: You are most likely a nonalcoholic.

4: You may be an alcoholic.

5 or more: You almost definitely are an alcoholic.

[The interpretation is what the original screening test says. I would say, however, that 4–5 or more points means mainly that alcohol is severely affecting your life. If this is the case for you, you should talk to a health professional about it.]

GROUP ACTIVITY OPTION

Form a group with two to four other students. Use the questions in this test to discuss *someone you know* (don't use names) who seems to have a drinking problem. Which "yes" answers seem to apply to him or her? Does that person admit to having a drinking problem? Why or why not, in your opinion? What is there about alcohol that makes problem drinkers so unwilling to admit they have a problem?

CALCULATING YOUR BAL. Panel 11.3 presents the approximate blood alcohol level (BAL) according to your body weight and the number of drinks consumed during 1 hour. A drink is defined as any of the following: (1) a can or bottle (12 ounces) of beer; (2) a glass (4 ounces) of wine; (3) a 1-ounce shot of 100-proof liquor; (4) a 1.5-ounce shot of 80-proof liquor.

For example, if you weigh 160 pounds and have four drinks in an hour, your BAL will be .12%—which makes you legally drunk everywhere. (In general, for men and women of equal weight, *women* experience a higher BAL after the same number of drinks.)

Marijuana & Cocaine

PREVIEW & REVIEW Drug dependence, the reliance on a substance, may give way to addiction, requiring increased dosages. Marijuana may lead to psychological dependence, lung problems, and other unpleasant side effects. Cocaine usually produces depression and anxiety after the high, as well as addiction and other hazards.

More than a third of Americans over the age of 12 have used an illicit drug at least once.[35] The largest group of users are those in the 18–25 age group.[36] However, the message discouraging drug use *does* seem to have gotten through. "The proportion of college students who smoked marijuana at least once in 30 days went from one in three in 1980 to one in seven" in 1993, says one report. Moreover, "cocaine users dropped from 7% to 0.7% over the same period."[37] Even so, many students still do use illegal drugs, particularly marijuana.

WHAT'S THE REAL STORY ON DRUG USE? A few years ago, some University of California, Berkeley, researchers created an uproar among drug counselors when they released the results of a 15-year study. The investigators found that teenagers who had experimented casually with drugs appeared to be better adjusted than adolescents who either abstained or regularly abused drugs.[38,39] The teenagers the researchers labeled "experimenters" used no drug more than once a month, and no more than one drug other than marijuana. The frequent users used marijuana regularly, at least once a week, and had tried several stronger drugs such as cocaine. The frequent users showed evidence early in life of psychological maladjustments, emotional mood swings, inattentiveness, stubbornness, insecurity, and other signs of emotional distress.

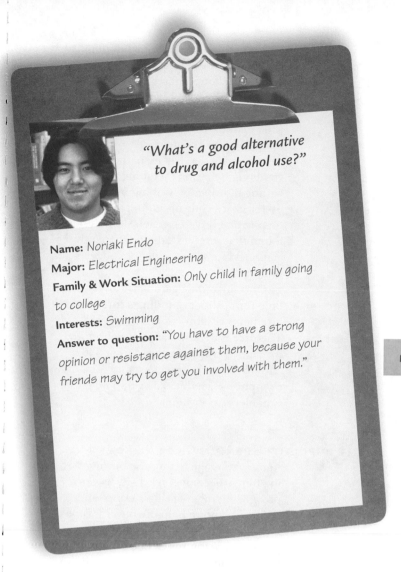

"What's a good alternative to drug and alcohol use?"

Name: Noriaki Endo

Major: Electrical Engineering

Family & Work Situation: Only child in family going to college

Interests: Swimming

Answer to question: "You have to have a strong opinion or resistance against them, because your friends may try to get you involved with them."

The Berkeley researchers insisted they did not mean to advocate drug experimentation, but many drug counselors were horrified anyway. Perhaps, though, three conclusions can be drawn:

- **Drug experimenters are not necessarily healthier:** Young people who experiment with drugs aren't necessarily psychologically healthier. Rather, the healthiest can survive the drug-experimentation years and are flexible enough to right themselves if they do experiment.

- **Drug experimentation is unnecessary:** It is not necessary to explore drugs in order to explore life or to combat stress. Techniques for achieving the "optimal experience" and for escaping tension are available without drugs.

- **Drug experimentation MAY lead to dependence or addiction:** Unfortunately, some beginning users don't survive. After all, how do you *know* you're "psychologically healthy" when you begin using? Clearly, some people who start out exploring life by experimenting with drugs do get caught in the trap of dependence or addiction.

    <u>Dependence</u> **refers to the reliance on or need for a substance.** The dependence may be physical, psychological, or both. <u>Addiction</u> **refers to a behavioral pattern characterized by compulsion, loss of control, and continued repetition of a behavior or activity in spite of adverse consequences.**

MARIJUANA. In the short run, marijuana acts somewhat like alcohol, producing feelings of relaxation and tranquility and, for some people, a heightened sense of perception.

The down side of marijuana use is as follows: (1) Among inexperienced users, marijuana may produce anxiety and paranoia.[40] In addition, some users also report headaches, nausea, and muscle tension. (2) It impairs psychomotor performance, so it's best not to drive a car while under the drug's influence. (3) It may produce some psychological dependence. Heavy users who stop show such signs as sleep disturbance, irritability, and nausea.[41] (4) It may cause respiratory problems, such as chronic bronchitis and pulmonary disease.[42] (5) Some regular marijuana users have shown such behaviors as apathy, difficulty concentrating, lost ambition, and decreased sense of goals.[43] Although it used to be thought that marijuana is not physically addicting, some individuals have been found to be as addicted to it as to any other mind-altering substance.

COCAINE. "Even among drugs of considerable addiction potential, cocaine stands apart," writes one psychologist who specializes in studying the drug. "It is, in its various forms, the most destructive drug in human history. Not heroin, not LSD, not marijuana, not alcohol, not PCP—

none of these drugs is as capable as cocaine of grabbing on and not letting go."[44] Cocaine exerts this powerful hold on people because, unlike other drugs, it *directly* stimulates the pleasure circuits in the brain.

Cocaine exists in several forms—regular, free-base, and crack. Regular cocaine is inhaled or injected. Free-base cocaine is smoked. Crack is often smoked.

The euphoria provided by the drug has a tremendous down side. (1) The cocaine high is followed by severe depression called a "crash," followed by anxiety, fatigue, shakiness, and withdrawal. (2) Cocaine use rapidly leads to addiction: in an attempt to recover the feelings of ecstasy, users require repeated and higher doses. The highs get higher but the valleys get deeper. (3) Repeated use can produce headaches, shakiness, nausea, lack of appetite, loss of sexual interest, and depression. Addiction leads to all kinds of life-threatening problems: paranoid delusions, hallucinations, seizures, heart attack, heart muscle damage, stroke—and finally overdose that can cause death.[45]

Gambling & Spending

PREVIEW & REVIEW "Process dependencies" or "process addictions" cover disorders such as compulsive gambling and compulsive spending.

In recent years, the words "dependence" and "addiction" have become broadly generalized to behavior other than drug use. That is, some experts now apply these terms to "processes" rather than chemicals—areas such as compulsive gambling, spending, eating disorders, sexual obsessions, and Internet overuse.[46] (Not all health-care professionals agree that these are true dependencies, however.)

COMPULSIVE GAMBLING. The rates of gambling by college students seem to be higher than among others in the adult population. A survey of 2,000 college students in six states found that 87% had gambled. Moreover, 25% had gambled weekly, and 11% had gambled more than $100 in one day. Some amounts ranged up to $50,000 in one week![47] About 5.7% were described as having pathological gambling behavior, including repeatedly betting in hopes of winning big to make up for losses and continuing to gamble despite inability to pay debts. The study found that several students frequently gambled money set aside for college tuition.[48]

Once-in-a-while gamblers can have a little fun without spending a fortune, as I do when I visit my friends in Nevada. The trick is to designate a certain sum for betting only (whether $10 or $50), and when that is gone to spend no more. Compulsive gamblers may find help with Gamblers Anonymous.

COMPULSIVE SPENDING. Compulsive spenders *repeatedly* engage in impulse buying. Buying things becomes an activity used to provide feelings of self-assurance and self-worth and to help the buyer escape feelings of anxiety and despair. Not surprisingly, compulsive spenders often become compulsive debtors, who continually borrow money from institutions, family, and friends to pay their bills.

Characteristics of compulsive buyers are the following.[49] (1) They are very anxious and depressed. (2) They often buy for other people. (3) They may be "binge buyers," "daily shoppers," or "multiple buyers." People who are binge buyers may go on a shopping binge only occasionally, perhaps triggered by an upsetting event. Daily shoppers go shopping every day and become upset if they do not.

Many people have trouble handling money. To guard against excess expenditures, you need to inject rationality into the shopping process. For example, you can draw up plans for shopping, ask others to do the shopping, shop only when feeling calm, or destroy all credit cards. Resources such as Debtors Anonymous are also available.

IDENTIFYING SOME LEGAL DEPENDENCIES

With other students in a small group, identify as many *legal* dependencies as possible. (Don't list illegal drugs.) Also identify the reasons you think people develop such dependencies. Select two from the list and develop plans for reducing dependence on them. Share your first list and your strategy with the rest of the class.

What are the major dependencies identified by the class? What do you think of the reasons suggested for why people develop dependencies? Do you think people choose dependencies of their own free will?

Looking Good: Weight & Energy Balance

PREVIEW & REVIEW Most women are self-critical of their looks, men are less so. Important factors in body image are size and weight. To maintain desirable weight, you need to understand the concept of energy balance.

If you're like most people, you think you're less than perfectly attractive. Even handsome people feel they're flawed.

You have only to look to advertising and the mass media for comparison. Today the average model, dancer, and actress, for example, weighs 23% less than the average American woman. Moreover, she is thinner *than 95% of women.*[50] Is that what ordinary people are supposed to aspire to?

HOW DO YOU FEEL ABOUT YOUR BODY?

Women and men college students have been found to have different kinds of feelings about their bodies.

- *Women:* In general, college women are highly self-critical, especially about their thighs, hips, and weight. Men are actually less critical of women than women are of themselves. Indeed, men actually prefer women who are heavier than women think is attractive.[51,52]

- *Men:* College men tend to overestimate their own attractiveness or are relatively tolerant of their physical drawbacks, such as being overweight.

When it comes to their looks, people may be self-conscious about their skin, hair, teeth, having to wear glasses, or other attributes. In general, however, the most important matters bearing on body image appear to be *size and weight.*

HOW TO LOOK GOOD: THE CONCEPT OF ENERGY BALANCE. *"Low on calories!"* We seem to see that claim wherever we go—in food ads and on the grocery shelves. A few years ago, however, I realized I wasn't sure what a "calorie" was, so I did a little research.

A *calorie* is the unit of heat used to measure the energy potential of food. *Energy* is defined as "the capacity to do work." This simply means that *the body takes in calories from food and expends them in work—namely, physical activity.* Ideally, you should have "energy balance." **Energy** ___balance___ **is the state in which the calories expended are the same as the calories consumed.** If the calories you eat are not expended in activity, you *gain* weight. If you don't consume enough calories for the energy you expend, you *lose* weight.

No doubt some people are obese because they eat too much. But that's only half the story. As we see from the concept of energy balance, the calories expended are as important as the calories consumed. Not being physically active enough, in fact, may be *the* most important reason that so many adults in the United States are obese.

So how many calories do you actually need from food in order to look good? That depends on your sex, age, frame, percentage of body fat, and level of activity. For example:

- *For women:* If you are 20 years old, 5 feet 4 inches tall, weigh about 120 pounds, and generally engage in only light activity, you need 1,700–2,500 calories a day to maintain your weight.

- *For men:* If you are 20 years old, 5 feet 10 inches tall, weigh about 154 pounds, and engage in only light activity, you need 2,500–3,300 calories a day.

"Light activity" means that you spend 2 hours a day in light physical activity, ranging from putting on your clothes to fixing dinner. Beyond that, it is assumed you walk for 2 hours a day, stand for 5, sit for 7, and sleep or lie down for 8. People who are more active will need more calories than the above; so will people who are taller. Shorter people will need less; so will older people.

Here, finally, is the bottom line—the formula for looking good.

1. Don't think you have to look thinner or weigh less than is appropriate for your height and size.

2. Observe the concept of *energy balance:* don't eat any more in calories than you can expend in physical activity.

3. To look muscular and fit, take part in physical activity.

How much physical activity is required? Energy-expenditure requirements vary for each person. Nevertheless, a study of men who expended only 2,000 *extra* calories per week in physical activity than their inactive counterparts found they were healthier and lived longer.[53] My guess is they also looked a whole lot better.

An extra 2,000 calories a week isn't a lot, and this kind of activity can easily be worked into your life. For instance, a 150-pound person could burn about this many calories just by mixing physical exercise and chores over the course of 5 hours in a week. Physical activity could be walking or bicycling to class. Chores could be housecleaning or gardening.

Feeling Good: The Benefits of Being Active

PREVIEW & REVIEW Physical activity can enhance your mood, energy, and creativity; keep weight down; and reduce heart-disease and cancer risks.

stated that being in college can be very stressful. But I also know from my experience that this is where physical activity can truly help. Indeed, I find activity a feel-good pill that can lift my spirits and my energy level.

HOW ACTIVITY MAKES YOU FEEL GOOD. Some of the benefits of activity are as follows:

■ *Anxiety and tension relief:* Physical activity provides a means of releasing yourself from anger, anxiety, and tension.[54–56] One study investigated men and women ages 30–49 who walked at slow, medium, fast, and self-selected paces. The researchers found that, regardless of the pace, all the walkers felt "immediate and significant decrease in anxiety and tension." Moreover, the improved moods lasted up to 2 hours after the workout ended.[57]

■ *Alleviation of depression:* In one experiment, a group of mildly and moderately depressed patients were assigned randomly to one of two groups—those who would receive psychotherapy and those who would take up running. The runners felt better after only a week, and were declared "virtually well" within three weeks, with the benefits lasting at least a year. The runners were reported to do as well as the patients receiving short-term psychotherapy and to do better than those receiving long-term psychotherapy.[58–61]

Staying power

■ *Increased energy:* Even a brisk 10-minute walk can increase energy and decrease fatigue for as long as 2 hours.[62] Thus, when you have an afternoon slump you'll probably find a short, vigorous walk will pick you up better than, say, a candy bar.[63]

Mindfulness

■ *Stimulation of creative thinking:* Some people who exercise are able to let their minds "take a vacation" from the worries at hand.[64] (I find this happening to me.) Studies suggest that exercise can sharpen mental skills and enhance creativity. Even a single 20-minute session of aerobic dance can increase creative problem-solving abilities.[65]

■ *Health benefits:* Physical activity is the principal way to keep your weight at its desirable levels. It also has a whole bunch of health benefits: It probably reduces the risk of heart disease.[66–70] It may reduce the risk of cancer and diabetes.[71] Among women, it may reduce the risk of osteoporosis, a bone-crumbling disorder that often leads to hip fractures in later life.[72]

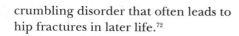

FITNESS & FUN. You notice that, in general, I have used the term "physical activity" rather than "exercise" throughout. A lot of people think that exercise is an "odious, sweat-soaked endeavor," to quote two writers on the subject. Physical activity, on the other hand, "can be any daily undertaking, work or play, that involves movement."[73]

Actually, exercise need not be unpleasant. Indeed, whatever you choose to call it, this kind of activity should be something you *want* to do. Personal fitness is not about punishment—forget the expression "No pain, no gain." Rather, it's about *fun* and *feeling good.* You need to remind yourself that exercise not only improves your health but also makes you *feel better.*

Perhaps, however, you want to go beyond various kinds of movement and into a *program* of physical fitness. **<u>Physical fitness</u> is defined as having above-average (1) flexibility, (2) aerobic endurance, and (3) muscle strength and endurance.** Here's what I mean:

■ *Flexibility: Flexibility* is suppleness of movement—your ability to touch your toes or twist your body without discomfort, for instance. Flexibility is achieved through various stretching exercises.

■ *Aerobic endurance: Aerobic endurance* describes how efficiently your body uses oxygen and is able to pump blood through your heart and blood vessels. Aerobic endurance is achieved by high-intensity workouts such as jogging or running or vigorous swimming, rowing, dancing, or bicycling. (I enjoy jogging and cross-country skiing.)

■ *Muscle strength and endurance: Muscle strength* is the ability to exert force against resistance, whether standing up from a chair or lifting a free weight. *Muscle endurance* is the ability to keep repeating those muscle exertions, so that you can scoop not just one but several shovels full of snow. Muscle strength and endurance is achieved through *resistance training:* doing sit-ups, lifting free weights, working out on weight machines.

If you're interested in getting into some of these activities, consider signing up for some classes.

Peak Performance with a Power Diet

PREVIEW & REVIEW Avoid fats and oil, which lower energy and make you gain weight. Avoid sugar, which provides energy but no nutrients. Eat complex carbohydrates, as in vegetables and fruits. Eat a variety of foods. Avoid salt and junk foods; women should take calcium and iron.

College takes a lot of energy and stamina. Physical activity helps, but a power diet will boost your productivity or athletic performance even further. It will also lower your chances of getting heart disease or cancer.

How good is your diet now? To find out, try Personal Exploration #11.3.

Here are some recommendations for a power diet.

1. GO EASY ON FOODS OF ANIMAL ORIGIN. Meat and dairy products are responsible for dietary fat, artery-clogging cholesterol, and a great many weight-adding calories. Try to revise your food choices so you eat less meat (particularly red meat), cheese (try low-fat cheese), greasy potato chips, ice cream (which contains fat), and the like. You'll probably feel the results in more energy.

Particularly to be avoided are *fats and oils*. Too much fat also makes people overweight and lowers their energy level. Fats and oils have been linked to cancer and heart and blood-vessel disease. Nutritionists feel strongly about the undesirability of fats and oils. Indeed, the Food Guide Pyramid says these are to not even be considered a food group and should be eaten only sparingly. Consuming no fats at all would be deadly, but fats are already available in the average diet.

Different foods have different amounts of fat. Fat is low or nonexistent in fruits, vegetables, and grain products and high in foods of animal origin. *Visible fats* are fairly easy to spot. They are almost anything greasy—butter, margarine, shortening, cooking and salad oils, and the "marbling" in steak and other red meat. *Invisible fats* are harder to identify. The major sources are meat, poultry, fish, and dairy products. Invisible fats are also frequently added during the preparation of food. Examples are fried foods, butter on baked potatoes, foods in cream sauces, or anything deep-fried in batter.

2. GO EASY ON SUGAR. Sugar provides energy but no nutrients. Moderate sugar intake with meals is all right. However, most of it should come not from high-sugar foods such as candy but from "natural sugar" sources, such as fruits. In addition, you should drink sugar-free soft drinks or juices without added sugar.

3. EAT PERFORMANCE FUEL: COMPLEX CARBOS. *Complex carbohydrates* **are foods such as whole grains, barley, whole-wheat pasta, vegetables, and fruit.** Athletes of all sorts eat large quantities of these to provide the body's main energy fuel, glycogen, to sustain intense physical activity. Fat and protein do not produce glycogen; carbohydrates do. (Complex carbos also provide *fiber,* helpful in preventing and alleviating constipation and certain intestinal disorders.) Sports nutritionists recommend a high-performance diet that is less protein and fat and principally carbohydrates—bread, cereal, pasta, vegetables, and fruits.[74,75]

4. EAT A VARIETY OF FOODS. Unless you have a highly imbalanced diet, you probably won't need vitamin and mineral supplements. Even athletes and other high-energy individuals can get needed vitamins from a low-fat, high-complex-carbohydrate diet—provided they eat a *variety of foods.* (This is what is called a "balanced diet.")

5. BE MODERATE WITH SALT, TAKE CALCIUM & IRON, & AVOID JUNK. A few other tips round out the recommendations for a power diet:

■ *Avoid salt:* Too much salt may raise blood pressure, at least in some people. High

THE EATING SMART QUIZ: HOW HEALTHY IS YOUR DIET?

How do you rate? This is a quick, simple eating quiz for all ages which looks at how your eating patterns compare to the American Cancer Society's guidelines. Below each category of food are examples. When rating yourself, think of foods similar to those listed that are in your diet.

■ DIRECTIONS

Circle the number of points for the answer you choose in the points column at the far right. Total your points. Compare your score with the analysis at the end of the quiz.

YOUR POINTS

Oils and fats: butter, margarine, shortening, mayonnaise, sour cream, lard, oil, salad dressing.

- I always add these to foods in cooking and/or at the table.   0
- I occasionally add these to foods in cooking and/or at the table.   1
- I rarely add these to foods in cooking and/or at the table.   2

- I eat fried foods 3 or more times a week.   0
- I eat fried foods 1–2 times a week.   1
- I rarely eat fried foods.   2

Dairy products:

- I drink whole milk.   0
- I drink 1%–2% fat-free milk.   1
- I drink skim milk.   2

- I eat ice cream almost every day.   0
- I eat ice milk, low-fat frozen yogurt, and sherbet.   1
- I eat only fruit ices, seldom eat frozen dairy desserts.   2

- I eat mostly high-fat cheeses (jack, cheddar, Colby, Swiss, cream).   0
- I eat both low- and high-fat cheeses.   1

- I eat mostly low-fat cheeses (2% cottage, skim milk mozzarella).   2

Snacks: potato chips, corn chips, nuts, buttered popcorn, candy bars.

- I eat these every day.   0
- I eat some occasionally.   1
- I seldom or never eat these snacks.   2

Baked goods: pies, cakes, sweet rolls, doughnuts.

- I eat them 5 or more times a week.   0
- I eat them 2–4 times a week.   1
- I seldom eat baked goods or eat only low-fat baked goods.   2

Poultry and fish:*

- I rarely eat these foods.   0
- I eat them 1–2 times a week.   1
- I eat them 3 or more times a week.   2

Low-fat meat:* extra-lean hamburger, round steak, pork loin, roast, tenderloin, chuck roast.

- I rarely eat these foods.   0
- I eat these foods occasionally.   1
- I eat mostly fat-trimmed red meats.   2

High-fat meat:* luncheon meats, bacon, hot dogs, sausage, steak, regular and lean ground beef.

- I eat these every day.   0
- I eat these foods occasionally.   1
- I rarely eat these foods.   2

Cured and smoked meat and fish:* luncheon meats, hot dogs, bacon, ham and other smoked or pickled meats and fish.

- I eat these foods 4 or more times a week.   0
- I eat some 1–3 times a week.   1
- I seldom eat these foods.   2

Legumes: dried beans and peas: kidney, navy, lima, pinto, garbanzo, split-pea, lentil.

- I eat legumes less than once a week.   0
- I eat these foods 1–2 times a week.   1
- I eat them 3 or more times a week.   2

Whole grains and cereals: whole-grain breads, brown rice, pasta, whole-grain cereals.

- I seldom eat such foods.   0
- I eat them 2–3 times a day.   1
- I eat them 4 or more times daily.   2

Vitamin C–rich fruits and vegetables: citrus fruits and juices, green peppers, strawberries, tomatoes.

- I seldom eat them.   0
- I eat them 3–5 times a week.   1
- I eat them 1–2 times a day.   2

Vegetables of the cabbage family: broccoli, cabbage, brussels sprouts, cauliflower.

- I seldom eat them.   0
- I eat them 1–2 times a week.   1
- I eat them 3–4 times a week.   2

Alcohol:

- I drink more than 2 ounces of 80-proof liquor daily. (Alcohol equivalents: 2 oz. of 80-proof liquor = 6 1/2 oz. wine OR 18 oz. beer OR 25 oz. 3.2 beer.)   0
- I drink alcohol every week, but not daily.   1
- I occasionally or never drink alcohol.   2

Personal weight:

- I'm more than 20 pounds over my ideal weight.   0
- I'm 10–20 pounds over my ideal weight.   1
- I'm within 10 pounds of my ideal weight.   2

*If you do not eat meat, fish, or poultry, give yourself a 2 for each meat category.

Total score: _____

■ HOW DO YOU RATE?

0–12 points: A warning. Your diet is too high in fat and too low in fiber-rich foods. It would be wise to assess your eating habits to see where you could make improvements.

13–17 points: Not bad! You're partway there. You still have a way to go.

18–36 points: Good for you! You're eating smart. You should feel very good about yourself. You have been careful to limit your fats and to eat a varied diet. Keep up the good habits and continue to look for ways to improve.

■ REMEMBER

A poor score does not mean you will get cancer, nor does a high score guarantee that you won't. But your score will give you a clue as to how you eat now and where you need to improve to reduce your cancer risks.

■ IMPORTANT

This eating quiz is for self-information and does not evaluate your intake of essential vitamins, minerals, protein, or calories. If your diet is restricted in some ways (for example, you are a vegetarian or have allergies), you may want to get professional advice.

GROUP ACTIVITY OPTION

In either large or small groups, discuss the results of this Personal Exploration. How much of your diet is based solely on the fact that "I only eat what tastes good"? How much is based on factors of cost? of availability? Suppose you were going to give up just *one* unhealthy food that you eat regularly (such as candy bars). What would you try to eat instead that would come close to providing the same reward?

---

blood pressure is an indicator of potential heart disease.

■ ***Women—take calcium and iron:*** To avoid the bone disorder of osteoporosis in later life, women should take calcium supplements. To forestall anemia, they should also take iron.

■ ***To avoid fatigue, eat frequently but avoid junk foods:*** You may prefer five or six smaller meals to three large ones if you expend a lot of energy. "Grazing" on low-fat, nutritious foods may help avoid that drowsy letdown that often follows a big lunch.[76] If you eat every few hours and eat before you get too hungry, it will keep you from being overwhelmed by hunger and gorging.

However, chips, ice cream, cookies, and the like are not low-fat and are not performance boosters. Better are fruit, vegetables, yogurt, bread sticks, unbuttered popcorn, juices, unsalted nuts, whole-grain crackers, and similar high-complex-carbohydrate items.

GROUP ACTIVITY #11.3

BEGINNING A POWER DIET

This activity requires that everyone in the class take a week to try *one* aspect of the "power diet" described above, then report the results.

With others in a small group of five, each take just *one* of the five recommendations for a power diet. Each of the five of you should take a different recommendation. (If you can't decide voluntarily, write the different recommendations on slips of paper and take turns drawing the folded slips out of a hat.) Practice that recommendation as conscientiously as possible for a week. Take notes on what temptations and difficulties you encounter.

At the end of the week, report your experience to your group. What was hard about it? What was easy? Could you keep it up for the rest of the school term? Which of the other five recommendations would you want to try next?

If the instructor requests, share some of your experiences with the class as a whole.

Recharging Time: Sleep & Rest

PREVIEW & REVIEW Many people neglect the sleep and rest they need, suffering a "sleep deficit" resulting in lowered performance. To get enough rest, you should follow regular sleep habits and bedtime rituals.

What's the best way to pull an all-nighter? This is a question I hope you won't have to address, because the whole purpose of this book is to make it so you don't have to. Nevertheless, suppose you find that you have roughly 24 hours to prepare for a test or write a paper. Should you plug in the coffeemaker, hit the books, and then catch a 4 A.M. snooze before going to class? Actually, if you take a short nap *before* staying awake all night, you'll avoid sleepiness and your performance will be better.[77]

This is an example of how a little knowledge can enable you to manipulate your internal clock to further your performance.

Sleep researchers say that people's sleep needs vary, although most adults seem to do their best work by sleeping 7–8 hours.[78] In general, most people need 7½–8½ hours of sleep per night. A small percentage, however, can get by on 5 or 6 hours and another small percentage need 9 or 10.

More than 100 million Americans get by with insufficient sleep—nearly every other adult and teenager.[79] Indeed, sleep experts have found that most people get 60–90 minutes less sleep each night than they should. This kind of "sleep deficit" can have important consequences. Even one night's loss of 2 hours sleep is not made up during the following 5–6 days of normal sleep.[80] Sleep deprivation can lead to difficulty in concentration, fatigue, and poor performance on a variety of tasks.[81]

Onward: Applying This Chapter to Your Life

PREVIEW & REVIEW Your body is not expendable.

Many people treat their bodies as if they were expendable, but find they are not. Probably the more you neglect or abuse your health, the less energy you'll have as well as less self-esteem.

Of course, on some level of consciousness you probably know this. Now's the time to put this knowledge into practice. What two specific things did you learn in this chapter that you could adopt for taking better care of yourself? Write them down here:

_____

_____

_____

_____

_____

Real Practice Activities for Real People

REAL PRACTICE ACTIVITY #11.1: HOW DOES WELLNESS REQUIRE PERSISTENCE?

Staying power

This practice activity, which may be performed in small-group or classroom-wide discussion, is designed to get students thinking about how they need to apply persistence to adapting positive health habits.

College requires that you take on a variety of new behaviors and responsibilities. Some of these may pertain to how you treat your health, which, if not managed properly, may affect not only your academic performance but your very life itself.

In small-group or class discussion, consider the following questions: How can you use the information presented in this chapter to develop and maintain wellness? What specific negative behaviors require perseverence in order to change them? What are the barriers to achieving optimum help and how can you overcome them?

REAL PRACTICE ACTIVITY #11.2: RELEARNING HOW YOU HANDLE STRESS.

Mindfulness

This practice activity may be done in small groups, with members helping each other develop stress management plans. Individuals may later write up the results as reaction papers to be handed in to the instructor.

Learning to handle stress is one of the most important things you'll ever do. Actually, you've already developed some specific coping or adaptation mechanisms. The important question is: Could they be better? Stress is governed by how you react to real or perceived threats or situations. However, some behaviors may become automatic—that is, mindless—with possible negative consequences to your health.

In this practice activity, you and other members of a small group are to take turns working out individual stress management plans for each of you. Use the

REAL PRACTICE ACTIVITY #11.3: USING THE WEB FOR HEALTH INFORMATION.

Information technology

This activity may be performed by individuals out of class, who may then submit a reaction paper to the instructor or report their results in class discussion.

The World Wide Web has become a terrific resource for health and medical information. For this practice activity, pick a health subject in which you're interested (for example, stress, allergies, diet, alcohol use) and then use the Web to find some reliable data about it. Report the information (reaction paper or class discussion) as directed by your instructor.

Whatever condition you're interested in, you can use a search engine to find statistics, support groups, and other data. The main caution you need to be aware of is that some sites are unbiased and legitimate and some are unreliable or are trying to sell you something. The following are some of the more reliable sites (but be wary of giving away too much information about yourself, since you don't know where it might end up):[82]

The American Medical Association's Health's Insight: *www.ama-assn.org/con-sumer.htm*

Health on the Net: *www.hon.ch*

Health Information Technology Institute: *www.mitretekorg/hiti*

The Mayo Clinic's Health Oasis: *www.mayohealth.org*

MedicineNet: *www.medicinenet.com*

The National Library of Medicine's Medline: *www.ncbi.nlm.nih.gov/PubMed*

Tuft University's Nutrition Navigator: *navigator.tufts.edu*

U.S. Department of Health and Human Services' Healthfinder: *www.healthfinder.org*

The Examined Life

JOURNAL ENTRY #11.1: HOW DO YOU REACT TO STRESS? What kind of psychological reactions do you have to stress (for example, irritability, impatience, depression)? What kind of physiological reactions do you have to stress (for example, insomnia, upset stomach, tiredness)? List your reactions and compare them to the reactions of other people you know.

_____

_____

_____

_____

_____

_____

_____

JOURNAL ENTRY #11.2: HOW DO YOU DEAL WITH STRESS? What kinds of things do you do to reduce the feelings of stress? What kinds of things _could_ you do?

_____

_____

_____

_____

_____

_____

_____

_____

JOURNAL ENTRY #11.3: IS THERE A RELATIONSHIP BETWEEN STRESS & "PARTYING"? Give some thought to the whole matter of "partying," or heavy drinking and/or drugging. How much of it do you see around you? Have you been affected by it? Is stress a contributor?

_____

_____

_____

_____

_____

_____

_____

_____

JOURNAL ENTRY #11.4: WHAT ARE YOUR DRINKING/DRUGGING HABITS? Do you routinely get intoxicated or high? Has it affected your academic work or relations with others? What do you think you should do about it?

_____

_____

_____

_____

_____

_____

_____

_____

JOURNAL ENTRY #11.5: WHAT ARE YOUR EAT-ING HABITS? Consider your eating habits. Do you have a balanced diet? Is it high in fats? Do you weigh too much? What is *one thing* you could do every day that would put you onto a healthier diet?

_____

_____

_____

_____

_____

_____

_____

_____

_____

JOURNAL ENTRY #11.6: HOW DO YOU FEEL ABOUT EXERCISE? Do you exercise regularly? If not, list all the reasons why you don't, such as feelings of embarrassment, don't know how to begin, and so on. What *one thing* could you do this week that would get your started?

_____

_____

_____

_____

_____

_____

_____

_____

_____

_____

_____

Relationships

Dealing Successfully with Other People

What are the two most important personal issues in life?

ove and work, said psychologist Sigmund Freud. Or *"romance and finance,"* as I've heard other people put it.

What about you? Are relationships and career issues important matters in *your* life? I know they certainly are for me. Ending war, poverty, and disease are certainly of greater significance for humankind in general, of course. However, for most people the two most important *personal* issues are love and work.

We considered money issues in Chapter 9 and take up career matters in the final chapter. Here let's look at that important other side of life: relationships.

Intimate Relationships: From Being a Friend to Being in Love

PREVIEW & REVIEW Intimate relationships include friendship but also various kinds of intimacy. Love may be of five types: passionate (romantic), erotic (sexual), dependent (addictive), friendship (companionate), and altruistic (unselfish). Loss of love means having to deal with feelings of rejection and rebuilding self-esteem.

any psychologists seem to measure mental well-being by the success of our relationships with others. Let us examine the range of relationship possibilities.

FRIENDSHIP & INTIMACY. <u>*Friendship*</u> is a relationship between two people that involves a high degree of trust and mutual support.

Friendship is important throughout your life. People's well-being seems to depend on the quality of social interaction they have with friends as well as with family.[1]

Many studies find better health among people who can turn to friends or family for affection, advice, empathy, assistance, and affirmation. They are more likely to survive major life challenges such as heart attacks and major surgery than those without such support. They are also less likely to develop cancer, respiratory infections, and other diseases.[2] Friends can help reaffirm your self-worth when you suffer life's disappointments or your good opinion of yourself is challenged.

Friendships can be close and may or may not involve intimacy. To some people, the word "intimate" means having

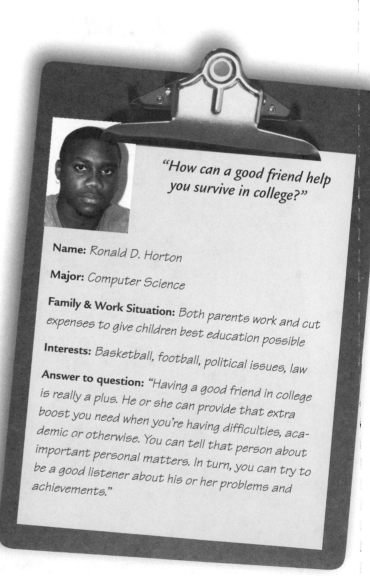

"How can a good friend help you survive in college?"

Name: Ronald D. Horton

Major: Computer Science

Family & Work Situation: Both parents work and cut expenses to give children best education possible

Interests: Basketball, football, political issues, law

Answer to question: "Having a good friend in college is really a plus. He or she can provide that extra boost you need when you're having difficulties, academic or otherwise. You can tell that person about important personal matters. In turn, you can try to be a good listener about his or her problems and achievements."

sex. However, _**intimacy**_ **is defined as a close, familiar, affectionate, and loving relationship with another person.**[3,4] Intimacy can take many forms. People may share interests, ideas, or recreational activities. They may share closeness of feeling or closeness developed through physical contact.

Many adult returning students are fortunate because they already have family who support their efforts. Others, however, find that school in fact negatively affects their relationships with family members, who may resent the time being taken away from them. Still others, such as the divorced or widowed, may look for supportive friends on campus, perhaps with students in similar circumstances. Regardless of age, going to college generally changes the nature of existing relationships.

LOVE. What is love? The reason there is so much confusion about love is that this one word is used to describe a multitude of feelings.

Professor F. Philip Rice describes five types of love—romantic, erotic, dependent, friendship, and altruistic. Together they make up what he calls _complete love._[5]

■ _**Infatuation, passionate, or romantic love:**_ When we experience that dizzying ecstasy and joy known as "falling in love" we are infatuated. _**Infatuation**_ **is passionate love, or romantic love: passionate, strong feelings of affection for another person.** This kind of love is real enough in its physiological manifestations: pounding heart, breathlessness, sometimes the inability to eat or sleep.[6]

The reasons people fall in love are probably proximity, commonality, and perceived attractiveness. People become attracted to those they see frequently and who share similar attributes.[7] Physical attractiveness is also often important at first. Attractiveness is sometimes heightened by the perception of dangerous circumstances (which is why secret love may be so intense).[8,9]

In the end, infatuation or romantic love cannot be sustained. It becomes less

wildly romantic and more rational, although deepening of feelings of love may continue to grow. Wildly emotional love evolves into the more low-keyed _**companionate love**_ **or friendship love, with feelings of friendly affection and deep attachment.**[10,11]

■ _**Erotic love:**_ _**Erotic love**_ **is sexual love,** but not necessarily romantic love. Many people can have sex without romantic love; indeed, some are unable to handle emotional involvement. Others find that having sex actually diminishes the feelings of romantic love. Yet others find that tensions that diminish loving feelings also adversely affect the sexual aspect of their relationship. Many couples, however, discover that their sexual and loving feelings blend and enhance their relationship.

■ _**Dependent love:**_ _**Dependent love**_ **is love that develops in response to previously unmet psychological needs.** For instance, someone who got little praise as a child may have an intense psychological need for appreciation met by the beloved. Or a studious person may welcome appreciation for his or her playfulness.[12]

At its extreme, this kind of love can become an addiction to another person as the source of security. Then love becomes a "mutual protection racket." The two people continue to hang on to avoid loneliness or to meet an extreme need for approval.

■ _**Friendship love:**_ As mentioned, _friendship_ or _companionate love_ is more low-key than romantic love. Friendship love is genuine _liking_ for the other person, which results in a desire to be together. Despite the mass media's emphasis on romance and sexuality, companionate love may be the most common and frequently experienced aspect of love.[13]

■ _**Altruistic love:**_ _**Altruistic love**_ **is unselfish concern for the welfare of another.** An example is a parent willingly and happily assuming care for a child. In a relationship such as marriage, altruistic love means accepting the beloved without insisting that he or she change.

■ **Build self-esteem:** Just as a love relationship builds self-esteem, being rejected lowers it. To raise your self-esteem, Phillips suggests you use index cards on which every day you write two good things about yourself. For example, write down things you have done recently or in the past that are positive. When negative thoughts creep in, say "Stop," and think one of these good thoughts about yourself.

If you are the one being let down, don't spend a lot of time speculating *why*. The other person may not even know why he or she is no longer in love. It won't help to torture yourself trying to figure it out. A helpful strategy may be to simply put some distance between yourself and the other person.

If you are the one trying to disengage from the relationship, remember how it feels to be rejected. Try to be honest but gentle: "I no longer feel the way I once did about you." Don't promise to try to "work things out," and don't try to take care of or "rescue" the other person. Do try to mobilize your support group and get involved with activities you enjoy.

GROUP ACTIVITY #12.1

WHAT KINDS OF SUPPORTING RELATIONSHIPS DO YOU HAVE?

"No man is an island, entire of itself . . .," the poet John Donne said. He might have said "man or woman," but the point is clear: we are not alone, isolated from other people.

Form a small group with other students in your class. Take turns describing people you know who will give you emotional and other support, if needed, to help sustain you. What kind of qualities do such people have? Are they good listeners? Do they express their feelings well? If you or others feel short on such support, where can it be found? How can one widen the circle of supportive friends?

THE END OF LOVE. Relationships can be a source of great joy, their loss a source of great pain. One difficulty in coping with the end of love is dealing with *rejection*. Rejection can be unreciprocated love in an attempted relationship or love that "grows old and waxes cold."

In *How to Fall Out of Love,* Debora Phillips suggests some steps for recovering from the loss of love:[14]

■ **Stop thoughts of the person:** You can learn to spend less and less time thinking about the loved one. Make a list of positive scenes and pleasures that do not involve the former beloved. When a thought about the person enters your mind, say "Stop," then think about one of the best scenes on your list.

Conflict & Communication: Learning How to Disagree

PREVIEW & REVIEW Five styles of dealing with conflict are avoidance, accommodation, domination, compromise, and integration. Committed couples must learn to address differences in several areas. Communication consists of ways of learning to disagree. In bad communication, you become argumentative and defensive and deny your own feelings. In good communication, you acknowledge the other person's feelings and express your own openly. Expert listening consists of tuning in to your partner's channel. It means giving listening signals, not interrupting, asking questions skillfully, and using diplomacy and tact. Most important, it means looking for some truth in what the other person says. To express yourself, use "I feel" language, give praise, and keep criticism specific.

Why can't people get along better? Must there always be conflict in close relationships, as between lovers, family members, roommates, or housemates? To see what your usual approach to conflict is, try Personal Exploration #12.1.

FIVE STYLES OF DEALING WITH CONFLICT.

Researchers have identified five styles of dealing with conflict, one of which is probably closest to yours.

1. *Avoidance: "Maybe It Will Go Away."* People who adopt this style find dealing with conflict unpleasant and uncomfortable. They hope that by ignoring the conflict or by avoiding confrontation the circumstances will change and the problem will magically disappear. Unfortunately,

PERSONAL EXPLORATION #12.1

WHAT ARE YOUR FEELINGS ABOUT CONFLICT?

Check which *one* of the following statements best describes your feelings when you approach a conflict with someone close to you.

1. ❑ I hate conflict. If I can find a way to avoid it, I will.

2. ❑ Conflict is such a hassle. I'd just as soon let the other person have his or her way so as to keep the peace.

3. ❑ You can't just let people walk over you. You've got to fight to establish your point of view.

4. ❑ I'm willing to negotiate to see if the other person and I can meet halfway.

5. ❑ I'm willing to explore the similarities and differences with the other person to see if we can solve the problem to both our satisfaction.

■ INTERPRETATION

Whichever one you checked corresponds to a particular style of dealing with conflict. They are: (1) avoidance, (2) accommodation, (3) domination, (4) compromise, (5) integration. For an explanation, read the text.

GROUP ACTIVITY OPTION

In a small or large group, discuss the style of conflict that you seem to gravitate to. How well does this seem to work for you? As a regular way of operating, what kinds of frustrations does it produce for you, if any? for the people with whom you're in conflict? What alternative style of conflict can you see yourself using?

avoiding or delaying facing the conflict usually means it will have to be dealt with later rather than sooner. By then, of course, the situation may have worsened.

2. *Accommodation: "Oh, Have It Your Way!"* Accommodation does not mean compromise; it means simply giving in, although it does not really resolve the matter under dispute. People who adopt a style of easily surrendering are, like avoiders, uncomfortable with conflict and hate disagreements. They are also inclined to be "people pleasers," worried about the approval of others. However, giving in does not really solve the conflict. If anything it may aggravate the situation over the long term. Accommodators may be deeply resentful that the other person did not listen to their point of view. Indeed, the resentment may even develop into a role of martyrdom, which will only irritate the person's partner.

3. *Domination: "Only Winning Matters."* The person holding the winning-is-everything, domination style should not be surprised if he or she some day finds an "I'm gone!" note from the partner. The dominator will go to any lengths to emerge triumphant in a disagreement, even if it means being aggressive and manipulative. However, winning isn't what intimate human relationships are supposed to be about; that approach to conflict produces only hostility and resentment.

4. *Compromise: "I'll Meet You Halfway."* Compromise seems like a civilized way of dealing with conflict, and it is definitely an improvement over the preceding styles. People striving for compromise recognize that both partners have different needs and try to negotiate to reach agreement. Even so, they may still employ some gamesmanship, such as manipulation and misrepresentation, in an attempt to further their own ends. Thus, the compromise style is not as effective in resolving conflict as the integration style.

5. *Integration: "Let's Honestly Try to Satisfy Both of Us."* Compromise views solution to the conflict as a matter of each party

meeting the other half way. The integration style, on the other hand, attempts to find a solution that will achieve satisfaction for both partners. Integration has several parts to it:

- *Openness for mutual problem solving:* The conflict is seen not as a game to be won or negotiated but as a problem to be solved to each other's mutual benefit. Consequently, manipulation and misrepresentation have no place; honesty and openness are a necessary part of reaching the solution. This also has the benefit of building trust that will carry over to the resolution of other conflicts.

- *Disagreement with the ideas, not the person:* There is an important part of integration, which we expand on below. This is that partners must be able to criticize each other's ideas or specific acts rather than each other generally as persons. It is one thing, for instance, to say "You drink too much!" It is another to say "I feel you drank too much last evening." The first way is a generality that disparages the other's character. The second way states that you are unhappy about a particular incident.

- *Emphasis on similarities, not differences:* Integration requires more work than other styles of dealing with conflict (although the payoffs are better). The reason is that partners must put a good deal of effort into stating and clarifying their positions. To maintain the spirit of trust, the two should also emphasize the similarities in their positions rather than the differences.

AREAS OF CONFLICT. It is said that no married couple hasn't thought about divorce. Likewise no other committed couple hasn't thought about splitting up. The number of subjects over which two people can disagree is awesome. One area about which couples must make adjustments are unrealistic expectations, such as who should do which household chores. Other matters have to do with work and career, finances, in-laws, sex,

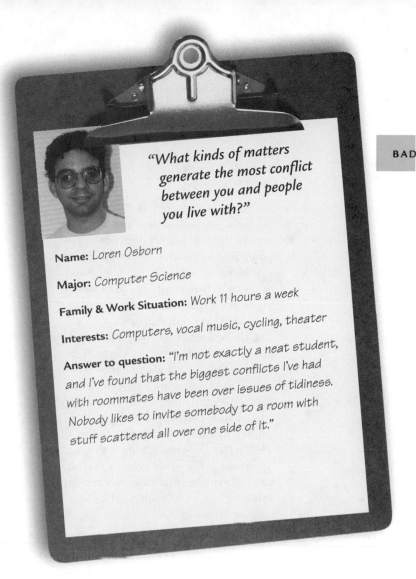

and commitment/jealousy.[15] Most of the foregoing problems can be overcome with effective communication. Indeed, good communication—to handle conflict and wants—is critical to the success of a committed relationship.

COMMUNICATION: THERE ARE WAYS TO LEARN HOW TO DISAGREE.

The fact that conflict is practically always present in an ongoing relationship does not mean that it should be suppressed. When handled constructively, conflict may bring problems out into the open, where they can be solved. Handling conflict may also put an end to chronic sources of discontent in a relationship. Finally, airing disagreements may lead to new insights through the clashing of

divergent views.[16] The key to success in relationships is the ability to handle conflict successfully, which means the ability to communicate well.

BAD COMMUNICATION.

Most of us *think* communication is easy, points out psychiatrist David Burns, because we've been talking since we were children.[17] And communication *is* easy when we're happy and feeling close to someone. It's when we have a conflict that we find out how well we really communicate—whether it's good or bad.

Bad communication, says Burns, author of *The Feeling Good Handbook,* has two characteristics:

- *You become argumentative and defensive:* The natural tendency of most of us when we are upset is to argue with and contradict others. The habit of contradicting others, however, is self-defeating, for it creates distance between you and them and prevents intimacy. Moreover, when you are in this stance you show you are not interested in listening to the other person or understanding his or her feelings.

- *You deny your own feelings and act them out indirectly:* You may become sarcastic, or pout, or storm out of the room slamming doors. This kind of reaction is known as *passive aggression.* However, it can sometimes be as destructive as *active aggression,* in which you make threats or tell the other person off.

There are a number of other characteristics of bad communication. One is *martyrdom,* in which you insist you're an innocent victim. A second is *hopelessness,* in which you give up and insist there's no point in trying to resolve your difficulties. A third is *self-blame,* in which you act as if you're a terrible, awful person (instead of dealing with the problem). A fourth is *"helping,"* in which instead of listening you attempt to take over and "solve" the other person's problem. A fifth is *diversion,* in which you list grievances about past "injustices" instead of dealing with how you both feel right now.

GOOD COMMUNICATION. "Most people want to be understood and accepted more than anything else in the world," says Burns.[18] Knowing that is taking a giant first step toward good communication.

Good communication, according to Burns, has two attributes:

- *You listen to and acknowledge the other person's feelings:* You may be tempted just to broadcast your feelings and insist that the other agree with you. It's better, however, if you encourage the other to express his or her emotions. Try to listen to and understand what the other person is thinking and feeling. (I expand on listening skills below.)

- *You express your own feelings openly and directly:* If you only listen to the other person's feelings and don't express your own, you will end up feeling short-changed, angry, and resentful. When you deny your feelings, you end up acting them out indirectly. The trick, then, is to express your feelings in a way that will not alienate the other person.

BECOMING EXPERT AT LISTENING. If communication is listening, how is that done? Some ideas are offered by Aaron Beck, director of the Center for Cognitive Therapy at the University of Pennsylvania. In his book *Love Is Never Enough,* he suggests the following listening guidelines:[19]

- *Tune in to your partner's channel:* Imagining how the other person might be feeling—putting yourself in the other's shoes—is known as *empathy,* trying to experience the other's thoughts and feelings. The means for learning what the other's thoughts and feelings are can be determined through the other steps.

- *Give listening signals:* Use facial expressions, subtle gestures, and sounds such as "uh-huh" and "yeah" to show your partner you are really listening. Beck particularly urges this advice on men, since studies find that women are more inclined to send responsive signals. Talking to someone without getting feedback is like talking to a wall.

- *Don't interrupt:* Although interruptions may seem natural to you, they can make the other person feel cut off. Men, says Beck, tend to interrupt more than women do (although they interrupt other men as often as they do women). They would do better to not express their ideas until after the partner has finished talking.

- *Ask questions skillfully:* Asking questions can help you determine what the other person is thinking and keep the discussion going—provided the question is not a *conversation stopper.* "Why" questions can be conversation stoppers ("Why were you home late?"). So can questions that can have only a yes-or-no answer.

  Questions that ask the other's opinion can be *conversation starters.* (Example: "What do you think about always having dinner at the same time?") Questions that reflect the other's statements help convey your empathy. (Example: "Can you tell me more about why you feel that way?") The important thing is to ask questions *gently,* never accusingly. You want to explore what the other person is thinking and feeling and to show that you are listening.

- *Use diplomacy and tact:* All of us have sensitive areas—about our appearance or how we speak, for example. This is true of people in intimate relationships as much as people in other relationships. *Problems in relationships invariably involve feelings.* Using diplomacy and tact in your listening responses will help build trust to talk about difficulties.

  An especially wise piece of advice about listening comes from David Burns: Find *some* truth in what the other person is saying and agree with it. Do this even if you feel that what he or she is saying is totally wrong, unreasonable, irrational, or unfair. This technique, known as *disarming,* works especially well if you're feeling criticized and attacked.

  If, instead of arguing, you agree with the other person, it takes the wind out of his or her sails. Indeed, it can have a calming effect. The other person will then be more open to your point of view. Adds Burns: "When you use the disarm-

ing technique, you must be genuine in what you say or it will backfire. You can always find some valid way to agree, no matter how illogical the person's accusations might seem to you. If you agree with them in a sincere way, they will generally soften and will be far more willing to listen to you."[20]

BECOMING EXPERT AT EXPRESSING YOUR-
SELF. It is often tempting to use the tools of war—attacking and defending, withdrawing and sulking, going for the jugular. However, these will never take you as far in resolving conflicts in intimate relationships as will kinder and gentler techniques.

In expressing yourself, there are two principal points to keep in mind:

■ *Use "I feel" language:* It's always tempting to use accusatory language during the heat of conflict. (Examples: "You make me so mad!" or "You never listen to what I say!") However, this is sure to send the other person stomping out of the room.

A better method is simply to say "I feel" followed by the word expressing your feelings—"frustrated"; "ignored"; "attacked"; "nervous"; "unloved." This way you don't sound blaming and critical. (Compare this to saying "You make me . . ." or "You never . . .") By expressing how you feel, rather than defending the "truth" of your position, you can communicate your feelings without attacking the other.

■ *Express praise and keep criticism specific:* Most of us respond better to compliments than to criticism, and most of us seek appreciation and fear rejection. In any conflict, we may disagree with a person's *specific act or behavior.* However, we need not reject the other as a person.

For example, you might want to say, "When we go to parties, you always leave me alone and go talk to other people." It's better, however, to combine criticism with praise. For example: "I'm proud to be with you when we go to parties, and I hope you are of me. However, I think we could have even more fun if we stay in touch with each other when we're at a party. Does this seem like a reasonable request?"[21]

Assertiveness: Better Than Aggressiveness or Nonassertiveness

Aggressiveness is expressing yourself in a way that hurts others. Nonassertiveness is not expressing yourself, giving in to others and hurting yourself. Assertiveness is expressing yourself without hurting either others or yourself. Both men and women have assertiveness problems, women sometimes being too passive, men too aggressive, although the reverse is also true. Developing assertiveness means observing your own behavior in conflict situations, visualizing a model for assertiveness, and practicing assertive behavior.

t's important to learn to express your disappointments, resentments, and wishes without denying yourself. Yet you also don't want to put other people down or make them angry. This means learning to be *assertive*.

Assertiveness doesn't mean being pushy or selfish but rather being forthright enough to communicate your needs while respecting the needs of others. Being assertive is important in intimate relationships, of course. However, it's also important in many other social interactions in which speaking out, standing up for yourself, or talking back is necessary.

AGGRESSIVE, NONASSERTIVE, & ASSERTIVE BEHAVIOR. Let us consider three types of behavior: aggressiveness, nonassertiveness, and assertiveness. (Distinctions among these behaviors have been put forth in two interesting, readable books by psychologists Robert Alberti and Michael Emmons. They are *Your Perfect Right* and *Stand Up, Speak Out, Talk Back!*[22,23]) The definitions are as follows:

- *Aggressiveness—expressing yourself and hurting others:* <u>Aggressive behavior</u> means you vehemently expound your opinions, accuse or blame others, and hurt others before hurting yourself.

- *Nonassertiveness—giving in to others and hurting yourself:* <u>Nonassertive behavior</u>—also called <u>submissive</u> or <u>passive behavior</u>—means consistently giving in to others on points of differences. It means agreeing with others regardless of your own feelings, not expressing your opinions, hurting yourself to avoid hurting others. Nonassertive people have difficulty making requests for themselves or expressing their differences with others. In a word, they are *timid*.

- *Assertiveness—expressing yourself without hurting others or yourself:* <u>Assertiveness</u> is defined as acting in your own best interests by expressing your thoughts and feelings directly and honestly. It means standing up for yourself and openly expressing your personal feelings and

opinions, yet not hurting either yourself or others. Assertiveness is important in enabling you to express or defend your rights.

It's important to learn to *ask for what you want in a civilized way, without hurting the feelings of the other person.* This is what assertive behavior is all about. Consider what happens if you try aggressive or nonassertive behavior. Aggressive behavior probably won't help you get what you want because your pushiness or anger creates disharmony and alienates other people. It may also make you feel guilty about how you treated others. Nonassertive behavior also may not help you get what you want. Though it may be an attempt to please others by not offending them, it may actually make them contemptuous of you.[24] In addition, nonassertive behavior leads you to suppress your feelings, leading to self-denial and poor self-esteem.

You need to know, however, that assertive behavior will *not* always get you what you want. Probably no one form of behavior will. Still, if performed correctly, it may improve your chances. The reason is that assertive behavior is not offensive to other people. This makes them more willing to listen to your point of view.

ASSERTIVENESS & GENDER STEREOTYPES. It has been suggested that behaving assertively may be more difficult for women than men. This is because many females have supposedly been socialized to be more passive and submissive than men.[25] For example, some women worry that acting boldly in pursuing success will make them appear unfeminine.[26] Indeed, by the college years, women may view an act of assertive behavior as more aggressive when done by females than by males.[27]

However, many men have assertiveness problems, too. Some males have been raised to be nonassertive, others to be aggressive rather than assertive. Some researchers suggest that actually more males than females need to be trained in assertiveness to modify their typically more aggressive behavior.[28]

To get an idea of your assertiveness, try Personal Exploration #12.2 (*opposite page*).

DEVELOPING ASSERTIVENESS. There are different programs for developing assertiveness, but most consist of four steps:[29]

- *Learn what assertive behavior is:* First you need to learn what assertive behavior is, so that you know what it is supposed to be like. You need to learn how to consider both yours *and* others' rights.

- *Observe your own behavior in conflict situations:* You then need to monitor your own assertive (or unassertive) behavior. You need to see what circumstances, people, situations, or topics make you behave aggressively or nonassertively. You may find you are able to take care of yourself (behave assertively) in some situations, but not in others.

- *Visualize a model for assertiveness:* If possible, you should try to find a model for assertiveness in the specific situations that trouble you and observe that person's behavior. Role models are important in other parts of life, and this area is no exception. If possible, note how rewarding such behavior is, which will reinforce the assertive tendencies.

- *Practice assertive behavior:* Of course the only way to consistently behave assertively is to practice the behavior. You can do this as a rehearsal, carrying on an imaginary dialogue in private with yourself. Or you can actually role-play the behavior, practicing the assertive behavior with a good friend, counselor, or therapist.

Unwanted Sex: From Sexual Harassment to Rape

PREVIEW & REVIEW Members of either sex may be victims of forced or unwanted sexual attentions or actions. Unwanted sex ranges from sexual harassment to sexual assault, including statutory, acquaintance, and date rape. It's important to learn techniques for preventing, resisting, or coping with acquaintance or stranger rape.

grave problem for both sexes, but particularly for women, is that of dealing with unwanted sexual attention or demands. This may range from listening to sexual remarks to experiencing rape.

SEXUAL HARASSMENT. Your instructor or supervisor puts a hand on your shoulder. "Can we discuss your coursework/possible promotion over dinner?" he or she says, then gives you a wink and glides away. You don't want to do it, but you're worried about your grade or promotion. This really isn't about sex, it's about power. What do you do?

Sexual harassment **is unwelcome sexual attention, whether physical or verbal, that creates an intimidating, hostile, or offensive learning or work environment.** Such harassment may include sexual remarks, suggestive looks, pressure for dates, letters and calls, deliberate touching, or pressure for sexual favors, but it's really about bullying, not sex.[30] The U.S. Supreme Court has ruled that sexual harassment constitutes employment discrimination as serious and illegal as racial or religious discrimination.[31]

Men and women may see each of these matters differently. For instance, in one study, 95% of women felt that "deliberate touching" by a supervisor constituted sexual harassment. However, only 89% of men felt this was so.[32] These differences seem to reflect a sexual double standard.

HOW ASSERTIVE ARE YOU?

Answer "Yes" or "No" to each of the following statements.

1. When a person is blatantly unfair, do you usually fail to say something about it to him or her?

   ❑ Yes   ❑ No

2. Are you always very careful to avoid all trouble with other people?

   ❑ Yes   ❑ No

3. Do you often avoid social contacts for fear of doing or saying the wrong thing?

   ❑ Yes   ❑ No

4. If a friend betrays your confidence, do you tell him or her how you really feel?

   ❑ Yes   ❑ No

5. Would you insist that a roommate do his or her fair share of cleaning?

   ❑ Yes   ❑ No

6. When a clerk in a store waits on someone who has come in after you, do you call his or her attention to the matter?

   ❑ Yes   ❑ No

7. Do you find that there are very few people with whom you can be relaxed and have a good time?

   ❑ Yes   ❑ No

8. Would you be hesitant about asking a good friend to lend you a few dollars?

   ❑ Yes   ❑ No

9. If someone who has borrowed $5 from you seems to have forgotten about it, would you remind this person?

   ❑ Yes   ❑ No

10. If a person keeps on teasing you, do you have difficulty expressing your annoyance or displeasure?

    ❑ Yes   ❑ No

11. Would you remain standing at the rear of a crowded auditorium rather than look for a seat up front?

    ❑ Yes   ❑ No

12. If someone kept kicking the back of your chair in a movie, would you ask him or her to stop?

    ❑ Yes   ❑ No

13. If a friend keeps calling you very late each evening, would you ask him or her not to call after a certain time?

    ❑ Yes   ❑ No

14. If someone starts talking to someone else right in the middle of your conversation, do you express your irritation?

    ❑ Yes   ❑ No

15. In a plush restaurant, if you order a medium steak and find it too rare, would you ask the waiter to have it recooked?

    ❑ Yes   ❑ No

16. If a landlord of your apartment fails to make certain necessary repairs after promising to do so, would you insist on it?

    ❑ Yes   ❑ No

17. Would you return a faulty garment you purchased a few days ago?

    ❑ Yes   ❑ No

18. If someone you respect expresses opinions you strongly disagree with, would you venture to state your own point of view?

    ❑ Yes   ❑ No

19. Are you usually able to say no when people make unreasonable requests?

    ❑ Yes   ❑ No

20. Do you think that people should stand up for their rights?

    ❑ Yes   ❑ No

■ INTERPRETATION

There is no scoring system. You can figure out what the answers *should* be. Now it becomes a matter of rehearsing the response so you'll be able to act assertively the next time it's required. What will you do the next time the landlord fails to make repairs? Or the people in your household don't do their fair share of cleaning? Or you need to ask the waiter to have your steak cooked some more?

However, men, too, occasionally experience harassment by women (or men).

So what do you do if you're confronted with sexual harassment by someone who has power over your college or work career? Proving harassment in court is difficult, and other institutional arrangements are predisposed to protect the harasser.[33,34] Thus, one needs to proceed deliberately. First keep a log, recording dates, times, nature of incidents, and any witnesses. According to one survey, just asking or telling the person to stop worked for 61% of the women. Telling coworkers, or threatening to, worked 55% of the time. Pretending to ignore the offensive behavior usually didn't work at all.[35] If the harassment persists, stronger measures may be required. *(See* ■ *Panel 12.1.)*

RAPE: DATE RAPE & OTHER SEXUAL ASSAULTS. Sex may be pleasurable, but forced sex is in the same category as any other attack. Assault is assault, whether it is with a gun, a club, a fist—or a penis. <u>*Rape*</u> **is defined as sexual penetration of a male or female by intimidation, fraud, or force.** Most rape victims are women;

indeed, more than 22% of women say they have felt forced by a man to have unwanted sexual contact.[36] However, one study of 3,000 randomly chosen Los Angeles residents found that one-third of victims of attempted sexual assault were men.[37] In one survey of Stanford University students, one in three women and one in eight men reported having unwanted sexual activity.[38]

Rape victims can be of all ages. However, it's a shocking fact that 61% of rape victims were under 18 when attacked, according to the National Victim Center.[39] In almost 80% of cases, the victim knew her rapist.

Three kinds of rape are particularly worth mentioning:

- *Statutory rape:* <u>*Statutory rape*</u> **is unlawful sexual intercourse between a male over age 16 and a female under age 12 or 21.** (The exact definition depends on the state.) As the National Victim Center report showed, 3 out of 10 rape victims had not reached their 11th birthdays.

- *Acquaintance rape:* <u>*Acquaintance rape*</u> **is rape by a person known by the victim,** whether related or unrelated. The National Victim Center report found

---

PANEL 12.1 **H**ow to fight sexual harassment.

If sexual harassment persists, here are some steps to take:

Document: Keep a detailed written record of the incidents, with dates, times, places, names, and quotes. Keep any notes you receive.

Confide in co-workers or friends: You may tell trusted co-workers, friends, family members, a minister, or others, saying you may have to file a grievance and that you want them to know what is happening.

Find witnesses or supporting evidence: If there are witnesses, ask them to write a statement for you. If you are receiving harassing phone calls, have someone be an "ear witness" by listening in and taking notes. Look for other people in your same situation who may have been harassed by the same person.

Confront the harasser: Say the behavior must stop immediately, and let him or her know you will file a complaint if it does not. If necessary, write a letter—or follow up your conversation with a memo summarizing your talk—and hand it to the harasser in the presence of a witness. Keep a copy.

Talk to the harasser's supervisor: Talk to an appropriate third party such as the harasser's supervisor or someone in the human resources department or equal opportunity office.

File a complaint: If your institution or company does not take steps to stop the harassment, file a legal complaint based on state or federal antidiscrimination laws. Your state may have a department of fair employment or you may take your case to the U.S. Equal Employment Opportunity Commission (call 800-USA-EEOC).

that 78% of rapists were known to their victims.

■ *Date rape:* In *date rape*, **the rapist is someone with whom the victim has had a date,** as on a college campus. At one time nonconsensual sex between men and women on dates was thought to be a form of female error or lack of resistance. Today, however, sexual activity that is abhorrent to females is considered assault by males.[40]

Some college students are still uncertain as to when sex is considered consensual or rape. One student, asked whether his date had consented to sex, replied, "No, but she didn't say no. So she must have wanted it, too."[41] He added that both had been drunk and the woman had struggled initially. The man's behavior may have been reinforced by pressure from other men to "score." Many men also assume that when a woman enters their bedroom it is an unspoken invitation to sex. Regardless, whatever one person's assumptions about the other or the state of intoxication, it is *always* rape if sex is not consensual.

AVOIDING & COPING WITH RAPE. Men and women interpret sexual cues differently. For instance, researchers asked students to judge several activities: going to a date's room, kissing, French kissing, removing one's shirt. More men than women interpreted these behaviors as indicating a willingness to have sex.[42] These are the kinds of misinterpretations of nonverbal cues that can hurt someone.

To cope with rape, here are some suggestions:

■ *To avoid acquaintance or date rape:* Be aware of your surroundings and intentions. Stay out of ambiguous situations (such as bedrooms) and be clear in communicating what you want and don't want. Learn to listen carefully to your partner's messages about what he or she wants and doesn't want. Use a neutral tone and speak in "I" statements—for example, "I want to be taken home."

Trust your instincts. If you're uncomfortable with a situation, follow your intuition. Don't be afraid of hurting somebody's feelings.

■ *To avoid stranger rape:* When on the street, be aware of your surroundings. Anticipate how you would respond to an attack. Look behind you, stay in the middle of the sidewalk, and walk with a confident stride. Use extra caution in parking garages. If you're alone on an elevator, get out if a stranger gets on and pushes the button for the basement. Have your keys in hand when you approach your car so you won't have to stand there fumbling.

■ *To resist rape of any kind:* Don't be too polite to fight. Be loud, be rude, cause a scene. Attackers count on the fear of embarrassment. Research shows that women who fight back have a better chance of escaping rape than those who plead or cry.[43] This is especially true if the person attempting rape is an acquaintance.

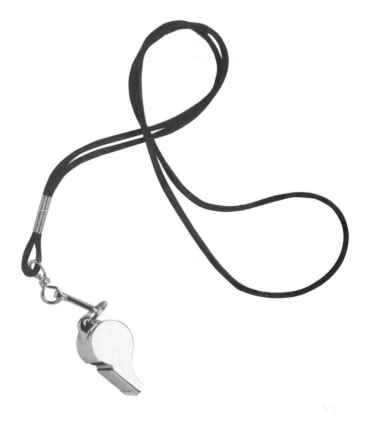

To cope with rape: Call the police and a rape crisis center or rape treatment center. Don't bathe or wash yourself or your clothes or touch anything in the location of the rape. If a condom was used, try to remember where it was discarded. Try to remember everything about the rapist: his car, clothing, scars, haircut, and things he said and did. Report any weapons or restraints used, and if bruises show up later, have photographs taken by the police. Go to a hospital and be tested and/or treated for sexually transmitted diseases.

Afterward, expect emotional aftershocks, even if you weren't hurt physically. Tell your physician and try to institute a health strategy that includes psychological as well as physical factors. Confide your feelings to a friend.[44] Many women at first blame themselves, especially if they were attacked by men they trusted. Then later—perhaps years later—they may decide they were sexually assaulted.[45]

GROUP ACTIVITY #12.4

AMBIGUOUS SITUATIONS

Form small groups divided equally between males and females. Discuss situations that you are aware of (or can conceive of) in which a man and woman might have different understandings about whether one is interested in having sex. (Don't feel you have to participate in this discussion if you'd rather not. Practice your assertiveness and say "I'd rather just listen.") Describe how you might have handled such situations in the past. Then suggest how they should be handled now.

Sexually Transmitted Diseases: HIV & AIDS

PREVIEW & REVIEW HIV (Human Immunodeficiency Virus) may progress over about 10 years into AIDS (Acquired Immune Deficiency Syndrome). HIV is diagnosed through an antibody test, but the test cannot predict if the virus will become AIDS. HIV may infect both sexes and is principally transmitted by unprotected sex and by shared drug needles.

Formerly called venereal diseases, _sexually transmitted diseases (STDs)_ **are infectious diseases that are transmitted as a result (usually) of sexual contact.** Although AIDS is the most serious, there are many other STDs. They include hepatitis B, herpes, human papilloma virus (HPV), chlamydia, gonorrhea, syphilis, and parasite infections *(See* ■ *Panel 12.1.)* These are growing rapidly, bringing considerable suffering and even death.

HIV & AIDS: THE MODERN SCOURGE. We will focus on HIV and AIDS because they are recent threats and because they have produced all kinds of misunderstandings. HIV and AIDS are two different things:

- _HIV_: _HIV_, or _human immunodeficiency virus_, **the virus causing AIDS, brings about a variety of ills. The most important is the breakdown of the immune system, which leads to the development of certain infections and cancers.**

- _AIDS_: _AIDS_ **stands for** _acquired immune deficiency syndrome_, **a sexually transmitted disease that is caused by HIV. It is characterized by irreversible damage to the body's immune system.** As a result, the body is unable to fight infections, making it vulnerable to many diseases, such as pneumonia. So far, AIDS has proven to be always fatal.

Sexually transmitted diseases. Although it's the most recent (and perhaps most dangerous) STD, HIV/AIDS is by no means the only one. Others are hepatitis B, herpes, human papilloma virus (HPV), chlamydia, gonorrhea, syphilis, and parasite infections.

Hepatitis B: A Disease of the Liver

Hepatitis covers five virus-caused inflammatory diseases of the liver (A, B, C, D, and E), which have similar symptoms but otherwise are different. Hepatitis B is transmitted through infected blood (or saliva, mucus, and semen), typically by sexual contact or sharing of drug needles. Symptoms include fever, chills, headache, nausea, diarrhea, loss of appetite, skin rashes, and sometimes the yellowing of skin and eyes called jaundice.

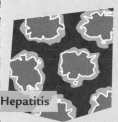

Hepatitis

Among Americans at risk for hepatitis B are the 10 million heterosexuals who have multiple partners or whose partners have multiple partners. Adolescents are particularly at risk because they tend to have sex more often with more partners, and many do not use condoms.

The disease lasts 2–6 months. People usually recover on their own, although in a small percentage of cases (1–3%) there are fatalities from liver failure. A drug called alpha interferon has shown promise of being effective in treatment. A vaccine has been available for about a decade which has been found to be 80–95% effective.

Herpes: The Secret Virus

Herpes is a viral infection that evades the body's immune defenses by hiding in the nervous system until reactivation of the virus occurs. A great number of people—30 million, or perhaps 16% of all Americans ages 15–74—have been infected with herpes, and perhaps as many as 1 million more join their ranks every year.

The most common strains are the *herpes simplex virus, types 1 and 2,* which are sexually transmitted and which produce cold-sore-like blisters in the areas of the genitals and mouth. In both types, one may experience numbness, itching, or tingling in the area where there has been contact with the virus, followed by an often painful eruption of water-filled blisters. Within 10 days of an initial exposure to the virus, people may feel flu-like symptoms: fever, chills, nausea, headaches, fatigue, and muscle aches. The eruption crusts and scabs over, and then in about 2 weeks the skin appears normal.

After the first episode, the virus seems to disappear. Thereafter it emerges from time to time—sometimes as frequently as four or more times a year. Sometimes it will produce no symptoms. At other times it will produce outbreaks of blistering sores. As time goes on, many people find that the duration of symptoms becomes shorter and less severe.

Among adults, apparently the principal effects of herpes are feelings of desperation and social inhibition. A great many herpes victims feel isolated and depressed and fear rejection in social situations.

There is no cure for herpes, and stress, depression, and other psychological upsets seem to trigger recurrences among people infected with the virus. People with herpes who have learned relaxation and other coping techniques seem to suffer fewer outbreaks. In addition, a prescription drug called *acyclovir,* if taken during the initial herpes outbreak, can ease the symptoms.

Herpes

Human Papilloma Virus (HPV): The Fastest-Spreading STD

HPV, short for *human papilloma virus,* which causes genital warts, is the fastest-spreading STD in the United States. There are presently an estimated 12–24 million cases of HPV in the United States, with 750,000 new cases being added every year. Indeed, some researchers found that nearly *half* of a sample of sexually active college women, each of whom had had sexual relations with an average of four lifetime partners, were HPV positive.

HPV should not be taken lightly. At one time, it was thought that HPV caused only *genital warts*—unpleasant but supposedly harmless fleshy growths in the areas of the genitals and mouth. However, some types of HPV have also been found to be associated with cancer (of the anus, penis, vulva, and cervix). Unfortunately, HPV also may be painless and show no symptoms, both in males and females.

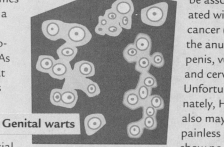

Genital warts

HPV is very contagious, being readily transmitted by sexual contact. On average the incubation period is 2–3 months after contact. One test for HPV infection is called the Southern blot technique.

Genital warts are treated by freezing, heat, cauterization, laser therapy, chemicals, or surgical removal. Treatment is required for one's sexual partner as well, who may otherwise reinfect the patient.

Chlamydia: The Most Common STD

If HPV is the fastest-growing STD in the United States, chlamydia is perhaps the most common, with as many as 4 million new cases appearing in the U.S. every year. *Chlamydia*—or more accurately *chlamydial infections*—consists of a family of sexually transmitted diseases caused by a bacterium (*Chlamydia trachomatis*). A major problem associated with this STD is that the organism *often does not cause any symptoms*. Yet if it is untreated it can cause lifelong damage, such as pelvic inflammatory disease in women, urinary tract infections in men, and sterility and blindness in both sexes.

About 50–70% of infected females and 30% of infected males show no signs of early symptoms. Those that do show signs may experience itching and burning during urination 2–7 days after infection. Diagnosis of chlamydia must be made by a health-care professional, and the standard treatment is antibiotics.

Gonorrhea: An Old Enemy

Once upon a time, when the phrase "venereal disease" was in use, when people thought of sexually transmitted diseases they thought principally of gonorrhea and syphilis.

Gonorrhea is caused by the sexual transmission of a bacterium (*Neisseria gonorrhoeae*). It is an organism that is easily transmitted. A man who has had sexual intercourse *once* with an infected woman has a 20–25% risk of getting the disease; a woman who has intercourse *once* with an infected man has a 50% chance of getting it.

Because the gonorrhea bacterium needs warmth and humidity to thrive, it is harbored principally in warm, moist areas of the human body. Thus, one may contract gonorrhea from an infected person through genital, anal, and oral contact. Toilet seats may harbor the gonorrhea bacterium for a few seconds; however, the evidence does not show this to be a means of transmission.

Symptoms appear 2–8 days after one has been infected. Some men, perhaps 10–20%, show no signs of infection at all. Otherwise, the main manifestation is burning pain during urination and later discharge (pus) from the urinary tract. Although the burning sensation may subside in 2–3 weeks, if the disease is not treated it spreads throughout the urinary and reproductive systems, causing scarring, obstructions, and sterility.

Early gonorrhea symptoms in women may be so slight that they are apt to be overlooked. Indeed, up to 80% of women show no symptoms at all, and women may only begin to suspect they have a problem when their partners are diagnosed. When symptoms appear, they may take the form of irritation of the vagina and painful and frequent urination.

Gonorrhea is primarily diagnosed through laboratory tests. The principal treatment is use of antibiotics, especially penicillin.

Syphilis: The "Great Imitator"

Syphilis, another old enemy like gonorrhea, is known as the "great imitator" because its sores and other symptoms mimic other disorders and diseases, such as cancers, abscesses, hemorrhoids, and hernias.

Syphilis is a sexually transmitted disease caused by a bacterium (a long, slender, spiral bacterium, or spirochete, called *Treponema pallidum*). Syphilis is serious because it can become a systemic infection, leading to possible brain damage, heart failure, and death.

Syphilis appears in four stages:

■ *Primary stage:* Within 10–90 days of infection, one or more pink or red dime-sized or smaller sores called *chancres* appear on the sex organs, mouth, or other parts of the body. Because the sores do not cause pain, they may not be noticed. The chancres disappear by themselves in 3–6 weeks, but this does not mean the disease has disappeared.

■ *Secondary stage:* About 6–8 weeks later, symptoms appear that may be mistaken for the flu: swollen lymph nodes, sore throat, headache, and fever. There may also be loss of hair. In addition, the disease produces a rash, which may appear on the hands or feet or all over the body and which does not itch. Finally, large, moist sores may appear around the mouth or genitals. The sores disappear in 2–6 weeks, but this only means the disease has entered the next stage.

■ *Latent stage:* In this stage, which may last from a few months to a lifetime, the disease goes underground. Although 50–70% of those with untreated syphilis remain in this latent stage for the rest of their lives and experience no further problems, the rest develop late-stage syphilis.

■ *Tertiary stage:* Years after the initial exposure, the effects of untreated syphilis may result in damage to the heart and major blood vessels, the central nervous system, or other organs. This may cause blindness, paralysis, and death.

Syphilis is diagnosed by means of blood tests. Penicillin is the most common treatment and can be highly effective if given during the primary stage.

Parasite Infections: Pubic Lice & Scabies

The STDs described so far are dangerous. However, the two parasite infections transmitted by sexual contact are mainly just annoying.

Called "crabs," because of their crab-like appearance, *pubic lice* are wingless, gray insects, about 1/16th inch long, that live in human hair. Pubic lice feed on blood, causing itching and skin discoloration. Female lice lay eggs, or *nits,* that are attached to the hair. *Scabies* are tiny mites that burrow under the skin and lay eggs, producing itching and discolored lines on the skin.

Besides being transmitted by sexual contact, both pubic lice and scabies may be picked up from infected clothing and bedding, which should be washed. Treatment is by washing oneself and others in the household with insecticide-containing shampoos and soaps available at pharmacies.

In the United States and Canada, HIV now affects 1.3 million people. For 449,000 people the HIV infections have developed into AIDS. In the 15-year history of the disease, 358,000 people in North America have already died of AIDS.[46] In the United States, presently as many as 27 out of every 100,000 adults die of AIDS.[47] Half of those infected are under age 25. AIDS is the second leading cause of death (after accidents) for men and women in the United States between the ages of 25 and 44.[48]

The really scary thing is that people with HIV *often show no outward symptoms of illness*—FOR PERHAPS AS LONG AS 10 YEARS! Thus, a person can be a carrier and infect others without anyone knowing it.[49] The estimated average time from HIV infection to first symptom is 5 years and to AIDS 8–10 years.[50]

Maybe you've heard these numbers thrown around before. What's interesting, however, is how little attention people pay to numbers. "So what?" you may think. "It's not going to be me. Anyway, I don't want to be preached to." Despite all the warnings, AIDS continues to spread among young gay men.[51,52] And despite all the widespread messages about the value of condoms, the use of condoms actually declines as teenagers get older—perhaps because older students switch to birth-control pills or other methods that protect against pregnancy, not realizing they are of no use against HIV.[53]

Many people can't put a face on AIDS. It's not the kind of glamorous disease portrayed on TV, which often edits out night sweats and diarrhea, making the symptoms not real at all.[54]

TESTING FOR HIV. How does a person find out whether he or she has HIV? The answer is by taking a standard blood test called the *HIV antibody test.* The test does not detect the virus itself. Rather it detects the antibodies that the body forms in response to the appearance of the virus. (Antibodies are molecules that are secreted into the bloodstream, where they bind to the invading virus, incapacitating it.)

Negative test results *can* mean positive news: the HIV may not be present. *Posi-* *tive* test results *can* mean negative news: the HIV may be present. Still, anyone taking these tests needs to be aware of certain cautions:

- *Antibodies to the virus may not develop immediately:* If the test results are negative, it may mean the body has not been exposed to HIV. But it may also mean that antibody formation has not yet taken place. The time it takes for most people to develop antibodies is about 1–3 months, though it varies. Some people do not develop antibodies until 6–12 months have elapsed since exposure to the organism. (Meanwhile the person may be infected and continue to infect others.)

- *Be aware that testing labs can make errors:* If performed correctly, the tests themselves can be highly accurate, detecting antibodies in 99.6% of HIV-infected people. The problem is that some medical labs have problems with high error rates in their testing.[55]

- *Tests cannot predict AIDS:* Currently, tests can show that a person has HIV. They cannot predict whether that HIV will develop into AIDS.

WHY IT'S IMPORTANT TO BE CONCERNED ABOUT STDS. The sexually transmitted diseases caused by viruses—HIV, hepatitis B, herpes, genital warts—cannot be cured, although they can in many cases be controlled. STDs caused by bacteria—chlamydia, gonorrhea, and syphilis—can be cured. Unfortunately, however, they are often difficult to detect, because many have no obvious symptoms, and thus may lead to grave difficulties later. Clearly, then, the wisest course is to do what's necessary to avoid getting STDs in the first place.

Some Rules for Safer Sex

PREVIEW & REVIEW One way to reduce the risk of exposure to STDs is to ask the right questions of prospective sexual partners. The answers, however, provide no guarantees. The safest form of sex for preventing transmission of STDs is abstinence and other behavior in which body fluids are not exchanged. The next least risky is protected sex, such as that using condoms. High-risk behavior involves sexual exchange of body fluids or use of intravenous needles. Long-term mutually monogamous relationships are an especially important consideration.

"Know your sexual partner," medical authorities advise. Concerned about STDs, many students have taken the advice to heart.

Unfortunately, they may go about it the wrong way, says psychologist Jeffrey D. Fisher.[56] Students try to gauge their risks by asking other students about their home town, family, and major. Or they try to judge their sexual chances on the basis of the other person's perceived "social class," educational level, or attractiveness.[57]

Do such external clues work? No, says Fisher. These are useless and irrelevant facts, not guides to safe sex.

How can you be sure that sex is really safe? The answer is: you can't. However, there are things that you can do to reduce your risks.

THREE LEVELS OF RISK: HIGH-RISK SEX, SAFER SEX, SAVED SEX. In general, there are three levels of risk in sexual behavior:

- *Very risky—unprotected sex and other behavior:* Behavior that is high-risk for the transmission of STDs includes all forms of sex in which body fluids may be exchanged. By body fluids, I mean semen, vaginal secretions, saliva, or blood (including menstrual blood). These are transmitted through unprotected vaginal, oral, or anal sex.

    High risks also include behavior having to do with the intravenous (IV) injection of drugs, a prime means of transmitting STDs. Certainly you shouldn't share IV needles yourself. Moreover, you should avoid sexual contact with someone who is an IV drug user or whose previous partner was. Avoid having sexual contact with people who sell or buy sex, who may be IV drug users.

- *Somewhat risky—"safer" sex:* The next best step to ensuring safe sex—actually, only saf*er* sex—is to use *latex condoms*. "Safer" sex is still somewhat risky, but at least it minimizes the exchange of body fluids. One example of safer-sex behavior is deep (French) kissing. Another is vaginal intercourse using latex condoms with **_nonoxynol-9_, a spermicide that kills STD organisms.** (Condoms are described on the next page.)

- *Lowest risk—"saved sex":* The safest kind of sex avoids the exchange of semen, vaginal secretions, saliva, or blood. The principal kind of "saved sex" is abstinence. **_Abstinence_ is the voluntary avoidance of sexual intercourse and contact with a partner's body fluids.**

    Saved sex includes massage, hugging, rubbing of bodies, dry kissing (not exchanging saliva), masturbation, and mutual manual stimulation of the genitals. In all cases, contact with body fluids is avoided. *The trick in practicing safe-sex activity is not to get swept away and end up practicing unsafe sex.*

SOME SEX, SOME RISK. If you've decided that abstinence is not for you, what should you do? The principal kinds of advice are as follows:

- *Use precautions universally:* If you choose to have sex, then CONSISTENTLY use safer-sex measures, such as a condom and spermicide, with ALL partners. This means ALL sexual partners, not just those you don't know well or those you think may be higher risk. Doing this means you'll have to learn to overcome any embarrassment

you may feel about talking with your partner about using condoms.

■ *Keep your head clear:* Be careful about using alcohol and other drugs with a prospective sexual partner. Drugs cloud your judgment, placing you in a position of increased vulnerability.

■ *Practice mutual monogamy:* Having multiple sexual partners is one of the leading risk factors for the transmission of STDs. Clearly, mutual monogamy is one way to avoid infection.

Be aware, however, that even apparent monogamy may have its risks. If one partner has a secret sexual adventure outside the supposedly monogamous relationship, it does not just breach a trust. It endangers the other's life—especially if the unfaithful partner is not using condoms.

In addition, you may be in a monogamous relationship but have no idea if your partner was infected previously. To be on the safe side, it's suggested the two of you wait several weeks while remaining faithful to each other. Then both of you should take a test to see if HIV antibodies are present. This gives some indication (though not absolutely) that the partner is currently free of infection.

ABOUT CONDOMS. A _condom_ is a thin sheath made of latex rubber or lamb intestine. (Though called "natural skin," lamb intestine is not as safe as latex.) A condom comes packaged in rolled-up form. It should then be unrolled over a male's erect penis, leaving a little room at the top to catch the semen. Some condoms are marketed with a "reservoir" at the end for this purpose.

A condom provides protection for both partners during vaginal, oral, or anal intercourse. It keeps semen from being transmitted to a man's sexual partner and shields against contact with any infection on his penis. It also protects the male's penis and urethra from contact with his partner's secretions, blood, and saliva.

These thin, tight-fitting sheaths of latex rubber or animal skin are available in all kinds of colors, shapes, and textures. They also come with or without a reservoir tip and are available dry or lubricated. Spermicide-coated condoms, including those with nonoxynol-9, have been shown to be effective in killing sperm.[58] When buying condoms, always check the expiration date. Also, don't store them in places where they might be exposed to heat (wallets, glove compartments), which causes latex to deteriorate.

Unfortunately, *condoms are not perfect protection.* They only *reduce* the risk of acquiring HIV infection and other STDs. Note that *reducing the risk is not the same as eliminating the risk.* If the condom is flawed or it slips off or breaks, there is suddenly 100% exposure.

Condoms break most frequently when couples use oil-based lubricants or engage in prolonged sex. A condom may also be weakened if couples attempt their own "quality testing" (such as blowing up condoms to test for leaks).

Choosing Among Birth-Control Methods

PREVIEW & REVIEW Methods of contraception vary greatly in effectiveness, side effects, cost, and other matters.

What are the chances of becoming pregnant? For a couple having unprotected intercourse over a 1-year period, the odds are 85–90%. About 1 million unplanned adolescent pregnancies occur every year in the United States. In addition, every year about 1.5 million abortions are performed. It's clear from these figures, then, that the gambling casino of reproduction all too frequently works in nature's favor.[59]

CONCEPTION & CONTRACEPTION. Avoidance of unwanted pregnancies requires the practice of *contraception* or *birth control*, **the prevention of fertilization or implantation.** Fertilization and implantation are two different matters. *Fertilization*, or *conception*, **occurs when the male reproductive cell, the sperm, meets the female reproductive cell, the egg or ovum.** This produces the fertilized egg (zygote). *Implantation* **is the act in which the fertilized egg burrows into the lining of the uterus.** In this location it grows into a fetus.

Only one method of birth control is *guaranteed* to avoid pregnancy—*complete abstinence*. All others have *some* risk of pregnancy, although some (such as tubal sterilization or vasectomy) are extremely slight.

Today concerns about preventing pregnancy often have to be linked with concerns about protection from STDs. For nonmonogamous, sexually active heterosexuals, these two concerns come down to a single method of contraception and protection: *condoms*. Heterosexual couples who need not worry about STDs, however, have a great many choices in contraception.

CHOICES AVAILABLE: THE VARIETIES OF BIRTH CONTROL. There are many criteria for choosing a method of contraception: availability, effectiveness, cost, personal comfort, effect on health, and religious beliefs. The accompanying box shows the effectiveness (or lack thereof) of various contraceptive methods in terms of preventing pregnancy. *(See ■ Panel 12.3.)* The various methods of contraception are explained within the box.

Onward: Applying This Chapter to Your Life

PREVIEW & REVIEW Ignorance about love and sex is not bliss.

Love and sexual passion are among the most powerful human forces. So powerful are they, in fact, that they lead people sometimes to take chances or make decisions they might not otherwise make. For instance, students who did not use a condom during sex often report they got carried away, "out of control." Or they say they did not plan ahead when they became sexually involved.[60]

We are surrounded by words and images about love and sex. However, a great many people, including many college-educated people, are surprisingly uninformed about these subjects. Unfortunately, we live in a time when ignorance in relationship and sexual matters can no longer be considered bliss.

Probably we all think we know quite a bit about human relationships. After all, we've grown up having relationships (of some sort) with other humans. Did you learn something new in this chapter? Write it down here:

_____

_____

_____

_____

_____

_____

Effectiveness of contraceptive methods.
The following are the principal types of birth-control methods, in order of effectiveness.

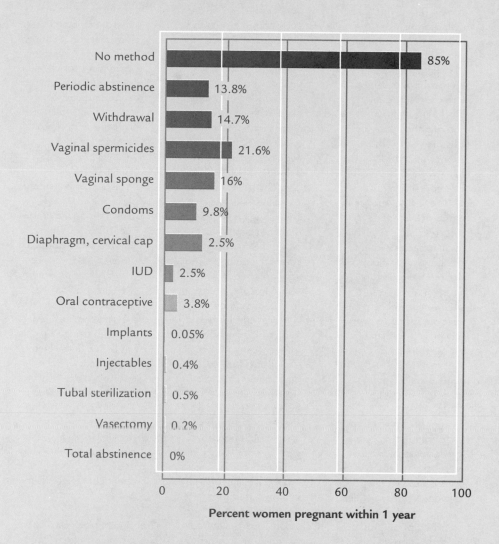

Method	Percent women pregnant within 1 year
No method	85%
Periodic abstinence	13.8%
Withdrawal	14.7%
Vaginal spermicides	21.6%
Vaginal sponge	16%
Condoms	9.8%
Diaphragm, cervical cap	2.5%
IUD	2.5%
Oral contraceptive	3.8%
Implants	0.05%
Injectables	0.4%
Tubal sterilization	0.5%
Vasectomy	0.2%
Total abstinence	0%

Percent women pregnant within 1 year

No Method at All. Intercourse in which no method of contraception at all is used has the highest failure rate for birth control. In one study, 85% of women ages 15–44 who didn't think they were infertile were estimated to have become pregnant within 1 year.

Douching. *Douching* is the practice of rinsing out the vagina with a chemical right after sexual intercourse. From the standpoint of birth control, it is almost worthless. Douching is an attempt to "wash out" the ejaculate. Instead, however, it often brings the sperm into contact with the cervix. Moreover, some sperm are able to enter the uterus within seconds of ejaculation, before a woman has a chance to begin douching.

Periodic Abstinence. *Abstinence* is the voluntary avoidance of sexual intercourse. *Complete abstinence* is the surest form of birth control. *Periodic abstinence* is another matter—it is not sure at all. Periodic abstinence refers to the avoidance of sexual intercourse during perceived fertile periods of the woman's menstrual cycle. Periodic abstinence goes under the names of *fertility awareness, natural family planning,* and the *rhythm method.*

This method cannot be used by women who have irregular menstrual cycles or who are at risk for STD exposure owing to unprotected intercourse. Moreover, using this method to prevent pregnancy requires a motivated, knowledgeable couple who has undergone training. The couple must be able to abstain or use another contraceptive method during those times the woman is estimated to be at risk for fertility.

Withdrawal. *Withdrawal* consists of removing the penis from the vagina prior to ejaculation, so that no sperm are deposited in or around the vagina. This method also seems to be flawed: nearly 15% of women are estimated to become pregnant with the technique. Not only does withdrawal require unusual willpower, but all it takes is the little bit of fluid released from the penis *prior* to ejaculation to send sperm into the vagina.

(continued next page)

Vaginal Spermicides Alone.
Vaginal spermicides are sperm-killing chemicals—such as spermicidal foam, cream, jelly, film, or suppositories—which are placed in the vagina within 30 minutes before intercourse. Some require the use of an applicator. Others, such as the suppositories, require a waiting time of 10–15 minutes after insertion before intercourse can take place.

Spermicides can be effectively used as lubricants during sexual intercourse. Those that contain nonoxynol-9 also kill bacteria and viruses in addition to sperm. It is recommended that these agents be used with other methods such as condoms and diaphragms. Spermicides can be purchased without a physician's prescription in many drugstores and supermarkets. Some people are sensitive to these agents. If burning or itching occurs, you may find switching to another brand will often alleviate the problem.

One of the newer spermicide contraceptives is the *vaginal contraceptive film (VCF)*, which consists of a thin, small (2-inch × 2-inch) film impregnated with nonoxynol-9. From 5 to 90 minutes before intercourse, the woman inserts the VCF into her vagina, where it dissolves into a gel-like material over the cervix. It is effective for up to 2 hours.

Vaginal Sponge. The *vaginal contraceptive sponge* is a soft, mushroom-shaped spongy disk saturated with spermicide (nonoxynol-9). Moistened and inserted into the vagina over the cervix up to 24 hours before intercourse, the device blocks sperm from entering the uterus and kills the sperm. The sponge must be left in place for 6–8 hours after intercourse.

The vaginal sponge is a one-size-fits-all method that is available in pharmacies without prescription and does not require individual fitting. It does require that users be able to feel that the sponge is properly placed so that it covers the cervix.

Condoms. *Condoms* are discussed in the text.

Diaphragm & Cervical Cap.
Diaphragms and cervical caps are barrier contraceptives that are always used with spermicidal creams or jellies. They are available only by prescription. Both come in various sizes and require a fitting by a health-care professional to determine correct size and style.

Diaphragms and cervical caps can be inserted up to 6 hours before intercourse (although a shorter time between insertion and intercourse may afford better protection) and must remain in place for 6–8 hours afterward. Both should be checked for holes after every use

(just hold them up to the light). Both increase the woman's risk of *toxic shock syndrome*—a severe, potentially life-threatening bacterial infection—if they remain in the vagina for prolonged periods of time.

To distinguish between the two devices:

■ *Diaphragms:* A *diaphragm* is made of a soft latex rubber dome stretched over a flexible metal spring or ring. The size varies from 2 inches to 4 inches, depending on the length of the vagina. When in place, the diaphragm covers the ceiling of the vagina, including the cervix. It works primarily by holding spermicide in contact with the cervix and by blocking sperm from entering the cervix.

If possible, diaphragms should be removed before 24 hours have elapsed from the time of insertion. They should not, however, be removed within 6 hours of the last act of intercourse. Diaphragms can be reused for a period of up to 1 year.

■ *Cervical caps:* The *cervical cap* operates in much the same way as the diaphragm. This is a much smaller, thimble-shaped rubber or plastic cap that fits directly onto the cervix. Insertion of the cervical cap tends to present more of a challenge to first-time users than does the diaphragm.

Unlike diaphragm users, cervical cap users do not need to reapply spermicide with each subsequent intercourse after insertion. In addition, they can leave the cap in place for up to 48 hours. Not all women can use the cap, owing to fitting problems or problems with cervical damage.

IUD. The *IUD* (for *intra-uterine device*) is a small plastic device that is placed inside the uterus. The IUD, which must be inserted by a health-care professional, may prevent fertilization in some women. Or, if fertilization takes place, the IUD prevents the fertilized egg from being implanted in the lining of the uterus. Once inserted, the IUD string must be located after every menstrual period to be sure the device remains in place. Depending on the type used, an IUD may remain in the uterus for 1–6 years.

Oral Contraceptives. The *oral contraceptive* or *birth-control pill,* famously known as simply The Pill, consists of synthetic female hormones that prevent ovulation or implantation. It is the most effective *reversible* birth control method available (surgery, for instance, may not be reversible). Nearly 14 million women use the pill in the United States, and it appears to be the contraceptive of choice among women ages 15–24.

The three basic types of pills are as follows:

■ *Combination pill:* The *combination pill* contains two hormones, estrogen and progesterone. These hormones, independently or together, prevent pregnancy in three ways: (1) They primarily prevent ovulation. (2) They change the mucus in the cervix, making it difficult for the sperm to enter the cervix. (3) They change the lining of the uterus, preventing implantation.

The combination pill provides a steady dosage of the two hormones, estrogen and progesterone. The pill is taken for 21 days, with 7 days off.

■ *Multiphasic pill:* The multiphasic pill is a variation on the combination pill. Whereas the combination pill provides a steady dosage of the two hormones, the *multiphasic pill* provides a changing dosage of estrogen and progesterone that more nearly mimics the body's natural cycle of hormones.

Like the combination pill, the multiphasic pill is taken for 21 days, with 7 days off.

■ *Minipill:* The *minipill* contains progesterone only. It thus has fewer side effects than the other two, but it is also less effective in preventing pregnancy. Because it contains no estrogen, the minipill does not consistently prevent ovulation. It does, however, change cervical mucus and change the lining of the uterus.

Unlike the combination and multiphasic pills, the minipill is taken every day.

It is important for users to check with their health-care practitioner regarding the pill-taking schedule and find out what to do in the event a pill is missed.

Women who are not good candidates for oral contraceptive use are those with a history of blood clots, stroke, heart disease, impaired liver function, or cancer. Those with diabetes, migraine headaches, hypertension, mononucleosis, or other problems should discuss the risks with a health-care practitioner.

Implant Contraceptives (Norplant). *Implants,* marketed under the brand name *Norplant,* consist of small, removable silicone-rubber rods or capsules filled with synthetic progestin, which are embedded in a woman's arm or leg. The capsules, which can be implanted surgically by a physician in 15 minutes using a local anesthetic, release low levels of synthetic progestin, preventing ovulation and restricting sperm from entering the uterus. The implants may stay in place for 5 years and can be removed surgically if a woman wants to become pregnant.

Implants are considered extremely effective, with less than one-half of 1% of women becoming pregnant in the first year.

Injectable Contraceptives (Depo-Provera). An *injectable contraceptive* known as *Depo-Provera* consists of a long-lasting progestin that is administered once every 3 months. During the time between injections, a woman has no menstrual periods or irregular ones. Fertility returns after the use of injectables is discontinued.

The risk of pregnancy from injectable contraceptives is extremely low—only 0.4% of women are estimated to become pregnant within the first year.

Tubal Sterilization—Female Sterilization. *Sterilization* is the surgical—and generally permanent—interruption of a person's reproductive capacity, whether male or female, preventing the normal passage of sperm or ova. Sterilization is the most popular contraceptive method among American couples.

In females, the procedure is called *tubal sterilization* and is accomplished by blocking or cutting the egg-carrying tubes called the fallopian tubes, thus preventing the passage of the egg from ovary to the uterus. Tubal sterilization may take the form of either *tubal ligation,* the cutting and tying of the fallopian tubes, or *tubal occlusion,* the blocking of the tubes by cauterizing (burning) or by use of a clamp, clip, or band of silicone.

Vasectomy—Male Sterilization. Male sterilization is accomplished by means of a vasectomy. A *vasectomy* is a surgical procedure that involves making a pair of incisions in the scrotum and cutting and tying two tubes (called the vas deferens) that carry sperm from the testes to the urethra, through which semen is ejaculated. After a vasectomy, sperm continue to form, but they are absorbed by the body. The man continues to be able to have erections, enjoy orgasms, and produce semen, but the ejaculate contains no sperm cells.

Vasectomies, which can be performed as a 20-minute procedure in a doctor's office with local anesthetic, are considered extremely effective: only 0.2% of women whose mates have had vasectomies are estimated to become pregnant in the first year.

A man contemplating a vasectomy should proceed as though the procedure were irreversible. Although 90% of the operations to reopen the tubes are successful, only 40–70% of these reversals result in the ability to father children.

Real Practice Activities for Real People

REAL PRACTICE ACTIVITY #12.1: MAINTAINING A HEALTHY RELATIONSHIP WHILE SUCCEEDING IN COLLEGE.

Staying power

This practice activity may be done in small groups or individually as a reaction paper written for the instructor.

Relationships are important. But so is your college work. What happens if the two are in conflict, as when academic demands drain time away from the person or people you are close to? Or, conversely, when the ending of a relationship results in one's dropping out of college (as happens with some traditional students)? Here's where staying power becomes important for both college and relationship skills.

Using information presented in this chapter (and others), identify 10 ways you can maintain a healthy relationship and still succeed in college.

REAL PRACTICE ACTIVITY #12.2: CAN YOU APPLY CRITICAL THINKING TO RELATIONSHIPS?

This practice activity may be done in small groups with no more than five people each. Each group is to consider the following questions, which later may be discussed in the class at large.

Mindfulness

Can mindfulness be applied to relationships? Can you think critically about people you're close to? When confronted by other kinds of problems (such as dealing with things or processes rather than people), can you take a rational approach to solving them? Or do you usually react in an emotional way? Do you find you react to problems differently if they involve someone close to you than if they are strangers? What can you do to apply critical thinking skills to relationship and people problems? Do most members of the group seem to show similarilities in the way they handle relationships?

REAL PRACTICE ACTIVITY #12.3: RELATIONSHIPS IN CYBERSPACE.

Information technology

This practical activity provides the basis for student discussion, either in small groups or in the class as a whole, as directed by the instructor.

The Internet provides many possibilities for finding community and relationships. For example, a parent of a child with diabetes and another predisposed to diabetes found that she made "wonderful and enduring friendships" through a chat room on a Web site devoted to children with diabetes.[61] On the other hand, a study by researchers at Carnegie Mellon University found that people who spend even a few hours a week online experienced higher levels of depression and loneliness than if they used the computer network less frequently.[62]

In small-group or classroom-wide discussion, consider the following questions: What is the most satisfying way to meet people? What do you think of online ways of meeting people? To what extent do you think your ideas are influenced by stereotypes? Why do you think people might be more depressed by the online experience? (Some suggested possibilities: The Net reduces social involvement. Face-to-face relationships provide more support and reciprocity. Online relationships are shallow, resulting in lost feeling of connection to others. Internet use is linked to sleep deprivation, which causes depression. Internet users of pornography may have unreal expectations.)

The Examined Life

JOURNAL ENTRY #12.1: HOW DO YOU HANDLE CONFLICT? Write a page or two of detail about an important relationship (such as parents, boyfriend/girlfriend, spouse, children, professor, boss). Are you satisfied with this relationship? What have you learned in this chapter that might help you to improve it?

_____

_____

_____

_____

_____

_____

_____

_____

JOURNAL ENTRY #12.2: ARE YOU PASSIVE OR AGGRESSIVE? Do you feel you're inclined to be aggressive or to be passive in conflict situations? Imagine yourself having a disagreement with someone (such as an instructor about a grade on a paper or a roommate about living arrangements). Write out a little script about some things you might say to express your point of view without hurting the other person or hurting yourself.

_____

_____

_____

_____

_____

_____

_____

JOURNAL ENTRY #12.3: IS THERE SOMEONE YOU CAN TALK WITH? Do you often feel lonely, unloved, unwanted? Why do you think that is? Who might you talk to about this? (An example is someone at the college counseling service.)

_____

_____

_____

_____

_____

_____

_____

_____

_____

_____

JOURNAL ENTRY #12.4: HAVE YOU HAD MIS- UNDERSTANDINGS ON A DATE? Have you ever had a dating experience in which another person seemed to mis- understand the nature of the occasion? That is, you may have thought there was/was not an invitation to have sex, but the other person thought the oppo- site? Describe the situation. (Note, inci- dentally, if there was any alcohol or other drugs involved.)

_____

_____

_____

_____

_____

_____

_____

_____

_____

JOURNAL ENTRY #12.5: HOW DO YOU FEEL ABOUT ABSTAINING FROM SEX? Because we live in the Age of AIDS, more and more students are abstaining from sexual relationships. Do you know anyone who has announced this? How do you feel about his or her decision?

_____

_____

_____

_____

_____

_____

_____

_____

_____

JOURNAL ENTRY #12.6: HOW DO YOU FEEL ABOUT BUYING CONDOMS? How difficult emotionally is it for you to buy condoms or to discuss their use with a prospective sexual partner? What are the impediments?

_____

_____

_____

_____

_____

_____

_____

_____

_____

_____

_____

18. Majors & Careers

Determining Your Future

IN THIS CHAPTER What will you do when you get out of college? What would you *like* to do? Is there necessarily a relationship between your major and your prospective career, and which should you decide on first? These are some of the most important questions you'll ever have to consider. And you're in the unique position of *being able* to consider them now. In this chapter, we consider the following:

- *Your future:* What is the purpose of work? What do you want to do when you get out of college, and how can you get career advice?

- *Vocational tests:* What vocational tests can help point you toward a career?

- *Job hunting:* What are the best ways to find a good job? How can you use a computer to help you in a job search? What are the best ways to write a résumé?

*"Everyone wants a
clear reason to get up
in the morning."*

So points out journalist Dick Leider. He goes on: "As humans we hunger for meaning and purpose in our lives. At the very core of who we are, we need to feel our lives matter . . . that we do make a difference."[1]

What is that purpose?

"Life never lacks purpose," says Leider. "Purpose is innate—but it is up to each of us individually to discover or rediscover it. And, it must be discovered by oneself, by one's own conscience."

Why Work?

PREVIEW & REVIEW Whatever you do to make money, you are trading your "life energy." To figure out the answer to the question "why work?" is to figure out the purpose of your life.

What is the purpose of your life? For most people, Freud said, the two biggest things that provide meaning and purpose are *love,* as we discussed in the last chapter, and *work.* For many students, in fact, the main reason they are going to college is because it will determine their future work.

Let us, however, consider a fundamental question: *Why work?*

Most people *think* they know the answer. To put bread on the table. To support their families. To afford what they want to do when they're *not* working. In other words, they work for money.

But what is it, exactly, that we are giving up in return for money?

MONEY & YOUR LIFE ENERGY. Joe Dominguez and Vicki Robin are authors of a wonder-ful book called *Your Money or Your Life.* In it they point out that money is something we choose to trade our "life energy" for. They write:

> *Our life energy is our allotment of time here on earth, the hours of precious life available to us. When we go to our jobs we are trading our life energy for money. . . . This definition of money gives us significant information. Our life energy is more <u>real</u> in our actual experience than money. You could even say money <u>equals</u> our life energy. So, while money has no intrinsic value, our life energy does—at least to us. It's tangible, and it's finite. Life energy is all we have. It is precious because it is limited and irretrievable and because our choices about how we use it express the meaning and purpose of our time here on earth.*[2]

Thus, they say, in considering what to do for a living, two questions become important:

- Are you receiving satisfaction and value in proportion to your life energy expended?

- Is the expenditure of life energy in alignment with your values and purpose?

Considering all the ways you might spend your future days, then, what would make you *feel most fulfilled while trading your irretrievable life energy?*

WORK & YOUR LIFE'S PURPOSE. Philosopher Jacob Needleman is the author of *Money and the Meaning of Life.*[3] He also gives frequent seminars about people and money. The most common question he hears, he reports, is "How do I engage in making a living and still keep my soul?"[4] Thus, to figure out the answer to "Why work?" is to begin to figure out the purpose of your life.

Unfortunately, for a great many people, work does not give them that sense of purpose. According to a Gallup Poll, only 41% of the respondents consciously chose the job or career they were in. Of the rest, 18% got started in their present job through chance circumstances, and 12% took the only job available. The remainder were influenced by relatives or friends. Perhaps the most important finding was this:

Nearly two-thirds said that, given a chance to start over, they would try to get more information about career options.[5]

Maybe, then, you are in a good position to take advantage of others' hindsight. Get as much information as you can about careers and jobs. Try to avoid aimlessness.

IF YOU DIDN'T HAVE TO WORK . . .

On a sheet of paper, write down three things you would prefer to spend your life doing. Assume you'd be getting a reasonably modest income and didn't have to work. (These are your dreams, so make them as detailed as possible.)

Now write down three more things you would like to do as work or career if money were no object. In a small group or classroom setting, discuss your choices. Why would you choose these directions? Do you think you could achieve any of these? How might you go about it?

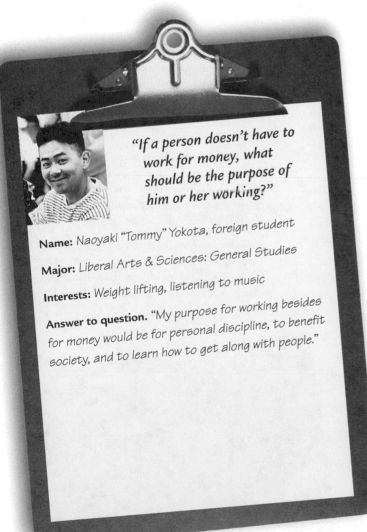

"If a person doesn't have to work for money, what should be the purpose of him or her working?"

Name: Naoyaki "Tommy" Yokota, foreign student

Major: Liberal Arts & Sciences: General Studies

Interests: Weight lifting, listening to music

Answer to question. "My purpose for working besides for money would be for personal discipline, to benefit society, and to learn how to get along with people."

What Do You Want to Be After You Graduate?

PREVIEW & REVIEW You'll probably change jobs and even careers often. Though people dream about glamorous jobs, in college they usually focus on careers with some connection to their abilities and interests. Some careers have a relationship to one's major, but many others do not. Often the additional training needed can be acquired in graduate school. Other competencies related to a career are related work experience, personal discipline, information-handling skills, and political and networking skills. It's best to decide on a career before a major; advice can be obtained at the college career counseling and job placement center.

n urging you to get career information, I also need to say this: Don't be afraid about making a mistake in a career choice. People make career changes all the time, in all phases of life. Moreover, in the beginning it's natural to go through some trial and error until you find what suits you. Indeed, columnist and business consultant Jack Falvey points out that most people do some casting about: "It is a rare person who knows with certitude what he [or she] wants to be and then follows that dream into the sunset for a lifetime. It is unrealistic to set that [ideal] as a standard."[6]

In fact, in the future the average person is expected to have *four career changes*—and several job changes within each career.[7] Statistically, people change jobs or assignments every 2½ years.[8] The best approach you can take, then, is to be flexible.

"I WISH I WERE A . . . " Television tends to give us a false impression of the work world. (For instance, one study of 90 programs watched by children found that 58% of the TV characters didn't have occupations. Or they had unrealistic occupations, such as vampire hunter and ghostbuster.[9]) Maybe this in part explains why the professions men and women say they choose in a *fantasy* life consist of the following:[10]

Men:

    Athlete—48%
    Business leader—38%
    Musician—29%

Women:

    Singer—35%
    Author—31%
    Doctor—29%

Of course, there's nothing wrong with aspiring to one of these occupations. One has to realize, however, that to reach the *top* of one of these professions—to achieve fame and fortune—is another matter altogether. The stars in their fields stand at the summit of a pyramid. But the nature of a pyramid, as Falvey points out, is that the further you

climb, the less space remains. Thus, the majority of pyramid climbers never get to the top.[11]

No wonder people have mid-life career crises in their mid-forties after having climbed as far as they're going to go. Clearly, then, the rewards of work should come not just from scaling the heights but from doing the job itself.

In any event, most first-year students think more about careers that are connected to their abilities and interests rather than that are glamorous.

IS THERE A RELATIONSHIP BETWEEN MAJORS & CAREERS? Many students assume that to enter most careers you must have the appropriate major. There are three possibilities here:

- *Relationship between career and major:* For some fields, there clearly *is* a relationship between the major and the career. To be an engineer, nurse, or musician, for example, you should major in engineering, nursing, or music, respectively. This is because the training for the occupation is so specific.

- *No relationship between career and major:* A great many fields require no specific major at all. You can be a sales representative, a store manager, a police officer, or the like with almost any major.

- *Relationship between career and graduate training:* For some fields—even seemingly specialized and technical ones—training can be obtained at the graduate level. For

example, you could major in history as an undergraduate, then get a master's degree in business, journalism, librarianship, or social work. The master's will enable you to enter one of these fields as a profession. (Some graduate programs may insist that you go back and make up particular undergraduate prerequisite courses that you might have missed.)

Quite apart from considering your career, however, is another important question: What do you want to *study*? For most people, college is a once-in-a-lifetime activity. Regardless of what you're going to do for a living, now's the time to study those things that truly interest you. Philosophy, English literature, ethnic studies, history of science, fine arts, and physical education might not seem directly connected to your career interests. But if you're interested in any of these subjects, the college years are the time to investigate them.

OTHER COMPETENCIES NEEDED FOR A CAREER. It's important to realize that a major and a college degree are only a *start* toward a career. Besides these, you need other competencies appropriate to the work you choose. Examples are:

■ *Related work experience:* It greatly helps to have acquired some skills related to the line of work you're entering. Such skills may be obtained from part-time work, internships, work-study programs, cooperative educational experiences, and cocurricular activities. These are matters I would strongly recommend looking into with a career counselor.

■ *Personal discipline:* You need to know how to dress appropriately, get to work on time, and be pleasant to coworkers and clients. You also need to be able to persist in completing your assignments come hell or high water. (You might not *want* to make 100 telephone calls a day, but it might be required in your job.) Here's where staying power is important.

Staying power

■ *Information-handling skills:* Most jobs these days that have a future to them require that you know how to handle information. This means knowing how to

Information technology

write a report, give a speech or presentation, and run a meeting. It probably also means knowing how to handle a computer—to do word processing or spreadsheets, for example.

■ *Political and networking skills:* Knowing how to handle organizational dynamics, otherwise known as office politics, is an important aspect of most career building. So is networking—the making, nurturing, and maintaining of personal contacts with people who can assist you. Indeed, developing these skills while in college can well help you get your foot in the door for a new career. (For example, you might get to know an instructor or fellow student who has connections to an industry you're interested in.)

WHAT DO YOU WANT TO DO FOR A CAREER?
Students often wonder what kind of work they can do with their major. A better question to ask—especially during your first year of college—is "What do I want to do for a career?" By taking the time to explore this question, you can then decide what majors (and minors) might be appropriate for you.

There are, of course, thousands of vocations. The *Dictionary of Occupational Titles*, published by the U.S. Department of Labor, lists over 20,000 occupations. How do you find which might be best for you? You can just leave things to chance, as many people do. Indeed, one out of three students puts off making a career decision until after graduation.[12] Then you can take whatever comes along, hoping everything will just work out for your future happiness.

But consider what it is that makes people want to succeed. University of Rochester psychology professor Edward L. Deci has studied human motivation for many years. According to his research, people do better when they are encouraged to pursue a task for its own sake. They also enjoy it more than those told to do the task for a reward, or those told they will be punished if they don't perform correctly.[13] Clearly, then, it's worth your while to seek out a career that you really want to do.

And remember what I said earlier about the working people interviewed for a Gallup Poll: *Nearly two-thirds said that, given a chance to start over, they would try to get more information about career options.*

Now's your chance.

CAREER COUNSELING & JOB PLACEMENT

CENTER. Career guidance starts with a visit to the career counseling center, which most colleges have. Often this is coupled with the job placement office.

Basically the career counseling and job placement center offers the following services:

■ *Vocational testing:* Tests such as those described in the next section ask you questions about your interests, abilities, and values. They also make suggestions about possible career areas that might interest you.

■ *Career counseling:* Career counseling offices usually have lots of information about what occupational fields are expanding. They also can tell you where the jobs tend to be concentrated geographically, the salary levels, and the training required. In addition, they can advise on transferring, as from community college to university.

You may get one-on-one advice from career advisors. Or you may be steered to job fairs attended by prospective employers or be introduced to alumni working in fields you're considering.

■ *Information about graduate school:* Some careers may require an advanced degree. Often the career counseling office provides information on graduate and professional programs and their admissions requirements and costs.

■ *Job placement:* Students of the 18–24 traditional college age may think of part-time or summer jobs as simply ways of making money to help get them through college. However, they can also provide valuable work experience that you can leverage later when you're trying to obtain a career-path type of job. The job placement office can also help you find out about internships or fieldwork jobs associated with your major.

Tests to Help Establish Career Interests

PREVIEW & REVIEW Vocational tests can help people establish their career interests and abilities. One presented here is the "career video" exercise. More formal tools include the Strong/Campbell Interest Inventory and the Edwards Personal Preference Schedule. Visiting the career counseling and job placement office can be a valuable and ultimately time-saving experience.

How can you identify which occupations might suit your abilities and interests? One way to do this is through tests. Let's consider some of these tests.

THE "CAREER VIDEO" EXERCISE. John Holland is a psychologist at Johns Hopkins University who has developed a system that divides career areas into six categories based on different interests and skills.[14] Here let us suppose that Holland's six career categories have been produced as a series by a "career introduction video service." (This is sort of a variation on those video dating services I'm sure you've seen ads for.) To see which careers appeal to you, try Personal Exploration #13.1.

THE "CAREER VIDEO": WHAT INTERESTS & SKILLS ARE YOU ATTRACTED TO?

DIRECTIONS

The accompanying description shows a summary of six career videos, labeled 1, 2, 3, 4, 5, 6. Read the description of all six videos. Then answer the questions below.

NUMBER OF VIDEO

a. Which video are you drawn to because it shows the group of people you would *most enjoy* being with? _____

b. Which second video are you drawn to because it shows the people you would *next most enjoy* being with? _____

c. Which video of the third rank are you drawn to because it shows people you would *enjoy being with*? _____

1. **Objects, things, animals:**

   People in this video are shown working with tools, machines, objects, animals, or plants. They may work outdoors. They have mechanical or athletic skills.

2. **Learning, analyzing, solving:**

   People in this video are shown analyzing and solving problems, learning, observing, discovering. They are curious and have good investigative skills.

3. **Innovating and creating:**

   People in this video are shown being intuitive, creative, imaginative, and artistic. They like to operate in unstructured environments.

4. **Helping and informing:**

   People in this video are shown training, developing, curing, enlightening. They like working with people and often have word skills.

5. **Influencing, performing, leading:**

   People in this video are shown persuading, performing, or managing people. They like working with people in achieving a goal.

6. **Data and details:**

   People in this video are shown executing tasks, following instructions, and working with numbers and facts. They like working with data.

INTERPRETATION

The numbers represent the following:

1 = *Realistic*

2 = *Investigative*

3 = *Artistic*

4 = *Social*

5 = *Enterprising*

6 = *Conventional*

In general, the closer the types, the less the conflict among the career fields. Here's what the six fields mean.

1. **Realistic:** People in this video consider themselves "doers." They are practical, down-to-earth, mechanically inclined, action-oriented, interested in physical activity.

   Interests may be mechanical or scientific. Examples of occupations: coach, computer graphics technician, electrical contractor, electronics technician, farmer, fitness director, health and safety specialist, industrial arts teacher, jeweler, navy officer, physical education teacher.

2. **Investigative:** If you're this type, you consider yourself a problem solver. You're probably rational and analytical, valuing intellectual achievement. You're thought-oriented rather than action-oriented. You may not be very people-oriented, indeed may be a loner.

   Sample occupations: cattle breeder, college professor, computer programmer, engineer, environmentalist, flight engineer, physician, scientist, urban planner.

3. **Artistic:** As might be expected, artistic people describe themselves as creative. They also consider themselves independent, unconventional, and emotional, valuing self-expression and disliking structure.

   Careers are apt to be in visual or performing arts. Examples of occupations: actor, architect, cartoonist, communications specialist, editor, illustrator, interior decorator, jewelry designer, journalist, librarian, orchestra leader, photographer, public relations person, sculptor.

4. **Social:** Social people value helping others and consider themselves socially concerned and caring and understanding of other people. They are drawn to associating with others in close personal relationships.

   Some careers: career specialist, caterer, convention planner, counselor, home economist, insurance claims specialist, minister, nurse, teacher, travel agent.

5. **Enterprising:** If you consider your-self adventurous, assertive, risk-taking, outgoing, and persuasive, you may be of the enterprising type. Power and prestige are important to you, and you prefer leadership to supporting roles.

   Examples of occupations: banker, city manager, FBI agent, labor negotiator, lawyer, market-ing specialist, politician, pro-moter, real-estate developer, sales representative, television announcer or producer.

6. **Conventional:** Conventional types see themselves as enjoying routine, order, neatness, detail, and struc-ture, as well as prestige and status. They are self-controlled and skilled in planning and organizing.

   Some occupations: accountant, auditor, database manager, hos-pital administrator, indexer, infor-mation consultant, insurance administrator, legal secretary, office manager, personnel special-ist, statistician.

Most people are not one distinct type but rather a mixture of types. That is why this Personal Exploration offers second and third choices.

With everyone else in your class, complete Personal Exploration #13.1. When everyone is done, join with oth-ers in a group corresponding to your first choice of career video. (If you find yourself the only one in a group, join the group of your second choice.)

Discuss the following questions: What qualities led you to this choice? What kinds of occupations men-tioned above seem attractive to you? Does the major (or majors) you're contemplating lead in this direction?

Now join with others in your sec-ond choice of career video. Discuss the same questions. If there's time, join the group of your third choice. Do you find yourself assembling with most of the same people as before? If not, what seems to account for the differences? What information of per-sonal value to you can you take away from this?

A more sophisticated version of the "career video" test is available under the name of the *Vocational Preference Inventory,* developed by John Holland. Holland has also written a *Self-Directed Search Assessment Booklet.* This contains a self-marking test that you can use to examine what occupa-tions you might begin to investigate. A career counselor can give you a further explanation of these valuable tests.

Three other tests used by career coun-selors are the Strong/Campbell Interest Inventory (SCII), the Edwards Personal Preference Schedule (EPPS), and the COPSystem Interest Inventory. The Strong/Campbell test enables students to compare their interests to those of people in various occupations. The Edwards test allows students to discover

what their personal needs and prefer-ences are—such as need for order, domi-nance, helping others, and social orientation. The COPSystem test divides interests into 14 career clusters and sug-gests information regarding college majors and the skills needed for success in certain careers.

GOING FOR AN APPOINTMENT AT CAREER COUNSELING. A visit to a career coun-seling center and the taking of a voca-tional test might take the better part of an afternoon. But the experience may well save you months or even years of wasted effort. In order to get started on establish-ing your career path—and the right major—do Personal Exploration #13.2.

WHAT CAN YOU LEARN FROM A VISIT TO THE CAREER COUNSELING & JOB PLACEMENT OFFICE?

The purpose of this assignment is to get you into the Career Counseling and Job Placement Office and have you talk to one of the counselors.

■ DIRECTIONS

Call the Career Counseling Center (or its equivalent on your campus) and make an appointment to come in. Explain to the counselor that you are doing a class assignment for this course. Ask if he or she can spare 15–20 minutes of time for a brief interview. Make an appointment to meet.

My appointment is at (date and time)

_____

_____

with (name of counselor)

_____

_____

at (location)

_____

_____

■ QUESTIONS FOR THE VISIT

Review the interview questions on this page and add two of your own. Ask the following questions and fill in the blanks.

GROUP ACTIVITY OPTION

After completing this Personal Exploration, discuss the results of your investigations in class. Then make an appointment to follow up on one of the components (such as taking a vocational test). Write a one-page report on your follow-up investigation to turn in to the instructor.

1. What kind of career counseling services do you offer?

_____
_____
_____
_____
_____
_____
_____
_____
_____
_____
_____

2. What kind of information do you have about occupational fields?

_____
_____
_____
_____
_____
_____
_____
_____
_____
_____

3. What kind of vocational tests do you offer? How long do they take?

_____
_____
_____
_____
_____
_____
_____
_____
_____

4. What kind of information do you have, if any, about graduate and professional schools?

_____
_____
_____
_____
_____
_____
_____
_____

5. If this office has a job placement component, what kind of services does it offer? Does it help students get internships or fieldwork placements?

_____
_____
_____
_____
_____
_____
_____
_____
_____
_____
_____

The Job of Looking for a Job

PREVIEW & REVIEW Everyone should train in the job of looking for a job. Two ways to investigate jobs are via the informational interview and internships. The computer can also be a job-search tool, as in hunting for online job openings and putting your résumé in an online database. It helps to know techniques for writing résumés, both recruiter-friendly and computer-friendly, chronological and functional. It's also important to know how to write a cover letter to accompany the résumé and how to behave in an interview.

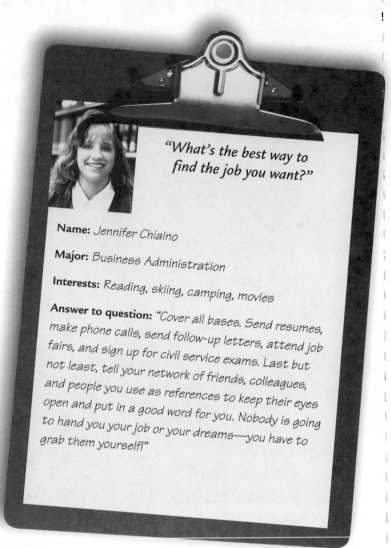

"What's the best way to find the job you want?"

Name: Jennifer Chiaino

Major: Business Administration

Interests: Reading, skiing, camping, movies

Answer to question: "Cover all bases. Send resumes, make phone calls, send follow-up letters, attend job fairs, and sign up for civil service exams. Last but not least, tell your network of friends, colleagues, and people you use as references to keep their eyes open and put in a good word for you. Nobody is going to hand you your job or your dreams—you have to grab them yourself!"

The average person will go job hunting *eight* times in his or her life," says Richard Bolles. A former clergyman, Bolles is author of *What Color Is Your Parachute?* and other writings about career searching.[15–17] Thus, today one needs to train for the task of *finding and getting* a job as much as for the ability to do the job itself.

Bolles offers several insights on finding that "lucky" job.[18] Luck, he says, favors people who:

- Are going after their dreams—the thing they really want to do most in the world.

- Are prepared.

- Are working hardest at the job hunt.

- Have told the most people clearly and precisely what they are looking for.

- Treat others with grace and dignity, courtesy and kindness.

THREE WAYS OF LOOKING FOR JOBS. Listing the various ways of finding jobs would take a book in itself. My suggestion is to go through the Career Counseling Center and find out everything you can about this subject. Three ways of making connections are as follows.

- **Networking:** I would agree with Jack Falvey when he says that contacts are everything. This means learning to "network" as a way of developing relationships that could pay off in a job. **Networking is making contacts, and making use of existing contacts, with people to find work and advance your career.**

 Suppose you're a bank manager looking to fill entry-level jobs such as teller, personal banker, and mortgage consultant. Whom would you be more apt to hire—applicants who were referred by your own employees or applicants who weren't? A two-year study of one large bank found that although applicants with referrals made up only 8% of all applicants, four out of five of them were interviewed and they received 35% of the jobs.[19] Why? First, the applicants who knew someone in the bank had important information about the bank and the skills it wanted. Second, it's more difficult for a manager to assess such qualities as dependability when he or she can't check out an applicant with other employees first.[20]

Networking can be *formal*, as when you make it a point to get to know instructors or others (as through internships or social organizations) in the industry in which you're interested in finding work. Or it can be *informal*, as when you're able to call upon friends, fellow students, or coworkers of yours to help you make connections (as through a relative) to a possible job.

Many people may wince at the mere mention of the word "networking," in part, according to one career consultant, because it goes back to one of the guiding principles of childhood: Don't talk to strangers. We may also be resistant because we want to feel it's not *who* we know but *what* we know in developing our careers.[21] Nevertheless, networking is important. "Part of an aggressive career strategy is making sure your accomplishments and skills are known within your company and within your industry," says the president of one national executive recruiting firm.[22]

■ *The informational interview:* Students have somewhat of a privileged status just by being students. That is, everyone knows that they are in a temporary position in life, that of *learning*. Consequently, it is perfectly acceptable for you to write a letter to a high-level executive asking for an *informational interview*. The letter should be written on high-quality paper stock, perhaps even on a letterhead printed with your name and address. (See ■ *Panel 13.1.*)

"You may find it hard to believe that some senior management types would clear their calendars for an hour or two just to talk to a student," Falvey observes, "but they do it all the time.[23] After sending the letter, you can make the follow-up phone call. This will probably connect you with a secretary who handles the appointment calendar. Simply remind him or her that you had written

I need your help. I am researching _____ industry (profession). If I could meet with someone of your experience, I am sure I could get enough information in a half hour to give me the direction I need to begin finding out how _____ really works.

As a first-year student studying _____, I find it difficult to understand how everything applies or fits together.

I will call your office in hopes of scheduling an appointment.

GROUP ACTIVITY #13.2

THE INFORMATIONAL INTERVIEW

Read the section at left, "The informational interview." Obtain an informational interview with someone, preferably an executive or administrator. He or she should be in an organization you're interested in working for, either as an intern or in a possible career capacity. Prepare a list of questions to ask the person you'll be interviewing. After the interview, write a one-page paper reporting your experience for your instructor.

to set up a meeting and ask how the executive's calendar looks.

- *Internships:* Summer interns are a segment of the labor force that, according to one report, "in a generation, has grown to encompass roughly a third of college students . . . ."[24] Essentially **an _internship_ is a temporary stint of on-the-job training that allows you to gain inside professional experience within a particular company or organization.** What the company gets in return is your labor (sometimes for a modest salary, sometimes for no salary). It also gets the opportunity to bid for your services after school if the people there decide they like you—an example of networking at work.

  Internships—sometimes called field experiences or cooperative educational experiences—may be as short as a few days during semester break or as long as a complete summer or school term. You can locate them through the career counseling center, of course. You can also simply ask guest speakers or other campus visitors. You might even be able to create your own internship, as by asking an executive during an informational interview.

WRITING A RECRUITER-FRIENDLY RÉSUMÉ. Writing a résumé is like writing an ad to sell yourself. However, it can't just be dashed off or follow any format of your choosing. It should be carefully designed to impress a human recruiter, who may have some fairly traditional ideas about résumés. (It should also be designed to be put into an employer's computerized database, as I'll describe.)

Some tips for organizing résumés, offered by reporter Kathleen Pender, who interviewed numerous professional résumé writers, are as follows.[25] *(See ■ Panel 13.2 for an example.)*

- *The beginning:* Start with your name, address, and phone number. (These days you could also add your fax number, your e-mail address, and even your Web site address, if you have one.)

  Follow with a clear objective stating what it is you want to do. (Example: "Sales representative in computer industry.")

Under the heading "Summary" give three compelling reasons why you are the ideal person for the job. (Example of one line: "Experienced sales representative to corporations and small businesses.")

After the beginning, your résumé can follow either a *chronological* format or a *functional* format.

- *The chronological résumé:* The chronological résumé works best for people who have stayed in the same line of work and have moved steadily upward in their careers. Start with your most recent job and work backward, and say more about your recent jobs than earlier ones.

  The format is to list the years you worked at each place down one side of the page. Opposite the years indicate your job title, employer name, and a few of your accomplishments. Use action words ("managed," "created," "developed"). Omit accomplishments that have nothing to do with the job you're applying for.

- *The functional résumé:* The functional résumé works best for people who are changing careers or are re-entering the job market. It also is for people who want to emphasize skills from earlier in their careers or their volunteer experience. It is particularly suitable if you have had responsibilities you want to showcase but have never had an important job title.

  The format is to emphasize the skills, then follow with a brief chronological work history emphasizing dates, job titles, and employer names.

- *The conclusion:* Both types of résumés should have a concluding section showing college, degree, and graduation date and professional credentials or licenses. They should also include professional affiliations and awards if they are relevant to the job you're seeking.

- *The biggest mistakes on résumés:* The biggest mistake you can make on a résumé is to *lie*. Sooner or later a lie will probably catch up with you and may get you fired, maybe even sued.

  The second biggest mistake is to have *spelling errors.* Spelling mistakes communicate to prospective employers a basic carelessness.

Examples of a basic résumé.

771 Randall Avenue
San Jose, CA 95190

(408) 555-4567

STACEY S. WILLIAMS

OBJECTIVE:

Sales representative in an electronics company in an entry-level position.

SUMMARY:

Experienced with working with general public and in retail selling during summer and Christmas jobs. Superb writing skills developed through college courses and extracurricular activities. Active volunteer in literacy program and discussion forums. Knowledge of Spanish.

BUSINESS EXPERIENCE:

Nov. 22–Dec. 24, 1998   FRY'S ELECTRONICS, San Jose, CA

SALESPERSON, television sets and VCRs.

Nov. 22–Dec. 24, 1997   MACYS, San Jose, CA

SALESPERSON, video games.

SUMMER JOBS:

1993–1997   DEPT. OF PARKS & RECREATION, San Jose, CA

June–Sept. 1997, GATE ATTENDANT, pool area; June–Sept. 1996, GATE ATTENDANT, pool area; June–Sept. 1995, LOCKER ROOM ATTENDANT; June–Sept. 1994, LOCKER ROOM ATTENDANT; June–Sept. 1993, PARK ATTENDANT. Collected tickets, checked residency, painted, cleaned pool area.

EDUCATION:

A. A. in International Business, minor in Journalism, San Jose Community College, San Jose, CA, 1998. Dean's List, 2 years.

Courses in International Relations: U.S., European, Latin America.

Additional courses in: Principles of Journalism, Feature Writing, Fundamentals of Public Speaking, Principles of Economics, Introduction to Business.

EXTRACURRICULAR ACTIVITIES:

Editor and reporter, college newspaper.

Member, debate team.

Volunteer, Project READ, a literacy program, and of National Issues Forums, network of forums to discuss national issues.

REFERENCES AVAILABLE ON REQUEST

Other résumé dos and don'ts appear in the box below. *(See ▪ Panel 13.3.)*

Information technology

Once upon a time, an employer would simply throw away old résumés or file them and rarely look at them again. Now a company may well use a high-tech résumé-scanning system such as Resumix.[26] This technology uses an optical scanner to input 900 pages of résumés a day, storing the data in a computerized database. The system can search for up to 60 key factors, such as job titles, technical expertise, education, geographic location, and employment history. Resumix can also track race, religion, gender, and other factors to help companies diversify their workforce. These descriptors can then be matched with available openings.

Such résumé scanners can save companies thousands of dollars. They allow organizations to more efficiently search their existing pool of applicants before turning to advertising or other means to recruit employees. For applicants, however, résumé banks and other electronic systems have turned job hunting into a whole new ball game. The latest advice is as follows:

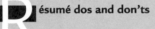

PANEL 13.3   **R**ésumé dos and don'ts

There are no hard and fast rules to résumé writing, but these are a few points on which the majority of experts would agree.

▪ **DO . . .**

- Start with a clear objective.
- Have different résumés for different types of jobs.
- List as many relevant skills as you legitimately possess.
- Use jargon or buzzwords that are understood in the industry.
- Use superlatives: biggest, best, most, first.
- Start sentences with action verbs (organized, reduced, increased, negotiated, analyzed).
- List relevant credentials and affiliations.
- Limit your résumé to one or two pages (unless you're applying for an academic position).
- Use standard-size, white or off-white heavy paper.
- Use a standard typeface and a letter-quality or laser-jet printer.
- Spell check and proofread, several times.

▪ **DON'T . . .**

- Lie.
- Sound overly pompous.
- Use pronouns such as I, we.
- Send a photo of yourself.
- List personal information such as height, weight, marital status or age, unless you're applying for a job as an actor or model.
- List hobbies, unless they're directly related to your objective.
- Provide references unless requested. ("References on request" is optional.)
- Include salary information.
- Start a sentence with "responsibilities included:"
- Overuse and mix type styles such as bold, underline, italic, and uppercase.

■ ***Use the right paper and print:*** In the past, job seekers have used tricks such as colored paper and fancy typefaces in their résumés to catch a bored personnel officer's eye. However, optical scanners have trouble reading type on colored or gray paper and are confused by unusual typefaces. They even have difficulty reading underlining and poor-quality dot-matrix printing.[27] Thus, you need to be aware of new format rules for résumé writing. *(See ■ Panel 13.4, right.)*

■ ***Use key words for skills or attributes:*** Just as important as the format of a résumé today are the *words* used in it. In the past, résumé writers tried to clearly present their skills. Now it's necessary to use, in addition, as many of the buzzwords or keywords of your profession or industry as you can.

Action words should still be used, but they are less important than nouns. Nouns include job titles, capabilities, languages spoken, type of degree, and the like ("sales representative," "Spanish," "B.A."). The reason, of course, is that a computer will scan for keywords applicable to the job that is to be filled.

Because résumé-screening programs sort and rank keywords, résumés with the most keywords rise to the top of the electronic pile. Consequently, it's suggested you pack your résumé with every conceivable kind of keyword that applies to you. You should especially use those that appear in help-wanted ads.[28]

Tips for preparing a computer-scannable résumé. Resumix Inc., maker of computerized résumé-scanning systems, suggests observing the following rules of format for résumé writing.

■ Exotic typefaces, underlining, and decorative graphics don't scan well.

■ It's best to send originals, not copies, and not to use a dot-matrix printer.

■ Too-small print may confuse the scanner; don't go below 12-point type.

■ Use standard 8½ × 11-inch paper and do not fold. Words in a crease can't be read easily.

■ Use white or light-beige paper. Blues and grays minimize the contrast between the letters and the background.

■ Avoid double columns. The scanner reads from left to right.

If you're looking for a job in desktop publishing, for instance, certain keywords in your résumé will help it stand out. Examples might be *Adobe Illustrator, Pagemaker, PhotoShop, Quark.*

USING THE COMPUTER TO LOOK FOR JOBS.

Information technology

Today there are many computer-related tools you can use to help you in your job search. These range from résumé-writing software to online databases on which you can post your résumé or look for job listings.[29-37] (*See* ■ *Panel 13.5, right.*)

Two types of online job-hunting tools are as follows:

■ **Online job openings:** You can search online for lists of jobs that might interest you. This method is called the "armchair job search" by careers columnist Joyce Lain Kennedy, coauthor of *Electronic Job Search Revolution*.[38] With a computer you can prowl through online information services, online job ad services, or newspaper online information services. (Examples of online information services are America Online, CompuServe, Microsoft Network, and Prodigy.)

■ **Résumé database services:** You can put your specially tailored résumé in an online database, giving employers the opportunity to contact you. Among the kinds of resources for employers are databases for college students and databases for people with experience.

PANEL 13.5

Computerized tools to help job searching. (Go to *http://csuccess. wadsworth.com* for the most up-to-date Web addresses.)

RESOURCES FOR CAREER ADVICE

You can find job-search advice, tips on interviewing and résumé writing, and postings of employment opportunities around the world by using your Web browser to use a directory such as Yahoo! (www. yahoo.com) to obtain a list of popular Web sites. In the menu, you can click on Business and Economy, then Employment, then Jobs. This will bring up a list of sites that offer career advice, résumé postings, job listings, research about specific companies, and other services.

Advice about careers, occupational trends, employment laws, and job hunting is also available through on-line chat groups and bulletin boards, such as those on the online services—America Online, CompuServe, Microsoft Network, and Prodigy. For instance, CompuServe offers career-specific discussion groups, such as the PR Marketing Forum. Through these groups you can get tips on job searching, interviewing, and salary negotiations. In addition, you might wish to check the U.S. Bureau of Labor Statistics Web site (*http://stats.bls.gov/emptabl. htm*), which contains employment projections and a list of fastest-growing occupations; Career Magazine (*www.careermag.com*); Job Search Advice for College Grads (*www.collegegrad.com*); and JobSmart Salary Survey Links for all fields (*www.jobsmart.org/tools/ salary/sal-prof.htm*).

WAYS FOR YOU TO FIND EMPLOYERS

Companies seeking people with technical backgrounds and technical people seeking employment pioneered the use of cyberspace as a job bazaar. However, as the public's interest in commercial services and the Internet has exploded, some online job exchanges have opened up for nontechnical people.

Some jobs are posted on Usenets by individuals, companies, and universities or colleges, such as computer networking company Cisco Systems of San Jose, California, and the University of Utah in Salt Lake City. Others are posted by professional or other organizations, such as the American Astronomical Society, Jobs Online New Zealand, and Volunteers in Service to America (VISTA).

ONLINE JOB LISTINGS

- **America's Job Bank:** A joint venture of the New York State Department of Labor and the federal Employment and Training Administration, America's Job Bank (*www.ajb. dni.us/index.html*) advertises more than 100,000 jobs of all types. There are links to each state's employment office. More than a quarter of the jobs posted are sales, service, or clerical. Another quarter are managerial, professional, and technical. Other major types are construction, trucking, and manufacturing.

- **Career Mosaic:** A service run by Bernard Hodes Advertising, Career Mosaic (*www.careermosaic.com*) offers links to nearly 200 major corporations, most of them high-technology companies. One section is aimed at college students and offers tips on résumés and networking. A major strength is the JOBS database, which lets you fill out forms to narrow your search, then presents you with a list of jobs meeting your criteria.

- **Career Path:** Career Path (*www.careerpath.com/*) is a classified-ad employment listing from numerous American newspapers, which you can search either individually or all at once. Major papers include the *Boston Globe*, the *Chicago Tribune*, the *Los Angeles Times*, the *New York Times*, the *San Jose Mercury News*, and the *Washington Post*.

- **E-Span:** One of the oldest and biggest services, the E-Span Interactive Employment Network (*www.espan.com*) features all-paid ads from employers.

- **FedWorld:** This bulletin board (*www.fedworld.gov*) offers job postings from the U.S. Government.

- **Internet Job Locator:** Combining all major job-search engines on one page, the Internet Job Locator (*www. joblocator.com/jobs*) lets you do a search of all of them at once.

- **JobHunt:** Started by Stanford University geologist Dane Spearing, JobHunt (*www.job-hunt.org*) contains a list of more than 700 sites related to online recruiting.

- **JobTrak:** The nation's leading online job listing service, JobTrak (*www.jobtrak.com*) claims to have 35,000 students and alumni visiting the site each day, with more than 300,000 employers and 750 college career centers posting 3,000 new jobs daily.

- **JobWeb:** Operated by the National Association of Colleges and Employers, Job Web (*www.jobweb.org/*) is a college placement service with 1,600 U.S. member universities and colleges and 1,400 employer organizations. It claims to have served over 1 million college students and alumni.

- **Monster Board:** Not just for computer techies, the Monster Board (*www.monster.com*) offers real jobs for real people, although a lot of the companies listed are in the computer industry.

- **NationJob Network:** Based in Des Moines, Iowa, NationJob Network (*www.nationjob.com*) lists job opportunities primarily in the Midwest. A free feature called P.J. Scout sends job seekers news of new jobs.

- **Online Career Center:** Based in Indianapolis, Online Career Center (*www.occ.com/occ/*) is a nonprofit national recruiting service listing jobs at more than 3,000 companies. About 30% of the jobs are nontechnical, with many in sales and marketing and in health care.

- **Workplace:** An employment resource offering staff and administrative positions in colleges and universities, government, and the arts (*http://galaxy.einet.net/galaxy/ Community/Workplace.html*).

RÉSUMÉ WEB SITES

- **E-Span:** Featuring paid ads from employers, the E-Span Interactive Employment Network (*www.espan.com*) also allows job seekers to post their résumés.

- **Internet Employment Network:** This free résumé referral service also allows you to search a database of all occupational categories (*garnet.msen.com:70/1/vendor/napa/jobs*).

- **Online Career Center:** This nonprofit job registry allows job searchers to post their résumés for free (*www.occ. com/occ/*).

- **Skill Search:** An online employment service that creates an applicant profile, Skill Search (*www.internetis.com/ skillsearch/*) works with 60 alumni groups.

You may wish to try Personal Exploration #13.3 *(opposite page)* to draft a résumé, using some of the principles just described.

WRITING A GOOD COVER LETTER. Write a targeted cover letter to accompany your résumé. This advice especially should be followed if you're responding to an ad.

Most people don't bother to write a cover letter focusing on the particular job being advertised. Moreover, if they do, say San Francisco employment experts Howard Bennett and Chuck McFadden, "they tend to talk about what *they* are looking for in a job. This is a major turn-off for employers."[39] Employers don't care very much about your dreams and aspirations, only about finding the best candidate for the job.

Bennett and McFadden suggest the following strategy for a cover letter:

■ *Emphasize how you will meet the employer's needs:* Employers advertise because they have needs to be met. "You will get much more attention," say Bennett and McFadden, "if you demonstrate your ability to fill those needs."

How do you find out what those needs are? *You read the ad.* By reading the ad closely you can find out how the company talks about itself. You can also find out what attributes it is looking for in employees and what the needs are for the particular position.

■ *Use the language of the ad:* In your cover letter, use as much of the ad's language as you can. "Use the same words as much as possible," advise Bennett and McFadden. "Feed the company's language back to them." This will produce "an almost subliminal realization in the company that you are the person they've been looking for."

■ *Take care with the format of the letter:* Keep the letter to one page and use dashes or asterisks to emphasize the areas where you meet the needs described in the ad. Make sure the sentences read well and— very important—that no word or name is misspelled.

THE INTERVIEW. The intent of both cover letter and résumé is to get you an interview. The act of getting an interview itself means you're probably in the top 10–15% of candidates. Once you're into an interview, a different set of skills is needed.

You need to look clean and well-groomed, of course. Richard Bolles suggests you also need to say what distinguishes you from the 20 other people the employer is interviewing. "If you say you are a very thorough person, don't just say it," suggests Bolles. "Demonstrate it by telling them what you know about their company, which you learned beforehand by doing your homework."[40]

Still, you shouldn't try to smooth-talk your way through the interview, suggests Max Messmer, head of Robert Half International, a big staffing services firm. Honesty counts, and you should mean what you say. Because personal references for job candidates are becoming more difficult to obtain, interviewers are now scrutinizing candidates more carefully for character and candor. Indeed, a survey by the firm found that nearly one-

HOW CAN YOU BUILD AN IMPRESSIVE RÉSUMÉ?

For this exercise, it doesn't matter whether you're of traditional college age or are a returning adult student. Its purpose is to get you accustomed to thinking about one important question: *What kinds of things might you be doing throughout your college years in order to produce a high-quality résumé?*

Fill in the lines below with your *present* experience. Then add ideas about *experience you might acquire* that would help you in the next few years.

■ 1. MY PRESENT EDUCATION:

_____
_____
_____
_____

Highlights of my present education (your most impressive accomplishments):

_____
_____
_____
_____

■ MY FUTURE EDUCATION:

_____
_____
_____
_____

Highlights of my education (impressive accomplishments you would like to be able to list):

_____
_____
_____
_____

■ 2. MY PRESENT WORK EXPERIENCE:

_____

_____
_____
_____
_____

Highlights of my present work experience (your most impressive accomplishments):

_____
_____
_____
_____

■ MY FUTURE WORK EXPERIENCE:

_____
_____
_____
_____
_____

Highlights of my work experience (impressive accomplishments you would like to be able to list):

_____
_____
_____
_____

■ 3. MY PRESENT CO-CURRICULAR ACTIVITIES:

_____
_____
_____
_____
_____

Highlights of my present co-curricular activities (your most impressive accomplishments):

_____
_____
_____

■ MY FUTURE COCURRICULAR ACTIVITIES:

_____
_____
_____
_____

Highlights of my cocurricular activities (impressive accomplishments you would like to be able to list):

_____
_____
_____
_____

■ 4. MY PRESENT HONORS AND AWARDS:

_____
_____
_____
_____

■ MY FUTURE HONORS AND AWARDS:

_____
_____
_____
_____

GROUP ACTIVITY OPTION

Brainstorming may help in putting together your résumé. In a small group, talk through your responses to the directions above. Ask for feedback and suggestions. Then listen to others read their responses to this Personal Exploration and offer your own comments.

third of executives polled rated honesty and integrity as the most critical qualities in a job candidate. "Without such attributes as trustworthiness and integrity, even the most highly skilled and articulate job seeker or employee will have limited success," says Messmer.[41]

Terry Mullins, dean of the School of Business Administration at the University of Evansville in Indiana, points out that most successful interviews follow a three-scene script. If you plan your moves to cooperate with the script, you'll increase your chances of being hired.[42]

■ *Scene 1: The first 3 minutes—small talk and the "compatibility" test:* The first scene of the interview, lasting about 3 minutes, consists of small talk. This is really a compatibility test.

Thus, as you shake hands, you should make eye contact and smile. Wait to be invited to sit down. Comment on office decorations, photographs, or views. Ask after objects in the interviewer's office that may reflect his or her personal interests. Show that you are at ease with yourself and the situation.

■ *Scene 2: The next 15–60 minutes—telling your "story":* Even though you may be uncomfortable about self-promotion, it's *expected* at a job interview. Indeed, employers estimate future accomplishments by past successes. Thus, before the interview you should have spent considerable time studying your accomplishments to reveal the best of your skills. You should examine your experience in terms of goals achieved, abilities developed, lessons learned—and then get comfortable practicing your "story."

In scene 2 of the interview, which may last anywhere from 15 minutes to an hour or more, you should explain your accomplishments, abilities, and ambitions, emphasizing your ability to add value to the employer. If you can claim credit for reducing costs, increasing sales, or improving quality in your previous jobs, you should stress this now. Also, if you have any blemishes on your record or holes in your experience, this is the time to explain them. As you come to the end of this scene, Mullins suggests, you should emphasize your willingness and capacity to perform at the highest level for your new employer.

■ *Scene 3: The final 1–2 minutes—closing the interview and setting up the next steps:* The end of the interview, which may last only a minute or two, is crucial, Mullins says. You don't want the interviewer to control the situation with the customary "We'll be in touch with you when we decide something." This statement takes away your power to influence the decision.

Instead, Mullins advises, you should end the interview by saying, "I'll keep you posted about developments in my job search." This final remark keeps you in control and enables you to follow up with additional information—such as a letter restating some of your accomplishments or providing news of other job offers—that may improve your prospects.

THE FOLLOW-UP LETTER. Regardless of how well or how poorly you felt the interview went, afterward you should *always* send a short thank-you note. The letter, advises Max Messmer, should accomplish three things:[43] (1) It should express your gratitude. (2) It should reinforce your interest in the job. (3) It should recap the two or three strongest points working in your favor.

Onward: Applying This Chapter to Your Life

PREVIEW & REVIEW Life is an endless process of self-discovery.

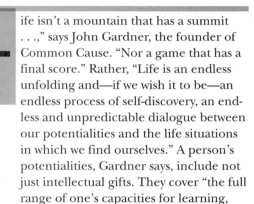

"Life isn't a mountain that has a summit . . .," says John Gardner, the founder of Common Cause. "Nor a game that has a final score." Rather, "Life is an endless unfolding and—if we wish it to be—an endless process of self-discovery, an endless and unpredictable dialogue between our potentialities and the life situations in which we find ourselves." A person's potentialities, Gardner says, include not just intellectual gifts. They cover "the full range of one's capacities for learning, sensing, wondering, understanding, loving, and aspiring."[44]

This, then, is not the end. It is the beginning. Explain what you can take from this chapter to help you on your journey:

_____

_____

_____

_____

_____

Real Practice Activities for Real People

REAL PRACTICE ACTIVITY #13.1: MAINTAINING A HEALTHY RELATIONSHIP WHILE SUCCEEDING IN COLLEGE. This practice activity may be done in small groups or individually in a reaction paper written for the instructor.

Staying power

Throughout the book we have emphasized the importance of staying power—persistence, perseverence, commitment, focus, conscientiousness—in achieving success, both in college and in life. Taking each quality of staying power discussed in Chapter 1—sense of personal control and responsibility, optimism, creativity, and the ability to take psychological risks—illustrate how you can personally use each quality in exploring career options.

REAL PRACTICE ACTIVITY #13.2: APPLYING MINDFULNESS TO YOUR CHOICE OF MAJOR OR CAREER. This practice activity should be done by individuals and expressed in a reaction paper to be handed in to the instructor.

Mindfulness

Reread the section "Why Work?" at the beginning of this chapter, particularly the paragraphs about life energy and your life's purpose. Many students spend more thought on buying cars, clothes, and sound systems than they do on how they will expend their "life energy." Putting so little effort into career planning means whatever job they end up in will be simply by default—that is, through mindlessness—and they might not like the result.

How much mindfulness have you applied toward making your choice of major or career? Show how you can apply the steps of critical thinking toward this investigation. Provide specific examples in your response.

Information technology

REAL PRACTICE ACTIVITY #13.3: YOU & INFORMATION TECHNOLOGY. This practical activity provides the basis for student discussion, either in small groups or in the class as a whole, as directed by the instructor.

How does an average starting salary of $41,561 plus choice of companies sound? That's what's available to recent college graduates in computer science. Companies have hundreds of thousands of openings for programmers, systems analysts, and computer engineers—openings going unfilled. Yet most first-year college students say they plan to stick with business, psychology, health services, law, and other career paths in which the opportunities or pay are less promising.[45]

Questions for discussion: How do you feel about computers, such as using them for word processing and e-mail? Why would you major or not major in computer science? How do you think information technology could help you in the present field in which you plan to major? How do you plan to keep up with new developments in computers and telecommunications?

The Examined Life

JOURNAL ENTRY #13.1: DREAMING WHAT YOU'D LIKE TO STUDY The best way to start thinking about your prospective career field or major is to dream your dreams. Your journal is the place to do this. Take 15 minutes to free-associate, and write as quickly (but legibly) as you can all your desires about things you're curious about or enjoy and would like to study. Then state what fields of study or majors might best serve your wishes.

JOURNAL ENTRY #13.2: DREAMING YOUR CAREERS You go through life only once. Yet it's possible to have more than one career—be a salesperson/musician, a travel agent/travel writer, a nurse/social activist, for example. Or you might have successive careers, each one different. When you "dream the impossible dream," what careers come to mind?

JOURNAL ENTRY #13.3: GETTING GOOD AT JOB INTERVIEWS Interviewing for jobs is a skill all by itself. This book did not have space to give this subject the coverage it deserves. What other kinds of skills do you think are needed for interviewing? What books can you find in the library that might help you refine your interviewing techniques?

JOURNAL ENTRY #13.4: WHAT IS THE MOST SIGNIFICANT ANALYSIS YOU'VE DONE IN THIS BOOK? Throughout this book, you've had many opportunities, in the section "The Examined Life," to examine what you really think about matters that are important to you. Which one of these was the most important? How will you translate your concerns into action?

_____

_____

_____

_____

_____

_____

_____

_____

_____

_____

Notes

CHAPTER 1

1. Survey by Caliper, Princeton, NJ, 1998. Cited in Fisher, A. (1998, May 25). Am I too old to be a tech expert? . . . What are employers really looking for? *Fortune*, p. 202.
2. Person, E. S. Quoted in Anonymous (1990, September). Motivation. *Self*, p. 215.
3. Adapted from Friday, R. A. (1988). *Create your college success: Activities and exercises for students.* Belmont, CA: Wadsworth, pp. 116–119.
4. Carter, C. (1990). *Majoring in the rest of your life: Career secrets for college students.* New York: Noonday Press, pp. 61–62.
5. Rotter, J. B. (1966). Generalized expectancies for internal versus external control of reinforcement. *Psychological Monographs, 80*(Whole No. 603).
6. Study of American College Testing, Iowa City, IA. Reported in Henry, T. (1996, July 11). College dropout rate hits all-time high. *USA Today*, p. 1A.
7. Saterfiel, T. Quoted in Henry, 1996 (see note 6).
8. Levitz, R., & Noel, L. (1989). Connecting students to institutions: Keys to retention and success. Pp. 65–81 in Upcraft, M. L., Gardner, J. N., & Associates (Eds.). *The freshman year experience: Helping students survive and succeed in college.* San Francisco: Jossey-Bass.
9. Passell, P. (1992, August 19). Twins study shows school is sound investment. *New York Times*, p. A14.
10. Reich, R. Interviewed in Belton, B. (1994, September 2). Reich: College education a buffer against recession. *USA Today*, p. 3B.
11. Research by Blau, F. D. Cited in Kleiman, C. (1998, May 31). Top 3 needs for getting off welfare—education, education, education. *San Jose Mercury News*, p. PC1; reprinted from *Chicago Tribune*.
12. Wessel, D. (1994, September 26). For college graduates, a heartening word. *Wall Street Journal*, p. A1.
13. U.S. Bureau of the Census. Cited in Healy, M. (1994, July 22). Time (in school) is money. *USA Today*, p. 1D.
14. Katz, J. (Ed.) (1968). *No time for youth: Growth and constraint in college students.* San Francisco: Jossey-Bass.
15. Kalat, J. W. (1990). *Psychology* (2nd ed.). Belmont, CA: Wadsworth, p. 440.
16. Rotter, J. B. (1966). Generalized expectancies for internal versus external control of reinforcement. *Psychological Monographs, 80*(Whole No. 603).
17. Findley, M. J., & Cooper, H. M. (1983). Locus of control and academic achievement: A literature review. *Journal of Personality & Social Psychology, 44*, 419–427.
18. Lefcourt, H. M. (1982). *Locus of control: Current trends in theory and research.* Hillsdale, NJ: Erlbaum.
19. McGinnis, A. Quoted in Maushard, M. (1990, October 22). How to get happy: What makes optimists tick. *San Francisco Chronicle*, p. B5. Reprinted from *Baltimore Evening Sun*.
20. McGinnis, A. L. (1990). *The power of optimism.* San Francisco: Harper & Row.
21. Szent-Györgyi, A. Quoted in von Oech, R. (1983). *A whack on the side of the head.* Menlo Park, CA: Creative Think, p. 7.
22. von Oech, 1983, p. 21.
23. Hyatt, C., & Gottlieb, L. (1987). *When smart people fail.* New York: Simon and Schuster, p. 20.
24. Garfield, C. Quoted in Rozak, M. (1989, August). The mid-life fitness peak. *Psychology Today*, pp. 32–33.
25. Anonymous. (1995, April). What's your biggest regret in life? *Health*, p. 14.

CHAPTER 2

1. Anonymous. (1993, June 28). Defining greatness. *Newsweek*, pp. 48-50.
2. Sternberg, R. Quoted in Chollar, S. (1996, April). Rethinking intelligence. *American Health*, pp. 80–83.

3. Gardner, H. (1983). *Frames of mind: The theory of multiple intelligences.* New York: Basic Books.
4. Gardner, H. Quoted in Crossen, C. (1997, June 5). Think you're smart? Then just try to sell a new kind of IQ test. *Wall Street Journal*, pp. A1, A13.
5. Crossen, 1997.
6. Goleman, D. (1995). *Emotional intelligence.* New York: Bantam.
7. Goleman, D. Quoted in Derrow, P. (1996, April). Thinking from the heart. *American Health*, pp. 82-83.
8. Guild & Garger, 1986. Cited in Ducharme, A., & Watford, L., Explanation of assessment areas (handout).
9. Ducharme & Watford.
10. Langer, E. J. Quoted in Hilts, P. J. (1997, September 23). A scholar of the absent mind. *New York Times*, pp. B9, B13.
11. Langer, E. J. (1997). *The power of mindful learning.* Reading, MA: Addison-Wesley, p. 4.
12. Langer, E. J. (1989). *Mindfulness.* Reading, MA: Addison-Wesley, pp. 12–13.
13. Langer, 1997, pp. 26–27.
14. Langer, 1989, pp. 16–17.
15. Langer, 1989, p. 69.
16. Randi, J. (1992, April 13). Help stamp out absurd beliefs. *Time*, p. 80.
17. Ruchlis, H., & Oddo, S. (1990). *Clear thinking: A practical introduction.* Buffalo, NY: Prometheus, p. 109.
18. Ruchlis & Oddo, 1990, p. 110.
19. Gerard, N. Quoted in Powers, L. (1996, November 25). A crusade against error: First, admit they happen. *USA Today*, p. 13B.
20. Kahane, H. (1988). *Logic and contemporary rhetoric: The use of reason in everyday life* (5th ed.). Belmont, CA: Wadsworth.
21. Rasool, J., Banks, C., & McCarthy, M.-J. (1993). *Critical thinking: Reading and writing in a diverse world.* Belmont, CA: Wadsworth, p. 132.
22. Rasool, Banks, & McCarthy, 1993, p. 132.
23. Farnham, A. (1994, January 10). How to nurture creative sparks. *Fortune*, pp. 94–100.
24. Farnham, A. (1994, January 10). Teaching creativity tricks to buttoned-down executives. *Fortune*, p. 98.
25. Osborn, A. (1953). *Applied imagination.* New York: Scribner's.
26. Higgins, J. M. (1995, September-October). Mind mapping: Brainstorming by oneself. *The Futurist*, p. 46; from Higgins, J. M. *101 creative problem solving techniques.*
27. Ray, M., & Myers, R. (1986). *Creativity in business.* Garden City, NY: Doubleday, p. 42.
28. Ray & Myers, 1986, p. 92.
29. Raudsepp, E. Quoted in Golin, M. (1992, April). Subconscious smarts. *Psychology Today*, p. 47; from Raudsepp, E. *Secrets of executive success.*
30. Golin, 1992.

CHAPTER 3

1. Stewart, T. A. (1994, April 4). The information age in charts. *Fortune*, pp. 75–79.
2. Mandel, T. in Anonymous. (1992, November 16). Talking about portables. *Wall Street Journal*, p. R18.
3. Campus Computing Project, directed by K. C. Green, Claremont Graduate University, reported in Guernsey, L. (1997, October 17). E-mail is now used in a third of college courses, survey finds. *Chronicle of Higher Education*, p. A30.
4. Stewart, 1994.
5. Baig, E. C. (1997, November 10). A little high tech goes a long way. *Business Week*, p. 154E10.
6. Himbeault-Taylor, S., quoted in Baig, 1997.
7. Robinson, P. (1997, September 14). There are many ways to pinch pennies on PCs. *San Jose Mercury News*, p. 2F.
8. Williams, R. (1993, April 10). On the hunt for a used computer. *The Globe & Mail* (Toronto), p. B13.
9. Claris survey of small businesses, reported in USA Snapshots. (1996, July 17). Small- business software. *USA Today*, p. 1B.
10. Brinkley, J. (1998, May 27). Microsoft has a stronghold in office suites. *New York Times*, pp. C1, C2.
11. Dataquest Inc. study, reported in Swartz, J. (1997, August 21). A rush to plug PCs into the Internet. *San Francisco Chronicle*, pp. A1, A15.

12. Tetzeli, R. (1994, March 7.) The Internet and your business. *Fortune*, pp. 86–96.
13. Landis, D. (1993, October 7). Exploring the online universe. *USA Today*, p. 4D.
14. Louis, A. M. (1997, April 1). What you should look for when shopping for an ISP. *San Francisco Chronicle*, p. D11.
15. Sandberg, J. (1996, December 9). What do they do on-line? *Wall Street Journal*, p. R8.
16. Odyssey Ventures Inc., cited in Sandberg, 1996.
17. Einstein, D. (1996, February 20). What they want is e-mail. *San Francisco Chronicle*, pp. B1, B6.
18. Crowe, E. P. (1995, August 8–21). The news on Usenet. *Bay Area Computer Currents*, pp. 94–95.
19. Marin, M. H. (1996, April 1). Digging data out of cyberspace. *Fortune*, p. 147.
20. Martin, 1996.
21. Scoville, R. (1996, January). Find it on the net. *PC World*, pp. 125–130.
22. Ihnatko, A. (1993, March). Right-protected software. *MacUser*, pp. 29–30.
23. Business Software Alliance, reported in Shapley, R. (1997, May 19). Corporate Web police hunt down e-pirates. *New York Times*, p. C5.
24. Rust, B., reported in Haworth, K. (1997, July 11). Publishers press colleges to stop software piracy by their students. *Chronicle of Higher Education*, pp. A19–A20.
25. Haring, B. (1997, May 27). Sound advances open doors to bootleggers. *USA Today*, p. 8D.
26. Blumenstyk, G. (1996, September 27). Comics and centerfolds on Web pages pose a copyright problem for colleges. *Chronicle of Higher Education*, pp. A29–A30.
27. Bynum, T., quoted in Hardy, L. (1995, August 1). Tapping into new Ethical quandaries. *USA Today*, p. 6D.
28. Hines, A. (1994, January-February). Jobs and Infotech. *The Futurist*, pp. 9–13.

CHAPTER 4

1. Myers, D. G. (1992). *The pursuit of happiness: Who is happy—and why.* New York: William Morrow.
2. Samuelson, R. J. (1996, July 1). The endless road 'crisis.' *Newsweek*, p. 47.
3. Robinson, J. P., & Godbey, G. (1997). *Time for life.* Quoted in Hirsch, A. (1997, July 26). Author says there's more free time than we think. *San Francisco Chronicle*, p. A21; reprinted from *Baltimore Sun*.
4. Beneke, W. M., & Harris, M. B. (1972). Teaching self-control of study behavior. *Behavior Research & Therapy, 10*, 35–41.
5. Kessinger, T. G. Quoted in: Marriott, M. (1991, April 12). In high-tech dorms, a call for power. *New York Times*, pp. A1, A8.
6. Rimer, S. (1991, October 27). Television becomes basic furniture in college students' ivory towers. *New York Times*, sec. 1, p. 14.
7. Moffatt, M. (1989). *Coming of age in New Jersey.* Rutgers, NJ: Rutgers University Press.
8. Marriott, 1991.
9. Ellis, D. (1991). *Becoming a master student* (6th ed.). Rapid City, SD: College Survival, Inc., p. 53.
10. Lakein, A. (1973). *How to get control of your time and your life.* New York: Peter H. Wyden.
11. Sapadin, L. (1997). *It's about time.* New York: Penguin.
12. Sapadin, L. Reported in Peterson, K. S. (1997, July 22). Helping procrastinators get to it. *USA Today*, p. 7D.
13. Zimbardo, P. G. (1977). *Shyness: What it is, what to do about it.* Reading, MA: Addison-Wesley, p. 14.
14. Robinson & Godbey, 1997.
15. Haron, D. (1994, June 23). Campus drinking problem becomes severe [letter]. *New York Times*, p. A14.
16. Hanson, D. J. (1994, September 28). Parents: Don't panic about campus boozers [letter]. *New York Times*, p. A11.
17. Wechsler, H. et al. (1994, December 7). Health and behavioral consequences of binge drinking in college. *Journal of the American Medical Association.*
18. Associated Press (1992, September 20). Study finds more drinking at small colleges than large ones. *New York Times*, sec. 1, p. 20.
19. della Cava, M. R. (1996, January 16). Are heavy users hooked or just on-line fanatics? *USA Today*, pp. 1A, 2A.
20. Howe, K. (1995, April 5). Diary of an AOL addict. *San Francisco Chronicle*, pp. D1, D3.
21. Hamilton, K., & Kalb, C. (1995, December 18). They log on, but they can't log off. *Newsweek*, pp. 60–61.
22. Yu, S., quoted in Hamilton & Kalb, 1995.
23. Kandell, J. J., quoted in Young, J. R. (1998, February 6). Students are unusually vulnerable to Internet addiction, article says. *Chronicle of Higher Education*, p. A25.
24. American Psychological Association, reported in Leibrock, R. (1997, October 22). AOLaholic: Tales of an online addict. *Reno News & Review*, pp. 21, 24.
25. Hamilton & Kalb, 1995.
26. Sanchez, R. (1996, May 23). Colleges seek ways to reach Internet-addicted students. *San Francisco Chronicle*, p. A16; reprinted from *Washington Post.*
27. Sanchez, 1996.
28. Belluck, P. (1996, December 1). The symptoms of Internet addiction. *New York Times*, sec. 4, p. 5.
29. Jacoby, B. (1989). *The student-as-commuter: Developing a comprehensive institutional response.* Ashe-Eric Higher Education Report 7.
30. Stewart, S. S., & Rue, P. (1983). Commuter students: Definition and distribution. In Stewart, S. S. (Ed.). *Commuter students: Enhancing their educational experiences.* San Francisco: Jossey-Bass.
31. Wright, S. E. (1996, October 13). Is there any hope for Silicon Valley's worst commute? *San Jose Mercury News*, pp. 1P, 3P.
32. Casteneda, C. J. (1996, August 16). Public transit: Competing against cars, and losing. *USA Today*, p. 8A.
33. Casteneda, C. J., & Sharn, L. (1996, August 16). Car pools: Too much time and trouble for a lot of riders. *USA Today*, p. 8A.
34. Hamilton, E. (1996, August 8). When should a teen get a car? *Point Reyes Light*, p. 6.
35. Tyson, E. (1996, August 18). Kicking the car habit. *San Francisco Examiner*, pp. D-1, D- 2.
36. King, J. E. (1998, May 1). Too many students are holding jobs for too many hours. *Chronicle of Higher Education*, p. A72.
37. Research by Department of Education, National Center for Education Statistics, reported in King, 1998.
38. Department of Education, *1995-96 National Postsecondary Student Aid Study*, reported in King, 1998.

CHAPTER 5

1. Haber, R. N. (1979). Twenty years of haunting eidetic imagery: Where's the ghost? *Behavioral & Brain Sciences, 2*, 583–629.
2. Cowley, G., & Underwood, A. (1998, June 15). Memory. *Newsweek*, pp. 48–54.
3. Gordon, B., quoted in Yoffe, E. (1997, October 13). How quickly we forget. *U.S. News & World Report*, pp. 53–57.
4. Lapp, D. C. (1992, December). (Nearly) total recall. *Stanford Magazine*, pp. 48–51.
5. Lapp, 1992, p. 48.
6. Crovitz, H. F., & Schiffman, H. (1974). Frequency of episodic memories as a function of their age. *Bulletin of the Psychonomic Society, 4*, 517–18.
7. Ebbinghaus, H. (1913). *Memory.* New York: Teachers College. (Original work published 1885.)
8. Survey by National Institute for Development and Administration, University of Texas. Cited in: Lapp, 1992.
9. Pauk, W. (1989). *How to study in college* (4th ed.). Boston: Houghton Mifflin, p. 92.
10. Pauk, 1989, p. 92.
11. Research by Salthouse, T., Georgia Institute of Technology, reported in Yoffe, 1997.
12. Cowley & Underwood, 1998.
13. Fogler, J., & Stern, L. (1994). *Improving your memory: How to remember what you're starting to forget* (rev. ed.). Baltimore: Johns Hopkins.
14. Minninger, J. (1984). *How to improve your memory.* Emmaus, PA: Rodale. Reprinted from Minninger, J. *Total recall.*
15. Cowley & Underwood.
16. Krueger, W. C. F. (1929). The effect of overlearning on retention. *Journal of Experimental Psychology, 12*, 71–78.
17. Weiten, W., Lloyd, M. A., & Lashley, R. L. (1990). *Psychology applied to modern life: Adjustment in the 90s* (3rd ed.). Pacific Grove, CA: Brooks/Cole.

18. Bromage, B. K., & Mayer, R. E. (1986). Quantitative and qualitative effects of repetition on learning from technical text. *Journal of Educational Psychology, 78*(4), 271–78.

19. Zechmeister, E. B., & Nyberg, S. E. (1982). *Human memory: An introduction to research and theory.* Pacific Grove, CA: Brooks/Cole.

20. Kalat, J. W. (1990). *Introduction to psychology* (2nd ed.). Belmont, CA: Wadsworth, p. 295.

21. Doner, K. (1994, March). Improve your memory. *American Health,* pp. 56–60.

22. Underwood, B. J. (1957). Interference and forgetting. *Psychological Review, 64,* 49–60.

23. Fowler, M. J., Sullivan, M. J., & Ekstrand, B. R. (1973). Sleep and memory. *Science, 179,* 302–304.

24. Thorndyke, P. W., & Hayes-Roth, B. (1979). The use of schemata in the acquisition and transfer of knowledge. *Cognitive Psychology, 11,* 83–106.

25. Craik, F. I. M., & Lockhart, R. S. (1972). Levels of processing: A framework for memory research. *Journal of Verbal Learning & Verbal Behavior, 11,* 671–84.

25. Raugh, M. R., & Atkinson, R. C. (1975). a mnemonic method for learning a second-language vocabulary. *Journal of Educational Psychology, 67,* 1–16.

27. Intons-Peterson, M. J., & Fournier, J. (1986). External and internal memory aids: When and how often do we use them? *Journal of Experimental Psychology: General, 116,* 267–80.

28. Bower, G. H. (1970). Organizational factors in memory. *Cognitive Psychology, 1,* 18–46.

29. Doner, 1994.

30. Bower, G. H., & Clark, M. C. (1969). Narrative stories as mediators of serial learning. *Psychonomic Science, 14,* 181–82.

31. Weiten, W., Lloyd, M. A., & Lashley, R. L. (1990). *Psychology applied to modern life: Adjustment in the 90s* (3rd ed.). Pacific Grove, CA: Brooks/Cole, p. 24. Adapted from Bower & Clark, 1969.

32. Paivio, A. (1986). *Mental representations: A dual coding approach.* New York: Oxford University Press.

33. McDaniel, M. A., & Einstein, G. O. (1986). Bizarre imagery as an effective memory aid: The importance of distinctiveness. *Journal of Experimental Psychology: Learning, Memory & Cognition, 12,* 54–65.

34. Crovitz, H. F. (1971). The capacity of memory loci in artificial memory. *Psychonomic Science, 24,* 187–88.

35. Limerick, P. (1997, April 16). In rapid-fire world, pupils listen better than read. *USA Today,* p. 13A.

36. Just, M., Carpenter, P. A., & Masson, M., reported in Meer, J. (1987, March). Reading more, understanding less. *Psychology Today,* p. 12.

37. Carver, R., quoted in Mindell, P. (1995, September 3). 'War and Peace' in 20 minutes? If you care what it says, read [letter]. *New York Times,* sec. 4, p. 2.

38. Robinson, F. P. (1970). *Effective study* (4th ed.). New York: Harper & Row.

39. Pauk, W. (1989). *How to study in college* (4th ed.). Boston: Houghton Mifflin, p. 181.

40. Pauk, 1989, 171.

41. Pauk, 1989, 171–84.

42. Ray, M., & Myers, R. (1986). *Creativity in business.* Garden City, NY: Doubleday, p. 42.

43. Donahue, P. A. (1989). Helping adolescents with shyness: Applying the Japanese Morita therapy in shyness counseling. *International Journal for the Advancement of Counseling, 12,* 323–32.

44. Zastrow, C. (1988). What really causes psychotherapy change? *Journal of Independent Social Work, 2,* 5–16.

45. Braiker, H. B. (1989, December). The power of self-talk. *Psychology Today,* 24.

CHAPTER 6

1. Lindgren, H. C. (1969). *The psychology of college success: A dynamic approach.* New York: Wiley.

2. National Study of Student Learning, study by Hagedorn, L. S., Nora, A., & Pascarella, E., reported in Henry, T. (1995, July 11). Organized lessons stick with students. *USA Today,* p. 1D.

3. Weiten, W., Lloyd, M. A., & Lashley, R. L. (1990). *Psychology applied to modern life: Adjustment in the 90s* (3rd ed.). Pacific Grove, CA: Brooks/Cole, p. 22.

4. Pauk, W. (1989). *How to study in college.* Boston: Houghton-Mifflin, p. 122.

5. Lucas, S. E. (1989). *The art of public speaking.* New York: Random House.

6. Zimbardo, P. (1977). *Shyness: What it is; what to do about it.* Reading, MA: Addison-Wesley, p. 12.

7. Zimbardo, 1977, p. 14.

8. Solomon, J. (1990, May 4). Executives who dread public speaking learn to keep their cool in the spotlight. *Wall Street Journal,* p. B1.

9. Bromage, B. K., & Mayer, R. E. (1986). Quantitative and qualitative effects of repetition on learning from technical text. *Journal of Educational Psychology, 78*(4), 271–78.

10. Bravman, J., quoted in Manuel, D., Salisbury, D., & Rapalus, P. (1995, Summer). What makes an award-winning teacher? *Stanford Observer,* p. 15.

11. Dave, T., quoted in Burdman, P. (1998, April 28). Part-time instructors busy working overtime. *San Francisco Chronicle,* pp. A1, A9.

12. Cage, M. C. (1996, February 9). Learning to teach. *Chronicle of Higher Education,* pp. A19–20.

13. Research by Greenwald, A., & Gillmore, G., reported in Archibold, R. C. (1998, May 24). Give me an 'A' or else. *New York Times,* sec. 4, p. 5.

14. Wilson, R. (1998, January 16). New research casts doubt on value of student evaluations of professors. *Chronicle of Higher Education,* pp. A12–14.

15. Wilson, 1998.

16. Mitchell, L. C. (1998, May 8). Inflation isn't the only thing wrong with grading. *Chronicle of Higher Education,* p. A72.

17. Wiesenfeld, K. (1996, June 17). Making the grade. *Newsweek,* p. 16.

18. Young, J. R. (1997, December 5). Invasion of the laptops: More colleges adopt mandatory computing programs. *Chronicle of Higher Education,* pp. A33–35.

19. Grenier, A., quoted in DeLoughry, T. J. (1993, October 6). Portable computers, light and powerful, gain popularity on college campuses. *Chronicle of Higher Education,* pp. A21, A24.

20. Pepper, J. (1996, August 22). In classroom or home, notebook computers come of age. *New York Times,* B5.

21. Branscum, D. (1997, October 27). Life at high-tech U. *Newsweek,* pp. 78–79.

22. Special advertising section, "The New Presentation Technology: How Business Puts It to Work," *Business Week,* November 10, 1997, pp. 23–34.

23. Henry M. Levin, quoted in Kate Murphy, "Pitfalls vs. Promise in Training by CD-ROM," *New York Times,* May 6, 1996, p. C3.

24. Richard Clark, quoted in Murphy, 1997.

25. Richard C. Hsu and William E. Mitchell, "Books Have Endured for a Reason . . ," *New York Times,* May 25, 1997, sec. 3, p. 12.

26. Jack McGarvey, ". . . But Computers Are Clearly the Future." *New York Times,* May 25, 1997, sec. 3, p. 12.

27. Graziadei, W. D., quoted in Guernsey, L. (1998, February 13). Educators ask whether interactivity works in on-line courses. *Chronicle of Higher Education,* p. A32.

28. Guernsey, L. (1998, March 27). Distance education for the not-so-distant. *Chronicle of Higher Education,* pp. A29–30.

29. Craig, C., quoted in Guernsey, 1998.

30. McCollum, K. (1998, June 12). Posting students' Social Security numbers on Web sites called a threat to privacy. *Chronicle of Higher Education,* p. A28.

CHAPTER 7

1. Walter, T., & Siebert, A. (1990). *Student success* (5th ed.). Fort Worth, TX: Holt, Rinehart and Winston, pp. 96–97.

2. Walter & Siebert, 1990.

3. Starke, M. C. (1993). *Strategies for college success* (2nd ed.). Englewood Cliffs, NJ: Prentice Hall, p. 82.

4. Bok, S. Cited in: Venant, E. (1992, January 7). A nation of cheaters. *San Francisco Chronicle,* p. D3; reprinted from *Los Angeles Times.*

5. Dobrzeniecki, A. Quoted in: Butler, D. (1991, March 2). 73 MIT students guilty of cheating. *Boston Globe,* p. 25.

6. Mason, C. Quoted in: Venant, 1992, p. D4.

7. Josephson, M. Quoted in: Venant, 1992, p. D3.

8. Himmelfarb, S. (1992, June 1). Graduates feel anxious, not just about jobs [letter]. *New York Times,* p. A14.

9. Woodell, M. L. (1991, November 24). Fraud? Imagine you're in the spotlight. *New York Times,* sec. 3, p. 11.

10. Tetzeli, R. (1991, July 1). Business students cheat most. *Fortune,* pp. 14–15.

CHAPTER 8

1. Ellis, M. E. Quoted in Mitchell, J. J. (1997, March 16). 'Soft skills' prized by tech firms. *San Jose Mercury News*, pp. 1E, 3E.
2. Walter, T., & Siebert, A. (1990). *Student success: How to succeed in college and still have time for your friends*. Fort Worth, TX: Holt, Rinehart and Winston, pp. 108–109.
3. Walter & Siebert, 1990, p. 103.
4. Guilford, C., quoted in McCollum, K. (1996, September 20). Web site treats writer's block. *Chronicle of Higher Education*, p. A33.
5. McBride, K. B., & Dickstein, R. (1998, March 20). The Web demands critical reading by students. *Chronicle of Higher Education*, p. B6.
6. Applebome, P. (1997, June 8). On the Internet, term papers are hot items. *New York Times*, sec. 1, pp. 1, 20.
7. De Cesare, L. (1997, June 10). Virtual term papers [letter]. *New York Times*, p. A20.
8. Leland, B., quoted in Applebome, 1997.
9. Dwyer, E. (June 10, 1997). Virtual term papers [letter]. *New York Times*, p. A20.
10. Zimmerman, M. (1997, June 15). How to track down collegiate cyber-cheaters [letter]. *New York Times*, sec. 4, p. 14.
11. Rukeyser, W. L. (June 15, 1997). How to track down collegiate cyber-cheaters [letter]. *New York Times*, sec. 4, p. 14.
12. Rothenberg, D. (1997, August 15). How the Web destroys the quality of students' research papers. *Chronicle of Higher Education*, p. A44.
13. Hecht, B. (1997, February 17). Net loss. *New Republic*, pp. 15–18.
14. Alessandra, T., & Hunsaker, P. (1993). *Communicating at work*. New York: Fireside, p. 169.
15. Wohlmuth, E. (1983). *The overnight guide to public speaking*. Philadelphia: Running Press, p. 119.
16. Wohlmuth, 1983, p. 118.
17. Theibert, P. (1993, August 2). Speechwriters of the world, get lost! *Wall Street Journal*, p. A16.
18. Wohlmuth, 1983, p. 31.
19. Walters, L. (1993). *Secrets of successful speakers: How you can motivate, captivate, and persuade*. New York: McGraw-Hill, p. 203.
20. Alessandra & Hunsaker, 1993, p. 179.
21. Alessandra & Hunsaker, 1993, p. 169.
22. Walters, 1993, p. 32.
23. Malouf, D., cited in Walters, 1993, p. 33.
24. Walters, 1993, p. 36.
25. Walters, 1993, p. 37.
26. Wohlmuth, 1983, p. 133.
27. Robinson, J. R. (1991, November 6). [Letter to editor.] U.S. students memorize, but don't understand. *New York Times*, p. A14.
27. Elder, J. (1991, January 6). A learned response. *New York Times*, sec. 4A, p. 23.

CHAPTER 9

1. Kramer, G. L., & Spencer, R. W. Academic advising. P. 97 in Upcraft, M. L., Gardner, J. N., & Associates (Eds.). (1990). *The freshman year experience: Helping students survive and succeed in college*. San Francisco: Jossey-Bass.
2. Crockett, D. S. Academic advising. Pp. 244–63 in Noel, L., Levitiz, R., & Saluri, D., & Associates (Eds.). (1985). *Increasing student retention*. San Francisco: Jossey-Bass.
3. Higher Education Research Institute, University of California at Los Angeles, survey sponsored by American Council on Education. Reported in: Associated Press (1992, January 13). College freshmen feeling pinch. *San Francisco Chronicle*, p. A3.
4. Kelly, D. (1991, February 19). Students leave in deeper debt. *USA Today*, p. 6D.
5. Rigdon, J. E. (1991, January 3). Student loans weigh down graduates. *Wall Street Journal*, p. B1.
6. Seligman, K. (1992, March 29). More and more college students on '7-year plan'. *San Francisco Examiner*, p. A-1.
7. Anonymous. (1995, April 18). The rich get richer faster [editorial]. *New York Times*, p. A16.
8. *Washington Monthly* (1993, March). Cited in: Ouellete, L. (1993, September/October). Class bias on campus. *Utne Reader*, pp. 19–24.
9. Kelly, 1991.
10. Phillips, M. (1974). *The seven laws of money*. Menlo Park, Calif., and New York: Word Wheel and Random House, p. 41.
11. Phillips, 1974, p. 32.
12. Astin, A. W., Dey, E. L., Korn, W. S. et al. (1991). *The American freshman: National norms for fall 1991*. Los Angeles: Higher Education Research Institute, Graduate School of Education, University of California, Los Angeles.
13. Gottesman, G. (1991). *College survival*. New York: Prentice Hall Press, pp. 13–14.
14. Gottesman, 1991, pp. 196–97.
15. Melia, M. K. (1992, May). Carry-out cash. *American Demographics*, p. 6.
16. Anonymous (1991, February 9). Credit cards become big part of life. *New York Times*, p. 16.
17. Brookes, A. (1994, November 5). Lesson for teen-agers: Facts of credit-card life. *New York Times*, p. 31.
18. Foren, J. (1991, December 1). College students piling on credit card debt. *San Francisco Examiner*, p. E-9.
19. Kutner, L. (1993, August 19). College students with big credit card bills may be learning an economics lesson the hard way. *New York Times*, p. B4.
20. Warner, J. (1992, July 20). It's chic to be cheap: A penny-pincher's primer. *Business Week*, pp. 94–95.
21. Madden, M. (1996, August 5). Colleges tighten belts. *USA Today*, p. 9B; citing report by American Council on Education, *Campus Trends 1996*.
22. Kiplinger's Changing Times (1988). *Success with your money*. Washington, DC: Kiplinger Changing Times, p. 132.
23. Nemko, M. (1992, June 28). A grown-up's guide to financial aid. *This World, San Francisco Chronicle*, pp. 11–12.
24. Manegold, C. S. (1994, September 19). U.S. has high hopes for a revamped student loan program. *New York Times*, p. A10.

CHAPTER 10

1. Hacker, A. (1995, May 11). Who should go to college? *New York Review of Books*, pp. 37–40.
2. Traub, J. (1995) *City on a hill: Testing the American dream at City College*. Reading, MA: Addison-Wesley. Cited in: Hacker, 1995.
3. Hacker, 1995.
4. Hacker, 1995.
5. Howard, D., quoted in McLeod, R. G. (1997, December 26). New rules for marking racial identity. *San Francisco Chronicle*, pp. A1, A21.
6. McLeod, 1997.
7. Cohen, M. N. (1998, April 17). Culture, not race, explains human diversity. *Chronicle of Higher Education*, pp. B4–5.
8. Cohen, 1998.
9. Hill, H. C. (1997, November 7). The importance of a minority perspective in the classroom. *Chronicle of Higher Education*, p. A60.
10. Hill, 1997.
11. Hudson Institute, Workforce 2000, U.S. Bureau of Labor Statistics, in Anonymous (1988, July). Jobs for women in the nineties, *Ms*, p. 77.
12. Naisbitt, J., & Aburdene, P. (1990). *Megatrends 2000*. New York: Morrow, p. 19.
13. Freedberg, L. (1993, November 12). Women outnumber men at college. *San Francisco Chronicle*, pp. A1, A9.
15. Adelman, C., U.S. Department of Education. *Women at thirtysomething*. Cited in: Stipp, D. (1992, September 11). The gender gap. *Wall Street Journal*.
16. Cage, M. C. (1993, March 10). Openly gay students face harassment and physical assaults on some campuses. *Chronicle of Higher Education*, pp. A22–A24.
17. Study by National Gay and Lesbian Task Force, reported in Goldberg, C. (1998, May 31). Acceptance of gay men and lesbians is growing, study says. *New York Times*, sec. 1, p. 15.
18. Freedberg, L. (1992, June 28). The new face of higher education. *This World, San Francisco Chronicle*, p. 9.
19. Beck, B. (1991, November 11). School day for seniors. *Newsweek*, pp. 60–65.
20. Kuemmel, D., quoted in Romell, R. (1997, June 1). Midlife career changes filling classrooms. *San Jose Mercury News*, p. 2PC; reprinted from *Milwaukee Journal Sentinel*.

21. Smeaton, D., quoted in Romell, 1997.
22. Simpson, J. C. (1987, April 3). Campus barrier? Black college students are viewed as victims of a subtle racism. *Wall Street Journal.*
23. Evans, G. (1986, April 30). Black students who attend white colleges face contradictions in their campus life. *Chronicle of Higher Education,* pp. 17–49.
24. Robinson, L. (1998, May 11). 'Hispanics' don't exist. *U.S. News & World Report,* pp. 26–32.
25. Robinson, 1998.
26. Barringer, F. (1991, June 12). Immigration brings new diversity Asian population in the U.S. *New York Times,* pp. A1, D25.
27. Marriott, M. (1992, February 26). Indians turning to tribal colleges for opportunity and cultural values. *New York Times,* p. A13.
28. Desruisseaux, P. (1997, December 12). Foreign enrollment rises slightly at colleges in the United States. *Chronicle of Higher Education,* pp. A42, A44.
29. Kotkin, J. (1993, February 24). Enrolling foreign students will strengthen America's place in the global economy. *Chronicle of Higher Education,* pp. B1–B2.
30. U.S. Census Bureau, reported in Anonymous. (1998, April 10). Immigrant population rising—almost 10% now born elsewhere. *San Francisco Chronicle,* p. A2; reprinted from *Washington Post.*
31. Jaschik, S. (1993, February 3). Backed by 1990 law, people with disabilities press demands on colleges. *Chronicle of Higher Education,* p. A26.
32. Shapiro, J. P. (1993). *No pity: People with disabilities forging a new civil rights movement.* New York: Times Books.
33. Hall, H. (1988, December). Trying on old age. *Psychology Today,* p. 67.
34. Belkin, L. (1992, June 4). In lessons on empathy, doctors become patients. *New York Times,* pp. A1, A13.
35. Jacoby, B. (1989). *The student-as-commuter: Developing a comprehensive institutional response.* Ashe-Eric Higher Education Report 7.
36. Stewart, S. S., & Rue, P. (1983). Commuter students: Definition and distribution. In Stewart, S. S. (Ed.). *Commuter students: Enhancing their educational experiences.* San Francisco: Jossey-Bass.
37. Gardner, L. F. (1994). *Redesigning higher education: Producing dramatic gains in student learning.* ASHE-ERIC Higher Education Report No. 7. Washington, D.C.: George Washington University, School of Education and Human Development.
38. Astin, A. W., et al., study at University of California at Los Angeles. Reported in: Henry, T. (1996, October 14). More in college, fewer graduate. *USA Today,* p. 1D.
39. Tyson, R. (1996, August 16). Travel time: For many, it's a longer, busier road. *USA Today,* p. 8A.
40. Tyson, R. (1996, August 16). Suburbs: Cities replaced as main work destinations. *USA Today,* p. 8A.
41. Nippert-Eng, C. (1996). *Home and work.* Chicago: University of Chicago Press.
42. Shellenbarger, S. (1996, July 17). Making the trip home from work takes more than just a car ride. *Wall Street Journal,* p. B1.
43. Tyson, E. (1996, September 1). If you must drive, consider all costs when buying a car. *San Francisco Examiner,* pp. C-1, C-6.
44. American Automobile Manufacturers Association, cited in: Tyson, E., August 18, 1996.
45. Tyson, E., August 18, 1996.
46. Eldridge, E. (1996, July 19). Thieves hog wild over motorcycles. *USA Today,* p. 1B.
47. Castaneda, L. (1996, July 4). Scooters—easy and economical. *San Francisco Chronicle,* pp. E1, E2.
48. Pam Dixon, *Virtual College* (Princeton, NJ: Peterson's, 1996).
49. Glenn R. Jones, *Cyberschools: An Education Renaissance* (Jones Digital Century, 1997).
50. Joseph B. Walther, quoted in William H. Honon, "Northwestern University Takes a Lead in Using the Internet to Add Sound and Sight to Courses," *New York Times,* May 28, 1997, p. A17.
51. Price, H. B. (1998, May 22). Fortifying the case for diversity and affirmative action. *Chronicle of Higher Education,* pp. B4–B5.

CHAPTER 11

1. Anonymous. (1987, October). The perils of burnout. *Newsweek on Campus.*
2. Lazarus, R. S. (1981, July). Little hassles can be hazardous to health. *Psychology Today,* p. 61.
3. Selye, H. (1974). *Stress without distress.* New York: Lippincott, pp. 28–29.
4. Holmes, T. H., & Rahe, R. H. (1967). The social readjustment rating scale. *Journal of Psychosomatic Research, 11,* 213–18.
5. Selye, 1974, p. 27.
6. Lazarus, R. S., & Forlman, S. (1982). Coping and adaptation. In W. D. Gentry (Ed.). *Handbook of behavioral medicine.* New York: Guilford Press.
7. Hinkle, L. E., Jr. (1987). Stress and disease: The concept after 50 years. *Social Science & Medicine, 25,* 561–66.
8. Kiecolt-Glazer, J., & Glaser, R. (1988). Major life changes, chronic stress, and immunity. *Advances in Biochemical Psychopharmacology, 44,* 217–24.
9. Kiecolt-Glazer, J. et al. (1987) Stress, health, and immunity: Tracking the mind/body connection. Presentation at American Psychological Association meeting, New York, August 1987.
10. Kannel, W. B. (1990). CHD risk factors: A Framingham study update. *Hospital Practice, 25,* 119.
11. Eliot, R., & Breo, D. (1984). *Is it worth dying for?* New York: Bantam Books.
12. McCulloch, A., & O'Brien, L. (1986). The organizational determinants of worker burnout. *Children & Youth Services Review, 8,* 175–90.
13. Girdano, D. A., & Everly, G. S., Jr. (1986). *Controlling stress and tension.* Englewood Cliffs, NJ: Prentice-Hall.
14. Matthews, A. (1993, March 7). The campus crime wave. *New York Times Magazine,* pp. 38–42, 47.
15. Anonymous. (1987, August). Dear diary. *American Health.*
16. Mee, C. L., Jr. (Ed.). (1987). *Managing stress from morning to night.* Alexandria, VA: Time-Life Books.
17. Zajonc, R. B. (1985). Emotion and facial efference: A theory reclaimed. *Science, 228,* 15–21.
18. Adelmann, P. K., & Zajonc, R. B. (1989). Facial efference and the experience of emotion. *Annual Review of Psychology, 40,* 249–80.
19. Zajonc, R. Cited in: Goleman, D. (1989, June 29). Put on a happy face—it really works. *San Francisco Chronicle,* p. C10. Reprinted from *New York Times.*
20. Donahue, P. A. (1989). Helping adolescents with shyness: Applying the Japanese Morita therapy in shyness counselling. *International Journal for the Advancement of Counselling, 12,* 323–32.
21. Zastrow, C. (1988). What really causes psychotherapy change? *Journal of Independent Social Work, 2,* 5–16.
22. Braiker, H. B. (1989, December). The power of self-talk. *Psychology Today,* p. 24.
23. Cousins, N. (1979). *Anatomy of an illness.* New York: Norton.
24. Dillon, K. M., Minchoff, B., & Baker, K. H. (1985–86). Positive emotional states and enhancement of the immune system. *International Journal of Psychiatry in Medicine, 15,* 13–18.
25. Long, P. (1987, October). Laugh and be well? *Psychology Today,* pp. 28–29.
26. Siegel, B. (1986). *Love, medicine, and miracles.* New York: Harper & Row.
27. Reifman, A., & Dunkel-Schetter, C. (1990). Stress, structural social support, and well-being in university students. *Journal of American College Health, 38,* 271–77.
28. Leerhsen, C., et al. (1990, February 5). Unite and conquer. *Newsweek,* pp. 50–55.
29. Snyder, M. (1988). Relaxation. In J. J. Fitzpatrick, R. L., Taunton, & J. Q. Benoliel (Eds.). *Annual review of nursing research, 8,* 111–28. New York: Springer.
30. Benson, H. (1989). Editorial: Hypnosis and the relaxation response. *Gastroenterology, 96,* 1610.
31. Wechsler, H. et al. (1994, December 7). Health and behavioral consequences of binge drinking in college. *Journal of the American Medical Association.*
32. Adler, J., & Rosenberg, D. (1994, December 19). The endless binge. *Newsweek,* pp. 72–73.
33. Center on Addiction and Substance Abuse, Columbia University (1994). *Rethinking rites of passage.* Cited in: Adler & Rosenberg, 1994.
34. Associated Press (1992, September 20). Study finds more drinking at small colleges than large ones. *New York Times,* sec. 1, p. 20.
35. Schuster, C., director National Institute of Drug Abuse. Cited in: Medical Tribune News Service (1991, January 25). High school seniors report less drug use. *San Francisco Chronicle,* p. A12.
36. National Institute of Drug Abuse (1988). *National Household Survey on Drug Abuse: Main findings 1988.* DHHS Pub. No. (ADM)90-1682. Washington, DC: U.S. Department of Health and Human Services.

37. Adler & Rosenberg, 1994.
38. Shedler, J., & Block, J. (1990, May). Adolescent drug use and psychological health. *American Psychologist*, pp. 612–624.
39. Perlman, D. (1990, May 14). Furor over report on teenage drug use. *San Francisco Chronicle*, p. A10.
40. Johnson, B. A. (1990). Psychopharmacological effects of cannabis. *British Journal of Hospital Medicine, 43*, 114–16.
41. Jones, R. T. (1980). Human effects: An overview. Pp. 54–80 in: R. C. Peterson (Ed.). *Marijuana research findings: 1980*. Rockville, MD: National Institute on Drug Abuse.
42. Maisto, S. A., Galizio, M., & Connors, G. J. (1991). *Drug use and misuse*. Fort Worth, TX: Holt, Rinehart and Winston.
43. McGlothin, W. H., & West, L. J. (1968). The marihuana problem: An overview. *American Journal of Psychiatry, 125*, 370–78.
44. Flynn, J. C. (1991). *Cocaine: An in-depth look at the facts, science, history and future of the world's most addictive drug*. New York: Carol Publishing Group, p. 14.
45. Chychula, N. M., & Okore, C. (1990). The cocaine epidemic: A comprehensive review of use, abuse and dependence. *Nurse Practitioner, 15*(7), 31–39.
46. Goleman, D. (1992, March 31). As addiction medicine gains, experts debate what it should cover. *New York Times*, p. B6.
47. Walters, L. S. (1990, June 18). Teen gambling is the latest addiction of choice. *San Francisco Chronicle*, p. B5; reprinted from *Christian Science Monitor*.
48. Associated Press. (1989, June 23). 1 in 20 college students are compulsive gamblers—survey. *Reno Gazette-Journal*, p. 6D.
49. Goleman, D. (1991, July 17). Reining in a compulsion to spend. *New York Times*, pp. B1, B8.
50. Wolf, N. (1991). *The beauty myth: How images of beauty are used against women*. New York: William Morrow, p. 184.
51. Britton, A. G. (1988). Thin is out, fit is in. *American Health, 7*, 66–71.
52. Hutchinson, M. (1985). *Transforming body image: Learning to love the body you have*. Freedom, CA: Crossing Press.
53. Anonymous (1991). The easy road to fitness. *University of California, Berkeley Wellness Letter, 7*, 6.
54. Tucker, L. A., Cole, G. E., & Friedman, G. M. (1986). Physical fitness: A buffer against stress. *Perceptual & Motor Skills, 63*, 955–61.
55. Sime, W. E. (1984). Psychological benefits of exercise. *Advances, 1*, 15–29.
56. Roth, D. L., & Holmes, D. S. (1987). Influence of aerobic exercise training and relaxation training on physical and psychological health following stressful life events. *Psychosomatic Medicine, 49*, 355–65.
57. Rippe, J. M. Quoted in: Cardozo, C. (1990, September). The new feel-great prescription: Even a few minutes of exercise can enhance creativity, self-esteem, and chase away the blues. *Self*, p. 124.
58. Greist, J. H., Eischens, R. R. et al. (1978). Running out of depression. *The Physician & Sportsmedicine, 6*(12), 49–56.
59. Monahan, T. (1986). Exercise and depression: Swapping sweat for serenity? *The Physician & Sportsmedicine, 14*(9), 192–97.
60. Morgan, W. P., & O'Connor, P. J. (1987). Exercise and mental health. In: Dishman, R. K. (Ed.). *Exercise adherence*. Champaign, IL: Human Kinetics Publishers.
61. Farmer, M. E., Locke, B. Z., Moscicki, E. K. et al. (1988). Physical activity and depressive symptoms: The NHANES I epidemiologic follow-up study. *American Journal of Epidemiology, 128*, 1340–51.
62. Thayer, R. E. (1988, October). Energy walks. *Psychology Today*, 12–13.
63. Thayer, R. E. (1987). Energy, tiredness, and tension effects of a sugar snack versus moderate exercise. *Journal of Personality & Social Psychology, 52*(1), 119–25.
64. Mott, P. (1990, October 7). Mental gymnastics. *Los Angeles Times*, pp. E1, E18–E19.
65. Gondola, J. C. Cited in: Cardozo, 1990, p. 124.
66. Martin, J. E., Dubbert, P. M., & Cushman, W. C. (1990). Controlled trial of aerobic exercise in hypertension. *Circulation, 81*, 1560–67.
67. Kelemen, M. H., Effron, M. B., Valenti, S. A. et al. (1990). Exercise training combined with antihypertensive drug therapy. *Journal of the American Medical Association, 263*, 2766–71.
68. Somers, V. Cited in: Associated Press. (1991, June 11). Study finds exercise alone can reduce blood pressure. *New York Times*, p. A6.
69. Hansen, H. S. et al. Cited in: Medicine Tribune News Service. (1991, September 25). Exercise lowers children's blood pressure. *San Francisco Chronicle*, p. D6.
70. Paffenbarger, R. S., Hyde, R. T., Wing, W. L. et al. (1986). Physical activity, all-cause mortality, and longevity among college alumni. *New England Journal of Medicine, 314*, 605–613.
71. Lee, I.-M., Paffenbarger, J. Jr., & Hsieh, C. (1991). Physical activity and risk of developing colorectal cancer among college alumni. *Journal of the National Cancer Institute, 83*, 1324–29.
72. Kirkpatrick, M. K., Edwards, R. N., & Finch, N. (1991). Assessment and prevention of osteoporosis through use of a client self-reporting tool. *Nurse Practitioner, 16*(7), 16–26.
73. Ornstein, R., & Sobel, D. (1989). *Healthy pleasures*. Reading, MA: Addison-Wesley, p. 103.
74. Clark, N. (1990). *Sports nutrition guidebook*. Champaign, IL: Leisure Press.
75. Applegate, L. (1991). *Power foods: High-performance nutrition for high-performance people*. Emmaus, PA: Rodale.
76. Applegate, L. (1991). Fast-track snacks. *Men's Health, 6*, 40–41.
77. Dinges, D. F., & Broughton, R. J. (Eds.) (1989). *Sleep and alertness: Chronobiological, behavioral, and medical aspects of napping*. New York: Raven Press.
78. Carlinsky, D. (1990, March 14). Not everyone needs eight-hour slumber. *San Francisco Chronicle*, pp. B3–B4.
79. Kates, W. (1990, March 30). America is not getting enough sleep. *San Francisco Chronicle*, p. B3.
80. Mass, J. Cited in: Kates, 1990, p. B3.
81. Johnson, L. C. (1982). Sleep deprivation and performance. In W. B. Webb (Ed.). *Biological rhythms, sleep and performance*. New York: Wiley.
82. Rogers, A. (1998, August 24). Good medicine on the Web. *Newsweek*, pp. 60–61.

CHAPTER 12

1. Ishii-Kuntz, M. (1990). Social interaction and psychological well-being: Comparison across stages of adulthood. *International Journal of Aging & Human Development, 30*(1), 15–36.
2. Claes, M. E. (1992). Friendship and personal adjustment during adolescence. *Journal of Adolescence, 15*(1), 39–55.
3. Stein, J. (Ed.) (1973). *The Random House dictionary of the English language*. New York: Random House.
4. Schaefer, M. T., & Olson, D. H. (1981). Assessing intimacy: The pair inventory. *Journal of Marital & Family Therapy, 7*, 47–60.
5. Rice, F. P. (1989). *Human sexuality*. Dubuque, IA: Wm. C. Brown.
6. Shea, J. A., & Adams, G. R. (1984). Correlates of male and female romantic attachments: A path analysis study. *Journal of Youth & Adolescence, 13*, 27–44.
7. Rubin, L. (1973). *Liking and loving*. New York: Holt, Rinehart & Winston.
8. Hatfield, E., & Sprecher, S. (1986). *Mirror, mirror . . . The importance of looks in everyday life*. Albany: State University of New York Press.
9. Dutton, D., & Aron, A. (1974). Some evidence for heightened sexual attraction under conditions of high anxiety. *Journal of Personality & Social Psychology, 30*, 510–17.
10. Hatfield, E., & Walster, G. W. (1978). *A new look at love*. Reading, MA: Addison-Wesley.
11. Rindfuss, R. Cited in: Larson, J. (1991, November). Cohabitation is a premarital step. *American Demographics*, 20–21.
12. Viorst, J. (1979). Just because I'm married, does it mean I'm going steady? Pp. 283–89 in: B. J. Wishart & L. C. Reichman (Eds.). *Modern sociological issues*. New York: Macmillan.
13. Saxton, L. (1977). *The individual, marriage, and the family* (3rd ed.). Belmont, CA: Wadsworth.
14. Phillips, D. (1980). *How to fall out of love*. New York: Fawcett.
15. Weiten, W., Lloyd, M. A., & Lashley, R. L. (1991). *Psychology applied to modern life: Adjustment in the 90s* (3rd ed.). Pacific Grove: CA: Brooks/Cole.
16. Weiten, Lloyd, & Lashley, 1991, p. 179.
17. Burns, D. D. (1989). *The feeling good handbook*. New York: Plume.
18. Burns, 1989, p. 371.
19. Beck, A. (1989). *Love is never enough*. New York: HarperPerennial.
20. Burns, 1989, p. 379.
21. Crooks, R., & Baur, K. (1990). *Our sexuality* (4th ed.). Redwood City, CA: Benjamin/Cummings, p. 268.
22. Alberti, R. E., & Emmons, M. L. (1970). *Your perfect right: A guide to assertive behavior*. San Luis Obispo, CA: Impact.

23. Alberti, R. E., & Emmons, M. L. (1975). *Stand up, speak out, talk back!* New York: Pocket.

24. Jakubowski-Spector, P. (1973). Facilitating the growth of women through assertive training. *Counseling Psychologist, 4,* 75–86.

25. Weiten, Lloyd, & Lashley, 1989.

26. Horner, M. J. Toward an understanding of achievement related conflicts in women. *Journal of Social Issues, 28,* 157–76.

27. Freundl, P. C. (1981, August). Influence of sex and status variables on perceptions of assertiveness. Paper presented at meeting of the American Psychological Association, Los Angeles.

28. Smye, M. D., & Wine, J. D. (1980). A comparison of female and male adolescents' social behaviors and cognitions: A challenge to the assertiveness literature. *Sex Roles, 6,* 213–30.

29. Weiten, Lloyd, & Lashley, 1991.

30. Bordo, S. (1998, May 1). Sexual harassment is about bullying, not sex. *Chronicle of Higher Education,* p. B6.

31. U.S. Supreme Court, *Meritor Savings Bank v. Vinson.* Cited in: Goldstein, L. (1991, November). Hands off at work. *Self,* pp. 110–13.

32. U.S. Merit Systems Protection Board. Cited in: Deutschman, A. (1991, November 4). Dealing with sexual harassment. *Fortune,* pp. 145–48.

33. Anonymous. (1991, October 12). Proving harassment is tough in court, lawyers say. *San Francisco Chronicle,* p. C10; reprinted from *New York Times.*

34. Karl, T. Cited in: O'Toole, K. (1991, November-December). How to handle harassment. *Stanford Observer,* p. 8.

35. U.S. Merit Systems Protection Board, 1991.

36. Michael, R. T., Gagnon, J. H., Laumann, O., & Kolata, G. (1997). *Sex in America: A definitive survey.* New York: Warner.

37. Anonymous. (1989, April). Offering resistance: How most people respond to rape. *Psychology Today,* p. 13.

38. Stanford Rape Education Project. Cited in: Anonymous. (1991, January-February). Men, women interpret sexual cues differently. *Stanford Observer,* p. 15.

39. National Victim Center. Cited in: Anonymous. (1992, May 4). Unsettling report on epidemic of rape. *Time,* p. 15.

40. Cells, W. 3d. (1991, January 2). Growing talk of date rape separates sex from assault. *New York Times,* pp. A1, B7.

41. Cells, 1991, p. B7.

42. Stanford Rape Education Project, 1991.

43. Coffe, J. (1993, January/February). To escape rape. *American Health,* p. 18.

44. Schroepfer, L. (1992, November). When the victim is a woman. *American Health,* p. 20.

45. Gross, J. (1991, May 28). Even the victim can be slow to recognize rape. *New York Times,* p. A6.

46. Global AIDS Policy Coalition, United Nations AIDS Program, reported in: Perlman, D. (1996, July 5). A bit less gloom in AIDS battle. *San Francisco Chronicle,* pp. A1, A17.

47. National Center for Health Statistics, reported in Russell, S. (1997, September 12). AIDS death rates fall among younger adults. *San Francisco Chronicle,* pp. A1, A17.

48. Russell, 1997.

49. Blattner, W. A. (1991). HIV epidemiology: past, present, and future. *Faseb Journal, 5,* 2340 - 48.

50. Giesecke, J., Scalia-Tomba, G., Hakansson, C. et al. (1990). Incubation time of AIDS: Progression of disease in a cohort of HIV-infected homo- and bisexual men with known dates of infection. *Scandinavian Journal of Infectious Diseases, 22,* 407–411.

51. Peyser, M. (1997, September 29). A deadly dance. *Newsweek,* pp. 76–77.

52. Krieger, L. M. (1998, January 4). Many no longer see unsafe sex as taboo. *San Francisco Examiner,* pp. D-1, D-3.

53. Painter, K. (1996, July 10). Push to abstain doesn't lower teen sex rates. *USA Today,* 1D.

54. Phillips, L. (1996, July 20). How teens handle the HIV virus. *San Francisco Chronicle,* p. A23.

55. Snell, J. J., Supran, E. M., Esparza, J. et al. (1990). World Health Organization quality assessment programme on HIV testing. *AIDS, 4,* 803–806.

56. Fisher, J. D. Cited in: Adler, J., Wright, L., McCormick, J. et al. (1991, December 9). Safer sex. *Newsweek,* pp. 52–56.

57. Montefiore, S. S. (1992, October). Love, lies and fear in the plague years . . . *Psychology Today,* pp. 30–35.

58. Hatcher, R., Guest, F., Stewart, F. et al. (1990). *Contraceptive technology: 1990–1992.* (15th ed.). New York: Irvington.

59. Forrest, J. D. (1987). Has she or hasn't she? U.S. women's experience with contraception. *Family Planning Perspectives, 19,* 133.

60. Workman, B. (1991, May 2). Sex at Stanford not always safe, poll finds. *San Francisco Chronicle,* p. A20.

61. Ullman, E. H. (1998, September 5). The Web as community [letter]. *New York Times,* p. A24.

62. Carnegie Mellon study, reported in: Harmon, A. (1998, August 30). Sad, lonely world discovered in cyberspace. *New York Times,* sec. 1, pp. 1, 22.

CHAPTER 13

1. Leider, D. (1988, July/August). Purposeful work. *Utne Reader,* p. 52; excerpted from *On Purpose: A Journal About New Lifestyles & Workstyles,* Winter 1986.

2. Dominguez, J., & Robin, V. (1992). *Your money or your life.* Bergenfield, NJ: Penguin.

3. Needleman, J. (1991). *Money and the meaning of life.* New York: Doubleday.

4. Needleman, J. Quoted in: Carman, J. (1990, June 26). Talking about money on PBS. *San Francisco Chronicle,* p. E1.

5. Gallup Organization October 1989 survey for National Occupational Information Coordinating Committee. Reported in: Associated Press (1990, January 12). Working at the wrong job. *San Francisco Chronicle,* p. C1.

6. Falvey, J. (1986). *After college: The business of getting jobs.* Charlotte, VT: Williamson.

7. Yate, M. J. Reported in: McIntosh, C. (1991, May). Giving good answers to tough questions. *McCall's,* pp. 38, 40.

8. Falvey, 1986.

9. McGregor, J., doctoral dissertation, Florida State University, Tallahassee. Reported in: Associated Press. (1992, July 21). TV gives kids false view of working, study says. *San Francisco Chronicle,* p. D5.

10. Lieberman Research Inc. 1990 mail poll of 2320 people for *Sports Illustrated.* Reported in: USA Snapshots. (1991, November 8). I wish I was a . . . *USA Today,* p. 1D.

11. Falvey, 1986.

12. Shertzer, B. (1985). *Career planning* (3rd ed.). Boston: Houghton Mifflin.

13. Deci, E. L., & Flaste, R. (1995). *Why we do what we do: The dynamics of personal autonomy.* New York: Grosset/Putnam.

14. Holland, J. (1975). *Vocational preference Inventory.* Palo Alto, CA. Consulting Psychologists Press.

15. Bolles, R. N. Quoted in: Rubin, S. (1994, February 24). How to open your job 'parachute' after college. *San Francisco Chronicle,* p. E9.

16. Bolles, R. N. (1994). *What color is your parachute?* Berkeley, CA: Ten Speed Press.

17. Bolles, R. N. (1990). *The 1990 quick job-hunting (and career-changing) map: How to create a picture of your ideal job or next career.* Berkeley, CA: Ten Speed Press.

18. Bolles, R. N. Cited in: Minton, T. (January 25, 1991). Job-hunting requires eyes and ears of friends. *San Francisco Chronicle,* p. D5.

19. Study by Stanford and Columbia universities. Reported in Koss-Feder, L. (1997, January 5). In a job hunt, it often *is* whom you know. *New York Times,* sec. 3, p. 8.

20. Popp, A. L. (1997, January 26). Getting a foot in the door: The fruits of networking [letter]. *New York Times,* sec. 3, p. 38.

21. Steinkirchner, K. Reported in Anonymous (1994, August). The 'N' word. *Psychology Today,* p. 13.

22. Judge, L. Quoted in Ross, S. (1997, June 15). Don't hide your light under a bushel: Network. *San Jose Mercury News,* p. 2PC.

23. Falvey, 1986.

24. Anonymous (1996, July 18). For students, internships becoming rite of passage. *San Francisco Chronicle,* p. A7; reprinted from *Los Angeles Times.*

25. Pender, K. (1994, May 16). Jobseekers urged to pack lots of 'keywords' into résumés. *San Francisco Chronicle,* pp. B1, B4.

26. Howe, K. (1992, September 19). Firm turns hiring into a science. *San Francisco Chronicle,* pp. B1, B2.

27. Bulkeley, W. M. (1992, June 23). Employers use software to track résumés. *Wall Street Journal,* p. B6.

28. Kennedy, J. L., & Morrow, T. J. (1994). *Electronic résumé revolution: Create a winning résumé for the new world of job seeking.* New York: Wiley.

29. Palladino, B. (1992, Winter). Job hunting online. *Online Access,* pp. 20–23.

30. Anonymous. (1992, October). Online information. *PC Today,* p. 41.

31. Strauss, J. (1993, October 17). Online database helps job seekers. *San Francisco Sunday Examiner & Chronicle,* Help wanted section, p. 29.

32. Murray, K. (1994, January 2). Plug in. Log on. Find a job. *New York Times,* sec. 3, p. 23.

33. Mannix, M. (1992, October 26). Writing a computer-friendly résumé. *U.S. News & World Report,* pp. 90–93.

34. Bulkeley, W. M. (1992, June 16). Job-hunters turn to software for an edge. *Wall Street Journal,* p. B13.

35. Anonymous. (1992, June). Pounding the pavement. *PC Novice,* p. 10.

36. Anonymous. (1993, September 13). Personal: Individual software ships ResumeMaker with career planning. *EDGE: Work-Group Computing Report,* p. 3.

37. Mossberg, W. S. (1994, May 5). Four programs to ease PC users into a job search. *Wall Street Journal,* p. B1.

38. Kennedy, J. L., & Morrow, T. J. (1994). *Electronic job search revolution: Win with the new technology that's reshaping today's job market.* New York: Wiley.

39. Bennett, H., & McFadden, C. (1993, October 17). How to stand out in a crowd. *San Francisco Sunday Examiner & Chronicle,* help wanted section, p. 29.

40. Bolles. Quoted in: Rubin, 1994.

41. Messmer, M., quoted in Honesty counts in job interview. (1997, July-August). *The Futurist,* p. 49.

42. Mullins, T., reported in How to land a job. (1994, September/October). *Psychology Today,* pp. 12–13.

43. Messmer, M. (1995). *Job hunting for dummies.* Foster City, CA: IDG Books, p. 307.

44. Gardner, J. W. 1991 commencement address, Stanford University, June 16, 1991. Quoted in: Gardner, J. W. (1991, May-June). You are what you commit to achieve. *Stanford Observer,* pp. 10–11.

45. Greene, R. (1998, August 20.) Students opting for low-tech majors. *San Francisco Chronicle,* p. D3.

Sources & Credits

CHAP. 1: **Prac Expl #1.3** adapted from Nowicki-Strickland Scale and results from Nowicki, S. Jr. & Strickland, B. R. (1973, February). A locus of control scale for children. *Journal of Consulting & Clinical Psychology, 40*(1), 148–54. Copyright (C) 1973 by the American Psychological Association. Adapted by permission. **Panel 1.1** adapted from McGinnis, A. L. (1990). *The power of optimism.* San Francisco: Harper & Row, p. xiv. CHAP. 2: **Prac Expl #2.1** adapted from "Modality Inventory" by Ducharme, A., & Watford, L., Middle Grades Department, Valdosta State University, Valdosta, GA 31698. Reprinted with the kind permission of Dr. Adele Ducharme and Dr. Luck Watford. **Pers Expl. #2.2** adapted from Adams, J. L. (1974). *Conceptual blockbusting.* Stanford, CA: Stanford Alumni Association (The Portable Stanford), p. 106. CHAP. 3: Chapter adapted from Williams, B. K., Sawyer, S. C., & Hutchinson, S. E. (1995). *Using information technology: A practical introduction to computers & communications.* Burr Ridge, IL: Irwin. Used with permission of Richard D. Irwin, a Times Mirror Higher Education Group, Inc., company. **Panel 3.1** adapted from Robinson, P. (1997, September 14). There are many ways to pinch pennies on PCs. *San Jose Mercury News,* p. 2F. Copyright San Jose Mercury News. Reprinted by permission. All rights reserved. **Panel 3.12** from Williams, Richard. (1993, April 10). On the hunt for a used computer. *The Globe & Mail* (Toronto), p. B13. **Pages 63–77** adapted from Williams, B. K., Sawyer, S. C., & Hutchinson, S. E. (1999). *Using information technology: A practical introduction to computers & communications,* 3rd ed. Burr Ridge, IL: Irwin/McGraw-Hill. CHAP. 4: **Panel 4.7** adapted from box from Sapadin, L. (1997). *It's about time.* New York: Penguin. Reported in Peterson, K. S. (1997, July 22). Helping procrastinators get to it. *USA Today,* p. 7D. Copyright 1997, USA TODAY. Reprinted with permission. **Panel 4.8** based on data from Wechsler, H., & McFadden, M. (1979). Drinking among college students in New England. *Journal of Studies in Alcohol, 40,* 969–96; Wechsler, H., & Isaac, N. (1991). Alcohol and the college freshman: "Binge" drinking and associated problems. Washington, DC: AAA Foundation for Traffic Safety; Wechsler, H., & Isaac, N. (1992). "Binge" drinkers at Massachusetts colleges: Prevalance, drinking style, time trends, and associated problems. *Journal of the American Medical Association, 267,* 2929–31. **Pers Expl #4.8** from box from Belluck, P. (1996, December 1). The symptoms of Internet addiction. *New York Times,* sec. 4, p. 5. From Young, K. S., Department of Psychology, University of Pittsburgh, Bradford, PA, in *University of Pittsburgh Research Review,* 1996. Copyright (c) 1997 by The New York Times. Reprinted by permission. CHAP. 5: **Pers Expl #5.1** adapted from Weintraub, P. (1992, March). Total recall. *American Health,* pp. 77–78. American Health (c) 1992 by Pamela Weintraub. **Panel 5.1** from Weiten, W. (1989). *Psychology: Themes and variations.* Pacific Grove, CA: Brooks/Cole, p. 254. Used with permission. Based on material from D. van Guilford, Van Nostrand, 1939. **Panel 5.2** adapted from Livermore, B. (1992, November). Four steps to remembering names. *Self,* p. 50; and Crook, T., with Allison, C. (1992, July). The art of remembering names. *Reader's Digest,* pp. 71–74, from *How to remember names,* copyright (c) 1992 by Thomas Crook and Christine Allison, published by HarperCollins, New York, NY 10022. **Page 130,** material beginning "A Rustler . . .; from Weiten, W., Lloyd, M. A., & Lashley, R. L. (1990). *Psychology applied to modern life: Adjustment in the 90s* (3rd ed.). Pacific Grove, CA: Brooks/Cole, p. 24. Adapted from Bower, G. H., & Clark, M. C. (1969). Narrative stories as mediators of social learning. *Psychonomic Science, 14,* 181–82. Copyright (c) 1969 by the Psychonomic Society. Adapted by permission of the Psychonomic Society. **Prac Expl #5.2** adapted from Cortina, J., Elder, J., & Gonnet, K. (1992). *Comprehending college textbooks: Steps to understanding and remembering what you read* (2nd ed.). New York: McGraw-Hill, pp. 3–4. By permission of McGraw-Hill. **Panel 5.3** reproduced from Weeks, J. R. (1992). *Population: An introduction to concepts and issues* (5th ed.). Belmont, CA: Wadsworth. **Panel 5.4,** page reproduced from Biagi, S. (1994). *Media/Impact: An introduction to mass media,* updated second edition. Belmont, CA: Wadsworth, p. 180. CHAP. 6: **Prac Expl #6.1** adapted from "Modality Inventory" by Ducharme, A., & Watford, L., Middle Grades Department, Valdosta State University, Valdosta, GA 31698. Reprinted with the kind permission of Dr. Adele Ducharme and Dr. Luck Watford. **Panel 6.1** adapted from Lindgren, H. C. (1969). *The psychology of college success: A dynamic approach.* New York: Wiley. CHAP. 8: **Panel 8.3 and Panel 8.7** adapted from from Williams, B. K., Sawyer, S. C., & Hutchinson, S. E. (1999). *Using information technology: A practical introduction to computers & communications,* 3rd ed. Burr Ridge, IL: Irwin/ McGraw-Hill. CHAP. 9: **Panel 9.1** courtesy Genesee Community College. **Panel 9.3** adapted from San Jose State University Police Department (1989). *Safety and security at San Jose State.* San Jose, CA: San Jose State University, Police Department, Investigations/Crime Prevention Unit. CHAP. 10: **Pers Expl #10.1,** The Quick Discrimination Index (QDI), is copyrighted by Joseph G. Ponterotto, Ph.D. No further reproduction or photocopying of this instrument is permitted without the written permission of Dr. Ponterotto. If you are interested in using this instrument for any purpose, write to Joseph G. Ponterotto, Ph.D. (at the Division of Psychological and Educational Services, Fordham University at Lincoln Center, Room 1008, 113 West 60th Street, New York, NY 10023-7478) and request the "User Permission Form," the QDI itself, and the latest reliability and validity information. CHAP. 11: Portions of chapter adapted from Williams, B. K., & Knight, S. M. (1994). *Healthy for life: Wellness and the art of living* (Pacific Grove, CA: Brooks/Cole), especially Unit 2. Used with permission. **Prac Expl #11.1** from Mullen, Cathleen, & Costello, Gerald. (1981). *Health awareness through self-discovery.* Edina, MN: Burgess International Group. **Panel 11.2** from Benson, H. (1989). Editorial: Hypnosis and the relaxation response. *Gastroenterology, 96,* 1610. **Pers Expl #11.2,** Michigan Alcoholism Screening Test, adapted from Selzer, M. L. (1971). The M-A-S-T. *American Journal of Psychiatry, 127,* 1653. Copyright 1971, the American Psychiatric Association. Reprinted by permission. **Pers Expl #11.4** reprinted from American Cancer Society (1989). *Eating smart,* 85-250M, Rev. 3/93. No. 2942. Courtesy of the American Cancer Society, Inc., and its Minnesota Division, 800-ACS-2345. CHAP. 12: Portions of chapter adapted from Williams, B. K., & Knight, S. M. (1994). *Healthy for life: Wellness and the art of living* (Pacific Grove, CA: Brooks/Cole), especially Units 8, 9, 11. Used by permission. **Pers Expl #12.1** from Sternberg, R. J., & Soriano, L. J. (1984). Styles of conflict resolution. *Journal of Personality & Social Psychology, 47,* 115–26; Weiten, W., Lloyd, M. A., & Lashley, R. L. (1991). *Psychology applied to modern life: Adjustment in the 90s* (3rd ed.). Pacific Grove: CA: Brooks/Cole; Williams, B. K., & Knight, S. M. (1994). *Healthy for life: Wellness and the art of living* (Pacific Grove, CA: Brooks/Cole), pp. 8.36–8.39. **Pers Expl #12.2** from Lazarus, A. A. (1971). Assertiveness questionnaire, in *Behavior theory and beyond.* New York: McGraw-Hill. Reproduced with permission of McGraw-Hill. **Panel 12.1** adapted from: Commission on the Status of Women. (1991). *How to create a workplace free of sexual harassment.* San Francisco: Commission on the Status of Women; Karl, T., cited in: O'Toole, K. (1991, November-December). How to handle harassment. *Stanford Observer,* p. 8; Goldstein, L. (1991, November). Hands off at work. *Self,* pp. 110–12. **Panel 12.2** from Williams, B. K., & Knight, S. M. (1994). *Healthy for life: Wellness and the art of living.* Pacific Grove, CA: Brooks/Cole, pp. 9.8–9.9. Used with permission. Based on data from Centers for Disease Control (1990). *Contraceptive options: Increasing your awareness.* Washington, DC: NAACOG. Hatcher, R., Guest, F., Stewart, F. et al. (1990). *Contraceptive technology, 1990–1992.* New York: Irvington. Leads from the MMWR (1988). Condoms for prevention of sexually transmitted diseases. *Journal of the American Medical Association, 259,* 1925–27. Harlap, S., Kost, K., & Forrest, D. (1991). *Preventing pregnancy, protecting health: A new look at birth control choices in the United States.* New York: Alan Guttmacher Institute. Anonymous (1991, December). Deconstructing the condom. *Self,* pp. 122–23. Consumers Union (1989, March). Can you rely on condoms? *Consumer Reports,* pp. 135–41. Consumers Union (1995, May). How reliable are condoms? *Consumer Reports,* pp. 320–25. **Panel 12.3** artwork reproduced with the permission of The Alan Guttmacher Institute from Kathryn Kost, Jacqueline Darroch Forrest, and Susan Harlap. (1991, March/ April). Comparing the health risks and benefits of contraceptive choices. *Family Planning Perspectives, 23*(2), 54–61, table 1. CHAP. 13: **Prac Expl #13.1** adapted and reproduced by special permission of the Publisher, Psychological Assessment Resources Inc., Odessa, FL 33556, from the *Self-Directed Search Assessment Booklet* by John L. Holland, Ph.D. Copyright 1970, 1977, 1985, 1990, 1994 by PAR, Inc. Further reproduction is prohibited without permission from PAR, Inc. The Self-Directed Search materials are available for purchase through PAR, Inc. by calling 1-800-331-8378. **Panel 13.1** from Falvey, J. (1986). *After college: The business of getting jobs.* Charlotte, VT: Williamson Publishing, p. 37. **Panel 13.3** from Pender, K. (1994, May 16). Résumé dos and don'ts. *San Francisco Chronicle,* p. B4. © San Francisco Chronicle. Reprinted by permission. **Panel 13.5** from Williams, B. K., Sawyer, S. C., & Hutchinson, S. E. (1999). *Using information technology: A practical introduction to computers & communications,* 3rd ed. Burr Ridge, IL: Irwin/ McGraw-Hill.

Photo Sources & Credits

Photos on following pages by Michael Garrett, Genesee Community College: 7, 13, 16, 25, 39, 40, 44, 53, 63, 91, 110, 114, 120, 122, 130, 138, 141, 142, 157, 162, 165, 174, 190, 194, 203, 206, 211, 213, 114, 217, 240, 253, 260, 261, 265, 280, 282, 284, 292, 294, 306, 313, 325, 338, 343, 345, 367, 374. *Photos on following pages from PhotoDisc, Inc.:* 3, 5, 15, 20, 22, 26, 29, 30, 31, 34, 35, 37, 42, 51, 54, 55, 65, 67, 71, 72, 75, 77, 78, 81, 82, 84, 86, 102, 103 (both), 104, 105, 116, 117, 125, 128, 132, 134, 144, 149, 155, 156, 160, 167, 168, 176, 185, 187, 188, 189, 193, 197, 218, 230, 237, 239, 242, 244, 251, 257, 269, 277, 278, 279, 289, 295, 299, 304, 312, 316, 318, 319, 320, 321, 327, 328, 337, 340, 357, 365, 368, 370, 380, 382, 384. Images copyright 1998 PhotoDisc, Inc.

Glossary/Index

browser, you can easily return to those pages in a future session, 70

penalties for cheating and, 206
on term papers, 212–214
Graduate school, 368, 370
Grammar, 214, 232
Grants are gifts of money, 283
Guaranteed Student Loans, 284
Guessing strategies, 196
Guided imagery is a procedure in which you essentially daydream an image or desired change, anticipating that your body will respond as if the image were real, 319
Guiding words are common words that instruct you in the tasks you are to accomplish in your essay-question answer, 199–200

Handbooks, 221, 223
Handouts, 186
Happiness, 15, 83, 268
Hassles are simply frustrating irritants, 313
Hasty generalization, 42
Health
diet and, 330–332
energy balance and, 327–328
exercise and, 329
habit patterns and, 312
sleep and, 333
stress and, 314
weight and, 327–328
Health insurance, 281
Health service, 261
Hepatitis B, 353
Herpes, 353
Higher education. *See also* College
fears about, 8, 10–12
happiness and, 15, 268
importance of staying power in, 6–7
income level and, 14, 268
life goals and, 22–24
personal development and, 14–15
High school
college compared to, 5–6
qualifications of teachers in, 173–174
Hispanic Americans, 302
History list records the Web pages you have viewed within a specified time period, 70
HIV (human immunodeficiency virus) is the virus causing AIDS. It brings about a variety of ills, the most important of which is the breakdown of the immune system, which leads to the development of certain infections and cancers, 352
testing for, 355
Holmes-Rahe Life Events Scale, 314
Homepage, or welcome page, is the main page or first screen you see when you access a Web site, 69
Homework. *See also* Study
preparedness for lectures and, 160–161, 164, 165
scheduling time for, 101
Homophobia is fear of, or resistance to,

the idea of homosexuality or of homosexuals, 298
Homosexuals, 298
Honesty, academic, 203–207
Hope, 317
Hopelessness, 343
Housing
expense of, 278, 306
on-campus, 266
Housing office is a campus office to help students find housing either on or off campus, 264
How to Fall Out of Love (Phillips), 340
How to Remember Names (Crook), 129
Human immunodeficiency virus. *See* HIV
Human papilloma virus (HPV), 353
Humor, 317
Hyperlinks, 70
Hypertension, 125
Hypertext is a system in which documents scattered across many Internet sites are directly linked, so that a word or phrase in one document becomes a connection to a document in a different place, 68, 238
Hypertext markup language (HTML) is the set of special instructions, called tags or markups, that are used to specify links to other documents, 68
Hypertext transfer protocol–which is expressed as http://–is the communications standard (protocol) used to transfer information on the Web, 68

IBM-compatible computers, 54–55
Idea cards, 225
Immediate perceptual memory is defined as a reflex memory in which an impression is immediately replaced by a new one, 122
Immediate reviewing, 145
Immigrants, 303
Implantation is the act in which the fertilized human egg burrows into the lining of the uterus, 358
Implant contraceptives, 361
Income indicates where your money comes from, 269
budgeting, 272–276
college education and, 14, 268
paying attention to, 269, 270, 271
sources of, 269
Incubation technique, 47
Index is an alphabetically arranged list of names and subjects that appear in the text, giving the page numbers on which they appear, 137
Index cards, 218, 223, 225–226, 240
Inductive argument is defined as follows: If the premises are true, the conclusions are *probably* true, but the truth is not guaranteed, 41, 42
Infatuation is passionate love, or romantic love; passionate, strong

feelings of affection for another person, 339
Infirmary, 261
Information
CD-ROM sources of, 224
high-tech collection of, 226
low-tech collection of, 223, 225–226
Informational interview, 375–376
Information cards, 225, 228
Information overload, 124
Information technology is technology that merges computers with high-speed communications links, 52–77
classroom use of, 177–180
computer software, 59–62, 74–76
ethics of using, 77
importance of skills in, 52, 77
the Internet, 63–68
online courses and, 179–180
personal computers, 53–59
the World Wide Web, 68–74
Initial research, 217
Injectable contraceptives, 361
Inkjet printers, 56
Instructor evaluations consider how fairly instructors grade and how effectively they present their lectures, 253
Instructors
academic help from, 259
grading system and, 176–177
high school vs. college, 173–174
interviewing, 175
negotiating with, 207
personal accounts of, 172–173
psyching out testing methods of, 186–187, 189
student evaluations of, 174–175
term paper topics and, 216
Insurance, 281–282
Integrated software packages combine the features of several applications programs into one software package, 62
Integration, 342
Intelligence
emotional, 31
seven kinds of, 30
Interference is the competition among related memories, 127
Interlibrary loan is a service that enables you to borrow books from other libraries, 220
Intermediate-range goals, 86–87
Internal locus of control is the belief that rewards and punishments are due to one's own behavior, character, or efforts, 31, 17
International students, 302–303
Internet, or simply "the Net," is an international network connecting approximately 140,000 smaller networks in more than 200 countries, 63–68
addiction to, 109–110
addresses used on, 66
features of, 66–67

hardware and software requirements, 63–64
job opportunities on, 380–381
services for connecting to, 64–66
as study-time distraction, 109–110
term papers and, 235–238

Internet addict is anyone who spends an average of 38 hours a week online, 110

Internet service providers (ISPs) are local or national companies that will provide unlimited public access to the Internet and World Wide Web for a flat monthly fee, 65–66

Internship is a temporary stint of on-the-job training that allows you to gain inside professional experience within a particular company or organization, 376

Interviews
employment, 382, 384
follow-up letter to, 385
informational, 375–376

Intimacy is defined as a close, familiar, affectionate, and loving relationship with another person, 339

Invisible fats, 330

Iron supplements, 332

Irrelevant attack on an opponent attacks a person's reputation or beliefs rather than his or her argument, 43

Irrelevant reason is a type of fallacy in which the conclusion does not follow logically from the supposed reasons stated earlier, 42

It's About Time (Sapadin), 106

IUD (intrauterine device), 360

Job-placement office is a campus office that provides job listings from employers who are looking for student help, 264, 370

Jobs. *See* Career; Employment; Work

Journal research, 221–222

Journal writing, 26

Jumping to conclusions is a type of fallacy. It happens when a conclusion has been reached when not all the facts are available, 42

Junk foods, 332

Keywords are important terms or names that you are expected to understand and be able to define, 220

Kilobyte, 56

Kinesthetic learners learn best when they touch and are physically involved in what they are studying, 34

Laboratory assignments, 16

Laptop computers, 114, 177–178, 226

Laser printers, 56

Later reviewing, 145

Latex condoms, 356

Learning
active, 37
demonstration of, 213–214
difficult subjects, 146–150
drill-and-practice, 126–127
mindful, 34–37, 128–131
reading for, 132–133, 139–145

Learning center or lab is a special center where students go to learn a specific subject or skill, 260

Learning objectives are topics the student is expected to learn, which are listed at the beginning of each chapter, 138

Learning styles are the ways in which people acquire knowledge, 31
lectures and, 34, 156, 157
personal exploration of, 32–33
textbooks and, 34
types of, 33–34

Leasing computer equipment, 58

Lectures
attendance at, 157, 159–160
career skills and, 15–16
class participation in, 160–161, 165–167
computer use in, 177–179
fighting boredom and fatigue in, 161–164
learning styles and, 34, 156, 157
note-taking system for, 167–172
online, 179–180
overcoming obstacles in, 164
taping, 114, 149, 164

Legal services, 264

Lesbians, 298

Librarians, 220, 259–260

Library computer lab, 54

Library research, 219–226, 260
book resources and, 220–221
CD-ROM information sources and, 223, 224
central library and, 219–220
collecting information in, 223, 225–226
computer networks and, 221, 223
government literature and, 221, 223
periodical resources and, 221–222
practical exploration exercise on, 227
reference materials and, 222–223, 224

Life goals
college education and, 22–24
examples of, 23

Lifted term papers, 213

Listening
active, 161–164
becoming expert at, 344–345

Listservs, 67

Loan is money you have to pay back, either as money or in the form of some work, 284

"Loaner" computers, 54

Locus of control refers to one's beliefs about the relationship between one's behavior and the occurrence of rewards and punishment, 17
personal exploration of, 18–19

Long-answer essay generally requires three or more paragraphs to answer, 197
strategy for handling, 198–203

Long-range goals, 22–24, 85

Long-term memory entails remembering something for days, weeks, or years, 123
cramming and, 122
forgetting curve and, 123–124
reading and, 134
strategies for improving, 126–131

Love
loss of, 340
types of, 339

Love Is Never Enough (Beck), 344

Lying is simply misrepresentation of the facts. It can occur by omission or by commission, 205

Lying (Bok), 205

Macintosh computers, 54–55

Magazine research, 221–222, 224

Mailing lists, 67

Major is a student's field of specialization, 258
relationship to career, 368–369

Margins
using for taking notes, 168–169, 171
using in 3Rs reading system, 143

Marijuana, 325

Martyrdom, 343

Massed practice is putting all your studying into one long period of time, 126

Master timetable, 91–94

Matching questions require you to associate items from one list with items from a second list, 196–197

Media center, 259–260

Meditation is concerned with directing a person's attention to a single, unchanging, or repetitive stimulus. It is a way of quelling the "mind chatter," 320

Megabyte, 56

"Melting pot," 296

Memory is defined as a mental process that entails three main operations: recording, storage, and recall, 120
cramming and, 122
forgetting curve and, 123–124
general health and, 125
impediments to, 124–125
personal exploration of, 121
strategies for improving, 126–131
types of, 122–123

Mental imagery is a procedure in which you essentially daydream an image or desired change, anticipating that your body will respond as if the image were real, 319

Menus (software), are lists of choices for manipulating aspects of your document, 59

Merit-based financial aid is based on some kind of superior academic, music, sports, or other abilities, 283

Method of loci is a memory technique that involves memorizing a series of places and then using a different vivid image to associate each place with an idea or a word you want to remember, 131

Microsoft Internet Explorer, 69

Microsoft Network (MSN), 64

Mind control, 243

Mindfulness is characterized by three features: (1) the creation of new categories, (2) openness to new information, and (3) awareness of more than one perspective, 35–37
  cultivating, 37
  learning process and, 34–37, 128–131
  money and, 269

Mindfulness (Langer), 34

Mindlessness is characterized by three features: (1) entrapment in old categories, (2) automatic behavior, and (3) acting from a single perspective, 35

Mind mapping, sometimes called clustering, is brainstorming by yourself with the help of pencil and paper, 45–46

Mind-sets, 38–39

Minipill, 361

Minor is a smaller field of specialization chosen by the student, 258

Minorities. *See also* Diversity
  racial and cultural, 294–296, 300–303

Mistakes
  admitting and reducing, 39
  fear of making, 44–45

Mixed-modality learners are able to function in any of three learning styles or "modalities"–auditory, visual, and kinesthetic, 34

Mnemonic devices are tactics for making things memorable by making them distinctive, 129–130

Modems are hardware devices needed to send messages from one computer to another via a phone line, 63–64

Money, 266, 268–285
  bank accounts, 279–280
  charge, credit, and debit cards, 280–281
  college costs and, 266, 268
  controlling spending of, 278–279
  financial aid, 282–285
  formulating a budget, 272–276
  insurance, 281–282
  keeping an expense record, 277
  managing income and expenses, 269–270, 271
  mindfulness about, 269, 270, 271
  personal diagnostic report, 271

Money and the Meaning of Life (Needleman), 366

Money plan, or budget, is simply a plan or schedule of how to balance your income and expenses. It helps you see where your money is going to come from and where it is going to go, 272–276
  monthly, 272, 274–276
  yearly, 272, 273

Monogamy, 357

Motivation, 6–7

Motorcycles, 306

Motor scooters, 306

Multiculturalism refers to cultural and racial diversity, 290

Multimedia, 68, 179

Multiphasic pill, 361

Multiple-choice questions allow you to pick an answer from several options offered, 195–196

Muscle strength and endurance, 329

Narrative story method is a memory technique that involves making up a narrative, or story. It helps students recall unrelated lists of words by giving them meaning and linking them in a specific order, 130

Native Americans, 302

Natural family planning, 359

Natural language queries, 74

Need-based financial aid requires you or your parents to fill out forms stating your resources. The school then determines how much aid needs to be made up from somewhere else, 283

Needs analysis document is a form for helping people prove their financial need to their schools, 283

Negative thoughts, 146, 147, 191

Negotiating with instructors, 207

Nervousness, reducing, 242–244

Netscape Navigator, 69

Networking is making contacts, and making use of existing contacts, with people to find work and advance your career, 374–375

Newsgroups. *See* Usenet newsgroups

Newspaper research, 221–222

News services, online, 236

Nonassertive behavior means consistently giving in to others on points of difference. It means agreeing with others regardless of your feelings, not expressing your opinions, hurting yourself to avoid hurting others, 346

Nonoxynol-9 is a spermicide that kills STD organisms, 356

Non sequitur, 42

Nontraditional students, sometimes called adult students or returning students, are post-secondary students who are older than 24 years, 299–300

Norplant, 361

"No shame, no blame" approach to mistakes, 39

Notes
  5R system for taking, 167–172
  leaving spaces in, 164
  preparing for oral presentations, 240
  sorting for term papers, 226, 228
  trading with classmates, 164

Objective questions are those that are true-false, multiple-choice, matching, and fill-in, 193, 194–197
  fill-in-the-blank questions, 197
  matching questions, 196–197
  multiple-choice questions, 195–196
  strategies applicable to, 194–195
  true-false questions, 195

101 Creative Problem Solving Techniques (Higgins), 45

Online computerized catalogs require that you use a computer terminal or microcomputer that has a wired connection to a database, 220

Online courses, 179–180

Online information services provide access to all kinds of databases and electronic meeting places to subscribers equipped with telephone-linked personal computers, 64

Optimism, 20, 317

Oral contraceptives, 360–361

Oral presentations, 239–244
  audience attention in, 242
  career skills and, 212
  delivering, 243–244
  preparing notes for, 240
  reducing nervousness in, 242–243
  stages in, 241–242

Order words, 163

Orientation program, 252

Originality, 213

Outgo indicates your monetary expenditures, 269

Outlines
  for long-answer essays, 200–201
  for oral presentations, 240
  for term papers, 218

Overdoers, 107

Overlearning is defined as continued rehearsal of material after you first appeared to have mastered it, 126

Papers. *See* Term papers

Paradigm Online Writing Assistant, 235

Parent Loans for Undergraduate Students (PLUS), 284

Participation in classes, 160–161, 165–167

Partying, 109, 321

Passive aggression, 343